S0-BZZ-304

BIBLICAL ARCHAEOLOGY TODAY

Organizing Committee

AVRAHAM BIRAN (Chairman), *Hebrew Union College–Jewish Institute of Religion*
SHIMEON AMIR, *The Israel Academy of Sciences and Humanities*
JOSEPH AVIRAM, *Israel Exploration Society*
MOSHE DOTHAN, *University of Haifa*
AVRAHAM EITAN, *Israel Department of Antiquities and Museums*
JONAS C. GREENFIELD, *The Hebrew University of Jerusalem*
MOSHE KOCHAVI, *Tel-Aviv University*
ABRAHAM MALAMAT, *The Hebrew University of Jerusalem*
BENJAMIN MAZAR, *The Hebrew University of Jerusalem*
ELIEZER D. OREN, *Ben-Gurion University of the Negev*
EPHRAIM STERN, *The Hebrew University of Jerusalem*
EPHRAIM E. URBACH, *The Israel Academy of Sciences and Humanities*
YIGAEL YADIN, *The Hebrew University of Jerusalem*

BIBLICAL ARCHAEOLOGY TODAY

Proceedings of the International Congress
on Biblical Archaeology
Jerusalem, April 1984

Israel Exploration Society
The Israel Academy of Sciences and Humanities
in cooperation with the
American Schools of Oriental Research

To Yigael Yadin, in memory

ISBN 965–221–004–8

EDITED by Janet Amitai
CONSULTING EDITOR: Rafi Grafman
COPY EDITOR: Robert Amoils

TYPESETTING: Yael Kaplan, Jerusalem
PLATES: Tafsar, Jerusalem
PRINTED IN ISRAEL by Ben Zvi Printing Enterprises Ltd., Jerusalem

Contents

Session III: Stratigraphy, Chronology and Terminology

Session IV: Israel's Neighbors in the Iron Age in the Light of Archaeological Research

Session VII: The Dead Sea Scrolls

Session VIII: Revealing Biblical Jerusalem

The Closing Session

Social Events, Exhibitions and Excursions

Acknowledgments

The Organizing Committee of the International Congress on Biblical Archaeology acknowledges with deep appreciation the generous support of the following:

Israel Ministry of Science and Development
Hebrew Union College–Jewish Institute of Religion
Israel Ministry of Education and Culture
Israel Ministry of Foreign Affairs, Division for Cultural and Scientific Affairs
The Jerusalem Foundation
Israel Ministry of Tourism

The publication of this book was made possible through the generous support of the following:

The Dorot Foundation
The S.H. and Helen R. Scheuer Family Foundation
Ophir Tours Ltd.

Honorary Sponsors

Akademie der Wissenschaften in Göttingen
Akademie der Wissenschaften und der Literatur, Mainz
W.F. Albright Institute for Archaeological Research—An Institute of the American Schools of Oriental Research
Bar-Ilan University
Bayerische Akademie der Wissenschaften
Ben-Gurion University of the Negev
The British Academy
British School of Archaeology in Jerusalem
Centre de Recherche Français de Jérusalem
Deutscher Verein zur Erforschung Palästinas
Deutsches Evangelisches Institut für Altertumswissenschaft des Heiligen Landes
École Biblique et Archéologique Française
Hebrew Union College–Jewish Institute of Religion
The Hebrew University of Jerusalem
Heidelberger Akademie der Wissenschaften
Institut de France—Académie des Inscriptions et Belles Lettres
The Institute for Advanced Study, Princeton
Institute of Holy Land Studies, Jerusalem
Israel Department of Antiquities and Museums
The Israel Museum, Jerusalem
The Jewish Theological Seminary of America
Koninklijke Nederlandse Akademie van Wetenschappen
Österreichische Akademie der Wissenschaften
Palestine Exploration Fund
Pontifical Biblical Institute, Jerusalem
Rheinisch-Westfälische Akademie der Wissenschaften
Society of Biblical Literature
Swedish Theological Institute, Jerusalem
Tel-Aviv University
University of Haifa

Preface

The need to evaluate, discuss and report on the present stage of the various studies which comprise biblical archaeology has long been felt. To fill that need the International Congress on Biblical Archaeology was convened in Jerusalem during the first week of April 1984. The date was chosen to mark the 70th anniversary of the Israel Exploration Society. Some 300 scholars from abroad and 400 from Israel gathered together to discuss the more than forty papers presented at the Congress.

During the five days of deliberations, time was set aside for visits to the excavations in Jerusalem, and an important part of the Congress program were the specially planned excursions and exhibitions which followed the deliberations. Here too the aim of the Organizing Committee was to present an up-to-date review of archaeological research carried out in Israel. The exhibitions presented recent finds and emphasis during the five days of excursions was placed on the newly excavated sites.

The Proceedings of the Congress are now published in this volume, and we would like to take this opportunity to thank all the institutions and individuals who made this publication possible. While the papers and responses follow the texts submitted by their authors, the discussions are based on the transcript of the tape recordings made at the time. It will be appreciated that this was, to say the least, not easy. In some cases, the recording was unclear and in others the discussion had to be condensed for lack of space. We hope, nevertheless, that we have published here a true representation of the discussions.

It will be noted that in this publication the spelling of place names is that used in the *Israel Exploration Journal*, while the transliterations follow in the main the manuscripts of the authors. We would like, however, to express our deep regrets for any mistakes resulting from technical difficulties.

It is with great sorrow that we note the untimely death of Prof. Yigael Yadin only a few months after the Congress. One of the last things he did was to review his paper before forwarding it for publication in this volume. It remains, therefore, the testament of his philosophy on the subject of biblical archaeology to which he devoted his professional career. We dedicate this book on biblical archaeology to his memory.

A. BIRAN
Chairman, Organizing Committee

Israel Exploration Society

Founded in 1914 as the Jewish Palestine Exploration Society (JPES), the Israel Exploration Society (IES) has lived up to its charter to further the exploration of Eretz-Israel, to conduct archaeological excavations, to publish archaeological and geographical studies, and to organize lectures, field trips, seminars, congresses and exhibitions.

The first excavation of the JPES was that of N. Slouschz in 1921–1922 at Hammath-Tiberias, the finds of which included a menorah carved in stone. This menorah was incorporated in the emblem of the International Congress on Biblical Archaeology. Since Hammath-Tiberias the Society has sponsored many archaeological excavations reaching into prehistoric times. Some of the highlights were those at the necropolis and synagogue of Beth-She‘arim and of the Philistine remains at Tell Qasile, the Hazor, Beth Yeraḥ, and Ramat Raḥel expeditions, the preliminary survey of Masada followed by its excavation and restoration, the exploration of the Judean Desert Caves, and the excavations at En-Gedi. Since 1967, the Society has been engaged in the monumental work in Jerusalem adjacent to the Temple Mount, in the Jewish Quarter and in the City of David. Other recent projects include Herod's palaces in Jericho and Herodium, and the ongoing work at Dor and Yoqne‘am.

In the 1930s when the Bezalel Museum was founded, the nucleus of its archaeological section was contributed by the JPES. Three decades later the IES also participated in the planning of the Israel Museum and the Shrine of the Book, where the Dead Sea Scrolls are housed. At the end of the British Mandate, when its Department of Antiquities ceased to function, the Society cooperated with the newly established State's government offices to set up the Israel Department of Antiquities and Museums.

The IES is administered by an executive committee representing the various archaeological institutions in Israel, scholars in fields related to the study of the Land of Israel, and public figures. The Society often represents these archaeological institutions in a joint effort to promote the case of the profession both in Israel and abroad. Close ties are maintained with the archaeology departments of the Israeli universities and other associations such as the Ben-Zvi Institute in Jerusalem and the Israel National Parks Authority, major museums and, of course, the Israel Department of Antiquities and Museums.

The Society's current membership approximates 4,000. Its offices are located in Jerusalem and there are branches in Haifa and Tel Aviv, in addition to the numerous affiliated study groups in the kibbutzim. Abroad, the American Friends of the IES, with chapters in New York and Washington, D.C., was established in the 1920s. The Anglo-Israel Archaeological Society in London also cooperates with the Society. Both groups sponsor archaeological lectures and distribute the Society's publications.

Since its inception, the Society has continuously published journals, pamphlets and books on archaeological subjects, some in cooperation with other institutions and publishers, particularly the Bialik Institute, Massada Press, Carta and Magness Press. From 1933 to 1967, the mainstay publication was the Hebrew *Yediot*, which was initially the bulletin of the JPES. *Yediot* was replaced by the more popular format *Qadmoniot*. Articles from the latter appeared in English in the "Holy Land Revealed" volumes: *Jerusalem Revealed*, *Ancient Synagogues Revealed*, and now in press, *Ancient Churches Revealed*. The Society's English quarterly, *Israel Exploration Journal*, has been Israel's archaeological window to the world since its inception in 1951. The *Eretz-Israel* series, the eighteenth volume of which has just been published, is basically in Hebrew, but includes English summaries and often features contributions in other languages. The character of the *Eretz-Israel* series is that of a Festschrift. The IES has also published major excavation reports such as *Hazor* (three volumes), *Beth-She'arim* (three volumes), *Early Arad*, *Hammath-Tiberias*, and *Judean Desert Caves* (two volumes). Other important works issued by the Society include N. Avigad's *Discovering Jerusalem*, Y. Aharoni's *Arad Inscriptions*, Y. Yadin's *The Temple Scroll* (three volumes), R. Amiran's *Ancient Pottery of the Holy Land*, and the monumental *Encyclopedia of Archaeological Excavations in the Holy Land* (four volumes).

The Israeli scholarly community's respect for the IES is demonstrated by the fact that the Israel Academy of Sciences and Humanities elected to cosponsor this International Congress on Biblical Archaeology. Although the framework of this Congress is intended to emphasize biblical archaeology, the program also gives expression to the major research activities carried out due to the encouragement and direction of the Israel Exploration Society over the past seventy years.

Jerusalem, 1985

J. AVIRAM
Honorary Secretary

THE OPENING OF THE CONGRESS

AVRAHAM BIRAN
Chairman, Israel Exploration Society
MENACHEM SAVIDOR
H.E. The Acting President of Israel
EPHRAIM E. URBACH
President, Israel Academy of Sciences and Humanities
TEDDY KOLLEK
Mayor of Jerusalem

The Opening of the Congress

Avraham Biran: On behalf of the Israel Exploration Society, and on behalf of the organizing committee, I would like to extend a hearty welcome to all of you who have come to take part in this International Congress on Biblical Archaeology which I trust will be the first of many to be held in Jerusalem.

The Israel Exploration Society is deeply gratified by this fantastic turnout honoring its 70th anniversary. Seventy years in the history of the lands of the Bible is but a fleeting moment, but in the history of archaeological research in Israel, these seven decades span two, almost three generations of scholars. The Society has to its credit over fifty excavations and hundreds of publications. It has a devoted membership of tens of thousands. This, perhaps, is one of its greatest and most amazing achievements. I recall at one of our annual conferences a number of years ago — I believe it was at Hanita in the north — Frank Cross was sitting next to me and watching the thousands of people sitting uncomfortably on the hard slopes of the mountain, avidly listening to lecture after lecture. He turned to me and said: "Look at them, they sit, they sit and listen, absorbed." Perhaps this ability to instill in the minds and hearts of our members the will to learn, the thirst for knowledge, a loving and deeper understanding of the Bible, archaeology and history, is the Society's greatest achievement.

This enthusiasm has culminated in this standing-room only conference; we could not accommodate all our members who wished to join this illustrious gathering. Illustrious it is. Over 800 have gathered here this evening, including 300 scholars and students from abroad from twenty different countries: from the United States to Japan; from Australia to Mexico; from South Africa to Finland; from Sweden to Canada; from Germany to Zimbabwe; from England to Italy, from Holland to Austria, from Ireland, France, Denmark, Scotland and Spain, and finally from Israel. To all of you, from near and afar, we extend the warmest of welcome.

Ladies and gentlemen, we are greatly honored this evening by the presence of the Acting President of the State of Israel, Mr. Menachem Savidor. Mr. Acting President, we would be grateful if you, Sir, would be good enough to officially open the First International Congress on Biblical Archaeology.

Menachem Savidor: I was just mentioning that I would not have come to this opening ceremony if a certain bill, restricting the activities of the archaeologists in our country, would have been approved by the Knesset. On behalf of the President of the State, I extend you warm greetings. We are living in an industrial and technological era in which social patterns are disrupted. We in the free world have a duty to find the way to render our society immune to the destructive currents that technology in our new consumer society is bringing upon us. We must therefore combine culture with technology, authenticity with modernity. Having said this, I would like to say that no other research and no other group of scholars work with such perseverance and profundity to contribute to the identification of our people with our authentic roots and culture. I have come here to salute all of those who have been engaged in this great enterprise for so many years. Ladies and gentlemen, no other nation on earth draws more from its past the reasons for its hopes and its fears. I think that Goethe was right when he said what one does not understand one does not possess. You, the archaeologists, enable the people of Israel to understand their past, to identify it, and to identify themselves with their past and culture.

I would like to conclude by saying that I am deeply honored and privileged to open this great gathering comprising so many scholars from the free world. I wish you fruitful deliberations and an enjoyable stay in our old/new homeland. Indeed there are days and moments which cast their light upon years. May I hope that such will be the days of your conference and your stay in Israel.

Avraham Biran: This Congress could not have been held without the active support of the Israel Academy of Sciences and Humanities, and especially without the inspiration and guidance of its distinguished President, Prof. Ephraim Urbach.

Ephraim E. Urbach: On behalf of the Israel Academy of Sciences and Humanities, I have the honor and pleasure to welcome all of you who have come from far and near to participate in the International Congress on Biblical Archaeology.

The Israel Exploration Society deserves to have a Congress convened to mark its 70th Anniversary. When one reads the first publication of the Society, one admires the pioneering spirit which animated its founding fathers, and helped them to overcome the tremendous difficulties and prejudices which they had to face. They and their followers succeeded in stimulating sympathy and collaboration in wide strata of our population. At the same time, the leading members of the Society became increasingly aware that in archaeology — as in other disciplines — enthusiasm is a good companion but not always a good guide.

Biblical archaeology is concerned with the material remains relating to the biblical period here and in the neighboring countries. Enthusiasm for the Bible provided the initial incentive for many of the earlier excavations. At the same time biblical scholars were rewarded by the broad picture of the historical, religious and ethical background made available from archaeological excavations, which has done much to explain, illustrate and corroborate the biblical record and counteract theories insufficiently based on facts. Of no lesser importance are the great discoveries relating to the Second Temple and Talmudic periods. Notwithstanding the witty remark attributed to Mommsen, referring to archaeology as "the illiterate science," biblical archaeology has yielded a rich literary crop: the Dead Sea Scrolls, the documents of the Judean Desert, and even a long Mishnaic-Talmudic inscription in Reḥov. These discoveries, which are of the utmost importance to the Jewish and Christian world as a whole, have aroused widespread interest. This interest finds expression in the participation of thousands of volunteers from all over the world in archaeological excavations in Israel, and will find its scholarly venue in the lectures and deliberations of the distinguished scholars participating in this Congress. Unfortunately, we do not see among them representatives of our nearest neighbors who are also engaged in archaeological research and share with us common cultural roots.

Abdullah H. Masry, Assistant Deputy Minister for Cultural Affairs in the Ministry of Education of Saudi Arabia, and editor-in-chief of *Atlal*, the Journal of Saudi Arabian Archaeology, does not include Israel in his article "Traditions of Archaeological Research in the Near East" [*World Archaeology* 13, no. 2 (1982): 221–237]. In that issue, Israeli archaeology is treated separately in an article by Ofer Bar-Yosef and Amihai Mazar (ibid., pp. 310ff.). Mr. Masry avoids mentioning Israel even when he writes: "Digging styles also contrast sharply in the Levant with paid local labor mainly being used in Syria and student volunteers taking their place elsewhere." However, he does quote approvingly Ruth Amiran's *Ancient Pottery of the Holy Land* and a publication of F. Asaro, I. Perlman and M. Dothan. In this interesting and informative article, Masry stresses several times the common links and problems of archaeology in the area, for example: "Recent work on early rock art styles in Saudi Arabia promises to link prehistoric cultures of the peninsula with those in the Negev, Sinai, Jordan and Egypt." At the conclusion of the article, he draws attention to the changing role of Near Eastern scholarship, which has developed from a marginal, almost passive form of learning to a science which assumes the direction of scholarly inquiry in the field. He points out the attempt to construct scientific models for cultural continuity between the ancient traditions and contemporary mores of societies in the region. Masry adds that this phenomenon "deserves understanding and encouragement, provided that a proper perception of the scientific priority is consistently maintained." I would add that perception of scientific priority includes also collaboration with archaeologists in Israel. Let me express our hope that such a call will not remain in the rendering of the Septuagint and other versions of Isaiah 40:3: "A voice of him that crieth in the wilderness"; but will be according to the masoretic text: "A voice that crieth: In the wilderness prepare the way of the Lord, make straight in the desert a highway for our God."

Once again: ברוכים הבאים, Blessed be all of you who have come to assist in fulfilling the prophecy of Isaiah, the son of Amoz: "Out of Zion shall go forth the law, and the word of the Lord from Jerusalem."

Avraham Biran: The city of Jerusalem and our mayor, Teddy Kollek, have long become synonymous. Among Mayor Kollek's many attributes is one which is less well known — he has been a member of the executive board of the Israel Exploration Society for the last thirty years. To bring Jerusalem's greetings, I call upon the person we all fondly know as Teddy.

Teddy Kollek: I am very proud to stand here, not only because I am the Mayor of Jerusalem — which is a source of special pride, and would be for anybody — but because I am proud to see that even during a government crisis when Parliament is being dissolved, the Speaker of the House, here serving as the Acting President of Israel, and at least one Cabinet Minister are present. Furthermore, there are more people here tonight to hear lectures on biblical archaeology than any party in Israel would be able to assemble at this moment.

Finally, I would like to draw a practical, political conclusion from archaeology. In the United States today, the major interest concerning Israel is not our inflation, nor the war in

Lebanon, nor what happens in Judea and Samaria, but the bill favoring moving the U.S. Embassy from Tel Aviv to Jerusalem. Jerusalem in the year 2000, only sixteen years from now, will celebrate 3,000 years of being made our capital by King David, so the Americans are 2,794 years too late with their legislation.

Let me wish you all a very good Congress and a very pleasant stay.

Avraham Biran: And now to our musical interlude: Zvi Avni's composition for Psalm 121, **אשא עיני אל ההרים**, "I lift up my eyes to the hills," for a string quartet and oboe, performed by young musicians studying at the Music Center of Mishkenot Sha᾽ananim under the supervision of the Rubin Academy of Music in Jerusalem.

SESSION I
BIBLICAL ARCHAEOLOGY TODAY

FRANK M. CROSS, *Harvard University*
The Biblical Aspect
BENJAMIN MAZAR, *The Hebrew University of Jerusalem*
The Historical Aspect
YIGAEL YADIN, *The Hebrew University of Jerusalem*
The Archaeological Aspect

Biblical Archaeology Today: The Biblical Aspect

Frank Moore Cross

As a representative of the scholars who live beyond the borders of this Holy Land, but whose eyes are focused upon it and upon its ancient heritage, I wish to bring greetings and congratulations to the Israel Exploration Society on the occasion of its seventieth anniversary. We are profoundly impressed by the energy, devotion, and achievements of the Society and the Israeli archaeological enterprise. We cannot forget the circumstances under which Israel's archaeologists have performed their tasks. They have overcome conditions of grave economic hardship, and have labored on during wars and threats of wars. They have persevered in their digging, and one archaeological tome after another has been brought to publication. The Israel Exploration Society has won the admiration of the scholarly world and rightly deserves its deep gratitude.

LITTLE MORE THAN a century ago the Bible was an isolated artifact of ancient Near Eastern civilization, a monument without known context or ancestry. Today, thanks to the archaeological exploration of Israel and neighboring lands, the history of Israel has become part of the history of the ancient world. Israel's ancient literature can be viewed as evolving out of the genres of kindred literatures and the religion of Israel described in its continuities with and contrasts to contemporary Near Eastern mythology and cult. The Bible in all its particularity and power is revealed as the ultimate achievement of the evolution of ancient Near Eastern culture.

At the same time, it must be said that the assimilation of the vast mass of new texts and monuments has only begun, and there is no diminution in the pace of discovery. *Pari passu*, we must reread biblical texts, discarding or refurbishing historical and literary constructs. New syntheses must be constructed to permit comprehension of new data for the history, religion, and literature of Israel.

The biblical scholar, wherever his special researches lead him, cannot afford to ignore the impact of the archaeological revolution.

The textual critic of the Hebrew Bible has been overwhelmed by the scrolls from the Judean Desert, perhaps the most spectacular discoveries of our generation. These manuscripts have lifted the veil obscuring the phase of textual development before the promulgation of the Rabbinic Recension of the first century C.E., the ancestor of the received text. The interpretation of the data from the manuscripts is still in progress. Efforts to reach a consensus on the early history of the Hebrew text of various biblical books have not been wholly successful, in part because of the failure of certain scholars to complete their editions of important Qumran texts. There have been secure conclusions reached on many long-debated issues. It is clear now, for example, that the Old Greek Bible underwent a series of recensions to bring it into closer conformity with a sequence of Hebrew texts. The oldest Greek text which we have recovered was certainly translated from a Hebrew text which differed considerably — and in some books extensively — from the textual base of the Rabbinic Recension. The textual criticism of the Greek Bible, long a dull if not moribund discipline, has been invigorated with new life and relevance. Freed from theories of the past, notably those of Paul Kahle, the textual critic can rejoin the critic of the Hebrew Bible in writing the history of the early development of the Hebrew biblical text, and ideally, in pursuing the ultimate goal of all textual criticism, the ferreting out of scribal errors.

The welter of new manuscripts of archaic date, some as early as the mid-third century B.C.E., combine with the steadily increasing corpus of inscriptional materials dating from the Late Bronze Age to Roman times, to afford other new tools for the textual critic. These materials throw new light on the history of the Hebrew language, the evolution of spelling styles, and the palaeographical development of the Old Hebrew, Palaeo-Hebrew, Aramaic, and Jewish scripts. The received Hebrew Bible is, in effect, a palimpsest, preserving many layers in its language, orthography, and script. In the centuries of copying, scribal schools shifted from script to script, modernized spelling from age to age, and even revised uncouth or forgotten items of grammar and lexicon. Fortunately, from the point of view of the textual critic, they were not wholly successful in removing traces of the past preserved in variant readings or perceptible in transparent scribal blunders. The detailed knowledge of the history of the language, its spelling styles and scripts — not to mention the disciplines of historical prosody and genre criticism — will, as such knowledge proliferates, aid the text critic in both of the primary branches of his discipline, *recension* and *emendation*. I am very much aware that these inseparable tasks of textual criticism are rarely pursued by the textual critic; emendation is performed by literary critics unschooled in recension, while the biblical textual critic restricts himself to the narrow task of recording variants, choosing between them, if at all, on limited recensional grounds. This separation of tasks is, as far as I know, unique to the study of sacred texts, and a scandal to scholars trained in the high tradition of classical textual criticism. Emendation and recension must be re-wedded in biblical textual study, and biblical archaeology is providing new materials to make such a reunion both practical and interesting.

I wish to make two further comments. Firstly, I am convinced that the study of the new materials for textual criticism will demonstrate that the text of biblical books crystallized early — in the case of the Octateuch, in the beginning of the Persian period. The subsequent history of their transmission is largely the history of variants arising in inadvertent scribal lapses or explicating additions. In instances where more than one edition of a book survives, as in the case of Jeremiah and the Chronicler's work (that is, Chronicles, Ezra and Nehemiah), the text of each appears to predate Hellenistic times. Secondly, I believe that there are sufficient data now available to argue that the fixation of the text and the canon of the Hebrew Bible were two aspects of a single endeavor made by Pharisees early in the first century C.E., in the time of Hillel and his school, and perhaps under the direction of Hillel himself.

The student of Hebrew literature and its prosodic forms, genres, tradition, and history is forced by the impact of archaeological research to place Israelite literature in the context of Semitic, especially Canaanite, literature. The results are shattering to the theories and constructs built up by generations of literary and form critics on the basis of internal biblical evidence alone. This result is not surprising. The shape of our theories has been structured by philosophical or theological dogma, the results of our circular inductive procedures already determined by presuppositions. I remain convinced that much form critical analysis remains an edifice of possibilities and speculation unless or until the genres of biblical literature in question are firmly linked up with comparable extra-biblical genres of Semitic literature.

In the case of early Hebrew poetry, for example, we find that Israel's repertoire of oral formulae, binary grammatical and semantic correspondences that provide the building blocks of orally composed song, stem from a common Canaanite poetic tradition. Moreover, verse forms and prosodic ornament (for example, numerical parallelism, climactic parallelism, impressionistic parallelism) follow identical or related patterns. The proper analysis of the meaning and mechanisms of Hebrew poetry is enormously facilitated by the study of extra-biblical poetic texts.

Again the study of the mythic cycles and epic texts of Ugarit prove that the early Israel narrative traditions — Israelite epic — share common orally shaped themes and story complexes: the march of the divine warrior to battle, his lightening bolts and thunderous voice convulsing nature; the coming of the victorious warrior to his mountain shrine where he appears in glory; the failure of an heir; the vision of ʾĒl in which blessing is given and an heir promised; the replacement of an older son by a younger.

Israel was heir to a rich literary heritage; to be sure she altered, and developed, and transformed this heritage. However, Israel's early literary works were not created in a vacuum. One recalls Gunkel's assertion that in early Israel, a song or poem comprised no more than "one or two lines" (more than that an early Israelite could not comprehend); or Wellhausen's statement that the early Israelite narrative could consist of only a single, simple story. Such notions, born of German idealism and romanticism, sound ludicrous when stated today against a background of contemporary literary works dug up from the earth. Yet the tendency to give a late date to long poems persists to this day, and the impulse to reduce complexes of epic tradition to theoretical and trivial units survives in uncritical tradition-historical analysis. This is often the case on the part of scholars who would reject analyst's views of the Homeric cycle as obsolete, or who would never apply such techniques to the Ugaritic cycles or to the Gilgamesh epic.

The historian of Israelite religion also must come to terms with the lore of contemporary biblical archaeology. In viewing patriarchal religion, we are forced to recognize that ʾĒl is the Patriarch of the gods, creator of the gods, of earth, and of man. Alt's *ʾēlīm*, genii of local shrines, are a figment of the scholarly imagination. The epithets of the gods of the fathers prove to be those of personal gods, epithets revealing the covenantal or kinship relation of the god to the Patriarch who keeps his cult. In West Semitic religion these kinship names usually applied to high gods. Despite the replacement of Alt's speculations with hard, new data, I heard a lecture recently by a distinguished European scholar who recited like a catechism Alt's notions of nameless gods and multiple, minor *ʾēlīm*. Alt's rightly famous paper was written in 1929, just when mounds at Ugarit and, shortly later, at Mari, began to divulge their texts. Thirty-five years later there is little excuse for scholars to stick their heads in the sands of older literature and ignore the newer resources. A single text recovered by the spade is often more valuable in the reconstruction of the history of Israelite religion than a hundred speculations of the past.

We could find illustrations in almost any era in the history of biblical religion. The covenant forms of Israel's religious literature and religious expression must be analyzed anew in the light of recent research. There is ample evidence that covenants and treaties imposing mutual obligations characterized the institutions of West Semitic society in both the second and first millennia B.C.E. They were alien both to Egypt and Mesopotamia save where Amorite and, later, Aramean influence penetrated. Hayim Tadmor's papers on these topics begin a new period in the study of biblical covenant and law. I am unable to resist adding a polemical remark: the claim that *bĕrīt* in early Hebrew meant "a unilateral obligation" is the feckless contrivance of a school of scholars striving consciously or unconsciously to salvage antinomian dogma.

We have dwelt on the possibility and importance of placing biblical literature, religion, and history into their Near Eastern context, the gift of biblical archaeology. In this fashion we perceive their continuities with their environment, and their distinctive features with new perspective.

Why did the religion of Israel become radically historical? Canaan had its historical epics. However, its mythic cycles, its cosmogony—the establishment of order in the universe of powers—appear to have been central to its religious perceptions and cultures. Certainly this was the case in Mesopotamia. But in Israel, the epic narrative of the events of the call, deliverance, and creation of the nation became the central focus of religious memory and rite. An epic of all-Israel, recited, and we believe, re-enacted in the pilgrimage shrines of the sacral league, replaced the festivals of Israel's neighbors which celebrated creation and kingship. To be sure, Israel called upon mythic themes to adorn her historic traditions. A Divine Warrior is the hero of the epic. In late prophecy and apocalypse, these mythic elements reassert their power. However, the transformations of the epic themes — the New War of Yahweh, the New Exodus and Way through the Desert, and the Recreation of the People of the Covenant — while identified at times with a new creation and a new victory over cosmic enemies, nevertheless maintain the integrity of a faith rooted in historical memory and historical hope. Can the historian trace the causes for Israel's transformation of minor historical themes in older Near Eastern religion into the central and dominant concern of religious faith and practice?

Again, one reads the prophecies of Mesopotamian prophets with little excitement. Why in Israel did there arise a prophetic poetry of incomparable power, whether judged by ethical or literary standards? Why the prophet's obsession with the righteous law of God and its impingement on historical existence?

I am not sure that the historian can give fully satisfactory answers to these questions. Ultimate explanations of the creativity of Israel's past can be said to be hidden in the mystery of human freedom, and some would add, in the mystery of the freedom of God. Yet I believe that the historian, or the archaeologist and biblical scholar in tandem, are capable, now and in the future, of penetrating many mysteries and in understanding increasingly the religious and literary development which produced the Bible.

Two dynamic societies, Israel and Greece, rose from the ruins of the ancient Near Eastern world. Evidently the relatively static and hierarchical societies of the Fertile Crescent had grown old and moribund. Israel was born in an era of extraordinary chaos. It was the *nepotes* of the great earlier civilizations who survived to oppress Israel. In biblical terms: "the iniquity of the Amorites is not yet complete."

Often overlooked is an invention, a cultural tool, which came into full use in the course of Israel's early history, which would have enormous impact on the evolution of civilization. I speak of the use of alphabetic writing. Literacy spread like wildfire, and with it the democratization of higher culture. Most obviously alphabetic writing made possible an immediate expansion of possibilities for accumulating knowledge and widely dispersing it. It multiplied the sources of learning and literature and history.

Further, the new mode of writing ultimately gave rise to new modes of viewing culture and new ways of thinking. Writing froze oral communication and made it visible, so to speak, to be examined and re-examined at leisure. Alphabetic writing vastly facilitated such reflective scrutiny. A text could be deliberately studied and with such study arose new possibilities for critical and logical analysis. The elitist and frozen societies of the Near East gave way to new historical societies, alphabetic societies which reached their pinnacle in the ancient world in Israel and Greece:

egalitarian Israel and its prophetic critique of state and society, and democratic Greece with its gift to man of logic and skepticism.

In short one can find elements in the era of Israelite origins which provide an occasion for change, and the tools for transformation. Clients and serfs, slaves and the dispossessed, could rise up in the midst of a decaying society. The covenant forms of patriarchal religion anticipate to some degree the institutions of the nascent Israelite faith. I must confess, however, that I do not find such elements of *praeparatio* or evident readiness for change, sufficient explanation for the religious and cultural revolution that in fact occurred with the rise of Israelite religious and literary life.

More satisfying to me in some ways is a naive explanation: the events which created a confederation of Israelite tribes, and the interpretation of these events by priest and poet, precipitated a new vision of divine reality and historical destiny. In other words, historical memories, preserved in poetry and legend, beyond the historian's powers to reconstruct from traditional and mythologically shaped lore, played an important, if not decisive role in initiating Israel's preoccupation with the historical. I doubt that biblical archaeology can ever establish that the traditional events of Israel's early epic are historical, and certainly the archaeologist cannot prove these events were truly interpreted, even if established as historical. Israel uniquely was plunged into history, into a perennial grappling with history as the realm of meaning, and it would not be surprising, I think, if this plunge were precipitated by Israel's own particular historical experience. In any case, Israelite preoccupation with history has created a Western civilization imbued with a like historical consciousness. In this we are all sons of Israel, slaves delivered from Egypt.

Let me turn finally to some practical problems which exist as we view the present state of the disciplines of biblical and archaeological research, and the interpenetration of these two disciplines. I detect in contemporary biblical scholarship an increasing narrowing of interest and training which is tending to produce a generation of scholars who are restricted to biblical studies, unable or unwilling to do primary research in new fields opened up by burgeoning new data won by the spade and trowel. Many tend to rally to the defense of familiar, older views (e.g., neo-Wellhausenism in Germany), or to pursue literary theory or structuralist inquiries which, they suppose, free them from historical and philological tasks. Admittedly, the tools and languages required to control new written and unwritten monuments at first hand place a not inconsiderable burden on the biblical scholar. Furthermore, programs in universities which provide the necessary tools for the biblical scholar are rare and becoming rarer. In many countries, Oriental studies are split apart from biblical studies, even placed in separate faculties.

In turn, there is a comparable, although more defensible, effort on the part of young archaeologists to free themselves from the hegemony of biblical studies and Semitic philology. They seek autonomy from these older disciplines, and with autonomy, increased specialization and linkage with the sciences. This is proper, or in any case, inevitable. I do fear an excessive reaction against their roots and progenitors. I have heard scholars, including those trained at my university, claim that biblical archaeology is a tainted term, and even that William Foxwell Albright was not an archaeologist. I am reminded of the remark attributed to the logical positivist, Rudolph Carnap, that "Plato was not a philosopher." In any case I am troubled by the tendency of biblical (or whatever they call themselves) archaeologists to abandon historical and humanistic interests and goals in their research and in their teaching. One cannot fault the specialist in prehistoric archaeology for seeking to solve purely scientific problems. It is quite another matter for an archaeologist, digging in historical times, to reduce his concerns to the same scientific problems imposed by unhappy necessity on the prehistorian. In Isaiah Berlin's words, "to say of history that it should approximate to the condition of a science is to ask it to contradict its essence." Archaeologists digging in historical periods have a responsibility to remember and to serve the historical and humanistic disciplines as well as the scientific. To do less is to betray their professional calling.

Biblical Archaeology Today: The Historical Aspect

Benjamin Mazar

A SIGNIFICANT ASPECT of modern biblical archaeology revolves around the complex problems of the period extending from the thirteenth to the tenth centuries B.C.E., the period embodying the full realm of Israelite history: the formative stage of the occupation and settlement of Canaan; its zenith; and the eventual decline of the United Monarchy.

The great progress made in the fields of stratigraphic archaeological excavations, archaeological-ecological surveys, and epigraphic research, especially Egyptian, has fundamentally influenced inquiry into biblical historiography and, in particular, the attempt to identify authentic historical data. Consequently, a major aspiration is to arrive at a synthesis between the collection and interpretation of archaeological evidence — which is not usually unambiguous — and the construction of an historical picture based upon the methodical and critical interpretation of written sources, biblical and non-biblical, and the determination of their chronological setting.

In particular, we must give our attention to developments during the crucial period from the thirteenth to the twelfth centuries B.C.E., namely the transition from the Late Bronze to the Iron Age. During this period the Hittite Empire collapsed, and Egypt's domination in the province of Canaan declined. The stage was thus set for the influx of immigrants from the Hittite Empire into Canaan, for the increasingly massive infiltration of nomadic tribes from both east and south, and for the onset of the maritime migratory movement of various ethnic groups called "The Sea Peoples." The same period saw the decline in the close trade relations linking the Aegean, Cyprus and Canaan, as reflected in the disappearance of Mycenaean IIIB pottery. The archaeological evidence from this period reveals the destruction of important cities throughout the Land of Canaan, and subsequently, the attempt by Rameses III (in the second quarter of the twelfth century B.C.E.), apparently after his victory over a coalition of "Sea Peoples," to restore and strengthen his control in southwestern Canaan and along the Via Maris. Simultaneously, there is the onset of a dynamic process of settlement activity in the mountainous regions on both sides of the Jordan, a phenomenon evidenced in the character of the settlements, with their almost uniform autonomous ceramics and architecture. In the coastal region, we witness the appearance of the "Sea Peoples," at sites such as Ashdod and Ekron, by the initial appearance of monochrome Mycenaean IIIC:1 pottery of local manufacture, and subsequently, apparently already in the time of Rameses III, by the advent and spread of the bichrome Philistine pottery and the establishment of Philistine settlements like Tell Qasile on the northern bank of the Yarkon River.

The predominant documents for understanding this period are of course the so-called Israel Stele from the fifth year of Merneptah, and its supposedly fragmentary duplicate at the Amon temple in Karnak presenting a series of battle scenes attributed to the reign of Merneptah by both Yurko and Stager. According to the lowest chronological determination, reached by Wente and Van Siclen, they are dated to 1207 B.C.E. The "Israel Stele" records Merneptah's conquest of the three important cities, apparently listed in geographical order, Ashkelon, Gezer and Yenoʿam (probably Tell el-ʿAbeidiyeh in the Jordan Valley), and then the eradication of Israel, whose name is prefixed with the determinative signifying a people. It seems that the three city-states had established an alliance in the province of *Kanaan-Ḥuru* in cooperation with the people of Israel, and then revolted against Egypt. The Merneptah victory hymn implies that Israel was already a unified national body, most likely similar in organization to Moab and Edom, both of which also make their first appearance in Egyptian sources in the thirteenth century B.C.E. It must be taken into consideration that these are names of specific peoples, and are different from the more general terms like *ʿApiru*, *Shusu* and *Ḥuru*.

The attempt to track down biblical sources illuminating this period draws our attention to the saga presented in Genesis 31–35 and which was perhaps entitled "The *Toledot* of Jacob" (Genesis 37:2). It includes stories concerning his sojourn in Gilead, the Vale of Succoth, and subsequently the hill country of Shechem, and as far south as the area of Bethel. Of special interest are two aetiological stories: one about Penuel, where Jacob received his name Israel, and the other about Succoth, where he built himself a "house" (ויבן לו בית), most likely a shrine, perhaps identical with the Late Bronze sanctuary discovered at Tell Deir ʿAlla, which is for good reasons identified with Succoth. Several other biblical traditions are connected with obscure sites in this area, including Adam (Tell ed-Dāmiyeh), near Jisr ed-Dāmiyeh, one of the important fords of the Jordan. It was known as the site of the damming up of the Jordan above the place where the Israelites crossed the river (Joshua 3:16). Apparently, this is the place of the large altar which, according to the old tradition preserved in Joshua 22, was built by the tribes of Gilead on the eastern bank of the Jordan, presumably as an alternative to Shiloh in Cisjordan. It was probably an altar surrounded by a temenos, like the impressive open air cult place of the twelfth century B.C.E. which was recently discovered by A. Zertal on Mt. Ebal. Adam plays apparently a significant role in ancient Hebrew poetry as an Israelite sacred place: in

Psalm 68:19, in a victory song reminiscent of the song of Deborah, "Thou hast carried off captives (שבית שבי), and has taken tribute" (*laqaḥtā mattānōt*) in Adam (instead of "among men"); in Psalm 78:60, "He [the Lord] forsook his dwelling (*miškān*) at Shiloh, the tent where he dwelt (אהל שכן) in Adam." Finally, in Hosea 6:7–8, relating an old tradition based on an event connected with both Gilead and Shechem, "... at Adam they [probably the priests] transgressed the covenant" (*wᵉhēmmāh bᵉādām* — instead of *kᵉādām* — *ʿavᵉrū bᵉrīt*). All of these verses are fragments of early Hebrew poetic compositions which were preserved in anthologies like "The Book of Wars of the Lord"; they echo events of the early days of the Settlement and also deeds of charismatic heroes.

These obscure traditions are a source reflecting a period during which Israel — a confederation of pastoral tribes whose eponym was held to be Jacob — was concentrated in the Jordan Valley, particularly in the Vale of Succoth, and extended to Gilead in the east and to the hill country of Shechem in the west. It may be assumed that at this time the Israelite tribes maintained symbiotic relationships and covenant ties with Canaanite cities which were subdued by Merneptah.

It seems that up to the end of the thirteenth century B.C.E., the Israelites and associated groups were mainly seminomadic tent dwellers, whose livelihood was dependent on extensive herds of sheep and cattle as clearly described in the sagas of the Patriarchs. It was only gradually that they adapted to the conditions of a settled life in permanent villages, and to an agricultural economy combined with pasture. They spread over large areas — as far as Upper Galilee in the north and the northern Negev in the south — as evidenced by archaeological excavations and surveys. This development was certainly eventful and characterized by treaties and covenants with the neighbors, as well as by clashes, raids and wars with city-states, political coalitions and ethnic groups. These events play a significant role in the late historiographic strata which depict the conquest of Transjordan and Canaan as an organized, well-coordinated action linked with the famous figures of the nation, Moses and Joshua. What the reports on early events and episodes embedded in the literary sources reflect *historically* — and they are often clarified or complemented by archaeological data — is basically the conquest and occupation of individual cities over a long period during the thirteenth–eleventh centuries B.C.E. These include the conquest and violent destruction of Canaanite Hazor by Naphtali (Joshua 11:13); of Laish in the north by Dan (Judges 18:27, Joshua 19:47); of Hivite Shechem by the Josephite tribe of Manasseh (Judges 9:45); of Hittite Luz-Bethel in the center of the country by the Josephites (Judges 1:22–25); of Hittite Hebron by Caleb, and of Debir-Kiriath Sepher by Othniel the Kenizzite, who was related to Caleb, both being part of the larger unit of Judah in the south; and lastly, of Jebusite Jerusalem by King David.

The process of vigorous rural and urban development continued "from Dan unto Beer-Sheba" as well as in Transjordan up to the time of the United Kingdom. In spite of the influence of Canaanite civilization, and the relations with the Philistines, Israel did not lose its sense of national-religious destiny and traditional way of life and tribal organization.

Another problem arises in connection with the zenith and subsequent decline of the United Monarchy in the tenth century B.C.E. The archaeological evidence, the vast quantity of biblical material, and the geographical list of Pharaoh Shishak (ca. 925 B.C.E.) engraved on the southern wall of the temple of Amon in Karnak, converge into a unified picture presenting a period of extensive construction of royal citadels, fortified cities, Levitical towns, and a variety of villages, especially along the main roads. The evidence also reflects an increase in population and widespread urban development in Israel during the United Monarchy. The destruction of cities by Shishak has also been confirmed in certain archaeological excavations such as Taanach, Megiddo, Yoqneʿam, Gezer, Tell Qasile and Tel Gerisa, as well as in archaeological surveys.

A significant fact is that the cities, including Succoth, Penuel, Mahanaim, Zarethan and Adam in the Vale of Succoth, were destroyed by Shishak's army and presumably remained deserted for many generations thereafter. Archaeological surveys and excavations also confirm the widespread destruction of settlements in the Negev, including seven forts (*ḥagarīm*), several cities, and a considerable number of camps and villages of semisedentary Negebite clans mentioned in the Shishak inscription, as well as settlements known from genealogical and geographical lists in Joshua and Chronicles.

Finally, I would like to support the universally accepted hypothesis that the biblical historiographic sources concerning this period and the contemporary archaeological evidence can be integrated, and do compliment each other. Nonetheless, we have to take into consideration the challenges of critical analysis and the complexity of the historical interpretation of abundant and heterogeneous material, and also to continuously revise accepted ideas.

About forty years ago, W.F. Albright, in his book *Archaeology and the Religion of Israel*, summarized his view on Near Eastern archaeology as follows:

> The material is so vast and its interpretation so far from being complete, that we have to exercise caution in selecting our data. Moreover, we have only grazed the surface of the available sources, both written and unwritten.

This statement is still valid today.

Select Bibliography

Aharoni, Y. *The Land of the Bible*, Part 2:II–III. 2d ed. Philadelphia, 1979.

Albright, W.F. *Archaeology and the Religion of Israel.* Baltimore, 1942.

——. *Archaeology, Historical Analogy and Early Biblical Tradition.* Baton Rouge, 1966.

Cohen, R. "The Iron Age Fortresses in the Central Negev." *BASOR* 236 (1981).

Dever, W.G. "Monumental Architecture in Ancient Israel in the Period of the United Monarchy." In

Studies in the Period of David and Solomon, edited by Tomoo Ishida. Tokyo, 1982.

Dornemann, R.H. "The Beginning of the Iron Age in Transjordan." In *Studies in the History and Archaeology of Jordan*, I, edited by A. Hadidi. Amman, 1982.

Dothan, Trude. *The Philistines and Their Material Culture.* Jerusalem, 1982.

——. "Some Aspects of the Appearance of the Sea Peoples." In *Griechenland, Die Agäis und die Levante während der "Dark Ages."* Vienna, 1983.

Goitein, S.D. "The City Adam in the Book of Psalms?" *Yedioth* 13 (1947).

Helck, W., Otten, H. und Bittel, K. "Geschichte des 13. und 12. Jahrh. v. Chr." In *Jahrbericht des Instituts für Vorgeschichte.* Frankfurt, 1976.

Kitchen, K.A. *The Third Intermediate Period in Egypt*, Parts 4 and 5E. Oxford, 1973.

Malamat, A. "The Monarchy of David and Solomon." In *Recent Archaeology in the Land of Israel*, edited by H. Shanks and B. Mazar. Washington: Biblical Archaeology Society; Jerusalem: Israel Exploration Society, 1984.

Mazar, A. *Excavations at Tell Qasile I, Qedem* 12 (1980).

Mazar, B. "The Campaign of Pharao Shishak to Palestine." *VT Suppl.* 4 (1957).

——. "The Historical Background of Genesis." *JNES* 28 (1969).

——. "The Early Israelite Settlement in the Hill Country." *BASOR* 241 (1982).

Sherrat, E.S. *The Pottery of Late Helladic IIIC and Its Significance.* Oxford, 1981.

Soggin, J.A. "The Davidic-Solomonic Kingdom." In *Israelite and Judaean History*, edited by J.H. Hayes and J.M. Miller. London, 1977.

Stager, L.E. "Merenptah, Israel, and Sea Peoples: New Light on an Old Relief." *EI* 18 (in press).

Strobel, A. *Der Spätbronzezeitliche Seevölkersturm.* 1976.

Tadmor, H., Weippert, M., Yadin, Y. and Dothan, M. In *Symposia, Celebrating the 75th Anniversary of the ASOR*, edited by F.M. Cross. Cambridge, Mass., 1979.

de Vaux, R. *Histoire ancienne d'Israel*, troisieme partie. Paris, 1971.

Weinstein, J.A. "The Egyptian Empire in Palestine: A Reassessment." *BASOR* 241 (1982).

Wente, E.F. and Van Siclen III, C.C. "A Chronology of the New Kingdom." In *Studies in Honor of George Hughes. SAOC* 39 (1976).

Yadin, Y. *Hazor, the Head of All Those Kingdoms.* London, 1972.

Yeivin, S. *The Israelite Conquest of Canaan.* Istanbul, 1971.

Yurco, F. *Mernephtah's Palestinian Campaign. SSE Journal* 8 (1978).

Biblical Archaeology Today: The Archaeological Aspect

Yigael Yadin

IT IS WITH AWE that I stand here to address this most important gathering of scholars in biblical archaeology. My shield is that tonight there are no respondents.

I am faced by a dilemma — whether to preach to the converted, to repeat commonplace facts, or to counterattack the politically motivated objections to "biblical" archaeology, or to stick my neck out and argue against the views of esteemed colleagues who also — but for legitimate reasons (although wrong, in my opinion) — would like to remove biblical archaeology from the academic disciplines; or whether I should use this opportunity to present my own views on specific archaeological and biblical problems. I shall succumb to all, to some briefly and to others in more detail.

The politically motivated objections are undisguised and perhaps should not even be mentioned here — were it not for the fact that they have recently infringed upon and curtailed scientific freedom, the *sine qua non* of our scholarly existence. As an archaeologist, I would like to call a spade a spade, and not only use it manually. However, since this paper is being presented at a scientific congress, this subject should be deferred for some other, more suitable forum.

More serious and more legitimate are the objections to biblical archaeology as a scientific discipline by some of our own colleagues. This, then, is our main concern. We are concerned, because these objections derive from persons who themselves in the past have contributed, often brilliantly — willingly or not — to this branch of research, and they now seem to be cutting off the very branch they were sitting on. I believe the main reason for these objections is embedded, strange as it may seem, in a basic misconception of what biblical archaeology is.

Biblical archaeology is sometimes portrayed as an antithesis of modern, advanced methods in field archaeology or of the interdisciplinary utilization of other sciences. This is of course wrong, for all these are the very basis of advanced research today, and biblical archaeology is abreast in this respect. Egyptology, Assyriology and classical archaeology are not the "pure" archaeology of Egypt, Iraq or Greece, respectively; they are disciplines integrating numerous means of research to attain the true goal of archaeology — the understanding of human mental activity in the past as crystallized in material remains and in its proper chronological sequence.

Therefore, biblical archaeology is not just a dialogue between experts in various disciplines. It is a branch of research in which any scholar engaged in the study of the past of the Land of Israel and its neighbors must be trained — if he or she is to perform the task properly and creatively, and not merely in a technical manner.

Today's scholar not only has a need for some degree of training in the tangent subjects of sociology, environmental studies, anthropology and geology — all hallmarks of up-to-date methods in archaeology — but must equally have a grounding in various other disciplines besides his own main specialization, all cognate to the main objectives, as shown by Prof. Cross and Prof. Mazar. Without such training, one is not capable of evaluating the various schools of thought in these ancillary disciplines.

With this in mind, I shall try to express my views as an archaeologist on the nature of biblical archaeology by means of definitions and examples of heuristic problems.

The nature and scope of biblical archaeology can best be illustrated by two sets of concentric circles, one geographical and the other chronological. The innermost geographical circle is the Land of Israel in its biblical connotation. It is clear that for certain periods (included in the innermost chronological circle to be discussed below), the main written source for the understanding of the religious, social and archaeological aspects of this land is the Bible. This will be best illustrated in the second session of this Congress, "The Israelite Settlement in Canaan — A Case Study." Three or four diametrically opposed and exclusive schools of thought will be presented and discussed, and only one of them (if any!) is correct. Some scholars totally negate the historiography of the biblical narrative of this episode. Some are not entirely free from presenting their views in a histrionic (nay, hysterical) rather than historical manner. Yet remove the Bible as the common denominator unifying these approaches and the entire edifice collapses — or could not even have come into being. This theme, therefore, based on the Bible and treated with the aid of archaeology, history, epigraphy and a host of supporting disciplines, is a superb, exciting case in point.

Yet, all the king's horses (including the archaeological horse I ride on) and all the king's men cannot give definite answers to the vital questions on how and precisely when the episode took place, and who brought it about. All we can say is that we are all convinced that it did take place. Nevertheless, three undeniable archaeological facts, already pointed out by Prof. Mazar, must be taken into account and not sidestepped:

1. All Late Bronze Age cities excavated to date came to a sudden end. In many cases they were burnt. True, we are not yet able to determine the exact dates or the identity of the destroyers, but we would not be too far off the mark if we were to say that this cataclysm occurred during the second half of the thirteenth century B.C.E.,

and that the sacking was carried out by the Egyptians, the Sea Peoples and Israelite tribes. In this connection, I believe that it is wrong to speak of an uninterrupted continuation of Canaanite culture from the Late Bronze Age into the early Iron Age at such cities as Megiddo, Beth-Shean, Lachish and others. What is relevant, foremost, is that at all of these sites, the last Late Bronze Age city was destroyed and then rebuilt by another factor. This is seen in Megiddo Stratum VIIB, Beth-Shean VII and, I believe, Lachish VII, separated from the subsequent post-Fosse Temple III (typified by Mycenaean IIIB ware) Level VI by a stratum of a temporary settlement with pits.

This destruction is an undeniable fact. It is true that at some sites, particularly those rebuilt — yes, rebuilt! — by Ramesses III, non-Israelite settlements are subsequently evident. But this leads to the second archaeological fact I wish to discuss.

2. The earliest Israelite settlements discovered date from the beginning of the Iron Age. Credit for revealing this stage, which is becoming more and more clear, is due to Albright, followed by the important survey work of Aharoni and, more recently, Kochavi, A. Mazar, Finkelstein, Zertal and others. All efforts to fix the date of these settlements within the accepted chronological framework of the Late Bronze Age so as to conform with certain theories, have failed. So far, not even one such site has been found with proper Late Bronze Age pottery, let alone the associated imported wares (such as Mycenaean IIIB or the Cypriote White Slip II and Base-Ring II wares). A single, isolated dubious scarab might at best indicate a *post-quem* date.

How can we explain these facts? This is surely the crux of the problem, and is a topic much to be discussed at this Congress. Since the Albright School, to which, by and large, I have the honor to subscribe, is not represented in the opening lectures on the subject, I shall take this opportunity to say a word or two on its behalf.

The Alt School sees in these remains the settlements of herdsmen originally coming from the desert and after a phase of coexistence with the urban Canaanite population — the famous "peaceful penetration" of Alt. This would be regarded as a negation of the Mendenhall–Gottwald sociological school of thought. Gottwald in the abstract of his paper to be presented here claims the opposite: "Bible and archaeology attest that the principal mode of production was crop cultivation, with secondary modes of production in animal husbandry.... Within the animal husbandry component, pastoral nomadism was a negligible mode of life for Israelites and for proto-Israelites."

The "conquest" or "destruction-first-and-settlement-later" school — not the "fundamentalist school," as it is sometimes wrongly labelled — could sit tight and utter: "Both are right in negating each other." But, more seriously, this school would point out, *inter alia*, the following, amazing facts.

Foremost, the Canaan which ceased to exist at the end of the Late Bronze Age was not as impregnable as previously imagined, a concept which misled many scholars into negating the ability of nomads to conquer the Canaanite cities. As already noted (at the Congress honoring the 75th anniversary of the American Schools of Oriental Research), Canaan in the days of the Egyptian New Kingdom was not strongly fortified. This was against the interests of the Egyptian overlords (as was also the case under the Twelfth Dynasty). The Egyptians either prevented the erection of new fortifications or, as their reliefs attest, they destroyed many existing ones. Scholars have been looking for Late Bronze Age city walls at Jericho in vain, since all the Late Bronze Age inhabitants had to protect them were the dilapidated fortifications of the Middle Bronze Age. This fact became a *cause celebre* against the "conquest" school. But where are the newly built Late Bronze Age city walls at Hazor? Where are those of Megiddo? And now it appears that the great city of Lachish was not refortified in the Late Bronze Age, but relied on the Middle Bronze Age glacis for its defense. Decaying Canaan of the Late Bronze Age, as revealed already in the Amarna Age, was relatively easy prey for the highly motivated and daring tribes penetrating the country. These attacks could be called *razzias*, if you wish — it sounds more romantic to the Western ear — but the traditional, social and economic ways of the Israelite tribes would have precluded their immediate resettling and rebuilding the cities. The conquest could have been swift, but the settlement process was a long one.

Finally, where are the contemporaneous Israelite remains of the Late Bronze Age required to support some of the other theories? They simply do not exist. This is a heuristic question, but again, without the Bible and the approach of biblical archaeology, it would never even have been raised.

Let us now turn to several "positive" cases concerning which there appears to be a more general consensus of opinion among scholars. The first instance which naturally comes to my mind is that of the Solomonic city gates and casemate walls of Hazor, Megiddo and Gezer. These discoveries without the Bible would have remained merely an interesting typological phenomenon with certain chronological value. In the context of biblical archaeology, however, they involve three further points of interest: (1) Solomon, a biblical personality who is not mentioned in any contemporaneous external source — and therefore a "candidate" for treatment as a myth — becomes an archaeological and historical reality; (2) these three cities — Hazor, Megiddo and Gezer — are now placed in their proper military, administrative and economic *Sitz-im-Leben*, and thus can serve as a firm chronological basis for dating both earlier and later strata at other sites; (3) an interesting point for the Bible scholar: at Hazor and Megiddo, at least, the Solomonic cities were covered and replaced in the ninth century B.C.E., thus shedding significant light on the date of the sources of 1 Kings. This and Shishak's invasion (discussed here by B. Mazar) were the only two clear-cut cases during the periods of the United and early Divided Monarchy. Now, of course, we can add to these the important discoveries made by A. Biran at Iron Age Dan. Here again, were it not for the advanced methods of biblical archaeology, one of the most important Israelite cult places would never have been revealed — let alone interpreted properly, at best as far as its true function and nature are concerned. Jeroboam's city and fortifications at Dan could be dated only through a combination of true field archaeology and the biblical data — pottery, stratigraphy and scripture. Otherwise, an earlier date, or a later one, would most probably have been suggested.

Another good example I wish to cite is the well-known controversy surrounding the dating of Lachish stratum III and the *lamelekh* jars. For nearly forty years, a scholarly battle over Lachish, nearly as fierce as that in 701 B.C.E., has continued to rage: Was stratum III destroyed by Sennacherib, or later? All the tools of biblical archaeology have been brought to bear on this question —pottery, stratigraphy and, above all, the textual evidence, biblical and cuneiform, supplemented by the famous reliefs from Sennacherib's palace. Now at long last, the question seems to have been settled as a result of the patient, methodical work of Ussishkin at this site. Finally we have a firm index for determining the "before and after" in Judah in all aspects of material culture. The date of the *lamelekh* jars — one of the most important and elusive discoveries of the Monarchy period — has now been clarified: both types (four-winged and two-winged) were produced prior to 701 B.C.E.; they were most probably used for food storage in the fortified cities in anticipation of sieges, as has previously been suggested. And as would appear from the meager finds from other sites of a later period, some of the remaining stock of jars was "reissued" under Manasseh, and only replaced by the rosette and two-triangle type jars, under Josiah. Yet many questions regarding Lachish still remain unanswered. The main questions concern the existence at the same time of two royal emblems and whether or not the gate of Stratum IV was built by Rehoboam. These problems with all their implications are a formidable and inviting challenge to meet.

Within the innermost geographical circle, the destruction wrought on Judah by Sennacherib in 701 B.C.E., and the total destruction inflicted by Nebuchadnezzar in 586 B.C.E. have left a traumatic imprint upon archaeologists. It has long been the fashion to ascribe any destruction in Judah during the latter part of the Monarchy to either Sennacherib or Nebuchadnezzar, that is, to either 701 B.C.E. or 586 B.C.E. Thus, the crucial reigns of Manasseh — the "Queen Victoria" of ancient Israel, who ruled for nearly sixty years—and of Josiah were, archaeologically speaking, practically nonexistent.

The period of the great campaigns of Esarhaddon and Assurbanipal to Egypt through Judah and Philistia, and the countermoves of Psamtik I, Necho I and Psamtik II were hardly noted in the field of archaeology. Furthermore, the clear biblical references to the fortifications of Manasseh and to Josiah's expansion and cultic reform have, with few exceptions, also largely been ignored. And suddenly, we find ourselves facing a paradox —a nearly nonexistent Judah between 701 and 586 B.C.E. As a result of this discrepancy, perhaps the greatest discovery of recent years has gone unnoticed. I refer to the extensive work carried out in the Negev and in southern Judah which has revealed —much to the astonishment of the excavators —that chief cities were actually built and fortified after 701 B.C.E., and that cities which had been lying in ruins for years were rebuilt during the seventh century B.C.E. This was found to be the case not only at ʿAroʿer, Tel ʿIra, Ḥorvat ʿUza, En-Gedi and Meṣad Ḥashvyahu, but also at such previously existing cities or forts as Beer-Sheba, Ashdod, Tell Malḥata, Kadesh-Barnea, Tel Seraʿ, Tel Gamma, Tell el-Ḥesi and, of course, Lachish — as well as others.

Moreover, at many of the above-mentioned sites two building phases were discerned within the seventh century B.C.E., the second of which did not always follow a total destruction. Today we possess the archaeological means to date fairly accurately the various stages of the seventh and sixth centuries B.C.E. The Assyrian Palace Ware, the eastern Greek pottery and the engraved tridacna shells (most probably used by Aegean mercenaries) are all from around 630–600 B.C.E.; local ware, including the distinguishing pointed base store–jars (some marked with the two triangles), long known at Beer-Sheba and Lachish, can now, following Oren's excavations at Tel Seraʿ and recently at Tell Abu Hureira, be assigned to the late seventh century; Edomite pottery and inscribed or marked weights are also of aid in resurrecting the Judah of Manasseh to Josiah, that is, of the seventh century B.C.E.

In a study which I have recently published jointly with Shulamit Geva, a new evaluation of seventh century B.C.E. Judah is proposed, dividing the period archaeologically into four phases: the early reign of Manasseh; the later part of his reign; the reign of Josiah; and the end of the seventh century and the very beginning of the sixth century B.C.E. This scheme is also of importance for the dating of Joshua 15.

I turn now to the outer geographical circle. The Land of Israel was a bridge or corridor between the great empires of the ancient Near East — a meeting point for the Mediterranean cultures and an emporium for their goods. It was a battlefield, one of the bloodiest in all antiquity. With the advent of the Sea Peoples, the Aegean cultures were introduced. Thus the past of this land cannot be studied scientifically without recourse to data from other lands on every flank. The archaeologist here, whatever his field of specialization, must muster — yes, muster! — the archaeology of one or more of the neighboring lands, as well as other disciplines relating to them.

This is the proper moment to refute another mistaken notion — one which would blend Israel (or Palestine) into the archaeology of Syria in its broadest sense. What may possibly have been right in Albright's heyday is no longer valid. All we have noted above clearly shows that the archaeology of Syria has little if any bearing on the crucial periods in the Land of Israel. Take, for example, the beginning of the Early Bronze Age. Some thirty years ago, it was first suggested that the initial massive penetration by Egypt into Canaan was carried out under Narmer and his successors. Subsequently, this concept has found support in the numerous inscribed jars bearing this royal name discovered in Early Bronze Age contexts, together with much daily ware of Egyptian origin, a clear indication, in my opinion, of Egyptian sovereignty. Today, no archaeology student can obtain a degree without having acquired a proper knowledge of Egyptian pottery of that period, as reflected in Ruth Amiran's "textbook" on pottery. From the scientific point of view, Syria was of secondary importance in the Early Bronze Age, and this is true of other periods as well, such as during the advent of the Philistines and during the Iron Age in general. Even for various phases of the Middle Bronze Age, it is not specifically to Syria that we turn for enlightenment. Reference can be made to the "Archaeology of the Levant," as is fashionable lately, but we should not be compelled to discover that in a book's index, Hazor, Megiddo or Lachish are listed under "Southern Levant!"

Let me now turn to the chronological set of concentric circles, and attempt to explain why it is legitimate to include the Early Bronze Age, and even earlier periods

— more or less "From Stone Age to Christianity," as one noted scholar has put it — within the framework of biblical archaeology.

A central, but still enigmatic problem in biblical archaeology is the so-called period of the Patriarchs (which B. Mazar touched upon). What better illustration of the problem can be found than the fact that scholars variously ascribe this period to MB I (or now with Ebla, even to the Early Bronze Age), to MB II and even to the Late Bronze Age. This broad range, and the absence of solid archaeological data, precludes even a brief discussion here, but whether or not the MB I is regarded as a continuation of the Early Bronze Age or as an independent, intermediate period, every archaeologist knows that it cannot be treated properly without a study of the Early Bronze Age, etc. Thus, not only is it legitimate to include these "pre-biblical" periods within the scope of biblical archaeology — it is imperative!

SESSION II

ARCHAEOLOGY, HISTORY AND BIBLE
THE ISRAELITE SETTLEMENT IN CANAAN: A CASE STUDY

DAVID N. FREEDMAN, Session Chairman, *The University of Michigan*

NORMAN K. GOTTWALD, *New York Theological Seminary*
The Israelite Settlement as a Social Revolutionary Movement
SIEGFRIED HERRMANN, *Ruhr-Universität Bochum*
Basic Factors of Israelite Settlement in Canaan
MOSHE KOCHAVI, *Tel Aviv University*
The Israelite Settlement in Canaan in the Light of Archaeological Surveys
AMIHAI MAZAR, *The Hebrew University of Jerusalem*
The Israelite Settlement in Canaan in the Light of Archaeological Excavations

Respondents

JOSEPH A. CALLAWAY, *Southern Baptist Theological Seminary, Louisville*
RUDOLF COHEN, *Israel Department of Antiquities and Museums*
ISRAEL FINKELSTEIN, *Bar-Ilan University*
LAWRENCE E. STAGER, *The University of Chicago*
MATITIAHU TSEVAT, *Hebrew Union College–Jewish Institute of Religion*

Discussion

The Chairman's Introduction

David Noel Freedman

On the basis of a growing body of data derived from numerous excavations conducted at a variety of sites on both sides of the Jordan River, and in the territory generally claimed for Israel in the Bible, a pattern and a picture of new settlement during the first phase of Iron Age I have emerged. These settlements share important common features: size and general plan; major installations and structures, as well as private dwellings; and objects and implements, whether tools or weapons, and above all pottery. While specific identification and direct evidence are so far lacking, there can be little doubt that these sites represent and reflect the Israelite Settlement in the Holy Land, beginning some time in the early phase of Iron Age I, presumably during the twelfth century B.C.E.

There is a striking contrast between these new settlements and those of the previous period (LB II); clearly a new element has entered the picture, that we can identify with the Israelites as opposed to the older population, which can be called Canaanite. At the same time, we must exercise caution in speaking of certain kinds of houses and pottery as Israelite, since these types were not limited to the Israelite areas of occupation nor to the Israelites only. We may agree that by the end of the twelfth century B.C.E., Israel was settled in various areas on both sides of the Jordan corresponding to the scriptural accounts, especially in the mountain country of the west bank (Ephraim and Manasseh in the north and Judah in the south), and on the plateaus of Gilead and Bashan on the east bank (that is, the territories of Reuben, Gad, and the other part of Manasseh).

There is considerably less agreement about the manner of the Settlement and the date of its initial stages. Any discussion of the Conquest, if that is what it was, brings with it the debate over the Exodus and the Wanderings and their historicity and chronology. It is clear that many of the cities of Canaan suffered severe damage if not total destruction at the hands of a variety of enemies during the last phase of the Late Bronze Age (roughly the last half of the thirteenth century B.C.E.). The number of possible perpetrators of these disasters, aside from the Israelites, is considerable: the Egyptians, Sea Peoples of different kinds including the Philistines, and other marauders from the eastern perimeter. It is difficult even under optimum conditions to pinpoint the destroying forces, and knowledge of the circumstances of these destructions, some involving the same cities over a relatively brief span of time, leaves much to be desired. In a substantial number of cases, no final and uncontested verdict has been or is likely to be reached. There is a good reason to believe that different cities were captured by different groups, and that there is no single or simple answer to the question of the urban devastation of Canaan in the thirteenth century B.C.E.

The chief positive conclusion that can be drawn from the welter of data is that the Israelite movement, which resulted in the Settlement in Canaan, was part of the general upheaval throughout the eastern Mediterranean, recorded in contemporary sources and widely attested by archaeological excavations. The changes were dramatic and drastic, and the new Israelite Settlement was one of a number characterizing the emerging order of things and state of affairs in the area. Almost at the same time as the appearance of Israel as a national entity, we have the settlement of the Philistines in the southwestern territory of Canaan, while the Arameans were taking firm hold in the northeastern regions, formerly part of the Hittite domain (cf. Amos 9:7, where the prophet compares the movements of the three peoples and implies that they were contemporaneous). Edom and Moab had already established states on the east bank, but not long before.

To what extent was the Israelite influx into and settlement of the new territories the result of military invasion, and to what extent was it a peaceful penetration? The answer may never be known with any certainty, but probably it will not lie in an absolute choice between the alternatives, but in a combination of both kinds of activity. It seems clear that Israel itself consisted of an amalgamation or congeries of groups, including those connected by blood ties and those who were attracted by the appeal of a new or radically reformed religion. In time, blood ties would be extended to include all the groups. No doubt also, while there must have been a core group of the faithful led by Moses out of Egypt, there must have been many others claiming descent from the Fathers, who remained in Canaan and joined their relatives at different stages or places in the course of movement from Egypt and Settlement in Canaan.

These developments, from the oppression in Egypt until the Settlement in the Land of Canaan, can be dated with considerable confidence to the period of the Nineteenth and Twentieth Dynasties of Egypt, or more particularly, from the time of Rameses II (ca. 1281–1215 B.C.E.) until that of Rameses III (1175–1144 B.C.E.) and his ephemeral successors. Of critical importance for historical determination and reconstruction is the well-known Merenptah Stele (ca. 1208 B.C.E.), which contains the one and only specific mention of Israel in ancient Egyptian records, and its first attestation in extra-biblical sources. The presence of a people bearing this name in the Land of Canaan toward the end of the thirteenth century B.C.E. is the pivot on which any and all theories of Israelite Settlement must hinge, as well as those concerning the Exodus and Wanderings. Doubtless, more information will be gleaned from time to time as the result of chance finds and controlled digging. Continuing and future excavations will fill in the picture of Settlement of the twelfth century B.C.E. along with the background and framework of destruction and devastation in the transition period from the Late Bronze to the early Iron Age.

Hand in hand with archaeological excavation will go biblical research. The latter is as indispensable as the former for a proper analysis and reconstruction of Israel's historical experience. Since different types of data are involved, different principles and methods of investigation and evaluation must be employed. The results obtained from the one source are no less significant than those from the other. I especially wish to emphasize the importance of the old traditions of Israel incorporated into the basic narrative of the Primary History, that is, the Books of Genesis through Kings, which contains the essential facts of its existence. While they were written down at a later time, and over the years were modified and adapted to suit contemporary interests and serve contemporary purposes, they contain a solid core of valid information handed down from earliest times, and should be accepted as substantially true. What has been said of the surviving prose materials is even more emphatically true for the old poetry now embedded in the same primary narrative. Much of it is a product of the earliest period of Israel's history, the same early Iron Age I of the Settlement in Canaan. Furthermore, there is good reason to believe that these poems, such as the Song of the Sea (Exodus 15), the Song of Deborah (Judges 5), the Blessing of Jacob (Genesis 49), and of Moses (Deuteronomy 33), and the Oracles of Balaam (Numbers 23–24), have been preserved practically unchanged in the Hebrew Bible. These, therefore, should be regarded as artifacts of the period of the Settlement as much as the four-room houses or collared-rim jars of the excavated sites.

Only by a judicious comparison and combination of strictly archaeological data with the results of biblical research, can we hope to recover the basic information we need to reconstruct the story of Israel's beginnings. If we dare to predict, the resultant picture will correspond in the main to the oldest biblical materials we have, while there may well be considerable shifting of details. Archaeological evidence should support the broad features, while modifying many of the particulars and making them more precise. There always remains the possibility of some sensational discovery which will tell us things we never imagined, settle long-standing controversies, open up new areas of investigation and inquiry in addition to raising new problems leading to new controversies. What could be better than that?

The Israelite Settlement as a Social Revolutionary Movement

Norman K. Gottwald

EVERY ACCOUNT OF *how* Israel "settled" in Canaan implicitly presupposes a view of *who* those first Israelites were, assigning them one or another identity, whether ethnic, socioeconomic, cultural, religious, or national.

There are four kinds of evidence pertinent to this inquiry: 1) the Hebrew Bible; 2) extra-biblical texts and inscriptions; 3) archaeological material remains; and 4) historical and comparative studies from the social sciences. The Bible is the primary source, for which extra-biblical texts provide a valuable supplement and balance. As we must work "backwards" through biblical texts with later overlays of interpretation, it is necessary to employ genre criticism, tradition-historical criticism, redaction criticism, and canonical criticism as well as the customary forms of older historical-literary criticism.

Data and theories from the social sciences can suggest illuminating controlled comparisons between Israel and other peoples in proportion to the exactness and completeness of our knowledge of early Israelite society. Archaeology's contribution to the partnership of disciplines necessary to unravel Israel's origins is to provide a material and sociocultural profile of the thirteenth to eleventh centuries B.C.E. Israelites, which can set parameters for reading the texts, and offer pointers to fertile analogies from the social sciences. The outlines of this long-needed cultural inventory are beginning to take shape as a result of the area surveys in the Upper Galilee, Judah, Samaria, Golan, and the Negev, together with the Iron Age I excavations at sites such as Sasa, Har Adir, Ḥorvat ʿAvot, Tell Qiri, ʿIzbet Ṣarṭah, ʿAi, Khirbet Raddana, Giloh, Tel Masos, and Tel Esdar. It should also be stressed that a broad knowledge of potentially comparable societies, and in particular the expression of social behavior in texts and material remains, will help us to avoid sociocultural misreadings of Israelite evidence which result in false leads and costly detours.

As my contribution to the Congress, I wish to highlight the role of social explanatory models, and some of their implications for the interpretation of archaeological evidence and perhaps for the shaping of strategies in the archaeological enterprise itself. I speak here not as an archaeologist, but as a biblical historian, indebted to archaeology as an indispensable source for the historical task. As one who is committed to the development of a social history of ancient Israel, I seek the light that archaeology can shed on social function and social process in earliest Israel.

My presentation is divided into three parts: 1) a statement of the heuristic questions that guide the inquiry into Israelite origins, together with provisional answers to these questions; 2) a sketch of the theoretical models from the social sciences that appear at present most appropriate for explaining Israelite origins; and 3) a reflection on how archaeology's contribution can best be interpreted and strengthened in the light of unreflected social presuppositions or more explicit social models entertained by scholars.

Heuristic Questions about Israelite Origins

These probative questions are addressed to all classes of evidence available. Each can be considered separately, but they form an integral set of issues which must be pursued in its many-sidedness before a plausible overall picture of how Israel began can be conceived. Here I give only a major outline of provisional "answers"; detailed argumentation can be found in *The Tribes of Yahweh* and other essays.[1]

What was the date of Israel's formation?
Israel took shape as an historically visible group in the period 1250–1150 B.C.E.

Where did Israel's formation occur?
The overwhelmingly attested immediate point of origin of the Israelites was in Canaan proper. Among these Canaan-based Israelites, there were traditions of extra-Canaanite origins or ventures which were part of the prehistories of subgroups in Israel and are of questionable historical credibility. The most prominent of these traditions, witnessing to the enslavement of Israelites in Egypt, also claims, however, that the earlier home of this enslaved group was in Canaan.

Did Israel have previous cohesive identity as a people prior to its confederation in Canaan?
The marks of a preconfederate or proto-Israelite identity, as expressed in the ancestor and Exodus-wilderness sagas, strictly concern only the identities of subgroups. Some of these identities may have been significant points of crystallization for the Israelite confederacy, but the peoplehood of Israel took form only as the Israelites came to power in the Land of Canaan. Accordingly, a recasting of our terminology for early Israel and its forerunners and subgroups is advisable.[2]

Can the historical steps in the formation of Israel in Canaan be reconstructed?
There is an indeterminate measure of historical plausibility in the biblical report that Israelites migrated from Egypt to Canaan. However, this saga-based evidence speaks only about a fraction of the full membership of Israelite society. How the entrance of this group to Canaan should be related to the histories of other subgroups in Israel is highly conjectural. None of the several reconstructions of the Settlement history passes beyond possibility. There is some reason to believe that an earlier, smaller Israelite association, perhaps of El-worshipping peoples, existed in Canaan prior to the entrance of the group from Egypt, and before an expanded reconstitution of the Israelite confederation.[3]

What was the dominant mode of production among the first Israelites?
The Bible and archaeology attest that the primary mode of production was crop cultivation, with secondary modes in animal husbandry and handcrafts. Within the animal husbandry component, pastoral nomadism was a negligible means of livelihood for Israelites as a whole, although it may have been the principal mode of production for certain small subgroups in the Israelite confederacy.

What was the social organization of the first Israelites?
Israelites comprised a coalition of village-based "tribes," with tendencies toward chiefdom. This coalition functioned to retain agrarian and pastoral surpluses in the hands of the cultivators and breeders in accordance with rough egalitarian principles.[4] Whether the family units were nuclear or extended, or some mixture of the two, is disputed. The amphictyonic analogy for this confederation is misconceived, not only in the detailed structural comparisons, but, even more seriously, in the analogy's overconcentration on religious unity to the neglect of a sufficient explanation of the sociopolitical and cultural basis of the Israelite people.

What was the stance or orientation of these first Israelites toward other inhabitants of Canaan?
The expressed Israelite opposition to Canaanites was not at the first based on territorial claims to Canaanite lands. Nor was it founded upon a preestablished Israelite ethnic identity that ruled out cooperation or merger *a priori* with all those who did not share it by birth or by a single common history. Impressions of territorial disputes and enmity based on nationality are the result of late redactional perspectives during the monarchy and exile. In the oldest sources, the Israelite quarrel with local inhabitants was a matter of outright rejection of the agrarian tributary system by which city-state apparatuses exacted taxes of compulsory labor, military service and in kind from their peasant subjects.[5]

The line of hostility and group division between Israelites and their enemies was a sharp cleavage between two forms of political economy that could not coexist. Military, ethnic, cultural, and religious divisions and clashes followed along the lines of this rupture. Apart from the issue of political economy and its attendant religious ideology, Israelites showed an extensive range of participation in Canaanite culture, and varying types of interaction and collaboration with Canaanites. The logical construction to be placed upon this social reality is that Israelites were themselves Canaanites, in the sense that they were those inhabitants of the land who took part in a broad-based movement from the underside of society, or from outside the circles of power, in order to create a new society and another type of power arrangement.

By which specific means did Israel come to power and gain self-identity and recognition by others? The Israelite popular movement used at least the following seven means of self-formation: 1) military and paramilitary actions; 2) propaganda, agitation, and psychological warfare; 3) treaty-making and intermarriage; 4) population growth; 5) cultivation of old and new lands with an adaptive technology and cooperative communal efforts; 6) mutual aid among tribes and tribal subsections; 7) development of a new culture and religion that fostered free agrarian institutions and reinforcing ideology.

Social Explanatory Models of Early Israel

On what explanatory lines should we conceptualize this Israelite movement? Are there tenable bodies of sociological and anthropological theory, which enable us to visualize and productively research this comprehensive, popular, eclectic, socially disruptive, inner-Canaanite movement, which managed to construct a new free agrarian formation involving mode of production, social organization, culture and religion? Four theoretical models, offering abundant sociohistorical comparative materials, seem especially appropriate.

Peasant rebellion

Earliest Israel shows many signs of having arisen through a series of peasant rebellions which united around a program of non-tributary agriculture and animal breeding, organization into a village-based tribal confederation, and devotion to the cult of the delivering and blessing deity Yahweh, who was a God both of history and nature. These peasant uprisings were joined by mercenaries, bandits, pastoral nomads, artisans, and priests. Some of these extra-agrarian recruits or converts served as leaders in the movement.[6]

Social Revolution

The specific effect of these successful rebellions was a social revolution — a new fusion of mode of production with social formation, replacing the city-state hierarchies and their tributary mode of production in large sections of the Canaanite highlands. The new society was free agrarian, and lacked a state form of government and class system, although it exercised political powers diffused through the social structure, and practiced social ranking in some degree. This revolution was protracted, ebbing and flowing over two centuries, with inhabitants of the land joining, opposing, or standing aloof, according to factors of class position and advantage, geographical location, and the varying strength of the Israelite movement.

As a model, social revolution is distinguishable from peasant rebellion, for not all peasant rebellions, even those that succeed in throwing off a given regime, actually bring about an extended change in ownership of the means of production. Those that have done so, notably in the twentieth century, deserve special attention in regard to the heuristic uses of their models for the study of early Israel.[7]

Frontier development

The new society eventually became indigenous in the highlands of Judah, Samaria, Galilee, and Gilead. Consequently, it had the distinctive shape of a developing frontier society possessing political autonomy, but vulnerable to reconquest by state power. The confinement of the uprisings and revolution to highland regions, and thus their limited success, seems to have been the result of complex factors of topography, technology, communication, internal conflicts, military balance of power, and perhaps limitations in strategy and tactics.[8]

Social banditry

The military irregularity and political confusion of the decentralized and decentralizing social revolution encouraged predatory actions by individuals and small groups. These bandit acts were typically directed against the city-states, but sometimes against fellow Israelites, in contradictory ways, which are understandable when considered against the background of the wide spectrum of social banditry as it tends to precede, accompany, and merge into rebellions and revolutions.[9]

To develop hypotheses about early Israel derived from models concurrently testable is a challenging prospect. Which of the models, or what combination of them, should be preferred for heuristic purposes is a moot point. The more we have reason to believe that the city-states of the Late Bronze Age collapsed from within, or were overthrown in some cases by non-Israelites, the more likely we are to stress frontier development and social banditry models. The more we have reason to believe that the gathering Israelite movement had to apply and sustain major force to push back the city-states, and internal persuasion to maintain socioeconomic equality, the more we are likely to stress the peasant rebellion and social revolution models. To date, the most balanced and lucid statement concerning the relevance of these explanatory models to the various classes of evidence about early Israel, is the essay of Marvin L. Chaney, completed in 1978 and only recently published.[10] The above-suggested societal models are by no means exhaustive. Aspects of early Israel may also be illuminated by models of segmentary tribal organization [11] and of military/ritual chiefdom.[12]

It is obvious that further and better hypothesized work on biblical texts and in archaeology will provide fuller testing of the heuristic validity of the above social science constructs, thereby enabling us to write a connected social history of the first Israelites.

Archaeology and Social Explanatory Models in the Study of Early Israel

Finally, I would like to make some observations about the relationship between archaeological interpretations and the social models and presuppositions held by scholars.

Expressed and unexpressed covering laws in the interpretation of archaeological data

It is clear that archaeologists and historians using archaeological materials definitely operate with mental pictures of early Israelite society, whether or not those pictures are consciously formed as arguable or testable hypotheses. This predisposition of the interpreter is often overlooked because so much archaeology and textual study proceeds inductively, rather than deductively. The social images tend to lie uncriticized in the background, or to emerge as generalizations which appear to stem strictly and incontestably from the artifactual or textual evidence without requiring rigorous scrutiny.

Some Palestinian archaeologists are stressing the value of formulating explicit deductive hypotheses as an aid to identifying and clarifying the assumptions and aims of excavators, and as a way of focusing strategy to test hypotheses. Thomas L. McClellan illustrates this by suggesting two possible deductive hypotheses or covering laws for explaining house sizes: they vary in proportion to the family's wealth and social status, *or* they vary in proportion to the number of household members.[13] McClellan presents a more complex covering law involving not only the size, but also the plan of the house in relation to other structures: extended families of unstable size will dwell in agglutinative architectural units, and often carry out remodelling; whereas nuclear families will live in well-defined households which are isolated by streets, alleys, courtyards and in architectural plan.[14] These covering laws are developed for Tell Beit Mirsim, but are formulated in a general enough way that they can apply to other sites. What is not so clear is how McClellan proposes to test his refined covering law archaeologically.

A more complicated application of covering laws is made by Frank S. Frick in an attempt to test for the presence of chiefdom in the archaeological data from Iron Age I at Tel Masos. Frick uses five archaeologically testable variables developed by Peebles and Kus,[15] and he concludes the presence of a ritual chief at Israelite Tel Masos. For the specifically *ritual* character of the chiefdom, he applies the work of Rappaport[16] on rituals as social homeostasis and communication devices to a model of how the early Levites presumably functioned. It is not clear, except by inference, whether this ritual dimension of the hypothesis about chiefdom is archaeologically tested.[17]

These examples of consciously formulated covering laws prompt one to puzzle about the normally unexamined covering explanations derived from uncriticized social presuppositions. They lead to monolithic and sketchily argued conclusions, and they foreclose other options which subsequently are never considered. The alleged pastoral nomadism of early Israel is a notorious generator of such *pro forma* explanations. The covering law seems to be as follows: as the first Israelites were pastoral nomads who lived apart from cities, disliked cities, and intruded on them when powerful enough to do so, and given the absence of any contrary information, we should conclude that the destruction of this particular city was the work of Israelite pastoral nomads. Moreover, because the cultural repertory of Israelite pastoral nomads was different from and, in certain respects, inferior to that of settled people, and given the absence of any contrary information, we should conclude that this settlement, with its new cultural items and its inferior execution of older cultural items, was indeed founded by Israelite pastoral nomads.

The pressures and skewing effects of these inchoate covering laws regarding pastoral nomadism color and shape work that in many of its details is resistant to them. For example, in separate interpretations of the excavation of Tel Masos, Aharoni, Fritz and Kempinski adopt a broad pastoral nomadic hypothesis about the builders of the Iron Age I village. Interestingly, however, all note features that do not obviously concur with the hypothesis, such as the well-developed traditions of building and pottery making, the high incidence of bovine animals, and the indications of extensive trade with the coastal plain and Transjordan.[18]

Fritz is so acutely aware of this tension between the model and the data that he sharply qualifies a pastoral nomadic explanation, arguing that the builders of Tel Masos had lived in coexistence with settled peoples, perhaps in the southern Shephelah, for decades or centuries before constructing the settlement at Tel Masos. He goes on to assert that the results at Tel Masos do not comfortably fit any of the existing Settlement models. The conquest model does not apply because there were no Late Bronze Age cities in the area to be destroyed. The social revolution model does not apply because new house types mean that the settlers did not form a group in Canaanite society. In his judgment, a group that had been for decades or centuries in the Shephelah would not qualify as a part of Canaanite society. The immigration model does not do justice to long-standing contact between builders of the village and the Late Bronze Age material culture.

It is worth taking a moment to reflect on Fritz's conclusions, as they are quite typical of the way social models are brought to bear on archaeological data. As far as I can see, the evidence from Tel Masos, when treated with flexibility, does not decisively rule out any of the models. Military conquest could have been the major overall strategy of the Israelites in order to secure settlement, but where no cities existed to attack, new settlement could proceed under the covering protection of military assaults elsewhere. Social revolution could have been the primary dynamic force which secured enough free space for settlements in unoccupied lands. The new house types may have been the work of long-settled people who developed the three- and four-room pillared house for a functional purpose, which we do not yet understand. Immigration is not invalidated per se, even on Fritz's terms, but merely qualified by recognition that the immigration of these particular pastoral nomads had occurred generations earlier. Also, the long-range trade at Tel Masos need not militate against pastoral nomadic origins per se, as the Midianite and Nabatean traders demonstrate.

It is instructive to examine alternative ways of interpreting the source of the three- or four-room pillared house at Tel Masos, now widely considered an innovation of the Israelite Settlement. Fritz sees its construction as an evolution of a broad-room house, also present at Tel Masos, and suggests that the broad-room house was an architectural rendering of the broad-roomed Bedouin tent known today, and presumably of very ancient use.[19] On the other hand, Kempinski offers the observation that stone monoliths were often used by people living in mountainous areas where such building materials are available, the basalt areas around the Sea of Galilee, the Golan and Transjordan providing excellent examples. He even speaks of the Tel Masos founders as "a people who already had a building tradition going back to the Bronze Age traditions of the mountainous areas."[20]

On the matter of buildings, Kempinski incidentally volunteers an interpretation of the material improvements in Stratum II at Tel Masos, which, if accepted, would neutralize at least one of the variables which Frick cites in his archaeological test for Israelite chiefdom at Tel Masos. Frick interpreted the large house of older Canaanite design in Stratum II (house 314), which contained the fine pottery and ivory lion's head, to be the house of a chief involved in long-range trade.[21] Kempinski believes that Tel Masos had probably been incorporated into the political and economic sphere of the Philistines before Stratum II, so that "some public buildings were also erected, apparently under the initiative of the city's Philistine overlords."[22] Obviously, if the "chief" posited by Frick at Tel Masos was installed by the Philistines, and perhaps even was a Philistine, this would tell us little or nothing about whether free Israelites recognized chiefs.

In short, we dare not move in a heavy-handed or monolithic way to apply our favorite social model, like a cooky cutter, to every archaeological problem, for a prescriptive use of the model debases its heuristic value and soon leads to dogma. This caution applies equally to all models. It can be illustrated by an inspection of the possible ways of explaining the destruction or non-destruction of cities in the formative Israelite period. Premature foreclosures of the identification of destroyers of Canaanite cities can be prevented if we systematically remind ourselves of the full range of possible explanations.

When cities are destroyed or deserted for long periods, it is common to argue that pastoral nomads were the destroyers, or that they wandered over the now deserted environs of the city, and that these nomads settled down gradually in the vicinity of the destroyed site, or even rebuilt the ruins in time. Without other evidence, these conclusions are not justified. The destroyers may not have wanted to settle the city, not merely because they were nomadic, but simply because they may have moved on to attack other cities or returned home, while the surviving former inhabitants dispersed into villages or went to other cities. Shifts in politics, trade or local agricultural conditions may have undermined the viability of the site for occupation, with the result that its former functions were obsolete or effete. Furthermore, it does not logically follow that an inferior building or rebuilding of a site must be attributed to culturally backward nomads. Sedentary rebuilders may not have had the expert masons or the ample building materials that the former state apparatus could muster, or in turbulent and insecure conditions, it may have been advisable to rebuild in haste and provisionally. Also, if the site was no longer to serve former administrative or commercial purposes, a modest rebuilding for a local populace may have been adequate.

In terms of the social revolution model, Paul Lapp and Edward Campbell Jr. have reasoned that cities involved in a civil war or internal uprising would not have been destroyed, since the victors would have had no reason to destroy their own home cities.[23] A complement to this claim is argued by John Bright. He observes that the absence of archaeological evidence of destruction may mean that a city was taken by internal revolt, and preserved by its inhabitants as part of the Israelite movement.[24] The implication is that many battles in the social revolution could have occurred without leaving any archaeological traces.

It seems to me that these observations presented alone are very one-sided and incomplete. Destruction of a city or the absence of destruction could be interpreted consistently as a military conquest from without or as a peasant revolt from within. Of course non-destruction may mean that a city was taken by internal uprising. It could also mean that no armed action occurred at the city, or that the city was taken by stratagem, or that it surrendered to conquerors or rebels to avoid destruction. Moreover, an exclusive focus on assaults on cities omits those situations where victory was won in open battle. I believe this was precisely the case with Shechem, whose armed forces appear to have been defeated by Israel in an open battle near Mt. Zalmon as poetically related in Psalm 68:11–14 and in Genesis 48:22; 49:23–24.[25]

In reply to Lapp and Campbell, in a social revolution, a city might also be destroyed because the local ruler held out in his fortified palace at the center of the city, making large-scale or total destruction necessary to topple him from power. Another credible explanation for the destruction of an administrative or commercial center is that there would have been no place for fortified administrative centers or trading emporiums in the tribal society of Israel. At least some of these centers may have been destroyed to prevent their reuse or to make a strong symbolic statement against hierarchy and luxury trade. It is likely that an aspect of the so-called "holy war" was a public defamation of the symbolic order of the defeated hierarchs (cf. Joshua 10:22–27).

Ethnicity and social behavior

The inquiry into Israelite beginnings would be greatly profited by a sharpening and clarifying of the elusive notion of ethnicity. C.H.J. de Geus, using the Latin concepts *connubium* and *forum*, hypothesizes the formation of Israelite ethnicity in an endogamous, long-resident, agrarian population, which developed by means of ethico-juridical and aesthetic-cultural community building processes.[26] He concludes with a summary observation:

> One might say, then, that a people is determined by the limits within which something is accepted, appreciated, admired or disapproved. In this context Von Grunebaum speaks of an admiring, disapproving or censuring "ever present public."

Kathryn Kamp and Norman Yoffee have drawn on social science literature concerning ethnicity to expose how imprecisely ethnic identities are ascribed by students of ancient Near Eastern history. They point out that a number of frequently occurring ethnic traits, including territorial segregation, single ecological or socio-economic adaptation, and a shared language cannot be uniformly relied upon. Reliance on a trait list may render archaeology incapable of spotting ethnicity. For example, the excavator of the Assyrian colony at Kültepe in Asia Minor remarked that, without the cuneiform tablets and seal impressions, the Assyrians at Kültepe were indistinguishable from their Hattic neighbors.[27]

Kamp and Yoffee propose that in a study of ancient Near Eastern ethnicity one should focus on the social behaviors that generate differences in material culture, on how boundaries between groups are established and maintained, and on how ethnic identity projects role expectations. They suggest looking for behavior that symbolizes ethnic identity, behavior that is learned in the group socialization process, and behavior that exhibits group economic and/or political strategy. They follow current social science theory about ethnicity by defining an ethnic group as "a number of individuals who see themselves 'as being alike by virtue of a common ancestry, real or fictitious, and who are so regarded by others.'"[28] With this kind of behavioral approach to ethnicity, what might ethnicity have meant among the first Israelites?

The Merneptah stele tells us that by about 1230 B.C.E. there was a group in Canaan called Israel by the Egyptians, and presumably self-named in the same way. We do not know, however, its size or social organization, unless the determinative sign for people, as opposed to that of land, should be taken to indicate that Israel at that moment did not securely hold one territory, or that it was distinguishable from other Canaanite groups by certain patterns of social organization and behavior.

The difficulty of our task is that we are inquiring about ethnic ascription at the fountainhead of its emergence. We are not looking at an ethnic ascription that developed slowly and continuously over a long period of time, even if some of the subgroups included in the formation of Israel had well-formed previous identities. Thus, for example, the objection of Jacob Milgrom to the model of social revolution for early Israel which is based on the treatment of converts to the Jewish community in the Deuteronomic and Priestly sources, is not in any way decisive, or even relevant, to the circumstances in the originating composition of Israel.[29] The process by which a freshly arising group "converts" people is not likely to be the same as that by which that group assimilates additional members *later* in its history.

We must, in short, divest ourselves of all assumptions regarding Israelite identity based on later biblical and post-biblical understandings. We must resolutely reject any application of a late "essentialist" or "normative" Israelite identity to the initial Israelite movement. Instead, we must search for behavioral and symbolic signs among the people of Canaan during the thirteenth to eleventh centuries B.C.E. as disclosed in texts and by material remains, which we can therefore call "Israelite." This shift in our way of conceiving the inquiry can put familiar data in a somewhat different light.

By way of illustration, quite a number of scholars, among them Joseph Callaway, George Mendenhall, and Benjamin Mazar, have in various ways pointed out the presence of other groups of people in Canaan at the time of Israel's emergence. These appear as "the seven nations" in Israelite texts, notably Hittites, Hivites, and Jebusites,[30] or they are surmised to have been the destroyers of some Late Bronze Age sites, or the builders of settlements later taken over by Israelites.[31] Using essentialist ethnic categorization, we are tempted to think of each of these as a fixed demographic and cultural entity, of which Israel is yet another in the series. Most scholars will acknowledge that some of these other peoples became Israelites or lived in the Israelite community,[32] but this is normally seen as a change in community membership. The already fixed core of Israelite identity is posited as present. We are reaching, however, for that earlier original moment or process when tribally confederate Israel came to be composed of people who were *all* something else previously, even if some had originated from a smaller-scale "Israel," perhaps non-Yahwist and more socially homogeneous. I take it that this is the point being made by Mendenhall in a very suggestive chapter in his book *The Tenth Generation*, whatever one makes of his detailed etymological explanations of the proper names and gentilics.[33]

Although de Geus made considerable progress in describing Israel's Canaan-based ethnicity in terms of ethico-juridical and aesthetic-cultural community processes, I do not think he reached the nerve center of that Israelite ethnicity which erupted with such force at the end of the thirteenth century B.C.E. I believe, on the contrary, that the most fruitful and promising hypothesis is that Israel's dawning self-ascription as a people took place in a precarious social organizational matrix, where peasants and other kinds of producers and providers of services struggled to take command of the agrarian means of production. This was the forge that brought them to extraordinary self-consciousness, as it propelled them into the consciousness and social world of others around them. This social organizational struggle for the control of the political economy also triggered the religious ideology and cult which in turn validated and energized their struggle. It was the mixture of this new political economy and new religion which pulled together peoples of varying previous identities, and initiated a new integral cultural development.

What does one do with such a hypothesis? I have a sense of how it can be tested by textual evidence. However, I am much less clear about how, and even if, it can tested archaeologically. Much will be gained if archaeologists, freed from naive social pictures of early Israel, are able to verify or refute the hypothesis with some degree of probability. For all of us, there is a lot of work to be done.

Notes

1. N.K. Gottwald, "Were the Early Israelites Pastoral Nomads?" *BAR* 42 (1978): 2–7; idem, *The Tribes of Yahweh: A Sociology of the Religion of Liberated Israel, 1250–1050 B.C.E.* (Maryknoll: Orbis, 1979); idem, "John Bright's New Revision of 'A History of Israel,'" *BAR* 8/4 (1982): 56–61; idem, "Early Israel and the Canaanite Socioeconomic System," in *Palestine in Transition: The Emergence of Ancient Israel*, eds. D.N. Freedman and D.F. Graf, The Social World of Biblical Anituqity Series, 2 (Sheffield: The Almond Press, 1983), pp. 25–37; idem, "Two Models for the Origins of Ancient Israel: Social Revolution or Frontier Development," in *The Quest for the Kingdom of God: Studies in Honor of George E. Mendenhall*, eds. H.B. Huffmon, F.A. Spina and A.R.W. Green (Winona Lake, Ind: Eisenbrauns, 1983), pp. 5–24.
2. Gottwald, "John Bright's New Revision" (see note 1), pp. 59–60.
3. Idem, *The Tribes of Yahweh* (see note 1), pp. 493–497.
4. Ibid., pp. 798–799, n. 635.
5. Ibid., pp. 498–554.
6. H.A. Landsberger, "The Role of Peasant Movements and Revolts in Development," in *Latin American Peasant Movements*, ed. H.A. Landsberger (Ithaca: Cornell University, 1969), pp. 1–61; idem, "Peasant Unrest: Themes and Variations", in *Rural Protest: Peasant Movements and Social Change*, ed. H.A. Landsberger (New York: Barnes and Noble, 1973), pp. 1–64; B. Moore Jr., *Social Origins of Dictatorship and Democracy: Lord and Peasant in the Making of the Modern World* (Boston: Beacon, 1966); E.R. Wolf, *Peasant Wars of the Twentieth Century* (New York: Harper and Row, 1969); M.L. Chaney, "*ḤDL*-II and the 'Song of Deborah': Textual, Philological, and Sociological Studies in Judges 5, with Special Reference to the Verbal Occurrences of *ḤDL* in Biblical Hebrew" (Ph.D. diss., Harvard University, 1976).
7. W.F. Wertheim, *Evolution and Revolution. The Rising Waves of Emancipation* (Baltimore: Penguin, 1974); Wolf, *Peasant Wars* (see note 6); Gottwald, "Early Israel and the Canaanite Socioeconomic System" (see note 1).
8. G.E. Lenski, "Review of N.K. Gottwald, 'The Tribes of Yahweh,'" *Religious Studies Review* 6 (1980): 275–278; Gottwald: "Two Models for the Origins of Ancient Israel" (see note 1); concerning the systemics of "risk-spreading" highland agrarian practices, see D.C. Hopkins, "The Dynamics of Agriculture in Monarchical Israel," *Society of Biblical Literature Seminar Papers* 22 (1983): 177–193.
9. E.J. Hobsbawn, *Bandits* (New York: Delacorte, 1969); idem, "Social Bandits," in *Rural Protest: Peasant Movements and Social Change*, ed. H.A. Landsberger (New York: Barnes and Noble, 1973), pp. 142–157; M.L. Chaney, "Ancient Palestinian Peasant Movements and the Formation of Premonarchic Israel," in *Palestine in Transition* (see note 1), pp. 72–83.
10. Chaney, "Ancient Palestinian Peasant Movements" (see note 9); on the relation of the social models to archaeology, see also P.J. King, "The Contribution of Archaeology to Biblical Studies," *Catholic Biblical Quarterly* 45 (1983): 4–11.
11. Gottwald, *The Tribes of Yahweh* (see note 1), pp. 237–341; C. Schäfer-Lichtenberger, *Stadt und Eidgenossenschaft im Alten Testament. Eine Auseinandersetzung mit Max Webers Studie 'Das antike Judentum.' BZAW* 156 (Berlin/New York: de Gruyter, 1983), pp. 323–367.
12. F.S. Frick, "Religion and Sociopolitical Structure in Early Israel: An Ethno-archaeological Approach," *Society of Biblical Literature Seminar Papers* 17 (1979): 233–253
13. T.K. McClellan, "Social Organization and Patterns in the Material Culture of Tell Beit Mirsim," paper presented to the Social World of Ancient Israel Group of the American Academy of Religion and the Society of Biblical Literature at the 1977 annual meeting, pp. 9, 11.
14. Ibid., p. 16.
15. C.S. Peebles and S.M. Kus, "Some Archaeological Correlates of Ranking Societies," *American Antiquity* 42 (1977): 421–447.
16. R.A. Rappaport, "The Sacred in Human Evolution," *Annual Review of Ecology and Systematics* 2

(1971): 23–44; idem, "Ritual, Sanctity and Cybernetics," *American Anthropologist* 73 (1971): 59–76.

17. Frick, "Religion and Sociopolitical Structure" (see note 12), pp. 235–236, 241–242, 248–249.
18. Y. Aharoni, "Nothing Early and Nothing Late: Re-writing Israel's Conquest," *BA* 39 (1976): 66–67; V. Fritz, "The Israelite 'Conquest' in the Light of Recent Excavations at Khirbet el-Meshâsh," *BASOR* 241 (1981): 68–71; A. Kempinski, "Israelite Conquest or Settlement? New Light from Tell Masos," *BAR* 2/3 (1976): 29–30.
19. Fritz, "The Israelite 'Conquest'" (see note 18), p. 65.
20. Kempinski, "Israelite Conquest or Settlement?" (see note 18), p. 30.
21. Frick, "Religion and Sociopolitical Structure" (see note 12), p. 244.
22. Kempinski, "Israelite Conquest or Settlement?" (see note 18), p. 30.
23. P.W. Lapp, "The Conquest of Palestine in the Light of Archaeology," *Concordia Theological Monthly* 38 (1967): 298–299; idem, *Biblical Archaeology and History* (New York: World, 1969), p. 110; E.F. Campbell Jr., "Moses and the Foundations of Israel," *Interpretation* 29 (1975): 152.
24. J. Bright, *A History of Israel*, 3d ed. (Philadelphia: Westminster, 1981), p. 132.
25. Gottwald, *The Tribes of Yahweh* (see note 1), pp. 550–552.
26. C.H.J. de Geus, *The Tribes of Israel: An Investigation into Some of the Presuppositions of Martin Noth's Amphictyony Hypothesis* (Amsterdam: Van Gorcum, 1976), pp. 156–164.
27. K.A. Kamp and N. Yoffee, "Ethnicity in Ancient Western Asia During the Early Second Millennium B.C.: Archaeological Assessments and Ethnoarchaeological Prospectives," *BASOR* 237 (1980): 94–96.
28. Ibid., p. 88, quoting T. Shibutani and K.K. Kwan, *Ethnic Stratification* (New York: Macmillan, 1965).
29. J. Milgrom, "Religious Conversion and the Revolt Model for the Formation of Israel," *JBL* 101 (1982): 175–176.
30. B. Mazar, "The Early Israelite Settlement in the Hill Country," *BASOR* 241 (1981): 76–80.
31. J.A. Callaway, "New Evidence on the Conquest of 'Ai," *JBL* 87 (1968): 315–320.
32. Mazar, "The Early Israelite Settlement" (see note 30), p. 79.
33. G.E. Mendenhall, *The Tenth Generation: The Origins of the Biblical Tradition* (Baltimore: Johns Hopkins University, 1973): pp. 142–173.

Basic Factors of Israelite Settlement in Canaan

Siegfried Herrmann

LAST YEAR A German journal, *Anfänge Israels*,[1] related to the Catholic journal *Bibel und Kirche*, was issued with a collection of articles concerning new hypotheses on the origins of Israel. On the first page, the term *Hypothesenumbruch* ("the breakdown of hypotheses") appears, and it is discussed by Helmut Engel in his article entitled "*Abschied von den frühisraelitischen Nomaden und der Jahweamphiktyonie. Bericht über den Zusammenbruch eines wissenschaftlichen Konsensus.*"[2] What was this *wissenschaftlicher Konsensus*, this scientific agreement? Engel states that the former consensus was represented by Alt, Noth, Fohrer, and S. Herrmann,[3] and later criticized by de Vaux, Zuber, de Geus, Rowton, and Gottwald.[4] I would not like to analyze the representation and grouping of these scholars, and I do not know whether the second group represents the new consensus. However, we can sense the intention of this German author — the former concept of the nomadic past of Israelite tribes and their amphictyonic organization should be replaced by new models, inspired mainly by sociological theories, with or without biblical evidence.

My impression is that we are actually living in a period of dramatic scientific development. The question is which theory or hypothesis can benefit us most in the understanding of Israel's first steps in the land during the so-called formative period?[5] I believe that we need theories with a closer connection to the biblical and extra-biblical texts, together with careful consideration of the archaeological results. The question is which source provides some certainty regarding the real Israelite Settlement in the premonarchical period? This is a very old question, but should be raised afresh in order to limit new theories and speculations.

* I wish to thank the Institute for Advanced Studies of the Hebrew University of Jerusalem for the fellowship awarded to me in the academic year 1983/84, during which I prepared this paper. I am very grateful to Prof. Alan R. Millard, who read this article and improved my English in the final stage of preparing the text for print.

In general, one is inclined to distinguish three settlement models in Canaan: conquest, immigration, and revolt — and to favor one of them. One of the first mistakes made, however, is the generalization of one model, and the assumption that the settlement process was characterized by the same presuppositions and conditions in every region. The Bible itself does not present such a simple picture, and surveys and detailed archaeological results strengthen the supposition that the process of the Settlement was a combination of several steps and several models adopted to suit the local conditions. The archaeological inheritance is undoubtedly manifold, but not so complete as to reveal the whole process of all the historical developments. We need, therefore, both support and confirmation by textual evidence, and we must admit that the combination of archaeological results on the one hand, and texts on the other hand, although sometimes impossible is sometimes successful. At least, the cooperation of archaeologists, historians and sociologists, each in their own discipline, and not forgetting the literary-critical analysis, can support the efforts to reveal the historical process with more probability.

What are the basic factors? The Bible tells us that the tribes came from outside the land. Undoubtedly, this is not an invention, but we cannot be sure that all tribes came from outside, nor do we know the point of their departure. I would not like here to delve into one of the most controversial fields of research and hypothetical assumptions: how to interpret the fact that the Patriarchs came from the north or from the northeast, and the so-called Moshe-group entered the land from the south. This is significant and characterizes the complexity of the Israelite formative period. However, one of the unanimously accepted presuppositions is the occupation of the coastal area by the Canaanite and Philistine population before or during the Israelite Settlement. At the same time, we do find in the hill country some fortified cities like Shechem, but the population is more widely dispersed in a more or less organized form. This is what Albrecht Alt called "*grössere territoriale Gebilde*" in the mountains during the Late Bronze Age in contrast to city-states in the plains.[6]

For the Negev, we have to conjecture a more complicated situation, as we have no convincing Canaanite settlement there during the Late Bronze Age. We have Early Bronze Age in Arad, but no Middle Bronze Age or Late Bronze Age. Resettlement took place only in Iron Age I at some places, like Arad, Tel Masos, Tel Esdar and Beer-Sheba, and in Iron Age II at Tell Malḥata and Tel ʿIra.[7] The biblical information relating to this area at the time of the Settlement is dispersed and without convincing coherence. This is not surprising when we compare the archaeological results. The conclusion for this part of the country is that the Settlement was mainly the result of a peaceful invasion not prevented or opposed by the Egyptian or the Canaanite forces.[8] Furthermore, it is an open question whether or to what extent we should include in this southern settlement process the so-called *Š3św*-movements. The Egyptian term *Š3św* seems to be the reflection, from the Egyptian point of view, of the population movements in this area. The texts are collected with commentary by Raphael Giveon,[9] and Wolfgang Helck pointed out that the *Š3św* are attested mainly for territories south of the Dead Sea.[10] Unfortunately, we are not able to define the ethnical provenance of these groups of *Š3św*. It is therefore impossible to identify with any certainty some of them with later Israelite tribes. We should bear in mind, however, the classical starting point of the southern Israelite tribal movements. This is the role of Kadesh-Barnea and the contribution of the Kadesh traditions, including the Negev traditions in Numbers 13 and 14 and Judges 1[11] concerning Caleb, Othniel, Judah and Simeon. Whatever these traditions can tell us about the historical background of early Israelite groups, these southern territories, according to the archaeological observations, seem to have been receptive during the Late Bronze Age, making possible forms of relatively independent settlements there.

In the western coastal plain and in the Plain of Jezreel, we have a completely different historical constellation with other geographical presuppositions. The well-known text in Judges 1:27–36 lists the territories and towns which remained inaccessible to Israelite tribes. There we have two main fortified lines which Thutmose III already recorded. They protected the land and served as barriers along the coastline, making difficult entry or ascent into the hill country of Judah and Ephraim. This is what Albrecht Alt called *die beiden Querriegel* — "the two barriers."[12] The northern one is mentioned in Judges 1:27 and includes Beth-Shean, Taanach, Dor, Jibleam, and Megiddo. The second one, to which pharaonic town lists testify, is equally convincing, and includes Yaffa, Ono, Aphek, Socoh and other places in the "plain of Ono" (Nehemiah 6:2). Judges 1:29 and 35 mention the following as inaccessible to Israel in this area and in the hill country: Gezer, Shaalbim, Aijalon, Har-Heres. Therefore the list in Judges 1 gives us some impression about the limitations of Israelite Settlement in the west and northwest, where the Canaanites or the Philistines occupied the chief settlements.

In the Galilee, the archaeological evidence shows that Hazor was destroyed in the Late Bronze Age during the thirteenth century B.C.E.[13] Then after the destruction of Hazor, according to pottery evidence,[14] settlement took place in the hill country of Galilee.

However, if our impression is correct, certain biblical traditions about the beginning of the settlement of these territories are problematic. Also what do we know and what can we reveal about the settlement process in Judah,[15] and what is the significance of the name "Israel" on the Merneptah Stele?[16] If we take it for granted that the Egyptian generic determinative at the end of the Egyptian hieroglyphs for the name "Israel" really refers to a "people" as opposed to "foreign country,"[17] we can conclude that there was a population group named "Israel," which was closely connected to the Ephraimite hill country. This could substantiate the older assumption that the hill country seems to have been the kernel of Israelite activities. However, where is the starting point or where is the origin of these activities in this area? The biblical tradition in the Book of Joshua really leads us into this part of the land. It is far from a fundamentalistic perspective if we accept the special Israelite activity in the center and in the eastern part of the hill country, as archaeological evidence supports the biblical tradition: after the decline of the Late Bronze Age culture, we can observe the increase of Iron Age settlements. I will not elaborate upon the archaeological details, because my impression is that the archaeologists have not yet spoken the last word about the hill country settlement and the interpretation of several strata at such sites of actual archaeological interest as Et-Tell, Raddana, ʿIzbet Ṣartaḥ, Shiloh and Giloh further south.[18]

Historically speaking, in the light of biblical texts, we have reason to believe that during the Iron Age or earlier, a new population penetrated into the territory of Benjamin and Ephraim, a population which was perhaps unified by a common origin — whether or not by the veneration of a common god is another question. We have reasons to assume, however, that this movement was a separate process from that in the Negev, and there is no indication that the population groups of this area penetrated further north. In Judges 1:8, Jerusalem was attacked and destroyed by Judean groups, but there was no settlement. Contrary to these traditions, we have the well-known collection of stories regarding the occupation of the Benjaminite and Ephraimite hill country in the form of a single campaign transmitted in the Book of Joshua. The special military operations in Joshua 1–10, however, are limited to the Benjaminite territory. The so-called digression to the south in Joshua 10:29–39, including the conquest of Libnah, Lachish, Eglon, Hebron and Debir, seems to be a special tradition and not connected originally with Joshua. His advance ended in the area of Aijalon and Beth-Horon, excluding the events near the mysterious cave of Makkedah (Joshua 10:16–28).

In the middle of this traditional complex, in Joshua 9:17, we have a league of towns which were not attacked by the Israelites: Gibeon, Chephirah, Beeroth and Kiriath-Jearim. The Israelites were ready to make peace with them in form of a *b^erīt*. The most important words in Joshua 9:15 describing the content of *b^erīt* are *shālōm* and *l^eḥayyōtām* which mean "peace" and "to let them live."[19] The kernel of this tradition is the peaceful agreement with the former population supported by treaties or other forms of cooperation. Whether this population of Gibeon was Hivite or Hurrian is a special question.[20] In any case, the Israelites met different population groups in the hill country, which had settled there prior to the Joshua invasion.

The crucial point is the interpretation of the military actions in the Book of Joshua. An old proposal to solve this difficult problem is that given by Albrecht Alt in his article "*Erwägungen über die Landnahme der Israeliten.*"[21] He dealt in the first place with his concept "*Die kriegerischen Vorgänge,*" proposing that warlike enterprises and conquests could not have been the characteristic features during the first stage of the Israelite Settlement, but rather the consequence of a later extension by some tribes into the border areas of their central territories. Alt named this second stage of settlement *Landesausbau*, a word not easy to translate into English.[22] Perhaps Alt's *Landesausbau* is the assumption that the consolidation of tribes and the successive expansion required military actions against the fortified settlements, mainly in the neighborhood of the newly settled areas. In this respect, the so-called *Landesausbau* was at the same time "*die Abrundung des Territorialbesitzes,*" which means the possession of tribal territory in its definite extent.[23]

The basic factors of the Israelite Settlement in Canaan summarized in this short paper are not absolutely new. However, many details and facts concerning the settlement process are again open for discussion. I would like to sum up some remaining questions:

1. Are archaeological finds like plastered cisterns or the innovation of agricultural terraces convincing elements for assuming a new development introduced by new ethnical groups?[24]
2. How can we explain the traces of violent destruction of places and towns, particularly in the last periods of the Late Bronze Age and at the beginning of Iron Age I?
3. Are we entitled to assume an increase in settlement during the twelfth century B.C.E. caused by the expansion of the population?[25]
4. Can we assume independent developments in settlement and culture in Judah, Ephraim and the north?
5. What can we say about the common presuppositions which led to the later unification of Israel, particularly concerning the common faith and the common cultural and ethnical consciousness?
6. All these questions culminate into one: What is specifically *Israelite* in the process of growing Israel in its so-called formative period? What were the leading factors in this process? A common starting point in the past, perhaps at Kadesh, or the powerful extension of leadership from smaller groups to other groups in or entering the land?

These are basic factors which we have to keep in mind in order to explain the complicated process of the installation of Israel in Canaan. These questions all demonstrate the complexity of facts and aspects which have to be considered in researching the beginnings of Israel.

Notes

1. *Bibel und Kirche,* 2. Quartal (1983, Heft 2). Thema des Heftes: "Anfänge Israels" (Stuttgart, 1983).
2. Ibid., pp. 43–46.
3. A. Alt, "Die Landnahme der Israeliten in Palästina," 1925; "Erwägungen über die Landnahme der Israeliten in Palästina," 1939, both reprinted in *Kleine Schriften,* I (1953, 1968), pp. 89–175; M. Noth, *Das System der zwölf Stämme Israels* (1930; reprint 1966); idem, *Geschichte Israels* (1950; reprint 1969); G. Fohrer, *Geschichte Israels. Von den Anfängen bis zur Gegenwart* (1977); S. Herrmann, *Geschichte Israels in alttestamentlicher Zeit* (1973, 2d ed. 1980).
4. R. de Vaux, *Histoire ancienne d'Israel,* II (1973); B. Zuber, "Vier Studien zu den Ursprüngen Israels" (1976); cf. *Biblica* 58 (1977): 108–110; C.H.J. de Geus, *The Tribes of Israel. An Investigation into Some of the Presuppositions of Martin Noth's Amphictyony Hypothesis* (Amsterdam, 1976); cf. *Biblica* 57 (1976): 436–440; M.B. Rowton, "Dimorphic Structure and Topology," *Oriens Antiquus* 15 (1976): 17–31, and other essays; N.K. Gottwald, "Domain Assumptions and Societal Models in the Study of the Premonarchic Israel," *VT Suppl.* 28 (1975): 89–100; idem, *The Tribes of Yahweh: A Sociology of the Religion of Liberated Israel 1250–1050 B.C.E.* (Maryknoll: Orbis, 1979).
5. Recently, the hypothesis of premonarchic Israel as a segmentary society has been defended by

Christa Schäfer-Lichtenberger, *Stadt und Eidgenossenschaft im Alten Testament. Eine Auseinandersetzung mit Max Webers Studie 'Das antike Judentum', BZAW* 156 (Berlin/New York, 1983). Another approach was presented by A. Malamat, "Tribal Societies, Biblical Genealogies and African Lineage Systems," *Archives Européennes de Sociology* 14 (1973): 126–136.

6. Alt, "Die Landnahme der Israeliten" (see note 3), pp. 107–113.
7. The data mentioned are presented in the excavation reports and in some books and articles on subjects of general archaeological and historical interest. See M. Avi-Yonah, and E. Stern, eds., *Encyclopedia of Archaeological Excavations in the Holy Land*, 4 vols. (Oxford/Jerusalem, 1975–78); B. Mazar, ed., *World History of the Jewish People, III: Judges* (1971); P.J. King, "The Contribution of Archaeology in Biblical Studies," *CBQ* 45 (1983): 1–16; Y. Aharoni, *The Land of the Bible. A Historical Geography* (1967).
8. Y. Aharoni, "Nothing Early and Nothing Late: Re-writing Israel's Conquest," *BA* 39 (1976): 55–76; V. Fritz, "Die kulturhistorische Bedeutung der früheisenzeitlichen Siedlung auf der Ḫirbet el-Mšāš und das Problem der Landnahme," *ZDPV* 96 (1980): 121–135; idem, "The Israelite 'Conquest' in the Light of Recent Excavations at Khirbet el-Meshash," *BASOR* 241 (1981): 61–73; N. Na'aman, "The Inheritance of the Sons of Simeon," *ZDPV* 96 (1980): 136–152.
9. R. Giveon, *Les bédouins Shosou des documents égyptiens* (Leiden, 1971).
10. Attested by texts since the middle of the Eighteenth Dynasty until the period of Ramses II; W. Helck, "Die Bedrohung Palästinas durch einwandernde Gruppen am Ende der 18. und am Anfang der 19. Dynastie," *VT* 18 (1968): 472–480; M. Weippert, "Semitische Nomaden des 2. Jahrtausends. Über die Š3św der ägyptischen Quellen," *Biblica* 55 (1974): 265–280, 427–433; idem, "The Israelite 'Conquest' and the Evidence from Transjordan," in *Symposia, Celebrating the 75th Anniversary of the Founding of the American Schools of Oriental Research* (Cambridge, Mass., 1979), pp. 15–34, especially pp. 30–34; M. Görg, "Namenstudien VII: Š3św-Beduinen und Sutû-Nomaden," *Bibl. Notizen* 11 (1980): 18–20; idem, "Punon — ein weiterer Distrikt der Š3św-Beduinen?" *Bibl. Notizen* 19 (1982): 15–21.
11. The classical work is Ed. Meyer, *Die Israeliten und ihre Nachbarstämme* (1906; reprint 1967). Recently H.F. Fuhs, "Qādeš — Materialien zu den Wüstentraditionen Israels," *Bibl. Notizen* 9 (1979): 45–70, especially 54–70; S. Herrmann, *A History of Israel in Old Testament Times*, 2d ed. (1980), pp. 77–81; H. Donner, *Geschichte des Volkes Israel und seiner Nachbarn in Grundzügen*, Part 1 (1984), pp. 102–104, follows Noth and others in reducing the value of the Kadesh traditions.
12. Alt, "Die Landnahme der Israeliten" (see note 3), pp. 100–107.
13. Y. Yadin, *Hazor* (London, 1972), pp. 129–132.
14. Y. Aharoni, *The Settlement of the Israelite Tribes in Upper Galilee* (1957) (Hebrew); idem, *The Land of the Bible* (1967), pp. 205–208.
15. R. de Vaux, "The Settlement of the Israelites in Southern Palestine and the Origins of the Tribe of Judah," in *Translation and Understanding the Old Testament*, eds. H.T. Frank and W.L. Reed (1970), pp. 108–134, especially pp. 119–134.
16. Some new publications concerning this subject are H. Engel, "Die Siegesstele des Merenptah," *Biblica* 60 (1979): 373–399; L.E. Stager, "Merenptah, Israel, and Sea Peoples: New Light on an Old Relief," *EI* 18 (in press); G. Fecht, "Die Israelstele, Gestalt und Aussage," in *Fontes atque Pontes (Festgabe für H. Brunner), Ägypten und Altes Testament*, 5 (1984), pp. 106–138.
17. After the name of "Israel," we find the signs: throw-stick, man, woman, and strokes designating the plural; the other names are only followed by a throw-stick and the sign for hill country, which mean "place in foreign country." The problems are discussed by Engel, "Die Siegesstele des Merenptah" (see note 16), pp. 383–387.
18. J.A. Callaway, "The 1966 ʿAi (Et-Tell) Excavations," *BASOR* 196 (1969): 2–16; idem, "New Evidence on the Conquest of ʿAi," *JBL* 87 (1968): 312–320; J.A. Callaway and R.E. Cooley, "A Salvage Excavation at Raddanah in Bireh," *BASOR* 201 (1971): 9–19; M. Kochavi and I. Finkelstein, "ʿIzbet Ṣarṭah 1976–78," *IEJ* 28 (1978): 267–268; cf. *RB* 86 (1979): 114–115, pl. 4; M. Garsiel

and I. Finkelstein, "The Westward Expansion of the House of Joseph in the Light of the ʿIzbet Ṣarṭah Excavations," *Tel Aviv* 5 (1978): 192–198; I. Finkelstein, Z. Lederman and S. Bonimovitch, "Shiloh 1981," *IEJ* 32 (1982): 148–150, pl. 19B–C; idem, "Shiloh 1982," *IEJ* 33 (1983): 123–126, pl. 16B; A. Mazar, "Giloh: An Early Israelite Settlement Site near Jerusalem," *IEJ* 31 (1981): 1–36.

19. The text in Joshua 9:15 including the term *b^e^rīt* is of later composition (Deuteronomistic?), but this is not relevant at the moment.
20. More information is given by J. Blenkinsopp, *Gibeon and Israel*, The Society for Old Testament Study. Monograph Series 2 (1972), especially pp. 14–27.
21. Alt, "Die Landnahme der Israeliten" (see note 3); idem, "Erwägungen über die Landnahme" (see note 3).
22. Cf. Alt, "Die Landnahme der Israeliten" (see note 3), pp. 137–139.
23. Ibid., p. 138: "Mit den Kämpfen gegen die Kanaanäerstädte ihrer Umgebung hatten die Stämme das Höchstmass der Ausweitung und Abrundung ihres Territorialbesitzes erreicht, dessen sie aus eigener Kraft fähig waren; jede Erzählung über einen Kampf und Sieg war für sie also ein wesentliches Dokument zur dauernd gültigen Begründung ihres Besitzrechts gerade an den vormals umstrittenen Grenzbereichen."
24. Cf. these and other comparable questions in Weippert, "The Israelite 'Conquest'" (see note 10), pp. 30–34.
25. In this respect L.E. Stager has recently collected some facts and suggestions in his article, "The Archaeology of the Family in Early Israelite Society," *BASOR* 257 (in press). I thank Prof. Stager for making it accessible to me as well as the article "Merenptah, Israel, and Sea Peoples" (see note 16).

The Israelite Settlement in Canaan in the Light of Archaeological Surveys

Moshe Kochavi

BIBLICAL SCHOLARS AND historians are well aware that the biblical story of the Israelite occupation of Canaan, as crystallized in the Book of Joshua, is a late historiographical work, remote in time from the events described, and requiring a critical approach in order to reveal its historical nucleus. The only historical data for the early appearance of *Israel* in the Land of Canaan come from the Merenptah Stele, now dated to 1207 B.C.E. — the transitional Late Bronze–Iron Age in archaeological terminology.

The proponents of the historicity of the Joshua narrative, as developed by the Albright school, see the wholesale destruction of most Canaanite cities, and their immediate occupation by people of a lesser culture by the end of the Late Bronze Age, as a corroboration of the biblical story of Joshua taking by force the Canaanite cities in a swift campaign, thereby inheriting the land.

Alt and his followers adopted the opposite approach to the problem, suggesting a longer process of settlement by nomads from the desert fringe who carried out transhumance. According to this model, the Canaanite cities in the lowlands were conquered only after the Israelites gained a substantial foothold in the sparsely populated highlands.

A more recent model, now in fashion, sees the peasant uprisings of Europe in the Middle Ages as the closest analogy to the cause for the downfall of Canaanite civilization. According to this conception, Canaanite cities did not meet their fate at the hands of desert marauders, as the desert of Canaan could never have supported such large numbers of nomads. The destruction of the Canaanite cities was caused by the revolt of the oppressed masses of peasants living in the villages outside the cities. These rebels turned then to the faraway mountains, settled there, and created liberated Israel.

The time is ripe to view the historical models against the background of the geographical setting, the ethnological comparisons from this country, and the immense body of archaeological data now in our hands. Excavation and surface survey have become more precise in chronological determinations, and many blank spots on the map of this country have been filled in. The archaeological evidence indicates that many of the Canaanite cities reputed to have been conquered by Joshua — or alleged to have been destroyed by the rebelling peasants — were simply not in existence at the end of the Late Bronze Age. These include Heshbon, city of Sihon the Amorite, Arad, Jericho and ʿAi, cities whose downfall is described in detail. Other cities, which were considered to have been destroyed as a result of a mass uprising or an overall conquest in a campaign of only a few years duration, were in reality destroyed gradually over a time span of several generations. Hazor met its fate around 1275 B.C.E., while Lachish was destroyed about one hundred years later around 1160 B.C.E. Other "cities," such as Dan/Laish, Gibeon and Jarmuth, mentioned as destroyed by the Israelites, have such meager Late Bronze Age remains that we may assume them to have been merely small hamlets or only burial grounds at that time.

The major change that occurred between the Late Bronze and Iron Age was not the sudden destruction of Canaanite urban civilization, which in some locales continued throughout the Late Bronze–Iron Age transitional period. The real revolution took place not in the cities, but in the pattern of settlement in the countryside. During the Late Bronze Age, and especially toward its end, no small unfortified settlements are known. However, with the beginning of the Iron Age, they suddenly appear by the hundreds. The study of this phenomenon, the interpretation of the plans of the various sites, their spatial dispersion, their economic base, and their social structure, in short, all the complex processes involved, is the objective of the archaeological approach to the problem of the Israelite Settlement in Canaan.

Shifts in settlement patterns are best studied by using the methods of settlement archaeology: regional surface exploration aimed at locating the sites and analyzing their *raison d'être* and inter-site relations, combined with excavations at key sites, in order to determine more precise dating and obtain better knowledge of their material culture in all its regional variations. Ecological, ethnographic and other data form indispensable elements for the final synthesis. In spite of the enormous amount of work invested in this study during the last decade, it is still far from complete. Entire regions, such as the Upper Galilee, are still virtually unexplored, and others, like most of the Transjordan, have been only partially surveyed. A summary of the evidence, such as the present one, which treats each region separately, cannot of course be considered as anything more than a report on the state of the art.

The principle advance in our knowledge comes from the main area of Israelite settlement, namely the hill country of Ephraim and Manasseh. Systematic surveys and excavations carried out by Finkelstein and Zertal in recent years enable us now to reach some conclusions. Here, like in all the inland regions, there was a significant occupational regression during the fourteenth–thirteenth centuries B.C.E. The entire region between Shechem and Bethel seems to have been void of any major Canaanite town at that time. There is slightly more continuity of occupation in the inner valleys of the territory of Manasseh, but even there the decrease in the number of sites and, consequently, of population is radical; only one out of four Middle Bronze Age sites continues into the Late Bronze Age. With the beginning of the Iron Age, however, the more or less empty hills of Ephraim were washed over by a wave of settlers moving from northeast to southwest, a wave that left in its wake almost a hundred settlements in this region alone. The movement from east to west is attested by the appearance of later ceramic forms and more developed sites. It may be understood as the progressive adaptation of Mediterranean agriculture by people who started out by growing cereals and herding flocks, types of subsistence better suited to the eastern desert fringes from which they very likely came. The change in the layout of their settlements — from an enclosure to a small village — as observed at ʿIzbet Ṣarṭah, for example, went hand in hand with the development of a new subsistence pattern based on horticulture, such as olive and grape cultivation, and the resultant social changes within the community.

The northern part of this region has the largest number of sites dating to this period as yet located. There seems to have been a tendency to cluster these settlements, some of them sharing the same ecological unit, an inland valley such as the Vale of Dothan. A common cult place, like the "Bull Site" excavated by Amihai Mazar, and the kinship of the people of the neighboring villages illustrate the social relationships between families and clans, best attested in the Gideon cycle. The cult place on Mt. Ebal, on the contrary, has no settlements in its immediate vicinity, and has an entirely different type of cult structure. Consequently, it may have been a cultic center for larger groups that came from farther afield. What emerges from the archaeological evidence from the territory of Manasseh supports the biblical passages alluding to it as the cradle of the Israelite clans and tribes that eventually migrated from there, but maintained connections with their kinfolk for generations thereafter.

The pattern of settlement in the Land of Judah shows an even sparser Late Bronze Age occupation than that of the region immediately to its north. In the Judean hill country, there were only two major Canaanite centers, Jerusalem and Debir, most of the Canaanite cities being located in the lower-lying areas of the Shephelah. Early Israelite settlement in Judah was concentrated in the hill country, while the few sites located in the Shephelah lie on its very border. The Negev of Judah — the Beer-Sheba–Arad Basin — was settled by the Israelites only at the end of the eleventh century B.C.E. The early levels at Arad and Beer-Sheba and the short-lived hamlet of Tel Esdar III are examples of the beginnings of Kenite and Simeonite settlement in this region. Mt. Giloh, with its enclosure-like plan, was interpreted by its excavator as a herdsmen's hamlet. The transition to a more settled way of life is reflected, in this case, by its abandonment in the early tenth century B.C.E., when nearby Jerusalem was captured by David, making it possible for Israelites from the surrounding countryside to settle within its walls. During its existence as a kingdom, Judah continued to supply settlers to its outer regions, the Judean Desert, the Negev, the

Shephelah and the Yarkon-Ayalon River Basin. Settlement in most of these regions was made possible only after the subjugation of Philistine, Amalekite, and what was left of Canaanite power. Is it not possible that this was the historical analogy on which "Joshua's conquests" depend?

Turning north, we find a different settlement history in the valleys of Acre, Jezreel and Beth-Shean. Surface surveys and the excavations at Beth-Shean, Megiddo, Taanach, and more recently Tell Keisan, Tell Qiri and Yoqneʿam, point toward an uninterrupted continuation of Canaanite culture during the Late Bronze–Iron Age transitional period, with floruit in the twelfth century B.C.E. under the Egyptian Twentieth Dynasty. Beth-Shean and Megiddo were still serving as the two main Egyptian strongholds on the northern border of the empire in the days of Rameses VI (1141–1133 B.C.E.), and Israelite occupation of the valleys did not begin before the tenth century. For a survey of early Israelite settlement, we have to turn again to the inland hill regions, such as the Galilee and Gilead.

In Lower Galilee, like in Manasseh, the Canaanites were concentrated in the inland valleys, but here, unlike in Manasseh, Israelite settlement sites were established mainly in the hills. Zvi Gal observed here several groups of sites, located near small springs, and although they have not as yet been excavated, they seem to be similar in size and layout to sites in the hill country of Ephraim and Judah. Lower Galilee is the northern border for the dispersion of the collared-rim jar, so typical of the central hill country. The fact that the plateau forming the southeastern tip of this area, the inheritance of Issachar according to Joshua 19, was not settled before the tenth century B.C.E., means that a different reconstruction for the early history of this tribe is required, and that Alt's theories on this subject should be abandoned. It also corroborates Kallai's viewpoint regarding the date of the territorial border lists of the Israelite tribes as preserved in the Bible.

The survey carried out by Aharoni in Upper Galilee some thirty years ago was the first to reveal the settlement pattern of the early Israelites. Since then only limited archaeological work has been conducted in this region, which by and large remains an archaeological *terra incognita*. Nevertheless, we are already in a position to correct one of Aharoni's misconceptions. It seems that the Upper Galilee was void of major Late Bronze Age sites, except Qedesh in Galilee, situated in a small inland valley on the region's eastern border. Another phenomenon, not encountered in any of the other regions, is the existence here of several large forts located on mountain peaks. The material remains from the fort of Har Adir date from the eleventh century B.C.E. and suggest a link with the Phoenician coast to the west.

In the Western Galilee, the survey carried out by Raphael Frankel revealed clusters of Early Iron Age settlements located between the Phoenician coastal strip to the west and the high mountains of Galilee to their east. It is suggested that these settlements represent the inheritance of the tribe of Asher, who "... dwelt among the Canaanites, the inhabitants of the land; for they did not drive them out" (Judges 1:32).

Not a single collared-rim jar of the type characteristic of the central hill country has been found in the mountains of the Upper Galilee. The two dominant pithoi types here are the Tyrian type and the local type. Both are derived from Late Bronze Age prototypes common in northern Canaan.

The situation in Transjordan is very difficult to grasp, especially for an Israeli scholar who is deprived, in this case, of his best research tool — an intimate knowledge of the area. All that we know about southern Gilead and the Mishor, inhabited by the Gadites "from time immemorial" (as stated by Mesha, king of Moab), is that the collared-rim jar of the central hill country is found there in abundance but with some local variations. It seems to be the dominant pottery type in northern Gilead as well, although it is difficult to judge, as Mittmann's survey of the area was published without pottery illustrations. The survey itself, however, shows a settlement pattern similar to that of some Cisjordanian regions. The Late Bronze Age population of the Gilead was sparse at the time, and in the mountainous forested parts, the ʿAjlun, it approached nil. The ʿAjlun was first inhabited during the Early Iron Age, more Iron Age settlements appearing only sometime later in the Irbid Plain, the Yarmuk River Basin and the Jordan Valley. An early stage of settlement for the Gileadites is thus suggested in the areas far removed from Canaanite control, with a later stage represented by the abandonment of the less economically viable region for the lower and more fertile grounds.

I end my cursory survey in the hope that I have succeeded in stressing the primary importance of the archaeological evidence for reconstructing the history of early Israel. We believe, in fact, that any such reconstruction must take advantage of this source — the only really authentic source for this period. Archaeological evidence, when treated scientifically, is by its nature free from theological, sociological or political prejudice.

In any research the following points should be borne in mind:

1. The first phase of the Israelite Settlement occurred in the hill country where there were no Canaanite cities, or where the settling herdsmen were at least tolerated. It is Alt's *Landnahme* that seems to be in accord with this phase.
2. The expansion of the settlers into the surrounding lowlands began later and gained momentum only with the Monarchy. It is in this period that we have to look for the *Sitz-im-Leben* of the biblical concept of the Conquest and Settlement.

We may therefore conclude that as a case study for biblical archaeology, the archaeology of the settlement of the tribes of Israel not only illustrates the Bible, but has proven to be essential for its understanding.

Select Bibliography

Aharoni, Y. "The Settlement of the Israelite Tribes in Upper Galilee." Ph.D. diss., The Hebrew University of Jerusalem, 1957. (Hebrew, English forthcoming)

——. "Nothing Early and Nothing Late. Re-writing Israel's Conquest." *BA* 39 (1976): 55–76.

——. "The Settlement of the Tribes in the Negev — A New Picture." *Ariel* 41 (1976): 3–19.

——. *The Land of the Bible, A Historical Geography*. 2d ed. London, 1979.

——. *Archaeology of the Land of Israel*. London, 1983.

Albright, W.F. "The Israelite Conquest of Canaan in the Light of Archaeology." *BASOR* 74 (1939): 11–23.

——. *The Biblical Period from Abraham to Ezra*. New York, 1963.

——. *The Archaeology of Palestine and the Bible*. Cambridge, Mass., 1974.

Alt, A. "Erwägungen über die Landnahme der Israeliten in Palästina." In *Kleine Schriften zur Geschichte des Volkes Israel*. Band I. Munich, 1959, pp. 126–175.

——. "The Settlement of the Israelites in Palestine." In *Essays on Old Testament History and Religion*. Oxford, 1966.

Beck, P. and Kochavi, M. "The Egyptian Governor's Palace at Aphek — A Dated Archaeological Assemblage from the End of the Late Bronze Age." *Qadmoniot* 62–63 (1983): 47–51; 64 (1983): 126. (Hebrew, English translation forthcoming)

Finkelstein, I. "The ʿIzbet Ṣarṭah Excavations and the Israelite Settlement in the Hill Country." Ph.D. diss., Tel Aviv University, 1983. (Hebrew)

Finkelstein, I., Bunimovitz, S. and Lederman, Z. "Excavations at Shiloh, 1981–1983." *Qadmoniot* 65 (1984): 15–25. (Hebrew)

Frankel, R. "Galilee in the Late Bronze and Iron Age." In *The Lands of Galilee*, edited by A. Shmueli, A. Sopher, and N. Cleiut. Haifa, 1984. (Hebrew)

Gal, Z. "The Settlement of Issachar: Some New Observations." *Tel Aviv* 9 (1982): 79–86.

Gonen, R. "Burial in Canaan during the Late Bronze Age." Ph.D. diss., The Hebrew University of Jerusalem, 1979. (Hebrew)

Gottwald, N.K. *The Tribes of Yahweh: A Sociology of the Religion of Liberated Israel, 1250–1050 B.C.E.* Orbis: Maryknoll, 1979.

Kochavi, M. "The Excavations of Tel Esdar." *ʿAtiqot* 5 (1969): 14–48. (Hebrew)

——, ed. *Judea, Samaria and the Golan, Archaeological Survey in 1968*. Jerusalem, 1972 (Hebrew)

——. "The Period of Conquest and Settlement." In *The History of the Land of Israel*, edited by I. Ephal, vol. 2. Jerusalem, 1985. (Hebrew)

Lapp. P. "The Conquest of Palestine in the Light of Archaeology." *Concordia Theological Monthly* 38 (1967): 283–300.

Macdonald, B. "The Late Bronze and Iron Age Sites of the Wadi el Hasa Survey 1979." In *Midian, Moab and Edom*, edited by J.F.A. Sawyer and D.J.A. Clines. Sheffield, 1983.

Malamat, A. "The Danite Migration and the Pan-Israelite Exodus-Conquest. A Biblical Narrative Pattern." *Biblica* 51 (1970): 1–16.

——. "The Proto-History of Israel: A Study in Method." In *The Word of the Lord Shall Go Forth*, edited by C.L. Meyers and M. O'Connor. Philadelphia, 1983.

Mazar, A. "Giloh: An Early Israelite Settlement Site Near Jerusalem." *IEJ* 31 (1981): 1–36.

——. "The 'Bull Site' — An Iron Age I Open Cult Place." *BASOR* 247 (1982): 27–42.

Mazar, B. "The Historical Background of the Book of Genesis." *JNES* 28 (1969): 73–83.

——. "'They Shall Call People to Their Mountain.'" *EI* 14 (1978): 39–41. (Hebrew)

Mendenhall, G.E. "The Hebrew Conquest of Palestine." *BA* 25 (1962): 66–87.

Miller, J.M. "The Israelite Occupation of Canaan." In *Israelite and Judean History*, edited by J.H. Hayes and J.M. Miller. London, 1977.

Mittmann, S. *Beiträge zur Siedlungs und Territorialgeschichte des nördlichen Ostjordanlandes*. Wiesbaden, 1970.

Na'aman, N. "The Inheritance of the Sons of Simeon." *ZDPV* 96 (1980): 136–152.

Noth, M. *The History of Israel*. London, 1958.

Rowton, M.B. "The Topological Factor of the Hapiru Problem." *Anatolian Studies* 16 (1965): 375–387.

——. "The Woodlands of Ancient Western Asia." *JNES* 26 (1967): 261–277.

de Vaux, R. *The Early History of Israel*. Philadelphia, 1978.

Weippert, M. *The Settlement of the Israelite Tribes in Palestine*. London, 1971.

——. "The Israelite 'Conquest' and the Evidence from Transjordan." In *Symposia*, edited by F.M. Cross. Cambridge, Mass., 1979.

Zertal, A. "Aruboth, Heper and Solomon's Third District." M.A. thesis, Tel Aviv University, 1981. (Hebrew)

The Israelite Settlement in Canaan in the Light of Archaeological Excavations

Amihai Mazar

A SERIES OF excavations carried out in the various parts of the country during the last fifteen years has greatly increased our knowledge concerning the archaeological aspect of the Israelite Settlement. It is the purpose of this paper to survey some of the results of this research, and to discuss several problems related to the subject.

The Identification of Sites as Israelite

The following sites can be considered relevant to our discussion, though some of them are problematic in their definition:

In the Galilee: Dan, Hazor, Ḥorvat Harashim, Sasa, Har Adir, Ḥorvat ʿAvot.
In the central hills: Taanach, the 'Bull Site,' Mt. Ebal, Shiloh, ʿAi, Bethel, Khirbet Raddana, Tell en-Nasbeh, Tell el-Fûl, Giloh, Beth Zur.
In the foothills and Shephelah: ʿIzbet Ṣarṭah, Beth Shemesh (?), Tell Beit Mirsim (?), perhaps also Tel Zeror and Burgeta in the Sharon.
In the northern Negev: Tel Masos, Arad, Beer-Sheba, Tel Esdar, and perhaps also the cluster of Iron Age sites in the central Negev.

The identification of a site as Israelite largely depends on the evaluation of two main factors. The most important one is the site's attribution to the pattern of settlement, which is considered the best indication for Israelite settlement. This subject, discussed in Prof. Kochavi's paper, is essential for identifying sites as belonging to the new settlement wave. The other factor is the nature of the material culture, to which we shall return later.

Even when these two factors are considered, and seem to point to definite identification, we still remain with serious doubts concerning the definition of some sites. This is exemplified by the site of Har Adir, excavated by D. Davis for the Department of Antiquities. Har Adir is located in the high mountains of Upper Galilee amid a cluster of sites, considered since Aharoni's pioneering survey as a safe indication for intensive Israelite settlement. Though the finds at this site are similar in nature to those at neighboring sites, Har Adir differs in its being a large fortified citadel of a form foreign to the Israelite pattern of settlement. It is tempting to identify it as a Tyrian border fort, built in the heartland of the Israelite occupation in Upper Galilee, in an excellent strategic position overlooking the coastal plain, and in particular Tyre. Yet, the similarity of the finds to those at other Settlement sites in Upper Galilee may lead to a different solution, namely, that the fort was built by Israelites during the eleventh century B.C.E., at a rather advanced phase of their settlement, as a stronghold against the rising power of Tyre.

The neighboring sites of Taanach and Megiddo provide other good examples of problematic identification. Both appear in the list of unconquered cities in the north, together with Beth-Shean and Dor (Judges 1:27). Yet, Taanach Period I, published recently by W. Rast, greatly differs from the contemporary Megiddo Stratum VIIA. The nature of the material culture at Taanach closely resembles that of typical Israelite sites in the central hill country, and permits us to suggest that during the twelfth century B.C.E. Taanach was already an Israelite town. The significance of this conclusion in light of the biblical data in Judges 1:27, and particularly in the Song of Deborah, is obvious, as the battle of Deborah against Sisera took place "...at Taanach, by the waters of Megiddo." In contrast to Taanach, Megiddo retained its Canaanite traditions throughout Iron Age I (Strata VII–VI). Y. Aharoni's suggestion that Megiddo Stratum VI be identified as an Israelite settlement must be rejected in the light of the nature of the material culture there.

Several years ago I excavated the so-called 'Bull Site' southeast of Taanach, which I suggested should be identified as an Israelite open cult place of the twelfth century B.C.E. This identification is based solely on pottery dating, and on the site's relation to a cluster of small Iron Age I sites located in the vicinity, which fit our assumed Israelite pattern of settlement.

Tel Masos in the northern Negev was described by its excavators, Aharoni, Fritz and Kempinski, as a superb example of an Israelite site. However, other scholars (Kochavi, Herzog and Finkelstein) now tend to suggest that it was non-Israelite, perhaps Amalekite. It is true that Tel Masos is exceptional both in its architecture and finds, but it still can be seen as a major site in the general process of Israelite settlement in the northern Negev, here accompanied by foreign activity (Canaanite or Philistine), perhaps in the form of traders settling side by side with Israelites, giving external stimulus to its development.

We shall probably never have an absolute answer to the question of ethnic identification of the settlers at every site, particularly since there is no agreement among historians as to the degree of self-identity reached by the Israelites in this period. Thus, any suggestion or interpretation in this matter, particularly concerning the fringe areas, should remain tentative.

Chronology

The chronological framework for the sites under discussion can be established only on the basis of thorough pottery research, and comparison of the finds there with material from multistrata excavations.

In each of the regions — the Upper Galilee, central hill country and the northern Negev — we find a selection of pottery types characteristic of the settlement sites. Many of these types retain Canaanite traditions of the Late Bronze Age, yet the typological details distinguish them from their Late Bronze Age predecessors. The older types are accompanied by new ones typical of Iron Age I. It should be recalled that developments in pottery typology occurred slowly, except in periods of sharp cultural breaks. Such a break did not occur at the transition from the Late Bronze Age to Iron Age I. There was a slow process of disappearance of types and appearance of new ones. We now know, for instance, that the sporadic appearance of collared-rim

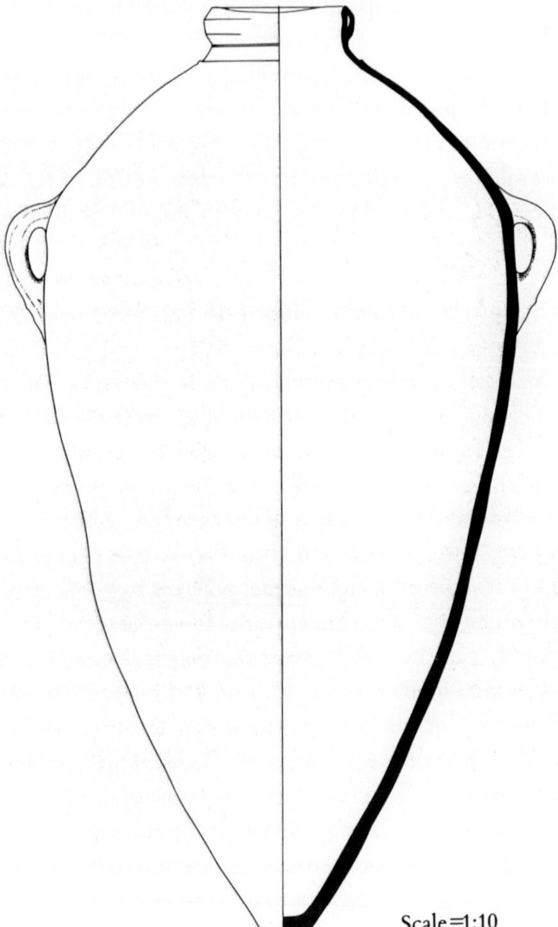

Drawing of a 'collared rim' pithos from Giloh

pithoi occurred at Aphek already in the Canaanite culture of the thirteenth century B.C.E., but this form only became common during Iron Age I. Cooking pots and storage jars manufactured in clear Canaanite tradition continued to appear during the first half of Iron Age I. The distinctions are sometimes very refined, and therefore we should not rely on the presence or absence of one specific type in a certain context. The entire assemblage should be discussed in detail, on the basis of quantitative relationships between the various types.

A close study of the pottery from the Settlement sites points to the conclusion that in fact none of these sites existed prior to Iron Age I. A number of them were founded during the twelfth century B.C.E., whilst most of them flourished during the eleventh century B.C.E. Many of these sites were deserted already during Iron Age I, perhaps toward the establishment of the Monarchy, when a slow process of urbanization was accompanied by the abandonment of some of the sites.

Our excavations thus in fact refer to the period of the Judges, and they cannot throw light on the debated question of Israelite presence in the country during the Late Bronze Age.

The recent finds in Upper Galilee, as well as excavations at Tyre and Tell Keisan, enable us to answer a long-debated question concerning the chronology of the Upper Galilee pottery assemblage, first identified by Aharoni at Ḥorvat Harashim. It is now clear that this assemblage, which postdates the destruction of Canaanite Hazor, is no earlier than Iron Age I, and perhaps is closer to the eleventh century B.C.E.

The Characteristics of the Material Culture in the Settlement Sites

Many of the sites are rather small villages of no more than 1–2 acres. Exceptions are Shiloh (4 acres), Tel Masos (12 acres) and Dan (50 acres). At Dan, Prof. Biran found evidence for Iron Age I pits in various parts of the tell, identifying them as evidence for the Danite settlement. Fortifications are almost unknown at these sites, yet in a few cases there is evidence for some sort of defense line. The most clear example is at Giloh, south of Jerusalem, where we found a defense line composed of several segments, each built in a different technique, perhaps by the family living adjacent to it. We have already mentioned the exceptional fort at Har Adir in Upper Galilee, yet there the ethnic identity of the builders remains enigmatic. Shiloh, the major Israelite center in the central hill country, remained unfortified, but was perhaps defended by the outer belt of houses forming the perimeter of the site. At Beer-Sheba, meager evidence for a casemate-walled settlement of the eleventh century B.C.E. was found; this might be regarded as a link to the casemated central buildings (so-called forts) of the central Negev dated to the late eleventh and tenth centuries B.C.E.

The inner planning of the settlements is only known from the few sites which have been extensively excavated. It appears that large open areas were incorporated to provide space for flocks, and grain was stored in sunken silos. Pens for livestock were found at Giloh, where a unit composed of a pen adjoined to a house was uncovered.

Pits and silos are most common at many of these sites, with vast numbers at Dan, ʿIzbet Ṣarṭah and Tell Beit Mirsim. The arrangement of houses in an outer belt is a common feature, for example at Ḥorvat ʿAvot (in the Galilee), Shiloh, ʿAi, Tell en-Nasbeh and ʿIzbet Ṣarṭah in the central hill country, and at Tel Masos and Tel Esdar in the northern Negev. This circular arrangement, leaving large open areas within the site, also provided a place for public activities (such as the Israelite shrine of Shiloh), probably located at the central and highest part of the town.

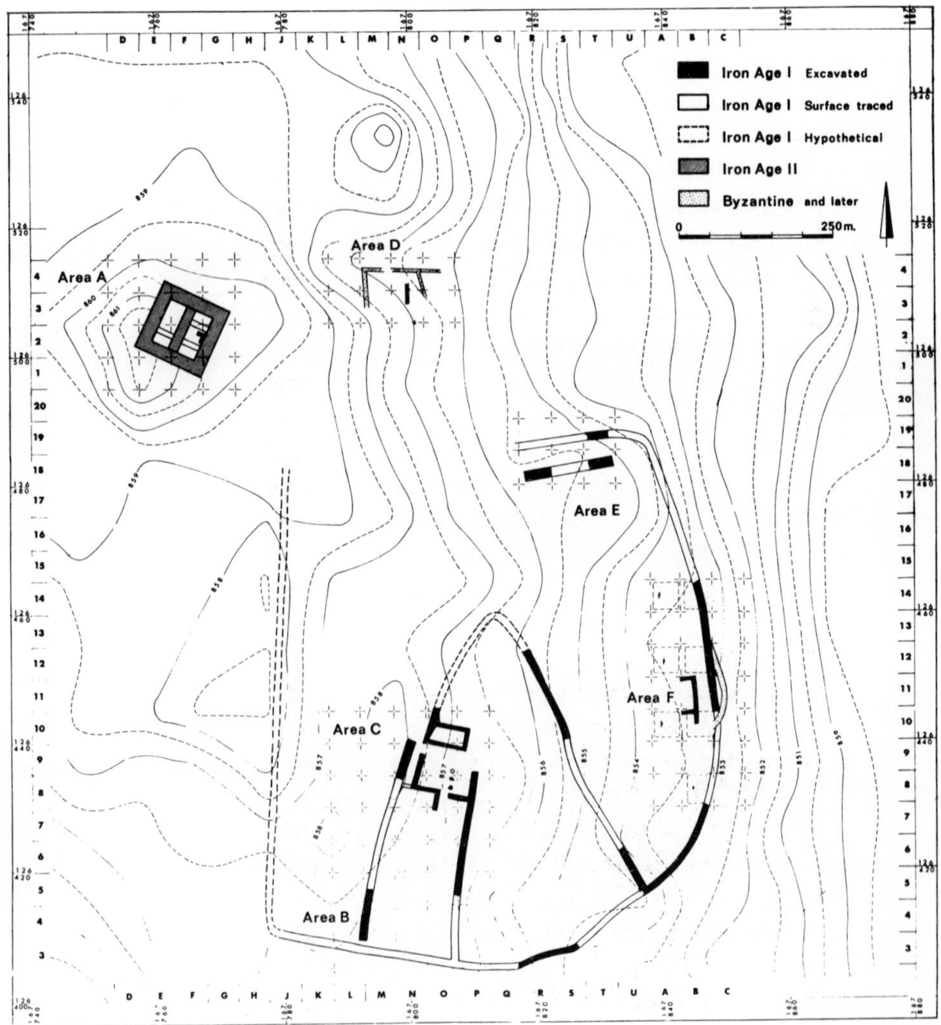

Plan of the Iron Age I site at Giloh, south of Jerusalem

This layout differs sharply from any known Canaanite plan and would appear to fit settlers living in a patriarchal society, the economic basis of which was combined pastoralism and simple agriculture. We may assume that most Settlement sites served a clan or some other tribal fraction totaling about 100 to 200 people. There were, however, several larger centers of population, such as Dan, Shiloh and Tel Masos.

The private dwellings in these settlements are in most cases pillared houses, buildings comprising a central courtyard divided by pillars, with rectangular rooms on one or more sides. These three-room and four-room houses are common at Israelite sites, particularly in the central hill country and the northern Negev. This has led several scholars to define them as an original Israelite innovation. Fritz and Kempinski have suggested that this house type developed from the tent of the seminomadic phase which preceded permanent settlement. We may, however, question both the origin of this house type and its attribution to the Israelites. After I excavated one of the earliest houses of this type at Giloh, I suggested that it was an example of the early stage in the development of the Israelite pillared house, which subsequently evolved into the stereotyped three-room and four-room house. Recent excavations at Tel Batash (Timnah), however, now lead me to suggest another

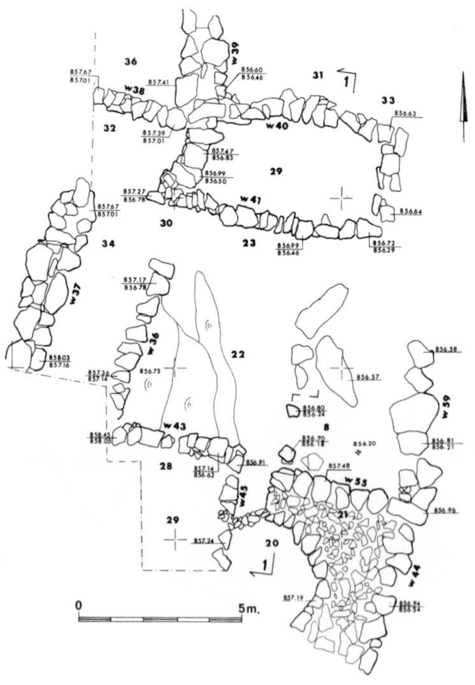

Plan of a dwelling at Giloh (twelfth century B.C.E.)

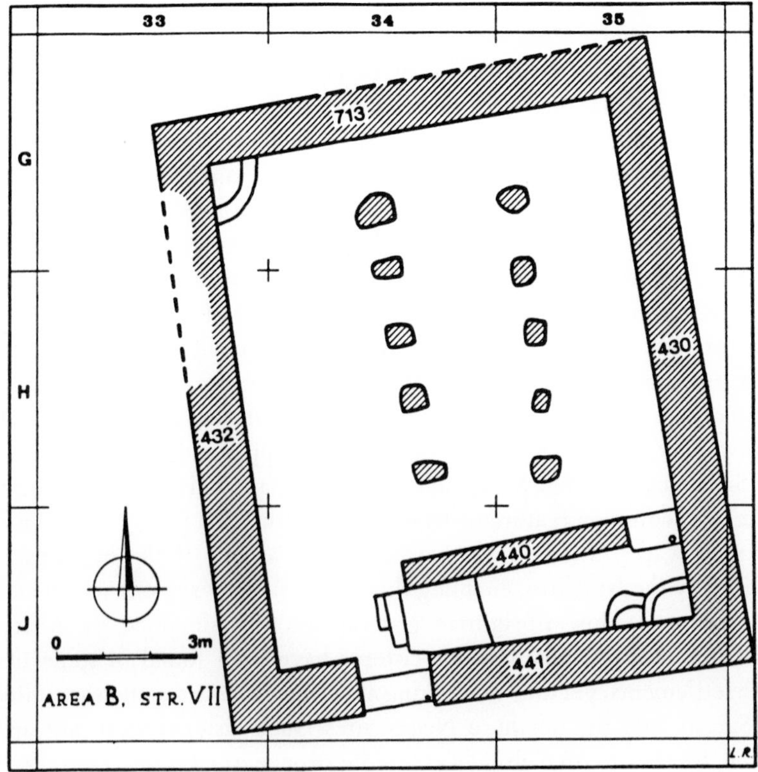

Plan of the Canaanite Late Bronze Age building from Tel Batash (Timnah) (fourteenth century B.C.E.)

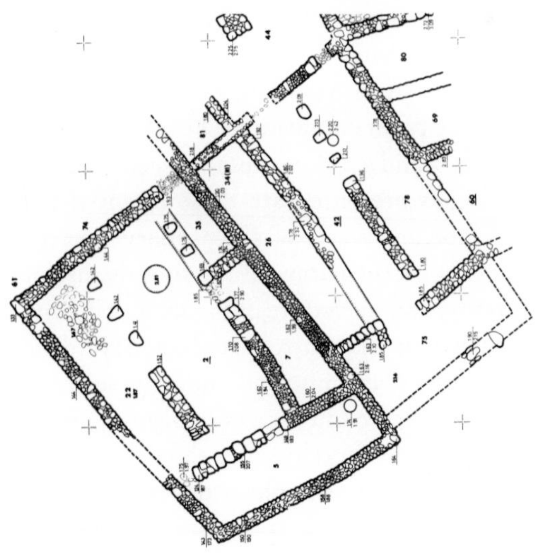

Plan of "four-room" buildings at Tel Masos. From *Tel Aviv* 1 (1974)

possibility. There, we discovered a pillared building in a Late Bronze Age II context (probably of the fourteenth century B.C.E.). This is a patrician house composed of two storeys: the ground floor was divided by two rows of five wooden pillars set on stone bases. We assume that this was a roofed storage area, while the second floor was the main living area. This division differs from that in the Iron Age houses, where the pillared area is assumed to have remained partly unroofed, but the Tel Batash building may be regarded as the closest Canaanite prototype of the pillared buildings which became so common in the Iron Age. It is thus possible that the pillared buildings of Iron Age I were inspired by a Canaanite architectural tradition, known so far only from isolated examples in the central part of the country.

The distribution of the pillared houses during Iron Age I is not limited to the Israelite Settlement sites. They are found in various regions of Palestine; thus we encounter them at Tell Keisan in the Plain of Acre; at Megiddo Stratum VIB; at Tell Abu Hawam IV; at Tell Qasile Stratum X; at Tel Ṣippor and Tel Seraʿin Philistia; and and at Sahab and Khirbet Medeineh in Transjordan. This house type may thus be regarded as a common feature of Iron Age I, not limited to any one ethnic group.

Plastered water cisterns have been regarded as one of the important features introduced by the Israelites, enabling them to settle new regions which lack natural water resources. This Albrightian generalization, maintained by Aharoni, now proves to be inexact. Lined water cisterns have been found in some Iron Age I Israelite settlements, yet they are lacking at various other sites, such as, Shiloh, Giloh, ʿIzbet Ṣarṭah, and the northern Negev sites. Such cisterns were not an Israelite invention, for they existed already at Middle Bronze Age Hazor. Thus the argumentation concerning their role in the Settlement process should be abandoned.

Turning to the finds at the Israelite sites, we have first to mention again the pottery repertoire. A survey of the pottery found reveals a great variety, indicating distinctive regional developments. One distinct aspect is the limited variety of types. Large pithoi and storage jars, as well as cooking pots, comprise most of the pottery assemblage at many of the sites. At Giloh, where a quantitative analysis was made, we found that these three types comprise 80% of the entire pottery assemblage. This proportion appears to be valid at other sites too, such as Shiloh, Bethel, ʿAi and in the Upper Galilee. The types presented are those essential to a subsistence economy where the storage of food and water was of primary concern. The minimal range of pottery types, together with the nature of the sites themselves, is the best indication of the economic situation and the nature of the society involved. We are dealing here with a poor, self-sufficient and introverted society, differing widely from the contemporaneous, wealthy Canaanite and Philistine societies dwelling in the plains.

Thus, the ethnicity is reflected in the assemblage as a whole, while the individual pottery types appearing at the Israelite sites should not be defined as limited to any particular ethnic group. A good example of this is the well-known collared-rim jar, which is considered to be a hallmark of the Israelite material culture of Iron Age I. These jars are abundant in a distinct geographic region: from the Jezreel Valley in the north to the Hebron region in the south. They are rarely found north of this area, and are totally absent from the Upper Galilee mountains as well as from the northern Negev sites. An exception is Dan, where a significant number of such jars was found, possibly reflecting the continuing connection of the Danites with the central hill country. The appearance of such jars at Megiddo, however, as well as in Transjordan, especially at the large site of Sahab, southeast of Amman, excludes any specific ethnic attribution to these jars. They should be regarded as a common feature in the central part of Palestine on either side of the Jordan; the specific suitability of these jars to the economic needs of the Israelite settlers made them dominant in the Israelite pottery repertoire. Yet they were never *exclusively* used by the Israelites.

The same economic needs which led to the common use of the collared-rim jar in the central hill country, made its counterpart, the Galilean pithos, a most common feature of the Israelite sites in Upper Galilee. Its typological ancestor is clearly attested at Canaanite sites in the north, from Hazor to Ugarit. During Iron Age I, the original Canaanite type underwent some development in form, such as a change in its proportions and the addition of handles, but much of the basic characteristic Canaanite shape was retained, and the type remained popular throughout the eleventh century B.C.E.

The Canaanite origin of other pottery types at the Israelite sites can be clearly attested. Thus the twelfth century B.C.E. cooking pots at Giloh, Bethel and other sites are very close to Late Bronze Age types known from Canaanite sites. These facts lead to the conclusion that the Israelite settlers had probably no clear tradition of pottery-making of their own. They settled sufficiently close to Canaanite centers to be able to obtain select pottery vessels, and perhaps later to produce them on their own, retaining the Canaanite traditional forms. Other Canaanite shapes, and the entire Canaanite decoration tradition, were abandoned by the new settlers.

We should mention the almost complete lack of art objects at the Israelite sites, except for a few clay moldings hinting at the existence of local artistic traditions. Other isolated pieces of art could well have been imported from Canaanite production centers, the most clear examples being the kernos found at Sasa, which is very similar to the one discovered at Megiddo; the lion-shaped handle found at Tel Masos; the bronze figurine of a seated male god found at Hazor; and perhaps also the unique bronze bull figurine found at what I assume is an open Israelite cult place in the Samarian hills.

The cult practices of the Israelite settlers are little known from archaeological excavations. We should mention the small high place found at Hazor in Area B, Stratum XI; the 'Bull Site,' which is a good example of an open cult place on a mountain ridge outside a permanent settlement; and finally the discovery by A. Zertal on Mt. Ebal, which appears to be an Israelite Iron Age I cult place. This latter excavation and the latest discoveries at Shiloh will perhaps add substantially to the information we have on the Israelite cult practices of this period.

Conclusions

The Israelite Settlement sites are defined mainly by the pattern of settlement to which they belong, and by the characteristic features of their material culture, which are unprecedented in the Late Bronze Age. Recent archaeological research increasingly stresses the Canaanite origin of various components of this material culture, such as details in architecture, pottery-making, artistic traditions and cult practices. Yet the Israelite material culture as a whole differs markedly from the previous and contemporaneous Canaanite culture. Various factors, such as the distribution of sites, their location and planning, the composition of the pottery assemblages, and the economic and social structure, are definitely non-Canaanite. Surveys and excavations thus reveal a material culture of a distinct character, which although inspired by Canaanite traditions, had an independent development of its own.

The permanent settlement phase reflected in the surveys and excavations may have been preceded by a seminomadic phase. During this early phase, probably at the very end of the Late Bronze Age and the beginning of the Iron Age (thirteenth–twelfth centuries B.C.E.), the Israelite tribes, coming into contact with the Canaanite culture of the country, absorbed existing material-cultural traditions, which continued to appear during the subsequent phase of permanent settlement. Unfortunately, this early phase has not left any archaeological evidence.

Select Bibliography

Aharoni, Y. *The Settlement of the Israelite Tribes in Upper Galilee.* Jerusalem, 1957. (Hebrew)

——. *The Archaeology of the Land of Israel.* Philadelphia, 1982, pp. 153–191.

Biran, A. "Tel Dan, Five Years Later." *BA* 43 (1980): 168–182.

Callaway, J.A. and Cooley, R.E. "A Salvage Excavation at Raddana, in Bireh." *BASOR* 201 (1971): 9–19.

——. "The 1966 ʿAi (et-Tell) Excavations." *BASOR* 196 (1969): 2–16.

Finkelstein, I. "The ʿIzbet Ṣarṭah Excavations and the Israelite Settlement in the Hill Country." Ph.D. diss., Tel Aviv University, 1983. (Hebrew)

——. "Notes and News," *IEJ* 32 (1982): 148–150; 33 (1983): 123–126, 267–268.

Fritz, V. and Kempinski, A. *Ergebnisse der Ausgrabungen auf der Hirbet el Masâs (Tel Masos) 1972–1975.* Wiesbaden, 1983.

Kochavi, M. "An Ostracon of the Period of the Judges from ʿIzbet Ṣarṭah." *Tel Aviv* 4 (1977): 1–13.

Miller, J.M. "The Israelite Occupation of Canaan." In *Israelite and Judean History*, edited by J.H. Hayes and J.M. Miller, London, 1977, pp. 213–284.

Mazar, A. "Giloh, An Early Israelite Settlement Site Near Jerusalem." *IEJ* 31 (1981): 1–36.

——. "The 'Bull Site,' an Iron Age I Open Cult Place." *BASOR* 247 (1982): 27–41.

Mazar, B. "The Early Israelite Settlement in the Hill Country." *BASOR* 241 (1981): 75–85.

de Vaux, R. *The Early History of Israel.* Parts III–IV. Philadelphia, 1978.

Weippert, M. *The Settlement of the Israelite Tribes in Palestine.* London, 1971.

Respondents

Joseph A. Callaway

For many years, the primary source for the understanding of the settlement in Canaan of the first Israelites was the Hebrew Bible, but every reconstruction based upon the biblical traditions has foundered on the evidence from archaeological remains. Therefore I do not agree with Prof. Gottwald's designation of the Hebrew Bible as the primary source. The primary source has to be archaeological remains because ultimately every hypothesis based upon the Bible, extra-biblical texts, inscriptions, or historical analogy has to find support in the material remains of the time.

Of the two older reconstructions of the Settlement, that of Albright and his followers, and that of Alt and his students, only the latter has found support for some of its main features in recent excavations. The Albright theory that, as Prof. Kochavi put it in his abstract: "...stressed the wholesale destruction of all the Canaanite cities by the end of the Late Bronze Age ... corroborating the biblical story of Joshua taking by force the Canaanite cities ... and thereby inheriting the land," has quietly expired from the lack of supporting evidence. This vindicates Alt's view reached in the early 1920s that repeated editing of the biblical traditions throughout the Old Testament period made a reconstruction of Israel's early history from those traditions impossible.[1]

Alt's significant discovery, working from Egyptian sources primarily, was that the central hill country between Jerusalem and the Valley of Jezreel was very thinly populated at the end of the Late Bronze Age. Shechem was the only city-state of importance in the region, which left wide gaps of territory both north and south virtually under no control.[2] This conclusion is supported by recent excavations and surveys of the central highlands.

Prof. Stager discovered in a survey of village sites from Hebron to Shechem that the density of permanent settlements increased dramatically in the transition from the Late Bronze to Iron Age I.[3] By about 1200 B.C.E., the number of villages in an area of 4,200 sq km had increased from twenty-three in the Late Bronze Age to 114 in Iron Age I. These are only the sites catalogued, which by no means is all of them. Kochavi notes that the "more-or-less empty hills of Ephraim were washed over by a wave of settlers moving from northeast to southwest, a wave that left in its wake hundreds of settlements." In any case, numerous small, unfortified villages of five acres or less were located on unoccupied older sites, or on hilltops that had never before supported permanent settlements.

It appears from the surveys of both Stager and Kochavi that Shechem exerted little or no regional influence in stopping the flow of settlers, when a century earlier, during the Amarna Age, the Labayu Dynasty had made its presence felt from Jerusalem to Megiddo. Lawrence E. Toombs shed some light on the impotence of Shechem in a paper given at the ASOR symposium in Jerusalem in 1975, in which he discussed the transition from the Late Bronze to Iron Age I. Reviewing the data from five principal areas of excavations conducted from 1957 to 1969, Toombs found that a major destruction of the city occurred late in the Late Bronze Age, ending a long period of considerable prosperity characterized by high population density, sophisticated building techniques, and impressive public works.[4] The agent of this destruction is not named, but Toombs notes that "Labayu's name had become a by-word for perfidy in the region" during the Amarna period, creating many enemies who would be willing to bring down the city when it weakened. Toombs dates the fall of Shechem to ca. 1300 B.C.E., a century before the advent of the Iron Age I settlers.[5]

Shechem seems to have been rebuilt after no significant break in occupation, but the buildings were poorer in materials and planning, and apparently only part of the city was repopulated. Other areas show evidence of agricultural activity and food storage, suggesting that the diminished city withdrew into the safety of its own fortifications.[6] This weakened state of affairs lasted through the transition from Late Bronze to Iron Age I in the central highlands, while the abandoned older sites and vacant hilltops north and south of Shechem were being planted with villages without interference.

Lacking specific evidence of the manner of infiltration and establishment of settlements in the highlands, Alt conjectured from historical analogy that "nomad" Israelites entered the land from the east, pasturing their flocks in the hills year after year until eventually they established villages and became sedentary.[7] This view appears in need of revision in the light of recent findings.

My excavations of the Iron Age I settlements at ʿAi and Raddana indicate that both villages were established from the beginning on a subsistence base of agriculture primarily and small cattle secondarily. That the newcomers were mainly farmers is indicated by an innovative, even revolutionary, new way of wresting a living from the arid, inhospitable hills of central Canaan. First, the hilltop villages were located away from natural water sources because each house had its own water supply in cisterns hewn in the solid rock underneath the structures. And second, steep hillsides which had never before been cultivated were cleared of underbrush and terraced to conserve water from rainfall needed for grain crops and gardens.[8]

Bell-shaped cisterns were hewn with bronze chisels in the thick layers of Senonian chalk exposed on most hilltops in the region. Even when ancient city ruins such as those at ʿAi (et-Tell) and Tell en-Nasbeh were settled, cisterns were dug by the newcomers, and the water sources used thousands of years earlier by the Early Bronze Age inhabitants were not restored. Wampler characterized the settlement at

Tell en-Nasbeh as "truly a place of cisterns" because a total of fifty-three was discovered.[9] At ʿAi, as many as three cisterns for each house were found in the most recent excavations.

The location of household cisterns underneath the walls and floors of the buildings suggests that they were excavated before the houses were built. In one house at ʿAi, two cisterns were located under the uphill side of the house, with openings outside the wall connected to surface drains cut in bedrock. A third cistern was underneath the greatroom of the house with a capstone in the middle of the floor. It was supplied with water from the two cisterns located on the uphill side of the house through openings in the sides about 50 cm above the bottom.[10] There would therefore be time for impurities in water collected in the first two cisterns to settle before the water spilled over into the third cistern from which the occupants drew their needs.

I have mentioned the probable sequence of building because, first, considerable time was required to establish a village, and second, the layout of houses in the village reflects a tradition of planning for sedentary life that the occupants brought with them. When we consider that a village of from two to five acres in size would have no more than about thirty to eighty men to do the building and defend their families, it seems obvious that nobody challenged the newcomers' claims to their sites.

Terracing of hillsides was another key element in the highlands subsistence strategy. Evidence for terracing during Iron Age I comes in part from excavations of the village at ʿAi, where terraces determined the settlement's size and limited it to the acropolis area. An Iron Age I agricultural terrace was discovered at Site G, on Contour 840, adjacent to Contour 845 on which the village structures ended.[11] The terrace followed broken edges of bedrock across half the width of the tell, from Site C to Site G, and covered the ruins of Early Bronze houses which had been destroyed and abandoned ca. 2400 B.C.E. The Iron Age I settlers had constructed terraces on the steep slopes of the acropolis, from Contours 845 to 850, as foundations for their houses, and the lower area of the tell from Contours 845 to 795 was terraced and cultivated.

How much of the valley and hills outside the ancient walls of ʿAi was planted with crops cannot be ascertained. The areas immediately east and south of the tell would have provided good soil for farming, although terraces on the slopes east of the tell would have been quite narrow and inefficient for the production of grain. Inside the Early Bronze Age city walls, up to 25 acres could have been planted. However, this 25 acres in addition to the limited patches outside would barely have provided bread for the village of 150 to 200 persons. The sources of subsistence from farming at ʿAi would have been inadequate for the villages.

It is now evident that a major supplement to the village subsistence was provided by small cattle which ranged the hills between ʿAi and the Jordan Valley. Their importance is indicated by a series of animal enclosures built adjacent to the houses in which the villagers lived.[12] In fact, only the house wall on the east side separated quarters of people from those of animals. And indeed, more space was given to animal enclosures than to the roofed areas of houses. Entrance to one of the rectangular enclosures was by way of a perfectly arched doorway 80 cm from floor to keystone.[13]

Considerable attention, therefore, was given to the care of sheep and goats, in providing shelter and safety from predators, and in having ready access to milk for yogurt and cheese. It is possible that up to one-half of a family's subsistence came from its animals. This does not mean, however, that the people were primarily shepherds. The evidence of permanent village settlements and a subsistence base of dry farming seems to point toward agriculture as the main source of food.

Although much of the above discussion has focused upon the site of ʿAi, it was only one of the ninety or so villages established in the central highlands at the beginning of Iron Age I, and is typical of most of them. The characteristic pillar houses equipped with household cisterns, terraced hillsides for dry farming, animal enclosures as part of the village structures, and an almost total lack of fortifications are among the shared features found at most sites.[14] These are features one would not expect from nomads who decided to settle down to village life because their presence was not contested.

This brings me to the question of the origins of the hill country newcomers. Prof. Gottwald has argued here from historical analogy that the first Israelites established an identity in a social revolt against their Canaanite overlords. This hypothesis does not seem credible now in view of the absence of Canaanite overlords in the central highlands at the beginning of Iron Age I, and it is also gainsaid by the evidence of small unfortified villages implying that nobody contested their claims to the land. The movement into the hills seems to have been peaceful, and indeed, the newcomers probably took refuge on their mountaintops to get away from strife and conflict.

Prof. Kochavi has concluded from his surveys of hill country sites that the newcomers entered the land in a movement from northeast to southwest. This movement, he notes in his abstract, "may be understood as the progressive adaptation to Mediterranean agriculture by people who started out by growing cereals and herding flocks, types of agriculture better suited to the eastern desert fringes from whence they most likely came." This seems to me to be an inadequate depiction of the people who came to the highlands with fixed patterns of house construction, a knowledge of cistern building and agricultural terracing, with highly developed bronze tools necessary for hewing pillars for houses and for digging cisterns, and a tradition of keeping small cattle in enclosures that were a part of the house compounds.

My research has taken the opposite direction to that of Prof. Kochavi because the material remains of villages that have been excavated seem to have their cultural background in the west and northwest of the highlands, that is, in the Shephelah and coastal plain, instead of the fringes of the desert in the east. The movement into the hill country at the beginning of Iron Age I, indeed was part of widespread population movements at the time, movements which reached northward to the Syrian coastal region and southward to the Egyptian delta. The newcomers who established villages in the highlands seem to have fled from conflict in the lowlands and coastal plain areas to escape more warlike newcomers to those regions.[15]

To some degree these conclusions are not new. In 1942 Albright noted the loss of much of the territory over which Canaanite culture had prevailed at the beginning of Iron Age I. By attributing the mass settlements of the central highlands to invading

Israelites, and the loss of Phoenicia and the coastal plains of Canaan to the Sea Peoples, he estimated that nine-tenths of the Canaanite culture area was lost.[16] Dispossessed along the Phoenician coast, Albright said that the Canaanites:

> ...were forced by circumstances and enabled by the march of civilization to exploit their mountain hinterland of Lebanon to an extent not previously possible. Thanks to the then recent discovery of the uses to which plaster made with slaked lime could be put, they were able to dig cisterns everywhere and to line them with true lime plaster, impervious to water. As in Israelite Palestine, this made it possible not only to develop intensive cultivation of the rich coastal lands of the Lebanese Riviera but also to build villages in the mountains.[17]

The displaced Canaanites are thus given credit for the development of cisterns which enabled them to move into the mountains of Lebanon and establish villages away from natural sources of water. Noth agreed with Albright's view, and noted the decisive influence of this new water source in the distribution of settlements in the land. But both Noth and Albright failed to associate the movement into the mountains between Jerusalem and Jezreel with the movement into the mountains of Lebanon. My view is that both were a part of the same population movements, and that the development of cisterns and agricultural terracing was common in both areas. The earliest references to terraces in the Levant are in the Ugaritic texts: "Mot, the god of death, is seized by vine-dressers who prune, bind, and drop him to the terrace."[18] Since Canaanites from the coastal cities south of Tyre carried on trade with Ugarit in the Late Bronze Age, and Canaanite merchants from Ashdod and other coastal cities actually lived in Ugarit or in its port city of Minet el-Beidah, terracing technology would have been known by people in the lowlands and coastal areas before the settlement of the highlands in Iron Age I.

Several discoveries of artifacts in the villages between Jerusalem and Jezreel also support the hypothesis that the central highlands were populated by Canaanites from the west rather than infiltrators or invaders from the east and south. A cuneiform tablet was found at Taanach by Lapp in destruction debris of the initial phase of a pillar-type building constructed at the beginning of Iron Age I. The destruction was dated to the first half of the twelfth century B.C.E.[19] Hillers published the tablet and reported that it is in alphabetic cuneiform, similar to three texts at Ugarit, and two other texts from Canaan. The text records a shipment of flour from Kokabaʿ, presumably to Taanach. Kokaba is identified with a ruin called Kaukab about 10 km south of Taanach by Hillers, who believes the tablet was written "in or near Taanach" by people who lived there in the early twelfth century B.C.E.[20]

In the Shephelah, a cuneiform tablet and two ostraca were found at Beth-Shemesh. The table is a birth incantation impressed by a stone or metal mold, and written in South Canaanite alphabetic cuneiform.[21] The tablet was reported to have come from indefinite Late Bronze Age strata, but the closest parallel to it is the Taanach tablet just discussed. The Beth-Shemesh tablet links the inhabitants of that foothill town with the larger cultural context of the Phoenician coastal region. The two ostraca, discovered in an area of Iron Age I pillar houses, are most closely parallel to an inscribed jar handle found in the destruction debris of a pillar house at Raddana. This suggests some relationship between the people of Beth-Shemesh who had a Canaanite background, and the settlement of Raddana in the highlands.

Numerous bronze and pottery artifacts, as well as a few iron tools at ʿAi and Raddana, have cultural parallels in the coastal and lowland regions also. Most of these have not been published so I shall mention them only in passing. The Raddana bowl with its twenty handles and bulls-head spouts has its parallels in many multi-handled kraters recovered in the unpublished Iron Age I Dothan tomb, and a jar from Macalister's excavations at Gezer has twin bulls-head spouts as well.[22] Numerous crucible fragments found at Raddana are exact parallels to objects published from Tell Qasile, a coastal site, as are an iron plowpoint and the haft of a mattock found at ʿAi.

Time and space do not permit extensive documentation of the lines of cultural connections between artifacts discovered in highland villages and those of the Shephelah and coastal plain area. These connections appear to me, however, to indicate a background for the highlanders in the more fertile lowlands and plains. In biblical terms, they have their origins among the Canaanites, participating in both the culture and religion of the Canaanites.

Notes

1. M. Weippert, *The Settlement of the Israelite Tribes in Palestine* (London: SCM Press Ltd., 1971), p. 2.
2. Ibid., p. 11.
3. L.E. Stager, "Highland Village Life in Palestine Some Three Thousand Years Ago," *The Oriental Institute Notes and News* no. 69 (1981): 1.
4. L.E. Toombs, "Shechem: Problems of the Early Israelite Era," *Symposia, Celebrating the 75th Anniversary of ASOR*, ed. F.M. Cross (Cambridge, Mass., 1979), pp. 68–93.
5. Ibid., p. 74.
6. Ibid., p. 75.
7. Weippert, *Settlement of Israelite Tribes* (see note 1), pp. 18, 41.
8. See J.A. Callaway, *The Early Bronze Age Citadel and Lower City at ʿAi (et-Tell)* (Cambridge: American Schools of Oriental Research, 1980), pp. 245–250.
9. J.C. Wampler, "Some Cisterns and Silos," in *Tell en-Nasbeh I*, ed. C.C. McCown (Berkeley: Palestine Institute of Pacific School of Religion, 1947), p. 129.
10. Publication in process.
11. Callaway, *Early Bronze Age at ʿAi* (see note 8); also J.A. Callaway and K. Schoonover, "The Early Bronze Age Citadel at ʿAi (et-Tell)," *BASOR* 207 (1972): 42, fig. 1.
12. J.A. Callaway, "The 1968–1969 ʿAi (et-Tell) Excavations," *BASOR* 198 (1970): 13, fig. 3; 14, fig. 4.
13. Ibid., p. 14, fig. 4.
14. See Y. Shiloh, "The Four-Room House — the Israelite Type House," *EI* 11 (1973): 277–285, for the pillar type house.
15. Stager, "Highland Village Life" (see note 3), p. 3.
16. W.F. Albright, "The Role of the Canaanites in the History of Civilization," in *The Bible and the Ancient Near East*, ed. G.E. Wright (Garden City: Doubleday & Company, 1965), pp. 456ff.
17. Ibid.
18. L.E. Stager, "Anatomy of a Highland Village" (unpublished paper).

19. W. Lapp, "The 1963 Excavation at Taannek," *BASOR* 173 (1964): 23.
20. R. Hillers, "An Alphabetic Cuneiform Tablet from Taanach (TT433)," *BASOR* 173 (1964): 45–50.
21. W.F. Albright, "The Beth-shemesh Tablet in Alphabetic Cuneiform," *BASOR* 173 (1964): 51–53.
22. J.A. Callaway and R.E. Cooley, "A Salvage Excavation at Raddana, in Bireh," *BASOR* 201 (1971): 9–19.

Rudolph Cohen

The archaeological excavations and surveys undertaken in Israel over the past decade have yielded an enormous amount of new data pertaining to the settlement of the ancient Israelites. As a number of prominent scholars have described in this session, this recent research has led to a new conception of the historical process involved, which is rapidly replacing that advanced by W.F. Albright, and developed by his followers. However, this revisionist reconstruction and Albright's, for that matter, fail to take into account the area south of the Beer-Sheba Basin. This region, including Kadesh-Barnea and the highlands of the central Negev, is of crucial importance in the biblical tradition of Exodus. It cannot, therefore, be ignored. Our surveys and excavations at Kadesh-Barnea[1] and in the central Negev, as well as those undertaken within the framework of the Negev Emergency Survey sponsored by the Israel Department of Antiquities and Museums,[2] have accumulated new material which, I believe, illuminates some of the issues under discussion.

The extensive excavations at Kadesh-Barnea have revealed three successive Iron Age fortresses, the earliest of which was erected in the tenth century B.C.E. No remains predating this period were found on the site.[3] It is interesting to note, however, that the regional survey of the Kadesh-Barnea area has discovered evidence of intensive settlement in the third millennium B.C.E. Numerous EB II and MB I sites have been recorded, in contradistinction to the total absence of remains from the period spanning the end of the Late Bronze and the onset of the Iron Age. The Negev Emergency Survey has verified a similar situation throughout the central Negev. The fifteen maps hitherto surveyed evince a vivid contrast between those periods in which the area flourished, and those of decline and abandonment.[4] It is now clear that EB II was a time of efflorescence in the central Negev and in the ʿUvda Valley. It was immediately succeeded by a comparable floruit in MB I. Hundreds of MB I sites have been surveyed in the central Negev, and many have been excavated over recent years, notably the large, centralized settlements of Beʾer Resisim,[5] Naḥal Niṣṣana[6] and En Ziq.[7] There is a concentration of settlements along the geomorphic line that runs from the Kadesh-Barnea region to north of Dimona. It is customary to view these MB I sites in the central Negev as the seasonal dwelling places of nomadic or seminomadic peoples who lived by herding and marginal farming.[8]

Following MB I, there was a settlement hiatus in the central Negev lasting over a thousand years, until Iron Age II. At this time, principally in the tenth century B.C.E., a basic transformation occurred in the area concerned: a widespread network of fortresses and associated settlements came into being.[9] The most typical building of the latter was the so-called four-room house,[10] generally connected with Israelite sedentarization. It appears that this network, serving to safeguard the vital desert trade routes, as well as the country's southern border, was established by King Solomon within the framework of his nation-building policies. Its destruction can be ascribed to Pharaoh Shishak, who (ca. 925 B.C.E.) launched a devastating attack against the kingdoms of Israel and Judah.[11] In the aftermath of his campaign, the southern border of Judah withdrew to the Beer-Sheba Basin, while the central Negev and adjacent regions were largely abandoned, until the emergence of the Nabatean Kingdom in the third–second centuries B.C.E. The fortress sequence at Kadesh-Barnea is extremely important, but has to be considered separately, and does not alter the general picture.

Thus, in considering the settlement history of the central Negev, we have the biblical tradition, which depicts a considerable Israelite presence around Kadesh-Barnea and the central Negev in the period of Exodus. Apart from this, we have the archaeological attestation of flourishing settlement during the third millennium B.C.E., followed by a settlement gap until the tenth century B.C.E.

At first sight, there is a clear contradiction between the biblical tradition and the archaeological data. There is no concrete indication of Israelite Settlement in the central Negev during the transition phase between the Late Bronze Age and Iron Age I, the period to which the coming of the Israelites is usually ascribed. This leaves the present-day scholar with a difficult choice between two logical alternatives. On the one hand, he can reject the biblical tradition as essentially unhistorical, as an ideological invention reflecting the actual conditions or purposes of later times. Or, on the other, he can seek to reexamine the currently accepted historical interpretation of the Israelite conquest. Most scholars have chosen the first alternative, and consider the biblical tradition to be a basically literary construct. I personally am inclined to give the second possibility a serious hearing. The settlement picture in the central Negev in the third millennium B.C.E. offers striking parallels to the description of the Israelite presence in this area as presented in the Old Testament traditions of the Exodus and Conquest. For this reason, I propose a reevaluation of the entire chronological scheme in which the Israelite Settlement in Canaan is normally studied.

Notes

1. R. Cohen, "The Excavations at Kadesh Barnea (1976–1978)," *BA* 44 (1981): 93–107; idem, "Excavations at Kadesh-Barnea, 1976–1982," *Qadmoniot* 41 (1983): 2–14. (Hebrew)
2. R. Cohen, "The Negev Archaeological Emergency Project," Notes & News, *IEJ* 29 (1979): 250–254.
3. R. Cohen, "Did I Excavate Kadesh-Barnea?" *BAR* (1981): 20–33. .
4. R. Cohen, *Archaeological Survey of Israel — Map of Sede Boqer East* (Jerusalem, 1981), no. 168.
5. R. Cohen and W.G. Dever, "Preliminary Report of the 'Central Negev Highlands Project,'"

BASOR 232 (1979): 29–45; idem, "Preliminary Report of the Second Season of the 'Central Negev Highlands Project,'" *BASOR* 236 (1980): 41–60; idem, "Preliminary Report of the Third and Final Season of the 'Central Negev Highland Project,'" *BASOR* 243 (1981): 57–77.
6. R. Cohen, "Naḥal Niṣṣana," *Hadashot Arkhaeologiyot* 83 (1983): 62–63. (Hebrew)
7. R. Cohen, "En Ziq," *Hadashot Arkhaeologiyot* 84 (1984): 55. (Hebrew)
8. R. Cohen, "The Mysterious MB I People — Does the Exodus Tradition in the Bible Preserve the Memory of Their Entry into Canaan?" *BAR* 9 (1983): 16–29.
9. R. Cohen, "The Iron Age Fortresses in the Central Negev," *BASOR* 236 (1980): 61–79.
10. Y. Shiloh, "The Four-Room House: Its Situation and Foundation in the Israelite City," *IEJ* 20 (1970): 180–190.
11. B. Mazar, "The Campaign of Pharaoh Shishak to Palestine," *VT Suppl.* 4 (1957): 57–66.

Israel Finkelstein

I would like to submit to this forum some ideas concerning the reconstruction of the Israelite Settlement process, which have crystallized following the recent excavations at ʿIzbet Ṣarṭah and Shiloh, and as a result of our comprehensive survey of the Land of Ephraim. For the purpose of clarity, I shall present these ideas in the form of numbered points:

1. It is clear today that the solution to problems regarding the Settlement process is to be found in regional research of the principal Settlement areas, that is, the hill country of Israel. Such work must entail detailed archaeological surveys, goal-oriented excavations, and a study of the ecologic background and economic potential of the Settlement regions, which is a crucial determinant of the Settlement pattern as revealed by surveys.

2. The two areas focused upon by previous research — the Upper Galilee and the Beer-Sheba Basin — are only of secondary importance to the Settlement phenomenon. Both regions are at the fringes of the area in which sedentarization occurred; the number of Settlement sites in both is relatively small; and the Israelite population reached these areas only at a fairly advanced stage of the process — at the end of the twelfth century or in the eleventh century B.C.E.

3. Even in the central hill country, settlement intensity varied. At the present juncture no more than ten Iron Age I sites are known in the Judean Hills; approximately twelve in Benjamin; ninety-five in Ephraim, and almost the same number in Manasseh. In other words, 90% of these sites are located between Ramallah and the Jezreel Valley (and these comprise approximately 65% of the sites known in all the area west of the Jordan).

4. When discussing the lands of Ephraim and Manasseh, the heartland of the Settlement area, one must take into account the significant geographical and archaeological differences between them. In Manasseh, a geographically amenable area, there was a great deal of activity in the Late Bronze Age; the archaeological and biblical evidence both indicate that a large Canaanite population continued to

flourish there in the Iron Age. Ephraim on the other hand, with much rougher terrain, was almost empty in the Late Bronze Age, and the early Iron Age inhabitants formed a more homogeneous population. This is one of the reasons why Shiloh, located in the heart of the region, became the main center for the Israelite population of the hill country.

5. A reconstruction of the sedentarization process in Ephraim, based on the data acquired in the survey, can also serve as an instructive model for other hill country districts (despite the regionality of the process). At the outset, most of the sites were established on the desert fringes and in the interior valleys of the northern uplands of the central range. These are the best areas for dry farming and grazing. Settlement of the western slopes of the Ephraim hill country occurred at the second stage. This part of the region presented several challenges to those who wished to settle it: it was further removed from permanent water sources, necessitated the clearance of a dense scrub forest, and required adaptation to hard rock and difficult terrain. Settlement in this geographical subunit brought about the growth of orchard agriculture. This pattern of settlement shows that the new settlers had a pastoral rather than urban or rural background. The second stage occurred at a time when the relatively amenable areas — the interior valleys and desert margins — were already populated with some density, but before the new settlers could sufficiently gather their strength to confront the Canaanites for control of the lower areas of the country. The more removed regions to the north and south — the Upper Galilee and the Beer-Sheba Basin — were also settled at this stage.

6. It is difficult to determine precisely when conflict between the settling population and Canaanite cities began, but it is reasonable to assume that it occurred as a result of the growing scarcity of available farmland. These confrontations are reflected in biblical traditions, aside from the description of the unified military conquest, which are all connected with the central hill country.

7. The process of Israelite expansion in Canaan, its intensity and date can now be traced with the aid of field data collected throughout the country. The initial Settlement took place mainly in Ephraim and Manasseh, and to some degree in Benjamin and Judah (so far, there is no archaeological evidence for Settlement sites earlier than the beginning of the twelfth century B.C.E.). From this core area the new population expanded southward to the Judean hill country and northward to the Galilee. This is in accordance with biblical material such as the description of the Danites' migration.

8. The southward expansion from the core area was complemented by a migration of the cultic center from Shiloh (which functioned as such from the second half of the twelfth century through the early eleventh century B.C.E.) to Benjamin at the end of the eleventh century and then to Judah in the early tenth century B.C.E. Judah, in fact, only attains its special significance in the history of Israel in the tenth century B.C.E.

9. We have at our disposal today enough data to make an estimate of the early Israelite population. This estimate is based on the number of sites found and their respective sizes. The result is doubled in order to anticipate what I would call "the

lacking data coefficient" in each area. Such a computation leads us to a figure of about 50,000 settled Israelites west of the Jordan at the end of the eleventh century B.C.E., on the eve of the United Monarchy. This estimate is many times lower than that suggested by scholars in the past, and has, of course, far-reaching implications for every aspect of the Israelite Settlement process.

10. As for the nature of the Settlement process, the field research, which includes socioecological work, indicates that Alt's approach was basically correct, although some of his ideas must be adapted to the archaeological data of today. The origin of at least part of the pastoral groups, which became sedentarized in the late thirteenth–early twelfth centuries B.C.E., after a long period of pastoralism, should be sought in the deterioration of the rural and urban system at the end of the Middle Bronze Age.

11. The Settlement process displays a great deal of regionality: in some areas settlement was carried out in the midst of an autochthonous Canaanite population, while in other regions, it took place in an area almost devoid of such. At times, at ʿIzbet Ṣarṭah for example, settlements were established next to Canaanite cities, while in western Galilee for instance, with a similar geographical background, new settlements distanced themselves from Canaanite centers.

12. The early Israelite archaeological material, similar to the pattern of Settlement, testifies to a clearly discernible cultural change in our region's history —contrary to what one may encounter in recent literature. Typical features of early Israelite settlements, such as the pillared buildings or collared-rim jars, should be analyzed from a geographic, quantitative and functional standpoint, and not solely on the basis of their appearance or absence at a given site. Having undertaken this sort of analysis, we still come to the conclusion that these features have their origins in the central hill country sites of the early Iron Age.

13. The development of early Israelite architecture was influenced by two major factors: the pastoral background of the settling groups, and the environmental determinants of the Settlement's heartland —the central hill country. The pottery of the early Israelite sites clearly expresses the socioeconomic status of their occupants: the paucity of types reflects a poor agricultural society, while the greater number of subtypes of this same repertoire indicates organization in isolated tribal entities.

Select Bibliography

Finkelstein. I. "The ʿIzbet Ṣarṭah Excavations and the Israelite Settlement in the Hill Country." Ph.D. diss., Tel Aviv University, 1983. (Hebrew)

——. *Archaeology of the Period of the Settlement and Judges*. Forthcoming. (Hebrew)

——, ed. "ʿIzbet Ṣarṭah — An Early Iron Age Site near Rosh Haʿayin." *Tel Aviv*. Forthcoming.

——. "Excavations in Shiloh 1981–1984, A Preliminary Report." Forthcoming.

Kochavi. M. "The Conquest and the Settlement." In *History of Eretz Israel*, II. Forthcoming. (Hebrew)

Mazar. A. "Giloh: An Early Israelite Settlement near Jerusalem." *IEJ* 31 (1981): 1–36.

Zertal. A. "The Israelite Settlement in the Hill Country of Manasseh." Ph.D. diss., Tel Aviv University. Forthcoming. (Hebrew)

Lawrence E. Stager

As Moshe Kochavi and Amihai Mazar have succinctly demonstrated, recent archaeological surveys (Israel Finkelstein in "Benjamin" and "Ephraim"; Adam Zertal in "Manasseh"; and Siegfried Mittmann in "Gilead") and excavations indicate a proliferation of unwalled villages in Iron Age I (twelfth–eleventh centuries B.C.E.). This phenomenon is especially pronounced in the central highlands of Palestine and Transjordan, both "frontiers" having been sparsely settled in the Late Bronze Age. The three- or fourfold increase in settled population, as indicated by surveys, seems incompatible with "natural growth" of the few Late Bronze Age city-states in the region. Consequently, some form of "immigration" into the highlands at ca. 1200 B.C.E. must be postulated.

Nevertheless, it is difficult for me to believe that all of these newfounded, early Iron I settlements derived from a single source —whether the former encampments (as yet unidentified archaeologically) in the "eastern desert" (Kochavi) of Late Bronze Age sheep/goat pastoralists settling down, or from disintegrating city-state systems (Gottwald), no longer able to control peasants bent on taking over lowland agricultural regimes for themselves or pioneering new, "free" lands in the highlands. When one considers the widespread phenomenon of small agricultural communities in Iron Age I, I find it all the more difficult to circumscribe it with the various historical and historiographic constructions of biblical and modern authors, who would limit this process to the "Israelites" exclusively.

Marc Bloch, the great historian of medieval Europe, has used the comparative method very effectively to test hypotheses and, in some cases, to eliminate "pseudo-local causes." For him (and other good historians), a general phenomenon must have equally general causes. Comparison with a similar, but widespread phenomenon often undermines purely local explanations. Now that archaeologists have collected the kinds of Settlement data that provide a more comprehensive pattern, we must widen our focus for a more comprehensive explanation than the regnant theories allow — whether they relate to Israelite "conquest," "revolution," or nomadic "sedentarization."

It would be oversimplistic to draw the boundaries of premonarchic Israelite Settlement so broad as to ascribe the change in the Settlement landscape to this historical force alone. This, of course, does not mean that particularistic, historical studies cannot be used to elucidate aspects of the broader processual framework.

Indeed, in the case of Israel, there is already by premonarchic times the eloquent testimony of the "Song of Deborah" (Judges 5), that a confederation of ten tribes was occupying a veritable mosaic of ecological niches on both sides of the Jordan, and carrying on a variety of professions, such as highland farming (Ephraim, Machir, Benjamin, Naphtali), sheep and goat herding (Reuben) as well as seafaring (Dan and Asher). In this early victory ode, the economic circumstances of the various tribes played an important, sometimes decisive role in whether they rallied to the muster against the Canaanites.

Textual sources indicate that premonarchic Israel was structured according to "tribal" principles of social organization. Concerning "origins," the basic question is whether this structure derived from the evolution of an already tribally structured group of pastoralists settling down (Alt and Noth) or from a radical "re-tribalization" of peasants, overturning or fleeing from Canaanite city-state societies (Mendenhall and Gottwald).

Archaeology is also providing support for understanding the social organization of premonarchic Israel as a kin-based, "tribal" society.[1]

In the Iron Age I highland villages, the heartland of early Israel, it is possible to distinguish multiple family compounds, such as those excavated by Joseph Callaway at Khirbet Raddana. These family compounds, comprised of two or three houses set off from their village surroundings by an enclosure wall, formed the basic socioeconomic units of the community, usually no more than 100–200 persons per village. In such villages, the extended or multiple family unit was the ideal type [cf. Micah's large household (*bêt*-Micah), comprised of various *bāttîm*, in Judges 18:22]. Such a household may have constituted a minimal *bêt ʾāb* (as Gottwald has suggested), or a small patrilineage.

Further clues to the composition of early Israelite villages can be deciphered from compound place names, which Benjamin Mazar has so astutely analyzed.[2] The first element of the place name reveals the settlement type, such as "hill," "enclosure," "diadem"; the second element, the name of the founding families or leading lineages. Examples are: *gibʿat šāûl, ḥašar ʾaddār, ʿaṭrōt, ʾaddār*, and *ʿaṭrōt bêt yôʾab*). In the Song of Deborah (Judges 5:7) such village inhabitants are called *pĕrāzôn*, no doubt after the general designation for unwalled villages, or hamlets, *pĕrāzôt* (cf. Ezekiel 38:11).

From the village to the regional or "clan" (*mišpāḥāh*) level of Israelite society, it is apparent that these territories took their names from the dominant large "families," either lineages or clans, living there. Samuel, a Zuphite, lived at his ancestral home Ramah, or Ramat(aim)-Zophim (named after his Ephraimite ancestor; 1 Samuel 1:1), in the land of Zuph (*ʾereṣ ṣûp*), through which Saul passed in search of his father's lost asses (1 Samuel 9). District or clan territories remained important subdivisions of tribal society even during the monarchical period, as the Samaria ostraca attest.

Given the low aggregate of the Late Bronze Age population throughout Canaan, it appears unlikely that the peasantry, even if they had all "revolted," could have been large enough to account for the total Iron Age I village population, where in the central highlands alone, I would put their number at about 40,000 (calculated on the basis of two hundred persons per ha. for the total occupied area; cf. Judges 5:8).

In Late Bronze times there must have been acute shortages of labor in the city-states, where attracting and retaining agricultural workers were an endemic problem. Evsey Domar[3] has developed an interesting hypothesis which could be relevant to an overarching explanation for the proliferation of agricultural villages in frontier areas, where such entities as Israel, Moab, and Edom were already known by the thirteenth century B.C.E. from Egyptian sources.[4] Domar contends that only two, but never all three elements — free land, free peasants, and non-working landowners — can coexist within the same agricultural structure. In the Late Bronze city-states, we know that free land (in the highlands and marginal regions), non-working landowners, and "serfs" did exist. With the decline of certain city-state systems, there would have been a centrifugal tendency for peasant farmers to settle beyond areas of state control, especially in the less accessible mountain redoubts (cf. Gottwald).

But for different reasons a similar trend might also have affected sheep-goat pastoralists. Recent anthropological research, such as that carried out by Emanuel Marx[5] among the Negev and Sinai Bedouin, has rendered obsolete the concept of the pastoral nomad who subsists on the meat and dairy products he produces, and lives in blissful solitude from the rest of the world. Even more outworn is the concept of seminomadism (still embraced by too many scholars of the ancient Near East) as a rigid ontological status, marking some cultural (pseudo-)evolutionary stage on the path to civilization, from desert tribesman to village farmer to urban dweller: in archaeological parlance, the "from tent-to-hut-to-house" syndrome.

So long as the Late Bronze markets and exchange networks were still operating, the sheep-goat pastoralists would have found specialization in animal husbandry a worthwhile occupation. However, with the decline of these economic systems in many parts of Canaan in the late thirteenth to early twelfth centuries B.C.E. — when "caravans ceased and travelers kept to the byways" (Judges 5:6) — the "pastoralist" sector, engaged in herding and huckstering, may also have found it advantageous to shift toward different subsistence strategies, such as farming with some stock-raising. This group undoubtedly formed part of the village population that emerged quite visibly in the highlands ca. 1200 B.C.E.

The trend was toward decentralization and ruralization especially in marginal "frontier" zones, brought about by the decline of the Late Bronze Age city-state and, in certain areas, of Egyptian imperial control. It is in this broader framework that we must then try to locate the more specific causes which led to the emergence of early Israel, which Benjamin Mazar and Siegfried Herrmann have addressed (see pp. 16–20 and 47–53).

Norman Gottwald has presented a seemingly comprehensive hypothesis to account for this change in his (and Mendenhall's) now well-known "peasant-revolt" model and concomitant "Yahwistic revolution." One of its most serious defects, however, seems to me to be its partial explanatory power. If these farming villages were the product of this Yahwistic revolution, then why do we find equally "egalitarian" villages outside the confines of premonarchic Israel? They appear over a much wider landscape than even the most maximalist views of early Israel could include, ranging from Ammon to Moab and even into Edom, not to speak of those settlements within Canaan itself, where the ethnic identity of their inhabitants is in question.

Without clear indications from texts, I seriously doubt whether any archaeologist can determine the ethnic identification of Iron Age I villagers through material cultural remains alone. For example, were the twelfth century B.C.E. inhabitants of Taanach "Israelites" or "Canaanites"? Even in contexts where collared-rim pithoi, storage pits, and three- or four-room pillared houses appear together (as they do in Iron Age I Taanach), these items do not in themselves provide an adequate indication of ethnos. The contrast between a twelfth-century city, such as Megiddo VII A, and a village, such as Taanach, during the same period reveals differences that derive more from socioeconomic than from ethnic factors. They reflect different settlement types of the same period.

These qualifications notwithstanding, it is also abundantly clear from the Merenptah Stele that Israel was a political-ethnic entity of sufficient importance to the Egyptians to warrant mention alongside its three Canaanite allies, the city-states of Ashkelon, Gezer, and Yenoʿam. Indeed, this event of ca. 1207 B.C.E. (according to the best Egyptian chronologies) was the nearest thing to a real revolution in Canaan — and it was against the Egyptians. The pictorial complement to the victory hymn of Merenptah can now be seen in the four battle reliefs (formerly attributed to Rameses II but now assigned with confidence to Merenptah), which depict the three city-states (Ashkelon is mentioned by name in the reliefs) and the "people" Israel.[6]

This new piece of evidence does not, of course, settle the perennial question concerning the "origins" of Late Bronze Age Israel, that is, whether it consisted predominantly of pastoralists, peasants, or new immigrants. It does, however, undermine the notion that the Israelites were really the Shasu, who had settled down in agricultural villages ca. 1200 B.C.E.[7] In the Merenptah reliefs, the Israelites are not depicted as Shasu, but wear the same clothing and have the same hair styles as the Canaanites, who are defending the fortified cities of Ashkelon, Gezer, and Yenoʿam.

From the detailed settlement maps which have been presented for the Late Bronze and Iron Age I periods, it seems to me that the changing pattern has more to do with the process of ruralization than revolution. Probably both "peasants" and "pastoralists" contributed to the Iron Age I village population.

As for the elusive problem of Israelite "origins" before the twelfth century B.C.E., I prefer for the time being to adopt the stance of the French sociologist François Simiand,[8] who nearly a century ago chided historians for bowing down before the "idol of origins," that is, showing an obsessive concern for when a phenomenon first began to appear rather than when it became important.

Notes

1. L.E. Stager, "The Archaeology of the Family in Early Israelite Society," *BASOR* 258, and his monograph, *Highland Villages: the Archaeology of Early Israelite Society* (forthcoming).
2. B. Mazar, "The Early Israelite Settlement in the Hill Country," *BASOR* 241 (1981): 75–85.
3. E.D. Domar, "The Causes of Slavery or Serfdom: A Hypothesis," *Journal of Economic History* 30 (1970): 18–32.
4. For example, J.B. Pritchard, ed., *ANET* (Princeton, 1950), pp. 243, 259.
5. E. Marx, "New Trends in the Study of Pastoral Nomads," *Nomadic Peoples* 10 (1982): 65–68; idem, "The Tribe as a Unit of Subsistence: Nomadic Pastoralism in the Middle East," *American Anthropologist* 79 (1977): 343–363.
6. F. Yurco, "Merenptah's Palestinian Campaign," *Society for the Study of Egyptian Antiquities Journal* 8 (1978): 70; L.E. Stager, "Merenptah, Israel, and Sea Peoples: New Light on an Old Relief," *EI* (in press).
7. For example, R. Giveon, "Les Bédouins Shosou des Documents Égyptiens (Leiden, 1971); M. Weippert, "The Israelite 'Conquest' and the Evidence from Transjordan," in *Symposia Celebrating the Seventh-Fifth Anniversary of the Founding of the American Schools of Oriental Research (1900–1975)*, ed. F.M. Cross (New Haven, 1979), pp. 15–34; W. Helck, "Die Bedrohung Palästinas durch einwandernde Gruppen am Ende der 18. und am Anfang der 19. Dynastie," *VT* 18 (1968): 472–480.
8. F. Simiand, "Méthode historique et science sociale," *Revue de synthèse historique* (1903): 1–22, 129–157.

Matitiahu Tsevat

Quid sum miser nunc dicturus, "What shall I, pitiable man, say now?" — "I," the biblicist, "now," almost a century and a half after the appearance of the second volume of the first scientific history of ancient Israel, the work of Heinrich Ewald. One-third of the volume is devoted to the periods of Joshua and Judges, the subject of this session. The biblicist, whether he shows self-pity or conceals it, is justified in asking this question (taken almost literally from the medieval sequence *Dies irae*), because the modern study of the Old Testament may be characterized in a major way as its historicization. The study of the Bible, a book that has come to us from the past, is, in part, a subject of the discipline that studies the past. The history of the literature and of the religion of Israel, the special interest of Wellhausen and his followers, probably comes to mind first, but it is the general history, the story of the life and fate of the people in all its manifestations, that provides the coordinates to any and all historical studies, the study of Old Testament literature and its growth not excluded.

From Heinrich Ewald to Roland de Vaux, the writing of that history consisted in no small part of the retelling of what the Bible tells. Dissatisfied with this state of affairs, and rightly so, modern historians have brought to bear on their research an ever-growing variety of approaches and aids, among them methods and models indigenous to other sciences; extra-biblical sources and sourcelike material; and results of the work of neighboring disciplines (history of the area, geography of Palestine, and others). These aids are employed to fill the lacunae left by the biblical record, to provide control for assessment of the factuality and accuracy of that record, and to evaluate data and reconstructions. The product often is a picture of the subject under study — an event or a period — that is at variance with the picture that the Old Testament paints.

As regards the periods of the Settlement of Israel in Canaan and of the Judges, the effort of the historians has not produced a result that the customer can accept with confidence and equanimity. "Customer" means anyone who does or may use the product of the historical research but had no part, or would not have been able to have a part, in its production. Therefore, I repeat my initial question: "What shall I, pitiable biblicist, say now?" with the word "now" this time marking the end of the endeavor of a century and a half designed to set Old Testament study on the ideal course of historicization. As concerns the periods of this session, I am constrained to say that the course has led the study and the student nowhere. The positions of Alt, Albright, Gottwald, Amihai Mazar, as well as of others do not contradict each other in every detail, but as integrated entities the four identified ones are irreconcilable. To the customer, the biblicist, four different positions means no position at all, because he sees no position that he can appropriate with confidence. The choice among the four and others may not and ought not to be left to him, since he will tend to pick the one that serves best his interpretation of a text or can be integrated most smoothly into his construct, which is not necessarily the best answer to the historical problem. Four variables instead of one means that the function of controlling the text or the interpretation of a given passage of the Bible, a service which historiography is expected to render to the exegete, is thus severely diminished.

Here I must be specific for I anticipate criticism. The situation, which I have described with disenchantment, may appear to others as praiseworthy. Continually expanding exploration and fresh methods, it will perhaps be argued, spawn new theories; and the study of Israelite history, including the period discussed, presents the picture of a vibrant science. The reason for my dissatisfaction is the continued peaceful coexistence of the old and the new. Adherents to the old theories are insufficiently impressed by the new. The quick and complete flip-flop, described by Thomas S. Kuhn in *The Structure of Scientific Revolutions*, with virtually everybody discarding the former and embracing the latter, does not characterize studies of ancient Israel, be they history, literature, or religion. (Archaeology seems to be an exception, but some archaeologists call it the archaeology of Palestine.) To be sure, Kuhn based his observation on the history of the natural sciences and the behavior of natural scientists. The flip-flop is generally not a mark of the humanities, and Old Testament study is a branch of the humanities. Nevertheless, I would be gratified to see in this area more rigor and determination. Longtime peaceful coexistence of conflicting theories is not a sign of health in any discipline.

Once more I am asking: *Quid sum miser nunc dicturus*? and my answer is a recommendation: For the study of the Old Testament, including and especially that of the historical books, deemphasize history, by which I mean the methods and results of modern historiography. The study of history and the study of literature undertake to answer different questions. The former asks: What was the case? The latter asks:

What is meant, or what is the sense, and how is the sense rendered? Biblical science is a historical science inasmuch as the knowledge of historical facts advances the understanding of the sense. (Here knowledge of the statics of history, such as general background, sociology, law, historical geography, etc., has precedence over the knowledge of particular events.) And even here, looking for background details in a text or supplying them when they are not there requires tact. Realism and naturalism are literary movements, artistic styles, aesthetic attitudes, the same as other movements, styles and attitudes. Not every author seeks to delineate sharp and detailed images. To the writings of those who do not, latter-day readers and interpreters should supply precision of imagery always with care and often not at all. The modern historian, on the other hand, loves the realism of his sources. He also strives for completeness and therefore notices with regret statements like the following: "What else Omri did and the exploits he performed are recorded in the annals of the Kings of Israel" (I Kings 16:27). Desire for completeness was not unknown to the biblical author, but for its satisfaction he sends the desirous outside of the Bible because the Bible has a different agenda.

A feature of the Old Testament that should give pause to the radical historicizer is that of the grand story that stretches from the beginning of Genesis to the end of Kings without giving the slightest indication that there is less reality, less actual happening in what we call the myths of Genesis and some other books than in the reports of Samuel and Kings. In *Mythische und historische Wahrheit* (1970, p. 93), Hugo Cancik admits that much, however half-heartedly. Certainly, the historian may legitimately mine Genesis or any other book of the canon for sources, even as the linguist may mine it for verb paradigms. But mining, especially surface mining, destroys the lay of the land. The number of differences between these two branches of the humanities can be augmented, and most of them can be traced to the different truths that the study of history and that of literature seek.

It might be interposed that these observations are not new or, if new, are insignificant. Although I do not at all accept this hypothetical criticism, I shall relate to it with this remark. Comparing the study of history with that of literature, the former is the hard science and the latter the soft one. People tend to defer to the hard sciences; the harder the science, the more reliable and powerful it is or is considered to be. To say it figuratively in terms of physics, the hardest of sciences: of two solids, the one that scratches the surface of the other is the harder one. The discipline of biblical study has been scratched all over by her sister disciplines, history among them. She would benefit from keeping at some distance from them for a little while, not in order to become ahistorical, forswear sociology, and so forth, but to take time out for reflecting on herself and her situation, especially regarding two points: (1) her essence and methods as a literary science vis-à-vis those of other sciences; and (2) the fact that the Bible has made its greatest impact on man when historical considerations about it have not been dominant. To be sure, these considerations have never been absent, nor should they ever be. Today they ought to profit from modern historiography. But history as a sequence of events has no intention, literature to a large extent has. The Bible certainly has, and this is its soul.

Discussion

A. Kempinski: I wish to comment on Prof. Gottwald's observations regarding archaeology in relation to his social theories. That these theories have very little to do with archaeological reality is obvious to anyone who heard the lectures of A. Mazar and M. Kochavi. The archaeological scenery includes not one single sign of Gottwald's social revolution or refugees of the Canaanite "feudal" system. As Tel Masos is one of the largest sites of the period of the Settlement, the results of our four seasons of excavation there are very indicative for every theoretical interpretation. To my mind, there is enough evidence of the foreign — non-Canaanite — elements brought by the earlier settlers to testify to their origin in the mountainous areas, and to what V. Fritz called "symbiosis," that is, their constant contact with the Canaanite culture in the period before their Settlement. This "symbiosis" is mainly based on the pottery analysis and the similarity of the proportions of animal bones (sheep, goats versus cows). However, I believe that the term "symbiosis" is misleading, "adaptation" being more suitable.

I do agree that we as archaeologists need a new model, but *one* model cannot be used for all Canaan, as the process of Settlement differs in various regions. With more information from excavations, the general picture will be split into even more local variations. We must first ascertain the situation in all the regions, and only later, if at all, decide on a general schema for all the country.

The last point I would like to mention is the problem of adaptation of pottery raised by A. Mazar. This process was a very long one and, to some extent, it shows that the Israelites, or whatever we call them, lived in contact for quite a long time with the Canaanites. We do, however, have a parallel case of a people who did not live in contact with the Canaanites developing their own pottery — the southern tribes of the central Negev highland and their Negebite pottery. When we compare these phenomena from an ethno-archaeological point of view, we obtain a clear picture: one group which was totally involved with the Canaanite culture and adopted its pottery forms, and another group which was totally isolated, each of them producing different pottery. As for chronology, I believe that this contact "adaptation" continued throughout most of the thirteenth century B.C.E.

C. Schäfer: Hearing all these lectures and having studied the social history of Israel for years, I am more and more convinced that we are posing the wrong questions. We are always looking for the origin of Israel and this is like asking "what is earlier — the hen or the egg?" Philosophers know that this question cannot be answered. I believe, therefore, when old models cannot be sustained due to archaeological finds, we should not look for a single new model, but for a new paradigm. When I try to compare the findings from the different regions of the Israelite country, I see that a revolutionary movement did not exist in all the country, nor was there a military conquest in all the country, but that very different social processes existed in the various regions.

The biblical text can be used as a basis for the interpretation of and for our search for a new paradigm. I have attempted to do so for four Israelite cities in the time of the Judges, because I believe this is to argue on secure ground. Secure ground for interpretation is the biblical text and not the archaeological data; they do not speak for themselves, we have to interpret them. If we read the biblical accounts regarding these four Israelite cities; Succoth, Gilead, Jabesh-Gilead and Gibeah of Saul, it seems that there were segmentary societies in these areas. The facts that Prof. Gottwald tries to interpret with his "peasant" model, would be better interpreted as the effect of a segmentary process. The main trait of segmentary processes is that there is no centralized organization, and that was true for the thirteenth century B.C.E. Organization existed on the level of cities and villages, but there was no retribalization. These cities and villages were practically independent political entities, as exemplified by the relations between Gideon and Succoth. Gideon could conquer Succoth without fear of reprisal from other Israelites as there were no stable political relations between the Israelite villages and cities. This is also demonstrated by the relations between Gibeah of Saul and Jabesh-Gilead, and in the attitude of Gilead to Jephthah and his band. I believe all these social groups belong to a kind of segmentary society. The dropouts from society, the "worthless fellows" (אנשים ריקים) in the Bible, could regroup and form bands. These bands of "worthless fellows" were part of the system. If this is taken into account, we see that there were various social structures in the thirteenth and twelfth centuries B.C.E.

If we use sociological methods in the study of the social history of Israel, we should remember the warning of Max Weber, one of the greatest sociologists, and not confuse and misinterpret sociological methods and tools with scientific aims. I believe this is Prof. Gottwald's mistake.

J. Walters: I would like to bring to your attention an identifying characteristic which is common to 90% of the characters in Genesis and which might be helpful in identifying the early Israelites. There is a pointer to this characteristic in the well-studied summary of Israel's history in Deuteronomy 26. "A wandering Aramean was my father." "Wandering" sometimes is translated as "fugitive" or "lost," or it could mean that the early Israelites were people who left an environment like Iran, a settled environment, an organized society, voluntarily or by force. Now, Adam and Eve were expelled from the Garden of Eden; Noah had to leave land to float on an ark; Cain was forced to leave his farm to become a wanderer; citizens of Babylon were scattered; Tara left Ur; Abraham left Haran; Lot left Abraham and later left Sodom and Gomorrah; Hagar and Ishmael left Abraham; Keturah's children leave Abraham; Isaac has to leave because of a famine; Jacob must flee from the family; Esau leaves; Judah eventually leaves; and Joseph is forcibly removed from his family. I am suggesting that the early Israelites were people who were forced out of organized society. This concept is in accordance with the idea of the Habiru and the Hebrew, and it really opens the door to the understanding of many other factors. For example, we can now identify who was the God or were the gods of these people; this explains why God treated Cain so well, and it also explains the story of the binding of Isaac and many others.

B. Levine: It seems to me, on the one hand, that the old objective of the early biblical archaeologist to verify the Bible, for whatever reasons —some of them very exalted —is still excessively upheld. On the other hand, biblical scholarship has dug itself one of those early Iron Age pits, or a series of them, and we are in what is called in Israel *botz* ("mud").

Prof. Tsevat's remarks were very erudite, succinct and exceedingly troubling to me. I am more worried about the attitude he expressed than about what I sometimes affectionately call "archaeological fundamentalism," by which I mean the task of the archaeologist to verify what is in the Bible, which I believe is spurious. He worries me more because he seems to be willing to live with the myth and to give up the search for reality. I do not blame "orthodox" people who tell me that everything in the Book of Numbers was written on the Plains of Moab or issued from the Tent of Assembly. But I do argue with more liberated people from the theological point of view, who are so willing to live with the literary myth as a way of avoiding the anguish that we are going through in trying to date biblical accounts, separate literary strata, to deal with perhaps the most poignant link between biblical studies and archaeology, namely *Sitz-im-Leben*. The argument of the conservative or the traditionalist against the scientist is: I am sure of what I have, while you keep changing your mind and cannot agree among yourselves. That can be a blessing. I will take all the abrasion that archaeologists, Semiticist, historians, Assyriologists can hand out, and hope that it will stimulate my bloodstream a little more when I come to meetings like this.

N.K. Gottwald: I am surprisingly concordant with Baruch Levine's statement. Although Social History, when compared to some other approaches to scripture, has tended to seem somewhat lucid or more mythological, it is history. I am interested in knowing how to date those texts, and how to locate them, and I am interested in the *Sitz-im-Leben* that involves not only individual texts, but the agglomeration of texts and streams of tradition and locations in society.

Let me try to answer specifically two of the objections I heard here, one by Prof. Callaway and one by Prof. Stager, and then make some more general remarks.

As to the point about the absence of overlords in the hills and in unfortified sites, it seems to me very clear that we must deal with the whole region, both the lowlands and the highlands. As pointed out by Prof. Callaway, we are dealing with the question of directions —perhaps multidirectional movements —during at least a two- to three-century time span. A particular moment and a particular set of data cannot simply be frozen and said to be the answer. I believe that we need to keep the arguments about a number of models alive and shôuld not foreclose too quickly. As to the question that Prof. Stager raises about the regions outside the revolt, I would prefer to ask: What about the regions outside the area within which the Israelite movement was indigenized in time, and why were there limitations to the movement whether it was really a revolt or not? I laid out at least four models and suggested some others to indicate that I am not particularly tied to one revolt model. There have been many peasant revolutions that varied a great deal from one another. In my book, *Tribes of Yahweh*, I suggest possible topographical factors relating to the limits of the Israelite movement in the highlands, that is from Gilead and Mishor into the tableland of Moab. This may provide an explanation for the indications that Ammonites and Moabites were in a limited way involved in the movement. They did not have the kind of terrain in which guerrilla warfare could be successfully fought, and therefore dropped out.

Now, we have to examine some of these key questions in terms of the text. Baruch Levine was right —we must study the literary traditions, not just as a world in itself, but as reflecting some ancient worlds. I am faulted for not having read the latest reports. However, what should be the interpretation if one has a situation where the populace was more or less indigenous, apparently not convincingly nomadic, and did not have to fight too hard for particular sites. What is the meaning of pre-Deuteronomistic biblical traditions about serious, major conflict in that society? We have to return to some of these questions. I think we need forums in which archaeologists, biblical scholars, and social historians can sit down together, and discuss them point by point, examining them like many-faceted jewels, and seeing how the different faces meet. We have to admit to each other that none of us knows all that needs to be known, rather than flay one another for what we do not know, and to bring into juxtaposition what we do know and try to see what progress we can make. We do not have to simply settle for myths about early Israel. Origins do not tell us everything, but I believe that in seeking them, we will know more.

A. Biran: I subscribe to what Prof. Gottwald said. We need a great deal of modesty. We have a great deal to learn and then perhaps we may reach some conclusions. Why don't we consider one case — Dan. I think all biblical scholars and historians agree that its story in Judges 18 is authentic, and describes a given situation. As a matter of fact, some people say that this illustrates or is the basis for the whole story of the Settlement in Canaan. Here archaeology has revealed a new settlement in a former Canaanite town. Obviously, the people who settled in these so-called settlement pits were not the people who were indigenous to the locality before that. Here we have an example of a change in the territorial *Geschichte* of a site. Why can't that same example be applied to the rest of the country?

J. Wilbar: I just hope that this forum does not overlook the possibility that the God of Israel does exist and that He operates in supernatural ways. It seems that the pattern of scripture is that God's model is not predictable and that, in fact, He could have enabled His people to win these lands with the kind of conflict that might be expected. The battle of Jericho would be an example.

Unidentified participant: I would like to ask Dr. Biran one question as I am really interested in the way by which archaeological interpretation is reached. You say that the new builders of Dan came from another site or another location. From how far away, in your judgment, would they have had to come? Can you answer this question?

A. Biran: They could have come from any distance. This is a case for biblical archaeology at its best. We have a record, Judges 18, so why not accept it? Therefore I tell you, they came from Zorah and Eshtaol, from the coast, and from there they moved up. There is no objective reason not to accept an historical document which tells about a group of people moving from one place to another. If we had not found a change in the material culture of the people at the time, then you could raise the questions: Is Judges 18 a myth or a story or was it written 500 years later, etc.?

The previous unidentified speaker: I understand your point there, but I am really interested in knowing how concrete is the material evidence regarding the distance from which they came, if you did not have a biblical record?

A. Biran: Kochavi pointed out that there are no collared-rim jars in the Galilee. Therefore I submit that the collared-rim jars at Dan were brought with the people when they came from the south through the hill country.

J. Balensi: Les repères éventuels de la migration des "Danites" sont loin d'être évidents. C'est une question de méthode. Je peux prendre comme exemple le site de Tell el-Far ͑ah (N). La culture matérielle qui le caracterise à la fin du II^{è} millénaire reflète une forte influence syrienne. Comment les biblistes ou les tenants d'une archéologie biblique peuvent-ils en rendre compte ? Les groupes qui se sédentarisent dans les collines de Samarie, véhiculant de tels modèles culturels, seront appelés plus tard, Israélites. Quatre modèles peuvent être évoqués:

1. Le prototype "en fer à cheval" de la *maison à quatre pièces* apparaître sur l'Euphrate au 15^{è}s.[1] Le bâtiment de Tell Batash[2] n'est pas antérieur à la période amarnienne. Le "temple du Bronze récent" de de Vaux à Fara ͑h a été publié par Chambon[3] comme une maison du Fer IB. Dans l'étude que je vais publier sur le Bronze Récent de ce site, je montrerai qu'au moins deux structures similaires l'ont précédé.
2. Le mode de *construction à piliers* est attesté dès le 14^{è}s. dans l'ouest du Croissant fertile, e.g. le domaine d'Ugarit.[4]
3. Albright avait proposé le *pithos à collier* comme spécifiquement israélite. Or ce type céramique, en Samarie, s'inscrit dans la tradition des pithoi qui remonte jusqu'au Bronze Moyen. Lorsque des empreintes de sceaux figurent sur la lèvre en bourrelet propre aux vases du Fer, elles trahissent une iconographie d'inspiration syrienne.[5]
4. Quelques figurines avaient été publiées par de Vaux[6] du type de l'Ashtart ornée de pastilles et d'incisions. Cet art est traditionnel dans la région entre Oronte et Euphrate.

L'influence syrienne ne fait pas de doute. A plus forte raison quand il ne s'agit pas d'un apport ponctuel, mais bien d'un lent processus à nouveau repérable à partir du Bronze Récent II. Il faut se défaire des assertions issues de considérations d'ordre ethnique. Les échanges culturels dans le Proche-Orient pendant le Bronze Récent sont tels que l'argumentation ethnique n'a guère de sens. Les modèles de *construction à pilier* et de *maisons à quatre pièces* appartiennent au Fer I, à des groupes ethniques différents, y compris les Philistins. La popularité croissante du *pithos à collier* dès la fin du Bronze Récent, tient à sa fonction de stockage dans une économie d'installations agricoles multipliées et dispersées, sur les deux rives du Jourdain. C'est l'attestation d'une profonde mutation dans la géographie humaine et économique de toute la région. Au dépeuplement latent succède un repeuplement progressif. Ce même phénomène est curieusement observable à Chypre à la fin du 13^{è}s.: immigration, dispersion des installations, prédominance des vases de stockage.

Notes

1. R.H. Dornemann, "The Late Bronze Age Pottery Tradition at Tell Hadidi, Syria," *BASOR* 241 (1981): 29s.
2. G. Kelm and A. Mazar, "Three Seasons of Excavations at Tell Batash —Biblical Timna," *BASOR* 248 (1982): 9s.
3. A. Chambon, *Tell el-Farʿah I. L'Age du Fer* (Paris, 1984).
4. J. Elayi, "Remarques sur un type de mur phénicien," *Riv. di Studi Fenici* 8 (1980): 165s.
5. M. Ibrahim, "The Collared-Rim Jar," dans, *Archaeology in the Levant, Essays for K. Kenyon* (Warminster, 1978), p. 106s.
6. R. de Vaux et A.-M. Stève, "La première campaigne de fouilles à Tell el-Farʿah, près Naplouse," *RB* 54 (1947): 585.
7. L. Badre, *Les figurines anthropomorphes en terre cuite à l'Age du Bronze en Syrie* (Paris: G. Geuthner, 1980); J. Margueron, "Maquettes architecturales de Meskéné-Emar," *Syria*, 53 (1976): 193s.

D.N. Freedman: I would like to make a small contribution now that everybody else has finished, and try to shift the pendulum a little back to non-Canaanite elements in the Israelite experience. There are factors here, it seems to me, that are not necessarily archaeological, but are certainly biblical. When did Yahwism become a movement? Where did it come from? The biblical tradition is quite clear about this. Whether we call it Canaan or not, it did not occur in the central heartland of Canaan. Yahweh, as far as we know, is one of the gods in the Canaanite pantheon. We have rather extensive literature on this. He came from Sinai and without saying just where that is, we know it is not in Canaan.

The second factor, curiously enough, is the language. Everybody knows that this is the strongest argument for identifying the Israelites as Canaanites. They spoke the same language —but did they? The so-called northern dialect is clearly Canaanite. You can hardly tell the difference between Israelite and Phoenician, but how about so-called Judah-ite? We have no attestation of this language before the Monarchy, but it is in the Israelite tradition. The Judah-ite dialect dominates the whole Bible. Where did it come from? It is clearly southern, and I would say Yahwism and the so-called southern dialect came from the same place —how far away from Canaan is not relevant, but not from inside Canaan.

Lastly, I would like to point to the prophetic tradition. Most people say the prophets are all contaminated by the Deuteronomic tradition. I believe that strictly speaking this is not true. It is an interesting phenomenon that Amos, who deals with all these peoples, identifies Israel, or compares Israel on the same basis with the Philistines and the Arameans. Nobody ever suggested that any of these groups were Canaanite. They all came from outside: the Arameans from Kir, the Philistines from Caphtor, and the Israelites from Egypt. He also talks about Edom, Moab and Ammon. We know that all have the same language as the Hebrews, the Israelites, but he separates those two groups and he puts Israel with the outsiders.

SESSION III
STRATIGRAPHY, CHRONOLOGY AND TERMINOLOGY

AVRAHAM BIRAN, Session Chairman, *Hebrew Union College–Jewish Institute of Religon*

SEYMOUR GITIN, *W.F. Albright Institute of Archaeological Research*
Stratigraphy and Its Application to Chronology and Terminology
RUTH AMIRAN, *The Israel Museum*
The Transition from the Chalcolithic to the Early Bronze Age
WILLIAM G. DEVER, *The University of Arizona*
From the End of the Early Bronze Age to the Beginning of the Middle Bronze
MOSHE DOTHAN, *University of Haifa*
Terminology for the Archaeology of the Biblical Periods
DAVID USSISHKIN, *Tel Aviv University*
Reassessment of the Stratigraphy and Chronology of Archaeological Sites in Judah in the Light of Lachish III

Respondents

AMNON BEN-TOR, *The Hebrew University of Jerusalem*
RAM GOPHNA, *Tel Aviv University*
AHARON KEMPINSKI, *Tel Aviv University*
PIERRE DE MIROSCHEDJI, *Centre de Recherche Français de Jérusalem*
ROGER MOOREY, *Ashmolean Museum, Oxford*
WALTER E. RAST, *Valparaiso University*
JOE D. SEGER, *Mississippi State University*

Discussion

The Chairman's Remarks

Avraham Biran: Sixty-two years ago W.F. Albright, J. Garstang and W.J. Phythian-Adams met together and agreed on a new chronological classification of Palestinian archaeology. Although their classification has, with modification, stood the test of time, it is quite proper that we here, at the first International Congress on Biblical Archaeology, should attempt a reevaluation of these terms.

Every chairman considers his session to be the most important, but this session *is* really the most important one, for I am daring enough — some would say foolhardy enough — to hope that out of our deliberations here, a new chronological classification will emerge, a classification that will be acceptable to all, and which will endure for another fifty years. If we succeed, I suggest that we call it the "Jerusalem Terminology."

Stratigraphy and Its Application to Chronology and Terminology

Seymour Gitin

BIBLICAL OR PALESTINIAN archaeology, from its inception, has been defined by the trinity of stratigraphy, chronology, and terminology. They have been the major focal points of archaeological research, and the structure by which the results of that research have been organized and interpreted. While this is true, in varying degrees, for the archaeology of all of the lands of the ancient Near East, stratigraphy has played a far greater role in determining chronology and terminology for the events which occurred in ancient Israel and the lands immediately adjacent to it, than in the other geographical areas of the Middle East.

For Egypt and Mesopotamia, stratigraphy has been of secondary importance. There, abundant epigraphic evidence has been the key to formulating chronology and terminology by providing astronomically fixed dates, correlated with king lists, chronicles and royal annals.

For the land described as Canaan, Palestine, or Israel, no treasure troves of documentary evidence, no royal archives have yet been uncovered from the first three millennia B.C.E. The only available textual evidence is the biblical record, limited by historical time reference, a corpus of ostraca, miscellaneous epigraphic data, and references in documentary evidence from Egypt and Mesopotamia. While important in any archaeological and historical reconstruction, this body of textual evidence, by itself, is insufficient for the writing of a comprehensive history. This conclusion is underscored in the popular textbook, *The Ancient Near East —A History*, in which the authors reconstruct the history of Egypt and Mesopotamia but not of Palestine. As for Palestine, the authors state there are only "material and artistic remains which add important dimensions to the evidence of the texts, but in the absence of texts they remain mute and enigmatic; they cannot constitute human history."[1] For these authors, and others working in ancient Near Eastern studies, history can only be written when there is a sufficient amount of textual evidence. As one of my colleagues is forever reminding me, five good cuneiform tablets are worth more than five good strata. That, of course, depends upon the contents of the tablets and the definition of the strata. In the absence of texts, however, it is unacceptable to assign the thousands of years of the Bronze and Iron Ages to prehistory or to purely anthropological study, and to ignore the task of reconstructing the history of the third, second and first millennia B.C.E. based on the archaeological record. It is precisely when the written record is weak that the anepigraphic part of the archaeological record, specifically the stratigraphic evidence, plays a more vital role than the secondary one assigned to it by some scholars. It is, therefore, no coincidence that the first significant step toward formulating a comprehensive chronological structure related to a system of periodization for ancient Israel, was the direct result of the earliest recognition of the value of stratigraphy sealed within the ubiquitous mounds of Palestine.

With the commencement of modern archaeological investigation at Tell el-Ḥesi, in 1890, Flinders Petrie observed that pottery found in different layers or strata represented different periods of history. Building upon his own experience in Egypt and that of Schleimann and Dorpfeld at Troy, he used stratigraphic sequence, that is, the relationship of different strata and their contents, as an index for deciphering the occupational history of a site. Linking the stratified ceramic evidence from Ḥesi with pottery forms he knew from Egypt and the Aegean, he drew the first isoglosses connecting Palestine and Egypt for the period of the Eighteenth Dynasty, and for what we consider today to be the Persian period. By means of this comparative approach to ceramic evidence, he produced a chronological classification with four periods: the Amorite, and the Early, Middle, and Late Jewish, which he dated from 1600 until 650 B.C.E.[2] The effect of Petrie's linkage of stratified and chronological data at one site was to create the possibility of extending that linkage to other sites with similar ceramic evidence. Thus, he set into motion a process which eventually would evolve into a universally acceptable schema of chronology and terminology.

During the next thirty-two years, this process continued, but with little real progress. New tels were excavated and important discoveries made, as enthusiasm grew for the exploration of the Holy Land. With each new excavation and publication, yet another proposal was made for the chronology and terminology of Palestinian evidence, none of which was based on well-stratified data, and none of which gained universal acceptance. Chaos reigned. In 1902, Bliss and Macalister published in their *Excavations in Palestine* a new terminology using "Pre-," "Early," and "Late Israelite," and "Jewish" and "Selucidan," based primarily on the presence or absence of Mykenaean or Phoenician pottery.[3] In 1912, Macalister published his *magnum opus* on Gezer. Gone were his Israelite periods. In their place, the First through Fourth Semitic periods appeared, followed by the Persian and Hellenistic periods, loosely dated by correlations with Egypt and inferences from biblical history.[4] Macalister reasoned that by using the Israelite designation too much weight was given to the Israelite immigration as a cardinal point. It did not affect Gezer and other cities that were outside the limits of Hebrew domination. On the other hand, "Semitic" was sufficiently general to include successive civilizations of Amorites, Hebrews, and other ethnic groups. He also moved to a numerical system, because it was analogous to Minoan periods used by Cretan explorers, and as it appeared more scientific.[5] With regard to these two points, Macalister's approach foreshadowed developments that ten years later were to form the basis for a system of chronology and terminology which eventually would be universally accepted.

A year later, Sellin and Watzinger published their finds from Jericho using the terminology "Canaanite," "Late Canaanite," and "Israelite."[6] Their dates were earlier by 400 years or more than those for comparable periods in Macalister's chronology. In 1916, Handcock, in his handbook *The Archaeology of the Holy Land*, tried the impossible by correlating all the chronological schema published to date in a single synthetic treatment.[7] The result was total confusion.

Following World War War I, the Department of Antiquities under the British Mandate for Palestine was established, and John Garstang became its first director. One of his earliest efforts was to bring together representatives of the American, British, and French schools of archaeology then active in Palestine, for the purpose of formulating a classification system of terms capable of specifying the phases of historical and archaeological evolution. In 1922 Garstang, Phythian-Adams, Vincent and Albright, in an historic meeting, agreed to a double-level classification system. The first level contained terms long-established in European archaeology: Palaeolithic, Neolithic, Bronze, and Iron, in addition to Arab, intended to be broad enough not to prejudice ethnographic complexities. At the second level, the Bronze Age was subdivided into Early, Middle, and Late Canaanite, and the Iron Age into Early, Middle, and Late Palestinian with internal subdivisions into Philistine, Israelite, Jewish, and Hellenistic.[8] The second level terminology was included to reflect the proper ethnographic nuances of the subdivisions of the larger categories. All levels of classification were grouped in numerical sequence following the principle which dominated the classification of Mediterranean civilizations, and which had then recently been fully developed by Carl Blegen in his publication *Korakou*.[9] Blegen had modeled his new chronological system of Helladic periods on Evans' earlier Minoan system.[10] Thus, the Palestinian classification system was compatible with the broader realm of Old World archaeology, and could be specifically paralleled to systems describing other Mediterranean cultures, thereby facilitating communication and the application of comparative analysis to artifactual evidence throughout the eastern Mediterranean basin.

However, while this new system represented a significant advancement in the process initiated by Petrie, its singular effect was on terminology and sequential perception. Many fundamental problems of chronology still remained to be solved. Specifically, the dark age between the Neolithic and the Bronze Age had yet to be properly described and dated. The dating and subdivisions of the third millennium for the most part remained problematic. Only the divisional outline for the Middle and Late Bronze Ages, linked to the Eygptian Twelfth and Eighteenth Dynasties, and isolated correlations with Egypt and Mesopotamia for the Iron Age had any chronological basis. What was needed was a coherent stratigraphic sequence for all periods established by evidence from several sites which could be related to each other and fixed in time by absolute dates available either from Egypt or elsewhere. This was to come, ten to fifteen years later, through the work of Albright and his student, G. Ernest Wright, based on the excavations at Tell Beit Mirsim, Megiddo, and other sites.

In the meantime, the Golden Age of archaeology was in its floruit. Sites were excavated throughout the country at an accelerated pace. Most archaeologists in their preliminary and final publications adopted the new classification system with its rough dating schema — Phythian-Adams at Ashkelon, Albright in his survey of the Jordan Valley in the Bronze Age, and Reisner at Samaria, to cite but a few.[11] There were, of course, some who still maintained their own chronology and terminology, like Petrie in his Ajjul publication, where he used the terms "Copper," "Bronze," "Canaanite," and "Hyksos" periods.[12]

By 1932, Albright, through his own excavation at Tell Beit Mirsim and his superior knowledge of Palestinian archaeology, was recognized as the leading exponent in developing chronology and terminology based on sound stratigraphic principles. In his classic volume, *The Archaeology of Palestine and the Bible*, he produced a table of archaeological periods which approximates in concept and detail similar charts used by archaeologists today. This classification system was to become the major focus, for the next thirty years, in the process of developing stratigraphically based chronologies and systems of terminology. In his periodical chart, Albright subdivided the third millennium B.C.E. into Early Bronze I, II, and III, beginning at 3000 B.C.E., with divisions at 2600 and 2300 B.C.E., and ending at 2000 B.C.E. Middle Bronze I and II began at 2000 and 1800 B.C.E., respectively; Late Bronze I at 1600 B.C.E.; LB II at 1400 B.C.E. His Early Iron Age I started at 1200 B.C.E., Early Iron Age II at 900 B.C.E., and Early Iron Age III extended from 600 to 300 B.C.E.[13]

Albright based his determination for most periods on the stratigraphic divisions related to typological changes in ceramic forms at Tell Beit Mirsim. However, for the beginning of the Early Bronze period, he relied on correlations between burnished platter bowls and Syrian forms found at other Palestinian sites, with First Egyptian Dynasty forms from the royal tombs at Abydos. The remainder of his Early Bronze subdivisions were not founded on any well-defined sequence of ceramic types. Given the lack of proper data, he felt that the establishment of such a ceramic typology was premature. In this, he followed Gjersted's approach to subdivisions for the third millennium in Cyprus.[14]

Albright's other subdivisions were more securely founded. A few examples will suffice. His Middle Bronze IIA was based on the correlation of the appearance of wheel-made pottery in strata G and F at Beit Mirsim with the royal tombs at Byblos, dated to the Twelfth Egyptian Dynasty.[15] His Late Bronze Age divisions were closely correlated with Cypriote and Mycenaean ceramic imports.[16] His Iron Age I divisions were related to the appearance of new ceramic groups such as those he associated with Israelites and Philistines.[17] In Iron Age II, his divisions were based on the appearance of red-slip and hand and wheel burnishing.[18] Throughout Albright's treatment of this classification system, he was always aware that his terminology was only a convenience, that is, the names for periods were irrelevant enough not to be controversial. For as he often stated, "the term Early Bronze is an unsatisfactory one since bronze was rarely used."[19] What was true for the Bronze Ages was also true for Early Iron Age I.

Immediately following Albright's work at Tell Beit Mirsim, new evidence was discovered that would finally clarify the ephemeral dark age that had existed for so long between the Neolithic and Early Bronze periods. Again, it was Albright who correctly saw that the Ghassulian culture was not to be dated from 3000 to 2000 B.C.E. as the excavators, Mallon and Koepel, believed, but that, in fact, it preceded the Early Bronze Age.[20] This was confirmed in 1935 by Garstang at Jericho, where he found Ghassulian type pottery below a thick stratum with Early Bronze wares.[21] The final piece of evidence which put this new Chalcolithic period in proper chronological perspective was found a year later at Afula by Sukenik and Avigad. There, Ghassulian pottery was excavated immediately below the grey burnished Esdraelon ware.[22]

The stage was now set for G. Ernest Wright to do for the third millennium what Albright had already accomplished for the second and first millennia B.C.E. In his 1937 doctoral dissertation, Wright established the key to the Early Bronze Age divisions by linking EB II with the First Dynasty of Egypt, a change from Albright's linkage with EB I. Using this as his point of departure, Wright formulated the chronological and terminological systems based on a summary of the best-stratified evidence for the Neolithic through the EB IV periods, from ca. the 6th millennium through the end of the 3rd millennium B.C.E. His EB I began at 3200 B.C.E., EB II at 2900, EB III at 2700, and EB IV ran from 2300 to 2000 B.C.E.[23] Wright's main problem with period classification was with the term "Chalcolithic," which in 1937 was still under attack as most scholars subsumed it under "Neolithic." Wright was in favor of maintaining the term "Chalcolithic," but in deference to his teacher, Albright, he suggested that if this term were to be given up, it should be replaced by "ceramolithic," a term that Albright continued to recommend as late as 1940.[24]

Albright and Wright's final definition of this entire classification system, built on the foundations of the decision by Garstang, Phythian-Adams, Vincent and Albright, minus the second level ethnic designations, now gained wide acceptance. It became the basis for the next stage of development in the process in which we find ourselves today, a stage in which there are two critical underlying issues.

The first issue concerns the basis for determining the choice of stratified evidence for describing and dating archaeological periods. In the past, the strength of personality, the force of argument of a particular scholar, and the format of the presentation were paramount. Those scholars who presented their ideas in the format of a textbook exerted a greater influence upon the selection and acceptance process of archaeological terminology and chronology than their colleagues, who published disparate articles scattered throughout numerous journals in a dozen different languages. Unfortunately, the attraction of a single authoritarian document purporting to tell all in 300 pages or less, has been seductive to the point of blindness to scholarly bias and the limitations of evidence.

There are three classic examples of this phenomenon. Albright's *The Archaeology of Palestine*, although based on the small, intrinsically insignificant site of Tell Beit Mirsim, tucked away in the southwest corner of the Shephelah, became for a generation of scholarship the primary divining rod for discerning the terminology and chronology of the entire country.[25] Kenyon's *Archaeology in the Holy Land*, the fourth edition of which appeared in 1979 shortly after her death, is still today a widely used text and an accepted authority — while based primarily on the author's experience at Jericho and Samaria.[26] Aharoni's volume, *The Archaeology of the Land of Israel*, recently published, is gradually gaining the same respect held in former days by its predecessors, even though its bias is blatantly clear with regard to its author's research in the Galilee and the northern Negev.[27]

A second criterion for data selection is the quality of the stratified evidence itself. Unfortunately, much depends on who is evaluating the data. As there are different approaches to field work, a scholar will evaluate the work of another in light of his own bias. Thus, information produced by a system stressing one set of values is rarely viewed favorably and used by proponents of another system. One can almost predict the review that will be written when a new archaeological report is published, depending upon the approach to excavation methods held by the reviewer. Is it then any wonder that different chronologies, terminologies, and perceptions of environment and history are often based on the same stratified data? Unless more objective criteria are established for such evaluation, and a consensus reached, this debilitating and counter-productive process will continue to overload literature.

The second critical, underlying issue is which terminology is most suitable for a classification system of archaeological periods — the traditional terminology of convenience or one which relates to the historical environment? There is a strong divergence of opinion on this question. Since World War II, the traditional terminology of convenience, with some internal adjustments at the subdivision level, has been supported in some of the more important synthetic articles such as: Wright's 1958 article "The Transition between the Chalcolithic and the Bronze Age";[28] his 1961 article "Archaeology of Palestine";[29] Lapp's 1967 treatment of "The Conquest of Palestine in Light of Archaeology";[30] Mazar's 1968 article "The Middle Bronze Age in Palestine";[31] Stern's 1975 article "Israel at the Close of the Period of the Monarchy — An Archaeological Survey";[32] and Holladay's 1976 treatment of late Iron II periods, "Of Sherds and Strata."[33]

Other scholars, however, while evaluating the same evidence, have attempted major modifications in the traditional system based on their conceptions of what actually occurred in a given period of history. In 1957, Kenyon proposed a new terminology for the traditional beginning of the Early Bronze Age, calling it "Proto-Urban" A, B, and C, followed by what she conceived as the real beginning of the urban period, her EB I.[34] In 1973, in the *Cambridge Ancient History* chapter on "The

Middle Bronze Age," she presented her strongest argument for beginning the Middle Bronze period with Albright's MB IIA and renaming it Middle Bronze I, since MB IIA was the real beginning of the Middle Bronze culture.[35] This has been supported by many scholars, most recently by Patty Gerstenblith.[36] With regard to the changing perception of the cultural extent of this period, and its relation to other phases of the Early Bronze and Middle Bronze Ages, conflicting proposals have been put forward. Dever, in numerous articles, has supported changing Albright's MB I to EB IVA, B, and C, based on his association of this period with the end of the Early Bronze culture and its discontinuity with the following Middle Bronze Age.[37] On the other hand, Dunayevsky and Kempinski have tried to show that there were cultural connections between the MB I or EB IV period and MB IIA.[38] Yadin and Kochavi's important contributions to the debate on the definition and chronology of the MB IIA period and its relationship to MB IIB, are based on different evaluations of when the urbanization process began in the second millennium.[39] Perhaps no other period better demonstrates that terminology is not a matter of mere convention, but rather an expression of discrete conceptions and perceptions of history.

Other treatments have dealt specifically with the Iron Age, like Aharoni and Amiran's "A New Scheme for the Subdivision of the Iron Age in Palestine," which as far back as 1958 reformulated the dates and subdivisions of Iron Age II according to historical perceptions and a well-defined evaluation of the stratigraphy and ceramic forms at Hazor, Samaria and other sites.[40]

The confusion generated by the response to the two critical underlying issues in the present stage of the process of applying stratigraphy to chronology and terminology, changed what had once been an orderly process in a relatively comprehensible discussion scattered through a handful of journals, excavation reports, dissertations, and handbooks, into a complex series of arguments of almost unmanageable proportions, appearing in an ever-growing body of multilingual periodical literature and monographs. Today the discussion on the traditional trinity has evolved into a polythetic paradigm composed of systems of multiple charts of intricate stratigraphic relationships depicted by triangular isoglosses connecting loci in Asia Minor, Egypt, Mesopotamia, and the Aegean, which require footnotes explaining the use of terms and dates often greater in length than the text itself.

The fact that we have not been able to produce a single objective textbook is indicative of the state of affairs in which we now find ourselves. For many of us who spend so much of our time coping with this growing body of literature, this may not be a problem, but just one of the more annoying aspects of our work. However, for new students, the problem is real and amounts to an unfair and often traumatic burden. If the goals of our research are definition, clarity, and the increase of productive and useable information, then we have failed ourselves, our students and colleagues in other areas of ancient Near Eastern studies, who must somehow relate to this confusing mass of overdigested data.

There is yet another dimension to this problem. Our colleagues in New World archaeology who are anthropologically oriented, have developed approaches to collecting, recording, and publishing data which have already had an impact on the way in which we direct and formulate our research. We have begun to explore in depth the ways the MB I (or is it the EB IVA, B, or C, or perhaps the transitional EB/MB?) man related to his environment. As such, the traditional trinity for organizing our excavations and publications —our very thinking about archaeological evidence —is being influenced. How are we to respond to this broadening of the structure of our discipline if there is no consensus on the traditional tripartite structure itself? How are we to expand if our foundation is not solid?

We are in a period of transition. Before we address the broader issues of a new agenda for archaeological research, the basic questions of our old agenda need to be answered. Our terminology and chronology need to be agreed upon, and a consensus established for evaluating stratified evidence produced by different excavation methods. The model of Garstang's 1922 gatherings could serve us well — small groups of responsible scholars working together on a common set of problems. One of the more positive outcomes of this Congress would be the organization of such groups, and agreement on the date of their meeting.

Notes

1. W.W. Hallo and W.K. Simpson, *The Ancient Near East. A History* (New York, 1971), p. 4.
2. W.F. Petrie, *Tell el-Hesy (Lachish)* (London, 1891), pp. 14–15, Pl. X.
3. F.J. Bliss and R.A.S. Macalister, *Excavations in Palestine 1898–1900* (London, 1902), p. 72.
4. R.A.S. Macalister, *Gezer*, vol. I (London, 1912), p. xxi.
5. Ibid., pp. 56–57.
6. E. Sellin and C. Watzinger, *Jericho* (Leipzig, 1913), p. 15.
7. P.S.P. Handcock, *The Archaeology of the Holy Land* (London, 1916), pp. 22–23.
8. L.H. Vincent, "Nouvelle Classification des Antiquités Palestiniennes," *RB* 32 (1923): 272–275; "Notes and News: A New Chronological Classification of Palestinian Archaeology," *PEFQS* (1923): 54, 55.
9. C.W. Blegen, *Korakou. A Prehistoric Settlement Near Corinth* (Concord, NH: American School of Classical Studies at Athens, 1921), p. 35f.
10. C.W. Blegen and A.J.B. Wace, "The Pre-Mycenaean Pottery of the Mainland," *Annual of the British School of Athens* 22 (1895): 175–189.
11. W.J. Phythian-Adams, "Report on the Stratification of Askalon," *PEFQS* (1923): 14; W.F. Albright, "The Jordan Valley in the Bronze Age," *AASOR* 6 (1924/25): 13–74; G.A. Reisner, C.S. Fisher and D.C. Lyon, *Harvard Excavations at Samaria*, vol. I (Cambridge, 1924).
12. W.F. Petrie, *Ancient Gaza I–IV* (London, 1931–34).
13. W.F. Albright, *The Archaeology of Palestine and the Bible* (Cambridge, 1932), p. 10.
14. Idem, *Tell Beit Mirsim I. AASOR* 12, no. 6 (1932): 4.
15. Idem, *Tell Beit Mirsim IA. AASOR* 13 (1933): 68, 70, 74.
16. Ibid., pp. 87–95.
17. Idem, *Tell Beit Mirsim III. AASOR* 21–22 (1943): 1–38.
18. Ibid., pp. 143–154.
19. Idem, "The Chalcolithic Age in Palestine," *BASOR* 48 (1932): 12.
20. Idem, "Palestine in the Earliest Historical Period," *Journal of the Palestine Oriental Society* (1935): 199ff.
21. J. Garstang, "The Early Bronze Age," *Annals of Archaeology and Anthropology* 22 (1935): 143ff.

22. M. Dothan, "Afula," in *Encyclopedia of Archaeological Excavations in the Holy Land*, vol. I, ed. M. Avi-Yonah (Jerusalem, 1975), p. 33.
23. G.E. Wright, "The Pottery of Palestine from the Earliest Times to the End of the Early Bronze Age" (Ph.D. diss., Johns Hopkins University, 1937), pp. viiiff.
24. Ibid., p. 4; W.F. Albright, *From the Stone Age to Christianity* (Baltimore, 1940), p. 132.
25. W.F. Albright, *The Archaeology of Palestine* (London, 1960).
26. K.M. Kenyon, *Archaeology in the Holy Land* (London, 1979).
27. Y. Aharoni, *The Archaeology of the Land of Israel* (Philadelphia, 1982).
28. G.E. Wright, "The Problem of the Transition between the Chalcolithic and the Bronze Age," *EI* 5 (1958): 37–45.
29. Idem, "The Archaeology of Palestine," *The Bible and the Ancient Near East* (New York, 1961), pp. 85–139.
30. P.W. Lapp, "The Conquest of Palestine in the Light of Archaeology," *Concordia Theological Monthly* XXXVIII, no. 5 (1967): 283–300.
31. B. Mazar, "The Middle Bronze Age in Palestine," *IEJ* 18 (1968): 65–97.
32. E. Stern, "Israel at the Close of the Period of the Monarchy — An Archaeological Survey," *BA* 38, no. 2 (1975): 26–54.
33. J.S. Holladay, "Of Sherds and Strata," in *Magnalia Dei. The Mighty Acts of God*, G.E. Wright Festschrift, eds. F.M. Cross, W.E. Lemke and P.D. Miller (New York, 1976), pp. 253–293.
34. K.M. Kenyon, *Digging Up Jericho* (London, 1957), pp. 93–102.
35. Idem, "Palestine in the Middle Bronze Age," in *Cambridge Ancient History* (Cambridge, 1973), pp. 77–116.
36. P. Gerstenblith, *The Levant at the Beginning of the Middle Bronze Age. AASOR*, Dissertation Series no. 5 (1983).
37. W.G. Dever, "New Vistas on the EB IV ('MB I') Horizon in Syria-Palestine," *BASOR* 237 (1980): 35–64.
38. I. Dunayevsky and A. Kempinski, "The Megiddo Temples," *EI* 11 (1973): 19, Fig. 33. (Hebrew)
39. Y. Yadin, "The Nature of the Settlements During the Middle Bronze IIA Period in Israel and the Problem of the Aphek Fortifications," *ZDPV* (1978): 1–23; M. Kochavi, P. Beck and R. Gophna, "Aphek-Antipatris, Tel Poleg, Tel Zaror and Tel Burga: Four Fortified Sites of the Middle Bronze Age IIA in the Sharon Plain," *ZDPV* (1979): 121–165.
40. Y. Aharoni and R. Amiran, "A New Scheme for the Subdivision of the Iron Age in Palestine," *IEJ* 8 (1958): 171–184.

The Transition from the Chalcolithic to the Early Bronze Age

Ruth Amiran

THE ESSENCE OF the thesis which I shall attempt to prove in this paper is that the Early Bronze culture evolved from the Chalcolithic culture, there being no sharp break between the two periods, and that such a development does not exclude or does not conflict with the existence of clear diacritical features of each of these two cultures. Indeed, this stands in total juxtaposition with the generally accepted hypothesis that the Chalcolithic culture, with all its advances in agriculture, herdsmanship, technology, art, etc., brusquely and completely disappeared before, or with, the beginning of EB I. New data accumulated in recent years both from regional surveys and from excavations, permit, in fact demand, some reevaluation or reinterpretation of the processes of development in the two periods under consideration. Yet, in anticipation of criticism and disagreement with some of the interpretations to be suggested here, I would like to quote a recent saying by Norman Yoffe: "Certitude is not the goal of science, progressive understanding is."[1]

The backbone of the analysis of transition in general is how to gauge or measure the weight of the element of *continuity* versus that of the element of *change*, and to achieve an all-encompassing conclusion with as much objectivity as possible. In the case of our present problem, we shall seek evidence showing that the factor of continuity is more pronounced than the factor of change in both realms of culture: the pattern of settlement, and the various categories of movable finds, such as pottery, stone vessels, flint tools, and others.

Work carried out during the last twenty years in various regions of the country has considerably increased our knowledge regarding both the density and the pattern of settlement of the Chalcolithic period and Early Bronze Age. In consequence, the map of the country is now well dotted with settlements dating to these two periods. Ram Gophna[2] has recently produced a careful analysis of the present situation. The general characterization of the economy of the Chalcolithic settlements as "agricoles-pastorales" (J. Perrot's definition of long ago[3]) is now being reevaluated in the light of many new discoveries, and indeed we must await the results of these studies.[4]

These studies in regard to the sociohierarchical structure of the settlements seem to indicate that the system consists of three types of settlements definable by size and with hierarchical dependency pointing to some social organization. When we compare the maps of the Chalcolithic and EB I periods, it is interesting to note that the map of EB I has undergone the greatest development in recent years. Furthermore, we realize the extent of continuity from the Chalcolithic period to EB I. I refrain from presenting these two maps, as data are still being processed and field work is still to be completed. Instead, I shall discuss some of the sites: large sites such as Megiddo, Beth-Shean, Tell el-Farʿah (N), Gezer, ʿAreini, and Lachish; and smaller ones, such as Afula, Diabeh, Tel Kitan (the latter two in the Jordan Valley); sites in the Shephelah like Lahav, Agra, Abu-Hof; and sites in the Arad Basin and Besor area. As a paradigm, we shall cast a brief look at the map of the immediate area of Arad, which indeed is also in a process of development. Its study is being carried out by the Arad expedition and units of the Archaeological Survey of the Department of Antiquities and Museums.[5] To date, the Arad map consists of some twenty sites within one-day walking distance from Arad, most of which produce sherds of both the Chalcolithic and the Early Bronze periods, thus constituting a history during these periods parallel to that of Arad. The sociopolitical differences between the center city, Arad, and the small settlements are beyond the scope of this paper.

The character of the small Chalcolithic–Early Bronze settlements is illustrated by two recently excavated sites located in different economic environments: Tel Kitan in the Jordan Valley near Beth-Shean, excavated by I. Eisenberg[6] of the Israel Department of Antiquities and Museums, and Small Tell Malḥata in the Beer-Sheba–Arad Basin, excavated by the Arad Expedition[7] as part of the Negev Emergency Project. Both sites are about seven to eight dunams in size (approximately two acres), but the different environments in which they are located affect the picture gained from the excavations. It seems that both in the Chalcolithic period and in EB I, the inhabitants of Tel Kitan built houses and made use of huge containers. Four houses of the Chalcolithic period and one or two of the EB I have thus far been uncovered. Due to the absence of Grey Burnished Ware, Eisenberg suspects a gap in the history of the site between the Chalcolithic and EB I. There could, however, be other interpretations of this absence, but we shall not elaborate upon this point now as the complex problem of the relationship between EB IA and EB IB, whether chronological or regional, is beyond our immediate concern here. (I do not see any evidence for the existence of the sub-period called EB IC.) The results of the excavations at Small Tell Malḥata provide a somewhat different picture: in the Chalcolithic period, the occupation is evidenced mainly by pits of various sizes, but also (thus far) one brick-made house. In EB I, the few houses were scattered, the emphasis being on large fenced areas containing round-platforms and other working installations. We must bear in mind that some large EB I settlements, such as Lahav, Abu-Hof,[8] etc., were discovered in the Shephelah, indicating some kind of hierarchical organization.

In reference to the nature of the economy of the settlements in the Chalcolithic period and in EB I, I should also like to emphasize the continuity between the two periods, mainly indicated by the inferences from and interpretations of movable objects. Besides being "agricoles-pastorales," the Chalcolithic economy shows another cardinal facet — incipient interregional/long-distance trade activity. I will mention only some of the evidence: two cylindrical Egyptian vessels, one made of alabaster excavated in the temple at En-Gedi,[9] the other made of ivory excavated in Tel Aviv;[10] a number of Canaanite pottery vessels found in Amratian-Naqada I contexts in Egypt; alabaster beads from Egypt found in Chalcolithic Gilat;[11] and a figurine of a donkey carrying two large vessels or baskets, excavated at Givatayim.[12] The two facets of Chalcolithic economy are discerned in an advanced form in the EB I economy: first and foremost, in the technology used to till the fields — mechanization, so to speak, with the invention or introduction of the animal-tracted plow substituting human labor. As stated by A. Sherratt,[13] this was the "second great achievement of human civilization." Two figurines clearly representing a pair of yoked oxen are certainly most plausible evidence for this development. With the animal-tracted plow, EB I field cultivation gradually surpassed that of the Chalcolithic culture in preparation for the emergence of urbanization.

In regard to trade, there was a considerable increase in long-distance commercial intercourse in EB I, reflected in imported and exported vessels (of course as containers of goods), which are uncovered in excavations in this country and in neighboring areas. In EB I, large quantities of figurines/statuettes of the loaded donkey were excavated in various sites throughout the country, from Qishyon in the Jezreel Valley to places along the main trade-traffic arteries, such as Aphek, Azor, etc. Pottery containers-vessels from both ends of the transaction routes, although mainly between Egypt and Canaan, also offer some indications of possible trade connections with northern Mesopotamia. The excavations at Minshat Abu-Omar in the Eastern Delta by D. Wildung[14] produced quite a considerable representation of Canaanite pottery. From excavations here, the considerable number of Egyptian jars bearing the incision with the name of Namer is a well-known and by now self-explanatory fact.

Some words are now in order in regard to the problem of the connections between Canaan and the cultures to the north. The EB I pottery, as is well known, manifests a certain flavor of the northern pottery repertoire of the Jamdat Nasr culture. The excavations at Habuba Kabira Sud on the Euphrates provided new evidence recently studied by the excavator, Eva Strommenger.[15] Habuba Kabira is a northern manifestation of the southern Uruk culture. Edith Porada[16] maintains that the distinction between the Uruk and Jamdat Nasr style (in the glyptic) now has to be eliminated. I believe this view corroborates my endeavor to trace a continuation of culture between the Chalcolithic period and EB I. Let us compare our pottery with that from Habuba Kabira Sud. At Tel Kitan, Eisenberg found a unique (until now) vessel,[17] which could have originated in the area of Habuba Kabira; at Habuba Kabira, the double-spouted vessels are quite common, and there also we find some single specimens of vessels showing a style of painting which is very reminiscent of the EB I group-painted style.[18]

We come now to the most intrinsically interesting point. Some of the objects discovered in clearly EB I assemblages do embody in their morphological features the very mixture of "old" Chalcolithic with newly developed EB I elements. These phenomena are perhaps decisive for more precise understanding of the processes which we can define as "continuity-plus-change." They may be considered as representing *the very moment* of transition as expressed in the hands of the craftsmen and artists. The following are some examples:

1. The line of development of the offering stand-bowl (designated as incense burner) from the Chalcolithic through to the end of the Early Bronze Age.
2. The basket-handled spouted bowl known from the EB I group-painted ware now goes back to the Chalcolithic period.
3. A jar excavated at Abu-Hof[19] clearly heralds the body shape and incipient ledge handles of EB I.
4. A bowl from Small Tell Malḥata has the EB I shape, while the painted decoration is still in the Chalcolithic tradition.
5. Vessels made of basalt present a most intricate and sophisticated phenomenon of continuity: the four-legged bowl of the Chalcolithic culture becomes the four-handled bowl of EB I.[20]

We shall conclude, or should I say culminate, with some of the cult and art objects. Here also, one can observe a conceptual continuity from the Gilat statuette of a female deity carrying a churn on her head to that from Bâb edh-Dhrâʿ, where the jar seems to have "swallowed" the head.[21]

In conclusion, it seems to me that the evidence of the material accumulated to date speaks for continuity between the Chalcolithic period and EB I. Continuity does not disallow development and change.

Notes

1. N. Yoffe, "Social History and Historical Method in the Late Old Babylonian Period," *JAOS* 102 (1982): 349.
2. R. Gophna, *History of Eretz-Israel. The Early Periods* (Jerusalem, 1982), pp. 76–118. (Hebrew)
3. J. Perrot, "La Prehistoire Palestinienne," dans *Supplément au Dictionnaire de la Bible* (1968), pp. 415ff.
4. Being carried out by D. Alon, Y. Gilead, T. Levi and others.
5. Special thanks are due to R. Cohen, the head of the Negev Archaeological Survey, and to Y. Guvrin of the survey unit working in the Arad area.
6. I am grateful to I. Eisenberg for this information.
7. An interim report on the first three seasons of excavation at Small Tell Malḥata prepared by Ornit Ilan, M. Saban and the writer is forthcoming.
8. Both these sites were discovered and excavated by D. Alon of the Israel Department of Antiquities and Museums.
9. D. Ussishkin, "The Chassulian Shrine at En-Gedi," *Tel Aviv* 7 (1980): 1–44 and especially 36.

10. The vessel was excavated by J. Kaplan, but is still unpublished. It is mentioned in my paper in *IEJ* 24 (1974): 9, with the kind permission of the excavator.
11. The find has not yet been published. I thank D. Alon, the excavator, for his permission to refer to it here.
12. J. Kaplan, *Ein el-Jarba* (Tel Aviv, 1969), p. 20 and Pl. 7. (Hebrew)
13. A. Sherratt, "Plough and Pastoralism: Aspects of the Secondary Products Revolution," in *Pattern of the Past: Studies in Honour of David Clarke*, eds. I. Hodder, G. Isaac and N. Hammond (Cambridge, 1981), pp. 261ff.
14. For general remarks regarding this excavation, see D. Wildung, *Ägypten vor den Pyramiden* (Mainz, 1981). Cf. R. Amiran, "Canaanite Merchants in Tombs of the EB I at Azor," *ʿAtiqot* 17 (in press).
15. For general remarks regarding this excavation, see Eva Strommenger, *Habuba Kabira* (Mainz, 1980).
16. Edith Porada, *Ancient Art in Seals* (Princeton, 1980), p. 6.
17. The vessel has not yet been published. I thank I. Eisenberg for his permission to include it here.
18. I am grateful to E. Strommenger for a good photograph of the vessel published with an incorrect representation of the base by D. Sürenhagen, "Untersuchungen zur Keramikproduktion innerhalb der Spät-Urukzeitlichen Siedlung Habuba Kabira-Süd in Nordsyrien," in *Acta Prahistorica et Archaeologica* 5/6 (1974/5), Tab. 19:161.
19. Excavated by D. Alon, but not yet published.
20. The line of development of the EB I four-handled basalt bowl from the Chalcolithic four-legged bowl is elaborated upon in Ruth Amiran and Naomi Porat, "The Basalt Vessels of the Chalcolithic and Early Bronze I Periods," *Tel Aviv* 11 (in press).
21. The Gilat statuette has been published by D. Alon, *ʿAtiqot* 11 (1976), pp. 116–118. The statuette from Bâb edh-Dhrâʿ is in the Semitic Museum of Harvard University.

From the End of the Early Bronze Age to the Beginning of the Middle Bronze

William G. Dever

THE TRADITIONAL Early Bronze IV–Middle Bronze I period, ca. 2400–2000 B.C.E., is a nonurban interlude between the first urban era in the Early Bronze Age in the third millennium B.C.E., and the renewed urban occupation in the true Middle Bronze Age in the second millennium B.C.E. Until recently it has been something of a "Dark Age," illuminated principally by isolated cemeteries and chance finds. Most of the major mounds of Palestine do not exhibit occupation throughout this period, and the few that do, have only shallow deposits (Fig. 1).

The phenomenon that confronts us is apparently due to a double-sided shift: (1) from the urban sites in the settled zone of northern and central Palestine to the marginal areas of Transjordan, the Jordan Valley, and the Negev-Sinai; and (2) from an economic strategy based on intensive agriculture, craft and industry, and trade, to one based rather on stock breeding, seasonal herding, and some dry farming (Fig. 2). The reasons for this period of profound socioeconomic change still elude us after two generations of research. The cause is not to be sought in "Amorite invasions," however, as scholars such as Albright, Glueck, and Kenyon thought, but rather in the collapse of the urban centers. This, in turn, was probably the result of an exceedingly complex combination of factors, such as overpopulation, exhaustion of natural resources, drought, famine, disease, and political corruption —all possibly related to the dramatic end of the Old Kingdom and the onset of the "First Intermediate" period in Egypt.[1]

All scholars agree on the transitional nature of this period in Palestine. However, various authorities, depending largely upon the degree of continuity they discern with the preceding and succeeding phases, have termed it "EB IV," "Intermediate" or "EB–MB," or "MB I." Here I shall use the EB IV terminology, as envisioned first by Wright and later advocated by Lapp, Oren, Olavárri, and myself for Palestine, and then by Matthiae for Syria.[2]

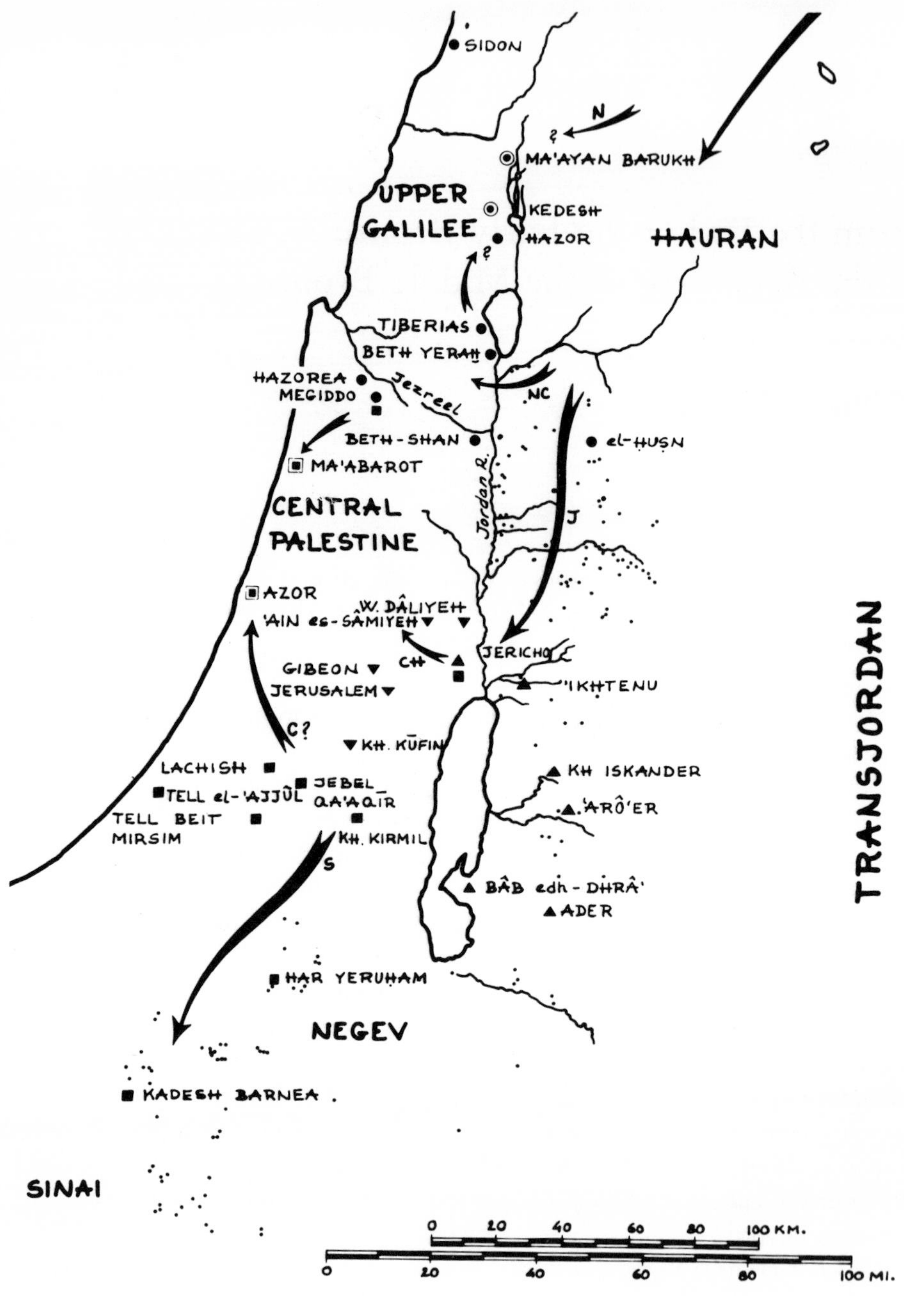

Fig. 1.
Map of principal EB IV sites. Unnamed sites are from surveys of Glueck, Aharoni, Cohen and others. Arrows indicate movements of cultural influence, not ethnic groups

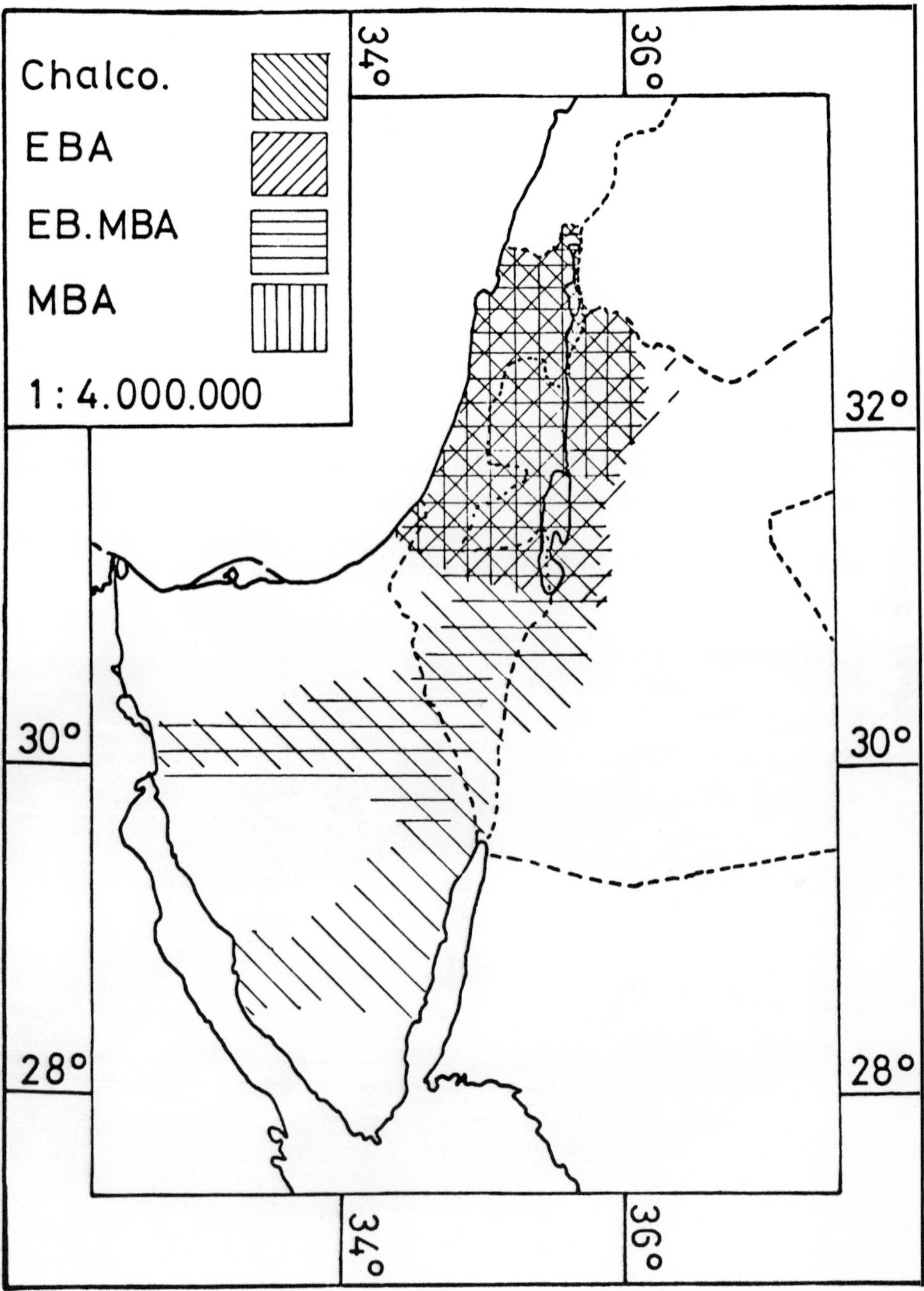

Fig. 2.
Comparative map of settlement patterns. From K. Prag, *Levant* 6 (1974), Fig. 2

In this brief synthetic treatment of EB IV, I shall focus on the exact nature of the period as a transition, presenting mostly new or unpublished material, and relying on my previous publications for overall detail.[3] I also include new material from Jordan and Syria, in the conviction that this period (like so many others in Palestine) can only be understood in a wider context. My approach in assessing socioeconomic change is *systemic*, assuming that culture is by and large the result of the interaction of a number of adaptive subsystems, all of which leave some traces in the archaeological record. Thus the categories of data at which we must look include not only pottery, as previous analyses stressed,[4] but also settlement patterns, village planning, architecture, subsistence systems, socioeconomic structure, tomb types, lithics, art and craft, and evidence for foreign relations.

Beʾer Resisim

An expedition of the "Central Negev Highlands Project," a joint American-Israeli undertaking in archaeology and arid lands studies, directed by myself and Rudolph Cohen in 1978–1980, excavated the better part of one of the largest and best-preserved of the several hundred EB IV settlement sites in the Negev-Sinai — Beʾer

Fig. 3.
Typical stone structure at Beʾer Resisim showing roof pillar, entrance, and other features
Photo: J. Kline

Resisim, situated in Naḥal Niṣṣana.[5] There the typical structure is a round or curvilinear stone shelter, about 2–4 m in diameter, as elsewhere in the Negev. These structures are built on bedrock, sealed with mudplaster, and roofed with timber, chalk slab, and plaster construction (Fig. 3). Since Beʾer Resisim is largely a one-period site, and was abandoned, rather than destroyed, at the end of the period, *in situ* materials were scant. However, ash deposits in communal food preparation areas with large quantities of predominantly sheep and goat bones, testify to dependence on herding as the mainstay of the economy. The presence of intact saddle-querns indicates also some dry farming of wheat or barley on the alluvial fans along the wadis below. A small hoard of copper ingots in one structure, as well as several Red Sea conch shells and polished pendants made from them, give evidence of trade over a considerable distance in metal, exotic raw materials, and finished products. Precisely such a mixed economy characterizes pastoral nomadic societies, both ancient and modern. As we shall see, such an economy is also in accordance with the long Early Bronze tradition of the Negev-Sinai.[6]

The Beʾer Resisim pottery (Fig. 4) also reveals widespread connections, both physical and temporal. Most of the pottery belongs, as expected, to my "Southern/Sedentary" family, and is undecorated or band-combed. But a painted teapot is one of just two painted EB IV pieces known in the south, the other very similar teapot coming from Jebel Qaʿaqīr in the Hebron Hills some 140 km to the north. A fragment of a gray wheel-made teapot has been shown by neutron activation analysis to be unique, and almost certainly comes from the "Caliciform" culture of the Orontes Valley in Syria, at least 500 km to the north. Although the surviving structures, and certainly the major occupational phase, appear to belong to late EB IV, there are small quantities of red burnished, earlier Early Bronze Age sherds in mixed debris and on bedrock (as are now known at most previous "one-period" EB IV sites in the Negev). Some may be EB II (below), but two burnished, rilled-rim neckless teapot sherds, one with a vestigial ledge handle, are paralleled only by identical vessels from EB IV sites in southern Transjordan. In addition, an undisturbed cairn produced an intact copper dagger and a red burnished EB IV amphoriskos. The above are the first traces of Transjordanian EB IV types clearly attested in Western Palestine.[7] And the other red burnished sherds probably take us back to the EB II repertoire of both Transjordan and the Negev-Sinai (below).

The site of Beʾer Resisim, at least 90% of which was excavated, reveals the first nearly complete EB IV village plan as yet published from a site on either side of the Jordan (Fig. 5). About eighty curvilinear structures are distributed over the central ridge, clearly grouped in distinct clusters, with large undifferentiated areas left open for domestic tasks, animal shelter, or the like. The individual structures have but one room, averaging well under 10 sq.m of floor space; they have no windows, a single entrance barely large enough to squeeze through, and a floor-to-ceiling space of under 1.5 m. They are not "dwellings" in the proper sense but simply sleeping shelters, each, to judge by demographic and ethnographic studies, for a single adult and one to three children. Each cluster of three to five structures is grouped around an

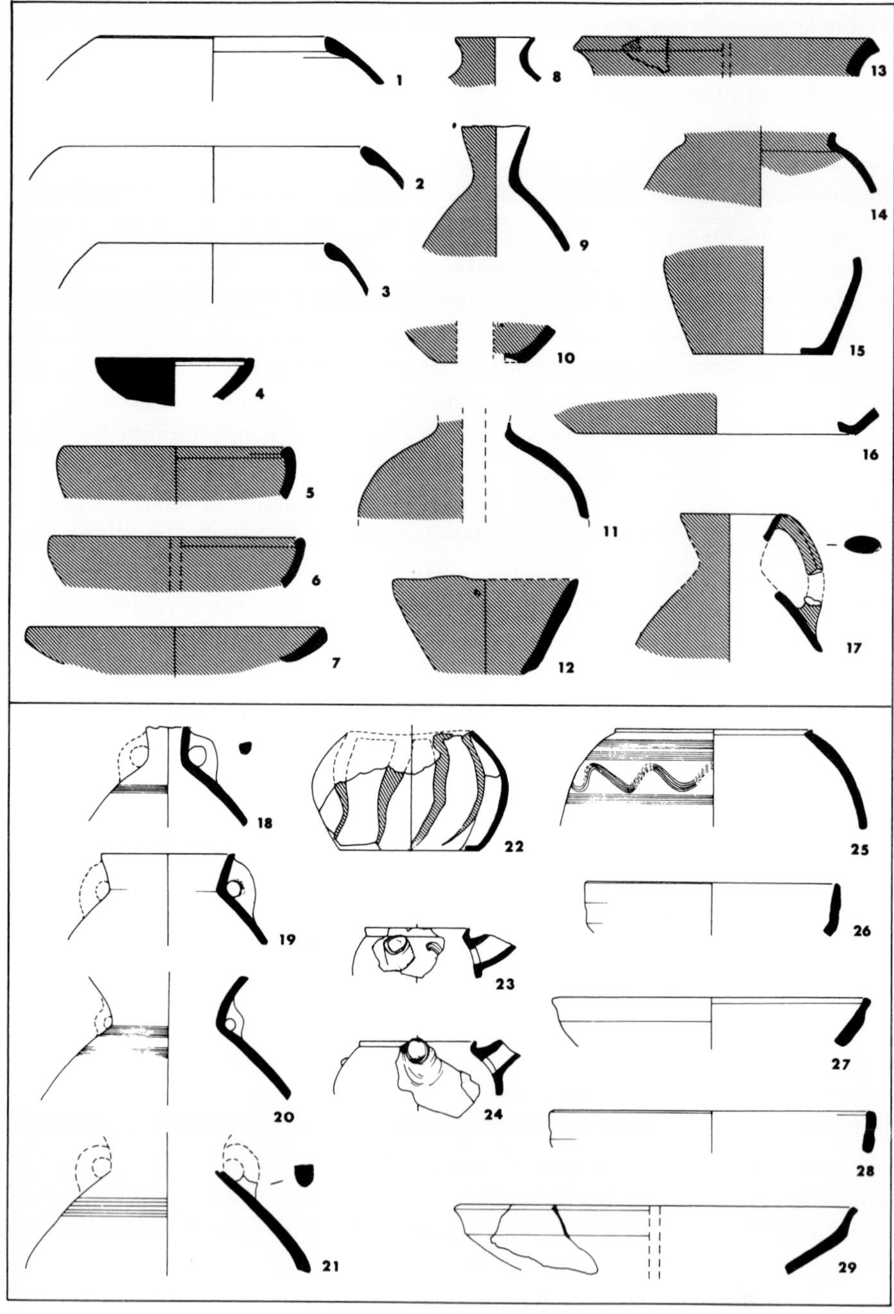

Fig. 4.
Representative EB II–EB IV pottery from Beʾer Resisim

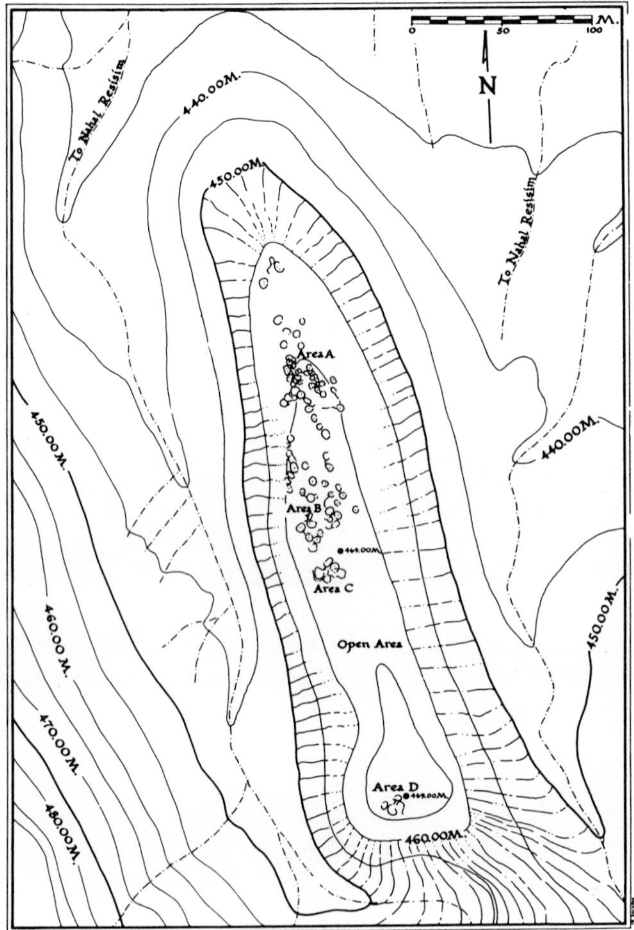

Fig. 5.
EB IV village of Be᾿er Resisim

open common courtyard, and probably represents a family unit consisting of one male, one to three females, and two to six children. Cross-cultural analyses have shown that similar village plans invariably characterize a society that is: (1) mobile rather than sedentary; (2) dependent on hunting-gathering and herding rather than intensive agriculture; (3) egalitarian in social structure; and (4) polygamous rather than monogamous. Thus at Be᾿er Resisim, we have a small kinship group or tribe of predominantly pastoral nomads, numbering perhaps seventy-five at any one time, which is well within the carrying capacity of this area, despite its minimal resources. If the pattern of seasonal movement was vertical (or elliptical) transhumance, Be᾿er Resisim was likely a winter encampment, the summer pastures being located in the Hebron Hills (below).[8]

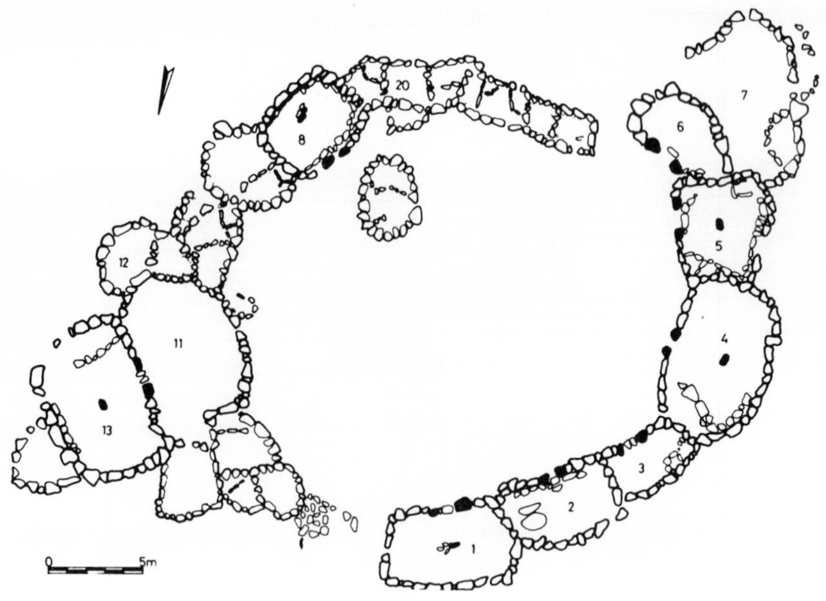

Fig. 6.
Typical structures of southern Sinai EB II sites. From I. Beit-Arieh, *BASOR* 243 (1981), Fig. 13

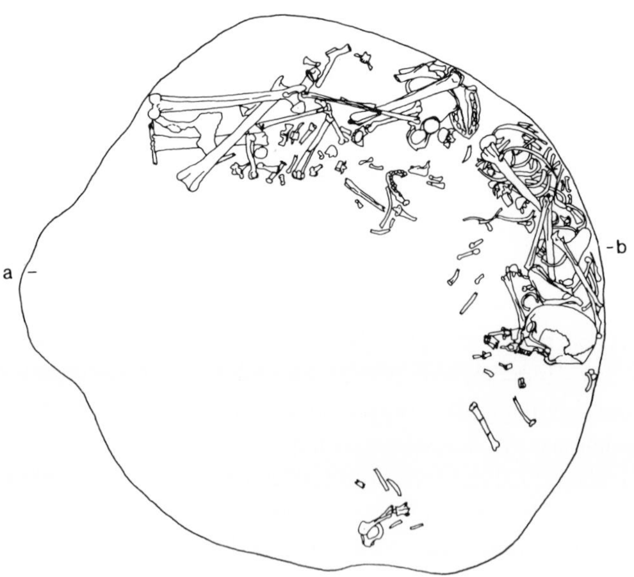

Fig. 7.
Typical EB IV shaft tomb and disarticulated burial at Jebel el-Qaʿaqīr

Again the direct prototype is found in the complex of EB II settlements in the Sinai, recently investigated by I. Beit-Arieḥ and others (Fig. 6). The individual curvilinear structures are very similar, although the "agglutinative" character of the overall plan of the Sinai sites shows more architectural sophistication than the ad hoc grouping at Beʾer Resisim. Furthermore, the Sinai sites, clearly related to large EB II sites like Arad in southern Palestine, may have been more permanently settled, that is, they constitute the marginal extensions of the urban Early Bronze Age of Palestine. The later EB IV Negev settlements like Beʾer Resisim, however, more primitive and transitory, mark the end of the Early Bronze Age — in fact, they represent the last vestige of the old Neolithic village type.[9]

Jebel el-Qaʿaqīr

We turn now to the Hebron Hills, where the one-period site of Jebel el-Qaʿaqīr (see Fig. 1), excavated by Hebrew Union College in 1968–1971, offers us what may be regarded as a summer encampment of the "Southern" Palestinian family.[10] The several large cemeteries of EB IV shaft tombs featured exclusively disarticulated burials (Fig. 7), which normally characterize nomadic societies exclusively. Occupational deposits were found only in a few natural caves. It appears that Jebel el-Qaʿaqīr, like many shaft tomb sites in the central and southern hills, was primarily a summer burial ground for various groups of pastoral nomads. Some of the copper weapons and the extensive pottery (Fig. 8) from the site are very close to those from Beʾer Resisim. We have already noted this in regard to the two unique painted teapots, and neutron activation analysis has shown the cooking pots from the two sites to be virtually identical in composition. Thus Jebel el-Qaʿaqīr belongs also to the last phase of the Early Bronze Age.

We have been attempting to characterize the "Southern" family of Palestine, both settlements and cemeteries, as belonging to the last nonurban phase of the Early Bronze Age, therefore "EB IV." The scheme I have developed over nearly twenty years, building on Ruth Amiran's brilliant intuition in 1960 regarding ceramic "families," divides the *whole* of EB IV Palestine and Transjordan into geographical-cultural families: N, NC, J, CH, TR, and S. I would argue that all of these can be regarded as belonging to the Early Bronze Age tradition. The ceramic evidence alone for these regional families is persuasive, as I have argued elsewhere, but there is more evidence.[11]

Transjordan

Let us now move northward and eastward to test our hypothesis of Early Bronze Age continuity at several recently excavated type-sites, beginning in southern Transjordan (my Family TR).

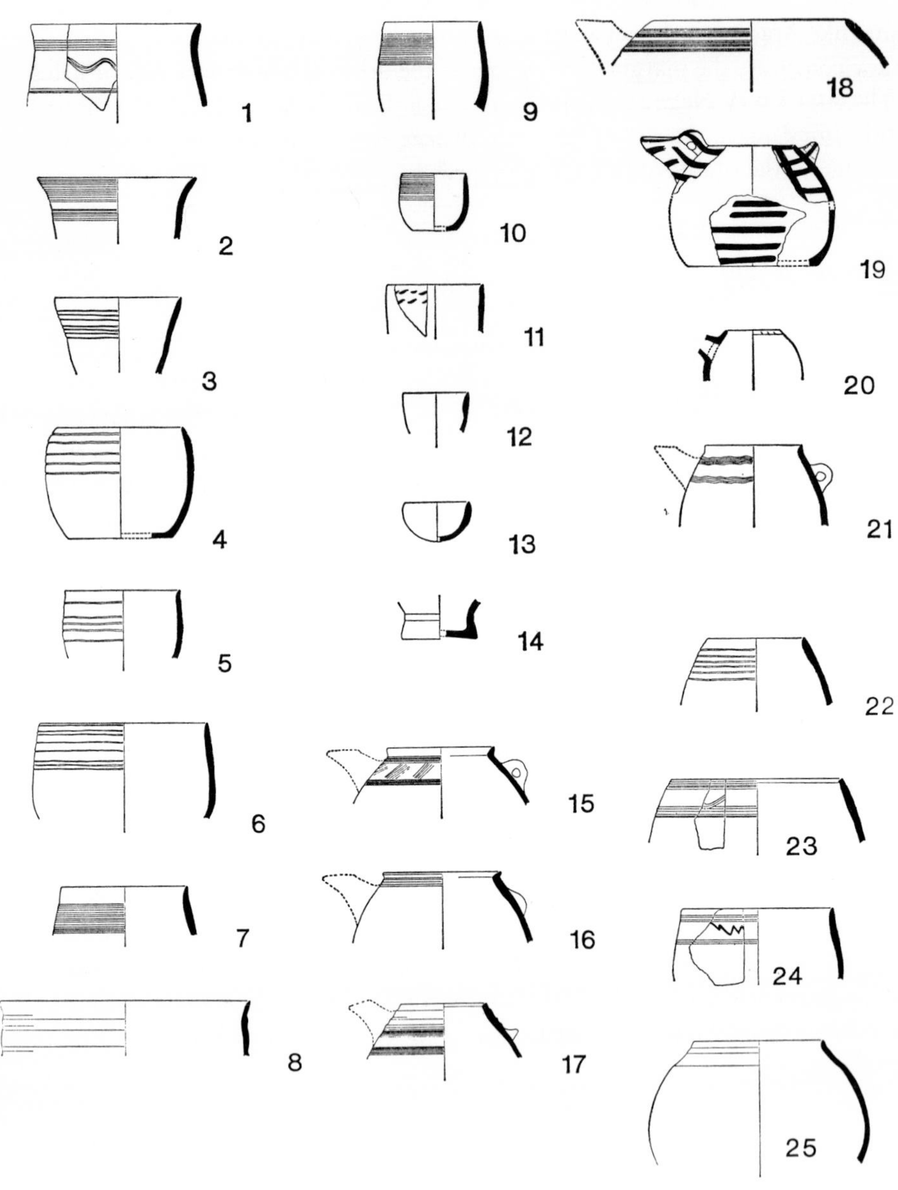

Fig. 8.
Pottery from Cave G23 at Jebel el-Qaʿaqīr. From S. Gitin, *EI* 12 (1975), Fig. 4

At Kh. Iskander, strategically located on a perennial stream in the Wadi Wala, north of Kerak (see Fig. 1), Peter Parr's excavations are currently being resumed and expanded by Suzanne Richard. This site now proves to be a large, fully *urban* EB IV site, extending back into EB III and probably earlier. The pottery and lithics of even the latest phase (my EB IVA–B) are without question in the long Early Bronze Age tradition. In addition, Early Bronze Age style broadroom houses persist into this phase. Still more significant is the perimeter defense wall, with a massive tower in the northwest, and what is almost certainly a chambered gate along the south stretch. It was clearly used (and may even have been built) in EB IV — the first EB IV town wall yet discovered in Transjordan or Palestine.[12]

Surprising as this extensive EB IV occupation in Transjordan may seem, the Bâb edh-Dhrâ' (see Fig. 1) excavations of P.W. Lapp, and since 1967 of W.E. Rast and R.T. Schaub, already anticipated this picture. The latest seasons have shown that after the destruction of the walled town-site in late EB III, there were several phases of EB IV occupation over much of the site and even outside the ruined city walls.[13] A number of EB IV shaft tombs were already known, one of which (T. A54), when studied by Schaub and myself in 1973, provided the long-sought "missing link" between the pottery of EB IV and EB III (the latter witnessed by the enormous repertoire of EB III in the charnel houses). We cannot go into detailed ceramic comparisons here, but on the basis of Bâb edh-Dhrâ', we can now demonstrate that a number of forms — bowls, teapots, jugs, small jars, chalices, cups, and lamps — show a continuous typological development from EB III into EB IVA–B and on into Albright's "MB I," after which they all cease (see Figs. 9 and 10).[14] Furthermore, most of these forms can be projected back to EB II prototypes. The same comparisons hold for EB II–IV lithic and metallic types. Even the distinctive shaft tomb of EB IV — previously thought to be unique and introduced from Syria — is now seen to derive from a long, local Early Bronze Age tradition, at least in Transjordan. At Bâb edh-Dhrâ' shaft tombs, virtually identical to those of EB IV, already characterized the EB I burials (see Fig. 11).

The results of the foregoing analysis, now confirmed by much further discovery and research, have far-reaching cultural implications.[15] We must now regard Albright's "MB I" as not Middle Bronze at all, but rather as the last, dying gasp of the Early Bronze Age (as G.E. Wright long ago suggested). And the direct continuity with EB II–III, together with the complete break at the end (below), renders the "Intermediate" (that is, partly intrusive) terminology of Kenyon and others untenable.

The composite EB IV–former "MB I" horizon, ca. 2400–2000 B.C.E., can be subdivided into three phases, EB IVA–C. EB IVA–B are now well represented at several sites in southern Transjordan, such as Iktanu, Ader, Iskander, 'Arô'er, and Bâb edh-Dhrâ'. In the north, we begin to find Glueck's older EB IVA–B material from surface surveys in the Jordan Valley in stratified contexts (below). EB IVC, the last phase, is largely missing in Transjordan and the Jordan Valley, but it is attested in Palestine by the many cemeteries in the central hills, and the hundreds of small

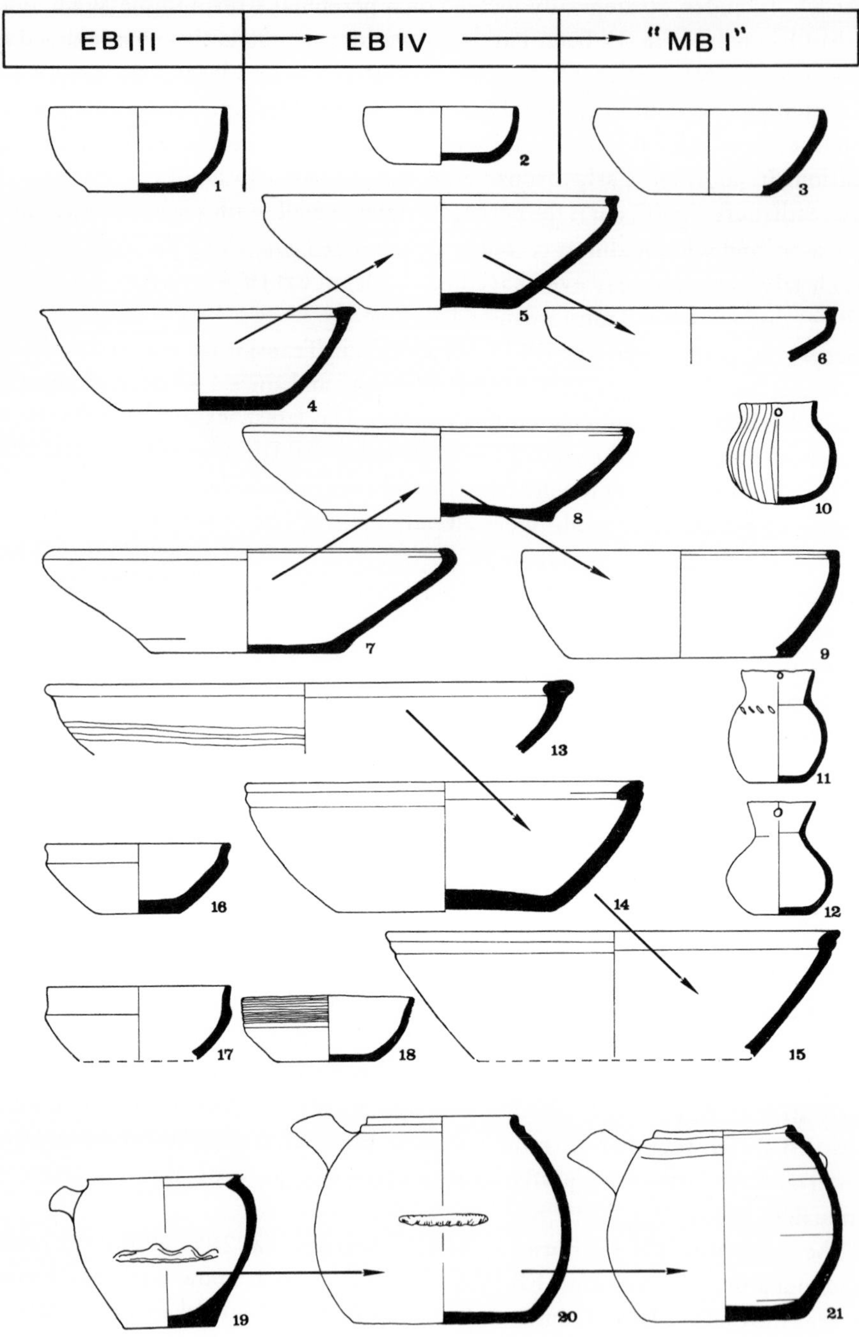

Fig. 9.
Ceramic comparisons between EB III, EB IV (from Bâb edh-Dhrâʿ T. A54), and "MB I" (= EB IVC).
From W.G. Dever, *BASOR* 210 (1973), Fig. 3

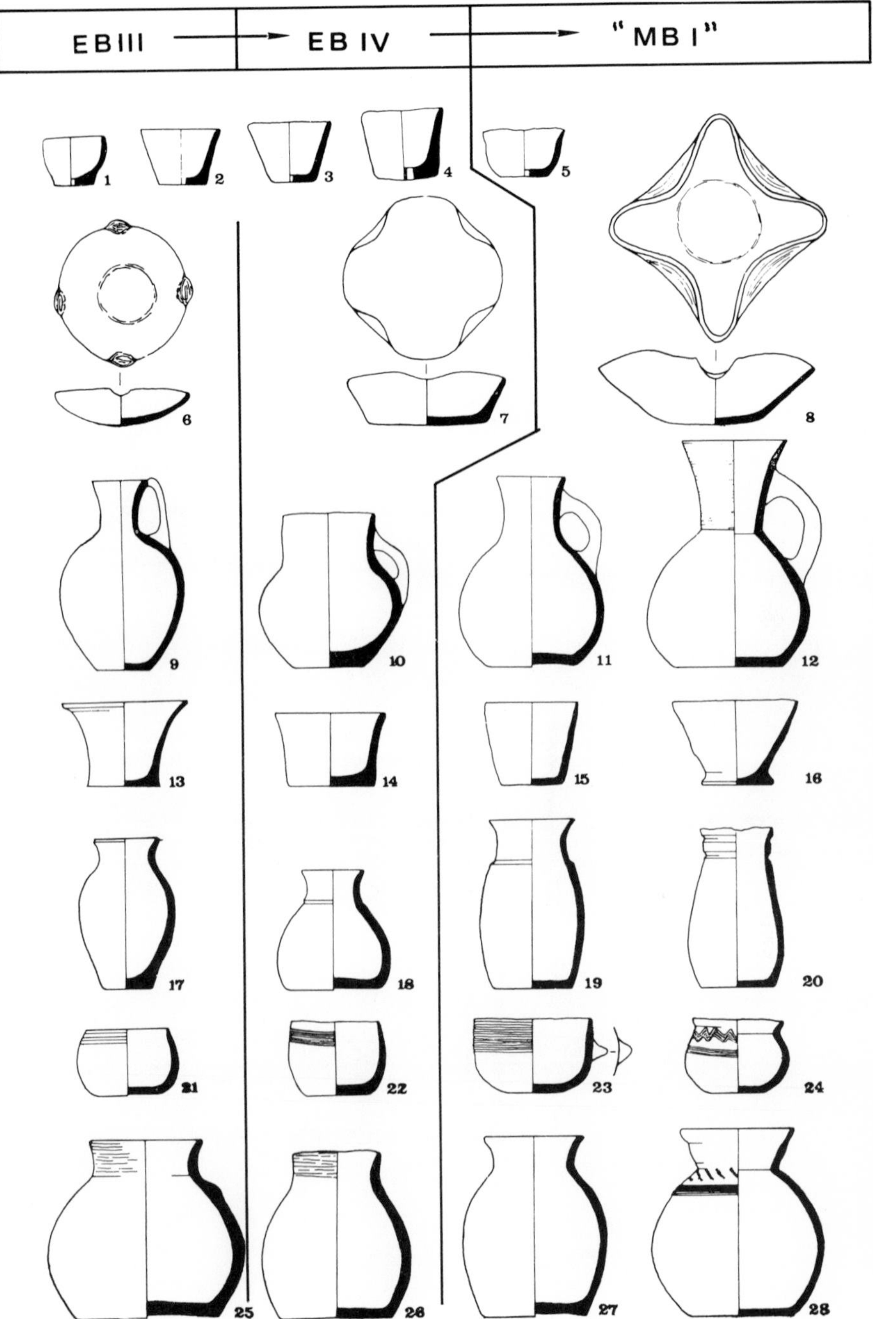

Fig. 10.
Ceramic comparisons between EB III, EB IV (from Bâb edh-Dhrâ' T. A54) and "MB I" (=EB IVC).
From W.G. Dever, *BASOR* 210 (1973), Fig. 4

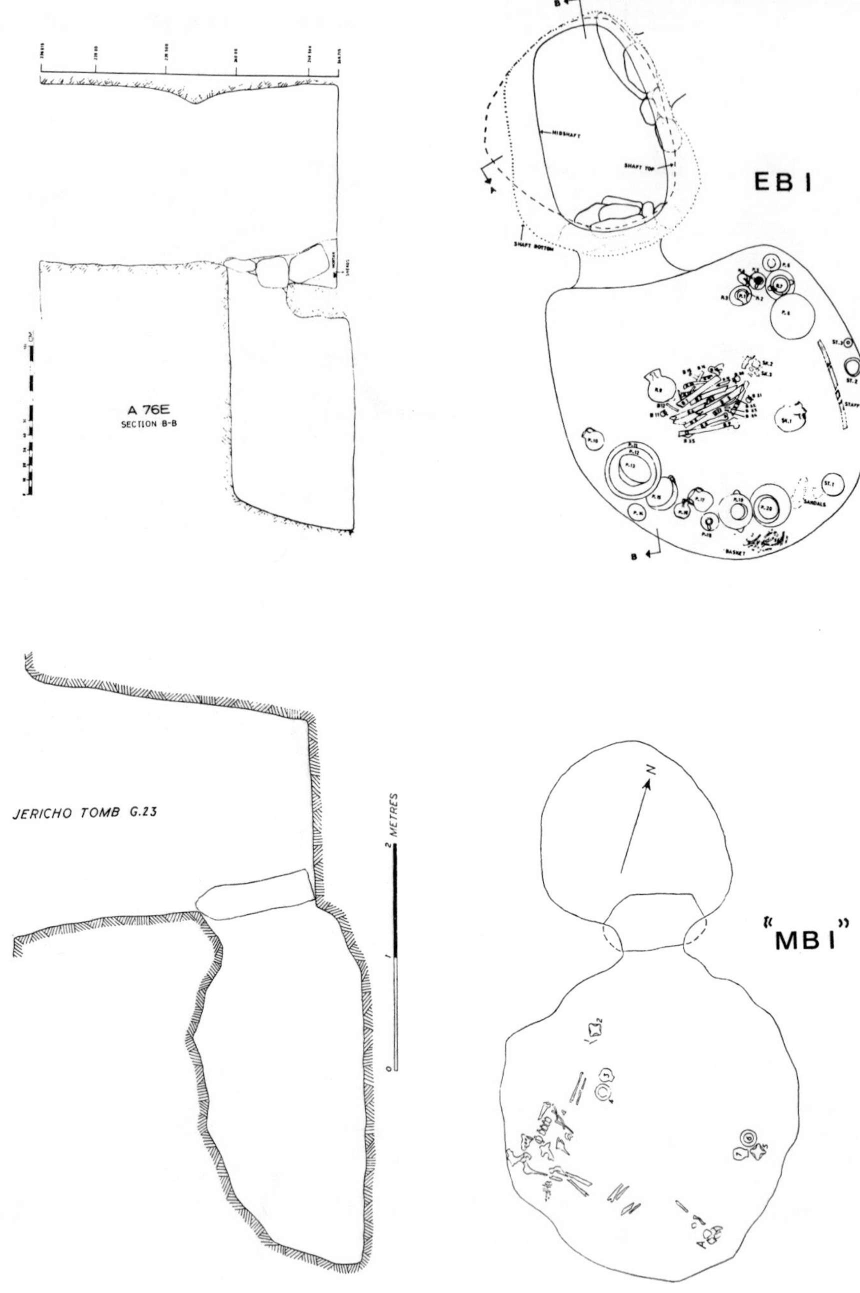

Fig. 11.
Comparison between EB I shaft tomb (Bâb edh-Dhrâʿ, T. A76A) and EB IV shaft tomb (Jericho, T.G 23). From P.W. Lapp, *BASOR* 189 (1968), Figs. 4, 5 and K. Kenyon, *Jericho*, 1, Fig. 99

settlements of the Negev-Sinai. This inevitably suggests that our EB IV, or "Southern" family (the pottery of which is typologically later than that of Transjordan), is the latest in the period, and is derived from the EB III–IV cultures of Transjordan. An alternate, but less likely view is that EB IVA–C are more geographical than they are cultural/chronological phases, and thus may all be partly contemporary.

The above hypothesis certainly needs further testing at stratified Early Bronze–Middle Bronze Age sites (although they are exceedingly rare). If confirmed, however, it would document the double-sided shift in settlement patterns and economic strategies that we posited above, to account for observable socioeconomic changes from late EB II through EB IV, especially the shift from sedentarism to pastoralism and back to sedentarism again, as well as the shift from Palestine to Transjordan and back. It would also close the long-assumed gap in EB III–early EB IV occupation in Palestine, since the "missing phases" are all present in Transjordan (as indeed EB III is now beginning to be in southern Palestine).

A new project of the University of Arizona at Tell el-Ḥayyāt,[16] in the Upper Jordan Valley near Pella, may help to resolve these issues, as the occupation at this site is largely confined to two periods, my EB IVA–B and Albright's MB IIA. Since the latter is by consensus the first phase of the true urban Middle Bronze Age, we may hope for a stratified sequence from the late Early Bronze Age into the early Middle

Fig. 12.
MB IIA levels at Tell el-Ḥayyāt

Bronze Age. The small (two and a half acre) low mound is located on the upper terrace of the east bank of the Jordan, below the perennial spring of Pella, adjacent to fertile alluvial lands. The 1982–1983 seasons uncovered near the surface a small, sedentary agricultural village with domestic architecture (see Fig. 12), a pottery kiln, classic MB IIA ceramic forms, and a good variety of domestic plant and animal remains. The lower levels, however, yielded quantities of combed, trickle-painted and other EB IV ceramic types of the "North Central" or Jezreel Valley family as expected, but absolutely no architectural remains. The "campsite" appearance may be purely fortuitous, for K. Prag has shown that many of the EB IVA–B villages in the Jordan Valley, although not located in areas of optimum rainfall, were nevertheless sedentary and agriculturally based.[17] In any case, future seasons of excavations at Tell el-Ḥayyāt may help to illuminate the question of continuity/discontinuity between the end of our Early Bronze Age and the true Middle Bronze Age.

Previously the above problem, by necessity, has been approached largely via comparative ceramic typology. Amiran, for instance, has argued for retaining the old "MB I" terminology on the basis of what she regards as direct links between several of my EB IV and Albright's MB IIA pottery forms.[18] Nevertheless, these are to my mind isolated and unconvincing comparisons. Suzanne Richard and I have both demonstrated that virtually all the links of the so-called MB I pottery are with the long EB I–III tradition, not with forms of the true Middle Bronze Age. Figures 13–14 present a number of comparisons showing a so-called MB I form, a typical EB II–III form, and an MB IIA form. Without going into discussion of details, I think it is nonetheless clear where the ceramic (and thus cultural) breaks lie. In every case, there is continuity between the general forms of EB II–III–IV, but none with the MB II forms following.[19]

A comparison of characteristic metallic types (see Fig. 15) illustrates very much the same sequence and relationships. Only the fenestrated crescentic axe exists through both late Early Bronze Age and early Middle Bronze Age phases, and even that changes rather sharply in both form and technology by MB IIA (now in true tin-bronze). Finally, we have already demonstrated that the EB I–III shaft tombs of Transjordan were in common use until EB IVC in Palestine (above), after which they disappeared completely. All these material culture comparisons, while limited in themselves, should be viewed within the larger setting of the distinctive EB II–EB IV urban-pastoral, dimorphic society already portrayed in the Negev-Sinai and in Transjordan, which also ends with our EB IVC, ca. 2000 B.C.E. None of these sites was occupied in MB II (or even later), which is perhaps the most dramatic confirmation of the discontinuity we have postulated at the end of the period in question.

Syria

Finally, we turn still farther north, to recent excavations in North Syria, in order to place Palestinian EB IV in a still larger historical and cultural setting, as well as to elucidate it partly by contrast.

The current Italian excavations at Tell Mardikh, ancient Ebla, have particularly shed light on the EB IV phase there. The terminology is borrowed from our designation for Palestine, but it is clear that the period in Syria is not marked by either urban collapse or discontinuity with the following MB II period.[20] On the contrary, Ebla reaches the zenith of its urban development in the third millennium B.C.E. precisely in this phase, the period of the well-known "Palace G" and its spectacular archive of cuneiform texts. The urban occupation continued, despite the destruction of the palace ca. 2250 B.C.E., right on into the second millennium, with strong architectural and ceramic continuity.[21]

The evidence of an urban phase in EB IV at Ebla is amplified by findings at a number of sites in northern Syria, particularly those excavated in the Tabqa Dam project on the Upper Euphrates. Tell Hadidi, excavated by R. Dornemann, may be taken as typical. Here again the third millennium B.C.E. occupation was at its peak in the EB IV period. Particularly significant are numerous chamber tombs recalling those of Palestine, with quantities of "Caliciform" (and more Mesopotamian style) pottery. Other sites on the Upper Euphrates duplicate the same picture.[22] It is thus clear that while the "Caliciform" pottery of central and northern Syria does indeed provide the distant prototypes for some of the Palestinian EB IV ceramic types (as the metallic types can also be paralleled), the overall contrast between the two cultural areas could hardly be more striking.[23]

Conclusion

In conclusion, what model can we propose that will accommodate the growing archaeological data for the transitional EB IV period, both in Palestine and in Syria? Elsewhere I have advocated the model of pastoral nomadism, rather than the old notion of "Amorite invasions," for explaining the socioeconomic changes in evidence.[24] This view is based on the accumulating archaeological data, renewed analysis of the Mesopotamian texts, and modern ethnographic studies of pastoral nomads. It argues that in Palestine we are dealing with a fairly large but nonnucleated population, much of which traversed considerable distances in their seasonal movements, and therefore came into contact with the urban centers of Syria. These peoples were not, however, raiders as earlier scholars thought, this view being based on a notion compounded of false analogy with modern camel nomads and nineteenth century romanticism. They were rather donkey nomads of the type portrayed in the Ur III and Mari texts dealing with the "Amorites."

As I have observed elsewhere:[25]

> ... the ascendancy of nomadic ways of life may be understood not as the *cause* but rather as the *effect* of the collapse of the urban centers. It has been observed that a shift from urbanism to pastoral nomadism in Western Asia has often been "triggered" by political misfortunes, economic reverses, a series of natural calamities such as drought or pestilence, by overpopulation of urban centers and exhaustion of natural resources, or

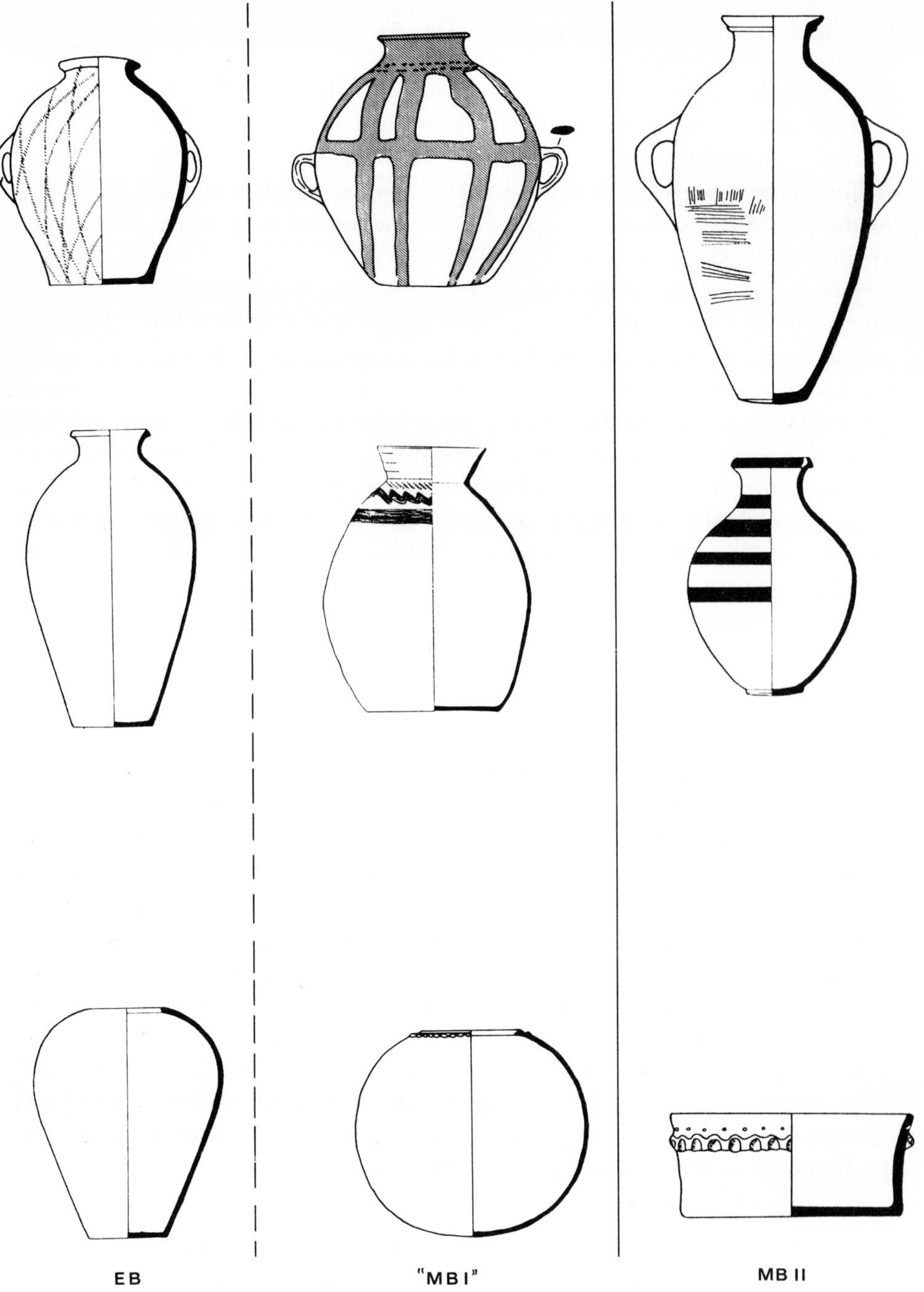

Fig. 13
Comparison between general ceramic forms of EB, "MB I" (= EB IV), and MB IIA. Scale = 1:5

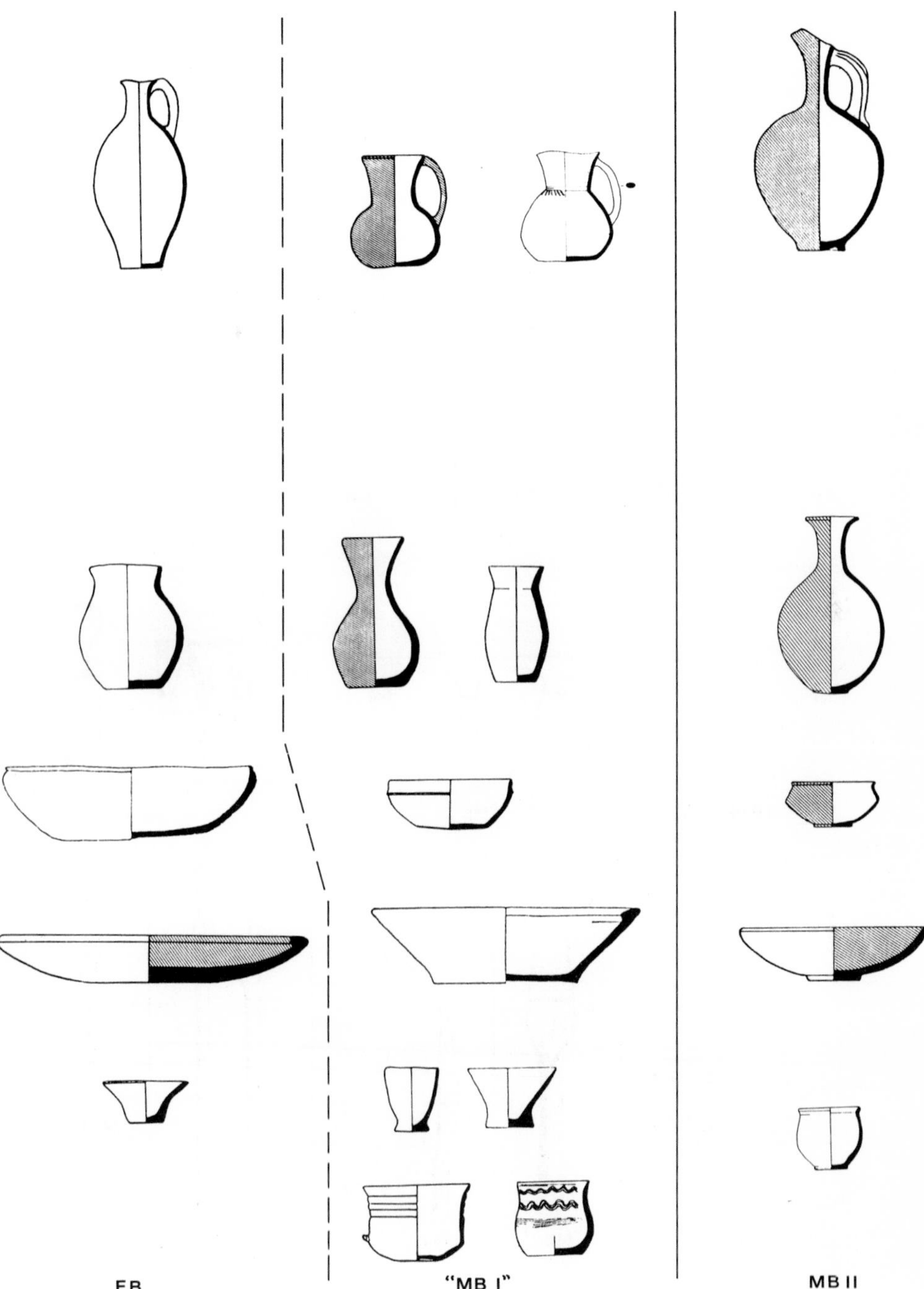

Fig. 14
Comparison between general ceramic forms of EB, "MB I" (=EB IV), and MB IIA. Scale = 1:5

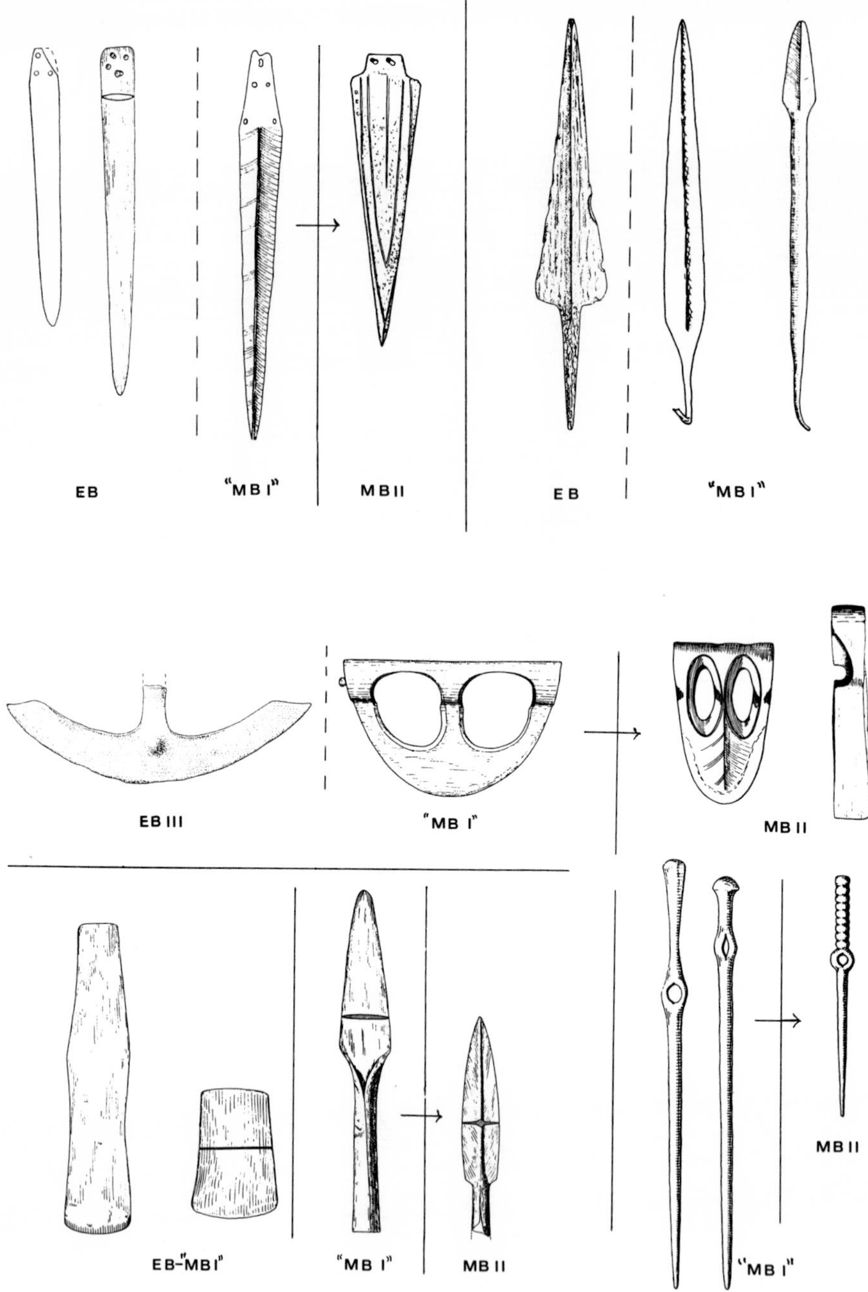

Fig. 15.
Comparison between general metallic forms of EB, "MB I" (= EB IV), and MB IIA. Scale = 1:2

some combination of these and other factors. The employment of the model of pastoral nomadism allows us to comprehend in EB IV what is really the last, post-urban phase of EB, rather than assuming as previous scholars did that Palestine was totally devastated and deserted for two or three centuries following the collapse of the urban centers.

The second question relates to the contrast we have observed between Palestine and Syria in EB IV. The basically pastoral economy of Palestine during the same period in which urban Syria sees the zenith of its prosperity (as evidenced at Ebla, for instance) is explicable if we posit that Palestine was a sort of "hinterland" in EB IV, dominated (perhaps having been reduced) by the powerful city-states to the north, and at the same time isolated from Egypt, which is now in its own "dark age" in the "First Intermediate" period. Palestine would then have been a relative backwater, populated largely by village peasants, herders, and itinerant traders.

Finally, the "Amorite" question may be resolved. The considerable linguistic evidence for an "Amorite" population in Syria-Palestine is now credible — not on the supposition that an "Amorite invasion" from Upper Syria and Mesopotamia had taken place, but by the recognition that the indigenous Bronze Age population had *always* been West Semitic or "Amorite." Movements of some population elements southward were not incursions of "foreigners," but part of the ebb and flow of peoples between the fertile zone and the steppe in Syria-Palestine from time immemorial. The EB IV period in Palestine simply witnesses the brief triumph of the "desert" over the "sown."

Notes

1. See further W.G. Dever, "The EB IV–MB I Horizon in Transjordan and Southern Palestine," *BASOR* 210 (1973): 37–63; S. Richard, "Toward a Consensus of Opinion on the End of the Early Bronze Age in Palestine-Transjordan," *BASOR* 237 (1980): 5–34.
2. For references, see Dever, "EB IV–MB I Horizon" (note 1), pp. 37–41.
3. See especially W.G. Dever, "The 'Middle Bronze Age I' Period in Syria-Palestine," in *Near Eastern Archaeology in the Twentieth Century: Essays in Honor of Nelson Glueck*, ed. J.A. Sanders (Garden City, NY: Doubleday, 1970), pp. 132–163; idem, "The Peoples of Palestine in the Middle Bronze I Period," *Harvard Theological Review* 64 (1971): 197–226; idem, "The Beginning of the Middle Bronze Age in Palestine," in *Magnalia Dei. The Mighty Acts of God: Essays on the Bible and Archaeology in Memory of G. Ernest Wright*, eds. F.M. Cross, W.E. Lemke and P.D. Miller (Garden City, NY: Doubleday, 1976), pp. 3–38; idem, "EB IV–MB I Horizon" (see note 1); idem, "New Vistas on the EB IV (MB I) Horizon in Syria-Palestine," *BASOR* 237 (1980): 35–64.
4. Especially Ruth Amiran, "The Pottery of the Middle Bronze Age I in Palestine," *IEJ* 10 (1960): 204–225; Dever, "EB IV–MB I Horizon" (see note 1).
5. For further details on the following, see R. Cohen and W.G. Dever, "Preliminary Report of the Pilot Season of the 'Central Negev Highlands Project,'" *BASOR* 232 (1978): 29–45; idem, "Preliminary Report of the Second Season of the 'Central Negev Highlands Project,'" *BASOR* 236 (1979): 41–60; idem, "Preliminary Report of the Third and Final Season of the 'Central Negev Highlands Project,'" *BASOR* 243 (1981): 57–77.
6. On the model of pastoral nomadism, see Dever, "New Vistas" (see note 3), pp. 56–58, and references there. See also the extensive bibliography in W.G. Dever, "Palestine in the Second Millennium B.C.E.: the Archaeological Picture," in *Israelite and Judean History*, eds. J.H. Hayes and

J.M. Miller (Philadelphia: Westminster, 1977), pp. 70–120.

7. See Cohen and Dever, "Second Season of 'Central Negev Highlands Project'" (see note 5), p. 54, Fig. 18:15, 17.
8. Further on the plan of Be'er Resisim, see Cohen and Dever, "Third and Final Season" (see note 5), pp. 60–62, 74; and especially, W.G. Dever, "Village Planning at Be'er Resisim and Socio-Economic Structure in EB IV Palestine," *EI* 18 (in press). On the model of pastoral nomadism and seasonal movements, see note 6 above.
9. See I. Beit-Arieh, "A Pattern of Settlement in Southern Sinai and Southern Canaan in the Third Millennium B.C.," *BASOR* 243 (1981): 31–55, and references there. Add now I. Beit-Arieh, "An Early Bronze II Site near Sheikh ʿAwad in Southern Sinai," *Tel Aviv* 8 (1981): 95–127; I. Beit-Arieh and R. Gophna, "The Early Bronze Age II Settlement at ʿAin el-Qudeirat (1980–1981)," *Tel Aviv* 8 (1981): 128–135; I. Beit Arieh, "An Early Bronze Age II Site near the Feiran Oasis in Southern Sinai," *Tel Aviv* 9 (1982): 146–156. For contrast of the Sinai EB II and Negev EB IV settlements, see Dever, "Socio-Economic Structure in EB IV Palestine" (note 8).
10. For further details on the following, see Dever, "'Middle Bronze I' Period" (see note 3), pp. 144–147; idem, "A Middle Bronze I Site on the West Bank of the Jordan," *Archaeology* 25 (1977): 231–233; idem, "Cave G26 at Jebel Qaʿaqīr: A Domestic Assemblage of Middle Bronze I," *EI* 15 (1981): 22–32; S. Gitin, "Middle Bronze I 'Domestic' Pottery at Jebel Qaʿaqīr — A Ceramic Inventory of Cave G23," *EI* 12 (1975): 46–62; Dever, "New Vistas" (see note 3), pp. 39–45, 48, 49, 56–58.
11. See Amiran, "Pottery of the Middle Bronze Age I" (note 4). On my EB IV "families," see note 3 — "Peoples of Palestine" and "New Vistas," pp. 35–49.
12. See further S. Richard and R. Boraas, "Preliminary Report of the 1981–82 Seasons of the Expedition to Khirbet Iskander and Its Vicinity," *BASOR* 254 (1984): 63–87. I am indebted to Dr. Richard for showing me the site and the materials on several occasions.
13. See now R.T. Schaub and W.E. Rast, "Preliminary Report of the 1981 Expedition to the Dead Sea Plain, Jordan," *BASOR* 254 (1984): 35–60, and full references there; also idem, *The Southeastern Dead Sea Plain Expedition: An Interim Report of the 1977 Season, AASOR* 46 (1981): 31–34.
14. See further R.T. Schaub, "An Early Bronze IV Tomb from Bâb edh-Dhrâʿ," *BASOR* 210 (1973): 2–19; Dever: "EB IV–MB I Horizon" (see note 1).
15. The latest synthesis, with full references, can be found in Dever, "New Vistas" (see note 3).
16. The project was cosponsored by the University of Arizona and the American Schools of Oriental Research, with additional financial support from the National Geographic Society and the Wenner-Gren Foundation. It was directed in the field by my students Bonnie Magness-Gardiner and Steven Falconer; see their "Preliminary Report of the First Season of the Tell el-Ḥayyāt Project," *BASOR* 254 (1984): 49–74.
17. K. Prag, "The Intermediate Early Bronze–Middle Bronze Age: An Interpretation of the Evidence from Transjordan, Syria and Lebanon," *Levant* 6 (1974).
18. Amiran, "Pottery of the Middle Bronze Age I" (see note 4), pp. 205–207, Fig. 1.
19. See further on this and the following, Dever, "EB IV–MB I Horizon" (see note 1), pp. 53–62; idem, "The Beginning of the Middle Bronze Age" (see note 3), pp. 4–8; S. Richard, "End of the Early Bronze Age" (see note 1); P. Gerstenblith, "A Reassessment of the Beginning of the Middle Bronze Age in Syria-Palestine," *BASOR* 237 (1980): 65–84.
20. For Ebla in EB IV, see provisionally P. Matthiae, *Ebla, An Empire Rediscovered* (Garden City, NY: Doubleday, 1981), pp. 65–111; see also idem, *Ebla in the Period of the Amorite Dynasties and the Dynasty of Akkad: Recent Archaeological Discoveries at Tell Mardikh (1975)* (Malibu, CA: Undena, 1979). For the use of the EB IV terminology in Syria and comparisons with Palestine, see references in Dever, "New Vistas" (note 1), pp. 49–52, and especially S. Mazzoni, "Elements of the Ceramic Culture of Early Syrian Ebla in Comparison with Palestinian EB IV," *BASOR* 256 (1984) (in press). I am indebted to Dr. Mazzoni for showing me the Ebla pottery in the spring of 1984.

21. See references in note 20 above.
22. See the discussion, with references to Hadidi and other sites, in Dever, "New Vistas" (see note 1), pp. 49–50. Useful preliminary reports will be found in D.N. Freedman and J.M. Lundquist, eds., *Excavation Reports from the Tabqa Dam Project-Euphrates Valley, Syria. AASOR* 442 (1979).
23. See Dever, "New Vistas" (see note 1), p. 52, with references; S. Mazonni, "Early Syrian Ebla" (note 20).
24. See above, note 6.
25. Dever, "New Vistas" (see note 1), p. 58.

Terminology for the Archaeology of the Biblical Periods

Moshe Dothan

TWO QUESTIONS WILL BE discussed in this paper: (1) What term should be used to describe archaeology in this country apart from the term "biblical archaeology," and (2) what terms should be employed for the basic divisions of the archaeology of the biblical periods?

Terminology is the scientific use of terms or a system of terms. Here the application of such a system involves the use of appropriate archaeological designations for a span of time from the end of the fourth millennium B.C.E. up to the Babylonian exile. During this time societies developed, great historical events took place and cultures in the ancient Near East, including the Lands of the Bible, replaced others. The term "biblical archaeology" is well suited to the *Land* of the Bible, but its definition should be broad enough to encompass the *Lands* of the Bible in general, as it may incorporate problems in areas as diverse as the Nile Delta and Ur of the Chaldeans, on the one hand, and Tarsus in the days of Paul, on the other. In many ways the scope and essence of biblical archaeology are parallel to those of "Homeric" and "classical" archaeology. These two terms, based largely on literary and historical documents, flourish side by side with the terms "Greek" and "Roman" archaeology, the latter essentially dealing with locally orientated material.

It seems that we need one specific term to describe this country in reference to its archaeology, instead of the various terms in use today, such as "Holy Land," "Near Eastern," "South Levantine," "Palestinian," "Syro-Palestinian," as well as "Israel" and "Land of Israel." The terms "Levantine" or "Near Eastern" are obviously too general. The connotations of the term "Holy Land" *a priori* narrow the scope of research mainly (though not entirely) to the biblical aspects of the past and to the holy places. We are left with only a few terms which can be divided into two groups on the basis of their geographical and ethno-historical (that is, archaeological) character. The first group consists of the terms "Palestinian" or "Syro-Palestinian"; the second includes "Israel" or "Eretz-Israel." Let us briefly analyze these alternatives in order to clarify which one is the most appropriate to describe the archaeology of this country.

Palestine was the official name of this country for only a mere thirty years under the British Mandate. Historically, this name – most probably based on the Hebrew *Pleshet* or on the Assyrian *Palashtu* which applied only to the southern coast – had its roots in the fifth century B.C.E. *Palaestine* is the Greek simplification and generalization known to us from Herodotus: Greek sailors and traders were certainly better acquainted with the Philistine coast than with any other part of the country. The Greeks used the term in reference to the southern coast, parallel to the use of *Phoinike* for its northern part. The use of *Palaestine* was discontinued for a long period which included that of the Second Temple when the name *Yehud* was first used, and the Hasmonean and Herodian periods when the country was called "Yehudah" (*Iudaea*). Hadrian reintroduced the name *Syria-Palaestina* or *Palaestina*, seeking to obliterate the name Judea, even as *Iudaea Capta*. Later, the epithet *Palaestina* covered various territories under the *Dux Palaestina*: *Palaestina Prima*, *Secunda* and *Tertia*.

With the Arab conquest, the country was divided into two parts, but only one was called *Jund Filastin*; the other was *Jund Urdun*. From the eleventh century C.E., the name *Palaestina* was almost forgotten. During the Crusader period the Kingdom of Jerusalem was also called the Kingdom of David, and once even Israel. Under Mamluk and Turkish rule the country was never a political unit; in the Mamluk period it was part of Syria, divided into districts named after the towns Damascus, Safed and Gaza. During most of the Ottoman period the country was part of the sanjaks of Damascus and Sidon, ruled by the Pasha of Damascus. Thus for nearly 700 years, the name *Palaestina* was hardly used. Only in the nineteenth century, with the awakening of European religious, historical and political interests, did the Latin name *Palaestina* reappear. We may conclude that the chronologically late and inconsistently used term "Palestine" was apparently never accepted by any local national entity. It therefore can hardly serve as a meaningful term for the archaeology of this country.

Let us now briefly examine the compound term "Syro-Palestinian." Lately it has become quite popular among some Near Eastern archaeologists. In antiquity, present-day Syria covered parts of Mesopotamia, Anatolia and Phoenicia, as well as other political and ethnic entities. Syria was first identified as such mainly in connection with Aram and the Arameans. Its name appears as "Syria" in Greek and Hellenistic sources (such as Herodotus), and was probably first used by the Persians in referring to "Athura" (Assyria), signifying "Eber Nahara," a general term for all the lands beyond the Euphrates. The archaeology of the political entity now called Syria comprises that of Assyrian, Dynastic Mesopotamian, Old Hurrian, Hittite, northwestern Canaanite and many other elements. Can such different, pluralistic cultures spread over such a large tract serve as partners to the archaeology of this country in the Canaanite and Israelite periods? Let us briefly examine whether evidence exists for such a partnership from the fourth until the middle of the first millennia B.C.E.

The only well-documented culture from the Chalcolithic period in this land, the Ghassulian-northern Negev culture and its branches, seems basically to be indigenous (though some scholars seek an origin in Ararat or the Caucasus for the inhabitants of the underground dwellings of the northern Negev). Some traces of influence and interrelations can be found in the contemporary Amratian and Gerzean cultures of Predynastic Egypt, and to some extent in the Ubaid and Uruk cultures of Mesopotamia.

For more than a thousand years, beginning in the last quarter of the fourth millennium B.C.E., the Early Canaanite (Bronze) Age is one of well-established agriculture and urbanization. There were direct relations with Early Dynastic Egypt, and influence of both southern and northern Mesopotamian city-states. If there was a relationship with Syria it was mostly with what may be called southern Syria, which actually comprised the coastal cities of northwestern Canaan (later Phoenicia), such as Byblos and Ugarit. Toward the middle of the third millennium B.C.E., new elements arrived in Canaan and traveled down this coast; they most probably originated in northeastern Anatolia or perhaps in Transcaucasia (cf. the Beth Yeraḥ culture).

Summing up this period, we can state that the archaeological remains in Canaan have little in common with those of "Syrian" archaeology. Much of the material culture, especially from the south of the country and along the coast, points to Egypt as the ultimate source.

At the end of the third millennium and in the first half of the second millennium B.C.E. – the Middle Canaanite (Bronze) Age in the archaeology of this country – there were certainly more northern and northeastern influences and connections than before. The last quarter of the third millennium B.C.E. (referred to as either EB IV, MB I, or "transitional") was a period of decline about which comparatively little is yet known, and whose population left relatively few permanent traces in Canaan. Here we may quote briefly one of the most prominent protagonists of the term "Syro-Palestinian archaeology," W.G. Dever, who in his article, "New Vistas on the EB IV–MB I Horizon in Syria-Palestine" [*BASOR* 237 (1981)], wrote:

> Syria is a highly urbanized culture while Palestine is completely non-urban (in the EB IV–MB I period, ca. 2300–2000 B.C.E.).... The material culture of the two areas is strikingly different.... On the basis of our analysis there can be no possibility of a direct or dominating cultural influence from Syria in the EB IV–MB I period.... The population [in Palestine] was largely indigenous and the material culture remained in the Palestinian Early Bronze tradition.

Later, in MB IIB, the "Syrian" elements are a mere part of the assemblage, which includes Mesopotamian, Hurrian, Hyksos and Egyptian elements merging with the local Canaanite. We possess only scanty "Syrian" archaeological evidence, which certainly cannot justify the term "Syro-Palestinian." In contrast to this lack of evidence, a little later Egyptian sources mention cities in Canaan by the hundreds, and this is reflected by the archaeological remains. For instance, at Lachish, the archaeology of the mid-second millennium B.C.E., could be called "Canaano-Egyptian." And in the fourteenth to thirteenth centuries B.C.E., with the growth of maritime trade with the Aegean and Cyprus, and with the increase of Hittite influence, even such a term as "Eastern Mediterranean" archaeology would be more suitable for this country than "Syro-Palestinian." We should recall that the archaeology of the vast area of present-day Syria during the third to second millennia B.C.E. is extremely rich and encompasses several different (and sometimes even incompatible) cultures. It would be arbitrary to tie Syria (even by hyphenation) to a comparatively small and poor country and its cultures, with which there were few relations during this period. Even these connections diminish sharply toward the end of the Late Bronze Age, and they are limited mostly to the northern coast of Canaan and the very southern part of Syria.

With the political and ethnic upheavals in the Eastern Mediterranean at the end of the thirteenth and beginning of the twelfth century B.C.E., we are confronted with a new situation in Canaan. The Israelite ethnic element slowly became dominant and finally absorbed the bulk of the diverse Canaanite population. The Israelites were the only ethnic group which, as a nation, succeeded in creating a state in this land, one that was neither dependent on some great empire nor belonged to a loose conglomerate of city-states like those of the Canaanite period. The Land of Canaan, according to the Bible, became Eretz-Israel – "the Land of Israel" (for example, Numbers 34; Ezekiel 47–48), though in reality its territory was much smaller than that implied in these sources (cf. for example, the phrase "from Dan to Beer-Sheba"). The archaeology of Eretz-Israel, from this period on, reflects a basically indigenous, originally Israelite material culture with Canaanite (Phoenician), Egyptian and Philistine (and other Sea Peoples') additions and, in a later phase, Aramean and Assyrian influences.

The weight of the evidence (including the period of the Second Temple, which does not fall within the present scope) clearly demonstrates that the only terms which can correctly be applied are "the archaeology of Israel" or "the archaeology of the Land of Israel." The term "archaeology of Israel," however, excludes regions outside the borders of the modern state. Therefore, "the archaeology of the Land of Israel" is preferable.

Turning now to the second question: what terms should we use for the basic divisions in the archaeology of the Land of Israel in the third and second millennia B.C.E. and the first half of the first millennium B.C.E.? The two most significant periods are now generally called the "Bronze" and "Iron" Ages.

These terms were adopted from the old European division and have become deeply entrenched in the archaeological research of Eretz-Israel. Sporadic attempts have been made to attach different names to parts of these periods, echoing the need for clarification with more meaningful, often ethnic or historical terms like "Semitic" or "Jewish." The terms "Bronze Age" and "Iron Age" became almost "official" during the British Mandate, when a prestigious committee suggested their combination with the parallel terms of Canaanite and Palestinian Ages. The Canaanite Age was divided into three phases; the Palestinian Age was subdivided into Philistine, Early, Middle, and Late Jewish, and Hellenistic. This terminology, though rarely used, shows that even sixty years ago some scholars were not content with "Bronze" and "Iron." Similar objections were again raised from the sixties on, mostly by such Israeli scholars as S. Yeivin, M. Avi-Yonah and Y. Aharoni. An extreme example of the prevailing inconsistency can be seen in *The Encyclopedia of Archaeological Excavations in the Holy Land,* which uses the terms "Canaanite" and "Israelite" periods in its Hebrew edition and retains the terms "Bronze Age" and "Iron Age" in the English version.

The terms "Bronze Age" and "Iron Age" are, in the author's opinion, no longer suitable, and at best may serve as general chronological labels. In many other countries, including some in Europe, they have been replaced, mainly by names of cultures deriving from archaeological and ethno-archaeological evidence. Most fields of Near Eastern archaeology, such as Mesopotamian and Egyptian archaeology, have never used these terms, their terminology being based on stages of civilization such as dynasties and intermediate (*Zwischenzeit*) periods.

Archaeological research of the cultures of the Mediterranean and Aegean has adopted ethnic, geographic or political terminology, for example, Helladic, Minoan, Mycenaean, Cypriote. There are still a few countries in the Near East which use the old "Bronze," "Iron" terminology, mainly Syria and Turkey, though changes are in evidence there too.

The long process of introducing bronze to the economy of the Near East was certainly not of such importance that it should still be used at this stage of our archaeological and historical knowledge in defining a mature and comparatively well-documented society. And this is in addition to the simple fact that bronze was not used, at any rate not in significant quantities, before the end of the third millennium B.C.E. Thus, we constantly use a misleading term, off by about a thousand years and nearly half of the duration of the period it denotes. The time is ripe for the final affirmation of the term "Canaanite" instead of the "Bronze" Age. The Canaanites were the only entity of the pre-Israelite period in this country well known to us at least from the beginning of the second millenium B.C.E. from Egyptian, cuneiform, and biblical sources and from excavations. Although the borders of Canaan changed, and although it included many ethnic groups (among these probably also the Amorites), these groups became part of Canaanite society. From the early period of its urbanization, this society possessed a shared material culture and cult. No other term can serve in this period as a common denominator for the country and its cultures.

With the gradual downfall of the Canaanite city-states and the Canaanite society, and the decline of the Egyptian hegemony, a new period began with settlement of the Israelite tribes and the final Israelite conquest. As stressed above, the Israelite culture (material and religious) became dominant a little later, and for the first time most of the country was united and independent. Iron was only one (albeit a significant) component of the material culture. Archaeologically (including the biblical aspects), the impact of Israel on the country was such that the period from around 1200 B.C.E. at least up to the Babylonian conquest and exile should be called "Israelite." This was illustrated vividly in the lectures of this session and in the results of the surveys and excavations carried out in recent years by the younger generation of archaeologists.

In conclusion, the author proposes the following terminology: the first term referring to the archaeology of this country, "Archaeology of the Land of Israel"; and the other two terms, "Canaanite Age" and "Israelite Age" to replace "Bronze Age" and "Iron Age," to faithfully reflect the two most significant periods in the history of this country and within the Near Eastern and biblical milieu.

Reassessment of the Stratigraphy and Chronology of Archaeological Sites in Judah in the Light of Lachish III

David Ussishkin

I BELIEVE THAT LACHISH, more than any other site, symbolizes the meaning and essence of biblical archaeology today, the cardinal topic of this Conference. Biblical archaeology, to my mind, is a combination of the archaeology of Syria and Palestine as conceived by W.G. Dever and his colleagues, and the archaeology directly associated with the biblical world and the Bible in the spirit and tradition of W.F. Albright and his school, with some variations. Archaeology is a technical independent discipline which should be practiced as such. It comprises the experience gained from excavations carried out in Israel according to the architectural method of excavation, and the experience gained from excavations employing the Wheeler–Kenyon method. Naturally, biblical archaeology is also influenced by the impact of the all-important developments in the fields of new archaeology. Lastly, I believe that biblical archaeology today must aim at achieving qualitative rather than quantitative results.

Archaeology of today, however, does not exist for itself. It is essentially an auxiliary tool to facilitate something more important: the study of history, and the study of human culture in the wider sense. When we deal with the Land of Israel, our main interest is, of course, to understand the history of the country, the Bible and the world of the Bible.

This concept of biblical archaeology as an independent discipline not based on but only connected with the study of the Bible, often contradicts old conceptions. I will present just two examples. The first relates to the famous biblical attribution to King Solomon of the gate at Megiddo. When we check the date and stratigraphy of the gate by archaeological means, we reach the conclusion that it was built after King Solomon's time. In other words, poor King Solomon never dreamt of erecting such a beautiful gate at Megiddo. The second example concerns the Siloam Tunnel in Jerusalem. Here again the biblical interpretation does not correspond to the independent archaeological study of the tunnel and its function. The same applies to Lachish and its Level III. Lachish is certainly a key site from the archaeological point of view, and it is now being studied again in the light of all the modern concepts of Syro-Palestinian archaeology. Our special interest, however, is directly related to the history of the biblical world and the biblical events with which Lachish is associated.

Excavations have been carried out at Lachish for the last ten years by the Institute of Archaeology of Tel Aviv University and the Israel Exploration Society. The physical effort made during this time is much less than that of Starkey's expedition in the 1930s. By a rough estimate, Starkey invested about 250,000 workdays in six years, as compared to our 25,000 workdays in nine years, and the amount of debris we have removed equals only about 5% of that which was removed in the 1930s. Recently, we have established the stratigraphy of the city in the first millennium B.C.E., and that of the Assyrian conquest by Sennacherib. This stratigraphy now provides us with a very good reference for studying many other sites in Judah. However, if we use the finds and pottery of Lachish III as a tool for dating and studying other sites, we have first to understand its limitations as such.

Lachish III was a very large city which was destroyed by a terrible fire. It seems that when the Assyrian army forced its way into the city, the soldiers went from one house to another and burned them down, evicting the inhabitants without giving them the opportunity to remove their pottery and other belongings. These objects were sealed and covered by the destruction debris, which in some cases reached a height of more than two meters. We now possess a large and versatile assemblage of pottery and other finds from Lachish III. Specifically, we should mention the *lamelekh* jars of all types, large storage jars stamped with a royal emblem and the letters למלך, "belonging to the king." Following the destruction of Lachish and the deportation of its inhabitants, the city was apparently abandoned and left in ruins until it was rebuilt, probably in the later part of the seventh century B.C.E., possibly during the reign of Josiah. This new fortified Judean city was in turn destroyed in 588–586 B.C.E. by the army of Nebuchadnezzar. Again a large assemblage of pottery vessels was found beneath the destruction debris. Therefore we have two large pottery assemblages consisting in the main of restored, complete vessels. They date to the last days of Lachish III, roughly the last decade of the eighth century B.C.E., and to the last days of Level II, namely the beginning of the sixth century B.C.E. Whatever happened in between is a good question, but Lachish does not provide the answer.

The limitations applying to the use of these finds are best illustrated by the case of the *lamelekh* jars. We know that there were many *lamelekh* jars in use at Lachish III at the end of the eighth century B.C.E., during the reign of King Hezekiah. We do not know, however, whether or not they were introduced beforehand as the city was destroyed in 701 B.C.E. Of course we do not know whether or not these jars continued in use in other parts of Judah. By 588–586 B.C.E., when the city was conquered by the

Babylonians, there were no *lamelekh* jars in Lachish II, thus leading to the conclusion that these jars were no longer in use at the beginning of the sixth century B.C.E.

Notwithstanding its limitations, Lachish can serve as a very good tool for determining chronology and reassessing many archaeological problems of other Judean sites. I will just mention two cases: Jerusalem's expansion and Tel Beer-Sheba. We know that Jerusalem expanded westward; the question is when did the process of spread begin, and when was the western side of the city fortified? Here, of course, the identification of the pottery types of Lachish III is significant for determining the date of construction of the western quarters of Jerusalem. This expansion was recently studied by Prof. N. Avigad in his excavations in the Upper City, and in other works, notably the doctoral thesis of G. Barkay.

The case of Tel Beer-Sheba, specifically its Level II, is more complicated. Level II was a Judean city destroyed by fire. Here also, the excavations, directed by Y. Aharoni, produced a large assemblage of pottery sealed by the destruction. There are similarities between the pottery assemblages of Beer-Sheba II and Lachish III, but they are definitely not identical. The various types of vessels are represented in different proportions, and there are even different types. Very notably, at Tel Beer-Sheba there are no *lamelekh* jars. The various explanations of this disparity demonstrate the difficulties in applying the evidence of Lachish III. We have the opinion of Tel Beer-Sheba's excavators, Y. Aharoni, A.F. Rainey and Z. Herzog, who claim that Beer-Sheba II was destroyed in 701 B.C.E. and corresponds to Lachish III. They attribute the differences in pottery at the two sites to the fact that *lamelekh* jars were not in use at that time in the south. Another opinion, expressed by N. Na'aman, holds that Beer-Sheba II was destroyed earlier than Lachish III, during the campaigns of Sargon, and this explains the absence of the *lamelekh* jars; their production began later, around the time of the siege and campaign of 701 B.C.E. A third explanation for the absence of *lamelekh* jars at Beer-Sheba II and the differences in the pottery between the two sites, was offered by Y. Yadin. He suggested that Beer-Sheba II was destroyed much later than 701 B.C.E.

Therefore, there are difficulties in reassessing the stratigraphy and chronology of archaeological sites in Judah in the light of Lachish III.

Respondents

Amnon Ben-Tor

The sequence of cultures in Palestine is a continuous chain of development, one period leading into the other. It is, therefore, not surprising that the most difficult problems of the research relating to this sequence are those connected with the three periods of transition: from the Chalcolithic to the Early Bronze Age, from the Early to the Middle Bronze Age, and from the Late Bronze to the Iron Age (the transition from the Middle to the Late Bronze Age is of a rather different nature).

In all periods of transition we face the difficulty of understanding the process of change, a difficulty reflected in the different terminologies used by various scholars to designate the same periods. Here we essentially deal with the personal preferences of the scholars in evaluating the data; the kind of judgments that have to be made are like debating: at dawn — is it still night, or is it already morning? The glass — is it half full or is it half empty?

It is not surprising that in regard to all periods of transition, the immigration into Palestine of people from outside was taken as an important factor: it is a most convenient way to explain a rather impressive number of changes occurring in a comparatively short period. It seems, indeed, that we should take into account ethnic movements during these periods of transition, even though their scope as well as importance occasionally may have been slightly exaggerated. It should also be remembered that there is a price which we have to pay for the convenience of being able to put the "blame" for changes on those newcomers, the price being the need to face problems such as: "Where did they come from?" "Did they enter the country peacefully or violently?" "What happened to the local population: — annihilation? assimilation?" etc. These are rather difficult problems for which, in most cases, so it seems, we still lack comprehensive answers.

Ruth Amiran has tried — rather successfully I must admit — to show that the glass is *half full*. I am going to try and suggest that the same glass is *half empty*. Indeed, I believe Amiran herself has given some weight to the half empty interpretation of the data, such as the introduction of the animal-drawn plough, extended trade, etc. — all appearing not before the Early Bronze Age. Taking into consideration the basic continuity in the sequence of cultures in Palestine, it seems to me that this particular transition represents one of the most clear-cut and fundamental changes in the entire history of this country. Even with all the elements of continuity and cultural resemblance between the Chalcolithic and Early Bronze Age which have been presented and stressed by Amiran, Palestine of the third millennium B.C.E. is substantially different from that of the fourth millennium. The two most significant aspects of change are the following:

The map of settlement: The story of EB I, and indeed of the subsequent history of the country for the millennia to come, takes place in sites like Jericho, ʿAi, Megiddo, Beth-Shean, Tell el-Farʿah and others. The story of Ghassul, Wadi Beer-Sheba, the Golan Heights' sites, and many other famous Chalcolithic settlements has forever come to an end. Never before, nor subsequently, has there been a change of such magnitude in the distribution of sites in this country.

The economy: With the movement of people to the mountains, to the Shephelah and the valleys — to regions in which the annual average rainfall is 350 mm and more — a substantial and far-reaching change in the economy of the country took place. In addition to modest agriculture and cattle, sheep and goat husbandry, we witness a sharp increase in the importance of various agricultural crops. Of particular importance is the domestication of the vine, the olive and several fruit-bearing trees — the so-called Mediterranean economy was born. This continued to be the economy of the country until modern times.

There are many other changes resulting from the above which then occurred. To name just a few: the rise in the standard of living, the increase of the carrying capacity of the land, and the increase in population and production of surplus resulting in the first real opportunities for long-range trade.

What we are dealing with is therefore clearly the first page of a new chapter and not the last page of an old one. Continuity — yes by all means, but clearly outweighed by novelty! Hence I find the term "EB I" most appropriate.

There are many important questions: What was the cause for all those changes? What was the role played by newcomers and/or cultural influences from the north, and perhaps also from the south? These and other questions are the problems that the present generation of scholars studying the Early Bronze Age must confront.

Ram Gophna

To R. Amiran: Ruth Amiran's efforts to convince us that the Early Bronze Age culture evolved and developed out of the Chalcolithic culture without any sharp break seem to me to be an overreaction to the first instinctive and unbiased impressions of those pioneer archaeologists who first encountered the phenomenon during the 1930s. Amiran's approach and presentation are an attempt to keep pace with the current anti-diffusionist school of thought prevailing in archaeological circles, which places greater emphasis on inner socioeconomic factors and processes than on ethnic movements, and considers these inner factors the main cause for cultural change in prehistoric times. But even today in the early 1980s, the conviction that a certain cultural gap exists between the Ghassulian-Chalcolithic and EB I continues to persist among some who work in the field. During various regional surveys carried out with young archaeologists of the "new generation," I frequently come across evidence that confirms the sharp distinctions between the Chalcolithic and EB I periods, which were observed so many years ago by experienced field archaeologists.

The most satisfactory explanation for the transition between the two cultures still seems to be that it resulted from a demographic disaster — prolonged drought, plague or whatever — that befell the Ghassulians, and ended with the large-scale penetration of a new population. These newcomers must have had certain affinities with the previous group — which should account for any similarities in the "moveables" (as Amiran calls them) of the two peoples. But the new population already had a different and more advanced agrotechnology, namely the plough, the evidence for which my colleague has recently pointed out. This new culture can be distinguished not only by its material aspects but by a settlement pattern entirely different from that of the previous Chalcolithic population. The settlement pattern of each period is a crucial indicator for determining the character of the transition between the two cultures existing in the second half of the fourth millennium B.C.E., and undoubtedly reflects certain important aspects of the social and economic structures and the way of life of each of these cultures.

A schematic depiction of the stratigraphical relationships common at many sites throughout the country shows the position of the EB I settlement in relation to the Ghassulian settlement. In some cases, the Ghassulian settlement is completely or partially covered by the remains of the EB I settlement, such as at Arad and Megiddo. In other cases, the Early Bronze Age settlement was established on a previously unoccupied site, for example, Beth Yeraḥ, or on the remains of a pre-Ghassulian site, such as Munḥata. A study of 185 sites located between the Upper Galilee and the Beer-Sheba Valley established that only 30% of the new EB I settlements were founded on a previous Ghassulian site, while 70% were erected on new or pre-Ghassulian sites. These figures are very strong evidence of an occupational gap between the two periods, from which we may infer that there was also a cultural gap between them.

The regional distribution of EB I sites as compared to those of the Ghassulians also illustrates the sharp shift in settlement pattern that occurred following the disappearance of the Ghassulian culture. Changes took place along the middle Jordan Valley, south of the Sea of Galilee, where the EB I settlements outnumbered by far the previous Chalcolithic sites. However, in the northwestern Negev and the Beer-Sheba Valley — the region that may be considered the "Ghassulian Paradise" — there were only three small, isolated EB I settlements, all established on previously unoccupied sites, as compared with scores of flourishing Ghassulian sites of various types and sizes.

It seems to me that Ruth Amiran has not taken into consideration the unique nature of our country due to its location at the extreme southern end of the Fertile Crescent on the fringe of the desert, and its vulnerability to the slightest environmental or social crisis. The geographical position of Eretz-Israel in the area supports my conviction that the demographic crisis that occurred here during the second half of the fourth millennium B.C.E. was so severe that most of the Ghassulian settlements were completely deserted when the first Early Bronze Age settlers arrived on the scene. Consequently, in spite of the continuity of a few minor elements of the material culture, I cannot accept the thesis that the Early Bronze Age culture evolved from the previous Ghassulian culture of the Chalcolithic period.

Aharon Kempinski

To R. Amiran: I would like to comment on Ruth Amiran's concept of "transition." To my mind all the examples she presented could also easily be explained by the contemporaneity of both cultures: the latest phase of the southern Chalcolithic (the Beer-Sheba Culture) and the northern EB IA (Gray Burnish–Red Burnish). This idea is an old cultural concept in Palestinian archaeology which was rejected by the Albrightians during the forties and the fifties, but upheld anew in the sixties by J. Perrot, K. Kenyon, R. de Vaux and M. Dothan.

Instead of showing that each of Amiran's examples could also prove the contemporaneity of both cultures,[1] I would like to emphasize an interesting methodical point in order to illuminate the concept of contemporaneity. It seems that in all three cultural breaks which occurred in the ancient cultural history of Palestine, the old culture coexisted for a time with the new. The best example is the "transition" of the Late Bronze Age to Iron Age I, or that between the Canaanite and the "Israelite" or "Philistine" cultures. Here it is easy to show, for example, that Megiddo VIIA (destroyed ca. 1140 B.C.E.) with its Late Bronze Canaanite culture must be contemporaneous with the Israelite small villages in the hill country to the south. We can clearly define two different pottery groups and building traditions, although there is already a kind of "osmotic" flow between both cultures. The same relations could also be shown between the later phase of MB I (the Intermediate EB–MB period) in the hill country and the Negev, and the MB IIA of the coastal region and the valleys — again as in the Late Bronze Age–Iron I relations a seminomadic culture vis-à-vis an urban one.

The southern Chalcolithic and the northern EB IA are just another example of the same pattern; the almost total lack of EB IA groups in the south and formation of the Arad IV settlement [EB IB!] directly after the late Beer-Sheba Chalcolithic Arad V is the best evidence proving such an argument.[2] There is no real gap between Strata V and IV; Stratum V at Arad fills the gap of the EB IA which is "missing" at this site.

To W.G. Dever: My response to W.G. Dever has been published in my article, "Early Bronze Age Urbanization of Palestine: Some Topics in a Debate."[3] I do agree with him that there is now some convincing evidence for the Transjordanian elements in the MB I culture of Palestine west of the Jordan. But there are other elements too, such as the central Syrian cultural influence (and see now the Qedesh cult cave published by M. Tadmor[4]), especially in the north of the country. Therefore, I cannot agree with Dever that all the developments were only internal and local; too many outer-Palestinian influences can be seen in the seminomadic MB I culture.

The other point on which I totally differ in view from Dever concerns his new hypothesis of the slow development to MB I seminomadism from EB IIB. This hypothesis simply disregards the recent finds throughout Palestine of the highly developed urban culture of EB IIIA and IIIB (the twenty-seventh–twenty-third centuries B.C.E.).

Notes

1. This will be done when Amiran publishes all her examples. Her main arguments were already published in her paper, "Pottery from the Chalcolithic Site near Tell Delhamiya and Some Notes on the Character of the Chalcolithic–Early Bronze I Transition," *EI* 13 (1977): 48–56 (Hebrew). It is quite strange that Amiran notes there (p. 54) three [!!!] contemporary cultures at the end of the Chalcolithic period and strong cultural differences between sites in the same region. Sequence and chronology must be clarified before dealing with "transitions."
2. Some northern pottery types do intrude into the south; see R. Amiran, *Early Arad* (1978), Pl. 4:4 and Pl. 8:21. This phenomenon is even more lucid at Tel Esdar and Tel Masos, as at these sites there was no EB IB/EB IIA settlement [contrary to R. Cohen's statements in *IEJ* 28 (1978): 185ff.]. See my note on the matter, "Tel Masos," *EI* 15 (1981): 178, no. 7.
3. A. Kempinski, *IEJ* 33 (1983): 235–241.
4. M. Tadmor, "A Cult Cave of the Middle Bronze Age I near Qedesh," *IEJ* 28 (1978): 1–30.

Pierre de Miroschedji

I shall focus my comments on the papers of Ruth Amiran and William Dever. Although they dealt with different periods separated by a millennium, they both investigated the problem of continuity versus discontinuity between archaeological periods, and they both covered periods which are comparable in several respects.

Indeed, both the Chalcolithic period and EB I on the one hand, and the so-called EB IV on the other, are nonurban periods during which a large percentage of the local population was composed of nomadic pastoralists not only in the semidesertic fringe of the country, but also in the Mediterranean zone. This similarity in way of life is supplemented by similarities in the pattern of settlement (the geographical distribution of sites and the type of sites), in the architecture and in the subsistence activities. The two periods also witnessed a strong cultural regionalism implying the existence of population groups which were culturally distinct. Last but not least, both periods are immediately antecedent to the floruit of an urban civilization during EB II–III and MB II, and both have experienced during their last phase, EB IB and

Dever's EB IVC respectively, a process of sedentarization and incipient urbanization.

I can only express my broad agreement with Ruth Amiran's thesis. It is lack of time, I presume, which prevented her from extending the list of arguments in favor of continuity between the Chalcolithic period and EB I. She spoke of pattern of settlement, trade relations, pottery, stone vessels and figurines. She could have also mentioned cultic architecture, a subject she developed herself in 1977 at a Symposium marking the 100th anniversary of the Hebrew Union College,[1] and continuity in burial customs, a fact conclusively argued by Jean Perrot in his recent publication of the ossuary tombs of the coastal plain of Israel.[2] Furthermore, she could have elaborated on way of life and cultural diversity during the two periods. All this would have further strengthened the impression of continuity between the Chalcolithic and EB I, at least in its initial phase, EB IA. At the same time, it would have given more prominence to the real change which took place, not so much with the transition from the Chalcolithic to EB IA, as with the transition from the EB IB to EB II, that is with the development of the urbanization process and the appearance of the first fortified cities.

The EB II and III periods appear then to have developed between two phases of nomadic pastoralism, and to represent an urban age which is the Early Bronze Age *stricto sensu*. Therefore, the demise of the Early Bronze Age civilization at the end of EB III and its replacement by a nonurban, largely seminomadic culture, marks a break of considerable magnitude. This break, however, is minimized by William Dever who argues that a large measure of continuity existed between EB III and the following period, which consequently should be viewed as the last phase of the Early Bronze Age and called EB IV, and that there is no continuity whatsoever between this EB IV and the following MB IIA.

This thesis has been upheld by Dever since 1973, and he is responsible for a considerable expansion of our knowledge concerning this period. In his lecture at this Congress, he mobilized an impressive array of arguments to demonstrate his point. It is now obvious that the break between EB III and the following period was less radical than previously believed. The strength of this conclusion, however, depends much on the perspective chosen, whether cultural, social, ethnic, or geographic. It applies mainly, if not only, to Transjordan, especially to its semidesertic fringe, where nomadic pastoralism was the prevailing subsistence strategy throughout the Early Bronze Age. Thus the picture gained there and described by Dever may well be distorted when extended to the whole area. A good example is provided by the comparison made between the architecture and the layout of EB II and so-called EB IV sites in the central Negev. Similarities are close indeed but can also be explained by the factors of location and way of life, and are not necessarily indicative of a cultural and social continuity, especially when dealing with seasonal settlements which remained unoccupied for several centuries. In any case, this kind of observation hardly applies to other parts of the country.

The present state of knowledge enables us to present no more than a plausible hypothesis which still requires much testing. It seems that we shall not be able to draw a balanced picture as long as we do not have for the Mediterranean zone a stratified settlement site for both the EB III and the following period, as with the case of Khirbet Iskander in Transjordan. Thus it remains doubtful whether the evidence at hand should necessarily be analyzed and interpreted as evidence of strong continuity except for marginal areas. Elsewhere the overall impression is still that of a sharp break between the Early Bronze and Middle Bronze Ages, both socially and culturally, although there are already clear indications of ethnic continuity.

In regard to the problem of terminology, I shall express my hesitations with a series of questions:

1. Is the fact that the period under consideration has no ties with MB II but some ties with EB III sufficient evidence to consider it as the last phase of the Early Bronze Age, and to call it EB IV? After all, Ruth Amiran has shown that there was a continuity between the Chalcolithic and EB I, so the same line of reasoning applies now to the Chalcolithic — but we cannot call it EB 0!
2. More generally, should we modify the terminology of archaeological periods just because our knowledge has increased and our understanding changed? If so, this is liable to happen with any archaeological period, and our terminology will become an ever-fluctuating system under a constant process of revision. The result will be utter confusion. Indeed, we have presently four different names — MB I, EB IV, EB–MB, Intermediate Bronze — to designate the same archaeological period. Is such a situation helpful to the archaeological debate?
3. Finally, should we ascribe so much importance to the formal aspect of terminology? What is important is the proper archaeological definition of a period, not the name given to it; this is a simple matter of convention. The present state of terminological confusion results from the hasty application of labels to insufficiently defined archaeological assemblages. As long as we shall continue to give precedence to terminology over archaeological definition, to form over substance, there is little hope that this situation will change. In regard to the transitional period from the end of the Early Bronze Age to the beginning of the Middle Bronze, I personally do not care whether we call it EB IV, MB I, EB–MB, Intermediate Bronze, or whatever. What I do care about is that all of us call it by the same name and that it applies to the same and clearly defined archaeological material.

Notes

1. R. Amiran, "Some Observations on Chalcolithic and Early Bronze Sanctuaries and Religion," in *Temples and High Places in Biblical Times*, ed. A. Biran (Jerusalem, 1981), pp. 47–53.
2. J. Perrot et D. Ladiray, *Tombes à ossuaires de la région côtière palestinienne au IVe millénaire avant l'ère chrétienne* (Paris, 1980).

Roger Moorey

I would like to respond to the varied papers we have heard in this session as illustrating together some general problems of interest to us all as archaeologists. I thought it would be most useful for me, not being a specialist in the archaeology of this area, to comment from a broad Near Eastern standpoint.

As a museum curator, I am perhaps also more concerned than my colleagues in field archaeology, with communicating our studies to the widest public. The fundamental dilemma is a familiar one: as the body of archaeological data, raw and processed, steadily grows, not only do the complexities of handling it increase, but the key intellectual problem of penetrating as far as possible to the essentials, by digesting rather than discarding the new details, is ever more formidable. Our predecessors were able to create the now familiar framework for study, designed on a traditional technological basis, with a simple uncluttered structure. Steadily accumulating details have inevitably obscured not only this basic outline, but more fundamentally, have tended to overweigh the original structure to a point at which remedial engineering, often radical, seems to be needed, as Dr. Gitin emphasized.

It happens that the problem is more acute for the archaeology of this area than, to the best of my knowledge, it is anywhere else in the Near East. The intensity of fieldwork and related study hereabouts has always been greater and more varied than elsewhere in the region, save perhaps in Egypt, and Egyptology is a law unto itself in its archaeological aspects. It has also been traditional to synthesize and structure the archaeology of Israel and Jordan more regularly and more brilliantly than has been the case for neighboring lands. As anyone who reads or teaches archaeology well knows, the general studies by Albright, Aharoni, Kenyon and de Vaux, to mention but the best known in the English-speaking world, are unparalleled in any other Near Eastern country. Ironically, our problem to some extent arises from the very excellence of these textbooks; by their very nature such works create dogmas: they are the tablets of our intellectual tradition; a point made by Dr. Gitin. We ignore them at our peril, whilst seeking to ensure that they are a living check, not a dead hand, on all our current endeavors.

The papers in this session have ranged over three increasingly intensive levels of archaeological categorization. I will briefly refer to each in turn. First Dr. Gitin and, more particularly, Prof. Dothan scrutinized our basic framework, the technological "Three Age System," a common heritage of Old World archaeologists from the pioneers of Scandinavian archaeology — and found it wanting, not for the first, nor no doubt, for the last time. The complexities of relating "historical time" to "archaeological time," material culture studies to documentary source studies, are such that I prefer to keep them entirely separate in terminology. My own experience of attempting to correlate archaeological phases and dynastic systems, the debris of dirt archaeology with the raw materials of cultural history in Egypt and in Mesopotamia, has left me very doubtful of the wisdom of using invariably ambiguous politico-cultural nomenclature in classifying material remains. At least the old technological terminology, if at times imprecise, arises directly from the primary material culture it is used to classify, not from concepts derived from wholly different source materials. It is anyway now little more than a convention. Do not we all use it as a code rather than as a series of truly descriptive categories? It is "EB III" / "MB IIC" / "IA II," or whatever, of which we think and talk. It is a shorthand or jargon that fixes immediately, and relatively unambiguously, in our minds a particular piece of local "archaeological time," uncluttered by preconceptions from other sources of information. If it is culture history, history, anthropological archaeology or biblical archaeology which we then go on to write for the public, we will at least have started unhampered by any particular, culturally biased terminology.

Both Profs. Amiran and Dever took us to my second level of classification by broaching more directly problems of explanation in periods where the archaeology is largely textless. It is not without significance that both were concerned with periods of transition, with assessing the relative roles of internal development and external stimuli in the causation of cultural change. So long as we were primarily interested in the geographical and chronological relationship of archaeological sites and cultures, and the traits characterizing them, we neglected internal organization. Consequently, changes were more often interpreted in terms of external rather than internal factors. The impact of the "new," or as I prefer, of "processual," archaeology has changed all that. The debate has only just begun and still, in this particular context, I would favor the concept of "intermediate" periods — that convenient noncommittal phrase used by Egyptologists. All periods of marked change have, to the retrospective eye, indications of the past, the present and the future; it is really a matter of where at any one time you choose to throw the emphasis. The more our data for such transitional periods increase, the more readily we shall see with precision where old traditions endured, where new ones emerged (or penetrated from elsewhere), and what the most distinctive features of the current situation were. As the most striking characteristic of such periods is this state of flux, it would perhaps be wisest to continue to recognize this in our classificatory terminology.

With Prof. Ussishkin's paper we reached the third and most intensive level of complexity and categorization. To a greater or lesser extent the main concerns of the two previous levels have been with coarse-grained comparisons, with broad categories, and with relatively crude standards of archaeological cross-dating. Prof. Ussishkin has skillfully and painlessly (were that it was always so) brought us to the crucial level of fine-grained archaeological analysis. It is here, particularly, it seems to me, that our current information explosion is in gravest danger of overwhelming us or, at the very least, leaving so few specialists in command of the details that scholars, let alone the interested public, will be increasingly baffled by a kind of archaeological algebra, constantly manipulated by those few scholars who have mastered the latest data. The relative relationships of the stratigraphy of sites, within small areas over a generation or two, are the level at which we are all now increasingly called upon to operate, as more and more becomes known. The distant days of the five major excavation reports, which everyone knew from student days and everyone continued to manipulate with ease, have long since passed. We have all read, indeed many of us have written, papers of such intricate detail that we know by name those half dozen or less colleagues, who may be hoped to read them *critically*. This is unavoidable, but if our understanding of cultural development, in the broadest sense, in any time or place, is to increase rather than diminish in real terms, it would seem vital in matters of stratigraphy and terminology to realize that greater apparent precision does not inevitably carry with it greater comprehension. If we continuously atomize our categories and multiply our labels without concurrent general synthesis, we run the risk not only of bewildering our colleagues working in other regions, but of losing our public, and it is they, after all, who keep us in business.

Walter E. Rast

To R. Amiran: As Amiran has shown with several illustrations from Bâb edh-Dhrâ ͨ, this site's evidence makes her thesis compelling. In fact, as we begin to reassess the transition from what has been called late Chalcolithic to the beginnings of EB I, the evidence from Bâb edh-Dhrâ ͨ makes it essential to reformulate the transition along the lines of her continuity and gradual progress model.

The crucial evidence is the great number of shaft tombs which have become well known at Bâb edh-Dhrâ ͨ, and which date to the first phase of usage of this site. Lapp's original dating of these tombs to EB IA has been vindicated by all subsequent excavation. He did not himself solve the problem of their relation to the late Chalcolithic, and so he tended to uphold the view set forth earlier by Albright and others that, following the Ghassulian, the region witnessed one of the clearest cultural breaks ever found in this area. This basic model gave rise to the common interpretation of the EB I or Proto-Urban groups as incursions of peoples from the outside.

As a matter of fact, the reason that the model proposed by Amiran can be adopted is because the entire assemblage from the shaft tombs, alongside the settlement patterns, suggests a continuity with late Chalcolithic culture.

At Bâb edh-Dhrâ ͨ the evidence shows that the real beginning of sedentary life on a broad scale, which we associate with the Early Bronze Age, occurred not during this EB IA phase, but rather in EB IB. It was during EB IB that the establishment of villages took place. Interestingly, such village life correlates with the practice of articulated burials, also a sign of more or less permanent settlement as opposed to the presence of mere camping evidence with disarticulated burials during the EB IA phase. A similar picture is found at Jericho and Tell en-Nasbeh, and other sites which have articulated burials in tombs of EB IB type, although not all sites with EB IB painted materials have produced evidence of actual settlement in this period.

The conclusion which can be drawn falls very much along the lines of what Amiran has presented. The unique EB IA phase at Bâb edh-Dhrâ ͨ has to be wedged between the late Chalcolithic and the Early Bronze proper. Not only the basalt tradition, but the punctate decoration on much of its handmade pottery, maceheads, shell bracelets and jewelry, and the disarticulated burials placed in shaft tombs in a way only perhaps locally variant from the caves with ossuaries at somewhat earlier periods, all suggest a perpetuation, probably in their latest form, of late Chalcolithic attributes. But just as there is continuity from late Chalcolithic into EB IA, so also there is a spillover into EB IB, so that our models must deal a great deal more with these indicators of transmission of traits and their cultural meaning.

On one point, however, a question needs to be raised. Is it valid to think of intricate "trade networks" in this period? This seems out of harmony with Amiran's proposal that we are dealing with essentially local components. The problem is how to explain materials whose source clearly lies elsewhere, such as ivory found in the carved pieces at Beer-Sheba Chalcolithic sites, and those more recently at En-Gedi, shells from the Red Sea, and stones (such as alabaster in the case of some maceheads) suggesting an Egyptian source. Do such items indicate expansive trade connections? Given the heavy factor of transhumance in this period, it may be better to conceive of the materials as having been obtained and returned by mobile groups rather than through trade mediation. Trade mediation, in any case, seems to presuppose a system with greater social differentiation than that which appears to have existed in the late Chalcolithic and EB I.

To W.C. Dever: Dever's paper, like Amiran's, illustrates the importance but also the subtlety of periods which lie between two well-defined cultural phases. What to call such interposed phases seems not as important as trying to model features which are characteristic of transitional phases. Is there a tendency for such phases to betray similar patterns? Do they all show signs of tailing out or degeneration, the "end of an era"? Do they suggest a context of hostile encounter and marks of destruction? What proportion of continuity and discontinuity can be meaningfully measured with its implications? In short, are we going to find a similar set of problematics to deal with in all such bridge time-spans and their cultural and human remains? It would seem that there are isomorphisms between the so-called transitional phases of different time periods, but obviously, since history does not repeat itself, each case has to be understood in its particularity.

The most important evidence we have for this period, as Dever has pointed out many times, is the clear distinction between Transjordan and Cisjordan. Clearly in Transjordan the EB IV phase was one of substantial settlements, possibly even in some cases walled ones. The clear evidence for such permanent agricultural settlements in this period is indicated not only in the structures and burials at Bâb edh-Dhrâʿ, but Aroer and Tell Ikfanu have been known for some time as indicating a similar arrangement, and now Kh. Iskander makes this unmistakable. By contrast, the EB IV (or MB I) of Cisjordan has comparatively sparse evidence for sustained settlement at the sites of this period, suggesting a stronger component of simple pastoralism than east of the Jordan. It is still difficult to tell for sure whether the EB IV in Transjordan for the most part is prior to that west of the Jordan, or whether they reflect two diverse situations during this period. I am inclined, as has been Dever, to see the Transjordan horizon as shortly predating that from Cisjordan.

If one poses the question in such a way that the crucial decision is whether the intervening phase of EB IV (MB I) is closer to the preceding Early Bronze or the succeeding Middle Bronze periods, there seems to be little doubt, as Dever argues, that the former is the case. That seems evident from the fact that EB IV evidence is commonly found where EB III settlements previously existed, at least as far as Transjordan is concerned. And, in terms of architecture EB IV buildings, where we have them, are little different from those of EB III, having a rectangular shape and built of fine mud bricks over stone foundations, just as in EB III. On the other hand, when material from this phase begins to appear in an excavation, it takes only a split second to identify EB IV pottery. This suggests that EB IV pottery is distinctive from that of EB III, despite the fact that some persistence of general motifs might be traced. Gone are the elegant EB III platters, often of large size, although a modified platter-type continues in EB IV. Gone also are the pitchers and juglets with spiked bases and many other forms typical of EB III. In their place are the "teapots" and simpler jugs with flattened bases, and the decorative technique of furrowing and wavy combing.

When these differences in the corpus of material are compared to other data, such as the entirely different type of tomb at Bâb edh-Dhrâᶜ in EB IV as opposed to the communal burial structures of EB III, the proposition of simple continuity raises problems. At Bâb edh-Dhrâᶜ we have to weigh the meaning of the fact that our EB IV settlement is for the most part around the edges of the previously abandoned or destroyed EB III town. Consequently, it will be important in future Early Bronze excavations, particularly in Jordan, to watch for the relation of the EB IV cultural horizon to that of EB III. While EB IV, then, has its linkages backward to that out of which it has come (the preceding Early Bronze phases), at the same time some substantial disjunctions also are indicated, and the efforts to explain these should also continue.

To M. Dothan: My question, in considering M. Dothan's proposal, may seem to be a *Kinderfrage*. Why call something something? Some of this might be subjective and based on personal preference. It seems, however, that the main concern in terminology is to facilitate correlation of data for historical, cultural and social studies. This is why we could all be much better served if, in such areas as classifications of ceramics, we would have terminologies and attribute lists which could be cross-referenced between sites, rather than having to expend energy on translating the idiosyncratic systems of each expedition or excavator.

I have no intrinsic objections to converting from the traditional technological terms to historical-political-ethnic designations, although for the periods prior to those dealt with by Dothan, we shall probably have to carry on with Chalcolithic, Neolithic, etc. My concern is whether such a change will expedite or hamper correlation, especially between rather contiguous regions.

For example, if Iron Age is replaced by Israelite, what should be used for the several areas east of the Jordan in the same period, which historically maintained some independence from the Israelite domination to which Dothan refers? Should they continue to be called Canaanite, which would be confusing since west of the Jordan that cultural epoch would be seen as having been succeeded by the Israelite? Or should a further localized breakdown, involving Edomite, Ammonite, and Moabite, be used, which is what we already seem to be doing, and which would seem to support Dothan's point?

It would seem that the technological designations have an advantage with respect to correlation. They are much more capable of broad, cross-cultural translation. Probably more than one of us has been frustrated by the problem of transposing what in Cyprus is called Early Cypriote into the better-known Early Bronze of the Levant, especially since the dates in Cyprus seem to be off. The designation Early Cypriote is fine for an inner understanding of the cultural development, but as soon as one seeks to make comparisons with other cultural regions, the relation to a more comprehensive standard arises naturally. The fact that there may be some time lags (Early Bronze might not have been synchronous in all the regions of comparison) does not negate the value of a more comprehensive terminology cutting across localized groupings. To speak of an American cultural epoch in recent centuries has value for an inner understanding of this culture, but if one wishes to make correlations with Europe and Great Britain, recognition of an Industrial or Atomic Age might be more useful.

Thus it seems that, even if localized terms are used and have some value, they cannot really repeat the technological terms since the latter serve functions not covered by the former.

Joe D. Seger

The struggles and controversies engaged in by archaeologists over appropriate and acceptable terminologies are a necessary and fundamental part of the archaeological discipline. At one level we can be satisfied simply with a "name" or "code word" that communicates a specific, recognized archaeological entity — one that as such facilitates discussion and review of data classes and cultural periods, etc. But at another level, we cannot be, and perhaps never should be, fully satisfied with the coinage of such terms without a persistent review of that to which they both explicitly and implicitly refer.

Our problems at this second level are especially severe when we seek to describe and define terms for overall periods of archaeological-cultural development. Here, as archaeologists, we concentrate *primarily* on questions of continuity versus discontinuity and on the extent to which we can adequately assess changes by reviewing the excavated data, such data including stratigraphic sequences, artifact types and development; and, increasingly in our day, ecological and environmental factors.

Secondarily, we, of course, also review relevant historical data, including "events" of a political or cultural nature, and related factors of more specific, "absolute" chronological assessment. *Finally*, to the extent possible, we also look to evidence of ethnic associations.

Perhaps, like all students, we yearn to have terms settled and clearly defined, so that we can easily embrace them and move on with consensus. However, it seems that today we find ourselves moving increasingly upstream. The situation is becoming more not less complex. Not only is the burden of actual excavation data accumulating at a bewildering pace, but newer, more discrete methodologies and interests in broader environmental and regional assessments are exacerbating the situation. For this reason my posture at present is to argue only for minimal changes in general nomenclature, though agreeing with Gitin that forums be fixed to facilitate ongoing dialogue.

G.E. Wright argued informally among his students for the construction of a simple, century-by-century reference system to be used irrespective of other names or terms. However, in truth, this is and has always been the universal, if unannounced, main frame for all discussions, and it would be counter-productive to opt for any generalized dismissal of otherwise recognized terms in favor of simple numerical chronology. It would seem equally unwise, however, to discard the broadly accurate — and more general terms — "Bronze" and "Iron" for those of "Canaanite" and "Israelite" as proposed by Prof. Dothan — although his arguments for use of these latter as parallel terms (as in Hebrew versus English, and in more popular reference situations) is not rejected. The argument here is threefold: (1) changes to these terms contribute nothing to the resolution of specific problems related to better understanding of cultural transition periods within the "Canaanite" era (for example from EB to MB) and may, in fact, serve to obscure those transitions; (2) such a change skews the reference too narrowly to the south Canaanite area during the Iron II/Israelite period and opens the way to the proliferation of the use of regionally and ethnically discrete terms during the early first millennium B.C.E.; (3) these changes emphasize ethnic associations which are archaeologically the most difficult to adequately identify and assess.

The above is not intended to suggest, however, that there is no room for some adjustment within the framework of the terminology currently used. The papers by Amiran, Dever, and Ussishkin provide excellent case studies for review, and I find myself in general agreement with all three. Here it is appropriate to add but a few supplementary footnotes.

1. Amiran's perception of cultural continuity from late Chalcolithic into EB I is substantially affirmed by evidence from the excavation of Cave I.3A at Gezer, the publication of which is forthcoming in the HUC-Gezer series. This cave represents second-phase occupation at the site, belonging to the EB I, "troglodyte" period settlement. It provides just one well-sealed assemblage of domestic remains including clearly defined EB I ceramic forms together with types of acknowledged Chalcolithic ancestry. A similar profile is likewise suggested by a modest collection of lithic

implements including transitional Chalcolithic/EB I flint blades and three basalt mortars.

2. Dever's view associating erstwhile MB I materials more closely with the Early Bronze continuum and thus redesignating it EB IV is also supported, howbeit with negative evidence, by recent excavations at Tell Halif in the northern Negev. There stratigraphy provides four substantial phases of EB III occupation and traces of EB IV (MB I) evidence, but no MB IIA–C occupation whatsoever.

3. Ussishkin's questions regarding correlations with Lachish Stratum III are also nuanced by recent work at Tell Halif, a site located at an intermediate geographical post between Lachish and Beer-Sheba. Stratum VIA at Halif shows extensive evidence of destruction which is presumed to be the result of Senacherib's 701 B.C.E. Judean campaign. The site was locally occupied for a brief time in the early seventh century B.C.E. and then abandoned. Until now only two *lamelekh* handles have been found at the site, neither in stratified deposits of the Iron Age. However, as the site was abandoned from the early seventh century until at least the late sixth century B.C.E., the presence of any *lamelekh* stamps adds weight to their usefulness as indicators of a late eighth century date on the model of Lachish Stratum III.

Are their arguments thus finally convincing? Perhaps, but Gitin has raised the prior question of how and on what grounds we can finally decide, and to this I return in conclusion. For my part, I am not sure that we can ever agree on any specific, universally applicable formula. However, I would argue that our considerations be weighed first, and heavily, in favor of the archaeological data; only secondly with reference to more general historical considerations, and rarely with respect to ethnicity. We must encourage the ongoing debates among us, and be satisfied only with that consensus of terminology that emerges on the basis of broadly accepted archaeological facts.

Discussion

L. T. Geraty: I listened carefully to Prof. Moshe Dothan's suggestion in his challenging paper, "Terminology for the Archaeology of the Biblical Periods." I am sympathetic to his concerns and can understand the motivation for them. I agree as well with many of his criticisms of the use of "Syro-Palestine." My problem is with the alternative he suggests — "Eretz-Israel." I understand that the term includes the adjoining territory around the State of Israel; however, to make the change suggested would be to politicize what should remain a scientific-humanistic discussion. Archaeologists working in the Middle East cannot afford to enter into politics if they are going to achieve for their disciplines the most that is possible and desirable. Of course the term "Syro-Palestine" may itself have political overtones, but that terminology at least has the advantage of being Albright's and of having been used before the establishment of any of the current political states in the region. To continue the term's use then is not necessarily to make a political statement.

I for one am not tied to the term "Syro-Palestine," but I cannot come up with anything better. I would have no objection at all to a conference or a committee that was charged to recommend viable and more acceptable alternatives.

With regard to Prof. Dothan's second suggestion to use the terms "Canaanite" and "Israelite" to replace "Bronze" and "Iron" respectively, I can see his logic, but it is misleading to use ethnic terms for periods in which those terms are not all-encompassing. Prof. Dothan is right in pointing out the problems with "Bronze" and "Iron." The question is whether it is worth giving up the broad terminology which we share with world archaeologists to gain the advantages associated with ethnic terms which have their limitations geographically and historically. The case for a change has not been argued strongly enough for me. Can you imagine trying to correlate Ammonite I, II, III with Edomite III and IV and with Israelite I–V, etc., knowing full well that such terms must cover other ethnic populations as well?

M. Eisman: I would like to respond to Prof. Dothan's second point and argue for the retention of the "Bronze" and "Iron Age" terminology. Prof. Dothan brought up the comparison with the Aegean civilization. I would like to point out that the terminologies there of Minoan, Mycenaean and Cycladic, for example, are in fact conveniences which are being shed more than they are being used. A number of years ago, an attempt was made to discard the traditional Minoan terminologies and replace them with "Palatial," "Pre-Palatial," "Post-Palatial." It failed miserably to gain more than passing interest, although the arguments offered by Prof. Hutchinson were compelling because of the Aegean's strong tradition of painted ceramic ware which allows very fine gradations of chronological assortment. Nevertheless, courses are increasingly being given in interrelations; people are looking for interaction not only within the Aegean but without. Aegean scholars are expanding into the Near East and increasingly giving up their particular designations to use the broad Bronze and Iron Age terminology. This is not the time to reverse the procedure at this end.

A. Biran: I would like to suggest that we ask the Israel Exploration Society to hold a special conference on this subject. I think Sy Gitin's point was well taken. We should discuss the probabilities or suggestions with other organizations and colleagues and then perhaps we will have a Jerusalem terminology.

SESSION IV

ISRAEL'S NEIGHBORS IN THE IRON AGE IN THE LIGHT OF ARCHAEOLOGICAL RESEARCH

RICHARD D. BARNETT, Session Chairman, *Professor Emeritus, The British Museum*

TRUDE DOTHAN, *The Hebrew University of Jerusalem*
The Philistines Reconsidered
JAMES D. MUHLY, *University of Pennsylvania*
Phoenicia and the Phoenicians
DONALD B. REDFORD, *University of Toronto*
The Relations between Egypt and Israel from El-Amarna to the Babylonian Conquest
JAMES A. SAUER, *University of Pennsylvania*
Ammon, Moab and Edom

Respondents

MANFRED BIETAK, Österreichisches Archäologisches Institut Zweigstelle Kairo
LAWRENCE T. GERATY, *Andrews University*
ORA NEGBI, *Tel Aviv University*
ELIEZER D. OREN, *Ben-Gurion University of the Negev*
EPHRAIM STERN, *The Hebrew University of Jerusalem*
DAVID STRONACH, *University of California, Berkeley*

Discussion

The Philistines Reconsidered

Trude Dothan

The sources for the study of the Philistines have presented the archaeologist and historian with a unique possibility of identifying and defining an ancient culture and people both in its local setting and in the larger framework of the Mediterranean world. The Bible, Egyptian records, and archaeological finds are the main sources for our knowledge of Philistine origins, cultural background, and history. Here I shall highlight the archaeological evidence of the material culture of the Philistines and attempt to place it within the chronological and cultural framework of the eastern Mediterranean. This evidence is multifaceted, encompassing patterns of settlement, architectural remains, urbanization, cultic architecture and vessels, glyptics, funerary practices, and, of course, the most prominent and well-known indicator of Philistine presence — their distinctive ceramic corpus. The archaeological evidence, which comes mainly from the rich finds in Israel and which forms the basis of our relative and absolute chronology, may also help to elucidate the origins and cultural affinities of other groups of Sea Peoples.

My emphasis is on the initial stages of Philistine culture when its distinctive character, not yet assimilated into other cultures, still reflected its origins. The ethnicon Philistines (for example, *prst*) first appears in ancient sources in the war reliefs of Ramesses III at Medinet Habu. They are mentioned as one of the groups of Sea Peoples whom he defeated in his eighth year and subsequently allowed to settle in southern Canaan. Other groups of Sea Peoples are known from earlier Egyptian texts such as the Merenptah inscriptions. I shall use the word "Philistine" as a generic term to include those related groups of Sea Peoples who settled in what was to become Philistia proper, and in other parts of Canaan, and whose identities are now emerging more and more clearly.

The events which occurred at the end of the thirteenth and the beginning of the twelfth century B.C.E. changed the history of Canaan and ushered in a new era. It was a period of transition that witnessed the collapse of the Hittite Empire, the end of the

Canaanite city-states, the decline of Egyptian political and military power in Asia, the arrival and settlement of the Israelite tribes and related entities, and the appearance of the Sea Peoples, mainly the Philistines, on the coast of Canaan.

The complexity of a period of dislocation, while characteristic of intermediate periods in general, is particularly well illustrated in Canaan during the transition from the Late Bronze to the Iron Age, for here the various cultural and ethnic elements coexisted and overlapped. In order to bring the events of this unstable period into focus, one must try to define and distinguish these different components.

At some sites, certain facets of local Canaanite culture continued into the early Iron Age, indicating the persistence of a local Canaanite population. Egyptian presence and influence can be discerned, revitalizing during the time of Ramesses III and continuing at some sites into the second half of the twelfth century B.C.E. The unsettled state of affairs of this period is further highlighted by the sudden interruption of sea trade and the cessation of the importation of Cypriote and Mycenaean vessels, which epitomized the cosmopolitan *koine* of the Late Bronze Age in the region. The settlement and diffusion of the Israelites is evident in the character and pattern of their new settlements. Finally, the Philistines, who remain the best documented of the Sea Peoples and who produced a highly distinctive and now well-known material culture, added new elements to this cultural melange, while recent archaeological research has made possible the identification of other groups of Sea Peoples, such as the Sherden and the Shikallu.

While the major settlement phase of the Sea Peoples following their defeat at the hands of Ramesses III in his eighth year has long been recognized from the literary and archaeological record, an ever-growing corpus of evidence from recent excavations in Canaan and on the coast of Syria, and in Cyprus is increasingly pointing not only to raids but to an initial wave of settlement in the eastern Mediterranean by Sea Peoples prior to their defeat by Ramesses III.

The sites in Israel containing Philistine cultural remains are found principally in the Shephelah and the southern coastal plain, but there is also evidence that Philistine culture spread to other areas of the country. Major excavations have established a clear stratigraphic sequence through which we can trace the initial appearance, then the flourishing, and finally the subsequent assimilation of Philistine material culture, a process which spanned the period from about 1200 to 1000 B.C.E.

Of the five capital cities of the Philistine Pentapolis, three — Gaza, Ashdod and Ashkelon — have been definitely located, and the identification of Tel Miqne with Ekron is greatly supported by the recent excavations there. These excavations are a joint American-Israeli project, sponsored by the W.F. Albright Institute of Archaeological Research and the Institute of Archaeology of The Hebrew University, and codirected by Dr. Sy Gitin and myself. The most extensive evidence of Philistine material culture has come from excavations at Tel Ashdod, Tel Miqne, and from a site on the northern border of Philistia whose ancient name we do not know — Tell Qasile (which is located within the city limits of modern Tel Aviv). These three sites, Ashdod, Miqne and Qasile, provide complementary data on the nature of the

Philistine urban settlement, and the facets of its material culture and cultic structure and practices.

Ashdod is situated on the southwestern coast of Canaan, on the main military and commercial route to Egypt through Gaza. Here, for the first time with the aid of a modern stratified excavation, the Philistine material culture can be studied in one of its principal cities, enabling us to follow its initial development and the transition from the Late Bronze Age (Stratum XIV) to the early Iron Age (Stratum XIII).

In Areas G and H, Stratum XIV, the important Canaanite city, most probably from the period of Ramesses II, was destroyed and newly settled in Stratum XIII. The rebuilt areas exhibit a new orientation, type of architecture, and material culture.

In Area G, on the northern perimeter of the acropolis, a huge, fortified Late Bronze Age structure from Stratum XIV was probably situated near a gate. It was abandoned and the character of the area completely changed between Strata XIV and XIII. In Stratum XIII, the parallel walls that had formed part of the Stratum XIV monumental building were destroyed, leaving only the thin inner partition walls. A structure, open to the sky — possibly a "high place" or cultic installation — was uncovered where part of the fortified building had previously stood.

South of this structure were several small rooms whose thin brick walls had been strengthened with large, dressed stones from Stratum XIV. Of special interest is the large amount of charred wood, probably from a kiln, found on the floor of these rooms. Twenty-seven pottery vessels were stacked upside down on the floor nearby. The entire area was probably a potter's workshop, and most of the relevant pottery from the lower phase of Stratum XIII was found on this floor. It consisted mainly of carinated or bell-shaped bowls, either undecorated or decorated with monochrome red bands, as well as fragments with spiral decoration, some of which were warped — undoubtedly kiln wasters. A basket-handled spouted jug was also found. The whole group has close affinities with Mycenaean IIIC:1b pottery from the Aegean, the eastern Mediterranean, and Cyprus.

The monochrome Mycenaean IIIC:1b pottery found here and in other parts of the site, especially in Area H, is of local manufacture. Even so, there is a clear distinction between this pottery and the typical Philistine bichrome ware. The Mycenaean IIIC:1b pottery, in forms, motifs, and color, is a faithful reproduction of the Mycenaean tradition. Most of the types were bell-shaped bowls and small kraters. The decorative motifs on the bowls consist of wavy, scalloped horizontal lines below the rim, a feature that is not typically encountered on Philistine bowls but that is well represented in the Mycenaean repertoire. The vertical zigzag pattern forming part of triglyphs, a typical Mycenaean decoration, is also foreign to the Philistine pottery. Fish motifs occur on two fragments at Ashdod (probably from the same krater), heralding the fish motif depicted on Philistine pottery.

In the upper phase of this stratum at Ashdod, Stratum XIIIa, differences from the lower phase (Stratum XIIIb) were noted only in minor details, such as a higher floor. The change is mainly discernible in the finds. In the upper phase, for the first time, we have a number of typical Philistine sherds (the one or two found in the lower phase seem to be intrusive). The same phenomenon occurs in other areas of the site where numerous sherds exhibiting these typical elaborate motifs were found.

Tel Miqne (Khirbet el-Muqanna ᶜ), identified with Philistine Ekron, is located on the southern bank of the Naḥal Timna. It overlooks the ancient network of highways leading northeast from Ashdod to Gezer and inland via the Naḥal Soreq to Beth Shemesh. Ekron was the northernmost city in the Philistine pentapolis and controlled the territory allotted to the tribe of Dan. Its eastern border, the western limit of the territory of Judah, was the scene of the events recounted in the Samson cycle.

The mound itself is some 200 dunams (50 acres) in size and has long been recognized as the largest Iron Age site in Israel. Its size, location, and rich ceramic corpus strongly support its identification with Ekron.

The main urban settlement at Miqne was founded at the beginning of the Iron Age, about the twelfth century B.C.E. This settlement, designated as Phase 9 by the excavators, boasts a 3.25 m wide mudbrick wall under which were sealed ceramic forms typical of the beginning of the Iron I period, including Mycenaean IIIC:1b and Philistine forms. The Mycenaean IIIC:1b pottery seems to appear in the initial stage of Phase 9. The high concentration of Mycenaean IIIC:1b and Philistine vessels continued through the three stages of Phase 8, all of which were associated with the mudbrick city wall.

At Miqne then, stratigraphic, architectural, and ceramic evidence join together to indicate that the earliest fortified center was established at the beginning of the twelfth century B.C.E., during the initial phase of penetration and settlement of the coastal and inner coastal plains by the Sea Peoples/Philistines. As at Ashdod, the ceramic evidence at Miqne indicates an initial appearance of Mycenaean IIIC:1b pottery followed closely by an overlapping and flourishing of elaborate Philistine bichrome ware.

The initial appearance of the monochrome Mycenaean IIIC:1b pottery at Miqne and Ashdod and throughout the eastern Mediterranean points to the immigration of numbers of people who had a common cultural background manifested primarily in their pottery. The unity of technique, style, and decoration in the many sites at which this pottery has been found indicates the short chronological period in which the dispersion of these invading elements took place. And, perhaps most startling, while one might assume that this pottery was brought to the many diverse areas in which it was found, testing by Neutron Activation Analysis of the materials from Cyprus and Canaan has indicated that in each place it was locally produced, reaffirming that the potters who made the ware shared a common background and ceramic tradition which they had brought with them and utilized in their new homes in a relatively short period of time.

Perhaps one of the most remarkable features of the appearance of Philistine material culture as seen in its most prolific manifestation — the pottery — is its sudden and rapid flourishing. It appears fully developed and with elaborate decoration in levels containing diminishing quantities of the monochrome Mycenaean IIIC:1b characteristic of the initial phase of settlement.

The finds from Strata XIIIa, XII and XI at Ashdod are characterized by impressive quantities of typical Philistine pottery —conclusive evidence that in Philistia proper this was the dominant pottery. Although plain Iron Age I pottery continued to be used for utilitarian purposes, a comparison with sites outside Philistia confirms the overwhelming predominance at Ashdod (and Miqne) of Philistine pottery.

The shapes and decorative motifs of Philistine pottery were a blend of four distinctive ceramic styles: Mycenaean, Cypriote, Egyptian, and local Canaanite. The dominant traits in shape and almost all the decorative elements were derived from the Mycenaean repertoire and point to the Aegean background of Philistine pottery. Philistine bichrome ware manifests, however, a far richer variety and combination of motifs and shapes than the Mycenaean IIIC:1b that precedes it in this country.

Philistine shapes of Mycenaean origin include bell-shaped bowls, large kraters with elaborate decoration, stirrup jars for oils and unguents, and strainer-spout beer jugs. Closed vessels are far more prominent in Philistine bichrome ware than in the Mycenaean IIIC:1b repertoire of this country, with examples coming not only from Ashdod and Miqne, but also from Beth-Shean and Akko.

The Philistine bichrome pottery exhibits a striking difference from that of the Mycenaean IIIC:1b monochrome found here. While Mycenaean IIIC:1b is typically fine, delicate, and well levigated, reflecting the firsthand know-how and the close Aegean ties of the potters who crafted it, the Philistine bichrome ware is, in many instances, much coarser and cruder. This changeover in ware, coupled with the increased proportion formed by Philistine pottery in the ceramic material culture, likely reflects production of the pottery on a large scale, utilizing mass-production techniques, and catering to a well-established population whose substratum was definitely Aegean in background.

The Mycenaean IIIC:1b pottery excavated up to the present in this country is executed primarily in "open-field" decoration, with only a few examples of the "elaborate" or so-called "Close Style" of Cyprus and the Aegean, while the extremely elaborate Philistine decorative style bears a closer relation to the "Close Style" of Mycenaean IIIC pottery generally. Philistine bichrome ware is executed in a two-tone decoration of red and black on a heavy white slip, a decorative technique divergent from the Mycenaean tradition. The most prominent motifs utilized in this pottery group are stylized birds, spiral loops, concentric half-circles, and scale patterns. Although Philistine vessels were richly decorated with motifs taken from the Mycenaean repertoire, these motifs were rearranged and integrated with other influences to create the distinctive signature known as "Philistine."

The singular and distinctive differences between Mycenaean IIIC:1b and Philistine bichrome pottery are best observed, therefore, in the shift from simple to elaborate decoration, the larger number of closed vessels produced, and the increased proportion formed by Philistine bichrome ware among the everyday utensils of the people. These changes may reflect a second influx of craftsmen, who shared a common Aegean background and familiarity with the ceramic craft of the Mycenaean IIIC:1b potters, but who, focusing on wide-scale production, introduced fresh and new elements into their own personal ceramic creation — Philistine bichrome ware.

The incorporation of an Egyptian shape and Egyptian motifs into the Philistines' ceramic repertoire is extremely important evidence for the settlement of Philistines in Canaan during the period of Egyptian dominance at the beginning of the twelfth century B.C.E., in Egyptian sites and strongholds such as Tell el-Farʿah (south). Egypt makes its most visible contribution to the Philistine ceramic repertoire with the tall-necked jug (Type 12) and with the stylized lotus motif which appears on Philistine pottery.

The excavations at Ashdod and Tell Qasile have provided new insights into the Philistine cult, cultic architecture, and cultic vessels. They have also helped to confirm the nature and attribution of many sporadic finds that in the past could only tentatively be attributed to the Philistine cult. The finds at Ashdod and Qasile also enable us to reappraise the contents of the Gezer cache and to add essential details lacking in the excavation report. The three sites of Gezer, Ashdod and Qasile have all yielded vessels which are definitely cultic in context and character, and have shed important light on our understanding of the original background of the Philistines.

R.A.S. Macalister's publication of the cache of objects from Gezer makes it difficult to relate it to any architectural remains. The *terminus a quo* of this group is provided by a fragment of an Egyptian faience vase bearing a cartouche of Ramesses III.

Philistine cultic buildings and temples are now more clearly understood in the light of the discoveries at Tell Qasile and the earlier phase at Ashdod. At Ashdod, the open-air high place (Area G) belonging to Stratum XIII included a brick altar and a stone base on which the statue of a god may once have stood. In Area H, the apsidal building (part of the northern complex) associated with the "Ashdoda" figurine may also have been of cultic significance.

The temples at Tell Qasile show a fusion of architectural styles, the principal elements of which are related to those of the well-known Canaanite temples at Lachish and Beth-Shean. Three phases of this temple complex, which was founded in the twelfth century B.C.E., were uncovered along with extremely rich cultic finds. Ever-growing evidence of cultic architecture in the Aegean world and its offshoots in the Mediterranean, especially that of the Late Cypriote III temples at Kition in Cyprus, the temple in the citadel of Mycenae, and the newest discovery, the shrines of Phylakopi on Melos, points to clear analogies with the Philistine temple at Qasile.

Philistine cult sites have produced a wide and rich variety of vessels with clear connections to Aegean cult. The kernos, a Philistine cultic libation vessel, was found in large numbers in Cyprus, and in Israel at Beth-Shean, Beth Shemesh, Megiddo, and elsewhere. Another distinctive vessel in the Philistine cult is the one-handled lion-head rhyton, a ritual or drinking cup, found thus far in Israel at Tel Zeror, Tell es-Safi, Megiddo, Tell Jerishe, and Tell Qasile. The Philistine pottery rhyton is the last echo of a long Mycenaean-Minoan tradition of metal and stone animal-head rhyta. These vessels have been found in the shaft graves at Mycenae and at Knossos on Crete, and are depicted in scenes of the ancient land of Keftiu on New Kingdom tomb walls in Egypt.

Female pottery figurines also reflect Philistine cult origins and beliefs such as the "Ashdoda," a schematic representation of a female deity and throne, a clear-cut stylistic continuation of the Mycenaean mother-goddess prototype. The female anthropomorphic vessel from the favissa in the Qasile temple may also hearken back to the matriarchal Mycenaean pantheon and to other similar vessels such as those found at Mycenae, Tiryns, and Phylakopi.

Hints of Philistine mourning customs can be gleaned from the terra-cotta female mourning figurine from Philistine contexts such as Tell ʿAitun and Azor. Most of this material comes from burials. These figurines stress hand gestures and were attached to the rims of Philistine kraters which are closely analogous to kraters with mounted female mourning figurines associated with the cult of the dead in the Aegean world and belonging to Mycenaean IIIC groups, such as those found at Perati and Ialysos.

The cult vessels from Ashdod reflect the Aegean background of the Philistines at a time when they were still closely linked with their Aegean homeland. The "Ashdoda" especially exemplifies this stage. At the other extreme, the cult vessels from Strata XI–X at Tell Qasile, while retaining an Aegean element, express the assimilation of different influences as well, some a marked departure from Aegean sources. These new developments could be innovations and inventions of the local potter, made to accommodate the Qasile cult to its provincial home.

The cult vessels clearly illustrate the evolution of the Philistine culture, whose Aegean base was gradually "diluted" by local cultural and religious influence. Moreover, these vessels provide some knowledge of the art of the early Iron Age, of which no monumental examples have been found.

Burial customs are generally a sensitive indicator of cultural affinities, and those of the Philistines show the same fusion of Aegean background with Egyptian and local Canaanite elements that distinguishes every other aspect of their culture. As yet, no burial grounds in any of the main Philistine centers have been found. However, several cemeteries that can be related to Philistine culture on the basis of tomb contents have been explored. In some cases, the Philistines perpetuated the indigenous funerary customs and tomb architecture; in others, they employed foreign modes of burial, such as the cremation interment found at Azor.

Two contemporary and interrelated features of Philistine burial customs — both of which borrowed from foreign traditions — are rock-cut chamber tombs and burial in anthropoid clay coffins. The chamber tombs of the "500" cemetery at Tell el-Farʿah clearly portray the highly assimilated character of Philistine burials. These tombs, built on the Mycenaean architectural model of a stepped *dromos* (passageway) leading to a rectangular chamber with shelves cut into the rock for placing the deceased and his or her goods, contained two complete anthropoid coffins and a mixture of Philistine and Egyptian pottery. While the tomb architecture reflects Mycenaean influence, the burial in anthropoid pottery coffins was originally an Egyptian practice and was taken over by the Philistines and incorporated into their own interment practices at Tell el-Farʿah.

Although there is no doubt that Philistines used clay anthropoid coffins, the great majority of clay coffin burials discovered in Palestine date to the period preceding the Philistines, the Late Bronze Age, when Egyptian garrisons and troops were stationed in Egyptian strongholds. This Egyptian presence has been confirmed through the excavation of Deir el-Balaḥ — an Egyptian Late Bronze Age stronghold with a subsequent Philistine occupation, whose LB cemetery has yielded over forty complete anthropoid pottery coffins through both licit and illicit digs. Clay coffin burials, then, are simply one more instance of the Philistines adopting and adapting Egyptian cultural traits after their mercenary service in or near Egyptian strongholds.

The northern cemetery at Beth-Shean, dating from the thirteenth–eleventh centuries B.C.E. (Levels VII–VI, Late Bronze Age–Iron I) has yielded fifty of these anthropoid coffins. A small number of Philistine bowl sherds were unearthed on the mound proper in connection with Level VI of the settlement. Five coffin lids, associated with the latest phase of the cemetery (Level VI; twelfth–eleventh centuries B.C.E.) have the distinctive feature of an applique headdress. One in particular, a headdress crowned by vertical fluting, is virtually identical to the feathered cap worn by the Peleset (Philistines), Shikallu, and Denyen on the Medinet Habu reliefs of Ramesses III. This headgear provides decisive evidence that the bodies buried in the grotesque coffins at Beth-Shean were those of Sea Peoples, most probably Philistines. The Bible (1 Samuel 31:8–13; 1 Chronicles 10:9–12) relates that Beth-Shean was occupied by Philistines after Saul's defeat at Gilboa in the late eleventh century B.C.E. The funerary objects associated with these headdress coffins at Beth-Shean confirm a date in the second half of the eleventh century, the time of Saul.

The presence of the Sea Peoples in the Egyptian stronghold at Beth-Shean again points to one of the distinctive settlement patterns associated with the Philistines in ancient Canaan — the incorporation into former and contemporary Egyptian settlements. Beth-Shean itself experienced a resurgence during this period, which was related to the last flourishing of Egyptian power in Canaan during the Twentieth Dynasty. The statue of Ramesses III from Beth-Shean and the accompanying building activity, the rebuilding of Tell el-Farʿah at this time, and the new finds from Lachish, including a cartouche of Ramesses III, indicate a definite resurgence of Egyptian military and political strength in Canaan during the Nineteenth and Twentieth Dynasties. The settlement of the Philistines in Canaan following their defeat in the eighth year of Ramesses III is one aspect of this final flourish.

The assignment of an absolute chronology to the events of this period is in a state of flux. Although the trend is toward the lower chronology, its use creates particular difficulties for the dating of the transition from the Late Bronze to Iron Age and for the early Iron Age in Canaan. Fortunately, the sequence of events remains unchanged, regardless of which chronology one adopts.

Data from a number of sites, both within Philistia proper and in surrounding areas, serve to establish a relative chronology for the period in question. The primary indicator of the end of the Late Bronze Age was the cessation of Mycenaean IIIB and Cypriote imports to Canaan. These vessels are not found in early Iron Age levels of

Canaanite sites. At Ugarit, a sword bearing the cartouche of Merenptah, found in the destruction level of the Late Bronze Age city, dates that level to his reign. The latest Mycenaean IIIB pottery at Ugarit occurs in this level, whose destruction was most likely carried out by Sea Peoples. At Tell Deir ʿAlla, Mycenaean IIIB pottery occurs in the destruction level of the LB II stratum, where a broken faience vase with the cartouche of Queen Tewosret was discovered. At both Ḥaruvit and Tell el-Farʿah, it makes its last appearance in a level prior to or contemporary with Seti II, that is, the end of the thirteenth century B.C.E.

The evidence from these sites indicates a date ca. 1200 B.C.E. for the final appearance of Mycenaean IIIB pottery in the Levant and provides a chronological backdrop for the dating of the earliest manifestation of Mycenaean IIIC:1 pottery in the eastern Mediterranean, which appears stratigraphically immediately after the disappearance of Mycenaean IIIB pottery. At ʿAkko, for example, local monochrome Mycenaean IIIC:1b was found in strata postdating the destruction of the Late Bronze Age city. A scarab with the name of Queen Tewosret, found in the ash layer, provides a *terminus ante quem* for the destruction of the Late Bronze city and a *terminus post quem* for the appearance of the Sea Peoples, again, ca. 1200 B.C.E.

Shortly following the introduction of monochrome Mycenaean IIIC:1b in this country by Sea Peoples, Philistine bichrome ware appears at a large number of sites in Canaan, first in Philistia proper and subsequently at various sites throughout the country. The diverse nature of the settlements in Canaan at this time necessitates care in the examination of the ceramic evidence, as the picture is far from homogeneous.

In Philistia proper, the two major pentapolis cities excavated provide a stratigraphic point of departure. At Ashdod, the monochrome Mycenaean IIC:1b phase immediately follows the destruction of the Late Bronze Age city about the beginning of the twelfth century B.C.E., and appears in a level (XIIIb) characterized by a series of apparently unfortified new structures. The ware, which reveals firsthand knowledge of Mycenaean techniques and is stylistically a short phase, precedes stratigraphically the first appearance of Philistine bichrome ware at Ashdod in Level XIIIa. Hence, the Mycenaean IIIC:1b at Ashdod is assigned to the period between Tewosret and the advent of the Philistines in the eighth year of Ramesses III.

At Miqne (Ekron), the second of the pentapolis cities to be excavated, the appearance of monochrome Mycenaean IIIC:1 pottery is associated with the first real urbanization of the city in the early Iron Age. Here as well, the picture repeats itself — the Mycenaean IIIC:1 pottery is soon followed by the appearance of Philistine bichrome ware.

At Ashdod and Ekron, the consolidation of Philistine bichrome ware was amazingly rapid. The pottery appears in its full floruit directly on the heels of monochrome Mycenaean IIIC:1b. It would be advantageous if further study could distinguish the phase of evolution from the monochrome Mycenaean IIIC:1b to full-blown Philistine bichrome ware with its characteristic white slip and red and black decoration, and a very few vessels may hint at this phase, such as those with white slip and monochrome decoration. However, because of the scarcity of intermediate vessels and the sudden flourishing of Philistine bichrome ware with its full repertoire of shapes and decorations, it appears that there had to be a second impact from outside which introduced the extremely close and elaborate style characteristic of Philistine pottery and basically foreign to Mycenaean IIIC:1b in this country.

The development of the elaborate close style of Philistine ware need not have taken a long time. Mycenaean IIIC:1b provided the nucleus of typology and the repertoire of motifs and shapes for Philistine bichrome ware. However, the proportions of types of vessels (open versus closed) changed with the appearance of Philistine bichrome ware, with closed types becoming more prominent, and Philistine bichrome ware proportionately representing a larger percentage of everyday ware at both Ashdod and Miqne than did Mycenaean IIC:1b in its previous stratum.

The Egyptian stylistic elements taken over by the potters of Philistine ware, such as the lotus motif on the high-necked jug, appear in the initial phase of Philistine pottery and serve as an indicator of the early date at which these elements were incorporated in the Philistine ceramic repertoire. These motifs were already common in Canaan in the Late Bronze Age, predominately in the thirteenth century B.C.E., and were therefore present upon the arrival of the Sea Peoples in Canaan. These motifs continued to be especially popular during the time of Ramesses III (the first half of the twelfth century B.C.E.) when Egypt experienced a resurgence of power, and are seen, for example, in the lotus-decorated alabaster vessels found in Megiddo Stratum VIIA.

The impact of local Canaanite influence is elusive except for the possibility of tracing back the tradition of bichrome decoration, and perhaps the white slip, to the Canaanite potters of the Late Bronze Age.

Within Philistia proper, a number of sites present alternate patterns of settlement, for they bear witness to the continuing Egyptian presence, especially strongly associated with the time of Ramesses III, and yet they do not individually boast a strong Philistine presence. This phenomenon was first observed at Tel Mor, an Egyptian fortress near Ashdod, which maintained an Egypto-Canaanite material culture simultaneously with the Philistine occupation of Ashdod, and only later featured a prominent Philistine presence.

At Tel Seraʿ, a similar picture emerges. The end of the Late Bronze Age is clearly marked by the cessation of Mycenaean and Cypriote imports in Stratum X at this site, located in Philistia. Stratum IX, dated to the reign of Ramesses III on the basis of hieratic bowls mentioning the "Year 22," bears a strongly Egyptian character. No Philistine influence is noted in Stratum IX, and Philistine pottery first appears in small quantities in Stratum VIII, following a gap in occupation between these two strata.

At Lachish to the east, the Mycenaean IIIB imports end with the destruction of the Fosse Temple, but this destruction was not associated with any clearly datable finds. On the mound itself, a bronze plaque bearing a cartouche of Ramesses III was found in Level VI and may bear witness to a new short-lived Egyptian settlement following the destruction of the Fosse Temple during his reign. After the destruction of this settlement the site was unoccupied until the tenth century B.C.E. Lachish, then, like

Tel Seraʿ, while confirming the basic sequence of the transition from the Late Bronze to the Iron Age during the early twelfth century B.C.E., remains a site which retained its Egyptian character, experienced a settlement gap in the early Iron Age, and was not taken over by the Philistines.

Conclusions

Settlement patterns similar to those seen in Canaan have been observed at sites to the north, such as at Ras Ibn Hani, the satellite of Ugarit. There, following the destruction of the Late Bronze Age city, as at Ashdod, a new wave of inhabitants swept in, bringing with them the now familiar monochrome Mycenaean IIIC:1b pottery, which was followed by the appearance of "Philistine-like bichrome ware." To the west, in Cyprus, the occupation of previously destroyed Late Bronze Age sites by Sea Peoples and the founding of new cities by them, closely parallel the settlement patterns observed in Canaan. Indeed, as we consider the overall picture of the Mediterranean world following the period of dislocation and the end of maritime trade and the cosmopolitan *koine* at the end of the Late Bronze Age, we witness rebuilding after destruction or the foundation of new settlements throughout the Mediterranean coast, the common denominator at these sites being the appearance of locally made Mycenaean IIIC:1b pottery.

The new discoveries in the Aegean and the Levant have enhanced our knowledge of the Philistines and have provided a sharper focus on this biblical people. We are now entering a new phase of research which may eventually allow us to distinguish the culture of the Philistines from that of other Sea Peoples, known to us from the Onomasticon of Amenope, who also settled along the coast of Canaan. The excavations at ʿAkko, postulated by M. Dothan to be a Sherden site, continue to shed light on the transition from the Late Bronze to the Iron Age and on the appearance of the Sea Peoples on the northern Canaanite coast. The growing number of Mycenaean IIIC:1b sherds found there immediately above the Late Bronze Age destruction level include a distinctive krater fragment with the depiction of a bird strongly reminiscent of those found on other Mycenaean IIIC:1b vessels. Some of the Mycenaean IIIC:1b sherds from ʿAkko came from a pottery kiln located near a metal reworking area. Of special interest is a stone altar(?) in the form of a mortar with incised drawings of ships, similar to those depicted on the walls of the Kition temple.

The new excavations at Tell Keisan, possibly belonging to the Sherden orbit, have yielded an exquisite, imported Mycenaean IIIC:1a stirrup jar from the early Iron Age levels, which could possibly be linked to the incursion of the Sea Peoples there. The Late Bronze Age levels at Keisan have not yet been reached, but will undoubtedly clarify the nature of the transition from the Late Bronze to the early Iron Age at the site. We can only anticipate that the excavation of the Shikallu port of Dor will also yield material that will enhance our understanding of the Sea Peoples and their movements and settlement on the coast of Canaan. The investigation of the Philistine material culture and its comparison with the written and historical sources continues, but the search for other Sea Peoples in Canaan and beyond has just begun.

Select Bibliography

Balensi, J. "Tell Keisan, temoin original de l'apparition du 'Mycenien IIICla' au Proche-Orient." *RB* 88 (1981): 399–401.

Bounni, A., Lagarce, J. Saliby, E. et Badre, L. "Rapport préliminaire sur la première campagne de fouilles (1975) à Ibn Hani (Syrie)," *Syria* 53 (1976): 233–264.

——. "Rapport préliminaire sur la deuxième campagne de fouilles (1976) à Ibn Hani (Syrie)." *Syria* 55 (1978): 233–301.

——. "Rapport préliminaire sur la troisième campagne de fouilles (1977) à Ibn Hani (Syrie)." *Syria* 56 (1979): 217–257.

Dothan, M. *Ashdod II–III. ʿAtiqot* 9–10 (1971).

——."ʿAkko." *IEJ* 31 (1981): 110–112.

——."ʿAkko." *IEJ* 33 (1983): 113–114.

——. "Sherden at Akko?" In *Sardinia in the Mediterranean: A Colloquium on Sardinian Archaeology*. Tufts University Symposium Volume (in press).

Dothan, M., Asaro, F., and Perlman, I. "An Introductory Study of Mycenaean IIIC:1 Ware from Tel Ashdod." *Archaeometry* 13 (1971): 169–175.

Dothan, M. and Dothan, T. "On the Mycenaean IIIC1 ware in Canaan" (forthcoming).

Dothan, T. *Excavations at the Cemetery of Deir el-Balaḥ. Qedem* 10 (1979).

——. *The Philistines and Their Material Culture*. Jerusalem, 1981.

——. "Some Aspects of the Appearance of the Sea Peoples and Philistines in Canaan." In *Griechenland, die Agäis und die Levante während der "Dark Ages" vom 12. bis 9. jh. v. Chr.*, Vienna, 1983, pp. 99–120.

Dothan, T. and Gitin, S. *Tel Miqne (Ekron) Excavation Project — Field Report I*. Jerusalem, 1982.

——. "Tel Miqne (Ekron), 1981." *IEJ* 32 (1982): 150–153.

——. "Tel Miqne (Ekron), 1982." *IEJ* 33 (1983): 127–129.

Hankey, V. "Mycenaean Pottery in the Middle East." *BSA* 62 (1967): 107–147.

——. "Late Mycenaean Pottery at Beth-Shan." *AJA* 70 (1966): 169–171.

Humbert, J.B. "Recents travaux à Tell Keisan (1979–1980)." *RB* 88 (1981): 373–398.

Mazar, A. *Excavations at Tell Qasile. Qedem* 12 (1980).

Wente, E.F. and Van Siclen III, C.C. "A Chronology of the New Kingdom." In *Studies in Honor of George Hughes*. *SAOC* 39 (1976): 218ff.

Phoenicia and the Phoenicians

James D. Muhly

IN THE FIELD of Old Testament studies the Phoenicians have received scant attention. While everybody is familiar with Hiram I of Tyre (961/0–928/7 B.C.E.) and his relations with Israel during the days of David and Solomon, and with the stories concerning the marriage of the Tyrian princess Jezebel, daughter of Ethbaal I, King of Tyre and Sidon (879/8–848/7 B.C.E.), to Ahab, King of Israel, little more is ever said regarding the role of the Phoenicians in biblical history or biblical archaeology. It is true, of course, that Phoenician religion represented a pagan celebration of obscene rites that was of great concern to various religious reformers, but such episodes tell us little about Phoenician archaeology or even about Phoenician history.

In 1967 the Society for Old Testament Study in England marked its jubilee with the publication of a volume on *Archaeology and Old Testament Study* (ed. D. Winton Thomas, Oxford, 1967). That collection of studies has almost no material on the Phoenicians, for the simple reason that it was arranged according to excavated archaeological sites, and in the mid-1960s there were no excavated Phoenician sites. The main Phoenician cities, such as Byblos, Beirut, Sidon and Tyre, were already major Canaanite cities in the Bronze Age and remained inhabited centers right into modern times. Whatever archaeological work could be carried out was in general concerned with levels no earlier than Roman times. Crusader Tyre has been the study of a marvelous two-volume work by Maurice Chéhab, but Phoenician Tyre has escaped the spade of the archaeologist.

The standard secondary works on the Phoenicians, by such scholars as Donald Harden, Sabatino Moscati and Giovanni Garbini,[1] really deal more with Carthage and the Western Phoenicians than they do with the Phoenicians in the Levant. The Phoenicians have, for long, been a people known only outside their homeland. In the Levant they appeared in historical texts, in their own inscriptions and in Assyrian royal inscriptions and letters, and were identified as being responsible for the production of a heterogeneous body of art work in ivory, metal, terracotta, faience and glass. Little of this material came from anything resembling a controlled or scientific investigation, and often the archaeological evidence for the Phoenicians was as far removed from a proper context in time and place as were the later literary testimonia.

One could, in fact, think of the eviden e for the Phoenicians as existing on a number of different levels, almost as if there were, for the modern scholar, different types of Phoenicians. These could be catalogued as:

— Historical Phoenicians, known from contemporary historical records (Phoenician inscriptions and Assyrian royal inscriptions and letters).

— Literary Phoenicians, known from the Old Testament and from Homer.

— Legendary Phoenicians, known from late classical writers, such as Josephus, Philo of Byblos and Lucian (all writing in Greek but claiming to have based their accounts upon authentic Phoenician sources).

— Artistic Phoenicians, known from work in ivory, metal (precious and base), terracotta, faience and glass, and from representations on funerary monuments and Assyrian reliefs.

— Archaeological Phoenicians, known from excavations at Phoenician sites (however limited) and from work at contemporary archaeological sites in the Levant.

— Colonial Phoenicians, known from chance discoveries throughout the Mediterranean and from modern archaeological work at Phoenician and Punic colonies in Cyprus, Sicily, Sardinia, Malta, North Africa and Spain.

What emerged from this was a confused, often distorted picture of what was taken to represent the history and culture of the Phoenicians. Many of the written "sources" were, in fact, highly tendentious in nature; there were major gaps in the surviving archaeological and historical record; and often works of art were regarded as being Phoenician or in a Phoenician style simply because they were eclectic in nature and not easily categorized as Syrian, Assyrian or Egyptian. Moreover, there was a great overbalance of evidence from Carthage and the western colonies, at the expense of evidence for the Phoenicians in their homeland, resulting in passages describing the burning of infants as sacrifices to the (supposed) god Moloch or Molek, straight from the pages of Gustave Flaubert's *Salammbô*.

Fortunately things have now started to change. In 1969 James Pritchard began work at the Phoenician city of Sarepta, modern Sarafand, the only site on the Phoenician coast with an occupational history that ended in Roman times and thus a site open to excavation down to Phoenician and even Canaanite levels. Unfortunately these excavations, conducted on behalf of the University Museum of the University of Pennsylvania, were interrupted by the civil war in Lebanon just at the point when the earlier levels at the site were about to be uncovered. We do, however, have information relating to the Iron Age and Bronze Age occupation of Sarepta from two soundings, denoted X and Y, that have been published as doctoral dissertations by two of Pritchard's former students, Issam Khalifeh and William Anderson.[2] Pritchard himself has edited a preliminary report on Sarepta and has also written a general book dealing with Sarepta and the Phoenicians.[3] The final multivolumed report is now in production in Beirut, with the first volume (Robert Koehl's study of the Late Bronze Age Mycenaean ware) already in page proofs. Despite the limited exposure of relevant levels, Sarepta has yielded a wealth of exciting material and has provided us with our first glimpse of the Phoenicians in their homeland. Prior to the excavations at Sarepta we knew of the Phoenicians only from the excavation of cemeteries at Khalde, Achzib (both only partially published) and Athlit[4] as well as the pottery rescued from four looted cemeteries in southern Lebanon.[5]

In 1973 Patricia Bikai was permitted to conduct a sounding within the perimeter of the original island of Tyre.[6] Working almost without interruption for the better part of a year (August 1973–July 1974), she was able to distinguish twenty-seven different strata going back into the Early Bronze Age. Following a break in occupation (corresponding roughly to the Middle Bronze Age), this area of Tyre was inhabited down to ca. 700 B.C.E., at which point a later Roman occupation removed all subsequent levels. This isolated area, in the Late Bronze Age, was occupied by a factory specializing in the production of red faience beads and, in Iron Age II, by a potter's atelier, with levels IV–I cutting through a pottery dump producing over 80,000 sherds. Although the archaeological record is skewed by limited exposure, this sounding at Tyre is of vital importance since it has provided a well-stratified ceramic sequence, covering the crucial transition from the Bronze Age into the Iron Age, that can now be correlated with the sequence established at Sarepta.

Detailed comparisons between the Tyre and Sarepta sequences, and of those sequences with others from contemporaneous sites in Syria and in Palestine, have already been made by Anderson, Bikai, and Khalifeh, and need not be repeated here. There are two aspects of the data, both rather unexpected developments, that do require further elaboration. The first is that during the period ca. 1150/1100–800/750 B.C.E., represented by Strata XIII–V at Tyre, by Periods VI and VII of Sounding X and Strata E and D of Sounding Y at Sarepta, there was only limited evidence for the existence of imported pottery or of imports of any type whatsoever.[7]

This is really quite remarkable. The great age of Phoenician mercantile activity, the time of Hiram I, of Solomon and the biblical accounts relating to Ezion-Geber, the Tarshish fleet and three-year voyages to the Land of Ophir, is simply not documented in the archaeological record from Tyre and Sarepta. What this has to tell us about Phoenician mercantile and maritime activity prior to the reign of Tiglath-Pileser III, only future archaeological work at the main Phoenician centers can clarify; but it certainly provides no evidence to support those who wish to push Phoenician expansion into the western Mediterranean back into the twelfth century B.C.E.[8]

The second aspect to be discussed here is, in fact, quite closely related to the first. Although the later Greek tradition placed the Phoenician colonization of the "far west" in a time-frame just after the Trojan War (with Cadiz being given a foundation date of ca. 1110 B.C.E. and Utica of ca. 1100 B.C.E.),[9] a century of archaeological exploration has produced no evidence for any Phoenician presence in Spain or North

Africa earlier than the eighth century B.C.E. This has been the state of affairs for some time now and nothing from the recent German work at Phoenician "factory" sites on the southern coast of Spain has altered the situation in any way.[10] Nor has any archaeological evidence been forthcoming in support of 814 B.C.E., the traditional date for the foundation of Carthage. Although it is true that modern occupation has hampered the excavation of early occupation levels there, there has now been extensive archaeological work at Carthage thanks to the international rescue effort sponsored by UNESCO, but nothing has been uncovered that can be dated any earlier than the latter part of the eighth century B.C.E.[11]

This late eighth century B.C.E. date for a Phoenician presence in the western Mediterranean now seems almost codified by the publication of the proceedings of the Cologne symposium, "Die phönizische Expansion in westlichen Mittelmeer-raum," held in April 1979. This massive volume (published in 1982) provides the most complete account to date of all the evidence relating to the Phoenician colonization of the Mediterranean world.[12] For the western Mediterranean we have only the isolated evidence of the Nora Stone(s) from Sardinia to take us back any earlier than ca. 800 B.C.E.[13]

What has not been appreciated, and what does not emerge from the papers presented at Cologne, is that the traditional Phoenician "facies," as known from numerous sites in the western Mediterranean — characterized by red-slipped and burnished jugs having a "mushroom lip" or trefoil rim, and by torpedo-shaped storage jars in a fabric designated by Bikai as "crisp-ware" — is not known from Phoenicia itself prior to the second half of the eighth century B.C.E.

It is with Stratum V, in the mid-eighth century B.C.E., that Bikai identified a definite change in the ceramic repertoire of Tyre, with the following strata dominated by those wares that go with the colonists to the western sites and that represent the "calling card" of the Phoenicians as far west as Mogador in Morocco.[14] In his excavations at Sarepta, Pritchard also recognized a decisive break in the archaeological record between City E and City D. Cities G–E provided a sequence of uninterrupted development from the end of the Late Bronze Age to ca. 800 B.C.E. The following period, City D, saw the introduction of a new city plan, a new style of architecture, and a new ceramic repertoire dominated by red-slipped, burnished jugs and torpedo-shaped amphorae or storage jars.[15]

The clear implication of this is that what we recognize as being distinctly Phoenician in the western Mediterranean did not exist in Phoenicia itself prior to the eighth century B.C.E. We can hardly expect to find "mushroom-lipped" jugs in Carthage, Utica or Mogador in any context earlier than the earliest evidence for such jugs in Phoenicia itself. What had been established as the chronology for the Phoenician colonization of the western Mediterranean is now supported by the stratigraphic evidence from Tyre and Sarepta.

In working out any ceramic chronology for the Iron Age world of the Mediterranean, the best evidence for absolute dating comes from the presence of imported Greek pottery. Just as the imported Mycenaean wares provide the evidence for dating the late Bronze Age in the eastern Mediterranean, so the Late Protogeometric and Geometric wares of Greece make it possible to assign absolute dates to archaeological strata throughout the Mediterranean. The chronological limitations of all non-Greek ceramic evidence are often not properly appreciated. Throughout the entire Iron Age of the Mediterranean world, local wares can at best provide only a relative dating. Only in Greece has a precise and (reasonably) secure ceramic chronological sequence been established.[16]

It has long been held that the earliest Greek pottery in the Levant can be seen in the famous skyphoi with pendant semicircles (known as PSC cups) identified at Tell Tayinat, Hama, Al-Mina, Tell Sukas, Tabbat al-Hamman, Tell Abu Hawam and Ashkalon. Dated to the second half of the ninth century B.C.E., this pottery has for the past twenty-five years been regarded as the hallmark of Euboean commercial and colonial expansion both east (to Al-Mina in North Syria) and west (to Pithekoussai [Ischia] in the Bay of Naples).[17] Writing in 1970, in the first volume of the publication of his excavations at Tell Sukas, Poul Riis could state that "no Greek Geometric pottery from the great Phoenician capitals is known."[18]

These pendant semicircle skyphoi were thought to have such a close association with Al-Mina that a special class of them became known as Al-Mina Ware.[19] The Iron Age site of Al-Mina, excavated almost as an afterthought by Leonard Woolley during his search for a Bronze Age harbor on the Syrian coast, thus became the focus for all Greco-Phoenician interconnections. Al-Mina came to be regarded as the most important Greek colony in the Levant and the place at which the Greeks most likely borrowed and adapted the Phoenician alphabet, during the years ca. 825–750 B.C.E., this despite the fact that the Iron Age levels there produced no inscriptions, Greek or Phoenician.

All contact between Greeks and Phoenicians was seen as taking place at sites in North Syria: at Al-Mina, Tell Sukas and Ras el-Basit (the best candidate for the Poseideion of Herodotus),[20] not in Phoenicia itself. This interpretation has dominated scholarship for the past generation, but major revisions are now under way. Classical archaeologists are themselves starting to revise their ideas regarding Al-Mina and the nature of the Greek presence in the Levant. More important, there is now evidence forthcoming from Phoenicia itself. Bikai's excavations at Tyre have produced sherds of Attic Late Protogeometric pottery, pieces with full concentric circles enclosing Maltese crosses, which must date to the latter part of the tenth century B.C.E.[21] This now becomes the earliest Greek pottery in the Levant.

Tyre has also produced a sherd from a Middle Geometric II krater or large pyxis that should date to the first part of the eighth century B.C.E., although its context at Tyre (in Stratum III) suggests a date in the second half of that century. This half-century lag between production in Greece and deposition in the Levant is true also for other finds of the same type of vase —at Hama, in Tomb 13 at Amathous, and in Royal Tomb 1 at Salamis —and probably for the unstratified MG II fragment from Huelva in Spain.[22]

Again we have the same style of imported pottery in Phoenicia and in Spain, and in a context dated to the second half of the eighth century B.C.E. What is truly remarkable is that an intact example of such a MG II ceremonial pyxis, used in the first instance for aristocratic funerals in Greece, has now turned up in a Phoenician tomb near Sidon.[23] Although the tomb itself was reused and thus provides no evidence for absolute dating, the Greek vase is undoubtedly a MG II pyxis of the same class as those discussed above and should date to the first half of the eighth century B.C.E. The absence of the typical Phoenician "mushroom-lipped" and trefoil-rimmed red-slipped jugs also supports the dating suggested above for such pottery. The tomb did contain an amphora with two horizontal handles of a class similar to Cypriot Geometric III ware, of the late ninth century B.C.E., and bearing a three-letter dipinto inscription that seems to be the earliest Phoenician inscription yet discovered on the Levantine coast.[24]

What has come to light here is evidence for the close relationship between Greece, Cyprus and Phoenicia in the early Iron Age. That relationship deserves to be examined in some detail. Our image of Iron Age Cyprus has been transformed just within the past few years, thanks to the work of Vassos Karageorghis. Although much of this material is still in the course of publication, enough is known in order to say what needs to be said here.[25] The Greek colonization of the island was well under way by the eleventh century B.C.E., concentrated in its western part. From Tomb 49, at the site of Palaepaphos-Skales, dating to the eleventh century B.C.E., comes a bronze spit or skewer (Greek *obelos*) inscribed with a personal name in the Arcadian genitive, thus supporting the later literary traditions that Agapenor, king of the Arcadians, came to Cyprus after the fall of Troy.[26] This is the earliest Greek inscription from Cyprus.

In the eastern part of the island, the site of Salamis replaced Bronze Age Enkomi as the dominant site in the area, with Kition seemingly an important religious center supporting at least five temples. These temples appear to have gone out of use around 1000 B.C.E. Then, after an hiatus of about 150 years, the area was resettled by Phoenician colonists from Tyre. The Phoenicians selected the site of the largest of the earlier Bronze Age temples, known as Temple 1, and built there a new Phoenician temple — the largest yet discovered — in honor of the goddess Astarte.[27] This temple was in use for a period of about fifty years and was then rebuilt, with minor modifications, following the destruction of the original temple in a fire. Associated with the rebuilding was a foundation deposit containing numerous small unguent juglets and bowls of Black-on-Gray Lustrous Ware, the former often thought to have a special association with the Phoenicians.[28] In a deposit from just prior to the destruction, there was a Red Slip bowl with an inscription usually identified as being in Phoenician but as yet defying all attempts at translation.[29] The only point upon which all would-be translators seem to agree is that the text does mention the goddess Astarte to whom the temple was dedicated.

The Tyrian identity of the Phoenician colonists in Cyprus was maintained for centuries thereafter. From the fourth–third centuries B.C.E. we have the funerary inscription of one ʾEšmunadon, identified as the "governor of Tyre" (*skn ṣr*),[30] confirming the close identity between the two sites. It has in fact often been argued that Kition is to be identified as the colony of *Qrtḥdšt*, known from Neo-Assyrian royal inscriptions and the Baʿal Lebanon inscriptions (KAI^{2}31) as a Phoenician city in

Cyprus. The problem is that a fifth century B.C.E. inscription from Kition (KAI²37) refers both to "the Carthaginian," *Hqrtḥdšty*, and to "citizens of Kition," *ʾš kty*, with the clear implication that Qartḥadašt and Kition are to be seen as two distinct locations.[31] This inscription also refers to "the temple of Astarte of Kition," *bt ʿštrt kt*, that certainly should be the Phoenician temple excavated at that site. Qartḥadašt must be identified with some other Phoenician site on Cyprus, perhaps with the unexcavated site at modern Limassol.[32]

If Kition is to be regarded as the first Phoenician colony, and the colonization of Cyprus as the first stage of Phoenician expansion into the Mediterranean, then that expansion must be placed no earlier than the latter part of the ninth century B.C.E. According to current interpretations of the archaeological evidence, Greek traders and merchants played a crucial role in that expansion, thus demanding a Greek presence in the Levant prior to the commencement of Phoenician expansion. That is exactly what the archaeological evidence now demonstrates, both in Cyprus and the Levant.

Recent British archaeological work in Crete at various Protogeometric and Geometric cemeteries in the vicinity of Knossos, and in Euboea, at the site of Lefkandi, has produced evidence for contact between Greece, Cyprus and the Levant going back into the eleventh century B.C.E.[33] The abundance of oriental imports and of jewelry and other artifacts made of gold from a period for which, up to only a few years ago, imports and gold were scarcely attested in the archaeological record, is now matched by finds from the Palaepaphos-Skales cemetery in southwestern Cyprus.[34]

What this evidence demonstrates is a flourishing trade between Greece, Cyprus and the Levant during what used to be known as the Dark Age of Greek history (ca. 1050–850 B.C.E.) and prior to the beginnings of Phoenician expansion. How, then, are we to account for the presence of Phoenician objects in the Aegean during this period? The obvious explanation is that they were brought from Phoenicia, or from Cyprus, by Greek merchants, but that solution has not met with favor among Aegean scholars, who prefer a more complex scenario. In a line of scholarly transmission — through J.N. Coldstream and J. Boardman back to T.J. Dunbabin — British archaeologists have argued for the presence of resident Phoenician (and even Urartian) craftsmen working in the Aegean, especially in Crete and the Dodecanese islands, and producing bronzes and gold jewelry for the Greek market.[35]

This interpretation depends in part upon a detailed and sophisticated art historical analysis capable of distinguishing true Phoenician imports from objects made by Phoenician craftsmen working in the Aegean, and from objects produced by a Greek apprentice trained by a Phoenician master-craftsman. Without going into detail here, I can only say that I find such distinctions lacking in conviction, and would reject the thesis of resident oriental craftsmen, and regard most of the items in question as true Phoenician imports.[36]

Most interesting is the bronze hemispherical bowl with a Phoenician inscription, from Teke Tomb J near Knossos, and dating to ca. 900 B.C.E. according to the archaeological evidence. (Attempts to date the inscription in the eleventh century

B.C.E. on the basis of palaeographic evidence must be regarded with skepticism.)[37] The bowl itself is certainly of Cypriot origin or inspiration. In Cyprus the type goes back into the Late Bronze Age and seems to have been introduced into the Aegean during the late tenth century B.C.E. There is nothing about this find that demands the presence of an early Phoenician resident at Knossos.

For many years the earliest Phoenician import in the Aegean was considered to be the hemispherical bronze bowl with embossed figured decoration from Grave 42 in the Kerameikos cemetery, dating to ca. 840 B.C.E.[38] Some years ago Irene Winter argued that this bowl was North Syrian, having nothing to do with the Phoenicians.[39] She went on to argue that the characteristic art style associated with the Phoenicians — the strong Egyptian influences best seen in the Layard group of ivories from Nimrud and in a series of decorated metal bowls —only developed during the course of the eighth century B.C.E. The Phoenician style continued into the seventh century B.C.E., in contrast to the North Syrian and South Syrian styles of ivory carving, which developed in the ninth century B.C.E. but had run their course by the latter part of the eighth century B.C.E.[40]

This reconstruction is in perfect agreement with the dating of Phoenician pottery discussed above. It suggests that, prior to ca. 800 B.C.E., the Phoenicians confined their interests and activities to the Levantine littoral, developing a local style in pottery and metalwork that, following the colonization of Cyprus, is often best described as Cypro-Phoenician. The best known product of this style is the Black-on-Red juglet, in a technique that has a tradition in Cyprus going back into the eleventh century B.C.E. Recent clay analyses have shown that many of these juglets from sites in North Syria (including Al-Mina) were actually made in Cyprus.[41]

Only with the colonial expansion of the eighth century B.C.E. did the Phoenicians develop the international art style that has for long been thought of as characteristically Phoenician. This style was brought by Phoenician colonists to the "far west," but because for such a long time so much of our evidence for the Phoenicians came from there, this style came to be regarded as "typically Phoenician." The important point is that it was not typically Phoenician before ca. 800 B.C.E. If we look at what other material went west with the Phoenician colonists, we find that once again the best evidence for dating is provided by imported Greek pottery. Leaving aside a few exotic finds in bronze, the earliest Greek material in the west consists of "SOS" amphorae and Proto-Corinthian kotylai, found together with Cypriot Bichrome IV ware. This presumes a dating for the presence of Phoenician colonists in the "far west" no earlier than the latter part of the eighth century B.C.E.[42]

Few vase types from Archaic Greece have attracted as much attention as "SOS" amphorae which, in the "far west," are known from contexts including Toscanos, Huelva and Mogador. There is now general agreement that such vases had a special association with Attica and were used as containers for shipping olive oil.[43] Exactly how these amphorae reached "far west" Spain and North Africa, is not clear as there certainly is little supporting evidence to suggest any active Greek trade with the region at such an early date. It is reasonable, therefore, to assume that they were brought by Phoenician colonists — but if that is the solution, it remains necessary to explain how the Phoenicians came into possession of Attic oil amphorae.

Excavations at the site of Pithekoussai on the island of Ischia, an Euboean colony founded in the early eighth century B.C.E. (perhaps ca. 770), have provided evidence that suggest a possible answer to that question. Pithekoussai has produced a considerable number of oriental imports, including "Lyre Player" scarabs of probable North Syrian origin, a Syrian flask with a human head modelled at the neck (known from an almost identical piece found at Zincirli), incised vase inscriptions both in Greek and in Phoenician, and a full assemblage of Phoenician ceramics (including red slip jugs with "mushroom lip" and red slip plates, and "torpedo" storage jars).[44] There can be little doubt regarding the Phoenician presence at Pithekoussai during the course of the eighth century B.C.E. and, as the site also produced a number of "SOS" amphorae,[45] it is quite possible that Phoenicians took some of these oil containers with them on their way to the "far west."

This brings us to the last question to be discussed in this paper, the reasons for Phoenician colonization, and Phoenician expansion into the "far west" as a possible background for Hiram I of Tyre and his Tarshish fleet. It will be recognized immediately that, in terms of the chronology used in this paper, there certainly was no Phoenician activity in the western Mediterranean during the tenth century B.C.E. In spite of much ingenious speculation, there is still no convincing interpretation of those biblical passages dealing with Hiram and Solomon and the Tarshish fleet.[46] Nor can we locate the land of Tarshish.[47] The Greek land of Tartessos is certainly to be placed in southern Spain, but no connection can be made between Tarshish and Tartessos.[48]

The famous description of the "ship of Tyre," in Ezekiel 27, is one of the most difficult passages in the entire Hebrew Bible. Whatever the exact details might be that make up the description of the ship,[49] the passage does show that metals played an important role in the trade between Tarshish and Tyre. According to Ezekiel, Tarshish was an important source of silver, iron, tin and lead. The references to silver and tin have attracted the most attention as they are both important metals of limited distribution, but they are available in Iberia, in Spain (silver)[50] and Portugal (tin).[51] As Greek traders also went west in search of Spanish silver, the silver of Tartessos, the Ezekiel passage has long been cited as evidence for equating Tarshish with Tartessos and for locating both in southern Spain, in particular the region of Huelva.

These problems have been dealt with in great detail in several recent publications,[52] and it will be possible here only to comment on selected aspects of some important points under discussion. The only direct connection between Phoenicians, Tartessos and silver comes in a late Hellenistic philosophical work attributed to Aristotle and known by the title *De mirabilibus auscultationibus*, "On Marvelous Things Heard." There it is stated:

> ... as is recorded in the Phoenician histories.... It is said that those of the Phoenicians who first sailed to Tartessos, after importing to that place oil, and other small wares of maritime

> commerce, obtained for their return cargo so great a quantity of silver, that they were no longer able to keep or receive it, but were forced when sailing away from those parts, to make of silver not only all the other articles which they used, but also all their anchors.[53]

As Brian Shefton already has recognized, the passage quoted seems to provide a faithful commentary on the archaeological evidence known through the distribution of "SOS" oil amphorae. But such evidence goes back no earlier than the late eighth century B.C.E. The earliest contemporary Greek reference to Tartessian silver comes in the *Geryonēis* of Stesichorus, a poet who lived in the early sixth century B.C.E. in the Sicilian city of Himera.[54] This evidence certainly indicates that the Spanish markets were not exploited much before the seventh century B.C.E.

According to Herodotus, the first voyage to Tartessos was that made by the Samian merchant Kolaios, who was blown off course on his way to Egypt and ended up in Tartessos. The voyage ended in great profit to Kolaios and his fellow Samians for, says Herodotus:

> This place had not at that period been exploited, and the consequence was that the Samian merchants, on their return home, made a greater profit on their cargo than any Greeks of whom we have precise knowledge, with the exception of Sostratos of Aegina, the son of Laodamas — with him, nobody can compare.[55]

This would be put down as another one of those wonderful stories told by Herodotus were it not for two unrelated discoveries that seem to confirm the basic historical credibility of his account. The first is the discovery just over ten years ago, at the site of Gravisca in southern Etruria, of a late sixth century B.C.E. inscribed stone cippus with a dedication reading "I belong to Aeginetan Apollo; Sostratos [son of...] had made me." The patronymic is missing but it is hard not to associate this text with Herodotus's Sostratos, although the lettering on the cippus suggests a date for Sostratos over a century later than that for Kolaios implicit in the literary record.[56]

The second notable discovery concerns a group of ivory combs excavated at the Heraion on Samos, Kolaios's native island, carved in a style very similar to that known from several ivory combs reputed to come from the site of Bencarron, near Carmona in Andalusia, Spain, and now in the possession of the Hispanic Society of America (New York). Both bodies of material can be dated to the third quarter of the seventh century B.C.E., and it has been argued that the Samos ivories are actually West Phoenician products, dedicated to Hera by Kolaios following his safe (and profitable) return from the land of Tartessos.[57]

No precise dates can yet be assigned to the remains of Iron Age mining and smelting in Iberia, where evidence for both copper and silver exploitation has been uncovered. Yet some Phoenician pottery, however fragmentary, has been found at these ancient metallurgical sites, and it seems reasonable to take this as evidence for actual Phoenician metallurgical activity in Spain.[58] The site of Toscanos has even produced fragments of ancient blowpipes or tuyeres (German *Blasebalgdüsen*), the piece that connected the bellows to the smelting furnace.[59]

Metals must have played a major role in the economy of the Phoenicians, as for the ancient Greeks, and the search for new mineral resources might have been a significant factor in the mercantile and colonial activities that opened up the western Mediterranean to Phoenician[60] (and Greek) exploitation. But the evidence for these activities goes back no earlier than the eighth century B.C.E. and, for the "far west," not much before ca. 700 B.C.E. This is some 250 years later than the time of Hiram of Tyre, Solomon and the Tarshish fleet.

Although Greek authors seem to have had fairly concrete ideas regarding the land of Tartessos, one has the impression that for biblical authors the land of Tarshish was some sort of "never-never-land," a far-off land of changing location. Connections with silver (Ezekiel 27:12; Jeremiah 10:9) might have something to do with Tartessos and Greco-Phoenician interests in Spanish silver, but other references (for example Genesis 10:4; Isaiah 23:1, 66:19; Jonah 1:3) cannot possibly be located in the western Mediterranean.

The Phoenicians of literature, as known from the Old Testament and Homer (especially the Odyssey), seem to have their "historical" background in the world of the eighth and seventh centuries B.C.E. Despite many learned and ingenious attempts, it is still not possible to reconstruct a *mise en scène* for Phoenicians in the Mediterranean world prior to ca. 800 B.C.E. The history of the Phoenicians in the Levant, especially in their Phoenician homeland during the period ca. 1200–800 B.C.E., is a history that remains to be written.

Notes

1. D. Harden, *The Phoenicians* (Harmondsworth, 1971); S. Moscati, *The World of the Phoenicians* (New York, 1968); G. Garbini, *I Fenici: storia e religione* (Naples, 1980).
2. I.A. Khalifeh, "A Stratigraphic and Ceramic Analysis of the Late Bronze and Iron Age Periods from Area II, Sounding X A/B–8/9, at Sarepta (Modern Sarafand), Lebanon" (Ph.D. diss., University of Pennsylvania, 1981); W.P. Anderson, "A Stratigraphic and Ceramic Analysis of the Late Bronze and Iron Age Strata of Sounding Y at Sarepta" (Ph.D. diss., University of Pennsylvania, 1979).
3. J.B. Pritchard et al., *Sarepta, A Preliminary Report on the Iron Age* (Philadelphia 1975); idem, *Recovering Sarepta, A Phoenician City* (Princeton, 1978). Of the many articles on Sarepta, special mention should be made of J.B. Pritchard, "The Phoenicians in Their Homeland," *Expedition* 14/1 (1971): 14–23.
4. R. Saidah, "Fouilles de Khaldé, Rapport préliminaire sur la première et deuxième campagnes," *Bulletin du Musée de Beyrouth* 19 (1966): 51–90; M.W. Prausnitz, "Die Nekropolen von Akhziv und die Entwicklung der Keramik vom 10. bis zum 7. Jahrhundert v. Chr. in Akhziv, Samaria und Ashdod," in *Phönizier im Westen*, ed. H.-G. Niemeyer (Mainz am Rhein, 1982), pp. 31–44; C.N. Johns, "Excavations at Pilgrims' Castle, ʿAtlīt, 1933," *QDAP* 6 (1937): 121ff.
5. S.V. Chapman, "A Catalogue of Iron Age Pottery from the Cemeteries of Khirbet Silm, Joya, Qrayé and Qasmieh of South Lebanon," *Berytus* 21 (1972): 55–194.
6. P.M. Bikai, *The Pottery of Tyre* (Warminster, 1978); idem, "The Late Phoenician Pottery Complex and Chronology," *BASOR* 229 (1978): 47–56.
7. Khalifeh, "A Stratigraphic and Ceramic Analysis" (see note 2), pp. 300f., 487 (Table 1c), 488 (Table 1d).
8. For early dating, see F.M. Cross, "Early Alphabetic Scripts," in *Symposia Celebrating the Seventy-Fifth*

Anniversary of the Founding of the American Schools of Oriental Research (Cambridge, Mass., 1979), pp. 97–123; idem, "Newly Found Inscriptions in Old Canaanite and Early Phoenician Scripts," *BASOR* 238 (1980): 1–20.

9. In the establishment of these dates we seem to be dealing with the first chronological argument based upon dendrochronology for, according to Pliny the Elder (*N.H.* XVI.216), writing in 77 C.E.., the cedar beams in the temple of Apollo in Utica were 1,178 years old. Cf. Moscati, *The World of the Phoenicians* (note 1), p. 99.
10. H.-G. Niemeyer, "Orient im Okzident — Die Phöniker in Spanien. Ergebnisse der Grabungen in der archäologischen Zone von Torre del Mar (Malaga)," *MDOG* 104 (1972): 5–44; idem, "Die phönizische Niederlassung Toscanos: eine Zwischenbilanz," in *Phönizier in Westen* (see note 4), pp. 185–206; H. Schubart, "Phönizische Niederlassung an der Iberischen Südküste," ibid., pp. 207–34. For recent French work on the Spanish coast, see J.M.J. Gran Aymerich, "Málaga: ville phénicienne," *Archeologia* 179 (1983): 34–40.
11. J.D. Muhly, "Homer and the Phoenicians," *Berytus* 19 (1970): 44–47; Bikai, *The Pottery of Tyre* (see note 6), p. 75. Of fundamental importance is R. Carpenter, "Phoenicians in the West," *AJA* 62 (1958): 35–53. C.R. Krahmalkov, "The Foundation of Carthage, 814 B.C. The Douimès Pendant Inscription," *JSS* 26 (1981): 177–191, offers an interesting attempt at defending the traditional chronology, but ignores the arguments presented by W. Culican, "Almuñécar, Assur and Phoenician Penetration of the Western Mediterranean," *Levant* 2 (1970): 35–36. For the UNESCO project cf. L.E. Stager, "Carthage: A View from the Tophet," in *Phönizier im Westen* (see note 4), pp. 155–166.
12. For this work, see note 4. Mention should also be made of G. Bunnes, *L'expansion phénicienne en Méditerranée. Essai d'interprétation fondé sur une analyse des traditions littéraires* (Brussels-Rome, 1979), which as indicated by the subtitle, is based upon an analysis of the literary sources. Such evidence is of great historical interest but of little value in attempting to date the Phoenician colonization of the western Mediterranean.
13. The first convincing interpretation of the famous Nora Stone inscription was by B. Peckham, "The Nora Inscription," *Or.* 41 (1972): 457–68. See also M. Delcor, "Reflexions sur l'inscription phénicienne de Nora en Sardaigne," *Syria* 45 (1968): 323–52; F.M. Cross, "An Interpretation of the Nora Stone," *BASOR* 208 (1972): 13–19. The remarks of J.C.L. Gibson, *Textbook of Syrian Semitic Inscriptions*, vol. III: *Phoenician Inscriptions* (Oxford, 1982), p. 28, are not to be taken seriously. The text is difficult to translate but even more difficult to place in a historical context.
14. A. Jodin, *Mogador, comptoir phénicien du Maroc atlantique* (Tanger, 1966), pp. 77–120.
15. Pritchard, *Recovering Sarepta* (see note 3), pp. 82–84.
16. See J.N. Coldstream, *Greek Geometric Pottery* (London, 1968); idem, *Geometric Greece* (London, 1977), p. 385 (chronological chart); A. Snodgrass, *The Dark Age of Greece* (Edinburgh, 1971).
17. J. Boardman, *The Greeks Overseas. Their Early Colonies and Trade*, 3d ed. (London, 1980), pp. 38–51 (east) and 162–169 (west). This subject has an enormous bibliography, but special emphasis must be given to the various publications of the Centre Jean Berard, Institut Français de Naples, especially the colloquia on *Les céramiques de la Grèce de l'Est et leur diffusion en Occident* (Paris, 1978); and *Nouvelle contribution à l'étude de la société et de la colonisation eubéennes* (Naples, 1981) and the paper there by D. Ridgway, "The Foundation of Pithekoussai," on pp. 45–56.
18. P.J. Riis, *Sukas I: The North-East Sanctuary and the First Settling of Greeks in Syria and Palestine* (Copenhagen, 1970), p. 158.
19. J. Boardman, "Greek Potters at Al Mina?," *Anatolien Studies* 9 (1959): 163–169. The vase in question is a skyphos with multiple-brush freehand decoration.
20. P. Courbin, "Une nouvelle fouille française sur la côte syrienne: a-t-on redécouvert l'antique Posideion à Ras el Bassit, site deux fois millénaire?," *Archeologia* 116 (1978): 48–62.
21. Bikai, *The Pottery of Tyre* (see note 6), Pls. XXII A.1, XXX.3, and see comments by J.N. Coldstream in *Phönizier im Westen* (note 4), p. 257.

22. B.B. Shefton, "Greeks and Greek Imports in the South of the Iberian Peninsula. The Archaeological Evidence," in ibid., p. 343 (and see comments there by J.N. Coldstream, p. 369).
23. For the tomb, see R. Saidah, "Une tombe de l'Age du Fer à Tambourit (région de Sidon)," *Berytus* 25 (1977): 135–146. For the MG II pyxis, see P. Courbin, "Une pyxis géométrique argienne (?) au Liban," ibid., pp. 147–157.
24. P. Bordreuil, "Épigraphie d'amphore phénicienne du 9è siècle," *Berytus* 25 (1977): 159–161.
25. See the annual for 1981, "Chronique des fouilles et découvertes archéologiques à Chypre," *BCH* 106 (1982): 685–744. For the Iron Age in particular, see V. Karageorghis, *Cyprus, from the Stone Age to the Romans* (London, 1982), pp. 114–127.
26. Karageorghis, ibid., pp. 120–121. For foundation legends relating to the Greek colonization of Cyprus, see M. Fortin, "Fondation de villes grecques à Chypre: Legendes et découvertes archéologiques," in *Mélanges d'Études Anciennes offerts à Maurice Lebel* (Quebec, 1980), pp. 25–44.
27. Karageorghis, *Cyprus* (see note 25), pp. 123–126.
28. F. Vandenabeele, "Quelques particularités de la civilisation d'Amothonte à l'époque du Cypro-Géometrique," *BCH* 92 (1968): 103–114.
29. M.G.G. Amadasi and V. Karageorghis, *Fouilles de Kition. III. Inscriptions phéniciennes* (Nicosia, 1977), pp. 149–160 (D 21, P1. XVIII, 1, 2; Fig. 23); M. Liverani, "Ciocca di capelli o focaccia di ginepro?" *Revista di Studi Fenici* 3 (1975): 37–41.
30. Amadasi and Karageorghis, *Fouilles de Kition* (see note 29), pp. 188–189 (F 6, P1. XXVIII, 3). For *Skn*, see E. Lipiński, "*Skn* et *Sgn* dans le sémitique occidental du Nord," *Ugarit-Forschungen* 5 (1973): 191–207; O. Masson and M. Sznycer, *Recherches sur les Phéniciens à Chypre* (Geneva-Paris, 1972), pp. 69–76. From the site of Cebel Ireş, in Cilicia, comes a Phoenician text of ca. 600 B.C.E., to be published by J. Russell and P.G. Mosca [a land grant text from one *ʾslprn*, the *skn* of *ylbš*]; see brief report by Russell and Mosca in *AJA* 87 (1983): 246.
31. B. Peckham, "Notes on a Fifth Century Phoenician Inscription from Kition, Cyprus (C1S 86)," *Or.* 37 (1968): 304–324, especially 321. For the various sites named "New City," see M. Sznycer, "Recherches sur les toponymes phéniciens en Mediterranee ocidentale," in *La toponymie antique. Actes du Colloque de Strasbourg, 1975* (Leiden, 1977), pp. 171–172.
32. H. Jacob Katzenstein, *The History of Tyre* (Jerusalem, 1973), pp. 207–210.
33. Coldstream, *Geometric Greece* (see note 16), pp. 55–71; idem, "Greeks and Phoenicians in the Aegean," in *Phönizier im Westen* (see note 4), pp. 261–275. For recent material from Lefkandi beyond that published in *Lefkandi I: The Iron Age. Plates and Text* (1979, 1980), see H.W. Catling, "Archaeology in Greece, 1981–82," in *Archaeological Reports for 1981–82*, 3–62, pp. 15–17; M. Popham, E. Touloupa and L.H. Sackett, "The Hero of Lefkandi," *Antiquity* 56 (1982): 169–174.
34. See illustrations in V. Karageorghis, *Ancient Cyprus, 7,000 Years of Art and Archaeology* (Baton Rouge, 1981), pp. 105–119.
35. T.J. Dunbabin, *The Greeks and Their Eastern Neighbours* (London, 1957), pp. 40–43; J. Boardman, "The Khaniale Tekke Tombs, II," *BSA* 62 (1967): 57–75; Coldstream, "Greeks and Phoenicians in the Aegean," in *Phönizier im Westen* (see note 4), pp. 261–275; R.O. Higgins, "Early Greeek Jewellery," *BSA* 64 (1969): 143–153; Boardman, *The Greeks Overseas* (see note 17), pp. 56–62.
36. For a critical rejection of the immigrant craftsmen interpretation, see A. Lebessi, "The Fortetsa Gold Rings," *BSA* 70 (1975): 169–176.
37. For the bowl and its inscriptions, see Coldstream, "Greeks and Phoenicians in the Aegean," in *Phönizier im Westen* (note 4), pp. 271–272; M. Sznycer, "L'inscription phénicienne de Tekke, près de Cnossos," *Kadmos* 18 (1979): 89–93. For a suggested eleventh century B.C.E. dating, see Cross, "Newly Found Inscriptions" (note 8). 8).
38. K. Kübler, "Eine Bronzeschale im Kerameikos," in *Studies Presented to David M. Robinson*, vol. II (St. Louis, 1953), pp. 25–29; idem, *Kerameikos V: Die Nekropole des 10. bis 8. Jahrhunderts* (Berlin, 1954), pp.

237f., Pl. 162. In *Phönizier im Westen* (see note 4) p. 264, Coldstream calls the bowl "Syro-Phoenician," but in *Geometric Greece* (see note 16), p. 60, he argues for manufacture by a Phoenician craftsman on Cyprus and thus dating to about the time of the Phoenician colonization of Kition.

39. I.J. Winter, "Phoenician and North Syrian Ivory Carving in Historical Context: Questions of Style and Distribution," *Iraq* 38 (1976): 16.
40. For the South Syrian school (Arslan Tash, Samaria), centered round Damascus, see I.J. Winter, "Is There a South Syrian Style of Ivory Carving in the Early First Millennium B.C.?" *Iraq* 43 (1981): 101–130. The basic distinction between North Syrian and Phoenician ivories goes back to F. Poulsen, *Der Orient und die frühgriechische Kunst* (Leipzig, 1912), pp. 38–53, and was elaborated in a number of publications by R.D. Barnett, especially in his *Catalogue of the Nimrud Ivories in the British Museum* (London, 1957).
41. J. Matthers et al., "Black-on-Red Ware in the Levant," *Journal of Archaeological Science* 10 (1983): 369–382. There is still great controversy regarding the chronology of these juglets; their first appearance in the Aegean, at the Seraglio cemetery on the island of Keos, can be dated just after 850 B.C.E. Cf. Coldstream, in *Phönizier im Westen* (see note 4), p. 268. For the several types of Black-on-Red ware, see W. Culican, "The Repertoire of Phoenician Pottery," in ibid., pp. 55–64.
42. B.B. Shefton, in ibid., pp. 337–370; and see the distribution map, p. 340, Abb. 1.
43. A.W. Johnston and R.E. Jones, "The 'SOS' Amphora," *BSA* 73 (1978): 103–141 (with examples from the "far west" on pp. 120–121).
44. G. Buchner, "Die Beziehungen zwischen der euböischen Kolonie Pithekoussai auf der Insel Ischia und dem nordwestsemitischen Mittelmeerraum in der zweiten Hälfte des 8 Jhs. v. Chr.," in *Phönizier im Westen* (see note 4), pp. 277–306; A. Rathje, "Oriental Imports in Etruria in the Eighth and Seventh Centuries B.C.: Their Origin and Implications," in *Italy Before the Romans*, eds. D. and F. Ridgway (London, 1979), pp. 145–183.
45. Johnston and Jones, "The 'SOS' Amphora" (see note 43), pp. 115–16. For "SOS" amphorae in Italy, see also I. Strøm, *Problems Concerning the Origin and Early Development of the Etruscan Orientalizing Style*, vol. 2 (Odense, 1971). pp. 233–236.
46. Cf. G. Bunnens, "Commerce et Diplomatie phéniciens au temps de Hiram Ier de Tyr," *Journal of the Economic and Social History of the Orient* 19 (1976): 1–31; idem, *L'expansion phénicienne* (1979), pp. 57–66.
47. Ibid., pp. 331–48; M. Elat, "Tarshish and the Problem of Phoenician Colonisation in the Western Mediterranean," *Orientalia Lovaniensia Periodica* 13 (1982): 55–69.
48. Contra U. Täckholm, "Neue Studien zum Tarsis-Tartessosproblem," *Opuscula Rom.* 10 (1974–75): 41–57; P. Cintas, "Tarsis-Tartessos-Gadès," *Semitica* 16 (1966): 5–37.
49. E.C.B. MacLaurin, "The Phoenician Ship from Tyre Described in Ezekiel 27," *The International Journal of Nautical Archaeology* 7 (1978): 80–83.
50. S.G. Checkland, *The Mines of Tharsis. Roman, French and British Enterprise in Spain* (London, 1967); B. Rothenberg and A. Blanco-Freijeiro, *Studies in Ancient Mining and Metallurgy in South-West Spain* (London, 1981).
51. C. Derré, "Caracteristiques de la distribution des gisements à étain et tungstene dans l'ouest de l'Europe," *Mineralium Deposita* 17 (1982): 55–77; D.J. Fox, "Tin Mining in Spain and Portugal," in *A Second Technical Conference on Tin*, vol. I (Bangkok, 1969), pp. 223–274; D. Thadeu, "Les gisements stanno-wolframitiques du Portugal," *Ann. Soc. Geol. Belg., Liège* 96 (1973): 5–30.
52. J.M. Blázques, *Tartessos y los orígines de la colonización fenicia en ocidente,* 2d ed. (Salamanca, 1975). Also the papers in *Tartessos y sus Problemas* (V Symposium Internacional de Prehistoria Peninsular) (Barcelona, 1969).
53. Pseudo-Aristotle, *De mirabilibus auscultationibus*, 134–135 [as quoted by B.B. Shefton in *Phönizier im Westen* (see note 4), p. 341].
54. New papyrus fragments of the Geryonēis were discovered in 1967; see P. Brize, *Die Geryonēis des Stesischorus und die frühgriechische Kunst* (Würzburg, 1980).

55. Herodotus IV.152, translated by A. de Selincourt (Harmondsworth, 1972).
56. D. Ridgway, "Archaeology in Central Italy and Etruria, 1968–73," in *Archaeological Reports for 1973–74*, 42–59 (Athens, 1974), pp. 49–50; M. Torelli, *La Parola del Passato* 26 (1971): 44–67. A.W. Johnston, "The Rehabilitation of Sostratos," *La Parola del Passato* 27 (1972): 416–423, dates Sostratos to the late sixth century B.C.E., on the basis of this inscription, but then attempts to associate him with the western Mediterranean oil trade. Herodotus makes no direct connection between Kolaios and Sostratos and there is no cause to associate the latter with Tartessos. Cf. B.B. Shefton, in *Phönizier im Westen* (note 4), p. 364, n. 79.
57. B. Freyer-Schauenburg, "Kolaios und die westphönizischen Elfenbeine," *Mitteilungen des Deutschen Archäologischen Instituts, Abteilung Madrid* 7 (1966): 89–108; Shefton, in *Phönizier im Westen* (see note 4), pp. 344–345.
58. Rothenberg and Blaco-Freijeiro, *Studies in Ancient Mining* (see note 50), pp. 171–173 (and for pottery, see p. 147, Fig. 165). It must be recognized that the main thrust of this research project was the recovery of evidence for prehistoric metallurgical activity.
59. H.G. Niemeyer, "'Phönizische' Blasebalgdüsen? Die Funde im spanischen Toscanos im zeitgenössischen Vergleich," *Der Anschnitt* 35 (1983): 50–58; idem, in *Phönizier im Westen* (see note 4), pp. 200–203.
60. Y.B. Tsirkin, "Economy of the Phoenician Settlements in Spain," in *State and Temple Economy in the Ancient Near East,* I and II, Orientalia Analecta 5–6 (Leuven, 1979), pp. 547–564; S. Frankenstein, "The Phoenicians in the Far West: A Function of Neo-Assyrian Imperialism," in *Power and Propaganda. A Symposium on Ancient Empires*, ed. M.T. Larsen (Copenhagen, 1979), pp. 263–294, especially p. 281 (and see comments there by R. McC. Adams, pp. 395–396).

The Relations Between Egypt and Israel from El-Amarna to the Babylonian Conquest

Donald B. Redford

THIS PAPER WILL BE DIVIDED into four parts, organized partly on thematic and partly on chronological lines. The overall purpose will be to explore the varying policies and attitudes of Egypt toward the southern sector of the Levantine coast within which the settlement and political evolution of Israel will prove meaningful.

The Egyptian Empire of the Nineteenth–Twentieth Dynasties and the Establishment of Proto-Israelite Elements in Palestine

While the New Kingdom inherited a unified concept of imperialism from its Middle Kingdom roots,[1] the application of this concept differed radically from region to region.[2] The practical organization and the mechanisms intended to establish Egyptian hegemony, which had proved workable in the Sudanese dependencies in the Twelfth, Thirteenth and early Eighteenth Dynasties, could in no way be applied to Asia. In the south a "king's son," or viceroy,[3] sat over an administration modelled exactly on that of Egypt. In the north the bureaucratic infrastructure was rudimentary in the extreme, and its control and responsibilities quite limited. No special offices were created here, the administration being parcelled out on an *ad hoc* basis among fortress-commandants, battalion-commanders, marshallers, charioteers, garrison-commanders and messengers. The ubiquitous, but vague, *imy-r ḫ3st* was more a courtesy epithet than a functional title,[4] and under no circumstances should it be equated with the Akkadian *rabiṣu* or *šākin mâti.*[5]

To a great extent the machinery for the reduction and control of the economy of the northern territories was adapted from that of Egypt proper. The tax system imposed on the Canaanite *ḫazanūti* was that of the "home counties,"[6] the working of fields as *khato*-lands of pharaoh was borrowed from the Nile,[7] and Egyptian "bailiffs" were to be found in Canaan as they were in Egypt.[8] As at home, the paramilitary Medjay force policed the Canaanite cities.[9]

Readjustments in the territories of the northern conquered lands were minimal or nonexistent. Although certain cities such as Gaza, Sumur and Kumidi (to name those in use at the end of the Eighteenth Dynasty)[10] were set aside for the residence of Egyptian commissioners, we cannot speak of "provinces," a concept alien to Egyptian thinking. The Egyptians conceived of control of conquered territory by recourse to the notion of the "circuit" (*pẖrt*) of a designated officer,[11] who thus became a "circuit official" (*pẖr.ty*).[12] All those Egyptians who appear in Amarna letters under the local rubric *rabiṣu* are nothing more than "circuit-officials," and to conjure up "provinces" out of their *ad hoc* assignments leads to confusion.[13]

Ramesside Egypt refused to consider its northern provinces desirable for the kind of active colonization it was practicing in Nubia and Kush. Palestine was valued for the routes which led through it to the north,[14] secondarily for the few resources it could contribute to the pharaonic exchequer. All means to secure these routes were employed, including the establishing of manned strong-points,[15] the dismantling of potentially hostile fortifications,[16] and the partial deportation of the population.[17] Except possibly for the southern coastal plain, few attempts were made to implant any immigrant Egyptian elements or to insinuate any Egyptian cultic practices. Certain coastal cities, such as Ashkelon and Jaffa, impressed the Egyptians with their commercial possibilities, and consequently were used as business centers vis-à-vis Syrian cities.[18]

The Canaanites for their part accepted the light Egyptian yoke relatively willingly. The sophisticated cities in the coastal plain and valleys had long since come to terms with Pharaoh. They continued to be governed, not only by the "laws of the palace" (as the Egyptians would have put it),[19] but also by their own customary law. They enjoyed commercial relations with Egypt outside of their tax obligations as members of the empire and, after the Egypto-Hittite peace, were able to trade up and down the Levantine coast almost at will.[20] Egyptians in small numbers frequented their cities[21] and, on the part of the Canaanites, a "descent" into Egypt was perfectly acceptable.[22] Egyptian luxury goods were to be seen in Canaanite *suqs*, Egyptian commercial agents made the rounds on behalf of their employers in the Egyptian temples,[23] and garrison troops, though chagrined at the prospect of long service abroad,[24] might even take to native cults and traditions.[25]

The sparsely populated hill country, however, already stripped of its inhabitants in the fifteenth century B.C.E., held no attraction for the Egyptian authorities who, even in the Eighteenth Dynasty, had shown a disinclination to police and control it. It was into this inhospitable upland, where it was still possible to enjoy an existence free of imperial authority, that the great folk-movement of the Late Bronze Age made its dramatic ingress.[26] If, as is becoming increasingly evident, the early Hebrews belonged to that amorphous community to which the Egyptians gave the loose designation *š3św*,[27] then they had always been and were to continue to be "beyond the pale" of Egyptian laws and cultural traditions.

It was the ambivalent attitude of the pharaonic administration toward these tribesmen from "beyond the pale" that informed the history of the area during the thirteenth century B.C.E. Not part of the original imperial structure in Palestine, and with no tradition of subservience to Egypt, the Shasu constituted a threat to the routes aforesaid, and at best an indigestible element in a Canaan which had long since come to terms with Egypt. The arrival by force of the Philistines and Tjekkel at key points on two of the three all-important routes to the north complicated Egypt's problems at a time of increasing political weakness. Like the Shasu, the Philistines were alien to the pharaonic imperial structure,[28] and it was only a matter of time before the refusal of these two groups to submit and be subverted in the traditional way brought the empire in the north to an end.

The Nature of Tanite Relationships with Palestine

Egypt entered the eleventh century B.C.E. in a state of military and economic decline, and there could be no question of maintaining traditional forms of imperial rule. The Ramesside house had wholly discredited itself.[29] Amun, in the oracular-juridical parlance of the day, had "appointed" as an "officer" for "the north of his land"[30] one Nesubanebdjed who had been in all probability nought but a trusted officer of the last Ramesside king. This worthy, catapulted (by marriage?)[31] to the kingship, and the four generations who followed him, ruled from Tanis, the new city which had arisen "phoenix-like" from the ruins of Pi-Ramesses in the northeast Delta.[32]

Whatever relationship the last Ramessides had attempted to perpetuate with the Asiatics, there could be no question of the Twenty-First Dynasty's inability to claim suzerainty over any territory east of the Delta. Even Byblos, the oldest state in the Levant to have been subverted by Egypt, demanded payment for its goods; and the present ruler averred strenuously that his ancestors had been paid for their services.[33] Unable to command compliance with their demands, the Tanite kings consciously fostered a commercial policy which involved them in cartels with the now-independent states of the coast.[34] Through the latter, diplomatic contact was still maintained with the great states of western Asia, including Assyria, whose thrusts toward the Syrian coast were now being felt in the Levant.[35] Military commands reminiscent of the exploits of old credited to the mighty Ramesside princes are indeed found at the Tanite court;[36] but whether they are evidence of military campaigns in Palestine is wholly unknown. Our sparse sources for the period occasionally throw up servants of Asiatic origin, but whether they arrived in Egypt as prisoners of war or through the slave-trade remains uncertain.[37] Egypt did, indeed, remember vividly the territory in the north over which she had once exercised sovereignty, as the detail of the geographical section of the Onomasticon of Amenemope clearly shows; but it was a region which no longer delivered taxes nor received Egyptian commissioners.[38]

Egypt, Israel and the Philistines under the Monarchy

The beginning of the first millennium B.C.E. witnessed the assimilation from an Egyptian point of view of the "indigestible" elements of the outgoing Late Bronze Age in West Asia into an at once familiar and manageable framework. This was not a "northern district of foreign lands" (as a New Kingdom scribe would have termed it), reduced to subservient status, but rather the ingredients of a "sphere of influence" encompassing a group of disunited states which Egypt gradually came to realize could be used as a buffer against the north.

For a relatively short period coeval with the last quarter of the eleventh and the whole of the tenth century B.C.E., there was a brief attempt to revive a New Kingdom policy of force. Even this was ambivalent. Egypt must have relished the sight of the birth of an Israelite state resulting in protracted hostilities with the Philistines;[39] the evidence of pharaonic attacks on the Shephelah,[40] trade with Israel,[41] and the diplomatic marriage of Solomon to an Egyptian princess[42] underscores an erstwhile alliance with Israel against the occupants of that most sensitive area from Egypt's point of view, viz. the coastal route to the north. But Pharaoh's court could also give aid and comfort to Israelite dissidents,[43] and could seriously contemplate preemptive strikes against a Solomonic kingdom grown too powerful in the view of the Egyptian administration. The rise of a new ethnic element within the ruling class in Egypt, viz. the Libyans,[44] whose role in Egyptian society for two centuries had been military, made such a policy of all-out belligerence to solve Egypt's "northern question" very attractive indeed.[45]

The outward manifestations of Sheshonq's Asiatic campaigning clearly show a conscious attempt to revive Ramesside forms: the stele announcing the *casus belli*,[46] the stele set up in conquered territory,[47] the head-smiting scene and toponym list.[48] But there can be no question that no matter what military expertise Sheshonq possessed, nor whatever long-range policy he had conceived, he nonetheless presided over an Egyptian establishment incapable of resurrecting the New Kingdom empire. The insinuation into the Egyptian countryside, especially in the Delta, of communities of soldiering Meshwesh tribesmen, not keen to assimilate themselves into native society, played havoc with the unity of purpose and the *élan vital* of the Egyptians. Very shortly after their coming to power with the accession of Sheshonq I, the intestate feuding of the chief families of the Meshwesh came to the fore, weakening the state. Osorkon II may well have flattered himself on his contribution to the coalition that fought at Qarqar, but his paltry 1,000 shows clearly how Egypt had lost the initiative, inclination and ability to fight abroad.[49] The ninth century B.C.E. witnessed two major attempts to rebel on the part of the Thebaid and, although the success of the Eleventh and the Seventeenth Dynasties was not to be repeated, the Libyan Twenty-Second Dynasty in the process was shown up as incapable of controlling the country, and Egypt was effectually divided.[50] It is not imprecise observation nor a hyperbolic cast of writing that makes Isaiah describe Egypt in chapter 19 as anarchic and disunited. In the mid-eighth century B.C.E. anyone proceeding from Judah to the

Delta and up the Nile would have encountered no less than seven fiefs of the great chief of the Me(shwesh) and two "kings" in Lower Egypt, two "kings" (Herakleopolis and Hermopolis) in Middle Egypt, and the temple estate of Amun in the Thebaid. The "legitimate" king of the Twenty-Second Dynasty directly controlled only Tanis and its environs and Athribis and Memphis; all other lords temporal, while they offered him lip service, ran their own bailiwicks independently.[51]

An investigation of Egyptian toponyms used in biblical texts of the eighth through sixth centuries B.C.E. (excluding the Exodus account) shows, as expected, that Israel and Judah were more familiar with the Bubasite reaches of the Delta, from Heliopolis to Tanis and Sile, than with the central or eastern parts of Lower Egypt. Interestingly, as is well known, the contemporary glyptic art of the Hebrews shows a preference for the "winged Khopry"[52] which was in fact a prominent icon of the Raᶜ-noufe district[53] around Sile.[54]

Egypt exchanged a passive for an active role in West Asian politics under the leadership of Sais, the city which more than any other was responsible for the risorgimento Egypt experienced in the seventh and sixth centuries B.C.E.[55] Nevertheless, Egyptian policy toward Israel, Judah and the coastal states shows a continuation of the ambivalent posture of the Twenty-First Dynasty; Egypt might be conspicuous by its absence (as at Samaria in 722 or Ashdod in 712 B.C.E.);[56] or unexpectedly on the scene in force (as in 720 under Tofnakhte at Gaza,[57] or in 701 B.C.E. under Sabaco at Eltekeh).[58]

If any single factor governed Egyptian policy, it was the age-old concern with the route leading through the Philistine plain. Shebitku and especially Taharqa, from 690 to 681 B.C.E., undertook to reduce the plain to Egyptian control, and to involve the chief Phoenician cities in anti-Assyrian alliances.[59] After the Assyrian withdrawal from Egypt, the Twenty-Sixth Dynasty attempted to continue the same policy, initially with some success.[60] It is important to keep in mind , however, that such a policy paid little attention to the inland states. True, a *modus vivendi* had been worked out between Judah and Egypt during the reigns of Hezekiah, Manasseh and Amon,[61] which prevented hostility, and even encouraged troop exchanges.[62] But one doubts whether, even from the standpoint of propaganda for home consumption, Egypt would have portrayed Judah as her vassal.[63] Necho II's attempt to go beyond the traditional sphere of the coast, and subvert the inland principalities,[64] was as exceptional as it was anachronistic, and in view of Egypt's limited capabilities vis-à-vis Mesopotamia, was bound to fail. Psammetichus II's enigmatic excursion to Asia,[65] and Apries' feint against the Babylonians before Jerusalem[66] were nothing but gestures. Apries' policy to the end of his reign was one of maintaining good relations with the coastal cities; the annihilation of Judah passed virtually unnoticed in Egypt.

The Influence of Egypt on Israel and Judah

Though the chronological parameters of the title of this paper would suggest that our concerns were primarily political, the subject of Israel's mutual relations with Egypt cannot be left without some nod in the direction of the spiritual debt of both nations to each other. When points of contact are determined, and laid out item by item, it will appear, as one might well have expected, that it is the erstwhile imperial power that has more often than not influenced its smaller neighbor. But what are these points of contact, and can we isolate them in time and place?

In the first place, it would be false to suggest that the direction of contact was a one-way street. The West Delta dialect we call "Late Egyptian," which was dominant as a literary dialect from 1300 to well after 700 B.C.E.,[67] is full of technical and literary terms borrowed either from classical Hebrew or the West Asian dialect ancestral to it.[68] The New Kingdom also knows, in its repertoire of *Novella*, the hero-god versus monster motif,[69] the plot of the goddess-emasculated god,[70] the allegory of Truth and Falsehood,[71] and the motif of the spurned wife.[72] It can be maintained convincingly that none of these topoi are native to Egyptian literature, but have been introduced from West Asia. Similarly, during the New Kingdom the corpus of Egyptian hymnody throws up a *Gattung* not seen before, viz. that of the Penitential Psalm, which bears a striking resemblance in its contents and oral formulaic composition to the "Complaint-Psalm" so familiar from the Hebrew Psalter.[73] Again, one need not posit any Hebrew "borrowing," but may rather detect an Egyptian indebtedness to Asia. But this is a reflection of the presence in Egypt during the Nineteenth and Twentieth Dynasties of people from Palestine, and not necessarily the natural attraction of the West Asian culture and norms.

Egyptian influence on Israel and Judah can be subsumed under four headings: 1) government mechanisms; 2) linguistic borrowings; 3) literary motifs; and 4) philosophical concepts. The first is the most difficult to demonstrate. It has been maintained that not only titles and court organization were in part derived from Egypt during the formative period of the Hebrew state, but also administrative procedures such as the tax and corvée exactions were modelled on Egyptian lines. But very often the organization of a government is an *ad hoc* procedure, and the mechanisms it devises are of a practical nature in order to meet *local* needs. Nevertheless, the proponents of Egyptian influence on Israelite government will insist that the "cabinet officer" of Solomon's administration,[74] the "assembly,"[75] the coregency as an administrative device,[76] or the mechanics of taxation and the corvée are clearly derived from Egyptian prototypes.[77] And one must admit that the phenomena of the "corvée" (מס) and the twelve taxation districts have excellent antecedents in Egypt; and while a ספך, מזכיר or רע־המלך sound no more Egyptian than native Canaanite or Israelite, an attempt at the sophistication of a court ranking system *may* owe something to Egypt.[78] On the other hand, government organization and tax mechanisms under Solomon share much in common with Canaanite practice.[79]

In examining the field of linguistic borrowings, the researcher may feel gratified at having come upon more solid evidence.[80] In the sphere of vocabulary Egyptian loan words are largely confined to those words Israel became familiar with through trade with Africa: river, papyrus, books, reeds, fine linen, red linen, lotus, ebony, natron, ape, alabaster, staff, ring, hin, ephah; or terms which drifted north as the baggage of folklore: Pharaoh, palanquin(?), wise man, king's-wife; or in the wake of the architect. This type of borrowing is understandable and quite convincing. It is more difficult in all cases, however, to concur with those who attempt to elicit Egyptian expressions as inspiration for idioms which now appear in wholly Hebrew guise. It is true that in some cases the similarity between the idiomatic usage in both languages is striking; but at first blush one is at a loss to explain how a language which had little or no vernacular currency in Israel should have insinuated itself in the jargon of semiliterate Israelite peasants.

Not so in the realm of literary motifs and genres. Few would deny the dependence, at scarcely more than a single remove, of Psalm 104 on the hymn to the sun-disc,[81] and of Proverbs 22:17–23:14 on Amenemope.[82] The Song of Songs belongs to the same basic genre, if it was not inspired by the lyric love poetry well known in New Kingdom Egypt.[83] Among other less specific motifs one might site: the sleeplessness of the ruler,[84] the image of the "hidden god,"[85] the idea of god as a "shepherd,"[86] the creation of man in god's image,[87] the "tree of life,"[88] the ethnical contrast between the "hot" and the "silent" man,[89] the *carpe diem* theme of the "Harpers' Songs."[90]

From any such list, however, we must strike out the so-called *Königsnovelle*, an infelicitous term coined by A. Herrmann forty-five years ago.[91] Not only is there no such word in ancient Egyptian, there is no genre or *Gattung* to which such a neologism might apply. The examples of the form elicited by Herrmann actually constitute a heterogeneous collection of genres which include speeches (*mdt*), the motif of king-in-council, the "royal-sitting," the "arrival of the messenger" theme, and embellished annals! What Herrmann has detected is nothing more than a *Tendenz*, a "mind-set," which produces in a variety of forms the contrast between the omniscience and omnipotence of the god-king and the mediocrity of his entourage. Needless to say, this finds no parallel in biblical literature, and I am at a loss to understand why certain scholars[92] raised the matter at all.[93] Certainly the fact that dreams should appear both in Egypt and Israel as vehicles for divine revelation proves nothing: the motif of the dream in ancient literatures is much too widespread to allow of any conscious borrowing.[94]

Israel is also alleged by some to owe a debt to Egypt in the broader realm of basic, "philosophical" concepts; but here I feel the argument often becomes tendentious and controversial. In the sphere of monarchical concepts, for example, a world of difference separates the god-king of Egypt from the "lord's anointed" of Israel. Some superficial parallels have been proposed in choice of terminology, but even these are not very convincing.[95] חכמה, "wisdom," is one of those concepts which, when once mentioned, conjure up a wide vista of innumerable shades of meaning which permeate a culture through and through. Egyptian too throws up a concept, similar in its breadth, which is conveyed by the term *m3ʿt*, "order, right-dealing, truth": but חכמה and *m3ʿt* have little in common. For the former surely we have to invoke parallels from among the other West Semitic cultures of the Levant. In the realm of cosmogony one can sometimes convince oneself that one is hearing strains of the sophisticated Memphite Theology in the Hebrew creation account of Genesis 1;[96] and it is certainly true that these documents demonstrate an occasional parallel of striking similarity. But additional evidence will have to come to light before we can speak of dependence.

Two problems concern the geographical centers which transmitted Egyptian influence in Palestine, and the period (or periods) when this influence was brought to bear most strongly upon the Israelites. It is interesting to note that most of the Egyptian expressions, motifs and ideas which appear "in Hebrew disguise" come from prophetic, psalmodic or "wisdom" books. They thus belong to a broad "literature" which, despite its close association with oral transmission, had early achieved a written, if not canonical, form.[97] Those who wrote, or read and passed on such works were the "literati," the scribes. In Asia we are dealing with a class of erudite individuals known collectively as the "wise." They flourished in Levantine cities where for over a thousand years before the fall of Jerusalem they had been ever and anon bombarded with ideas, and the idioms that expressed them, from the Nile Valley. At this distance in time it is difficult to pinpoint specific "centers of transmission" in which the requisite spiritual ties to Egypt remained strong; but we would be safe in including within a list of candidates such towns as Gaza and Ashkelon in the south,[98] and Tyre and Byblos in the north.[99] One would dearly love to know to what extent, if at all, the cities in the central highland such as Jerusalem or Shechem were exposed to the influence of Egyptian language and literature prior to the establishment of the Hebrew monarchy. Presumably the intensity of such influence ebbed and flowed over the centuries. One is safe in assuming that, while the Egyptian empire held sway, the educated Canaanites would to a certain degree pride themselves on their awareness at least of the content and scope of Egyptian wisdom and *belles lettres*; but after the invasion of the Sea Peoples it is questionable whether the newcomers, Philistines and Israelites, would have or (*could* have) maintained this tradition.

The reign of Solomon is often singled out as the period when, for exigencies of state, a scribal school was established in Jerusalem on Egyptian models, and when Egyptian influence on Israel's culture was strongest. *A priori* the suggestion is a plausible one, but the evidence often adduced for it leaves something to be desired.[100] In particular the problem has to do with the general tenor of the chapters in 1 Kings which purport to give an account of Solomon's reign.

From the close of the Ramesside period in Levantine history a tradition had developed, with the Egyptian "Pharaoh" as the obvious focus, of the "romantic world-monarch." The latter is made out to be a great kingly model from the past, who conquered numerous foreign countries, and to whose court scores of foreign kings present themselves as vassals. His troops are legion and his horses innumerable. The whole earth brings him tribute, and he is renowned for his wisdom. Slave-labor toils on his vast construction projects, thus freeing his own people to pursue their own lives in happiness and satiety. At home he reorganizes the government and the provinces, and engages in works of public welfare; abroad he sends out trading expeditions, especially southward along the Red Sea to Africa. Not least is he remembered for his marriage to the beautiful princess, daughter of a foreign king.[101]

Such is the Egyptian Sesostris, in the eyes of both native and foreign authors of the Late Period;[102] and such also is Solomon to the Deuteronomic author of 1 Kings. Solomon too ruled over numerous conquered states, from the Euphrates to the River of Egypt; he too received the tribute of the whole earth and was renowned for his wisdom. Like Sesostris, Solomon too employed slave-labor on vast building projects, so that the native Israelites could live free and happy lives. He too reorganized the administration, sent trading expeditions down the Red Sea to Africa, and married the daughter of a foreign king. In short, as the Deuteronomist portrays him, Solomon is the Israelite "Sesostris."

Now, "Sesostris" is a mélange of three historical individuals, viz. Senwosret III, Thutmose III and Ramesses II; and in the tales told of him one can still dimly discern historical events. But they are often distorted and misinterpreted, and one would be naive to use them solely as the source for a history. And in the case of Solomon, for whom we do not have the advantage of possessing contemporary sources, one might be wise in withholding judgment until a sober and uncommitted analysis of these later traditions has been undertaken. Then we might see that our confident belief in his reign as a period of intense scribal and intellectual activity, induced by mimicry of whatever foreign culture, is an unconscious assumption based solely upon a tendentious "reading" of the "Sesostris-like" traditions of 1 Kings.

Notes

1. Studies on the concepts, causes and mechanisms of empire, as they apply to Egypt, have begun to proliferate in the past decade. See in particular D. Lorton, *The Juridical Terminology of International Relations in Egyptian Texts through Dyn. XVIII* (Baltimore, 1974); B. Kemp, in *Imperialism in the Ancient World*, eds. P.D.G. Garsney and C.R. Whittakers (Cambridge, 1978), pp. 7ff.; J.P. Frandsen, in *Power and Propoganda: A Symposium on Ancient Empires*, ed. M.T. Larsen (Copenhagen, 1979), pp. 167ff; J. Leclant, in *Le concept d'empire*, ed. M. Duvoyer (Paris, 1980), pp. 49ff; E.J. Bleiberg, "Aspects of the Political, Religious and Economic Basis of Ancient Egyptian Imperialism during the New Kingdom" (Ph.D. diss., University of Toronto, 1984).
2. "To extend the frontier" is the phrase which best connotes the spatial concept of empire held by the Egyptians (cf. *Wb.* IV, 75: 2–4), from the Middle Kingdom [E. Blumenthal, *Untersuchungen zum ägyptischen Königtum des mittleren Reiches* (Berlin, 1970), p. 187] to Graeco-Roman times [O. Firchow, *Thebanischen Tempelinschriften aus griechisch-römischer Zeit* (Berlin, 1957), pp. 8, 10f., 15, 54, etc.]. In general see C. Desroches-Noblecourt, *Le petit temple d'Abou Simbel* (Paris, 1968), vol. I, p. 173, n. 201.
3. On the eccentric use of *s3-nsw* to designate a paramilitary and plenipotentiary function in the First Intermediate Period, see B. Schmitz, *Untersuchungen zum Titel S3-Njsw "Königssohn"* (Bonn, 1976), pp. 255ff.; R. el-Sayed, *BIFAO* 79 (1979), n. *y*; literature in A.R. Schulman, *JSSEA* 8 (1978): 43, n. 1.
4. *Wb.* III, 235: 10; see M.A.K. Mohammed, *ASAE* 56 (1959): 114f.; W. Helck, *MDOG* 92 (1960): 8f.; idem, *Die Beziehungen Ägyptens zu Vorderasien im 3. und 2. Jahrtausend v. Chr.*, 2d ed. (Wiesbaden, 1971), p. 260; M.S. Drower, *CAH* II, ch. 1 (Cambridge, 1973), pp. 417f.
5. *AHw.* II, p. 935; A.L. Oppenheim, *JAOS* 88 (1968): 178f.; *AHw.* III, p. 1141; cf. EA 7:76–77; KUB III, 57, rev. 2–4; E. Edel, in *Geschichte und Altes Testament*, ed. W.F. Albright (Tübingen, 1953),

pp. 44ff.; A. Alt, *Kleine Schriften zur Geschichte des Volkes Israel*, vol. I (Munich, 1953), pp. 187ff.

6. On *inw* and *b3kw*, see Bleiberg. "Basis of Ancient Egyptian Imperialism" (note 1); on *htr*, see D.B. Redford, *Studies in the Ancient Palestinian World* (Toronto, 1972), pp. 144ff.
7. On the *Khato*-lands (mainly temple-owned), see A.H. Gardiner, *The Wilbour Papyrus* II (Oxford, 1948), pp. 165ff.; W. Helck, *Zur Verwaltung des mittleren und neuen Reichs* (Leiden, 1958), pp. 129ff.; H. Kees, *Ancient Egypt, a Cultural Topography* (London, 1961), p. 72; B. Menu, *Le régime juridique des terres et du personne attaché à la terre dans le papyrus Wilbour* (Lille, 1970), pp. 92ff.
8. On the ubiquitous *rwḏw*, "bailiff," in an Asiatic context, cf. *Urk*. IV, 667:11 where the grain-bearing fields of the Esdraelon are assigned to these officers; cf. also 1442:20, R. Lepsius, *Denkmaeler* III (Leipzig, 1900), p. 140c; on the meaning of the term see Gardiner, *The Wilbour Papyrus* II (note 7), p. 21; D.B. Redford, in *The Akhenaten Temple Project*. I. *The Initial Discoveries*, eds. R.W. Smith and D.B. Redford (Warminster, 1977), pp. 108f.; cf. also D. Meeks, *Année lexicographique*, vol. I (Paris, 1980), p. 214; vol. II (Paris, 1981), p. 220; vol. III (Paris, 1982), p. 168.
9. Cf. EA 133:16–17; H. Klengel, in *Ägypten und Kusch* (Berlin, 1977), pp. 227ff.
10. Helck, *Beziehungen* (see note 4), pp. 249, 304ff.
11. Cf. D. Dunham, *Second Cataract Forts*. I. *Semna, Kummeh* (Boston, 1960), R.I.S. 1 (pl. 93A), R.I.S. 9 (pl. 93D); Z. Zaba, *The Rock Inscriptions of Lower Nubia* (Prague, 1974), no. 53, p. 75: *pẖrt m ḥ^{3}t-sp 7 ibd [1] prt*; no. 58, p. 85: *spr pẖrt r nw r nw*.
12. *Urk*. IV, 1112: 5–6.
13. De Vaux's hypothesis that biblical "Canaan" is a reflection of the old, imperial Egyptian usage with reference to its "province" of that name [*JAOS* 88 (1968): 23ff.; cf. A.F. Rainey, *BA* 28 (1965): 106] is ingenious but quite wrong.
14. S. Aḥituv, *IEJ* 28 (1978): 93ff.
15. Cf. J. Weinstein, *BASOR* 241 (1981): 1ff.
16. Cf. D.B. Redford in *Studies in the History and Archaeology of Jordan*, vol. 1, ed. A. Hadidi (Amman, 1982), p. 117.
17. Cf. the author's *King-Lists, Annals and Daybooks* (Toronto, 1984). No one should be deceived into interpreting some of these figures as misplaced "census" results: *pace* J.M.A. Jannssen, *JEOL* 17 (1963): 141ff.
18. Cf. S. Aḥituv, *IEJ* 28 (note 14): 95; D.I. Owen, *Tel Aviv* 8 (1981): 1ff.
19. Cf. K.A. Kitchen, *Ramesside Inscriptions*, vol. I (Oxford, 1975), 9:5; cf. also the "laws of Him-that-is-in-the-Palace," i.e., the king: *Urk*. IV, 903:13, and the "law of Pharaoh" (P. Boulaq X, 11). This "statutory law" is in contradistinction to local, customary law which is called the "laws of this land": K. Sethe, *Ägyptische Lesestücke* (Leipzig, 1928), no. 21:81, 22.
20. The evidence of the past three decades suggests a lively exchange of goods and people throughout the Levant. In general, see Helck, *Beziehungen* (note 4), pp. 428ff.
21. See Helck, *Beziehungen* (note 4), pp. 432ff; cf. *Pahi* [C. Schaeffer, *Le palais royal d'Ugarit* III (Paris, 1955), p. 142 (16.136, lines 9, 11)], and *Ḫeḫea* [ibid., p. 19 (15.11, lines 8–9)], both resident at Ugarit; for the house of an Egyptian merchant (?) at the same site, see *Syria* 51 (1974): 21.
22. Trading expeditions to Egypt by Canaanites, both royal and private, seem to have been common: cf. EA 101:15–17 (ships of Arvad); for the Ugaritic evidence, see C. Virolleaud, *CRAIBL* (1955): 77; Schaeffer, *Palais royal* V (Paris, 1965), p. 116; VI (Paris, 1970), no. 14. The scene of the visiting Canaanite merchant is sometimes the subject for an Egyptian artist in a tomb painting: cf. T. Save-Soderbergh, *Private Tombs at Thebes* I (Oxford, 1957), pl. 23; N. de G. Davies, *JEA* 33 (1974): 40ff. For the Memphite settlement of Canaanite merchants, centered upon the "House of Baʿal," see W. Helck, *Oriens Antiquus* 5 (1966): 2ff.; R. Stadelmann, *Syrisch-Palästinensische Gottheiten in Ägypten* (Leiden, 1967), pp. 32ff.
23. For Egyptian merchants making journeys to Syria (*H3rw*), see Bologna 1094, 5:5–6 [=A.H. Gardiner, *Late Egyptian Miscellanies* (Brussels, 1937), 5:8]. On merchants in general, see D. Meeks, *Hommages Sauneron*, vol. 1 (Cairo, 1979), pp. 249f.

24. Ramesside texts paint a bleak picture of service in garrisons abroad which could be deemed punishment: B.M. 10053, 5:4–24; J. Wilson, *JNES* 7 (1948): 138:51.
25. Cf. the veneration of Mekal by Amenemope, a member of the Beth-Shean garrison: H.O. Thompson, *BA* 30 (1967): 121, fig. 5: cf. idem, *Mekal, the God of Beth-Shan* (Leiden, 1970), but such was generally frowned upon: cf. Anast. I, 20:2–4; J. Černý, *JNES* 14 (1955): 161ff.
26. See R. Giveon, *Les bedouins Shosou des documents égyptiens* (Leiden, 1971), passim; D.B. Redford, *JSSEA* 12 (1982): 74, n. 155.
27. Giveon, ibid., pp. 235ff.; W. Helck, *VT* 18 (1968): 477f.; M. Weippert, *Biblica* 55 (1974): 270f. The presence of toponyms compounded with *Š3św* [cf. *ʿyn-Š3św*: E. Edel, *Ortsnamenlisten aus dem Totentempel Amenophis III* (Bonn, 1966), p. 25; M. Görg, *JNES* 38 (1979): 199ff.; W.A. Ward, in *Festschrift Elmar Edel* (Bamberg, 1979), pp. 29f.] in Lebanon and Syria hardly proves the *Š3św* to have been indigenous there.
28. For recent treatment of the Sea Peoples, see W.F. Albright, "The Sea Peoples in Palestine," in *CAH* II, ch. 33, 2d. ed.; T. Dothan, *The Philistines and Their Material Culture* (New Haven, 1982); W. Helck, *Die Beziehungen Ägyptens und Vorderasiens zur Ägaïs* (Darmstadt, 1979), pp. 132ff. [cf. D.B. Redford, *JAOS* 103 (1983): 481ff.]; A. Malamat, "The Egyptian Decline in Asia and the Sea Peoples," in *World History of the Jewish People* (Tel Aviv, 1971), vol. III, pp. 23ff.; R. Stadelmann, *Saeculum* 19 (1968): 156ff.; A. Strobel, *Der Spätbronzezeitliche Seevölkersturm* (Berlin-New York, 1976).
29. Cf. P. Berlin 10487: E.F. Wente, *Late Ramesside Letters* (Chicago, 1967), p. 53; A.H. Gardiner, *JMEOS* 2 (1912): 61.
30. Cf. Wenamun 2:35 [= A.H. Gardiner, *Late Egyptian Stories* (Brussels, 1932), p. 70]. The term "officer" (*snn<ty>*) was originally the military "chariot-warrior" [A.H. Gardiner, *Ancient Egypt Onomastica* I (London, 1947), *28; A.R. Schulman, *JARCE* 2 (1963): 87f.; Meeks, *Année lexicographique* (see note 8), vol. II, pp. 332f.; vol. III, p. 258]; but here it means something like "the official in charge."
31. Tant-amun was daughter of a simple "esquire (s^3b)," Nebseny: H. Gauthier, *Livre des rois* III (Cairo, 1907–1917), 258(L); P. Montet, *Le drame d'Avaris* (Paris, 1941), p. 189, n. 4. But cf. A. Niwinski, *JARCE* 16 (1979): 50f.
32. The name Tanis first appears in Wenamun 1.3 [= Gardiner, *Stories* (see note 30), p. 61] of Twentieth Dynasty date. Pi-Ramesses was still the residence under Ramesses III [cf. A.H. Gardiner, *JEA* 5 (1920): 192, no. 23, 192f., no. 25; Kitchen, *Ramesside Inscriptions*, vol. V (see note 19), p. 230], and was still in existence at the close of the dynasty [On. Am. 410 = Gardiner, *Onomastica* II (see note 30), *171ff.], thus overlapping with Tanis for a short time: J. van Seters, *The Hyksos, a New Investigation* (New Haven, 1966), pp. 128ff.; M. Bietak, *Tell el-Dabʿa* II (Vienna, 1975), pp. 179ff.; idem, in *Proceedings of the British Academy* 55 (1979): 278f.
33. Wenamun 2:5–13 [= Gardiner, *Stories* (see note 30), pp. 67f.].
34. Albright, *JAOS* 71 (1951): 260f.; idem, in *Robinson Studies* I (St. Louis, 1951), pp. 223ff.; idem, *CAH* II (see note 28), pp. 36f.; J. Leclant, in *The Role of the Phoenicians*, ed. W. Ward (Beirut, 1968), pp. 9ff.
35. For Tiglath-Pileser I's incursion into the Phoenician coast, see *ANET*, 2d ed., p. 275a.
36. Cf. the "chief generalissimo of His Majesty, chief steward of Amunrasonther, chief charioteer of His Majesty... Onkhefenmut," P. Montet, *Les Constructions et le Tombeau de Psousennès à Tanis* (Paris, 1951), p. 59, fig. 21, pl. 39; "general and commander (*ḥ*^{3}*wty*) of pharaoh's archers ... Wenbanebdjed," ibid., p. 84, fig. 31; see further, D.B. Redford, *JAOS* 93 (1973): 4f.
37. Cf. Akh-amun-nekhy and Akh-ptah-nekhy, specifically referred to as "Syrian servants" in a stele of Sheshonq son of Namlot from Abydos: A. Mariette, *Catalogue générale d'Abydos*, no. 1225, 10–11; A.M. Blackman, *JEA* 27 (1941): 92.
38. Cf. R.A. Caminos, *A Tale of Woe* (Oxford, 1977), p. 67 (if indeed *Nhr<n>* is to be read!).
39. On the Philistine role in uniting the Hebrew tribes, see A.D.H. Mayes, *VT* 23 (1973): 151ff.; cf. also K. Koch, *VT* 19 (1969): 78ff.
40. Cf. 1 Kings 9:16; and see A.R. Green, *JBL* 97 (1978): 353ff.; cf. also A. Malamat, in *Studies in the Period*

of David and Solomon, ed. T. Ishida (Tokyo, 1982), pp. 198f.

41. Cf. J.A. Soggin, "The Davidic–Solomonic Kingdom," in *Israelite and Judaean History*, eds. J.H. Hayes and J.M. Miller (London, 1977), pp. 374f.

42. On this marriage see, *inter alia*, J.R. Bartlett, *ZAW* 88 (1976): 222; A. Malamat, *JNES* 22 (1963): 10ff.; idem, *Biblical Archaeology Reader* (New York, 1964), pp. 91f.; idem, in *Studies in the Period of David and Solomon* (see note 40), pp. 198ff.; Redford, *JAOS* 93 (see note 36), p. 5, n. 20, 21; Soggin, *Israelite and Judaean History* (see note 41), p. 375; A.R. Schulman, *JNES* 38 (1979): 187f.

43. K.A. Kitchen, *The Third Intermediate Period in Egypt* (Warminster, 1973), pp. 274f.; B. Halpern, *JBL* 93 (1974): 523; Bartlett, *ZAW* 88, 205ff.; H. Donner, "The Separate States of Israel and Judah," in *Israelite and Judaean History* (see note 41), p. 386; R. North, *Homenaje a Juan Prado* (Madrid, 1975), pp. 200ff.

44. On the Libyans, see G. Moller, *ZDMG* 3 (1924): 36ff.; W. Holscher, *Libyer und Ägypter* (Gluckstadt, 1937); J. Yoyotte, *Mélanges Maspero* IV, ch. 1 (Cairo, 1961), pp. 121ff.; F. Gomaa, *Die libyshen Fürstentümer des Deltas* (Tübingen, 1974); J. Osing, *LdA* 3 (1980): col. 1015ff.

45. Redford, *JAOS* 93 (see note 36), p. 7.

46. G. Legrain, *ASAE* 5 (1904): 38f.; B. Grdseloff, *RHJE* 1 (1947): 95f.; Kitchen, *The Third Intermediate Period* (see note 43), p. 294.

47. Ibid., p. 299, n. 303.

48. G.R. Hughes, *Reliefs and Inscriptions* III, *The Bubastite Portal* (Chicago, 1954).

49. On Osorkon II's pretense at interference in Asian affairs, see Redford, *JAOS* 93 (note 36), pp. 14ff.; on the identification of *Musri* with Egypt, see A.T. Olmstead, *History of Assyria* (New York, 1923), p. 134; idem, *History of Palestine and Syria* (New York, 1931), p. 384; E. Meyer, *Geschichte des Altertums*, Vol. II,2 (Stuttgart and Berlin, 1928), p. 333; H. Tadmor, in *Unity and Diversity*, ed. H. Goedicke (Baltimore, 1975), p. 39.

50. See R.A. Caminos, *The Chronicle of Prince Osorkon* (Rome, 1958).

51. See especially Yoyotte, *Mélanges Maspero* (note 44), ch. 4, pp. 127ff., and Gomaa, *Die libyshen Fürstentümer* (note 44).

52. On the winged scarab on Israelite seals, see the literature cited in A.D. Tushingham, *BASOR* 200 (1970): 71ff.; A.F. Rainey, *BASOR* 245 (1982): 57ff.

53. Piankhy Stele, lines 19, 114 [see Grimal, *La stele troimphale de Pi(ankh)y* (Cairo, 1981)]; possibly the environs of Tanis [Yoyotte, *Mélanges Maspero* (see note 44), ch. 1, p. 129, n. 2; J. Vandier, *RdE* 17 (1965): 170ff.], applied as a designation of Osorkon IV's kingdom between Sile and Bubastis [W. Helck, *Die altägyptische Gaue* (Wiesbaden, 1974), p. 190; H. Gauthier, *Dictionnaire géographique* I (Cairo, 1931), p. 190; III, p. 130; P. Montet, *Géographie de l'Egypte ancienne* (Paris, 1959), vol. I, p. 201], and closely associated with the cults of the eastern frontier [*Edfu* 1, 130f.; P. Montet, *Kemi* 8 (1946): 64, Pl. 15; G. Daressy, *BIFAO* 11 (1914): 35f.].

54. See J. Vandier, *RdE* 17 (1965): 172ff.; on Khopry's solar identification, see K. Mysliwiec, *Studien zum Gott Atum* I (Hildesheim, 1978), pp. 75ff.; E. Brunner-Traut, *Gelebte Mythen* (Darmstadt, 1981), pp. 7ff.

55. See H. Brunner, *LdA* 1 (1975): col. 386ff.; idem, *Saeculum* 21 (1970): 151ff.; R.A. Fazzini, *Miscellanea Wilbouriana* (Brooklyn, 1972), pp. 64f.; H. Kees, *Das Priestertum im ägyptischen Staat* (Leiden, 1953), p. 198; J. Yoyotte, *Histoire de l'art*, vol. I (Paris, 1961), p. 238.

56. On סוא of 2 Kings 17:4 without doubt a transcription of *s3w* (=Sais), see H. Goedicke, *BASOR* 171 (1963): 64ff.; D.B. Redford, *JSSEA* 11 (1981): 75f. We have no indication that this appeal on Hoshea's part ever elicited Egyptian support. On the events of 712 B.C.E., see W. Hallo, *BA* 23 (1960): 56; H. Tadmor, *JCS* 12 (1958): 79ff.; idem, *BA* 29 (1966): 94; A.J. Spalinger, *JARCE* 10 (1973): 95ff.; cf. N. Naʾaman, *BASOR* 214 (1974): 25ff.

57. On the Gaza campaign, see *ANET*, 2d ed., p. 285; Tadmor, *BA* 29 (see note 56): 91; N. Naʾaman, *Tel Aviv* 6 (1979): 68ff. That Tefnakhte was indeed involved in military activity in the desert east of the Delta is supported by the tradition in Diodorus i.45; cf. Plutarch, *De Iside et Osiride*, 8.

58. To take 2 Kings 19:9 seriously in its reference to Taharqa [cf. among others, N. Naʾaman, *VT* 29 (1979): 65, and K.A. Kitchen, *RdE* 34 (1982–83): 65 and n. 33] is to introduce untold confusion. That the king in question was Sabaco (and not Shebitku) can be proven on chronological grounds: see the present author in *JSSEA* (forthcoming).
59. On Taharqa's policy, see in particular A.J. Spalinger, *CdE* 53 (1978): 22ff.
60. On Psammetichus I's appointment, see A.J. Spalinger, *JAOS* 94 (1974): 323ff. On his control of Philistia, and perhaps the Assyrian province of Megiddo [not extended before 648 B.C.E.: see R.A.S. Macalister, *The Excavations of Gezer* (London, 1911), pp. 23ff.], see A. Malamat in *The Age of the Monarchies*, vol. IV (Jerusalem, 1979), p. 205; idem, *VT Suppl.* 28 (1975): 125; also B. Otzen, *Studien über Deuterosacharja* (Copenhagen, 1964), pp. 78ff.; also D.B. Redford, *JAOS* 90 (1970): 477.
61. On possible pro- and anti-Egyptian factions in Judah, see A. Malamat, *VT Suppl.* 28 (note 60): 125f.; T. Ishida, *Annual of the Japanese Biblical Institute* 1 (1975): 23ff.; but cf. idem, *The Royal Dynasties in Ancient Israel* (Berlin, 1977), p. 164, n. 44.
62. Cf. Deuteronomy 17:16. This can only be viewed in the light of the policy of the Twenty-Sixth Dynasty to take foreign contingents into its armed forces pursuant to the treaty with Gyges [see M. Streck, *Assurbanipal und die letzten assyrischen Könige* II (Leipzig, 1916), pp. 20ff; A.J. Spalinger, *JARCE* 13 (1976): 134ff.]. On the Egyptian officers assigned to such foreign contingents, see F.K. Kienitz, *Die politische Geschichte Ägyptens vom 7. bis zum 4. Jahrhundert vor der Zeitwende* (Berlin, 1953), pp. 41ff.; H. Schaeffer, *Klio* 4 (1904): 157, pl. 2; J. Leclant, *BIFAO* 48 (1949): 187; idem, *BIFAO* 50 (1950): 171, n. 2; H. de Meulenaere, *BIFAO* 63 (1963): 21ff.; J. Vercoutter, *BIFAO* 48 (1949): 175. The tradition of Judeans being part of this foreign military presence in Egypt may be preserved in Diodorus i. 66.
63. The Philistine cities seem to have been reduced to vassalage by Egypt: cf. טבתה in the Adon letter, and the use of עבדך by the writer: J.A. Fitzmyer, *Biblica* 46 (1965): 52ff.; on the identity of the town in question, see B. Porten, *BA* 44 (1981): 36ff. But Josiah's entering into treaty with Egypt is doubtful.
64. See A.J. Spalinger, *Or.* 47 (1978): 19ff.; D.B. Redford, *LdA* 4 (1981): col. 379ff.
65. P. Rylands IX, xiv, 16ff; Redford, *JAOS* 90 (see note 60): 479f.
66. Jeremiah 37:5–11; B. Oded, "Judah and the Exile," in *Israelite and Judaean History* (see note 41), p. 473.
67. H.J. Polotsky, in *Textes et languages de l'Egypte pharaonique* (Cairo, 1972), pp. 133ff.
68. See M. Burchardt, *Die altkanaanäischen Fremdworte und Eigennamen in Ägyptischen* (Leipzig, 1909); Helck, *Beziehungen* (see note 4), pp. 505ff.
69. Amherst Fragments [=Gardiner, *Stories* (see note 30), pp. 76ff.]; cf. G. Posener, *AIPHOS* 13 (1953): 61ff.
70. P. D'Orbiney (= Gardiner, ibid., pp. 9ff.); see J. Assmann, *ZAS* 104 (1977): 1ff.; E. Blumenthal, *ZAS* 99 (1972): 1ff.; cf. also M.C. Astour, *Hellenosemitica* (1965): 257f.; D.B. Redford, *A Study of the Biblical Joseph Story* (Leiden, 1970), pp.91ff.
71. P. Chester Beatty II (= Gardiner, ibid., pp. 30ff.); see E. Meltzer, *JNES* 33 (1974): 154, n. 7.
72. Redford, *Joseph* (see note 70), pp. 91ff.
73. No recent comprehensive study of this genre has yet appeared; see A. Erman, *Sitzungsberichte der Bayerischen Akademie der Wissenschaften* (1911): 1088ff.; B. Gunn, *JEA* 3 (1916): 83ff.; among others, see S. Allam, *MDIAK* 24 (1969): 10ff.; J. Assmann, *RdE* 30 (1978): 22ff.; J.J. Clère, *RdE* 27 (1975): 70ff.; G. Posener, ibid., 195ff.; R.J. Williams, *JSSEA* 8 (1978).
74. Cf. R. de Vaux, *RB* 48 (1939): 394ff.; Leclant, *The Role of the Phoenicians* (see note 34), p. 11, and n. 21; Redford, *Ancient Palestinian World* (see note 6), pp. 141ff.; E.W. Heaton, *Solomon's New Men* (London, 1974); T.N.D. Mettinger, *Solomonic State Officials* (Lund, 1971).
75. See J. Wilson, *JNES* 4 (1945): 245.
76. E. Ball, *VT* 27 (1977): 268ff.; cf. E.R. Thiele, *JBL* 93 (1974): 174ff.
77. Redford, *Ancient Palestinian World* (see note 6), pp. 141ff. On the corvée, see the discussion and references in Soggin, in *Israelite and Judaean History* (note 41), pp. 376ff.
78. I have often wondered whether the Davidic and Solomonic lists of government officers (see

2 Samuel 8:16–18; I Kings 4:2–6) were not taken from monuments surviving in the time of the Deuteronomic writer.

79. Cf. J. Gray, *The Legacy of Canaan* (Leiden, 1964), pp. 224f.
80. See especially the works of R.J. Williams and the references there: in *The Legacy of Egypt*, ed. J.R. Harris (Oxford, 1971), pp. 257ff.; *VT Suppl.* 28 (1975): 231ff.; in *Studies in Honor of John Wilson*, ed. G.E. Kadish (Chicago, 1969), pp. 93ff.; see also M. Görg, *Biblische Notizen* 11 (1980): 7ff.; 13 (1980): 17ff.; 18 (1982): 15ff.; W.G. Simpson, *VT* 19 (1969): 128ff.
81. See P. Auffret, *Hymnes d'Egypte et d'Israel* (Göttingen, 1981), pp. 135ff.
82. Cf. above all, R.J. Williams, *JEA* 47 (1961): 100ff.; idem, *JAOS* 101 (1981): 10f.
83. Cf. Williams, *Legacy* (note 80), pp. 284ff.; G. Gerleman, *Ruth, Das Hohelied* (Neukirchen-Vluyn, 1965), pp. 89f.; R.E. Murphy, *VT* 29 (1979): 441; M. Görg, *Biblische Notizen* 21 (1983): 101ff.
84. B.G. Ockinga, *Biblische Notizen* 11 (1980): 38ff.
85. Williams, *Studies in Honor of John Wilson* (see note 80), pp. 95f.
86. D. Muller, *ZAS* 86 (1961): 126ff.
87. Williams, *Legacy* (see note 80), p. 288; T.N.D. Mettinger, *ZAW* 86 (1974): 403ff.
88. *Ḫt n ʿnḫ*: R.A. Parker and others, *The Edifice of Taharqa by the Sacred Lake at Karnak* (Providence, 1978), p. 71, n. 29; see also *Edfu* VII, 153:2, 290:7; *Esna* II, 45 (44), 121.
89. Williams, *Legacy* (see note 80), pp. 278f., 281f.
90. Ibid., 283f.
91. A. Herrmann, *Die ägyptische Königsnovelle* (Leipzig, 1938).
92. Cf. S. Herrmann, *W.Z. Karl-Marx Univ.* III, 1 (1953–54): 51ff; Soggin, in *Israelite and Judaean History* (see note 41), pp. 365ff. (and the literature cited there).
93. Cf. J. Van Seters, *In Search of History* (New Haven & London, 1983), pp. 160ff.
94. Ibid., p. 307.
95. Williams, *Legacy* (see note 80), p. 274; idem, *VT Suppl.* 28 (see note 80): 233ff.; W. Zimmerli, *VT* 22 (1972): 249ff.
96. On the Memphite Theology, see in particular K. Sethe, *Dramatische Texte zu altägyptischen Mysterienspielen* (Leipzig, 1928), pp. 1ff.; H. Junker, *Die Götterlehre von Memphis* (Berlin, 1940); K. Koch, *ZThK* 62 (1965): 251ff.
97. See most recently Williams, *JAOS* 101 (note 82): 1ff., and the literature there cited.
98. Gaza had an Egyptian temple which survived at least into the Twentieth Dynasty: P. Harris I, 9:1; see Alt, *Kleine Schriften* (note 5), pp. 216ff.; R. Giveon, *The Impact of Egypt on Canaan* (Göttingen, 1978), p. 23. For the alleged temple of Ptah at Ashkelon, see G. Loud, *The Megiddo Ivories* (Chicago, 1939), pl. 63; A. Alt, *ZDPV* 67 (1944): 5f.; Weinstein, *BASOR* 241 (see note 15): 19.
99. Byblos maintained contact with Egypt throughout the Iron I and II periods; Leclant, *The Role of the Phoenicians* (see note 34), pp. 9ff.
100. See Mettinger, *Solomonic State Officials* (note 74), pp. 140ff., and the literature there cited; on the so-called "Solomonic Enlightenment," see now Van Seters, *In Search of History* (note 93), pp. 216ff.
101. On the conquests, see Herodotus ii.104–111; Diodorus i.53.6–7, 55.1; Strabo xvii.1.5. On the taxation of conquered lands, see Diodorus i.55.10–11. On the conquered kings bringing tribute, see Diodorus i.58.1–2. The tradition of the marriage, which is not in the classical authors, lived on in the popular imagination, and surfaces in such late texts as the Bentresh Stele: cf. P. Tresson, *RB* 42 (1933), pl. 1; K.A. Kitchen, *Ramesside Inscriptions*, vol. II (Oxford, 1979), pp. 284ff.; A.J. Spalinger, *JSSEA* 8 (1977): 11ff. (where full bibliography will be found).
102. On Sesostris, see K. Sethe, *Sesostris* (Leipzig, 1900); G. Maspero, *JdS* (1901): 593ff., 665ff.; H. Kees, in *RE*, II, 2d ser., eds. P. Pauly, G. Wissowa, W. Kroll, K. Mittelhaus, K. Ziegler and W. Gärtner, pp. 1861ff.; K. Lange, *Sesostris, ein ägyptischen König in Mythos, Geschichte und Kunst* (Munich, 1954); M. Malaise, *CdE* 41 (1966): 244ff.

Ammon, Moab and Edom

James A. Sauer

IT HAS BEEN ALMOST fifty years since Nelson Glueck's pioneering work was carried out in Transjordan. That work was the basis of a synthesis of the archaeological history of Transjordan in the Bronze and Iron Ages, including ancient Ammon, Moab and Edom (see map on page 207).

During the last twenty years, extensive surveys and some excavations have been carried out in Jordan. Although the archaeological picture is still anything but clear, there are many substantial changes which need to be made in the synthesis which Glueck fostered.

Glueck's Synthesis

In Glueck's classic original synthesis it was argued that Transjordan was densely occupied during the latter part of the Early Bronze Age (ca. 2300–1900 B.C.E.). The steep decline at the end of the Early Bronze Age (Glueck's MB I) was associated by him, following Albright, with the Sodom and Gomorrah traditions of Abram/Abraham in Genesis 13–19. In the Middle and Late Bronze Ages, ca. 1900–1250 B.C.E., most of Transjordan (especially south of the Zerqā River) was abandoned. Although Canaanite culture flourished in Palestine during the Late Bronze Age, Glueck argued that most of Transjordan was still nomadic or seminomadic at that time. Only during the thirteenth century B.C.E. did resettlement begin in Transjordan with Iron Age sites which reflected the early Israelites, Ammonites, Moabites, and Edomites. Glueck used the Middle–Late Bronze Age gap in Transjordan as one part of an argument to support the "late" (thirteenth century B.C.E.) Exodus–Conquest date,

* The editors regret that due to lack of space it was impossible to print the extensive bibliography and references meticulously compiled by Prof. Sauer for publication with this paper.

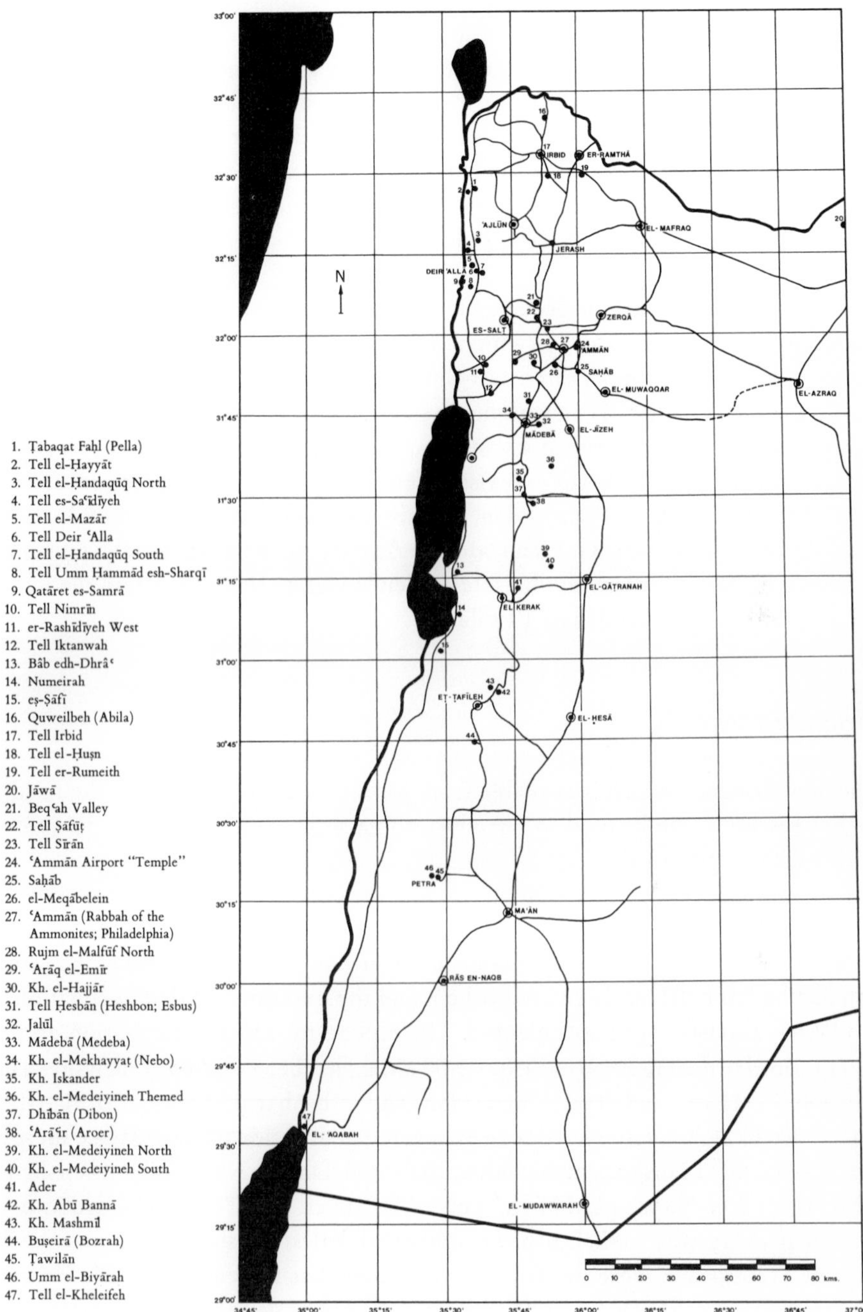

Map of western Transjordan, showing locations of relevant archaeological sites.
Road system is only approximate.

since there would have been essentially no one in Transjordan prior to that time. For the Iron I period in the thirteenth century B.C.E., Glueck reconstructed the growth of major kingdoms in Transjordan, and he saw those kingdoms continuing to prosper into the Iron II period. However, his original synthesis emphasized the fact that most of the Iron II remains in Transjordan should be dated prior to ca. 800 B.C.E. He also argued that a full gap in occupation existed in most of Transjordan from the end of the Iron II period down to the Nabatean and Hellenistic periods (ca. 300 B.C.E.). This gap included most of the Neo-Babylonian (ca. 605–539 B.C.E.) and Persian (ca. 539–332 B.C.E.) periods.

During his later work, it became clear that certain features of Glueck's original synthesis had to be revised. His emphasis on the Middle–Late Bronze Age gap in Transjordan had to be moderated, but Glueck and many others did not generally give up the overall principle. For example, the Late Bronze ʿAmmān Airport "Temple" was still interpreted by some as a seminomadic shrine for a twelve-tribe league. For the Iron II period, Glueck had to revise his emphasis on the pre-eighth century B.C.E. date of the materials in Transjordan, because of numerous discoveries which were from the seventh century B.C.E. and later. In Ammon, such late materials came mostly from tombs, and in Edom, similar late evidence was forthcoming from the excavations at Umm el-Biyāarah and Ṭawilān.

New Directions

The new evidence which is available from Jordan today, coupled with the results of earlier research, can be used to introduce some significant changes in the synthesis which Glueck proposed.

The Early Bronze Age

First, in essential agreement with Glueck, the urban character of much of Transjordan during EB I–III has been established, and the extension of that occupation into EB IV has also been well documented. The process by which urbanization occurred in Transjordan during EB I (ca. 3300–2900 B.C.E.) has been studied at such sites as Bâb edh-Dhrâʿ, Jāwā, and Tell Umm Ḥammād esh-Sharqī. Major EB II–III (ca. 2900–2300 B.C.E.) city sites have been excavated or are known from surface surveys in many parts of Transjordan, including Bâb edh-Dhrâʿ, Numeirah, Kh. Iskander, Dhībān, Tell el-Ḥandaqūq North, Tell es-Saʿīdīyeh and Tell el-Ḥandaqūq South. Similar in every way to their urban neighbors in Palestine, such as ʿAi, most of these sites in Transjordan were destroyed or abandoned at the end of EB III. However, several phases of EB IV (ca. 2300–1950 B.C.E.) succeeded the EB III occupation in Transjordan, at such sites as Bâb edh-Dhrâʿ, Ader, ʿArāʿir, Dhībān, Kh. Iskander and Tell Iktanwah. This EB IV occupation was also sedentary, unlike the seminomadic phase which Kenyon and others reconstructed for Palestine due to the tomb evidence there. The pottery of EB IV includes certain new features, such as teapots, cups, rilled rimmed bowls, and envelope ledge handled jars. It probably corresponds to the urban EB IV at Ebla and other sites in North Syria. Ceramic parallels also exist from the declining First Intermediate period in Egypt.

The EB III and EB IV remains in Transjordan should be interpreted on their own grounds, and in the context of solid contemporary archaeological evidence from such nearby regions as Palestine, Egypt, Syria, Mesopotamia, and Arabia. The evidence from Transjordan fits into that overall framework, and should not be viewed as strikingly different from it.

The Middle–Late Bronze Ages

The occupational gap which Glueck claimed to exist during the Middle and Late Bronze Ages in much of Transjordan has been disproved in northern and central Transjordan, although the situation in southern Transjordan is still unclear. In the north, major Middle Bronze and Late Bronze sites are well attested, with occupational histories which are again very similar to what is known from contemporary sites in Palestine.

From the Middle Bronze Age, excavated MB I (= IIA) remains are known from Ṭabaqat Faḥl, Tell el-Ḥayyāt, Saḥāb, and Jāwā. Urban MB II–III sites have been excavated or surveyed, and they have included major fortifications or glacis defenses at such sites as ʿAmmān Citadel, Saḥāb, and Tell Ṣāfūṭ. Numerous tombs are known, including those dating from MB II at Kh. el-Mekhayyaṭ and at Ṭabaqat Faḥl. MB III–LB IA tombs, containing fine cream wares, are known at ʿAmmān Citadel, Beqʿah Valley, Tell el-Ḥuṣn, and Ṭabaqat Faḥl. In addition, MB III–LB IA occupational remains are known at Tell Deir ʿAlla, and possibly at Ṭabaqat Faḥl. The Middle Bronze Age was very well represented in the East Jordan Valley Survey and surveys in northern Transjordan have also encountered it. Middle Bronze sherds have been reported at Jalūl, and I have found some on the surface of es-Ṣāfī. However, the period is only weakly attested in the recent surveys of Moab, Edom and southernmost Transjordan.

The Late Bronze Age is also very well attested in northern and central Transjordan, with major cities at such sites as Saḥāb, Jalūl, Tell Ṣāfūṭ, Tell el-Ḥuṣn, Tell Irbid, Ṭabaqat Faḥl, Tell es-Saʿīdīyeh, Tell el-Mazār, and Tell Deir ʿAlla. The ʿAmmān Airport "Temple" now fits into a context of major Late Bronze cities, and cannot be considered an isolated seminomadic shrine. Late Bronze remains, mostly tombs, have also been found at Mādebā, ʿAmmān, Beqʿah Valley, Quweilbeh and Qatāret es-Samrā. The Late Bronze Age was also well represented in the East Jordan Valley Survey, and in surveys in northern Transjordan. The international character and the quality of these finds agree fully with the character of such sites in Palestine, Lebanon and coastal Syria. It is clearly incorrect to continue arguing that Transjordan was largely seminomadic in the Late Bronze Age. Instead, a system of major city-states like that found in Palestine is much easier to document, primarily in central and northern Transjordan. In southern Transjordan, possible Late Bronze sherds have been published from ʿArāʿir, but, in agreement with Glueck, the Late Bronze Age has been only weakly attested in new surveys there. In southernmost Transjordan, recent surveys have produced "Midianite" sherds which have parallels with possible Late Bronze or Iron I sites like Qurayyah in northwest Arabia.

Thus, the Late Bronze culture in Transjordan is in every way identical to that which is known from Palestine and coastal Syria, long ago recognized to be the high point of "Canaanite-Amorite" culture. The Amarna Letters and the Ugaritic texts make clear what the physical archaeological remains also show, namely that the population in Syria-Palestine (including Transjordan) was predominantly "Canaanite-Amorite" in character, and not Israelite. It has long been recognized that the Middle Bronze destructions probably reflect the reconquest of Palestine by the New Kingdom Egyptian pharaohs, who then dominated Palestine and Transjordan during the Late Bronze Age. The argument for a substantial Israelite population in Palestine and Transjordan during the Late Bronze Age falls apart on the question of the character of the Late Bronze occupation itself, which is demonstrably and predominantly "Canaanite-Amorite."

Iron Age I

In regard to Iron Age I, Glueck, although correct in many ways, was mistaken about certain factors. On the side of error, he attributed most of the Transjordanian Iron Age remains, especially the "Ammonite," "Moabite," and "Edomite" painted potteries, to the earliest Iron I phases of their histories. Although certain types of Edomite painting might belong to the Iron I period, it is now well established that most of these painted wares belong primarily in Iron II, possible beginning in Iron IC (see below).

Glueck correctly noted, however, proper ceramic and architectural evidence for an Iron IA (ca. 1220–1000 B.C.E.) occupation throughout the hilly regions, and he identified this as the earliest Israelite, Ammonite, Moabite, and Edomite remains in Transjordan. This early Iron IA occupation was correctly identified by Glueck, despite numerous arguments by others to the contrary. Many have claimed, for example, that Edom was not occupied prior to ca. 800 B.C.E., because the major excavated sites (Umm el-Biyāarah, Ṭawilān, Buṣeirā) did not attest remains earlier than ca. 800 B.C.E. This objection has now been shown to be incorrect, because several recent surveys in northern Edom have encountered clear Iron IA sites (such as Kh. Abū Bannā and Kh. Mashmīl) with typical primitive Iron IA pottery and pillared houses. It is also likely that Iron IA pottery will someday be found at sites like Buṣeirā, in bedrock areas off the high acropolis of the site, as happened during the excavations at Tell Ḥesbān. In that regard, it should be noted that some possible Iron I sherds have already been published from Buṣeirā. Iron IA pottery has also been found throughout Moab, and at major defended sites like Kh. el-Medeiyineh North and South, where Iron I pillared houses are also known. It also seems to be attested at the sites of Dhībān, and ʿArāʿir. In north-central Transjordan, typical Iron IA pottery has come from excavations at Mādebā, Saḥāb, Tell Ḥesbān, Kh. el-Hajjār, ʿAmmān Citadel, and the Beqʿah Valley. It has also been found at many other sites during surface survey work, apparently including northern Transjordan. In the Jordan Valley, Iron IA pottery has been positively found only in the south, at a one-period site in Wādī Nimrīn, er-Rashīdīyeh West.

The character of these small Iron IA sites in Transjordan is similar in all aspects to that which is found in the hill country of Palestine, at such sites as Tell Beit Mirsim, Raddana, ʿAi, Bethel, Shiloh, and Taanach. The Iron IA sites in Moab and Edom are more substantial, as was noted by Glueck, and the pottery of the south is slightly different. We cannot positively determine whether these southern sites are contemporary with those to the north, or whether they are slightly earlier or later. As there is evidence of tomb use and (declining) ceramic continuity between the LB IIB and Iron IA periods at several sites in Transjordan, such as the Beqʿah Valley and Mādebā, it is possible that the Iron IA sites in Transjordan reflect an ongoing "Canaanite-Amorite" population in the hilly regions. However, it would also seem likely that Glueck was correct when he argued that these sites represent the earliest Israelite, Ammonite, Moabite and Edomite occupations in the country. It is at this time that ancient Israel is mentioned for the first time in an extra-biblical source, in the ca. 1220 B.C.E. Stele of Merenptah. The distribution and character of the Iron IA settlements in Palestine and Transjordan conform to the period of the Judges. The processes by which the transition from Late Bronze IIB to Iron IA took place are still unclear. On the one hand, the presence of a Late Bronze "Canaanite-Amorite" occupation in Transjordan would agree more with Albright's original theory of an Israelite conquest than did the Middle–Late Bronze Age gap theory of Glueck. On the other hand, alternate processes, especially within the Iron IA period itself, cannot be eliminated.

Published but not interpreted by Glueck was the Iron IB occupation in the north of the Jordan Valley, which differed significantly from the Iron IA occupations in the Transjordanian hill country and in the south of the Jordan Valley. The Iron IB culture, found at many sites in the north Jordan Valley, has been excavated at Tell Deir ʿAlla, Tell el-Mazār, Tell es-Saʿīdīyeh, and Ṭabaqat Faḥl. The culture attests urban architecture, smelting activities, rich tombs and distinctive painted pottery with bird and spiral motifs. This culture is clearly related to the "Sea People" or "Philistine" occupation along the coast of Palestine and Syria (at Ibn Hani), and it penetrated the Jordan Valley by way of Megiddo and Beth-Shean. It should probably be dated (with the ca. 1175 B.C.E. inscription of Ramesses III) to ca. 1175–1000 B.C.E.., and it clearly dominated the plains of Palestine and Transjordan during that time, in agreement with the biblical traditions from the period of the Judges. Although the LB IIB occupation suffered a severe destruction at Tell Deir ʿAlla, there is evidence of occupational continuity between LB IIB and Iron IB at other sites, including Tell es-Saʿīdīyeh, Ṭabaqat Faḥl and Beth-Shean. It would still seem likely, from the Iron IA evidence at Taanach, that there should be a brief Iron IA phase between the LB II and Iron IB occupations, as Albright argued at Tell Beit Mirsim.

The Iron IC period, ca. 1000–918 B.C.E., corresponding to the period of the United Monarchy in Israel, is not yet well documented in Transjordan, although several relevant sites have been excavated. According to biblical tradition (2 Samuel 8–12), Ammon, Moab and Edom came under Israelite domination at this time. The red-polished pottery of the tenth century B.C.E. has been found stratigraphically above the Iron IA remains at sites in the hill country of Transjordan, such as Saḥāb and Kh. el-Hajjār. It has also been found above the Iron IB materials at sites in the Jordan Valley, such as Tell Deir ʿAlla and Tell el-Mazār, where a tenth century B.C.E. sanctuary has been uncovered. Red-polished pottery has also been revealed at Tell Nimrīn in the south of the Jordan Valley, and perhaps at Ṭabaqat Faḥl in its northern part. In northern Transjordan, tenth century ceramics and casemate walls were excavated at Tell er-Rumeith, and very similar pottery came from several tombs at nearby Irbid and Mafraq. These northern sites have their best ceramic parallels at Hazor. In central Transjordan, Iron IC materials have come from tombs at Mādebā and Kh. el-Mekhayyaṭ. It is difficult to document Moab or Edom archaeologically during the tenth century B.C.E. In Edom, some tenth century B.C.E. finds have come from Buṣeirā, and perhaps also from Tell el-Kheleifeh. It was during this period that Cypro-Phoenician painting was introduced into Transjordan, the influence of which on local Ammonite, Moabite and Edomite painted potteries can be detected, primarily, during Iron II.

Iron Age II

In the Iron IIA period, northern Transjordan especially seems to have prospered. Sites that could be mentioned include Tell er-Rumeith, Irbid, Ṭabaqat Faḥl, Tell es-Saʿīdīyeh, and Tell Deir ʿAlla. It seems to be clear that the ceramic evidence from these sites has its best parallels at northern Israelite sites such as Samaria, Tell el-Farʿah, Megiddo, Beth-Shean, and Hazor. This period in northern Transjordan seems to have come to an end in the 734/21 B.C.E. Assyrian conquests, when north Israel was defeated and taken into exile. Tell er-Rumeith and other sites were destroyed and largely abandoned after 734/21 B.C.E., but this was not found to be the case in central and southern Transjordan. Iron IIA pottery is not easy to isolate in the region of Ammon, although it seems to be present in some of the largely later Iron II tomb groups (see below). The tombs at Mādebā and Kh. el-Mekhayyaṭ seem to extend down from Iron IC into the Iron IIA period. Moab expanded to the north under Mesha during the Iron IIA period, and Moabite pottery from that period has come from Dhībān, from ʿArāʿir, and from Kh. el-Medeiyineh Themed. In Edom, the Iron IIA period is very well represented at Buṣeirā, at Tell el-Kheleifeh and perhaps at Ṭawilān.

During the Iron IIB, Iron IIC and Persian periods, northern Transjordan seems to have been sparsely occupied, while central and southern Transjordan prospered. As a vassal of Assyria, then Babylonia, and then Persia, Ammon in particular seems to have grown as a result of the decline of north Israel in 721 B.C.E. and of Judah in 586 B.C.E. Artifacts are now abundant in the region of ʿAmmān, including pottery, inscriptions, sculpture and tombs. Sites attesting these Ammonite materials include ʿAmmān, el-Meqabelein, Saḥāb, Kh. el-Hajjār, Tell Sīrān, Tell Ḥesbān, Beqʿah

Valley, Tell Deir ʿAlla, Tell el-Mazār, and Tell es-Saʿīdīyeh. The geographical spread of these Ammonite artifacts would seem to indicate expansion to the west (to the Jordan River), with movements also northward (for example, Beqʿah Valley) and southward (for example, Tell Ḥesbān). The situation in Moab during these periods is very unclear, because of the limited number of new projects which have been carried out there. In Edom, the excavated sites of Buṣeirā, Ṭawilān, Umm el-Biyāarah, and Tell el-Kheleifeh have all produced Iron Age IIB (ca. 721–605 B.C.E.) materials. But, there is also strong evidence at most of these sites of continued occupations into the Iron Age IIC (ca. 605–539 B.C.E.) and into the Persian (ca. 539–332 B.C.E.) periods.

Thus, the original position taken by Glueck, followed by many others, that most of Transjordan was essentially abandoned during the Neo-Babylonian and Persian periods (ca. 605–332 B.C.E.), is today in need of great revision. It has often been argued, on the basis of Josephus' *Antiquities of the Jews*, 10.9.7, that when Jerusalem was destroyed by the Neo-Babylonians in ca. 586 B.C.E., Ammon, Moab and Edom were destroyed shortly thereafter, or that they at least declined rapidly. In fact, the archaeological and historical evidence for Ammon in particular (see below), but also for Edom, shows that they continued to thrive and indeed fared much better than did Judah during the Exile and Return. Rather than there being a major gap in occupation throughout Transjordan during these centuries, parts of central and southern Transjordan flourished more than ever before.

The argument for extending the late history of Ammon down into the Neo-Babylonian and Persian periods rests primarily on new archaeological evidence from Transjordan, but it also involves dating certain materials later than most scholars have done in the past. The Adoni Nur tomb in ʿAmmān was originally dated to the eighth–seventh century B.C.E. Neo-Assyrian period, on the basis of the famous seal from the tomb which mentioned the Ammonite king Amminadab. It can now be argued that although use of the tomb may well have begun in the Neo-Assyrian period, it certainly continued much later, especially into the Neo-Babylonian and Persian periods. The following evidence can be cited in support of the later dating of much of the materials from the sites near ʿAmmān (see above): (1) a Phoenician coin of ca. 400 B.C.E., found inside the circular Ammonite tower at Kh. el Hajjār; (2) the circular shapes of some of the Ammonite towers; (3) an uncalibrated radiocarbon date of ca. 400 ±50 B.C.E. from the organic contents of the sealed Tell Sīrān Bottle; (4) ostraca found at Tell Ḥesbān, dated ca. 500 B.C.E.; (5) black Attic imports of ca. 500 B.C.E.; (6) sand-core glass of ca. 500 B.C.E.; (7) late ceramic typology, including white smooth unburnished wares; black-slipped burnished wares; very widely spaced wheel burnishing; deeply flanged Persian lamps; very elongated alabastra and "Assyrian" bottles; forms and decorations which seem to herald Nabatean types, such as thin, rilled-rim bowls, forms with double bases, and forms decorated with crowstep paint; (8) artifact parallels with the Neirab cemetery in northern Syria, which included texts from the time of Nabonidus as well as the early Persian period; (9) artifact parallels with Neo-Babylonian and Persian Samaria.

Turning to the literary sources, it is feasible to interpret this archaeological evidence as a major flourishing of culture in the Ammonite region of Transjordan during the Neo-Babylonian and Persian periods. It was to Transjordan that people from Jerusalem fled during the ca. 586 B.C.E. destruction, implying that Transjordan was then a place of safety (2 Kings 24–25, Jeremiah 39–41). It was the people of Ammon, Moab and Edom, as well as others, who were castigated in Israelite prophetic and apocalyptic literature for rejoicing in the destruction of Jerusalem (for example Psalm 83; Isaiah 11; Jeremiah 49; Ezekiel 25; Zephaniah 2). Transjordan would have prospered during the time that Nabonidus maintained his residence at Teima in northwest Arabia, since the route through Transjordan would have then been especially important to the Neo-Babylonians. When the Jews in exile returned to Jerusalem, they found among their hostile (and successful) neighbors, primarily Tobiah the Ammonite, Sanballat of Samaria, and Geshem the Arab, but also the Ashdodites, Idumeans, and perhaps Moabites (Nehemiah 2–13; Josephus, *Antiquities of the Jews*, 11.2–8). The ultimate end of Ammon is not clear, but it would seem to have continued as a Semitic tradition well into the Hellenistic period, after the ca. 332 B.C.E. conquests of Alexander the Great. The Tobiads continued to exist until they died out at ʿArāq el-Emīr in the second century B.C.E. (Josephus, *Antiquities of the Jews*, 12.4.11), and there are also other references to the Ammonites at about this time (1 Maccabees 5; 2 Maccabees 5). The name of their capital city was changed to Philadelphia during the Hellenistic period, but the old name ʿAmmān was reinstated about a thousand years later when the Semitic Arabs drove Hellenism out in ca. 630–640 C.E.. The names of Dhībān and Buṣeirā, former capitals of Moab and Edom, were likewise remembered, but the kingdoms and peoples themselves were absorbed and lost forever in the long classical and Islamic periods.

This is a provisional and very brief outline of the archaeological history of Ammon, Moab and Edom within the context of the broader history of Transjordan, Palestine and the Near East. Work in Transjordan is actually just beginning, and this outline will certainly be modified by new discoveries in the future. While Glueck would undoubtedly not agree with everything that I presented here, he would certainly be delighted to see the exciting results of the research being carried out in Transjordan.

Respondents

Manfred Bietak

To J.D. Muhly: Egypt offers ample evidence, scarcely studied thus far, for the phenomenon of Phoenician expansion in the first millennium B.C.E. Herodotus (II.112) tells us of a "quarter of Tyrennians" behind the Ptah temple in Memphis, and he also indicates that there were established Canaanite cults in the area, such as in the temples of Proteus and of the foreign Aphrodite.

Another source of information is the settlement strata and tomb artifacts of the seventh, sixth and fifth centuries B.C.E. and later, which include an enormous amount of imported pottery, especially Phoenician amphorae, some of which are inscribed.

As we go back in time we see repeated evidence of a close commercial maritime relationship between Egypt (Tanis) and the coastal Phoenician cities as reflected in the tale of Wen Amun. It seems that in the eleventh century B.C.E. the whole foreign traffic of Egypt was in the hands of Phoenicians besides the former Sea Peoples. This would have required the presence of Phoenician sailors and representatives in Egyptian harbors, especially in Tanis.

It is illogical to separate from the Phoenicians their predecessors in the coastal towns of Phoenicia, the Canaanites, particularly from the area of Byblos. Their significant presence in the famous New Kingdom harbor of *Peru-nefer* with cultic installations for Baal, Astarte and Qudshu is well known. Also in Piramesse we have evidence of temples of Baal, Anat and Astarte during the Nineteenth Dynasty.

Canaanites from Phoenicia were also responsible for the development of a foreign colony during the late Middle Kingdom, which led to the rise of the Hyksos rule in Egypt.[1] Half a millennium before, during the Old Kingdom, the many imports from Phoenicia, particularly timber and pottery as containers of goods, were not only the result of trade organized by the Egyptian crown, but of Canaanite demand. Epigraphical evidence shows that Canaanites from Byblos and elsewhere settled in Egypt.[2] Thus Canaanite/Phoenician enterprise and expansionism should not be considered as an isolated phenomenon of a certain period. It has a long history as seen in Egypt, making an especially strong impact during the late Middle Kingdom, the Eighteenth Dynasty and the Late Period. This long repetitive tradition has never been adequately explained, but most surely had environmental reasons as well as economic ones. The search for metals was only one of several factors.

Circumstances similar to those in Phoenicia can probably be found in the Aegean Islands, where an enterprising and intrepid people with birth surplus rates and little possibility to expand into the hinterland took again and again to the sea.

To T. Dothan: Sea Peoples known from Egyptian sources since Amenophis III and who raided the Egyptian coast already in the second year of Ramesses II's reign may have been present at the eastern border of Egypt as early as the fifth year of Merenptah. An obscure passage at the beginning of the famous victory inscription of this king at Karnak refers to preparations to protect Heliopolis against an attack.[3] Before this passage, there is reference to the enemies of Egypt in this campaign. The Libyans obviously were in coalition with the Sea Peoples: *Trš, Šrdn, Šklš, Jqjjwš, Lk(k)*. It is generally assumed that the thrust of the foreign force came from the edge of the west delta, as the main antagonists were the Libyans. However, this passage refers, in connection with defense preparations for Heliopolis at the eastern apex of the delta, to the *Jtj* waters at Bubastis and to tents at the *Jtj* waters. Unfortunately this passage is damaged and incomplete.

The *Jtj* waters can be identified, according to textual evidence, as a) the branch of Heliopolis; and b) the backwaters of the most eastern nome, to be identified with the channel of the biggest drainage system in the eastern delta, the Bahr el-Baqar. Obviously, the *Jtj* waters of Heliopolis and the most eastern nome were the same and were connected to each other. They formed a natural strategic barrier for Egypt on its eastern border.

It is unlikely that the Libyan forces had been transferred to the eastern desert, but more probable that Sea Peoples began roaming the northeastern border of Egypt during the fifth year of Merenptah's reign. It is difficult to assess whether they inflicted serious damage on the Egyptian installations in Canaan or whether this engagement was just a raid or first attempt to enter Egypt from the east.

The last passage on the Israel Stele of Merenptah, dealing in particular with the Libyan invasion of the western delta, at least shows us that there were problems in Canaan which forced the Egyptian authorities to react:

> Plundered is Canaan with every evil, carried off is Ashkelon, seized upon is Gezer, Yenoam is made as that which does not exist, Israel is laid waste, his seed is not.

The Stele mentions, besides Israel, only those places destroyed, with no indication about an engagement with Sea Peoples as a cause of Egyptian intervention. On the other hand, it is difficult to explain all the turmoil by the appearance of proto-Israelite tribes beyond Yenoam, as Ashkelon on the coast is directly north of Gaza, the capital of the Egyptian province Canaan. Gaza is not mentioned on the Stele, so it had obviously remained intact.

Concerning the Philistine seizure of the coastal area of Palestine, we have heard an entirely satisfactory and clear account by Prof. Trude Dothan, in keeping with the archaeological evidence and the accepted interpretation of the textual records from

Egypt. However, close scrutiny of this written evidence, as carried out by Rainer Stadelmann some time ago,[4] may produce an historical picture which is different from that introduced by Albright, Alt and others. According to their thesis, the Philistines and the Tjekker were placed in garrisons along the Horus road (the "road of the Philistines") after capture, in order to pacify them and to create a buffer zone against an area which became increasingly troublesome. The main textual support is a passage in Papyrus Harris (I.76.5–9) stating that Ramesses III had placed the captured prisoners of war in garrisons and fed them. There is, however, no word that this event took place in Palestine.

An important point of this historical reconstruction is that the land battle of year 8 of Ramesses III's reign occurred far from Egypt, in Syria. However, the Medinet Habu inscription mentions that the Sea Peoples' coalition, after destroying Hatti, Kedi, Carchemish, Arzawa and Alashiya, established itself in a place in Amurru and crushed its population. Then they proceeded to Egypt, a blast of flames going before them. Another passage relates that the prince of Amurru was "turned to ash," while his people were taken prisoner. There is an indication of people fleeing to Egypt.

On the other hand, the account of Egypt's move to meet the approaching enemy only mentions that the king and his army started to move toward Djahi (at that time the common New Kingdom designation of Syria/Palestine). It does not stipulate specific places of the campaign route as on previous occasions (Thutmose III, Ramesses II). However, to understand the situation of Djahi, we have to consider a text, the "Glorification of Piramesse" in Papyrus Anastasi IV, in which the city is said to be situated "at the boundary of Egypt and Djahi." According to this description, Djahi bordered Egypt directly in the area of the Isthmus of Suez.

In the Medinet Habu inscription, the statement of Ramesses follows: "Those, who reached my boundaries, their sons [or rather their offspring] are not existent." This clearly suggests that, in addition to the invasions by sea, the attack on Egypt by land was met at the eastern boundaries of Egypt and not at the southern edge of Amurru. The fact that there is no mention of stations in the battle itinerary strongly supports this suggestion. This situation alone would logically explain how the king was able to meet the sea force probably entering the Pelusiac branch of the Nile (representation of "Migdol of Ramesses"), while nearly simultaneously repulsing an invasion by land.

This evidence would indicate the seizure of Palestine, at least the coastal plain and the Via Maris, by the Sea Peoples before they attacked Egypt by land. The second conclusion is that they, after having been repulsed by the Egyptians, would have stayed there.

Next we must ask to what extent Ramesses III was able to restore his authority and administration in the province of Canaan. The data are conflicting in this respect.

The dedication of the temple of Gaza and the presence of a statue of Ramesses III in Beth-Shean (in secondary position in stratum V) may date from early in his reign. It is remarkable, indeed, as pointed out by R. Stadelmann,[5] that Gaza, Ashkelon, Megiddo and Beth-Shean are not mentioned at all in both the list of towns of Ramesses III at Karnak and in the administrative texts of this period. Furthermore we do not know about a single overseer of the northern foreign countries from this time in any administrative text.[6] The lack of evidence of official administration from the time of Ramesses III onwards is a notable omission when compared with the evidence from the previous period.

The textual evidence seems therefore to suggest that the province of Canaan was largely lost during the time of Ramesses III, and that the Sea Peoples (the Philistines and the Tjekker) took hold of the coastal plain prior to their attack on Egypt, organizing a land and sea attack from close range. When this attack was repulsed they settled along the coastal plain of Palestine, establishing states independent from Egyptian hegemony.

When textual and archaeological interpretation are in conflict, the evidence must be reexamined in order to verify if there are other possible interpretations. For example, at Deir el-Balaḥ, the supraposition of the abandoned New Kingdom fortifications, the Philistine pits and the absence of refortification do not accommodate the idea of resettling Philistines in garrisons. It is also highly unlikely that a major body of defeated enemies would have been posted at a remote and sensitive frontier location, where it would have been difficult to properly supervise them. This would have required major units of Egyptian forces; however, their destroyed garrisons along the Via Maris were not rebuilt, nor do we have evidence of new fortifications in that region.

A certain degree of Egyptianization among the Philistines does not necessarily indicate their domination by the Egyptians. This phenomenon could also have been due to a local Egyptianized substratum, to the proximity to Egypt, and to Sea Peoples finding their way back after a period of residence in Egypt.

There is, however, some epigraphical evidence for an Egyptian administration in the southern part of Palestine after the eighth regnal year of Ramesses III. An ostracon of the twenty-first year of a king, who according to epigraphical dating by Orly Goldwasser may be identified as Ramesses III,[7] would suggest that at least in some parts of the south, in the inland area of Tell esh-Shariaᶜ (Tel Seraᶜ) and Lachish, Egyptian authority was maintained or restored.

North-south routes may also have been maintained for some time inland, avoiding the coastal strip occupied by the Philistines and Tjekker. The Beth-Shean statue of Ramesses III and the evidence of Egyptian occupation during the time of the late New Kingdom can probably be explained as the remains of a stronghold to maintain north-south connections behind the Philistine territory. This theory and the lack of Philistine pottery at Beth-Shean contradict Trude Dothan's identification of anthropoid clay coffins from Beth-Shean as Philistine.

The Megiddo epigraphical evidence relating to Ramesses VI (Stratum VIIa) in secondary position is not cogent evidence for a continuous Egyptian occupation until that period. It may, however, signal, in connection with the proposed theory of an Egyptian-controlled inland route, that Megiddo was, at least for a short time, a part of this Egyptian system behind the backs of the Sea Peoples. This system, if it existed at all during that time, seems to have been very unstable and obviously broke down immediately after Ramesses VI.

Future research, especially excavations at Beth-Shean and Megiddo, will show if the proposed explanations of the evidence hitherto collected are helpful. In this connection I would like, as a *post scriptum*, to pay tribute to the late Prof. Yigael Yadin who already initiated further excavations at those sites, which may yield the expected sources for this obscure period.

Notes

For her kind assistance in editing this text I am indebted to Mrs. Joan Huntoon, Columbia University.

1. M. Bietak, "The Origin of the Asiatics and the Hyksos in the Eastern Nile Delta," *Abstracts of the IIIrd International Congress for Egyptology. Toronto, 1982* (in press); idem, "Some News about Trade and Trade Warfare in Egypt and the Ancient Near East," *Marhaba* 3/83 (Vienna, 1983): 41–43.
2. H.G. Fischer, "A Scribe of the Army in a Saqqara Mastaba of the Early Fifth Dynasty," *JNES* 18 (1959): 264–265; idem, "The Nubian Mercenaries of Gebelein," *Kush* 9 (1961): 75.
3. B. Porter and R.L.B. Moss, *Topographical Bibliography of Ancient Egyptian Hieroglyphic Texts, Reliefs and Paintings. II. Theban Temples*, 2d ed. (Oxford, 1972), p. 131.
4. R. Stadelmann, "Die Abwehr der Seevölker unter Ramses III," *Saeculum* 19 (1968): 156–171; idem, "Seevölker," *Lexikon der Ägyptologie* V.6 (1984): 814–822.
5. Ibid.
6. Ibid.
7. I thank Orly Goldwasser for this information. It may be dangerous to ascribe an exact date to the inscription on the basis of the palaeography of a single sign. Probably the date refers to the twenty-first year of Ramesses II.

Lawrence T. Geraty

I was fascinated by Trude Dothan's new conception of "Mediterranean archaeology" which *raises* the dates for the Sea Peoples in the east. This contrasts with James Muhly's conception which *lowers* the dates for the Phoenicians in the west. J. Muhly seems to generalize from insufficient data. To use only two recent examples, Ora Negbi's article in *Levant*[1] and Émile Puech's publication of new eleventh and twelfth century B.C.E. Phoenician inscriptions from the islands of the Mediterranean in *Revue Biblique*[2] would seem to supply data whose interpretation would conflict with the view we heard (at least for the eastern Mediterranean). But both these authors are here and can speak for themselves.

Donald Redford's analysis of why Israel/Judah did not even count in Egypt's "Mediterranean focus" with respect to Canaan, at least until the tenth century B.C.E., makes very good sense. I was glad that he added a fifth section to what was available in his abstract: "Israel and Judah's Influence on Egypt." Montet long ago suggested Israelite influence on Egyptian literature. Is it possible, for instance, as Green suggested,[3] that Solomon's reorganization influenced that of Shisak? Apparently during this time Israel was actually stronger than Egypt — or so the Gezer episode has been interpreted.

But it is concerning James Sauer's paper on "Ammon, Moab, and Edom" that I feel best qualified to comment. In fact, I can claim at least some credit for his having taken a permanent interest in the subject — but that story cannot be related here.

Up until Sauer's recent move to Philadelphia, he was in the enviable position (so far as this topic is concerned) of living in the heartland of ancient Israel's eastern neighbors where he was either personally involved or served as advisor to, or close observer of, every pertinent archaeological project of note for a dozen years. His new synthesis of the evidence which he has shared with us today, much of it based on unpublished data, can thus be termed authoritative.

Even as late as thirty years ago, all we knew about Jordan came basically from four sources. The most important were certain ancient literary sources, foremost of which was the Bible of course. Next were the accounts left by travelers to the region over the centuries. Third, after 1868, we had the Moabite Stone — still the longest single extra-biblical literary document dealing with the history of Transjordan in the Iron Age. Fourth, after World War I we had the results of Nelson Glueck's surface surveys in the 1930s and 1940s. It was the synthesis achieved after *that* effort that Sauer has used as his point of departure.

Concerning Sauer's own synthesis, I have a few minor comments on details or emphases. 1) While the ʿAmmān Airport "Temple" may very well fit into a context of major Late Bronze Age cities in Transjordan, there is no such immediate context for it.[4] 2) While the argument for an Israelite population in Palestine and especially Transjordan during the Late Bronze Age may fall down on the question of the character of the Late Bronze occupation itself, I am not sure we know enough about that character to be dogmatic. Ceramic traditions do not necessarily settle the matter. And absence of dense urban settlements does not mean absence of people — Israelites included. 3) Sauer's neo-Albrightian view of the conquest is one way to interpret the evidence, but it has its problems in light of what some speakers have suggested about the Merenptah Stele, for instance. Furthermore, if Iron IA in Transjordan conforms with the period of the Judges, where were their predecessors? 4) Sauer's suggestion that Iron IA should always be sandwiched between the Late Bronze Age and Iron IB in the plains has yet to be tested.

A more substantive question relates not to the Transjordan ceramic evidence and how it should be interpreted — something for which Sauer has no peer — but rather to the processes which account for the transience in sedentary occupation east of the Jordan. Might it be profitable, for instance, to focus on the more recent beduinization (and thus resettlement of Transjordan) as a means of generating insights and hypotheses which in turn could be employed to elucidate the archaeological evidence pertaining to the question of change during the occupational history of the country. For example, a food system perspective (settlement, land use, water management, food processing and storage, transportation, diet, environment, etc.) would give due recognition to the way of life of the pastoral nomad as one among several strategies for exploiting the natural resource represented by the land east of the Jordan. Unfortunately, I do not have the time to work this out here, but I think looking at the data for Transjordan in this way has implications for relating the archaeological evidence to biblical history.

In any case, Sauer's new evidence suggests a picture of the history and culture of Transjordan in the biblical period that can be characterized by sedentarization, mixed farming, importance of cattle, central government planning, international trade, and literacy. The literary finds in Ammon, Moab and Edom are out of proportion to their contemporaries across the river (recently Jordan's first cuneiform tablet was found in Edom, at Ṭawilān, a sale contract for livestock drawn up in Ḫarran in the region of Darius). These regions appear to be very international and cosmopolitan in their outlook and not at all a cultural backwater when compared to Cisjordan. They may be seen as worthy neighbors and sometimes, yes, even rivals of Israel and Judah in the Iron Age.

Notes

1. O. Negbi, "Evidence for Early Phoenician Communities on the Eastern Mediterranean Islands," *Levant* 14 (1982):179–182.
2. É. Puech, "Présence Phénicienne dans les Isles à la Fin du IIe Millénaire," *RB* 90 (1983): 365–395.
3. A.R. Green, "Israelite Influence at Shishak's Court," *BASOR* 233 (1979): 59–62.
4. L. Herr, "The Amman Airport Structure and the Geopolitics of Ancient Transjordan," *BA* 46 (1983): 223–229.

Ora Negbi

To J.D. Muhly: The old controversial question whether it was the Phoenicians or the Greeks who were the first to move into the Mediterranean has been raised again at this Congress by Prof. Muhly in his paper.[1]

One of the main issues put forward by him is the claim for a Greek presence in the Levant prior to the Phoenician expansion. It seems very likely that there was a distinctive group of Mycenaean Greeks among the Sea Peoples who had settled along the Syro-Palestinian coast at the end of the Late Bronze Age.[2] But these peoples were not the only ones who were settling on foreign soil at that time. What about the Canaanites who left their homeland and immigrated to Cyprus? Are they not to be regarded as the first Phoenician colonists overseas?[3]

During the early Iron Age, there were population movements between the Aegean and the Levant. Recent archaeological discoveries indicate that trade activity was reestablished in the eleventh century B.C.E., when a certain degree of stability had been reached in the eastern Mediterranean.[4] From the written documents, it seems likely that there was more than one ethnic group in this region that possessed maritime capacity. This is well attested by Wenamun's report, which refers to certain mercantile organizations of Phoenicians and Sea Peoples working in cooperation along the Levantine coast in the eleventh century B.C.E.[5] A common colonial enterprise of Achaeans and Sidonians is assigned to Teucer and Belos who, according to Virgil, founded the city of Salamis on Cyprus.[6] Although this is merely a legend, it is just as legitimate a source as those used by others to prove that only one maritime power was prevalent in the Mediterranean during the Dark Age.

There are some scholars who dwell on the tradition of the Dorian invasion and the new cities founded by the heroes of the Trojan War, in order to prove that Greek colonization in the eastern Mediterranean took place about 1100 B.C.E.[7] They thoroughly reject other classical references to Phoenician colonization in the western Mediterranean in the same period, although it seems unlikely that the Greeks would have credited the Phoenicians with such an enterprise, unless it was based on fact.

Other scholars prefer to reject legends of Greek founders of Salamis and Paphos (Teucer and Agapenor, respectively), and to adhere to the version adopted by Josephus, according to which Kition, the first Phoenician colony on Cyprus, was already in existence in the tenth century B.C.E.[8]

And then there are those who try to demonstrate that the classical tradition of early Phoenician colonization in Utica and Cadiz corresponds well with the biblical references to the voyages of the Tarshish fleet of Hiram and Solomon.[9]

Prof. Muhly argued today that there is no archaeological evidence to support this maritime enterprise since, according to him, there is no indication of Phoenician activity in the western Mediterranean during the tenth century. It is true that there are no substantial architectural remains of Phoenician settlements overseas which can be dated before the mid-ninth century B.C.E., but Phoenician pottery and metal artifacts dating as early as the eleventh century B.C.E. are recorded not only from Cyprus and Crete, but also from Sicily and Sardinia.[10]

Prof. Muhly assumes that these early Phoenician objects were brought from the Levant by Greek merchants, presumably in Greek ships. If so, it is difficult to explain the almost complete absence of Greek pottery and other Greek imports in the Levant before the late ninth century B.C.E.[11] Therefore, there appears to be no alternative but to assume that these Phoenician objects were brought from Phoenicia, mainly from the port of Tyre, by Phoenician traders, presumably on their own ships.

The number of early Phoenician objects found overseas has increased lately due to new studies by Dr. Maria Bisi and Prof. Frank M. Cross.[12] Of special interest are two inscriptions, both of the eleventh century B.C.E., one engraved on a bronze bowl from Tekké in Crete and the other on a fragmentary stele from Nora in Sardinia.[13] According to these studies, the Nora fragment is about two hundred years older than the famous Nora stone. The new date of the Nora fragment supports the assumption that the Phoenicians did reach the western Mediterranean well before the tenth century B.C.E. I therefore see no reason to question the biblical references to the voyages of the Tarshish fleet of Hiram and Solomon at that time.

Notes

1. W.F. Albright, "The Role of the Canaanites in the History of Civilization," in *The Bible and the Ancient Near East*, ed. G.E. Wright (London, 1961), pp. 343–349; S. Moscati, *The World of the Phoenicians* (London, 1968), pp. 94–95; J.D. Muhly, "Homer and the Phoenicians: The Relations

between Greece and the Near East in the Late Bronze and Early Iron Ages," *Berytus* 19 (1970): 35–36; J. Boardman, *The Greeks Overseas* (London, 1980), p. 38.

2. N.K. Sandars, *The Sea Peoples* (London, 1978), pp. 164–174; see also T. Dothan's paper "The Philistines Reconsidered" in this volume (pp. 165–176).
3. O. Negbi, "Evidence for Early Phoenician Communities on the Eastern Mediterranean Islands," *Levant* 14 (1982): 179–182; É. Puech, "Présence Phénicienne dans les Îles à la Fin du IIe millénaire," *RB* 90 (1983): 365–395.
4. M. Yon, "Chypre et la Crete au XI[è] s.," in *Acts of the International Archaeological Symposium: The Relations between Cyprus and Crete, ca. 2000–500 B.C.* (Nicosia, 1979), p. 248; V. Karageorghis, "Cyprus between the Orient and the Occident in the Eleventh Century B.C.," in *Archéologie au Levant* (Lyon, 1982), pp. 173–178.
5. Albright, "The Role of the Canaanites" (see note 1), p. 103; B. Mazar, "The Philistines and the Rise of Israel and Tyre," *Proceedings of the Israel Academy of Sciences and Humanities*, vol. I, no. 7 (Jerusalem, 1964), pp. 2–5.
6. Moscati, *The World of the Phoenicians* (see note 1), p. 103.
7. J.L. Benson, "The Necropolis of Kaloriziki," *SIMA* 36 (Göteborg, 1973): 23; Boardman, *The Greeks Overseas* (see note 1), pp. 35–36; and recently V. Karageorghis, *Cyprus* (London, 1982), pp. 114–121.
8. Albright, "The Role of the Canaanites" (see note 1), pp. 341–342; Mazar, "Rise of Israel and Tyre" (see note 5), pp. 15–16; H.J. Katzenstein, *The History of Tyre* (Jerusalem, 1973), p. 64; P.M. Bikai, *The Pottery of Tyre* (Warminster, 1978), pp. 174–175.
9. Albright, "The Role of the Canaanites" (see note 1), pp. 342–345; Moscati, *The World of the Phoenicians* (see note 1), pp. 99–100; Mazar, "Rise of Israel and Tyre" (see note 5), p. 17; and recently Puech, "Présence Phénicienne" (see note 3), p. 395.
10. A.M. Bisi, "La Diffusion du 'Smiting God' Syro-Palestinien dans le Milieu Phénicien d'Occident," *Karthago* 19 (1980): 5–14; Boardman, *The Greeks Overseas* (see note 1), pp. 36–37; Negbi, "Early Phoenician Communities" (see note 3); Karageorghis, *Archéologie au Levant* (see note 4).
11. P.J. Riis, *Sukas I: The North-East Sanctuary and the First Settling of Greeks in Syria and Palestine* (Copenhagen, 1970), pp. 126–127, 159–162; J.N. Coldstream, *Geometric Greece* (London, 1979), pp. 199–200; Boardman, *The Greeks Overseas* (see note 1), pp. 39–44.
12. Bisi, "La Diffusion du 'Smiting God'" (see note 10); F.M. Cross "Newly Found Inscriptions in Old Canaanite and Early Phoenician Script" *BASOR* 238 (1980): 17.
13. J. Naveh, *Early History of the Alphabet* (Leiden, 1982), pp. 40–41; Peuch, "Présence Phénicienne" (see note 3), pp. 374–387.

ELIEZER D. OREN

I would like to remark on two interrelated issues, Prof. Redford's paper on the relations between Egypt and Canaan, and Prof. Dothan's paper on the early Sea Peoples.

Prof. Redford presented persuasively his view concerning Egypt's inability during the Empire period to apply its concept of imperialism in Canaan.[1] This conclusion certainly holds true for the Eighteenth Dynasty, but is hardly the case during the Nineteenth and Twentieth Dynasties. A reevaluation of the literary record in the light of the ever-growing volume of archaeological material from Palestine and Sinai warrants, in my opinion, a different perspective on the Egyptian Empire in Canaan.[2]

Late Bronze Age strata in Palestinian sites have yielded impressive evidence of the Egyptian impact on Canaan in a broad spectrum of fields, for example in art and architecture, funerary rites, cult and administration. Egyptian forts and residencies, remains of ceremonial city gates, numerous stelae, statues and architectural details with hieroglyphic inscriptions, as well as administrative documents that deal with produce taxes,[3] all bear conclusive evidence of the Egyptianization of Canaan under the Nineteenth and Twentieth Dynasties. This picture is now augmented by the results of our own systematic research in northern Sinai.[4] The north Sinai survey indeed testifies to the extensive military and administrative system that was established by Egypt along the "Way of Horus," including forts and granaries, way stations, administrative centers and industries.[5] In short, this was a carefully designed system that enabled Egypt to extend its domination over Canaan.

Under Rameses III, Egypt's involvement in Canaan, and in particular in southern Canaan, reached a degree not previously known. Moreover, we witness, for the first time, a concerted effort to institute in Canaan the Egyptian structure of government and perhaps also Egyptian cults. The evidence from Megiddo, Beth-Shean, Lachish, Ashdod and Tel Seraᶜ, to mention only a few sites, demonstrates clearly that Canaanite cities began a new cultural floruit — a sort of "swan song" of the Egypto-Canaanite culture. It is indeed to this period that all the known governors' residencies of Egyptian type belong, as well as the Egyptian epigraphic material dealing with the tax system instituted by Egypt in Canaan.

The famous Harris Papyrus presents a picture of overinvolvement of the Egyptian temples in the affairs of the province, and of cities in the land of Khuru actually becoming the property of the god Amun. Gaza, Egypt's administrative capital in southern Canaan, was selected as the site for the temple of Amun, as was most likely Ashkelon for the temple of Ptah. It may therefore be concluded that the increasing intervention of Egypt in Canaan brought about a new concept, according to which Khuru was considered in every way the crown property of the Pharaohs. The new concept was manifest in the reorganization of the administration in Canaan after an Egyptian pattern, and in the strong Egyptian influence on the local culture, including that of the newcomers, the Sea Peoples. In the light of the above we may conclude that during the Empire period, and in particular under the Nineteenth and Twentieth Dynasties, Canaan became an eastern extension of the Egyptian culture and its imperial administration.

Owing to the evidence from sites such as Beth-Shean, Tell Deir ᶜAlla, Tell el-Farᶜah (S) and two sites which were explored lately by the respondent (Tel Seraᶜ in the western Negev and the Ḥaruvit fort in northeastern Sinai), the chronological position of the related ceramic groups — Mycenaean IIIB, Mycenaean IIIC and Philistine pottery — is now firmly established.[6] Accordingly, the latest possible date for Mycenaean IIIB is in the last decade of the thirteenth century B.C.E., that is, in the reigns of Seti II and Queen Teosert.[7] The date of Mycenaean IIIC is fixed in the early twelfth century B.C.E., during the reign of Rameses III. Consequently, the Philistine pottery — itself a derivative of Mycenaean IIICb and of local manufacture — could not possibly predate the mid-twelfth century B.C.E. This is supported by the well-stratified evidence from Beth-Shean, Tel Seraᶜ and southern Tell el-Farᶜah.[8]

In Beth-Shean Stratum VI (early), the regional headquarters of Rameses III is represented by Mycenaean IIIC ware, but hardly any Philistine pottery is recorded at this site.[9] Similarly, no Philistine pottery is registered in Stratum IX at Tel Seraᶜ, which is dated by Egyptian administrative texts to the reign of Rameses III.[10] Philistine ceramics become plentiful, on the other hand, in the succeeding Stratum VIII. The reference to "year 20 + X" in one of the inscriptions from Tel Seraᶜ ascertains that Philistine pottery cannot be earlier than the late years of Rameses III.[11] Finally, the tombs of Aegean type at Tell el-Farᶜah (Cemetery 900) contain a rich collection of thirteenth–twelfth century B.C.E. ceramics,[12] yet not a *single* Philistine vessel is recorded in any of the tombs. The time span of the cemetery is indicated by the numerous scarabs that cover the entire list of Rameside kings including Rameses VI and VIII.[13] That Tell el-Farᶜah was a flourishing Philistine settlement, postdating, however, the Rameside dynasty, is attested by the abundance of painted Philistine wares both in funeral and occupational contexts.[14]

In conclusion, contrary to the view expressed today, I propose that the confrontations of Rameses III with the Sea Peoples in his fifth and eighth year can in no way be taken as a chronological pivot on which to hang the early production of Philistine pottery. It was rather the eventual settlement of the Philistines and other Sea Peoples in Canaan and their interaction with Canaanite and Egyptian cultures that resulted in the emergence of a new class of pottery in the mid-twelfth century B.C.E.

Notes

1. For Egypt's imperialism in Nubia and Asia, see P.J. Frandsen, "Egyptian Imperialism," in *Power and Propaganda — A Symposium of Ancient Empires*, ed. M.T. Larsen (Copenhagen, 1979), pp. 167–190.
2. For studies on Egyptian administration in Canaan, see A. Alt, "Das Stützpuntsystem der Pharaonen an der phönikischen Kuste und im syrischen Binnenland," in *Kleine Schriften zur Geschichte des Volkes Israel*, vol. III (Munich, 1959), pp. 107–140; W. Helck, "Die ägyptishche Verwaltung in den syrischen Besitzungen," *MDOG* 92 (1960): 1–13; M. Abdul-Kader Mohammed, "The Administration of Syro-Palestine during the New Kingdom," *ASAE* 56 (1969): 105–137.
3. J.M Weinstein, "The Egyptian Empire in Palestine — A Reassessment," *BASOR* 241 (1981): 18–21.
4. E.D. Oren, "North Sinai before the Classical Period," in *Sinai, Pharaohs, Miners, Pilgrims and Soldiers*, ed. B. Rothenberg (Bern, 1979), pp. 181–191.
5. For literary sources, see A.H. Gardiner, "The Ancient Military Road between Egypt and Palestine," *JEA* 6 (1920): 99–116.
6. For bibliography, see T. Dothan, *The Philistines and Their Material Culture* (Jerusalem, 1982), pp. 27–33, 81–82, 84–86; E.D. Oren, *The Northern Cemetery of Beth-Shan* (Leiden, 1973), pp. 146–150; idem, "Ziklag — A Biblical City on the Edge of the Negev," *BA* 45 (1982): 155–166; idem, "Egyptian New Kingdom Sites in Northeastern Sinai," *Qadmoniot* 49 (1980): 26–33. (Hebrew)
7. V. Hankey, "Mycenaean Pottery in the Middle East," *ABSA* 62 (1967): 127–128. Mycenaean IIIB (late) pottery turned up in Phase II of Ḥaruvit Fort alongside Canaanite and Egyptian vessels including a large jar with cartouches of Seti II; see O. Goldwasser, "An Egyptian Store-jar from Ḥaruvit," *Qadmoniot* 49 (1980): 34. (Hebrew)
8. Contra Dothan, *The Philistines* (see note 6), pp. 289–296.
9. V. Hankey, "Late Mycenaean Pottery from Beth Shan," *AJA* 70 (1966): 169–171; Oren, *Cemetery of*

Beth-Shan (see note 6), p. 147.

10. Oren, "Ziklag" (see note 6), p. 166.
11. A comprehensive study by O. Goldwasser on the inscriptions from Tel Sera^c is to appear shortly in *Tel Aviv*.
12. Dothan, *The Philistines* (see note 6), pp. 29–33; J.C. Waldbaum, "Philistine Tombs at Tell Fara and Their Aegean Prototypes," *AJA* 70 (1966): 331–340.
13. F.M. Petrie, *Beth Pelet* II (London, 1932), pp. 23–27.
14. Dothan, *The Philistines* (see note 6), pp. 27–29; see my forthcoming article, "Governors' Residencies in Canaan under the New Kingdom: A Case Study of Egyptian Administration," *EI* 18 (in press).

EPHRAIM STERN

To J.D. Muhly: Prof. Muhly's comprehensive study touched upon many major topics and problems; I find myself obliged to concentrate on but a few.

Evidently his suggestion regarding the date of the Phoenician expansion to the west is not quite new. It was presented twenty-five years ago by Riis Carpenter in his famous study, "Phoenicians in the West," but Carpenter, unlike Muhly, based his late dating exclusively on the archaeological material of the western Mediterranean. At the time he did not find it appropriate to cast doubt on the validity of the detailed biblical account regarding the flourishing state of the Phoenician people in their homeland during the Solomonic Age. But as I said before, my main concern is with the conclusions reached by Muhly regarding the eastern Phoenicians.

Let us first examine the archaeological basis for Prof. Muhly's proposition. It seems that in his opinion there are but two major excavations on the entire Phoenician coast on which we can rely — Tyre conducted by Patricia Bikai, and that at Sarepta by J.B. Pritchard. Both have testified to the poor condition of the country down to 750 B.C.E. Moreover, the famous "red-burnished ware," so characteristic of the Phoenician colonies, is missing prior to this period, and therefore the Phoenician expansion to the west could not have taken place earlier.

The Tyre excavation is no more than a trial pit and that of Sarepta was limited to a small area. Any experienced excavator knows how dangerous it is to conclude general historical interpretations based on such limited data. The chance character of the finds of the Tyrian excavation is manifested by the absence of the red-burnished jug with a conical neck and pinched mouth — one of the commonest shapes found in Phoenician expansion assemblages elsewhere.

All other excavations carried out along the Phoenician coast are not mentioned, or simply dismissed by Muhly as "cemeteries." I wonder whether the excavators of Achzib, Akko, Tell Keisan, Tell Abu Hawam, Shiqmona and even those sites along the Carmel coast (which were under Phoenician influence), Tel Dor and Tel Mevorakh, would agree with this hypothesis. It is interesting to note that in most of the above-mentioned sites, flourishing towns of the tenth century B.C.E. have been unearthed, in which many imported vases — mostly from Cyprus — have come to light. Others — very few — were from Greece. In 1983 a most interesting discovery was made by Zvi Gal who partly excavated a Phoenician fortress dated by him from the end of the tenth down to the mid-ninth century B.C.E. at the site of Cabul, the same town which according to the biblical account was given to Hiram I by King Solomon. During the first excavation season, the site yielded many pottery vessels, one of the earliest Phoenician assemblages to be uncovered, including dozens of red-burnished (Achzibian) vases dated by Bikai and Muhly so much later. This is true of many of the sites mentioned above where the same red-burnished material has been found in the tenth century context. I can testify for this in regard to my own excavation at Tel Mevorakh which has already been published.[1] It is true, however, that in the tenth century B.C.E., red-burnished ware was but a small part of the entire repertoire.

If Prof. Muhly draws the border between Phoenicia and Israel along the same lines as the modern border between Lebanon and Israel, he may be right in attributing such exaggerated significance to the excavations at Tyre and Sarepta. But, if more plausibly, at least ʿAkko Plain is added, the entire picture which he portrayed must be altered, and the tenth century B.C.E. is placed in a different light. By the way, the tenth century B.C.E. was the subject of three articles written years ago by W.F. Albright[2] dealing with the monumental art of the Solomonic period both in Israel and in Phoenicia.

I would like here to caution against drawing assumptions in regard to periods for which there is a lack of archaeological data. Yadin, in his lecture during the opening session, mentioned such a period relating to Judah — the seventh century between 701 and 586 B.C.E. This was in fact the subject of our M.A. Seminar at The Hebrew University. To a similar gap in our knowledge, pertaining to the ninth century B.C.E. in Judah, we devoted a seminar this year, calling it "The Disappearing Ninth Century." These gaps, of course, are not part of the archaeological development of the country — they are rather the products of error in our own methods.

Finally, it seems to me that at a gathering dedicated to biblical archaeology, it is hard to accept a conception that dismisses such detailed written evidence as that relating to the Phoenicians and their role in the history of the country in the tenth century B.C.E., even on the basis of much sounder archaeological evidence.

Notes

1. E. Stern, *Excavations at Tel Mevorakh (1973–1976). Part One: From the Iron Age to the Roman Period. Qedem* 9 (1978).
2. See for example, W.F. Albright, "Was the Age of Solomon without Monumental Art?" *EI* 5 (1958): 1–9.

DAVID STRONACH

Whether we search for the Sea Peoples, the early Israelites, or indeed the Phoenicians, the old question of the degree to which pots and peoples can be equated inevitably arises. Here I would only second the quite numerous caveats that I have already heard on this subject at this meeting, not least from Dr. Amihai Mazar, on the importance of context — and the need to look with all due rigor at the total assemblage of cultural traits.

As Prof. Muhly has rightly pointed out, it is only rather recently that we have been able to cite stratified evidence for the Phoenicians from their own homeland. But I wonder if it is not premature to dismiss Phoenician mercantile capabilities not only in the tenth century B.C.E., in the time of Hiram I and Solomon, but even as late at 850 B.C.E.? After all, wherever the land of Tarshish may have lain, we are told that Hiram did possess a fleet. Furthermore, it seems a little hard to suggest that the Phoenicians were dependent on Greek vessels for the shipment of their goods as late as 850 B.C.E., when certainly by the seventh century the Phoenicians had established their colony at Mogador in Morocco, well beyond the Straits of Gibraltar. No Greek colony ever existed so far from home.

The fact that the traditional Phoenician ceramic markers that are found on sites in the West Mediterranean are not so far represented in Phoenicia itself before the second half of the eighth century B.C.E. could prove to be an artifact of the very limited nature of modern archaeological investigation within the Phoenician homeland. At Serepta, Prof. Pritchard's excavations covered an area not much larger than 500 sq m; and at the site of Tyre, the one deep, controlled excavation only opened up an area of 100 sq m.

Not long before I left Berkeley to come here, I received a copy of Patricia Bikai's treatment of the early Iron Age pottery from the site of Palaepaphos-Skales in western Cyprus. Bikai points out that the chronological ties of much of the Phoenician pottery from this recently excavated site lie with Tyre XIII and Tell Keisan 9a–b, both of which can be placed in the second half of the eleventh century B.C.E. Other parallels in this same time range come from Qasile X and Megiddo VI.[1] This evidence has in fact persuaded Bikai to retract her earlier view[2] that the western expansion of the Phoenicians did not begin until the eighth century B.C.E. Indeed, she now ventures the thought that the eleventh century trade route to Palaepaphos-Skales may not have ended at that location.

I must add that this new information makes it all the more interesting that the international art style of the Phoenicians did not begin until the eighth century B.C.E. It must now be concluded, in other words, that this style was not an outgrowth of those early centuries which witnessed an expansion of mercantile trade alone; instead it bids fair to have been a direct product of the period of colonization.

To conclude these remarks on the interaction between Israel and its neighbors in the Iron Age, it is appropriate to remember that much remains to be explored. For example, more needs to be done toward the documentation of the various levels of interaction between Israel and Phoenicia in the early first millennium B.C.E. Second, there is a need for a thorough, up-to-date review of the Neo-Assyrian presence in Israel, particularly in the south where, thanks to a number of recent excavations, it is now beginning to be possible to grasp the remarkable extent of the Assyrian investment. Third, it is worth stressing, as Prof. Yadin already has, that seventh and early sixth century B.C.E. Judah is deserving of closer inquiry. And finally, as some of you may be expecting me to point out, the discovery of Israel in the Persian period is also at a certain threshold. Prof. Ephraim Stern has succeeded in pulling together, with admirable industry, so much of what is available from earlier studies and excavations; but now, as I hardly need stress, many sites with strata of the Persian period are being excavated with a new degree of precision — and there is, therefore, a real prospect of placing hitherto isolated materials in a better documented setting.

Notes

1. See P.M. Bikai, "The Imports from the East," in *Palaepaphos-Skales. An Iron Age Cemetery in Cyprus*, ed. V. Karageorghis (Universitätsverlag Konstanz GMBH, 1983), Appendix II, pp. 396–405.
2. Cf. P.M. Bikai, *The Pottery of Tyre* (Warminster: Aris & Phillips, 1978), p. 75.

Discussion

M. Weinfeld: I would like to link this session with that of yesterday on the subject of the Conquest. The famous picture depicting the Sea Peoples wandering together with their wives and children has been compared to Maḥane Dan, "the camp of Dan." The whole process of conquest is depicted against this background of shifting encampments, which were left only to carry out operations. This pertains especially to Gilgal, but also to Shiloh and Makkedah. Perhaps there were parallel Sea People/Israelite settlement movements. One must bear in mind that the biblical texts regarding Maḥane Gilgal, Maḥane Shiloh and Maḥane Makkedah have nothing to do with Deuteronomic late stratum. They were based on tradition, and must be considered valid.

Yesterday, we heard several alternative theories regarding the Conquest. Alt wrote an article in which he recognized as authentic Joshua's victorious leadership in the battle against the Amorite coalition in the Valley of Aijalon. Therefore, in spite of his peaceful infiltration hypothesis, Alt did not negate the possibility of military campaigns. If he had lived to see the Hazor excavations, he perhaps would have accepted the possibility that Joshua defeated a northern coalition. In both these expeditions, the tactic was one of sudden attack and not continuous fighting. The third alternative — the peasant revolt — was, in my opinion, not a peasant revolt but the joining of the Israelites by some of the local inhabitants.

Now in regard to Hiram and Solomon. It is true that the sources are complex, but we must remember that the Deuteronomic editor did not invent new material but adopted earlier sources.

I would now like to refer to the rhyton which Trude Dothan mentioned as an example of a borrowing from Sea Peoples. There are rhyton vessels which date much earlier than the Sea Peoples. In Ugarit, we have a rhyton in the form of a lion with an inscription which reads: *pn arw dš ʿly* PN *lršp gn*, "the face of a lion which PN offered to Reshef Gan." We also have a Hittite example where the elders of Ura pledge to bring a rhyton to the god, Yarri. Therefore, material which appears to be connected with the Sea Peoples may in fact come from the area of Anatolia.

D. Ussishkin: I would like to add a brief note about Lachish in reference to Trude Dothan's lecture. Lachish, to my amazement, was presented as a Philistine site. We know Lachish as a large Canaanite city flourishing during the first half of the twelfth century B.C.E., in the time of Rameses III. It was influenced by Egyptian culture and exemplified all the ceramic traditions of the Late Bronze Age. This city was destroyed sometime during the mid-twelfth century B.C.E. and the site was abandoned for a long period. Hardly one sherd of Philistine origin has been found at Lachish in all the extensive excavations carried out since the 1930s. It is quite obvious that it had no connection with the Philistines and their pottery. Not far from Lachish to the north is Tel Ṣafit, now identified with Gat. A little further north is Tel Miqne, ancient Ekron, about which we heard today. At these sites, Philistine pottery was found in modern stratigraphic excavations, but ḥardly any Late Bronze Age pottery was uncovered. It is difficult to understand how Lachish and Ekron could have coexisted without some pottery from one site passing to the other. The only feasible conclusion is that Ekron-Tel Miqne and Gat-Tel Ṣafit were founded after Canaanite Lachish ceased to exist. Consequently, Philistine pottery cannot be dated earlier than the middle of the twelfth century B.C.E. This is another indication that a radical change is called for in the conception and chronology of the Philistine culture as perceived by Prof. Dothan.

M. Prausnitz: I would like to refer to the Iron Age relations between Phoenicia, Cyprus and Israel. In the tenth century B.C.E., we find the first appearance in quantity of early red polished burnished ware in Palestine. I believe that a distinction should be made between the areas north and south of Acre, as we have the bichrome and white painted pottery in the north and in Cyprus, and the red polished burnished ware in the south. The excavations at Achzib prove without doubt that there was a change in the pottery associated with burials, probably during the ninth century B.C.E. The famous red polished burnished so-called Phoenician ware replaces the white painted bichrome traditions.

I believe that there should be a distinction between the commercial activities of the Phoenicians and their colonial expansion. Only the later types of red burnished jugs dating to the eighth century B.C.E. appear in the west in quantities.

A. Mazar: I would like to ask what is the significance of the appearance of Mycenaean IIIC:1 pottery at Ashdod and at Tel Miqne. At these sites there are large quantities of this ware, whereas at other sites like Beth-Shean and Tell Keisan, we find only a few examples. In previous publications of both Moshe and Trude Dothan, they referred to Mycenaean IIIC pottery at Ashdod and Tel Miqne as representing an early phase of non-Philistine Sea Peoples. Is this suggestion still valid? It seems to me that we can see in this Mycenaean pottery the real initial phase of Philistine settlement. This first wave of settlement should be dated to the time of Rameses III. I fully agree with the chronological framework presented here by Eliezer Oren, which, in fact, I suggested about nine years ago, and which can also be based on other sites and in particular on Meggido VIIa. The attribution of Philistine bichrome pottery to this stratum should be abandoned. During the first phase of Philistine settlement, the traditional Mycenaean IIIC pottery brought from Cyprus was still produced. Only later, after the time of Rameses III, and perhaps even after the total collapse of the Egyptian presence in this country, do we find the fully developed Philistine pottery, the bichrome ware.

M. Dothan: I do not need to defend Trude here. If she has the opportunity she will not doubt defend herself. But I do want to clarify certain points regarding Ashdod, which is really the only site with a stratified sequence from the Late Bronze Age of an extent which can be relied upon. The city of Ashdod, eighty dunams in size, was destroyed sometime toward the end of the second half of the thirteenth century B.C.E. Immediately afterwards, resettlement of a completely different nature took place, not dating later than the twelfth century B.C.E. Suddenly, we find for the first time in this country Mycenaean IIIC:1b pottery from Cyprus. There Karageorghis has found evidence at two or three sites of at least two waves of intruders — perhaps two waves of Sea Peoples. Everything that happened in Cyprus happened here also. The appearance of the Sea Peoples there is dated by the pottery to the end of the thirteenth century, perhaps the beginning of the twelfth century B.C.E.

There could not have been such a long time gap between the use of this Mycenaean IIIC pottery and the ware that followed it — the Philistine bichrome pottery. Those who worked with me at Ashdod, including Amihai Mazar, know that in some cases we encountered only two stages and two floors, which proves that no more than a generation passed. This brings us to the beginning of the twelfth century B.C.E.

In regard to Ussishkin's argument that two cities in close proximity could not have coexisted with such different characters, Ashdod and Tel Mor did coexist, each having a completely different culture, so this argument is invalid.

My last point is in reference to ʿAkko. We have there a completely new type of pottery, connected with some other Sea People. The evidence indicates that it is probably Sherden.

SESSION V
CUNEIFORM ARCHIVES FROM THE LANDS OF THE BIBLE

JACQUES TOURNAY, O.P., Session Chairman, *École Biblique et Archéologique Française*

ABRAHAM MALAMAT, *The Hebrew University of Jerusalem*
Mari and Early Israel
HENRI CAZELLES, *École Pratique des Hautes Études, Paris*
Ugarit et la Bible
DIETZ OTTO EDZARD, *Universität München*
Amarna und die Archive seiner Korrespondenten zwischen Ugarit und Gaza
HAYIM TADMOR, *The Hebrew University of Jerusalem*
Nineveh, Calah and Israel: On Assyriology and the Origins of Biblical Archaeology

Respondents

PINḤAS ARTZI, *Bar-Ilan University*
MICHAEL HELTZER, *University of Haifa*
LOUIS D. LEVINE, *Royal Ontario Museum*

Discussion

Mari and Early Israel

Abraham Malamat

JUST OVER FIFTY years have passed since Mari, situated on the Middle Euphrates slightly north of the Syrian-Iraqi border, was discovered accidentally, like Ugarit and El-Amarna. Since 1933, the French have exposed significant parts of the site, initially under the direction of the late André Parrot, who conducted twenty-one seasons of excavations, and since 1979 under Jean Margueron. The excavations have yielded a virtual treasure house of archaeological and epigraphical finds, and the results have exceeded all expectations.

Here we shall concentrate on the royal archives discovered in the magnificent palace of the Old Babylonian period, at which time Mari came under West Semitic control. It is this textual material which is of prime relevance to our subject. Of the 20,000 odd tablets unearthed in the palace, dating from the first or the second half of the eighteenth century B.C.E., depending on which chronological system one adopts, only a quarter or so have been published in a score of volumes, the most recent of which is *Archives royales de Mari* (henceforth *ARMT*), vol. XXIII (Paris, 1984). Even this fraction of the documentary material from Mari is sufficient to reveal the enormous potential of the discovery.

After half a century, what have we gained from these Mari texts? How have they contributed to the study of ancient Palestine, the history of early Israel or the earliest stratum of the Hebrew language? In short, how have they benefited biblical research as a whole? For our purposes, in contrast to Ugarit, for example, the main impact of Old Babylonian Mari is felt in the elucidation of Israel's protohistory, placing it in a perspective so far not attained from any other extra-biblical source.

Mari, like Palestine, is situated on the fringe of the Syro-Arabian Desert — albeit on an entirely different flank. The city-states of the so-called Fertile Crescent were

* This study was made possible through a grant from the Fund for Basic Research administered by the Israel Academy of Sciences and Humanities, and was carried out during my term as a fellow of the Institute for Advanced Studies at The Hebrew University of Jerusalem.

frequently infiltrated, and the West Semitic groups with whom we are concerned here, often simply called Amorites, were just one more of these intrusive movements. Old Babylonian Mari apparently did share ultimate origins with the early Israelites and many other peoples of the West. Thus, a comparison between early Israel and Mari can, should, and must be made. Indeed, the broad spectrum of the Mari archives — the largest extra-biblical body of material within this West Semitic milieu — actually invites such a comparison.

But first a cautionary word on the comparative method in regard to Mari and the Bible. Valid, meaningful comparisons can yield significant results, and can preclude shallow or extreme conclusions. Lack of discretion on this point has been a pitfall in the past, the outstanding example being the somewhat sensational hullabaloo surrounding the early announcements of the epigraphic finds at Ebla, although these finds are quite remarkable in themselves. I would reject any romanticist or neofundamentalist approach to the Mari documents, such as were adopted by some scholars soon after their discovery. André Parrot, the French excavator of Mari, never really freed himself of this attitude, and this fever was rampant in other lands as well. Such an approach tends to relate Mari *directly* with the Israelite cradle, almost as if there had been an initial, genetic connection between the tribal populations reflected in the Mari documents and the Patriarchs of the Hebrews.

Avoiding any such "genetic" view, the comparative method which I advocate could best be called "typological" or "phenomenological." In other words, efforts should be concentrated on examination of typical phenomena, seeking out common sets of concepts, and elucidating institutions and practices which were more or less parallel at Mari and among the Israelites. This approach can place our comparisons on a firm, constructive basis.

Valid comparison, however, also involves a contrastive approach, and the basic difference underlying Mari and the Bible must not be neglected. This difference — surprisingly ignored in most research —lies in the very nature of the two sources, for, in quality, they are as different as "the raw and the cooked," to use a phrase of Levi-Strauss. The Mari documents are everyday, firsthand material directly reflecting the reality of their matrix. Further, they were intended for limited, internal consumption. In decided contrast, the biblical material — mainly in the genre of folk narrative —has been "processed," that is, edited and re-edited, and in part indeed composed, centuries after the events described. Nonetheless, this latter point would in no way preclude, *a priori*, some erstwhile historical connection with Mari, though there is nothing in the data presently available which would support such an assumption.

We can now embark on a comparative study of Mari and the Bible, based on these assumptions and reservations. Mari at first appears to be remote from the Bible, in terms of time and space. Indeed, the earliest parts of the biblical text can go back little more than the twelfth century B.C.E., so we are faced with a gap of approximately half a millennium between the time Hammurabi sacked the Mari palace and the time when the earliest parts of the Bible, as we have it, were set down. However, it seems that reminiscences in the patriarchal narratives hark back much earlier than the twelfth century. The problem is —how much further back? This, as you are aware, is a major bone of contention among scholars.

Chronological Aspect

The most difficult problem arising from the patriarchal narratives is probably that of chronology. The so-called Patriarchal Age has often been ascribed to the first quarter, or third, of the second millennium B.C.E. — in archaeological terms, the Middle Bronze Age I (as held foremost by Nelson Glueck and W.F. Albright), or the Middle Bronze Age II (as held, *inter alia*, by Père R. de Vaux and E. Speiser). As the Mari documents are regarded by some authorities as more or less "contemporaneous" with Abraham, Isaac and Jacob, scholars could readily be enticed into adopting a "genetic" approach, leading to overevaluation of the extra-biblical evidence for the historicity of the Israelite Patriarchs. Another school of thought has gone to the opposite extreme, contending that the "Patriarchal Age" and the "Patriarchs" are no more than pure fable, a creation of the later biblical authors, and consequently, possessing no particular time of their own.

My own attitude is that the Patriarchs should not be assigned to any specific, well-defined set of dates, in other words, to a "Patriarchal Age." Hence, this oft-used term is of doubtful legitimacy. I am not suggesting the negation of the very essence of the Patriarchs, but I do, with certain other scholars, regard the Genesis narratives as an artificial construct, based on a limited three-generation scheme. This was the product of later biblical historiographers, who used the scheme to formulate what was actually a prolonged historical process. By such tendentious means as what we call "telescoping," the entire complex of Israel's protohistory was compressed into a simplistic and narrow chronological framework. The cycle of patriarchal narratives must originally have spanned hundreds of years, and probably preserved isolated reminiscences of an even dimmer past, of the early days of the Amorite tribes in Syro-Palestine at the end of the third millennium B.C.E. The literary end product of all this artifice resembles, by way of metaphor, an accordion which has been closed; in order to recover the full historical span, one must expand the accordion.

It is precisely this elasticity which should allay our suspicions concerning the Ebla discoveries and their historical consequences for the patriarchal narratives. If, indeed, the Ebla material does prove relevant to Hebrew origins, then our accordion should simply be extended somewhat further, to accommodate another half millennium or so.

How does all this affect an intelligent, considered comparison with Mari? With all due reservation, the Old Babylonian material at Mari could lie within the "reconstituted" or "untelescoped" purview of the protohistory of Israel, and hence be relevant for comparison with the Bible.

The Ethno-Linguistic Aspect

Viewing the problem from another angle, what can we find to strengthen the chronological basis for comparison? One prominent means is the onomasticon common to Mari and early Israel, a most potent argument in favor of the antiquity of Israel's protohistorical kernel. We shall limit our discussion solely to the members of the patriarchal family, some of whom find their namesakes at Mari. The best documented of these biblical names is *Yaʿaqob* (Jacob), the common occurrence of which at Mari can serve as hard evidence for its antiquity. It appears in tens of cuneiform documents in various forms, such as *Yahqub-El, Haqbu-El, Haqba-ahu* and *(H)aqba/a-Hammû*. The biblical form, as with many other names in the Book of Genesis, is truncated, a sort of nickname lacking its theophoric component, which was apparently El. Significantly, the name Jacob is also found somewhat later among the Semitic rulers of Egypt, the famous Hyksos kings, but there it appears with a different theophoric component.

Other "biblical" names at Mari are: Ishmael in the form *Yasmah-El*; Laban with theophoric elements, as in *El-Laban* or *Ahi-Laban*; and finally, Abram or Abraham in the form of *Abi-Ram*. A recently published Mari text (*ARMT* XXII, No. 328) contains the personal name *Bi-ni-ya-mi-na*, that is, Benjamin. This is the first time that this name appears in its full form in syllabic spelling, leaving no doubt as to its reading, and it is very significant to those initiated into this intricate problem. Admittedly, these names also occur in later periods, a fact which has often been offered as an argument negating an early date, especially by Th.L. Thompson and J. Van Seters. However, we cannot overlook the fact that they are used extensively, particularly in Old Babylonian and Hyksos contexts, and that, with the exception of the name of Abram, they are (especially the name Jacob) much less common in later periods.

Thus our comparison is of twofold significance. On the one hand, it demonstrates the horizon on which the patriarchal names should be evaluated; the majority of these names surely represent early models of personal names among the Israelites. On the other hand, these names are clear indicators of the ethnic affinity of Israel's ancestors, the West Semitic or Amorite stock. Therefore, personal names can often serve, in effect, as ethnic "calling cards," although serious limitations must be taken into account when using this as an isolated criterion.

We certainly have additional criteria of even greater weight for determining the West Semitic character of many of the population groups reflected in the Mari documents, on the one hand, and of the early Israelites, on the other. Foremost at Mari is a linguistic factor. The Mari texts are basically written in a chancery style Babylonian of the Hammurabi period. However, this language is permeated with West Semiticisms in grammar and, more significantly, in vocabulary and idiom. Numerous terms and expressions betray the everyday speech of the scribes, who frequently resorted to typical West Semitic words, or gave specifically West Semitic nuances to standard Akkadian terms.

Many of these very same West Semitic idioms are present in the Hebrew Bible as well, particularly in poetic or exalted language. I could readily cite numerous examples, especially concerning the conceptual world and lifestyle of the West Semites — idioms having no true equivalents in standard Akkadian since their referents are entirely foreign to the Assyro-Babylonian social and ideological milieu.

Since the details are somewhat tedious, we shall mention very few examples, slightly elaborating on one of them later on. Limiting ourselves to West Semitic terms in the realm of tribal society, we find the Mari terms: *gayum*, Hebrew *goy* — originally a tribal unit of perhaps modest extent, already organized into a territorial, administrative framework (there is even mention of a *gāyu Amurru*, that is, an Amorite clan); *ummatum*, Hebrew *ummāh* — another tribal entity derived from the word for "mother," apparently a unit originally attributed to a matriarch, like the Leahite and Rachelite tribes among the Israelites; *hibrum*, Hebrew *ḥeber* — an association of clans, but linked by communal wanderings; *nihlatum*, Hebrew *naḥ^a^lāh*— "patrimony," an inalienable family property; and *šāpiṭum*, Hebrew *šōfēṭ* — conventionally translated "judge" in the Bible, but as we can clearly learn from Mari, the term had a much broader sense — a person not merely dispensing justice, but ruling in general.

The Societal Aspect

All this West Semitic terminology, in one way or another, reflects a thoroughly tribalistic milieu, mainly of nonurban populations, but to some extent also of urban society. This is so at Mari as well as in early Israel, and it is only in these two sources — among all the documentary evidence of the ancient Near East till Islamic times — that tribal society manifests itself in full bloom.

If modern sociology and comparative anthropology are still very much groping about in their treatment of present-day societies, they are confounded all the more so in their attempt to grasp ancient, extinct societies. Despite this serious shortcoming, the variegated patterns and mechanisms of tribal structure and organization are often parallel in our two sources, though in other facets they diverge widely.

In such patrilineal tribal regimes as in the case of Mari and early Israel, the basic social and economic unit is the extended family — the *bet ab* of biblical Hebrew, and the Akkadian *bit abim* at Mari. Such units aggregate to form a clan and, subsequently, broader tribal associations. The best documented of the latter at Mari are the more or less sedentarized Haneans and the seminomadic Yaminites. The Yaminites, unattested outside Mari, are seen as a still somewhat unruly and independent group. Their name, literally meaning "sons of the right," that is, southerners, is outwardly identical with the name of the Israelite tribe of Benjamin, a fact which has occasionally been entirely blown out of proportion. For the present, however, I can see no connection between the two entities, beyond the similarity of name.

The process of tribal settlement as revealed at Mari can be seen to range over a broad spectrum of simultaneous stages of sedentarization, from the nomadic to the permanently settled. In the Bible, we see a diachronic view of this gradual process, the progressive stages depicted as if in sequence: entrance of the early Israelites into Canaan, roving about it, taking possession of parts of the land and, finally, settling it as a permanent, sedentary population. However, at Mari, we see this variegated process as a synchronous, side by side picture at one single, brief point in time. The stereoscopic picture obtained by viewing these two depictions — the synchronic and the diachronic — yields a depth and perspective otherwise unattainable. Mari provides "raw facts in the field," so to speak, almost like modern fieldwork, while the Bible, with its historical perception, has broken the process down into typified stages.

Throughout the biblical narratives we read of the encounter between tribal society and well-established urban culture, an ambivalent relationship of friction and symbiosis. At Mari too, such a picture is projected, and in this light we are now in a better position to assess the mode by which the Israelites were able to penetrate into urbanized Canaan and succeed in their process of *Landnahme*. In the Israelite-Canaanite encounter, it would seem that, more often than not, friction developed between the two rival social and political systems. A single indicative episode in this context, even if only of symbolic nature, was Jacob's encounter with the town of Shechem after the rape of his daughter, Dinah. Though the inhabitants of the city welcomed him and offered him land and connubial relations, Jacob and his sons, despite the fact that their rejection of the offer entailed a considerable loss of potential economic advantage, preferred to avenge the family honor.

That Israelite tenacity won out is history. This is in contrast to the experience in Mesopotamia, where there seems to have been much more mutual assimilation amongst the rival societies; the Akkadian-Babylonian culture on the one hand, and the various tribal, West Semitic elements on the other.

In Israel's protohistory we also encounter a symbiotic relationship of mutuality and cultural sharing between tribe and city. This sort of dimorphic society seems to be mirrored by recent archaeological discoveries from the Middle Bronze Age II in Palestine. Most significant in this respect are the various open satellite villages, mainly rather small and short-lived, found adjacent to Middle Bronze Age towns. The biblical traditions concerning the encampments of the Patriarchs alongside Canaanite cities such as Shechem, Bethel (Genesis 12:6,8) and Hebron (Genesis 13:18), fit in well with such an archaeological picture.

In the Mari documents, this mode of life is best illustrated in the concept of the *nawûm*. In standard Akkadian, this word means "desert, steppe, uncultivated field," but in its specialized West Semitic usage, it denotes semifertile pasturage and, by association, encampment there. Such a meaning can also be seen in the biblical Hebrew form of this word, *nāweh*. This word, although it does not appear in the patriarchal narratives, is found, in retrospective use, in poetic passages such as Psalms 79:7 and Jeremiah 10:25, as in the expression *n^{e}weh Ya^{ʿa}qob*, the "habitation" of Jacob.

Occasionally, a *nawûm* is mentioned as being attached to a city, as is implied by such phrases as "the *nawûm* of Carchemish" or Sippar and its *nawûm*. This is quite reminiscent of the depictions of the Patriarchs dwelling on the outskirts of Canaanite towns, which we have just noted. On the other hand, the outlying *nawûms* of the Mari texts are reflected in the biblical narrative regarding Jacob's sons (Genesis 37:12ff.), who pastured their flocks as far away from their father's base at Hebron as Shechem and even Dothan.

An interesting series of values emerges from a study of this word, *nawûm/nāweh*, in the Mesopotamian-Syrian-Palestinian sphere. The attitude toward the *nawûm* in the standard urban-orientated Assyrian-Babylonian culture is negative, regarding it as disruptive to civilization. At Mari, in the midst of the mixing bowl of Mesopotamian and West Semitic cultures, the general attitude is practical and sympathetic, accepting the *nawûm* as a fact of life. In the Bible, we see a sort of internal, self view of the *nāweh*, fully identifying with it and its way of life. Indeed, among the Israelites, the *nāweh* even assumed a theological dimension, as can clearly be seen in the best known of all the Psalms, Psalm 23: "The Lord is my shepherd, I shall not want; he makes me lie down in green *nāwehs*," that is, in green pastures!

The Geographical Aspect

Turning now to the geographical side of our subject, we find that the Mari documents are of value on several planes. First and foremost, they encompass the region known in the Bible as Aram-Naharaim, and today called the Jezireh in northeastern Syria. This was the land from which, traditionally, the Patriarchs came to Canaan. In this context, it is most significant that the two cities which were erstwhile habitats of the patriarchal clan — Haran and Nahor — find frequent mention in the Mari letters, specifically as focal points of nomadic tribal activity. Haran, in the Upper Balikh Valley, was a central station in the itinerary of the Hebrews on their way to Canaan. Nahor, on the western arm of the Habur River, east of Haran, is noted as the residence of Laban, a relative of the patriarchal clan, from whose family both Isaac and Jacob took their wives.

No less significant than the appearance of the early patriarchal habitat is the light shed on the dynamic dimension of mobility in the entire region. The comings and goings of the Patriarchs, between Aram-Naharaim and Canaan, are thus now brought into comprehensible perspective. The numerous references in the Mari documents to merchant caravans, official missions and, especially significant, the movements of tribal groups making their way from the Middle Euphrates region to as far away as northern Canaan, provide a much more convincing and reliable backdrop than the simple, almost naive picture reflected in Genesis. The obsolete view of a centrifugal flow from the Arabian Desert into the surrounding areas must now give way to another model. Metaphorically, we can now grasp the major tribal movements as a sort of "alternating current." Such a model exactly fits the descriptions of the patriarchal migrations between Aram-Naharaim and Canaan.

What other points of contact with the "Holy Land" do we find at Mari? Actually, very few. The name Canaan seems to appear in a recently published letter, in the form LÚ *Ki-na-ah-num*^{MEŠ}, that is, "Canaanites," and it occurs in connection with the term *habbātum*, "marauders," a synonym of *Habiru/ʿApiru*. This, then, is the earliest attestation of Canaan, pushing the documentation some three centuries further back than the hitherto known earliest reference to this name. Besides this, Hazor in northern Canaan is mentioned in some ten published Mari texts (including *ARMT*, vol. XXIII), all but one of them from the days of Zimri-Lim, the last ruler of Mari. Hazor, excavated during the 1950s and 1960s by Yigael Yadin, grew to greatness in the Mari period, having an "acropolis" and a lower city totaling 200 acres (700 dunams) in area (about the same size as Qatna and Ebla). What is significant for us is the fact that several cuneiform documents were also found there, raising our hopes that one day a royal archive of this period will be discovered at Hazor.

What did Mari and Hazor seek from one another? Hazor was beyond Mari's normal political sphere of influence, but it was on the very edge of its horizon of commerce. There are several Mari texts which deal in particular with a "strategic" commodity — tin, the metal which was alloyed with copper in a ratio of about one to eight in order to yield bronze. Trade in tin was brisk in this period, and Mari was a major tin emporium. In one Mari document alone, 500 kg of tin are listed, and other smaller quantities are noted as being received from or despatched to several destinations and persons in the West. Besides consignments to the king of Aleppo, quantities were apparently sent to Ugarit, to a Caphtorite there (that is, a merchant from Crete), and to a *ta-ar-ga-ma-an-num*. This is one of the earliest occurrences of this *Kulturwort* which is still used, after almost 4,000 years, in more or less the same meaning, "dragoman." What is of greatest concern to us in this document, is the fact that it includes three consignments of tin for Hazor, totaling over 35 kg, sufficient for the manufacture of some 300 kg of bronze. Furthermore, it is consigned to "Ibni-Adad, King of Hazor," revealing the personal name of the ruler of the city.

In this same tin text, we find mention of perhaps another city in Palestine — Laish, some 30 km north of Hazor. In recent years, Laish has been the object of extensive excavations directed by A. Biran. These excavations have revealed a large city of 200 dunams, encompassed by massive fortifications of the Middle Bronze Age II, that is, the Mari period. It is therefore likely that Mari, especially under Zimri-Lim, might have been responsible for the intensification of bronze manufacture in the Canaanite sphere.

Not long ago, I was privileged to publish a Mari text indicative of the commerce between Mari and Hazor. It seems that one of Zimri-Lim's servants was sent to Hazor, to purchase precious materials for use in the Mari palace. To quote: "This man took away from Hazor silver, gold and precious stones and made off," apparently without paying for them. In retaliation, the Hazor authorities detained a caravan from Mari. Matters were further complicated when the servant from Mari was assaulted and brutally robbed on his way home, at Emar on the Euphrates — claiming that both the goods and the sealed receipt for them had been stolen from him. Zimri-Lim appealed to Yarim-Lim, King of Aleppo, who enjoyed considerable influence throughout Syria, apparently to obtain release of his caravan at Hazor and to recover his property stolen at Emar. We shall never know the outcome of the affair, but it does provide a fascinating glimpse into the trials and tribulations of international trade at that time, especially in the West.

Another important realm which can contribute toward an understanding of the ancient Israelite experience can only briefly be referred to —religious manifestations and ritual practices, such as the covenant-making ceremony, enforcement of the ban as penalty for certain types of transgression, and the more controversial census-taking and ritual expiation. In all of these, certain essential similarities between Mari and Israel are evident. More important is the appearance at Mari of intuitive prophecy, that is, prophetic revelation without resort to mantic or oracular devices and techniques. Despite the considerable ideological hiatus between prophecy at Mari and in the Bible, the early manifestation of intuitive prophecy at Mari should not be belittled. We can see in existence there prophetic emissaries among West Semitic tribes many centuries before the similar, though more mature manifestation among the Israelites. In my opinion, however, the outstanding element in this comparison is twofold. Firstly, the unsolicited nature of the revelations, neither the "prophet" nor the addressee deliberately seeking them, and secondly, the sense of mission borne by the medium. We can now regard this sort of divine revelation as another facet of the pantographic relationship between Mari and early Israel — the parallelism between their ethnically and socially analogous population groups.

Treasure house that it is, Mari cannot for the present serve as anything more than indirect or circumstantial evidence for Israel's protohistory. Mari is not the Patriarchs, but it is of their world and it is closer to them than any other extra-biblical source.

For further material, see the author's articles:

1. *Mari and the Bible, A Collection of Studies* (17 Hebrew and English papers), 2d ed. enl. The Hebrew University of Jerusalem, 1980.
2. "'Silver, Gold and Precious Stones from Hazor': Trade and Trouble in a New Mari Document." *Essays in Honor of Y. Yadin. Journal of Jewish Studies* 33 (1982): 71–79.
3. "A Forerunner of Biblical Prophecy: The Mari Documents." In *F.M. Cross Jubilee Volume*. In press.
4. "'Doorbells' at Mari — A Textual-Archaeological Correlation." *Proceedings of the 30th Rencontre Assyriologique Internationale, Leiden, 1983*. In press.

Ugarit et la Bible

Henri Cazelles

Traiter des rapports entre Ugarit et la Bible en une demi-heure est une entreprise désespérée; toutefois, c'est ce qu'il convient de faire dans un congrès comme celui-ci. Il ne s'agit pas d'ajouter un numéro de plus à la bibliographie de Dietrich-Loretz-Sanmartín, déjà copieuse et déjà dépassée après les fouilles d'Ibn-Hani, ni de démontrer une fois de plus que l'une féconde l'intelligence de l'autre et réciproquement, mais de dégager les données fondamentales qui permettent une confrontation solide et fructueuse. Nous ne reprendrons pas le titre donné par Del Medico à son étude d'Ugarit: "La Bible cananéenne." Nous éviterons aussi de nous exposer au commentaire humoristique des Psaumes, par ailleurs si suggestifs, de notre regretté ami M. Dahood: "Le Psautier selon Ugarit." Puisque ce congrès traite d'archéologie et d'archives notre propos ne sera pas de traiter de littérature religieuse, mais d'Ugarit et Bible considérés comme archives, et des lieux antiques d'où nous viennent ces deux blocs de textes.

1. Ces deux blocs ne se ressemblent ni dans leur forme ni dans leur processus de composition. La Bible forme un livre, tout en admettant de nombreuses éditions à l'intérieur même de ses sections. La littérature ugaritique est faite de plusieurs bibliothèques provenant de différents temples, palais et maisons. A l'intérieur même du palais central nous avons des archives est, ouest, et centrales. Dans la maison privée de Rapʾanu nous trouvons des documents de caractère officiel. Toutes ces archives ont été enterrées ensemble après le grand désastre de la fin du Bronze Récent. La Bible n'a jamais été enterrée et a été soumise à des additions successives pendant un millenaire jusqu'à ce que le canon de l'Ecole pharisienne la considère comme close.

Le contenu, de plus, est différent. A Ugarit, pas de récits de création, pas d'oracles prophétiques, pas d'Annales ni de lois; peu d'hymnes et peu de sagesse. Dans la Bible peu de mythes, peu de lettres et peu de documents administratifs comme dans la cité amorite à présence hurrite.

2. Ces deux littératures sont fonction de la vie d'une capitale. Pour la Bible nous avons

peu à tenir compte de Samarie dans la composition du livre, même si la chute de cette ville a été un moment important dans l'histoire israélite. La Bible se developpe autour de Jérusalem et de son Temple "lieu choisi par le Seigneur pour y mettre son Nom." Ugarit est le centre de la culture ugaritique même s'il y avait des archives à Ibn-Hani, si Kochavi a trouvé une lettre en cunéiforme venant d'Ugarit à Aphek, et si des tablettes alphabétiques ont été trouvées au Liban (Sarepta), en Syrie (Tell Nebi Mend) et en Canaan (Beth Shemesh, Tabor, Taʿanak).

Mais combien différentes sont ces deux cités! Jérusalem, la vieille ville cananéenne conquise par David après une longue vie tribale en Israël, près de deux siècles après la destruction de l'Ugarit cananéo-phénicienne. Jérusalem solidement établie dans ses montagnes, loin de la mer et de cette voie militaire que fut la côte, ville épargnée par Sheshonq et Sennachérib, conquise par Nabuchodonosor et souvent depuis, mais toujours vivante, alors que malgré une timide réoccupation du site, Ugarit disparaît. Ugarit, un port en relations par terre avec la Mésopotamie, par mer avec l'Egypte et les îles, point de la côte le plus proche d'Emar et de l'Euphrate. Jérusalem, capitale qui ne fut jamais riche sauf l'année où, sous Salomon, lui arrivèrent 670 talents d'or; le même Salomon sera obligé de céder Kabul et ses villes pour 120 talents au roi de Tyr. Il faudra ensuite attendre Hérode. Ugarit, cité somptueuse avec ses nombreux palais et quartiers résidentiels. Elle laisse après sa destruction des restes qu'on ne peut comparer avec ce que Weil, Miss Kenyon et Shiloh ont trouvé sur l'Ophel.

3. Toutefois alors que les deux cités et leur littérature ne sont pas du même ordre, la connaissance de l'une aide puissamment à l'intelligence de l'autre.

a) C'est grâce à la Bible que l'ugaritique a pu être déchiffré, les bilingues accado-ugaritiques n'étant découverts que plus tard. Le vocabulaire et les éléments de grammaire ont pu être établis rapidement grâce à l'hébreu biblique.

—On ne lit plus Térah et Ashdod dans les légendes, mais que de toponymes bibliques comme Carkémish, le Siyannu, Gebal et d'autres!

—On ne savait que faire du *šṯʿ* d'Isaïe 41.10. Voilà qu'Ugarit nous donne le parallèle en CTA 5:2, 7; 6:6, 30: *yrʾ* "craindre." Une riche collection d'expressions psalmiques trouvent leurs parallèles. Quoiqu'on en ait discuté, le *mishpaṭ hammelek* de 1 Samuel 10.25 a un correspondant plus ou moins proche dans le *mṯpṭ yld* d'Ugarit V.

—Plus important —Les déités connues par la Bible, El, Baal, Ashtart, Reshef, voire Ashéra, deviennent des entités concrètes qui font image. Avec Eissfeldt on comprendra mieux pourquoi le Dieu d'Abraham peut être identifié à El tandis qu'il rejettera Baal au temps d'Elie.

b) Cependant nous savons par la Bible qu'au temps de Saül et David, Baal avait sa place et qu'Ishboshet fut d'abord un Ishbaal. Nous sommes ainsi confrontés avec les problèmes de la fondation de l'Etat monarchique en Israël. L'Etat dans l'Ancien Orient n'est pas seulement une administration militaire, civile et judiciaire. C'est un peuple qui a des problèmes de rois et de dynasties. Je regrette qu'on ait un peu négligé ces derniers temps les études des écoles scandinave et anglaise (Hooke). Il faut prendre très au sérieux ce qui est dit sur la fondation de la monarchie "à l'instar des peuples" voisins en 1 Samuel 8.5–20. C'est très justement que Z. Kallai a intitulé un de ses articles: *The United Monarchy in Israel. A Focal Point in Israelite Historiography*. Il y avait des Etats monarchiques dans le Canaan prébiblique, dans les lettres d'El Amarna; Abdi-Hepa de Jérusalem connu sous le titre "Ami du roi" qu'on retrouve dans l'entourage de Saül est probablement le *mudu* ugaritique. La Bible nous donne peu sur l'administration monarchique mais suffisamment par certaines listes et par les plaintes des Prophètes pour nous faire voir qu'il y avait là en Israël une pratique et un problème. L'abondance des archives d'Ugarit nous permet de mieux percevoir la nature de ces problèmes que seront à l'arrière plan des écrits bibliques. Mendelsohn a utilement comparé les privilèges du roi en 1 Samuel 8 et la pratique ugaritique. Alt a éclairé le sens des *Menschen ohne Namen* de 1 Rois, 4, mais les préfets de Salomon ne sont pas "celui" d'Ugarit. Alors que Temple et Palais sont intimement liés à Jérusalem comme à Khorsabad et Medinet Habu, il n'y a pas semblable lien entre les palais d'Ugarit et les temples de Baal ou de Dagan. Les archéologues auront leur mot à dire. Si nous ne savons rien des palais de David et de Salomon nous pourrions avoir des comparaisons grâce à Ramat-Rahel et Megiddo. Il y aura sans doute de grandes divergences puisque Y. Shiloh a souligné la différence entre les constructions à orthostates d'Ugarit et les murs israélites en *ashlar*. Les tombes mycéniennes d'Ugarit ne correspondent pas aux sépultures israéliennes de l'Age du Fer, et, à ma connaissance, il n'y a pas de chapiteaux proto-éoliques à Ugarit.

A Jérusalem comme à Ugarit on eut à affronter les problèmes de succession dynastique, de défaut d'héritier et de tensions familiales. C'est le thème fondamental des légendes ugaritiques de Keret, Aqhat et même de certains textes sur Baal; à Jérusalem c'est le problème de la succession de David, apparemment si pauvre du point de vue religieux, comme des vieux récits familiaux de la Genèse. Dans les deux cités on dut faire appel aux anciennes traditions tribales pour situer le présent: appel à Ditanu à Ugarit; évocation d'Abraham et des fils d'Israël à Jérusalem. Sur cet arrière plan nomade, Ugarit nous donne moins que Mari et la Bible. Mais on sait les contacts des tribus phéniciennes, montant vers le nord de la Syrie, avec l'Ah-Samak de Galilée, avec l'Harnem libanais de la légende d'Aqhat, enfin, près de Baal Saphon, avec les tensions entre une vieille culture de chasse représentée par le Dieu El (cf. Esaü) et la société sédentaire agricole d'Anat, Baal, Reshef, voir Ashérat de la mer (cf. Jacob).
c) Nous pouvons enfin constater comment la civilisation phénicienne d'Ugarit et celle d'Israël ont évolué différemment. La dynamique n'est pas la même. L'une aboutira à Sanchuniaton, à la mythologie phénicienne de Philon de Byblos en passant par la sagesse du roi de Tyr condamnée par Ezechiel 28.17, Chérubin dans un jardin. Cette *ḥokmah* du roi de Tyr, héritée de celle du dieu El d'Ugarit, fut reconnue à Salomon par tout Israël (1 Rois 3.28), et à David par la femme de Tekoa qui voit en lui la sagesse de l'ange du Seigneur (2 Samuel 14.20) Azitawadda de Karatepe comme Panammu de Carkémish étaient également loués pour leur sagesse. La Bible est plus réservée et n'apprécie guère la *ʿormah* du serpent de Genèse 3.1 la *ḥokmah* de Pharaon en Exode 1.10, ni celle de Jonadab en 2 Samuel 13.3. Cette *ḥokmah* aboutit à des désastres et ce n'est pas avant Isaïe 31.2 qu'on reconnaît explicitement au Seigneur le titre de *ḥâkam*;

il est encore plutôt dangereux. C'est un autre type de *ḥokmah* qui se manifestera en Proverbes 3.19–20, 8.12 ss.

Toutefois la Bible n'a jamais répudié ce que J. Gray a appelé *The Legacy of Canaan*. Avant Ugarit nous connaissions peu de ce qu'avaient légué Sidon, Tyr, voire les Jébuséens d'Abdi-Hepa. Les *Ras Shamra Parallels* nous donnent maintenant une grande abondance de matériel, trop aux dires de certains. Ce ne sont pas les textes les plus anciens de la Bible qui nous donnent le plus. L'index de J. Gray ne donne que quarante-huit cas dans la Genèse pour 126 dans les Psaumes. Le cas le plus curieux reste celui d'Isaïe 27.1–4. Dans cette Apocalypse d'Isaïe, qui est un des textes les plus récents du livre d'Isaïe, nous trouvons la description de Léviathan dans les termes précis dont en parle CTA 5.1–2. C'est une preuve que la Bible ne s'est pas developpée en ghetto et qu'elle a su à toutes les époques assimiler ce qu'elle trouvait de plus adéquat à son but dans les cultures ambiantes.

Amarna und die Archive seiner Korrespondenten zwischen Ugarit und Gaza*

Dietz Otto Edzard

I

MAN KÖNNTE VON einer "Überinterpretation" der in Tell al-ʿAmārna gefundenen Keilschrifttafeln sprechen, da diese fast 400 Texte und Fragmente nahezu unsere einzige Keilschrift-Quelle sind für das Bild, das wir uns vom kanaanäischen Zweig der semitischen Sprachen in der zweiten Hälfte des II. Jts. v. Chr. machen; für die Kenntnis der internationalen Beziehungen zwischen Ägypten, Syrien, Palästina, dem Hethiterland, Mesopotamien, Zypern; für die mit den politischen Beziehungen eng verknüpften Handelsbeziehungen; für die Struktur der ägyptischen Verwaltung in Asien. "Überinterpretation" insofern, als wir die Angaben der Briefe nur äusserst selten anhand anderer Keilschriftarchive nachprüfen können. Mit anderen Worten: Hundert Jahre nach der Entdeckung und siebzig Jahre nach J.A. Knudtzons meisterhafter Bearbeitung (VAB 2, 1915)[1] wissen wir von vielen "Amarna-Korrespondenten" immer noch nicht, wo sie residierten, da ihre Städte noch nicht identifiziert werden könnten; und in den Fällen, wo uns diese Residenzen bekannt sind, fehlen uns doch die Archive, die denen von Amarna entsprochen haben müssen (wenn auch sicher oft in einem viel beschränkteren Rahmen).[2]

Seit den vierziger Jahren haben Gelehrte wie W.F. Albright, W.L. Moran, A.F. Rainey, P. Artzi und viele andere gleichsam in zweiter und dritter Forschergeneration zur Deutung der Amarna-Briefe beigetragen.[3] Albright drückte 1944 die Hoffnung aus, "There is no reason to doubt that continued excavation in such rich sites as Megiddo and Lachish will yield a rich harvest of written documents from the latest pre-Israelite period."[4] In der Tat sind *einige* Tontafeln der Amarna-Zeit ans Licht gekommen. Aber wenn wir alle Texte und Fragmente zusammenzählen, so erreichen

* Der Titel des Vortrags lautete "Amarna — and What Else? Overevaluation of an Archive?"

wir—rein stückmässig—nur etwa ein Fünfzehntel des Amarna-Archives; umfangmässig bleiben wir weit unter einem Prozent. Unser Urteil bleibt also ganz und gar auf Amarna angewiesen, und diese Disproportion ist beunruhigend.

Eine solche Disproportion ist für den Assyriologen aber nichts Ungewohntes. Wir denken an Mari und Ebla im III. Jts. v. Chr. Ebla ist in den letzten fünfzehn Jahren übermächtig geworden. Auf Grund der ausserordentlich glücklichen Funde ist das zeitgenössische Mari in den Schatten gestellt. Das entspricht freilich nicht der historischen Wirklichkeit.[5] Nichts liegt näher, als denen von Ebla ähnliche Archive auch in Mari zu vermuten.[6]

Wir könnten uns auch vorstellen, man hätte noch vor der Entdeckung von Amarna reichhaltige "Amarna-zeitliche" Schriftfunde in Byblos gemacht. Man hätte dann sicher bei den 300 km südlich von Kairo entdeckten Tontafeln von "Byblos-Tafeln" gesprochen.

II

Wir wollen einen Rundgang machen durch zwischen den Breitengraden von Ugarit und Gaza gelegene Orte, an denen Keilschrifttafeln und -fragmente gefunden worden sind — "Amarna-zeitliche" wie auch ältere. Daran sollen dann einige Fragen und Betrachtungen angeschlossen werden.

1. Ugarit selbst heben wir hier nicht hervor. Seit 1969 ist der Ugarit-Philologie und -Archäologie im weitesten Sinne die Zeitschrift "Ugarit-Forschungen" gewidmet, und es gibt eine vielpfündige "Ugarit-Bibliographie."[7] Ugarit, das lange vor seiner Entdeckung dem Namen nach aus den Amarna-Briefen bekannt war,[8] sei hier nur erwähnt im Zusammenhang mit dem geheimen Wunsch jedes "Amarna-Philologen", es möge doch auch "Sidon-Forschungen", "Kumidi-Forschungen", "Askalon-Forschungen" und viele weitere geben.

2. Keilschriftfunde aus der bedeutenden Hafenstadt Byblos beschränken sich bisher auf eine einzige Tontafel, ein Syllabarfragment aus der Ur III-Zeit, wenn nicht gar noch älteren Datums.[9] Diese Tafel beweist wenigstens, dass es in Byblos schon gegen Ende des III. Jts. eine Keilschrift-Schreiberschule gegeben hat. Byblos wird auch in zwei Ur III-Urkunden erwähnt.[10]

Umso reicher der Befund in Amarna. Über ein Sechstel der Amarna-Briefe stammt aus Byblos. Das Byblos-Corpus hat sich, wie gut bekannt, als eine unschätzbare Quelle erwiesen nicht nur für die Kenntnis der politischen Zeitgeschichte, sondern vor allem für die Kenntnis des Kanaanäischen und für die Interferenz zwischen der Umgangssprache der Schreiber und ihrem Brief-Akkadisch.[11]

Byblos dürfte als Hafen und Handelsort mit Ugarit mindestens gleichrangig gewesen sein. So haben wir sicher auch mit einer Mehrzahl anwesender Völker und Sprachen zu rechnen. Politisch war Byblos freilich von Ägypten abhängig —anders als Ugarit mit seiner eigenen Dynastie. Auf jeden Fall aber muss Byblos mit einer ins III. Jts. hinaufreichenden Keilschrifttradition auch ein Zentrum lebhafter geistiger Tätigkeit gewesen sein. Nachdem in Tel Aphek (s. unten II 8) ein dreisprachiges lexikalisches Fragment entdeckt worden ist und in Anbetracht der reichen lexikalischen Funde aus Ugarit (Bilinguen, Trilinguen, Quadrilinguen), [12] wird man kaum daran zweifeln, dass es entsprechende lexikalische Texte auch in Byblos gegeben hat — von literarischen Keilschrifttexten abgesehen. Dagegen können wir nicht sicher vermuten, dass sich auch die Verwaltung in Byblos — teilweise — der mesopotamischen Keilschrift bedient habe. Auf jeden Fall können nur neue Ausgrabungen in Ǧubayl über Spekulation hinausführen.

3. Noch auf dem Boden Libanons, aber im Biq̄aʿ, liegt Kāmid al-Lōz, dessen Gleichsetzung mit dem alten Kumidi zuerst von H. Guthe vorgeschlagen wurde.[13] Kumidi ist "Amarna-Korrespondent" (EA 198). In Kāmid al-Lōz wurden bisher sieben Keilschrifttafeln gefunden.[14] Nr. 1 und 2 sind Rundschreiben des Pharao, eines an Zalaja, den "Mann von Damaskus", das andere an Abdi-Milki, den "Mann von Šazaena". Inhaltlich sind beide Briefe identisch. Pharao fordert die Empfänger auf, Ḫapiru-Leute nach Ägypten zu schicken; Pharao will sie in Nubien (*Ka-a-ša*, Kuš) ansiedeln im Austausch gegen von dort zu deportierende Bevölkerung. Es war ein Glücksfall, dass beide Tafeln zusammen gefunden wurden. Hätte man nur die an den "Mann von Šazaena" adressierte entdeckt, so hätte man, einem unausweichbaren Schluss folgend, Kāmid al-Lōz mit Šazaena gleichgesetzt.

Hier seien kurz die 1970 (s. Anm. 13, S. 57f.) gestellten Fragen resümiert: Warum wurden diese Pharao-Briefe in Kāmid al-Lōz entdeckt? Haben sie ihren Bestimmungsort nie erreicht? Gelangten sie in die Archive von Kumidi, nachdem sie von den Adressaten zur Kenntnis genommen worden waren? Oder sind es Duplikate? Die dritte Hypothese hat am meisten für sich. Es müssen freilich Duplikate sein, die der Absender bereits angefertigt hatte; denn der Schriftduktus der beiden Tafeln ist derselbe wie der von EA 162, einem in Amarna verbliebenen Duplikat eines Pharao-Briefes an Aziru von Amurru.

Wir wissen nicht, warum derartige Duplikate in Kumidi hätten deponiert werden sollen. Aber wir müssen betonen, dass uns die Annahme von Archivduplizierung das gesamte Korrespondenzsystem noch weit komplizierter erscheinen lässt.

Nr. 3 und 4 sind unverwertbare Brieffragmente. Nr. 5 aus Kumidi ist gleichsam "S. 2" eines Briefes; man zog offenbar relativ kleine Tafeln einem grösseren Format vor. Nr. 6, der Brief eines Eši-rabi an einen ägyptischen Beamten, weist eine sehr interessante Verbindung kanaanäischer Interferenz und hurritischen Syllabars auf. Nr. 7 ist vielleicht eine Schreibübung, und das wäre dann der erste Beleg für eine Schule in Kumidi.

4. Wir begeben uns nach Hazor, [15] ca. 250 km südlich von Kāmid al-Lōz. Hazor ist "Amarna-Korrespondent" (EA 227 f.; s.a. 148:41), und es kommt auch schon in der Königskorrespondenz des altbabylonischen Mari vor (*ARMT* 16/1, 14 f.). Aus Hazor

stammen beschriftete Tonlebermodelle der spätaltbabylonischen Zeit,[16] eine altbabylonische Gerichtsurkunde[17] und ein lexikalisches Fragment.[18] Bisher zwar nichts in situ aus der Amarna-Zeit; doch dürfen wir wohl von dem altbabylonischen Befund auf eine mehrere Jahrhunderte lange Schreibertradition schliessen.

5. Megiddo ist assyriologisch berühmt geworden durch das dort gefundene mittelbabylonische Gilgameš-Fragment,[19] das inhaltlich der VII. Tafel der klassischen Version des Epos entspricht. Das Bruchstück wurde leider ausserhalb jeden Schichtzusammenhanges gefunden, so dass es — streng genommen — noch nichts über ein lokales Schreiberzentrum aussagen könnte. Doch spricht nicht das Geringste gegen die Annahme, dass die sehr bedeutende Stadt auch eine Stätte geistiger Tätigkeit gewesen ist. Wir hätten dann das erste Beispiel für einen literarischen Keilschrifttext von einem Ort, der mit der Verwaltung in Amarna korrespondierte (EA 242–246; s.a. 234:19).

In Megiddo wurden in Schichten des 13. oder 12. Jahrhunderts auch Tonlebermodelle gefunden; sie sind aber — im Gegensatz zu denen von Hazor — nicht beschriftet.[20]

6. Knapp 10 km südöstlich von Megiddo liegt Tell al-Taʿannaḫ, von wo zwölf Keilschriftdenkmäler stammen.[21] Sie datieren in die Zeit vor Amarna,[22] und zwar in die Regierung Amenophis II., wenn Landsbergers Vermutung zutrifft.[23] Der Lokalfürst als der Empfänger der Briefe ist Re-ja$_8$-šur.[24] Die Taʿannaḫ-Texte Nr. 3 und 4 könnten Fragmente von Personenlisten irgendwelcher Art sein.

7. Aus Sichem (Tall al-Balāṭa) stammt ein Privatbrief,[25] dazu ein Tafelfragment, von dem nur eine Liste mit Personennamen, zum Teil mitsamt Vatersnamen, erhalten ist.[26] Da allen Namen *ši-bu* und Personenkeil vorangehen, läge es nahe, eine Zeugenliste zu vermuten und in dem Text einen Vertrag oder eine Gerichtsurkunde. Es wäre dann das bislang südlichste Beispiel für eine Rechtsurkunde in Keilschrift. Leider ist das aber unbeweisbar; das Tafelformat spricht dagegen.[27]

8. In Aphek (Antipatris) wurden bisher acht Tontafeln und Fragmente gefunden, darunter (Nr. 6) ein Brief des LÚ *ša-ki*<*-in*>(?) URU *Ú-ga-ri-it* an seinen "Vater und Herrn", den LÚ.GAL *Ḫa-a-ja*.[28] Der Absender macht Ansprüche auf Getreide geltend. Auffällig ist die grosse Entfernung zwischen Ugarit und dem Bestimmungsort (ca. 350 km).

Die lexikalischen Fragmente (Nr. 1, 3) sind —von Amarna selbst abgesehen —die ersten, die südlich von Ugarit gefunden wurden. Wenn richtig ergänzt, unterscheiden sie sich aber von den Multilinguen aus Ugarit. Nr. 3 enthält in Kol. I der beiden erhaltenen Zeilen jeweils ein Logogramm: [(...)A].MEŠ, [GEŠTIN].MEŠ, "Wasser", "Wein"; Kol. II enthält die akkadische Aussprache: *ma-wu*, *ka-ra-nu* (=*māwū*, *karānu*); Kol. III schliesslich die Umsetzung in die örtliche kanaanäische Sprache: *mu-mi*, *je-nu* (= *mōmi*, *jēnu*).

Leider lässt sich nicht sicher feststellen, ob Nr. 2 ein Verwaltungstext ist; denn die Zahlen zwischen 200 und 5000 in den vier Zeilenanfängen könnten durchaus auch aus einem Brief stammen.[29] Nr. 8 ist m. E. völlig unbestimmbar.

9. Das Brieffragment aus Gezer beim heutigen Ramla erinnert stellenweise an Brief Nr. 6 aus Tall Taʿannaḫ, soweit man das bei dem kümmerlich erhaltenen Text sagen kann.[30]

10. Lachis ist als "Amarna-Korrespondent" gut bezeugt (EA 328 f.; s.a. EA 287: 15, 288:43, 335:10, 16); aber eine Tontafel wurde bisher nur auf dem benachbarten Tall al-Ḥasi, 30 km südöstlich von Askalon, gefunden. Es ist EA 333 (nicht aus Amarna!), der durch Albright erschlossene "lèse-majesté"-Brief.[31] Nach Rainey wäre Tall al-Ḥasi das antike Jurṣa gewesen,[32] während Aharoni und Avi-Yonah Jurṣa südlich von Gaza lokalisieren.[33]

11. Der Vollständigkeit halber sei am Ende dieses Überblicks auch das Keilschrift-fragment aus Jericho genannt. Leider lässt es sich nicht näher bestimmen, und so müssen wir es ganz ausser Betracht lassen.[34]

III

An diesen Rundgang seien einige praktische Fragen angeschlossen. Es lohnt sich, sie zu stellen, auch wenn wir sie zur Zeit kaum schon beantworten können:

1. Addieren wir die Keilschrift-Fundplätze des 14. und 13. Jahrhunderts südlich von Ugarit und ferner die Orte, die wir aus Amarna als Korrespondenten in den betreffenden Landstrichen kennen, so kommen wir auf nahezu vierzig[35] Orte: Akka,[36] Akšapu,[37] Aphek (s. II 8), Askalon,[38] Beirut,[39] Byblos (s. II 2), Damaskus,[40] Dubu,[41] Ēni-šaṣi,[42] Gadašūna,[43] Gezer (s. II 9), Ginti-ašna,[44] Ḫašabu,[45] Hazor (s. II 4), Ḫazi,[46] Irqata,[47] Jericho (s. II 11), Jerusalem,[48] Jurṣa,[49] Kumidi (s. II 3), Lachis (s. II 10), Megiddo (s. II 5), Muḫišūna,[50] [N]a-x-ḫ[a-...][51] Naziba,[52] Qanû,[53] Qatna,[54] Ruḫizza,[55] Šamḫūna,[56] Šazḫimi/Šazaena,[57] Sichem (s. II 7), Sidon,[58] Tall al-Taʿannaḫ (s. II 6), Tunip,[59] Tyros,[60] Ziri-Bašani.[61]

Das ist ein Ortsnetz von zum Teil bemerkenswerter Dichte. Ein solches Ortsnetz haben wir uns vorzustellen, wenn wir den "Reisepass" EA 30 wörtlich nehmen wollen, den ein Herrscher von Mitanni an die "Könige von Kanaan" adressiert hatte.[62] Der Mitannier bittet den jeweiligen Empfänger —oder "Leser" —um Hilfe und Unterstützung für seine Gesandten auf ihrem Wege nach Ägypten. Mit anderen Worten: wo immer sich ein solcher Lokalherrscher befand, durfte man sicher sein, dass ein des Akkadischen mächtiger, Keilschrift lesender Schreiber zur Stelle war.

2. Wie wir wissen, unterschieden sich die "Amarna-Schreiber" qualitätsmässig sehr. Es gibt Briefe von hoher Schreiberkunst, Briefe mit geradezu literarischer Ambition

wie EA 147[63] oder 252.[64] Dem stehen höchst kümmerliche Handschriften gegenüber[65] sowie ganze Briefgruppen von einer langweiligen Monotonie und einer frappierenden Formelhaftigkeit. Die sieben Briefe des Jidija von Askalon (EA 320–326) sind ein Beispiel. Nur EA 326 unterscheidet sich vom Rest durch die Erwähnung von Pharaos Kritik am *rābiṣu*. So wenigstens sehen wir diese Briefe heute. Wir müssen uns aber hüten, diese Dokumente mit unserem literarischen Geschmack anzugehen. Es war ja gerade jene devote Regelmässigkeit der Vasallenberichte, auf die die ägyptische Verwaltung zählte.

Trotzdem ein statistisches Beispiel: EA 141 des Ammunira von Beirut enthält in 48 Zeilen 197 Wörter und Namen; es kommen jedoch nur 60 individuelle Wörter (und zwei Namen) vor, so dass im Durchschnitt jedes Wort über dreimal vertreten ist.

Aber nochmals: Wir dürfen die Schreiber nicht schelten, dass sie nicht wortschöpferisch gewesen seien. Waren sie doch meistens streng gebunden an ein Formular, dessen Nichtbeachtung womöglich als Majestätsbeleidigung aufgefasst worden wäre. Im Übrigen waren viele Schreiber sicher sehr beschränkt in ihrer Kenntnis schreibbarer Wörter. Wir dürfen keinen Vergleich mit den literarischen Schulen Mesopotamiens ziehen.

3. Die Schreiber wurden in Schulen ausgebildet — aber wieviele gab es ? Hatte jeder Ort, von dem wir bisher Keilschrifttexte besitzen, seine eigene Schule? Wir können das nicht beantworten. Vielleicht wurde in bestimmten Fällen ein fertig ausgebildeter Schreiber nach auswärts gesandt, um dort Dienst zu leisten. Oder es bediente sich umgekehrt ein Lokalfürst eines nahegelegenen Schreiberzentrums.[66] Mangels näherer Kenntnis der Verhältnisse erscheint es empfehlenswerter, nur von "Schulen" im abstrakten Sinne zu sprechen, d.h. unter einer "Schule" Schreibergruppen zusammenzufassen, die sich derselben Formulare bedienten. Hier ist noch Arbeit zu leisten. Es folgt ein relativ einfaches Beispiel:

Der Absender tut seine Huldigung dar mit der Verbalform *amqut* "ich fiel nieder" bei Briefen aus dem 'Norden'[67] und mit der Verbal *uš͟he͟hin* "ich warf mich zu Boden" (viele Spielformen)[68] im 'Süden'. *amqut* kommt in Byblos, Sidon, Tyros und in vielen weiteren Städten vor (s. oben III 1 mit Anmm.), *uš͟he͟hin* mit Varianten in Akko, Megiddo, Gezer, Jurṣa, Askalon. *amqut* findet sich auch in Jerusalem. Bei einem Absender, Šipṭi-Ba'la, finden wir jedoch einmal *amqut* (EA 330) und einmal *ištu͟ha͟hin* (EA 331). Ich möchte daraus schliessen, dass sich der Absender für den jeweiligen Brief verschiedener Schreiber bedient hatte, die bei der Begrüssung des Adressaten je ihrer Schultradition folgten.

In einer Briefgruppe nennt sich der Absender *qartappu* "Pferdeknecht" seines Herrn. Diese Gruppe ist identisch mit derjenigen, wo wir der *uš͟he͟hin*-Formel begegnen. So kommt denn in Šipṭi-Ba'las Brief EA 331 *qartappu* vor, während es in EA 330 (*amqut*) fehlt. Solche Beobachtungen lassen uns vermuten, dass der Schreiber in seiner Rolle eines regelrechten Sekretärs zwar den Wortlaut des Briefes nach allgemeinen Instruktionen seines Herrn formulierte, jedoch völlig frei in der ihm geläufigen, erlernten 'Briefsprache'. Wenn das zutrifft, dürfen wir keine Rückschlüsse auf die Sprache des Absenders ziehen, sondern nur auf die des Schreibers. Nicht ohne Grund sprach Moran von "The Scribe of the Jerusalem Letters" (s. Anm. 48).

4. In der Tat ist die Frage nach der Sprache — oder nach den Sprachen — der Korrespondenz ziemlich kompliziert, und wir müssen hier wieder wie so oft die Antwort schuldig bleiben. Wer konnte wessen Sprache verstehen, schreiben, lesen und sprechen? Und wie weitgehend? War Zweisprachigkeit (oder Mehrsprachigkeit) weit verbreitet? Wen-Amun erwähnt in seinem Reisebericht Dolmetscher erst nach Erreichen von Alašia.[69] Konnte er bis dahin mit Ägyptischkenntnis der ihm Begegnenden rechnen, oder sprach er selbst ein wenig kanaanäisch?

In welcher Sprache wurden die "Amarna-Briefe" Pharao (oder seinen Beamten) vorgetragen? Wir haben keinen Beweis dafür, dass der gebildete Ägypter der Zeit akkadisch konnte — und wenn wir hören, dass Potiphar den jungen Joseph auf akkadisch fragte "Woher weisst du denn alle diese Geschichten? Bist du von Karduniasch?", so ist unsere Autorität Thomas Mann.[70]

Andererseits sei an die Postskripte in den Briefen des Abdi-Ḫepa von Jerusalem (EA 286–289) erinnert, wo der Absender den Schreiber bei Pharao anspricht und ihn unterwürfigst bittet, seinen Brief so günstig wie möglich vorzutragen. Das heisst doch wohl, dass der lesende Schreiber den Inhalt in einer ihm passenden Form vortrug, nicht aber Wort für Wort vorlas.[71]

5. Wie häufig wurden "Amarna-Briefe" geschrieben? C. Kühne hat sich ausführlich mit dem "Zeitproblem" befasst und versucht, Kriterien dafür zu finden, welchen Zeitraum eine bestimmte Korrespondenz umfasste, wie lange ein Bote unterwegs war und welche Strecke er durchschnittlich pro Tag zurücklegte.[72] Meine Frage betrifft dagegen den Zeitabstand zwischen einem bestimmten und dem folgenden Brief. Abdi-Milki von Tyros versichert Pharao (EA 147:66–69), dass Zimreda von Sidon *ina ūmi u ūmi*[*m*]*a* "tagtäglich" au Aziru über das berichtet habe, was er über Ägypten erfuhr. Ist das wörtlich zu nehmen? Oder bedeutet es nur, dass Zimreda eben öfters als nur ein- oder zweimal im Monat geschrieben hätte? Derlei Fragen sind natürlich von Bedeutung, wenn wir wissen wollen, wie stark ein bestimmtes Schreiberzentrum mit Arbeit ausgelastet war.

6. Wer waren die Schreiber in Amarna selbst? Die Briefe aus Ägypten sind in einem anderen akkadisch abgefasst als die aus dem Raum zwischen Ugarit und Gaza einlaufenden. Sie mögen grammatische Fehler aufweisen,[73] und sie haben fast immer eine andere Wortfolge als die im akkadischen übliche;[74] doch sind sie im grossen Ganzen frei von Besonderheiten, die wir als Kanaanismen bezeichnen würden.[75]

K. Riemschneider hat die Keilschriftschreiber Pharaos mit der mitannisch-hurritischen Schule in Verbindung gebracht.[76] Ich weiss nicht, was seine einzelnen Argumente waren. Sofort ins Auge springt der häufige Gebrauch von Vokal-plene-Schreibungen in der Amarna-Version von "Adapa" (EA 356) und von "Nergal und Ereškigal" (EA 357), d.h. in den beiden am besten erhaltenen akkadischen literarischen Texten der Amarna-Schule. Schreibungen wie *E-re-eš-ki-i-ga-a-al* (EA 357:2) oder *ma-a-ar ši-i-ip-ri* (EA 357:3) lassen sich von der Orthographie des hurritischen "Mitanni-Briefes" nicht trennen. Häufige Vokal-plene-Schreibung ist aber auch charakteristisch für die Briefe Tušrattas, wie H.-P. Adler gesehen hat,[77] ohne allerdings eine Verbindung zu den literarischen Amarna-Texten zu ziehen. Wir müssen auf der anderen Seite zugeben, dass die wenigen uns in antiker Kopie erhaltenen Briefe, die aus Amarna abgesandt wurden, sowie die Pharao-Briefe von anderen Orten die genannte orthographische Eigentümlichkeit der Tušratta-Briefe nicht teilen.

7. Was die oft behandelten kanaanäischen "Glossen" in den Amarna-Briefen[78] betrifft, so sind noch viele Fragen offen. Sind sie ein unmittelbarer Beweis dafür, dass die Schreiber auf der ägyptischen Seite im Zweifelsfall auf eigene Kanaanäischkenntnisse zurückgreifen konnten? Oder sind sie ein Zeichen für Unsicherheit im Schreibgebrauch beim absendenden Schreiber, ohne dass eine Erläuterung für den lesenden Empfänger impliziert wäre?[79]

So spärlich das "Amarna-zeitliche" Keilschriftmaterial zwischen Ugarit und Gaza auch sein mag, so hat es uns doch zu vielen Fragen angeregt. Eine letzte Frage: Waren alle unsere Fundorte schon seit Jahrhunderten Stätten der Keilschrifttradition? Oder war die so weite Verbreitung und Dichte der Bezeugung eine vorübergehende Erscheinung? Wir könnten noch einmal die Situation Eblas zum Vergleich heranziehen: Zur Zeit seiner Archive hat es in Nordsyrien zweifellos viele Orte gegeben, an denen man die damalige Form der Keilschrift praktizierte. Ob es aber überall eine Kontinuität der Schreibfertigkeit und womöglich Gelehrsamkeit gab, wissen wir nicht.

Vielleicht ist es kein Zufall, dass die südlich von Ugarit gefundenen Keilschrifttexte zum allergrössten Teil Briefe sind. Zwar haben wir deutliche Hinweise auf Schulbetrieb und literarische Tätigkeit, wie sie mit einer Schule verbunden war, dagegen keinen Beweis dafür, dass Keilschrift auch in der örtlichen Verwaltung oder im Gerichtswesen verwendet wurde.[80]

Wenn also Keilschrift in "Amarna" in allererster Linie der lokalen und internationalen Korrespondenz zu dienen hatte, dann könnte ihr so umfangreicher Gebrauch in der Tat etwas Ephemäres gewesen sein, zu erklären durch die vorherrschenden politischen Strukturen. Es ist jedoch gefährlich, von wenigen Zeugnissen ausgehend weitreichende Schlüsse zu ziehen. Der mit den Quellen Mesopotamiens vertraute Historiker ist hier gewitzt und gewarnt.

Wir warten folglich geduldig darauf, dass eines Tages doch noch weitere "Amarna-zeitliche" Archive entdeckt werden — in Byblos oder wo auch immer. Ich bin überzeugt, dass sich die Assyriologie dann eine Zeitlang ganz einer solchen neu entdeckten Welt widmen wird.

Anmerkungen

1. Fortgesetzt durch A.F. Rainey, *El Amarna Tablets 359–379, AOAT* 8 (1970).
2. Einen Überblick "The Amarna Tablets from Palestine" bietet W.F. Albright in *CAH* II/2 (Cambridge, 1975), Kap. XX, S. 98–116. Textliste bei R. Borger, in K. Galling, E. Edel, R. Borger, *Textbuch zur Geschichte Israels* (1968), S. 5f.
3. J.-G. Heintz, *Index documentaire d'El-Amarna* (Groupe de Rech. et d'Études Sémitiques Anciennes, 1982) ist ein Hilfsmittel bei der Arbeit mit Amarna-Texten, selbst wenn es nicht auf Vollständigkeit ausgeht. So ist z.B. nicht angegeben, dass EA 256 und 274 neu von W.F. Albright, "Two Little Understood Amarna Letters from the Middle Jordan Valley," *BASOR* 89 (1943): 7–17 bearbeitet wurden. Zu EA 147 wäre ein Hinweis auf W.F. Albright, "The Egyptian Correspondence of Abimilki, Prince of Tyre," *JEA* 23 (1937): 190–203, nützlich gewesen (s. unten Anm. 63). Auch fehlen Hinweise auf die Autographien der einzelnen Texte.
4. W.F. Albright, "A Prince of Taanach in the Fifteenth Century B.C.," *BASOR* 94 (1944): 27.
5. Vgl. F. Pomponio, *Vicino Oriente* 5 (1982): 191–203.
6. Die — bisher nur wenigen — präsargonischen Tontafeln aus Mari sind nunmehr in der Herausgabe begriffen. Dank G. Dossin konnte ich in "Pantheon und Kult in Mari," *Compte Rendu, La Rencontre Assyriologie Internationale* 15/1966 (Liège, 1967), S. 51–71 einige der Texte verwenden.
7. M. Dietrich, O. Loretz, P.R. Berger und U. Sanmartin, *Ugarit-Bibliographie 1928–1966. AOAT* 20/1–4 (1973).
8. O. Weber und E. Ebeling, *Die El-Amarna Tafeln,* 2, II Teil (Leipzig: Vorderasiatische Bibliothek, 1915) (im folgenden *VAB* 2/II), S. 1581.
9. G. Dossin, *Mélanges de l'Université Saint-Joseph* 45 (1969): 245–249; vgl. auch D.O. Edzard, "Der Aufbau des Syllabars 'Proto-Ea,'" in *Society and Languages of the Ancient Near East, Studies in Honour of I.M. Diakonoff* (Warminster, 1982), S. 58.
10. E. Sollberger, "Byblos sur les rois d'Ur," *AfO* 19 (1959/60): 120–122. Da beide Texte [s.a. D.O. Edzard und G. Farber, *Die Orts-und Gewässernamen der 3. Dynastie von Ur, Répertoire Géographique des Textes Cunéiformes* 2 (Wiesbaden, 1974), S. 66] noch andere von Babylonien weiter entfernte Orte erwähnen: Marḫaši, Mari, Tuttul, Ebla, dürfte es keinen Zweifel an der Gleichsetzung des genannten *Ku-/Ǧu*$_5$*-ub-la*^{ki} mit Byblos geben. Zu Byblos aus assyriologischer Sicht vgl. B. Hrouda/W. Röllig, "Gubla" in *RlA* 3 (Berlin/New York, 1957/71), S. 673–675.
11. Nach F.M.Th. Böhl, *Die Sprache der Amarna-Briefe, Leipziger Semitische Studien* 5/II (Leipzig, 1909); E. Ebeling, "Das Verbum der El-Amarna-Briefe," *BA* 8/2 (1910), s. vor allem die Arbeiten von W.L. Moran, "An Unexplained Passage in an Amarna Letter from Byblos," *JNES* 8 (1949): 124f.; "The Use of the Canaanite Infinitive Absolute as a Finite Verb in the Amarna Letters from Byblos," *JCS* 4 (1950): 169–172; "New Evidence on Canaanite *Taqtūl(na)*," *JCS* 5 (1951): 33–35; "Amarna *Šumma* in Main Clauses," *JCS* 7 (1953): 78–80; "Early Canaanite *Yaqtula*," *Or.* 29 (1960), 1–19; "*Taqtul* — Third Masculine Singular?" *Biblica* 45 (1964): 80–82; "The Dual Personal Pronouns in Western Peripheral Akkadian," *BASOR* 211 (1973): 50–53.
12. J. Nougayrol, *Ugaritica* 5 (1968): 210–251.
13. In hsg. Ed. Meyer, *Ägyptiaca, Festschrift Georg Ebers* (Leipzig, 1897), S. 72; vgl. Weber, *VAB* 2/II, S. 1214f.; ausführlich R. Hachmann, in D.O. Edzard, R. Hachmann, R. Maiberger und G. Mansfeld, *Kāmid el-Lōz — Kumidi* [= *Saarbrücker Beiträge zur Altertumskunde*, 7 (1970): 63–94].
14. Nr. 1–4 (Briefe): *Kāmid el-Lōz* (s. Anm. 13), S. 55–62; Nr. 5 (zweiter Teil eines Briefes): G. Wilhelm, "Ein Brief der Amarna — Zeit aus Kāmid el-Lōz," *ZA* 63 (1973): 69–75; Nr. 6 (Brief): D.O. Edzard, "Ein Brief an den 'Grossen' von Kumidi aus Kāmid al-Lōz," *ZA* 66 (1976): 62–67 und *Saarbr. Beiträge...* 32 (1982): 131–135; Nr. 7 (Übungstext?): D.O. Edzard, "Ein neues Tontafelfragment (Nr. 7) aus Kāmid al-Lōz," *ZA* 70 (1980): 52–54.
15. Y. Yadin et al., *Hazor I–IV* (Jerusalem, 1958/61); Y. Yadin, *Hazor. Schweich Lectures 1970* (London, 1972).

16. B. Landsberger and H. Tadmor, "Fragments of Clay Liver Models from Hazor," *IEJ* 14 (1964): 201–217 [bei D.O. Edzard, *RlA* 4 (1972/75), S. 135 übersehen!].
17. W.W. Hallo and H. Tadmor, "A Lawsuit from Hazor," *IEJ* 27 (1977): 1–11.
18. H. Tadmor, "A Lexicographical Text from Hazor," *IEJ* 27 (1977): 98–102.
19. A. Goetze and S. Levy, "Fragment of the Gilgamesh Epic from Megiddo," *ʿAtiqot* 2 (1959): 121–128.
20. Zur Klassifizierung vgl. J.-W. Meyer, "Lebermodelle," *RlA* 6 (1980/83), S. 523. G. Loud, *Megiddo* II (Chicago, 1948), Tf. 255: 1–2.
21. Erste Veröffentlichung durch Fr. Hrozný, in E. Sellin, *Tell Taʿannek*, (Wien, 1904), S. 113–122. Neubearbeitung der Briefe 1, 2, 5 und 6 durch W.F. Albright, *BASOR* 94 (s. Anm. 4): 12–27, mit einleitendem kritischen Überblick über die Grabung und ihre Publikation.
22. Vgl. die Diskussion bei Albright, ibid., S. 26f.
23. B. Landsberger, "Assyrische Königsliste und 'Dunkles Zeitalter'," *JCS* 8 (1954): 59, Anm. 124; zurückhaltender A. Malamat, "Syrien-Palästina in der zweiten Hälfte des 2. Jahrtausends," in *Die altorientalischen Reiche*, II (Fischer Weltgeschichte 3, 1966), S. 187.
24. Lesung Landsbergers (s. Anm. 23), der Albrights Lesung *Re-wa-aš-šá* stillschweigend korrigiert.
25. F.M.Th. Böhl, "Die bei den Ausgrabungen von Sichem gefundenen Keilschrifttafeln," *ZDPV* 49 (1926): 325–327 (Kopie Tf. 46); neubearbeitet von W.F. Albright, "A Teacher to a Man of Shechem about 1400 B.C.," *BASOR* 86 (1942): 28–31, und s. wieder F.M. Th. Böhl, "Der Keilschriftbrief aus Sichem (Tell Balâṭa)," *Deutsches Archäologisches Institut Abteilung Bagdad* 7 (1974): 21–30. Nach Böhl (und eindeutig Kopie) Z.11 *il-ta-na-pá-tù* "sie schreiben immer wieder" statt *il-ta-na-ma-du* "sie studieren" (Albright).
26. Böhl, *ZDPV* 49 (s. Anm. 25): 322–325 (Kopie Tf. 45); die Namen diskutiert von Albright (s. Anm. 25), S. 29f., und — mit Verbesserungsvorschlägen — von Landsberger (s. Anm. 23), S. 59, Anm. 123.
27. Vgl. das Photo, *ZDPV* 49, Tf. 44. Das Fragment mit der "Zeugenliste" ist unförmig gerundet. Es fehlt kaum mehr als die Hälfte, so dass man sich fragt, ob auf dem fehlenden Teil genügend Platz für den Wortlaut eines Vertrages oder eines Gerichtsprotokolls gewesen ist. Zwei Zeilen der "Zeugenliste" sind über den Rand hinaus weit auf die Rückseite fortgesetzt. Wir fragen uns, ob wir es nicht eher mit einem Übungstext zu tun haben.
28. Nr. 1 (5837, lexikalisch): A.F. Rainey, "Two Cuneiform Fragments from Tel Aphek," *Tel Aviv* 2 (1975): 125–128, Tf. 24; Nr. 2 (5936, "administrative"): ders. ibid., S. 128, Tf. 24; Nr. 3 (8151, lexikalisch): ders., "A Tri-Lingual Cuneiform Fragment from Tel Aphek," *Tel Aviv* 3 (1976): 137f., Tf. 9; Nr. 4 (8552, Fragment): ibid., Tf. 10; Nr. 5 (8436, Fragment): ibid.; Nr. 6 (27386/1, Brief): D.I. Owen, "An Akkadian Letter from Ugarit at Tel Aphek," *Tel Aviv* 8 (1981): 1–17, Tf. 2. Dazu jetzt I. Singer, "Takuḫlinu and Ḫaya: Two Governors in the Ugarit Letter from Tel Aphek," *Tel Aviv* 10 (1983): 3–25; Nr. 7 (52055, Brieffragment): W.W. Hallo, "A Letter Fragment from Tel Aphek," *Tel Aviv* 8 (1981): 18–24, Tf. 3; Nr. 8 (52060/1, "administrative?"): Owen, ibid., S. 15, Tf. 2 (auf dem Photo lassen sich keine Keilschriftzeichen erkennen).
29. Vgl. etwa den Brief Aphek Nr. 6 (s. Anm. 28), Z. 14, 19.
30. W.F. Albright, "A Tablet of the Amarna Age from Gezer," *BASOR* 92 (1943): 28–30, 28, Anm. 6. Vgl. sonst für Briefe aus Gezer an Pharao, EA 297–300, 378; Pharao an Milk-ili von Gezer, EA 369. S. dazu S. Izreʾel, "Two Notes on the Gezer Amarna Tablets," *Tel Aviv* 4 (1977): 159–167.
31. W.F. Albright, "A Case of Lèse-Majesté in Pre-Israelite Lachish with Some Remarks on the Israelite Conquest," *BASOR* 87 (1942): 32–38.
32. A.F. Rainey, "The Administrative Division of the Shephelah," *Tel Aviv* 7 (1980): 197.
33. Y. Aharoni und M. Avi-Yonah, *The Macmillan Bible Atlas*, rev. ed. (Jerusalem, 1977), Karte 38; Y. Aharoni, *The Land of the Bible* (Philadelphia: Westminster Press, 1979), S. 153: "apparently Tell Jemmeh" mit Verweis (S. 186, Anm. 51) auf B. Maisler (Mazar), *Bulletin of the Israel Exploration Society* 16 (1951): 38–41 (Hebrew); ders., "Yurza, the Identification of Tell Jemmeh," *PEQ* 84 (1952): 48–51; ders., *Cities and Districts in Eretz-Israel* (Jerusalem, 1975), S. 141–146 (Hebrew).

34. S. Smith, "A Note on an Inscribed Tablet," *AAA* 21 (1934): 116f.
35. Zu der folgenden Liste keine erschöpfenden Literaturangaben. Vgl. grundsätzlich H. Klengel, *Geschichte Syriens*, II–III (Berlin, 1969/70); W. Helck, *Die Beziehungen Ägyptens zu Vorderasien im 3. und 2. Jahrtausend v. Chr.* (Wiesbaden, 1971); Aharoni, *The Land of the Bible* (s. Anm. 33); Heintz, *Index Documentaire* (s. Anm. 3), und auch, soweit schon erschienen, *RlA*.
36. EA 232–234.
37. EA 367: Pharao an Intarʾuta.
38. EA 320–326, 370: Pharao an Jidija.
39. EA 141–143; s.a. *VAB* 2/II, s.v. Bêruta.
40. S. oben II 3 *Kāmid-al-Lōz*, Nr. 1; vgl. *VAB* 2/II, S. 1573, s.v. Dimaska.
41. EA 205. Der Brief bedient sich des 'nördlichen' Grussformulars (s. dazu unten III 3). Klengel, *Gesch. Syriens*, III (s. Anm. 35), S. 101.
42. EA 363, 187:12. 'Nördliches' Grussformular, EA 187. Neubearbeitet von M. Weippert, "Die Nomadenquelle," in *Archäologie und Alttestament. Festschrift für K. Galling* (Tübingen, 1970), S. 267–272. Die Umsetzung des ṢI (EA 187:12) bzw. ZI (EA 363:4) in si_{20} bzw. *sí* ist m.E. nicht so unproblematisch, wie Weippert es annimmt. Bis zum letzten Beweis eines anderen sollte *-šaṣi* gelesen werden.
43. EA 177. 'Nördliches' Grussformular. Vgl. Klengel, *Gesch. Syriens*, III (s. Anm. 35), S. 63, auch zur Lesung.
44. EA 319. 'Südliches' Grussformular. Vgl. Rainey (s. Anm. 1), S. 92.
45. EA 174. 'Nördliches' Grussformular. Neubearbeitet von Weippert, "Die Nomadenquelle" (s. Anm. 42), S. 267–272.
46. EA 175, 185f. 'Nördliches' Grussformular. Neubearbeitet von Weippert, ibid.
47. EA 100. 'Nördliches' Grussformular.
48. EA 285–290. 'Nördliches' Grussformular(!). Vgl. W.L. Moran, "The Syrian Scribe of the Jerusalem Amarna Letters," in *Unity and Diversity*, hsg. H. Goedicke and J.J.M. Roberts (Baltimore, 1975), S. 146–166.
49. EA 314f.; vgl. oben II 10 mit Anm. 32f.
50 EA 182–184. 'Nördliches' Grussformular.
51. EA 272. 'Nördliches' Grussformular.
52. EA 206. 'Nördliches' Grussformular. Vgl. Klengel, *Gesch. Syriens* III (s. Anm. 35), S. 102.
53. EA 204. 'Nördliches' Grussformular.
54. EA 52–55. 'Nördliches' Grussformular. Vgl. Klengel, *Gesch. Syriens* II (s. Anm. 35), S. 96–113.
55. EA 191–192. 'Nördliches' Grussformular.
56. EA 225. 'Nördliches' Grussformular.
57. URU *Ša-az-ḫi-mi*, EA 203:4 = (?) URU *Ša-za-e-na*, *Kāmid al-Lōz*, Nr. 2 (s. Anm. 14). 'Nördliches' Grussformular. Zur Frage der Identität vgl. Edzard, *Kāmid el-Lōz* (s. Anm. 13), S. 58.
58. EA 144. 'Nördliches' Grussformular; s. sonst *VAB* 2/II, S. 1582, s.v. Ziduna.
59. EA 59. 'Nördliches' Grussformular; vgl. *VAB* 2/II, S. 1123f.; Klengel, *Gesch. Syriens*, II (s. Anm. 35), S. 75–95.
60. EA 146–155; *VAB* 2/II, S. 1580, s.v. Ṣurri. 'Nördliches' Grussformular.
61. EA 201. 'Nördliches' Grussformular.
62. Vgl. zuletzt P. Artzi, "El-Amarna Document No. 30," in *Actes du 29ᵉ Congrès des Orientalistes* (Paris, 1975), S. 1–7.
63. Albright, "Egyptian Correspondence of Abimilki" (s. Anm. 3), S. 196–203 spricht im Zusammenhang mit "Egyptianisms" von "poems" (Z. 5–15, 41–56) als Widerspiegelung ägyptischer Lyrik. In der Schärfe lässt sich das allerdings nach freundlicher Auskunft von Klaus Baer (Chicago) nicht begründen.
64. Neubearbeitung von. B. Halpern und J. Huehnergard, "El-Amarna Letter 252," *Or.* 51 (1982): 227–230.

65. Vgl. *Kāmid al-Lōz*, Nr. 6 (s. Anm. 14), und s. besonders das Photo 81, Tf. 41.
66. EA 174 aus *Ḫašabu*, 175 aus *Ḫazi* und 176 aus [...] sind ganz offenbar von ein und demselben Schreiber an ein und demselben Ort geschrieben; vgl. Weippert, "Die Nomadenquelle" (s. Anm. 42), S. 267–272. Ähnliches lässt sich vermuten von EA 203 aus *Šazḫimi*, 204 aus *Qanû*, 205 aus *Dubu* und 206 aus *Naziba*; vgl. Klengel, *Gesch. Syriens*, III (s. Anm. 35), S. 102; E.F. Campbell, *The Chronology of the Amarna Letters* (Baltimore, 1964), S. 113, nimmt auf Grund eines Vergleichs von EA 321 (Askalon) und 329 (Lachis) an, dass auch hier derselbe Schreiber am Werke war (freundlicher Hinweis von A. Lemaire).
67. Eine weitere Aufschlüsselung nach umgebendem Wortlaut innerhalb der Grussformel ist unbedingt nötig und sicher ergebnisreich.
68. *VAB* 2/II, S. 1508. Belege aus Ugarit, *Ḫattuša* und *Nuzi*, s. in *AHw. šukênu* 2 d–f.
69. Vgl. F.E. Wente, in *The Literature of Ancient Egypt*, hsg. W.K. Simpson (New Haven and London: Yale University Press, 1972), S. 154f.
70. Th. Mann, *Joseph und seine Brüder*, I (Stockholm, 1952), S. 990.
71. Vgl. A.L. Oppenheim, "A Note on the Scribes in Mesopotamia," *Assyriological Studies* 16 (1965): 254f. Anders zu beurteilen sind die offenbar von Schreiber zu Schreiber ausgerichteten "Grüsse" in EA 170:36–43; vgl. auch EA 12:23–26; mir unklar EA 316:16–25.
72. C. Kühne, *Die Chronologie der internationalen Korrespondenz von El-Amarna, AOAT* 17 (1973): 105–124.
73. Nichtbezeichnung des "Subjunktivs" in EA 1:28, 35 als ein Beispiel für viele.
74. *anumma ašteme awatam ša tašpura muḫḫiše ana jāši* "nunmehr habe ich das Wort gehört, das du an mich gesandt hast," EA 1:10 diene als Beispiel.
75. Aber z.B. jittadin, EA 369:28.
76. Vortrag am Oriental Institute, Chicago, kurz vor seinem Tode 1975.
77. H.P. Adler, "Das Akkadische des Königs Tušratta von Mitanni," *AOAT* 201 (1976): 13–16.
78. Nach Böhl und Ebeling (s. Anm. 11) und Ebelings "Glossar" in *VAB* 2/II vgl. als zusammenfassende Arbeit, P. Artzi, "The 'Glosses' in the Amarna Tables (and in Ugarit)," *Bar-Ilan* 1 (1963): 24–57 (Hebrew) mit englischem Resümee, S. XIV–XVII. Nach Artzi wären Glossierungen "signs of quasilexicographical activity" gewesen. Vgl. auch J. Krecher, "Glossen," *RlA* III (s. Anm. 10), S. 437f., §5 b 2.
79. Anregung von E. Reiner.
80. Vgl. oben II 8 mit Anm. 29. Ein Verwaltungstext in Keilschrift aus neuassyrischer Zeit wurde jüngst in Tell Kaysan südöstlich von Akko gefunden; s. R. M. Sigrist, "Une tablette cunéiforme de Tell Keisan," *IEJ* 32 (1982): 32–35.

Nineveh, Calah and Israel: On Assyriology and the Origins of Biblical Archaeology

Hayim Tadmor

IN THE LATE AUTUMN of 1913, the year in which the Jewish Palestine Exploration Society was founded in Jerusalem,[1] the Society of Biblical Archaeology was closing its forty-third session in London. During the session, divided into seven meetings, the following papers were read: "A Neo-Babylonian Astronomical Treatise in the British Museum" by L.W. King; "Yuia the Syrian" by H.R. Hall; "New Light on Sequence-dating" by F. Legge (criticizing Petrie's dating technique); "Semiramis in History and Legend" by F.C. Lehmann-Haupt; "Some Recent Discoveries in the Sudan" and "Babylonian Influence in China" [*sic!*] by A.H. Sayce, the president of the Society; "Some Amorite Personal Names in Genesis XIV" by W.T. Pilter; and "A Sumerian History of the World, and Its Possible Relations to Hebrew Tradition" by L.W. King.[2]

One can continue for some time to reflect upon the variety of topics discussed over seventy years ago by the learned savants at the meetings of the Society of Biblical Archaeology. The above, however, will no doubt suffice to illustrate the assertion that at that time biblical archaeology — at least in England — encompassed the whole cultural spectrum of the ancient Near East.

The Society was founded on December 9, 1870, with Dr. Samuel Birch, Keeper of Oriental Antiquities at the British Museum, in the chair. Its objectives were to forward:

> ... the investigation of Archaeology, Chronology, Geography and History of Ancient and Modern Assyria, Arabia, Egypt, Palestine and other Biblical Lands, by the promotion of the

* I am grateful to Mrs. Sue Gorodetsky for her editorial remarks.

> study of antiquities of those countries and the preservation of a continuous record of discoveries, now or hereafter to be in progress.[3]

The name "Society of Biblical Archaeology" was suggested by Dr. Birch. This, as Sir Wallis Budge, Birch's successor at the British Museum, put it, "... was a stroke of genius, for it appealed not only to philologists, but to theologians of all shades of thought."[4] A modern scholar will be amused to discover that the predecessor of this newly founded society bore the name "Syro-Egyptian Society." Four years later, the Society of Biblical Archaeology included among its members almost every Assyriologist, Egyptologist and leading biblical scholar in England, as well as some public figures — the most notable being Gladstone, the former prime minister, who served as one of its four vice presidents. The list includes 385 members, forty-three lady members (listed separately) and twenty-six honorary foreign members. Among the latter, one finds the names of noted scholars, pioneers in Assyriology, Egyptology and Semitic Philology, such as Brugsch of Cairo, Ebers of Leipzig, Ewald of Göttingen, Lepsius of Berlin, Schrader of Jena, Clermont-Ganneau of Jerusalem, Mariette Bey of Cairo, and de Longpérier, Maspero, Ménant, Oppert and de Saulcy, all of Paris.[5]

At one of the monthly meetings of the Society, on December 3, 1872, George Smith, a young Assyriologist, whose genius for deciphering and intuitive understanding of texts made him one of the greatest scholars in the field of Assyriology, announced the discovery of the cuneiform tablet from Nineveh which contained the Babylonian account of the Deluge.[6] This startling discovery prompted the proprietors of the *Daily Telegraph* to finance a further expedition to the site of Nineveh to find the "missing" parts of the Deluge story.

Admittedly, at that time — in the last quarter of the nineteenth century — it was not only the antiquarian quest for ancient cultures, but to a great extent the wide interest in the Bible, which provided the impetus for Assyriological research. This is not surprising; one should remember that only two or three decades earlier, the sensational discoveries made by Botta, Layard and Rassam at Khorsabad, Nineveh and Nimrud had stirred up wide public interest and aroused hopes for even greater revelations. The speedy decipherment of the Assyro-Babylonian cuneiform script by Henry Rawlinson, Edward Hincks, Jules Oppert and other scholars was no less sensational. The bearing of the Assyrian inscriptions upon the Bible, and especially upon the history of Israel and Judah, was quickly disseminated. In no time, the new finds became subjects of scholarly debate, as well as welcome topics for the daily press, literary journals and popular editions.

This paper, although it is presented at a session devoted to cuneiform archives, will draw little upon archival evidence, mainly as the thousands of cuneiform tablets from Nineveh offer relatively little toward a reliable reconstruction of the historical connections between Israel and Assyria. On the contrary, the royal inscriptions discovered at Nineveh and Nimrud (the site of ancient Calah), written on stone, clay prisms and cylinders, affected — if not transformed — the traditional presentation of biblical history. We shall turn our attention, therefore, to the evidence of these inscriptions — "The Monuments" in the parlance of the nineteenth century — and comment only in brief on the relevance of the Assyrian epistolary and administrative documents to biblical history.

Paradoxically, at the inception of Assyriology in the late forties and early fifties of the last century, it was the biblical evidence that illuminated the newly discovered cuneiform documents. The Books of Kings and the historical chapters in Isaiah became instrumental in the decipherment of the royal inscriptions of ancient Mesopotamia, as at times they provided the required bilingual version. After all, the biblical account preserved a careful transcription of the names of the Assyrian kings: Shalmaneser, Tiglath-Pileser, Sargon, Esarhaddon, and of the capitals of Assyria: Calah and Nineveh. In fact, the first name of an Assyrian king to be deciphered was that of Sargon, with the help of the biblical Hebrew transcription. In 1848, the French scholar Adrian de Longpérier, on the basis of the achievements of Paul Émile Botta, read the name *Sar-gin* on a monument from Khorsabad, and identified it with Sargon of Isaiah 20:1: "In the year that the commander in chief, who was sent by Sargon the king of Assyria, came to Ashdod ...."[7] De Longpérier also correctly read the word *Ashur*, and even ventured to offer a translation (about half of which is correct) of the text: "Glorious is Sargon, King, Great King, King of Kings, King of the country of Ashur."[8]

In spite of these bold efforts, everything was still obscure. Even the original names of the ruins of Khorsabad, Nimrud and Kouyunjik were unknown. Which of these monumental ruins concealed the site of ancient Nineveh, the great city of the Book of Jonah? Was it the twin mound of Kouyunjik/Nebi Yunis near Mossul (the traditional site of Jonah's burial); or was it Nimrud, 29 km southeast of Mossul; or Khorsabad, 22.5 km north of Mossul? To illustrate the state of confusion, we need only note that Botta entitled the report of his excavations at Khorsabad, the site of Dur-Sharrukin (the royal city of Sargon of Assyria): *Monument de Ninive*; whereas Layard named the account of his excavations at Nimrud, the site of ancient Calah: *Nineveh and Its Remains*. Unable to resolve the discrepancy between the archaeological evidence on the one hand, and the biblical account and the classical traditions on the other, Rawlinson suggested that apparently all three formed a "group of cities which in the time of the Prophet Jonah were known by the common name of Nineveh."[9]

With the publication in 1849 of Layard's magnificent volume *The Monuments of Nineveh*, and in 1851 of his folio *Inscriptions in the Cuneiform Character from Assyrian Monuments*, a new stage was inaugurated. Of special significance was the inscription on the Black Obelisk of Shalmaneser III, found at Nimrud and published in these volumes. Rawlinson deciphered the long inscription, an account of Shalmaneser's military campaigns, and published his translation in 1850.[10] He read correctly many names of cities and countries, but could not identify the name of its author. He transcribed it *Te-men-bar* (which approximately corresponds to what we know as the logographic writing of *Šulmanu-ašaredu*, Shalmaneser), and placed him in the twelfth or thirteenth century B.C.E. A few months later, it was the elderly Grotefend, the first decipherer of the Old Persian cuneiform writing, who suggested that the name should be read Shalmaneser.[11] He of course was thinking of the Shalmaneser of 2 Kings 17, who conquered Samaria (Shalmaneser V in our terminology).

About the same time, however, another brilliant decipherer, Edward Hincks from Ireland, identified on that monument the name of "Yaua, son of Humri" with that of Jehu of Israel.[12] Hincks observed that Shalmaneser of the Obelisk must therefore have reigned more than a century before the Shalmaneser who conquered Samaria. In the course of 1851, Rawlinson deciphered the historical inscription on the colossal bull of Sennacherib found by Layard at Kouyunjik. There, to general amazement, he read the names of Hezekiah, Jerusalem and Judah.[13] It was the account of Sennacherib's third campaign which described in detail his wars in the West, the defeat of Hezekiah, and the latter's tribute to Assyria — events narrated in extenso, though from an entirely different point of view, in 2 Kings 18–19 and Isaiah 36–37. This discovery finally convinced Rawlinson that Kouyunjik must be the site of Nineveh, and that Sennacherib was the son of Sargon, the Khorsabad king (Rawlinson still believed that the latter was identical with Shalmaneser of 2 Kings 17). He concluded his communication about Hezekiah and Sennacherib by expressing the hope — if not conviction — that, very shortly, he would be able to point out on the bas-reliefs that had been brought from Nineveh "the bands of Jewish maidens" which were delivered to Sennacherib, "and perhaps to distinguish the portraiture of the humbled Hezekiah."

At the beginning of the following year, Hincks announced that he had found the name of Menahem of Samaria on the slabs from the northwestern palace at Nimrud, thus proving that the slabs belonged to the Assyrian king named Pul in 2 Kings 15.[14] Like everybody else at that time, Hincks thought that Pul was different from Tiglath-Pileser III, mentioned in the same chapter in Kings. Incidentally, Hincks believed that Pul was Sargon!

In 1852 the decipherment of cuneiform had greatly advanced, so that Layard in his new book *Discoveries in the Ruins of Nineveh and Babylon*, published in 1853, was able to produce a list of kings, countries and cities mentioned in the Bible, that appear in the Assyrian inscriptions from Nineveh, Nimrud and Khorsabad. This list, compiled with the help of Hincks and Rawlinson, contains fifty-five names among which were: Jehu, Omri, Menahem, Hezekiah, Hazael, Merodach-Baladan, Judah (*Yaudi*), Jerusalem, Samaria, Ashdod, Lachish, Ekron, Ashkelon, Carchemish and Gozan. Each name was reproduced in cuneiform and in Hebrew.[15] Five years later, when Hincks, Oppert, Rawlinson and Talbot, independently and almost identically, deciphered a long inscription of Tiglath-Pileser I inscribed on a clay prism from Kalaʿat Sherghat (the site of the ancient Assur), Assyriology was officially acknowledged to be a legitimate discipline.[16]

Nonetheless, the intrinsic ties with biblical studies were not severed and they remained close till the twentieth century. Several scholars of the new discipline, the most notable among them Oppert (who became the first professor of Assyriology in Europe in 1869), even transcribed the Assyrian texts into Hebrew letters. Assyriologists, as well as Egyptologists, were deeply immersed in the questions of biblical history, and especially in those of biblical chronology, a topic which, even now, has not lost its appeal. This was to be expected. After all, a major contribution of the finds from Nineveh and Calah was in the realm of chronology, both Assyrian and biblical. The monuments provided the names of biblical kings who came in contact with the Assyrian monarchs; and the tablets of the *limmu* lists from Nineveh, or the "Eponym Canons" as they were known at that time, enabled a reconstruction of a chronological scheme of Assyrian history of the ninth, eighth and early seventh centuries B.C.E.

In 1862, Rawlinson announced the discovery of these tablets, the chronological value of which had already been recognized by Hincks about a decade earlier. These were published in 1866 by Norris, another of the founding fathers of Assyriology, a modest though very competent scholar, who copied the texts for the first of the two monumental volumes of the *Cuneiform Inscriptions of Western Asia*, edited by Rawlinson. In the most detailed of the series of these tablets, the "Canon V," it is stated that a solar eclipse took place in the month of Siwan in the "eponym year of Bur-Sagale." This was identified, with the help of astronomers, with the eclipse on June 15, 763 B.C.E., though some other earlier astronomical possibilities were also suggested.[17]

The solution for the Assyrian chronology offered by the new evidence prompted other scholars, including Egyptologists like Lepsius and classicists like Brandes, to contribute to the ensuing debate. The main participants were George Smith, Jules Oppert and Eberhard Schrader. In *The Assyrian Eponym Canon*, which was published in 1875, a year before he died, Smith offered a conclusive chronological framework for Assyrian history, based on the eponym lists from Nineveh. Notwithstanding the fact that over a century has passed, that framework — although modified by subsequent finds — remains virtually unaltered. A new and definitive edition of these eponym lists, in preparation by Alan Millard, will no doubt advance the study of Assyrian chronology, but probably will not substantially alter the dates established by Rawlinson and Smith.

Smith's book reflects the problem that faced scholarship at that stage of research. The chronological material of the tablets from Nineveh put biblical chronology to the test. The inconsistency between the two became widely recognized. The dilemma was which was more trustworthy — the dates of the Eponym Canon and the monuments of Nineveh and Nimrud or the biblical chronology.

Let me exemplify the problem by a single case, that of Pul, mentioned in 2 Kings 15:19 as a king of Assyria to whom Menahem king of Samaria paid a heavy tribute. The Assyrian royal inscriptions contain no record of a king by that name. However, those of Tiglath-Pileser III mention the tribute received from Menahem (*Minihimmu*) of Samaria; they also mention the death of Pekah (*Paqaha*) of Israel (*Bit-Humria*), and the enthronement of Hoshea (*Ausi'*). According to the Assyrian chronology, these events related in 2 Kings 15 can be dated to the years 738 and 732 B.C.E. respectively. How can one accommodate twenty years for Pekah, as well as two years for Pekahiah the son of Menahem, in the brief period between 738 and 732? Rawlinson,[18] and independently Lepsius[19] the noted Egyptologist, suggested that Pul was another name for Tiglath-Pileser. This suggestion, which was convincingly explored by Schrader,[20] solved the problem from the Assyriological aspect, but did not explain the excessively long reign assigned to Pekah in the Bible.

Smith did not resort to the solution of Oppert, namely to assume that forty years were missing in the Eponym Canon, and that there were two Menahems: the father, who paid tribute to a certain Pul, and his grandson, also Menahem, who yielded to Tiglath-Pileser.[21] Smith identified Pul with Adad-Nirari III, at that time read *Vul-Nirari*, who reigned about fifty years before Tiglath-Pileser. As to the mention of Menahem in the annals of Tiglath-Pileser, Smith suggested that the Assyrian scribe had made an error, and that the correct name should be Pekah, not Menahem. Aware of the weakness of such proposals, he wrote:

> I am differing from the opinion of Sir Henry Rawlinson, Canon George Rawlinson, Professors Schrader and Brandes, who accept as correct the Assyrian statements. In noticing this difference, I must confess that the view held by the two Rawlinsons and the German professors is more consistent with the literal statements of the Assyrian inscriptions than my own, but I am utterly unable to see how the biblical chronology can be so far astray here as the inscriptions lead one to suppose.[22]

Smith's dilemma illustrates the problem facing biblical scholarship both then and now. The Assyriologist, not burdened by the authority of Scripture, left the irreconcilable biblical problems to the biblical scholars. The symbiosis of Assyriology and biblical studies was disrupted and the disciplines drifted apart. Nowadays, some of us are trying to bridge that gap.

At the close of this paper, a brief comment on some of the most recent evidence from the letters and administrative documents bearing on our topic is in order. Naturally, these less spectacular documents did not attract scholars to the same extent as the royal inscriptions. Only much later, in fact mostly in our generation, have they become an object of methodical research — both the vast archives of Nineveh uncovered long ago by Rassam, Smith and Campbell-Thompson, and the less copious, but no less significant archives of Nimrud, excavated over two decades ago by Mallowan.[23] The paucity of documents from Israel and its neighbors in these archives has recently been explained by the supposition that correspondence with the West was conducted not in Akkadian but in Aramaic, and on perishable materials.[24]

Among the tablets from Nimrud, several relate to the administration of the Assyrian Empire west of the Euphrates, mostly in Phoenicia and Philistia;[25] a few others mention Israelites in Assyria proper, for example, *Hilqiya* and *Yasuri.*[26] A number of additional names appear on tablets from Nineveh.[27] Thus, for instance, one letter known long ago, and republished recently with a new fragment "joined" to it, illustrated the involvement of certain Israelites, by the name of *Niriyau, Palṭiyau*, in the urban life of Gozan, one of the centers to which the population of Samaria had been deported.[28] In connection with letters, a most important contribution has been made by the works of K. Deller and S. Parpola, which have greatly advanced our understanding of the Assyrian dialect of Akkadian and of the imperial correspondence composed in that dialect. On a different level, though no less significant, are the systematic studies in prosopography and Assyro-Babylonian onomastics, such as those carried out today by M. Fales and R. Zadok,[29] which have enhanced our ability to discern Israelites and their close neighbors among the conglomeration of peoples, many of them deportees, which formed the population of the Assyrian Empire.[30]

As more avenues of research open, there is little doubt that further contacts between Assyria and Israel will be detected, and it is hoped that the ties between Assyriology, biblical studies, and archaeology will thus be renewed. Such a rapprochement is to be warmly welcomed, provided that each discipline retains its own methodology and refrains from infringing upon the conceptual autonomy of the other.

Notes

1. The Society, which was the predecessor of the Israel Exploration Society, was unable to pursue its activities owing to the outbreak of World War I. It was reconstituted in 1920; see A.J. Braver, "From the Early Days of the Israel Exploration Society," in *Western Galilee and the Coast of Galilee, Papers of the Nineteenth Archaeological Convention* (Jerusalem: The Israel Exploration Society, 1965), pp. 231–233. (Hebrew)
2. *Proceedings of the Society of Biblical Archaeology* 35 (1913): 41–56, 101–113, 140, 164, 205–220, 250; W.T. Pilters' paper was continued in ibid., 36 (1914): 125–142, 212–230.
3. *Transactions of the Society for Biblical Archaeology* (henceforth *TSBA*) 1 (1872): ii. For the full text of the charter, see ibid., pp. xxv–xxvi.
4. E.A. Wallis Budge, *The Rise and Progress of Assyriology* (London, 1925), p. 262.
5. *TSBA* 3 (1874): 629ff.
6. *TSBA* 2 (1873): 213ff.
7. *Revue Archéologique* 4 (1848): 584.
8. Ibid., p. 508. The text is the beginning of the Bull Inscription from Khorsabad; D.G. Lyon, *Keilschrifttexte Sargon's König von Assyrien* (Leipzig, 1883), p. 13, line 1.
9. *JRAS* 12 (1849–50): 417.
10. Ibid., pp. 431–448. Though deciphering correctly many proper names, Rawlinson could not yet identify the names of Hazael of Damascus and Jehu 'son of Omri,' read by him as 'Khazakan of Atesh' and 'Jahua the son of Hubiri' (ibid., p. 447). Cf. also A.H. Layard, *Nineveh and Its Remains*, vol. II (London, 1850), p. 192. Also at the same time — the beginning of 1851 — Rawlinson still could not decipher Sennacherib's name on the rock inscription at Bavian (he read it 'Bel-Odonim-sha'), and voiced his opinion against the identification of this king — the "son of the builder of Khorsabad" — with Sennacherib [*JRAS* 12 (1849–50): 470].
11. *Gottingeschen Gelehrten Anzeigen* 13 (August 26, 1850).
12. *Athenaeum* (December 27, 1851): 1384. A comprehensive bibliography of Hincks' publications has been prepared by K.J. Catheart and Patricia Donlon, *Orientalia* 52 (1983): 325ff.
13. *Athenaeum* (August 23, 1851): 902ff. Hincks translated independently Sennacherib's annals. His translation has been followed by Layard, *Discoveries in the Ruins of Nineveh and Babylon* (London, 1853), pp. 139ff.
14. *Athenaeum* (January 3, 1852): 26.
15. Layard, *Nineveh and Babylon* (see note 13), pp. 626–628.

16. *Proceedings of the 34th Anniversary Meetings of the Royal Asiatics Society: The Annual Report* (May 1857), pp. ix–x [=*JRAS* 17 (1859)]; published separately as *Inscription of Tiglat Pileser I, King of Assyria as Translated by Sir Henry Rawlinson, Fox Talbot esq., Dr. Hincks and Dr. Oppert* (London, 1857).
17. See, most conveniently, in A. Ungnad, "Eponymen," *Reallexikon der Assyriologie* II (Berlin-Leipzig, 1938): 414.
18. *Athenaeum* (August 22, 1869): 245.
19. *Abhandlungen der Königl. Akademie der Wissenschaften zu Berlin* (1869), p. 56.
20. *Keilinschhriften und Geschichtsforschung* (Giessen, 1878), pp. 422ff.
21. *Revue Archéologique* 18 (1862): 319.
22. *The Assyrian Eponym Canon* (London, [1875]), p. 182.
23. M.E.L. Mallowan, *Nimrud and Its Remains*, vols. I–II (London, 1966); see also K. Deller's review in *Orientalia* 35 (1966): 179–191.
24. S. Parpola, "Assyrian Royal Inscriptions and Neo-Assyrian Letters," in *Assyrian Royal Inscriptions: New Horizons*, ed. F.M. Fales (Rome, 1981), p. 132.
25. H.W.F. Saggs, *Iraq* 17 (1955): 126–131.
26. B. Parker, *Iraq* 23 (1961): 27–28 (ND. 2443, IV:4 and ND. 2621, II:11).
27. I. Ephʿal, "On the Identification of the Israelite Exiles in the Assyrian Empire," in *Excavations and Studies, Essays in Honour of Prof. Shmuel Yeivin*, ed. Y. Aharoni (Tel Aviv, 1973), pp. 201–203 (Hebrew). For a list of Israelites/Judeans in Assyrian sources, see R. Zadok, *Jews in Babylonia in the Chaldean and Achemenian Periods* (The University of Haifa, 1979), pp. 35–38.
28. S. Parpola, *Cuneiform Texts from Babylonian Tablets in the British Museum. Part 53: New Assyrian Letters from the Kuyunjik Collection* (London, 1979), no. 46; and F.M. Fales, *AfO* 27 (1980): 142–146. For the name *Halabišu Samerinaya* in that document (rev. 90), see Ephʿal, "Israelite Exiles in the Assyrian Empire" (note 27), p. 281, no. 5
29. F.M. Fales, "West Semitic Names from the Governor's Palace," *Annali di Ca' Foscari* XIII/3 (1974): 179–188; R. Zadok, "Historical and Onomastic Notes," *Die Welt des Orients* 9 (1977): 35–56; idem, "Notes on the Early History of the Israelites and Judeans in Mesopotamia," *Orientalia* 51 (1982): 391–393.
30. H. Tadmor, "The Aramaization of Assyria: Aspects of Western Impact," in *Mesopotamien und seine Nachbarn. XXV Rencontre Assyriologique Internationale, Berlin, 1978*, eds. H.J. Nissen and J. Renger (Berlin, 1982), vol. I, pp. 449–470.

Select Bibliography on the Discovery and Decipherment of Cuneiform

Booth, A.J. *The Discovery and Decipherment of the Trilingual Cuneiform Inscriptions.* London, New York and Bombay, 1902.

Catheart, K.J. and Donlon, Patricia. "Edward Hincks (1792–1866): A Bibliography of His Publications." *Orientalia* 52 (1983): 325–356.

Driver, S.R. *Modern Research as Illustrating the Bible.* The Schweich Lectures 1908. London, 1909.

Hilprecht, H.V. *Explorations in the Bible Lands during the 19th Century.* Edinburgh, 1903.

Wallis Budge, E.A. *The Rise and Progress of Assyriology.* London, 1925.

Postscriptum

While this volume was in final page proofs, significant new evidence pertaining to archival texts from Calah came to my attention. In the publication by Stephanie Dalley and J.N. Postgate, *The Tablets from Fort Shalmaneser*, CTN Vol. 3 (London, 1985), Text No. 99 lists thirteen names, probably of charioteers originating from or perhaps stationed at the city of Samaria (URU *Sa-miri-ni*). Most of these names are Aramaic.

Dalley and Postgate's publication also mentions messengers from Judah, Ashdod, Edom and Gaza in a new wine list (Text 135) dating from either the reign of Tiglath-Pileser III or Sargon II. This and other similar texts previously published by J.V. Kinnier-Wilson [CTN 1 (London, 1972)] and now reexamined by Dalley and Postgate shed new light on the political relations between Samaria and neighboring states and the Assyrian empire at the zenith of its expansion to the West.

Respondents

Pinḥas Artzi

In principle, I accept Edzard's challenging thesis that in our evaluations we should strike a balance between the Amarna Archive itself and the Canaanite scribal centers. Therefore, our attention should focus on the activities of the Canaanite cuneiform scribe in about thirty towns as a basis for later developments. At the same time, far beyond the brief survey and evaluation of these centers, as carried out by Edzard, we should encourage the investigation into the knowledge and adaptations of the Canaanite cuneiform scribes during the Amarna period and after.

However, the necessary Assyriological groundwork (palaeographic, syllabaric, linguistic, lexical and stylistical) for the study of the El-Amarna documents is still incomplete. Thus, Schroeder's *Zeichenliste* (1915) excluded most of the Canaanite literary settlements from his palaeographic-syllabic analysis. Only Knudtzon (1915) and Moran (1975) contributed to filling part of this vacuum. Until this groundwork is mastered we will not understand the pattern of activities of the Canaanite cuneiform scribe in the various literary centers, the number of these scribes and their relation to the centers, the differences between various types of scribes ("Canaanite," "Hurrian," "Hittite"), their official positions and, chiefly, their level of education.

There are, however, a few studies — one of which prepared by the writer (1963) is sadly unfinished — on the regional system of the "glosses" in the Akkadian documents of Ugarit and Amarna, and *inter alia*, on the language of the Canaanite-West Semitic Amarna documents (beginning with the works of Albright and continuing with those of Moran and Rainey; see also Isreʾel, 1978; Sivan, 1978). These, together with observations on the lexical documents discovered at Aphek (see below), and added to Edzard's presentation here, enable us to determine a transition between the earlier, Mesopotamian peripheral phase of cuneiform literacy in Canaan, and the later, Western peripheral phase, represented by West Semitic "glosses," morphology, grammar, syntax and style, lexicon and bilingual/multilingual dictionaries (see Rainey, *Grammar*).

* This study was prepared during my term as a fellow of the Institute for Advanced Studies at The Hebrew University of Jerusalem.

Now what of cuneiform literacy in Canaan in the extended Amarna age up to 1200 B.C.E. (Artzi, 1978)? Edzard's survey shows that up to the late fifteenth–early fourteenth centuries B.C.E., certain cuneiform centers still existed in Canaan. The "Megiddo fragment" (Goetze and Levy, 1959) containing a variant of tablet VII of the Gilgamesh Epic, signifies the turning point. Though still representing literary-scholarly and editorial capability, and related to another peripheral version from Hattuša (Landsberger and Tadmor, 1964; cf. Beckman, 1984), the poor cursive script and certain syllabic phenomena introduce the cuneiform ductus at the verge of the Amarna Age in Canaan. Moreover, on the basis of Levy's palaeographic chart (1959), it may be pointed out that the scribe of the Gilgamesh variant fragment originated in the Byblos region, as did the scribe of a small historical-literary Amarna fragment (EA 340). These literary works were inscribed at the end of a period. Thus the entire picture of former literary-scholarly centers surveyed by Edzard constitutes a summary of an earlier situation from the point of view of Mesopotamian-metropolitan and even Mesopotamian-peripheral standards. The earlier, relatively high level of skill gave way to the "decline" evidenced throughout the entire Canaanite area in the Amarna period.

Among the cumulative causes for this decline, interest should concentrate on the significance of the location of the Canaanite cuneiform scribal area between two important scholarly centers, brilliant Ugarit in the north and imperial Amarna in the south. Possibly an aspect of the influence of both of these centers on Canaan was a "brain-drain" — the voluntary or forced emigration of learned scribes. EA 340 and the general organization of the Amarna Archive (in both its clerical and its scholarly capacities) seem to indicate this: its scribes were able to communicate in a wide variety of styles and languages from "International Akkadian" to "Canaanite." At the same time, they and some Egyptian colleagues were engaged in the study of foreign languages, of lexical texts and of Babylonian (and other) literary writings. This resulted in the innovative creation of Egyptian/foreign glossaries, such as EA 368 (other glossaries may also have been prepared, for example, Egyptian/Hittite; Starke, 1971). Moreover, while the Mesopotamian lexical texts in use at Amarna display a close affinity with the Ugaritic (and partly Hattuša) versions, certain literary texts at Amarna indicate incorporation of literary creations from far and near. One group of texts represents Babylonia [cf. EA 356, Adapa; EA 357, Nergal-Ereškigal; EA 358 (Artzi, 1982), a "triad" of mythic-epic tales written down at Amarna by a Babylonian scholar for instructional purposes].

I must disagree with Edzard's observation that the abnormal *plene* writing of EA 357 (and EA 356) recalls Mitannian orthotactics. The ductus of the "triad" is clearly Middle Babylonian, not Mitannian. The purpose of the *plene* writing in these texts was purely didactic.

How did the Canaanite cuneiform scribe react to this situation of "desolation"? In this regard, Edzard's call to turn attention from the Amarna Archive to the Canaanite scribal centers themselves is very felicitous, for thus the nature of the emerging process during the late fifteenth–thirteenth centuries B.C.E. can now be directly perceived. This was a compulsive process to seek compensation, primarily in resorting to the familiar: by turning to their own lingual resources, the scribes produced a West-Semiticized, hybrid-balanced, Canaanite-Akkadian literary system —the first (though partial) introduction of the Canaanite spoken language to a literary framework. This dramatic, crucial process encompassed virtually the entire sphere of scribal activity in Canaan (Moran, 1961; Rainey, *Grammar*).

Only after further intensive research will it be possible to understand the mechanisms and initial motives of this process correctly. Nevertheless, it can be surmised that it initially derived from a desperate need for continuity, and that, to a certain extent, it was guided by the old-established Canaanite cuneiform centers from the coastal Byblos region to Aphek. The example and influence of Ugarit also surely played a role in this process. Evidence (still to be fully evaluated) of its monitorship (and later formalization) can be found in the fourteenth–thirteenth centuries B.C.E. multilingual glossary fragments from Aphek — an epochal find (Rainey, 1976). It should be observed that (1) these glossaries give evidence of a systematic, *glossenkeil*-ed Canaanite translation system, using a Hattuša-Ugaritic-Phoenician type of double *glossenkeil* (Artzi, 1963); (2) the same lexical memory system (with other types of *glossenkeil*) is used throughout the contemporary cuneiform Canaanite correspondence; and (3) the possible date of the Aphek glossaries (which does not exclude the thirteenth century B.C.E.) may indicate that the Canaanite cuneiform scribe may have continued his work down to this period and even improved it.

On this point, I must note that Edzard's quite reserved attitude to the gloss (and *glossenkeil*) system in the Canaanite Amarna letters does not take into account their unique role and value in the process of literalization of the Canaanite.

The destiny of this corpus of Canaanite cuneiform scribes was really fulfilled only when the "alphabetic revolution" (Cross, 1979; Millard, 1979; Naveh, 1982; Haran, 1982) in Canaan came about. Although the writing system was fundamentally changed, and along with it the writing material (Haran, 1982), the tradition survived thanks to the Canaanite cuneiform scribes: the scribes of this newly emerging alphabetic era were the descendants of a generation which had already learned Canaanite literary skills both in cuneiform and alphabetic. Surely, this generation of scribes had its share in the establishment of the ancient Israelite spiritual, cultural and linguistic achievement represented by the Old Testament and by a slowly growing body of *in situ* documents in Canaan-Israel.

The earliest alphabetic document, already from the period of the Israelite Settlement, is the ʿIzbet Ṣarṭah ostracon, of the twelfth–eleventh centuries B.C.E. Without attempting any new readings, I would like to point out that the composition of this inscription is (a) static —that is alphabetic; (b) dynamic —an exercise in administrative procedures, including names of materials and personal names, apparently written already in Hebrew (Dotan, 1981). Such a composition seems to find its prototype in cuneiform composite exercises known at Amarna (EA 350) and Ugarit (Artzi, 1983). Thus, this ostracon *may* represent a modified continuation of certain scribal traditions.

Finally, we arrive at the famous passage in Judges 8:14 regarding the *naʿar* of the people of Succoth, who writes down the personal names of the officials and prominent citizens of the town. This "official of the town council" was a junior (?) scribe, and his standard ability to note down personal names points again to the administrative continuity of the cuneiform/alphabetic scribe in Canaan-Israel (cf. Malamat, 1971).

Select Bibliography

Albright, W.F. "A Teacher to a Man Shechem about 1400 B.C.E." *BASOR* 86 (1942).

——. "The Amarna Letters from Palestine." In *The Cambridge Ancient History*. Vol. II.2, Ch. XX, 3d ed. Cambridge, 1975.

Altman, A. "The 'Deliverance Motif' in the 'Historical Prologues' of Šuppiluliuma I's Vassal-Treaties." *Bar-Ilan Studies in History* 2 (1984).

Artzi, P. "The 'Glosses' in the Amarna Tablets (and in Ugarit)." *Bar-Ilan* 1 (1963). (Hebrew with English summary)

——. "Some Unrecognized Syrian Amarna Letters (EA 260; 317; 318)." *JNES* 27 (1968).

——. "Evidence of Lexical Knowledge in the Amarna Letters." *Bar-Ilan, Decennial Volume* 2 (1969).

——. "The Rise of the Middle Assyrian Kingdom." *Bar-Ilan Studies in History* 1 (1969, 1978).

——. *Berliner Beiträge zum Vorderen Orient* 1.1 (1982).

——. "The Library of the Amarna Archive." *RAI* 30 (in press).

Beckman, G. "Mesopotamians and Mesopotamian Learning at Hattuša." *Journal of Cuneiform Studies* 35, nos. 1–2 (1984).

Cassuto, M.D. "Biblical and Canaanite Literatures." In *Biblical and Canaanite Literatures*. 1942, reprint 1972. (Collected papers in Hebrew)

Cross, F.M. "Early Alphabetic Scripts." In *Symposia, Celebrating the on 75th Anniversary of the American Schools of Archaeological Research*. Cambridge, MA, 1979.

Demsky, A. "Literacy in Israel." Ph.D. diss., The Hebrew University of Jerusalem, 1976.

Dotan, A. "New Light on the ʿIzbet Ṣarṭah Ostracon." *Tel Aviv* 8 (1981).

Goetze, A. and Levy, S. "Fragments of the Gilgamesh Epic from Meggido." *ʿAtiqot* 2 (1959).

Haran, M. *Journal of Semitic Studies* 33, nos. 1–2 (1982).

Isreʾel, Sh. "The Gezer Letters of the El-Amarna Archive—Linguistic Analysis." *Israel Oriental Studies* 8 (1978).

Knudtzon, J.A. *Die El-Amarna Tafeln*. Leipzig, 1915.

Kochavi, M. "The Canaanite Palace at Aphek and Its Inscriptions." *Qadmoniot* 10 (1977). (Hebrew)

Kühne, C. *Die Chronologie der Internationalen Korrespondenz von El-Amarna*. Neukirchen-Veuyn, 1973.

——. "Mit glossenkeit markierte fremde Worter in Akkadischen Ugarittexten." *Ugarit-Forschungen* 6 (1974); 7 (1975).

Lambert, W.G. "Interchange of Ideas between Southern Mesopotamia and Syria-Palestine as Seen in Literature." *Berliner Beiträge zum Vorderen Orient* 1.1 (1982).

Landsberger, B. "Zur virten and siebenten Tafel des Gilgamesh-Epos." *Revue d'Assyriologie* 62 (1968).

Landsberger, B. and Tadmor, H. "Fragments of Clay Liver Models from Hazor." *IEJ* 14 (1964).

Malamat, A. "The Period of Judges." In *The World History of the Jewish People*. Vol. III. Jerusalem, 1971.

Millard, A.R. "The Ugaritic and Canaanite Alphabets — Some Notes." *Ugarit-Forschungen* 2 (1979).

Moran, W.L. "The Hebrew Language in its North-West Semitic Background." In *The Bible and the Ancient Near East. W.F Albright Festschrift*. London, 1961.

——. "The Syrian Scribe of the Jerusalem Amarna Letters." In *Unity and Diversity*. Baltimore, 1975.

Naveh, J. *The Early History of the Alphabet*. Jerusalem, 1982.

Rainey, A.P. "A Tri-Lingual Cuneiform Fragment from Tel Aphek." *Tel Aviv* 3 (1976).

——. *Grammar*. In press.

Schroeder, O. "Die Tontafeln von El-Amarna in Berlin." *VAS* 11–12 (1915).

Sivan, D. "Grammatical Analysis of the Northwest Semitic Vocables in Akkadian Texts of the Fifteenth–Thirteenth Century from Canaan and Syria." Ph.D. diss., Tel Aviv University, 1978.

Starke, F. "Zur Deutung der Arzara-Briefstelle. °VBOT 1, 25–27." *Zeitschrift für Assyriologie* 71 (1981): 224.

Tadmor, H. "A Lexicographical Text from Hazor." *IEJ* 17 (1977).

Michael Heltzer

Among the epigraphic remains from Ugarit there are no law codes as in the Old Testament, but there are many legal documents which enable restoration of the legal practices of that city, and the international treaties and correspondence provide a comprehensive insight into international law in the second half of the second millennium B.C.E.

From the social point of view, Ugarit should be considered in the light of contemporaneous societies such as Alalakh in Middle Assyria, Nuzu-Arrapkha, the Hittite Empire and Mycenaean (Linear B) Greece. The Israelite conquest of Canaan, the Aramaization of Syria, the destruction of the Hittite Empire and the "Dorian invasion" combined to destroy the existing social order of the rural community, along with the professional "royal dependents" (*bnš mlk*). The new order which resulted from this ethnic constellation was a more or less "barbaric" society with strong tribal elements and influences. Villages of landed peasantry and free artisans, partly organized into guilds, evolved. Naturally, the circumstances at the beginning of the Israelite monarchy forced its kings to adopt much of the administrative organization of the preceding Late Canaanite period. The data from Ugarit facilitate a better understanding of certain biblical passages and historical features, but the Canaanite-Ugaritic patterns cannot be depended upon entirely to explain Israelite history.

Louis D. Levine

Responding to a paper entitled "Nineveh, Calah and Israel" at a congress dedicated to biblical archaeology is somewhat daunting, not only because of the very stature of the author of that paper, but also because I am hard pressed to see how a sometime Iranian archaeologist and Assyriologist can hope to make much of a contribution to the general theme of the Congress itself. Thus, I am heartened by Prof. Y. Yadin, who defines biblical archaeology as covering virtually any of the disciplines of ancient Near Eastern studies, thereby including my remarks within the purview of this meeting. In what follows, I will also make some general comments in my role as both archaeologist and Assyriologist.

H. Tadmor has demonstrated that it is not enough to look at the products of a discipline when seeking to understand it. The very history of the discipline is an equally important subject for serious investigation. Indeed, many of the speakers at this Congress have made us keenly aware of how the modern historical dimension of biblical archaeology has shaped the very questions which it asks, and the way in which it asks those questions. This is so much the case that to an outsider it appears that many of the issues raised are as rooted in the way in which the material is studied as they are in any perceived or imagined ancient reality.

There is little doubt that for the history of Israel, no extra-biblical source has been more important than the records of the Neo-Assyrian kings and their empire. They have been around far too long to be considered spectacular, as are the finds from Ebla or Mari or Ugarit, but like old friends, the Neo-Assyrian texts continue to stand by us and to provide us with certain profound insights that all the other sources lack. Prof. Tadmor has already demonstrated that they are unrivaled for unraveling biblical chronology, the very cornerstone of biblical history. Abraham may wander over a millennium, according to one's tastes, as one speaker observed. Menahem wanders over less than a decade. That alone, for the historian, speaks volumes.

The value of the Neo-Assyrian records, however, is not confined to chronology, nor to the chronicling of contacts between Assyria and Israel in the Levant, nor to identifying Israelites or Judahites in Assyria *magna*. H. Tadmor has demonstrated this in publication after publication, but the limits of time prevented him from expanding his story for the present Congress. Thus, I would like to take up where he left off, albeit briefly, and bring the record up to the present. As he has done this for the epistolary and administrative texts and archives, I will concentrate on the royal inscriptions.

After the initial work on the decipherment of Akkadian had been completed, much of the remainder of the nineteenth century and the first half of the twentieth were taken up with the preparation of editions of the royal inscriptions, starting with George Smith's groundbreaking *History of Assurbanipal* (London, 1871) and proceeding through David G. Lyon's *Keilschrifttexte Sargon's* (Leipzig, 1883) to Eberhard Schrader's *Keilinschriftliche Bibliothek* II (Berlin, 1890), E.A.W. Budge and L.W. King's *Annals of the Kings of Assyria* I (London, 1902), M. Streck's masterful *Assurbanipal* (Leipzig, 1916), D.D. Luckenbill's *The Annals of Sennacherib* (Chicago, 1924), and T. Bauer's *Das Inschriftenwerk Assurbanipals* (Leipzig, 1933), to choose but a single example for each decade before the outbreak of World War II.

At the same time, histories of Assyria were being written, but in retrospect, they lack somewhat in sophistication. It would no longer be acceptable to change all of the pronouns in Sennacherib's eighth "campaign" from first person to third and leave it ambiguous that this is the account of what happened on the battlefield,[1] nor would a historian ever write today: "It is unfortunate that there are variant accounts of Sennacherib's arrangements for the government of the country at the conclusion of the campaign in Chaldaea."[2] But Assyriology was a young discipline, with limited resources and much to accomplish. One must not forget that the basic tools of the trade, von Soden's *Grundriss der akkadischen Grammatik* (Rome, 1952), Labat's sign list *Manuel d'épigraphie akkadienne* (Paris, 1959), and the two great dictionaries, *The Chicago Assyrian Dictionary* and the *Akkadisches Handwörterbuch,* are all post-World War II products.

These advances, plus further hard work preparing the basic texts, have continued to occupy the field in the postwar period. Here, one must mention the edition of R. Borger, *Die Inschriften Asarhaddons* (Graz, 1956), and the major project recently begun at the University of Toronto, called the Royal Inscriptions of Mesopotamia Project, whose aim is to collate and publish all known royal inscriptions from Mesopotamia. It is thanks to this research that some scholars currently working in the field have had the opportunity to raise questions which reinstate the link between Assyriology and biblical archaeology.

The Neo-Assyrian texts, whatever their peculiarities, provide us with an invaluable source not only for biblical history, but for biblical historiography as well. In the royal inscriptions, we are not faced with centuries of transmissions and redaction. When we look at a Sennacherib prism or a stele of Tiglath-Pileser III, we look at an original, an autograph. And when we follow the changes made from "edition" to "edition," or analyze how the material in a text is organized, or observe changes in style and language from the nearly poetic to the flatly pedestrian in one and the same text, we cannot lay this at the feet of an invisible and benighted redactor sitting in Babylon or an unreconstructed Jerusalem. We come face to face with an ancient reality that was, quite literally, fit for a king.

To understand this reality in all its manifestations is the task that many have set themselves. Tadmor and Ephʿal in Jerusalem, Cogan in Beersheba, some in North

America, and the Roman group founded by Liverani, to name but a few, have set out to examine the ideological, compositional, literary and historical dimensions of the enormous corpus of Neo-Assyrian royal texts. A glance at the volume edited by M. Fales, *Assyrian Royal Inscriptions: New Horizons* (Rome, 1981), or by H. Tadmor and M. Weinfeld, *History, Historiography and Interpretation* (Jerusalem, 1983), will suggest to the biblicist just how important this material will prove to be, in ways not touched upon until recently.

There is one other point worth raising about the value of the renewed study of the Neo-Assyrian material. The impetus for this came from a disenchantment with the nature of the questions being asked of the material, and a reassessment of the potential of this large data base. In this, Assyriology shares much in common with biblical archaeology of the 1980s. Here, too, the data base has grown at what some would claim to be an alarming rate, but this growth contains the very seeds for new questions and new approaches. While listening to the debates over biblical archaeology versus Syro-Palestinian archaeology, or EB IV versus MB I versus EB/MB, or sociopolitical versus religio-ethnic approaches, I could not but wonder if the terminological dispute was not beside the point, and only served to obscure the real problems in the field. In thinking about it, I was reminded of a remark made by Kent Flannery, who will, I hope, forgive the paraphrase. He said: "In the end, there is no such thing as new archaeology or old archaeology [or, as I am sure he would say, biblical or Syro-Palestinian archaeology], there is only good archaeology and bad archaeology."

Notes

1. A.T. Olmstead, *History of Assyria* (Chicago: University of Chicago Press, 1923; Midway Reprint, 1975), pp. 293ff.
2. S. Smith, "Sennacherib and Esarhaddon," in *The Cambridge Ancient History. III. The Assyrian Empire*, eds. J.B. Bury, S.A. Cook and F.E. Adcock (Cambridge, 1925), p. 64.

Discussion

J.-G. Heintz: I would insist on one single point, namely to respect the balance between the different corpora of ancient Semitic languages, and avoid over-evaluation of any one archive in reference to the Bible. In the same way archaeologists have to build a common terminology, Assyriologists have to harmonize efforts in documenting the epigraphical data in an accurate and pertinent way (perhaps by a computer-aided data bank) in order to broaden the comparative study of the Bible. But perhaps I am here speaking in a rather utopian way.

S. Parpola: I wish to refer to H. Tadmor's paper on "Nineveh, Calah and Israel," and in particular to its conclusion. I would like to stress that despite the heightened interest in the Assyrian archives during the past decades, we are still very much at the beginning of their analysis. When Prof. Tadmor cites new evidence from letters and administrative texts bearing on Israelites and biblical studies, we must keep in mind that the evidence has been culled mainly from isolated excavations and, like puzzle pieces, it has not yet been placed in proper context. I venture to say that once we have proceeded a little further in the analysis of the archives, and when these archives have been edited properly and put into proper perspective, we will be able to add considerably to our present knowledge and to better understand the bearing of the texts on biblical studies in general.

I also would like to add a note of caution. With the increased awareness of western impact on the Assyrian Empire, there is a danger of exaggeration and of seeing western influences where there is absolutely none. An example is the Assyrian prophetic phenomenon. As many of you certainly know, there exists a corpus of Assyrian prophetic utterances from Sargonid times which closely parallels the corresponding biblical phenomenon, and has for this reason often been cited as an example of western influence on the Assyrian culture and religion. I am afraid I must disagree with this interpretation. For one thing, texts recently published by Freydank have brought to light attestations from the Middle Assyrian period of the words for prophet that occur in these texts (*mahhû, mahhūtu* = *raggimu, raggintu*). Then we have several references to ecstatic prophets in Mesopotamian omen literature, which indicate that the phenomenon of ecstatic prophecy was not something extraordinary in Mesopotamia even prior to the Sargonid period. Lastly, if you examine these Assyrian prophecies in more detail, you will notice that their language is more or less pure Neo-Assyrian, and that the themes — the parallels used by the prophets — are more or less Mesopotamian. Most important of all, the ecstatic prophets came from circles that have very little in common with western elements of population, namely from the Ishtar cult. Therefore, despite the fact that we have occasional western words in these texts, and that some of the prophets have western names, I would consider this as a Mesopotamian phenomenon which has parallels in the west, but still is independently Mesopotamian. In picking out this example I do not want to strike a negative note. I would only like to say that, in my opinion, when we analyze the new evidence, we should refrain from any romantic or fundamentalist views, as Prof. Malamat pointed out in his lecture today, and retain a sober and impartial attitude to the texts. If we proceed in this way, I believe that the Assyrian archives have much to offer biblical studies.

SPECIAL SESSION AT THE KNESSET

YUVAL NE'EMAN
Minister of Science and Development
ALFRED GOTTSCHALK
President, Hebrew Union College–Jewish Institute of Religion

THORKILD JACOBSEN, *Professor Emeritus, Harvard University*
The Temple in Sumerian Literature
SAMUEL NOAH KRAMER, *Professor Emeritus, University of Pennsylvania*
Sumerian Mythology Reviewed and Revised

Special Session at the Knesset

Avraham Biran: Ladies and Gentlemen, we are deeply grateful to Prof. Yuval Ne᾽eman for inviting us to hold this meeting in the Knesset. His assistance and interest in our work is greatly appreciated. It gives me great pleasure to introduce the Minister of Science and Development, Prof. Yuval Ne᾽eman.

Yuval Ne᾽eman: Ladies and Gentlemen, it gives me great pleasure to host you on behalf of the Government of Israel and its Parliament which meets in this house — or should I say in deference to tonight's topic, *hekhal*. We are very happy that the Congress is being held in Jerusalem, but it is unfortunate that during your stay here, you have had to experience an unpleasant facet of our lives. (A terrorist attack took place in Jerusalem on April 2, 1984.) However, as you can see, life and scientific activity continue.

Now I would like to explain to you the Ministry of Science's connection with this Conference. The Ministry of Science was created in Israel two years ago to further the development of science-based industry and high technology on which this country stakes its future. My colleague, the Minister of Finance, and his staff were rather shocked when I told them a short time after I entered office that I was going to spend some money on archaeology as well. They insisted that I should spend money only on electronics and computers, etc. I argued that archaeology was a science. The matter was brought before the State Comptroller who declared a verdict that archaeology is a science. Consequently, archaeology is supported by the Ministry of Science and we have been able to increase archaeological activities in this country by about 25%, in addition to contributing to the organization of this Congress.

Many religions have shrines and burial places in this country and we respect all of them. Unfortunately, the location of burial places sometimes creates clashes between archaeologists and others. I have always believed, however, that with goodwill, it is possible to respect the dead and holy sites, and at the same time carry out scientific and archaeological research.

Let me now tell you something about Israel and its Parliament. In order to portray to you the strength of democracy in this nation, I looked for the earliest source I could find, knowing that the earlier the example, the more convincing it would be for archaeologists. I have chosen to read from *Baba Meẓi῾a*. This is the central gate which is the middle tractate in the Book of Torts of the Mishnah and of the Talmud. This is a story about a discussion which took place around the end of the first century C.E. The two main disputants are Rabbi Joshua and Rabbi Eliezer. I identify with Rabbi Joshua. He was an astronomer, and I am a physicist who has dealt with astronomy. I am reading the Hebrew (BT. *Baba Meẓi῾a* 59b) first so that my Israeli colleagues who may not be familiar with the text, will enjoy the literary aspects.

> תנא באותו היום השיב רבי אליעזר כל תשובות שבעולם ולא קיבלו הימנו אמר להם אם הלכה כמותי חרוב זה יוכיח נעקר חרוב ממקומו מאה אמה ואמרי לה ארבע מאות אמה אמרו לו אין מביאין ראיה מן החרוב חזר ואמר להם אם הלכה כמותי אמת המים יוכיחו חזרו אמת המים לאחוריהם אמרו לו אין מביאין ראיה מאמת המים חזר ואמר להם אם הלכה כמותי כותלי בית המדרש יוכיחו הטו כותלי בית המדרש ליפול גער בהם רבי יהושע אמר להם אם תלמידי חכמים מנצחים זה את זה בהלכה אתם מה טיבכם לא נפלו מפני כבודו של רבי יהושע ולא זקפו מפני כבודו של ר״א ועדיין מטין ועומדין חזר ואמר להם אם הלכה כמותי מן השמים יוכיחו יצאתה בת קול ואמרה מה לכם אצל ר״א שהלכה כמותו בכ״מ עמד רבי יהושע על רגליו ואמר לא בשמים היא מאי לא בשמים היא אמר רבי ירמיה שכבר נתנה תורה מהר סיני אין אנו משגיחין בבת קול שכבר כתבת בהר סיני בתורה אחרי רבים להטות אשכחיה

The English translation is as follows:

> It has been taught: On that day R. Eliezer brought forward every imaginable argument, but they did not accept them. Said he to them: "If the *halachah* agrees with me, let this carob-tree prove it!" Thereupon the carob-tree was torn a hundred cubits out of its place — others affirm, four hundred cubits. "No proof can be brought from a carob-tree," they retorted. Again he said to them: "If the *halachah* agrees with me, let the stream of water prove it!" Whereupon the stream of water flowed backwards. "No proof can be brought from a stream of water," they rejoined. Again he urged: "If the *halachah* agrees with me, let the walls of the schoolhouse prove it," whereupon the walls inclined to fall. But R. Joshua rebuked them, saying: "When scholars are engaged in a *halachic* dispute, what have ye to interfere?" Hence they did not fall, in honour of R. Joshua, nor did they resume the upright, in honour of R. Eliezer; and they are still standing thus inclined. Again he said to them: "If the *halachah* agrees with me, let it be proved from Heaven!" Whereupon a Heavenly Voice cried out: "Why do ye dispute with R. Eliezer, seing that in all matters the *halachah* agrees with him!" But R. Joshua arose and exclaimed: "*It is not in heaven.*" What did he mean by this? — Said R. Jeremiah: That the Torah had already been given at Mount Sinai; we pay no attention to a Heavenly Voice, because Thou hast long since written in the Torah at Mount Sinai, *After the majority must one incline.*

This is really the essence of democratic tradition. As this story claims, even a revelation cannot undo what the majority vote decides. We have been able to realize this tradition in the modern State of Israel, and this building embodies that realization. I think that R. Joshua would have enjoyed being with us tonight under the auspices of his Knesset.

Alfred Gottschalk: It is with a special sense of privilege and appreciation that I rise to express the profound thanks and delight of the participants in this historic First International Congress on Biblical Archaeology. The chairman, members of the organizing committee, the sponsoring agencies, institutions and support staffs have done a remarkable job in providing for the necessities and many amenities that have made this Congress so memorable. The many scholarly offerings, diverse in nature, challenging in theme, often provocative in content, gave rich evidence above ground that what has been discovered beneath it is far from moribund. The vigor and liveliness of our debates, the imaginative and controversial disputations over the nature of our discipline, have given rich testimony to the fact that the field of biblical archaeology is not only alive and well but thriving. The overflow audience of lecturers, respondents and visitors at session after session also indicates how important it was that this Congress be held, that the soft-spoken premise that there continues to exist such a discipline as biblical archaeology be lifted from the bedrock level and raised to banner height, for all to see. The many erudite presentations of the Congress also revealed a sense of passion usually absent from dry as dirt archaeological excavations. The ambience of Israel and Jerusalem, the heartland of our civilized world, no doubt fanned those passions. For here everything matters. Every *mapiq* and *dagesh* assumes universal dimensions. We have sensed here that passion which reaffirms the centrality of Israel as the Land of the Bible. While there are adjoining Bible lands, we have come to sense and know again that without Israel at the heart of the biblical experience the adjacent lands would merely form the backdrop of a stage set without a center stage motif.

So we are grateful for this opportunity to reaffirm the existence of the discipline, the passionate discipline of biblical archaeology, and to reassert that belief, here in this eternal city, undaunted by terrorists (a terrorist attack was carried out in Jerusalem on April 2, 1984) and detractors, resolute and firm as the enduring stones which give foundation to Jerusalem itself.

To the Israel Exploration Society on the occasion of its seventieth anniversary we pay special tribute. No more fitting accolade could have been given it than the outpouring from all over the world of the delegates to this Congress. The society has been the *moreh derekh*, the pathfinder in our discipline of biblical archaeology. May the society continue to thrive and serve. We wish you the biblical עד מאה ועשרים — until 120! — and toast you here spiritually — *leḥayyim* — to life!

The Temple in Sumerian Literature

Thorkild Jacobsen

THE ANCIENT MESOPOTAMIAN TEMPLE was from the very first a house, an abode for the deity who owned it. Its plan, accordingly, was that of a private house, originally T-shaped, later simplified to that of Andrae's rectangular "Herdhaus." (Its further development can here only be summarily sketched.) By the time of the Dynasty of Akkadê, presumably, the "Herdhaus" plan was abnormally enlarged. A crosswall broken by a wide door opening — perhaps reflecting earlier curtains — shielded the podium at the end of the room, thus creating the later southern "broadroom" cella. The remainder of the room, now too wide to roof, became an open court with rooms around its sides. More important temples were situated on artificial platforms surrounded by protective oval walls lined by rooms. The deity's living quarters on top of the platform were kept dark and were known as "the dark house" or "the house knowing no daylight." The lower rooms lining the oval walls were used as kitchens, shops for craftsmen, storerooms, etc. At the place where these rooms were constructed, the shape of the oval walls was changed to rectangular.

The economic base of the temple was extensive landholdings worked by temple personnel and sharecroppers. Local economies such as herding, fishing, orchardry, etc. were prominent.

The temple thus functioned as and was in fact a great estate. What set it apart was that it was sacred. Passages from Sumerian literature clearly show that temples aroused in contemporaries feelings of response to Otto's *Numinous, Mysterium, Tremendous et Fascinosum.* This holiness of the temple was no mere passive quality; rather, it was power upholding and strengthening nature and society. The great Enlil Hymn lists the cosmic effects of the demolition of É-kur; Gudea's Cylinders stress the power of É-ninnu to bring rains and prosperity. The powers of temples are thus specific, and generally they are the same as those of the deity of the temple in question. Moreover,

* The above is an abstract of the Prof. Jacobsen's lecture.

the identity of powers extends in many cases to identity of being. Temple and deity are one. [In my full lecture, the identity of É-ninnu with Ningirsu was discussed and temple names such as É-kur ("house mountain") belonging to the god Kur-gal ("Great mountain"), É-babbar ("the house of rising son") belonging to the god Babbar ("Rising sun") were considered.]

The power of the temple made it a major and central benefit to man. However, obtaining it and its blessings was possible only by divine gift. If the god allowed it, the finished temple remained as a visible daily sign of divine favor and divine presence of the gods as members of the community with a definite stake in it. If, on the other hand, the gods did not grant permission, all man could do was persevere with prayer in sackcloth and ashes. Self-willed Naram-Suen began rebuilding Enlil's temple, É-kur, without divine permission and thus, according to a —not historically correct— tradition, called down utter destruction on all of the country.

Destruction of temples, however, if we may trust the texts, was only rarely caused by human sins. Mostly the gods, for unknown reasons, let enemies destroy their sanctuaries and cities. Laments aimed at persuading the gods to have a change of heart and allow rebuilding, form a characteristic and well-exemplified branch of Sumerian literature. In their varied appeals to the gods to remember their possessions, joyous festivals, and human servants tending to their needs, one may see a reflection also of the human love for, and reliance on, the Temple as a symbol of peace and prosperity (various passages from laments illustrating these points were quoted in my full paper).

Sumerian Mythology Reviewed and Revised

Samuel Noah Kramer

FOR THE PAST SEVERAL YEARS I have been reviewing, revising, retranslating, and bringing up to date some twenty extant Sumerian myths in preparation for a volume on Mesopotamian Mythology to be published jointly with the French scholar Jean Bottéro. I have therefore had occasion to sift, probe and analyze their contents and to reflect and ponder on their nature and character; on the motives and goals that inspired their compositions; on the method and procedure utilized by their authors in originating, evolving, and developing their plot scenarios. I should like to share with you some of my conclusions, inferences, and surmises relating to this complex, abstruse and esoteric Sumerian literary genre created and developed some four thousand years ago not so very far from where we are gathered — "by the waters of Babylon" — to resort to an anachronism.

The extant Sumerian myths are fictitious tales, composed by imaginative, inventive poets and bards educated in the Sumerian academy of learning, the Edubba, who after graduation, served in the personnel attached to the temple, palace, or the Edubba itself. The point of departure, the motivating spark for each of these poetic tales, was the need to explain the origin of some theological credo, such as the puzzling fate of certain death-doomed deities; the birth and lot of a number of rather minor deities; the superiority of one deity over another; the investiture of a deity with powers relating to man's vital needs; the divine role in the rise or restoration of certain cities to power and glory; the divine role in important political events; the divine role in the origin of certain artifacts, plants, and commemorative chants; the divine role in one man's apotheosis to god-like immortality; the divine role in events related to the seasonal stagnation and revival of nature, and the death of the king and his reincarnation. In the course of explaining and illuminating these theological credos, the poet introduces themes, motifs, ideas, incidents, and episodes, some of which may have been of his own invention and creation, but many of which were generally current in the theological and literary circles of his days, not a few of which were no doubt survivals from hoary tradition, both written and oral.

The plot-scenarios of the Sumerian mythographer consisted primarily of episodes and incidents, actions and motivations, transplanted from the human scene to the world of the gods. The poets who composed these factitious and fictitious divine tales were not profound thinkers or metaphysical philosophers — by and large they accepted current theological credos and dogmas without speculating seriously and meaningfully about their origin and validity. Nor were they visionaries imbued with pristine archetypal, cosmic insights — the fact that they lived some four to five thousand years ago hardly brings them closer to the primitive archetypal *Homo sapiens* than is the modern writer of fiction. The extant Sumerian myths, moreover, have little if any connection with temple rituals — by no means can they be characterized as the rite "spoken." Nor will they reveal any cooking recipe, tasty or otherwise, to the modern structuralist, no matter how many layers he peels from their sense and meaning. In short, to judge from their contents, the Sumerian myths are appealing, inspiring, entertaining, edifying divine tales, aetiologically motivated, which, except for the fact that they were composed in poetic form by polytheistic mythographers, have much in common with the biblical myths revolving about the creation of the universe, the creation of man, the Garden of Eden, the Babel of Tongues, and the Flood. They resemble even more closely the haggadic and midrashic tales invented by the Rabbis of Talmudic days. In the pages that follow I shall analyze some of the more important and complex Sumerian myths[1] step by step in order to follow the author as he evolved his imaginative and fictitious tale to explain some extraordinary event in the world of the gods, especially as it related to the human scene.

Enlil and Ninlil: Transgression and Retribution

The text of this myth begins with a twelve-line poetic passage that is unique in Sumerian literature. In it the author introduces the locale of the divine action as well as the age and sex of the three main divine characters in virtually human terms — the place is the well-known Sumerian city Nippur with its river, canal, two docks and sweet-water well, and the principal characters are the youth Enlil, the young maiden Ninlil and the old woman Nunbaršegunu.

The plot of the tale begins with a nine-line passage relating that Ninlil's mother, Nunbaršegunu, had instructed her daughter to have herself impregnated with child by the great god Enlil, and to do so by bathing in the Idnunbirdu Canal and strolling along its bank where, taken with her beauty, that holy-eyed deity will penetrate her and leave his luxuriant seed in her womb.

Ninlil, continues the poet, carried out her mother's instructions to the letter, and Enlil, sexually aroused, presses her to have intercourse with him. But she refuses, protesting that she is too young, and that moreover her parents will punish her, and her companions will scorn her.

Despite Ninlil's objections, Enlil is determined to have his way with her. He therefore has his *sukkal*, the god Nusku, bring up a boat and having presumably invited Ninlil to join him, he has intercourse with her against her will, and pours into her womb the seed of Sin-Ašimbabbar (the moon-god as the New Moon).

Having raped the youthful Ninlil and satisfied his sexual passion, Enlil returned to Nippur, seemingly unaware that the great gods had met and judged him guilty of a serious transgression of the moral code for which he, king of the gods though he be, must suffer due retribution. One day as he was strolling about in the *kiur* alongside the Ekur, the gods seized him and commanded him to leave the city, and (though this is not stated explicitly in the text) to proceed to the Nether World where he would join the company of the other dead gods.

Unable to escape the fate to which he was doomed by the gods, Enlil left his city and proceeded to the Nether World. On arriving at the city gate, having observed that Ninlil was following him, he commanded the gatekeeper not to reveal his whereabouts to the inquisitive goddess. Ninlil arrives at the city gate, and, as Enlil had predicted, demands that the gatekeeper tell her where Enlil had gone. Evidently fearful that the gatekeeper might betray him, Enlil assumes the shape of the gatekeeper and tells Ninlil that he cannot reveal Enlil's whereabouts since he was threatened by the god with dire consequences if he did so. But Ninlil persists, protesting that while it is true that Enlil is his king, she is his queen, and therefore presumably equally entitled to be obeyed. By this time, however, Enlil's libido seems to have been aroused and he is eager to have it satisfied. So much so that when the reluctant goddess informs him that the seed of the moon-god is already in her womb, he counters with the assertion that while the seed of Sin will go up to heaven, the seed which he will pour into her womb will go down to earth, evidently implying that there is room for both. And without more ado he proceeds to penetrate Ninlil, and to pour into her womb the seed of the chthonic deity Nergal-Meslamtaea.

The action continues with Enlil, presumably having thrown off his human form, resuming his journey to the Nether World with Ninlil in close pursuit. This time he arrives at the bank of Nether World River, and there encounters the man in charge. From here on the events recounted in the preceding passage are repeated verbatim except that "the man of the Nether World River" is substituted for "the man at the gate." The seed that Enlil pours into Ninlil's womb this time is that of the chthonic deity Ninazu, the king of the Egidda temple.

Once again now Enlil, having resumed his divine form, continues his journey to the Nether World, with Ninlil in close pursuit. This time he encounters Silulim, the Sumerian Charon, who is to ferry him across the Nether World River. The events recounted in the preceding two passages are repeated once again virtually verbatim, except that "the man of the ferryboat," is substituted for "the man of the gate" and "the man of the Nether World River." And this time it is probably the seed of Enbilulu,[2] the canal inspector, that Enlil pours into the womb of the goddess.

With the begetting of the three chthonic deities the action of the myth comes to an end. But the poet, perhaps uncomfortable with the thought of concluding his tale on so dismal a note as Enlil's becoming a dead god, adds a eulogistic epilogue extolling Enlil as a mighty, powerful god who ensures fertility and prosperity in both heaven and earth, and whose command is forever unalterable.

So much for the plot-scenario of the myth, a tale obviously composed by a poet interested primarily in resolving the enigmatic problem relating to the deities Nergal, Ninazu and Enbilulu who as tutelary deities of important Sumerian cities were glorified in hymns and psalms as sons of the mighty Enlil, and yet, according to the theological credo of his day, were conceived as doomed to death and the Nether World. His answer was that these three deities were destined to their dismal fate from birth, since they were engendered by Enlil in human form and were conceived by their mother Ninlil as she followed her husband-to-be to the Nether World. Let us now try to reconstruct the thinking and reasoning of the author that led him to this imaginative conclusion.

The tragic fate of these three deities, it was not unreasonable to assume, must certainly be due to some transgression against one of the *me*, the divine norms that guided and controlled all behavior, both human and divine. But since there was no inkling of any wrongdoing on the part of these deities in the theological lore of his day, the author concluded that the cruel fate they suffered must have been due to some transgression on the part of their parents, and one that was probably sex-related, since no other kind of parental guilt could reasonably be assumed to be responsible for the affliction of the offspring.

Once persuaded that this was so, the author turned consciously and explicitly to the human scene about him in order to determine the specific nature of the sex-related parental misdeed that was responsible for the wretched fate of the three sons. Here, he virtually says in so many words, is his city Nippur, through which flow several large canals in which young women often went bathing at the behest of their mothers in order to find a suitable husband from among the men strolling along the banks. From time to time, as might be expected, one of these young ladies was raped by some sex-driven male, who was then no doubt punished severely by the city authorities, and perhaps banished or even put to death. Transplanting this type of human episode to the divine level, the poet visualized the god Enlil as a young man who at the sight of Ninlil, envisaged as a young seductive maiden, could not restrain his passion, and forced her to have intercourse with him against her will — an immoral act for which he was punished by banishment from Nippur and doomed to a ghastly existence in the Nether World.

Our poet-mythographer now had one major essential component of the plot of his tale: the rape of Ninlil and the banishment of Enlil to the Nether World, which was responsible in some way for the current belief that three of his sons were to be Nether World deities. (To be sure there was a fourth son, the luminous moon-god Sin, who, despite the rape of his mother, was destined to be an impressive sky-god and not a Nether World deity. This, however, presented no problem to our author. For while it was true that he was engendered and conceived after the misdeed had been committed by his father, this occurred while Enlil was still in Nippur and before he had been sentenced to the Nether World by the gods). But there was still a missing link in the plot of the tale, and this related to the events that followed the rape and banishment that brought about the birth of the three Nether World sons. And it was in this connection that the author utilized a motif not found in any other extant literary source, one that may therefore be of his own invention: the metamorphosis of Enlil[3] as a mortal resulting in the loss of the divine gift of immortality by his seed and offspring.

But who were these mortals and how did Enlil actually come to impersonate each of them. In answer to these questions the author envisaged the following scenario. Ninlil, the victim of the rape, was, as might have been expected, determined to follow Enlil closely no matter where he was going lest he escape her altogether and she would never become his duly married spouse. Enlil, on the other hand, was only too eager to get away from her, probably to save her and the son she was already bearing, the moon-god Sin, from his own fate. Now on his way from Nippur to the Nether World, it was clear to any imaginative mythographer, Enlil would have to make three stops in order to identify himself: the first as he left the city gate was under the charge of "the man of the gate"; the second, upon his arrival at the Nether World River, which was under the charge of "the man of the Nether World River"; the third, when he came to the ferryboat that was to transport him across the Nether World River, which was under the charge of "the man of the ferryboat." Fearing that any one of these mortals might betray his whereabouts to Ninlil who was close on his heels, Enlil assumed the shape of each in turn. However, in the course of trying to persuade the goddess of his ignorance of the raper's location, his libido got the best of him and he penetrated her. Thus it was that his three Nether World sons were engendered: Nergal by Enlil as "the man of the gate"; Ninazu by Enlil as "the man of the Nether World River"; Enbilulu by Enlil as "the man of the ferryboat."

Enki and Ninhursag: A Sumerian Paradise Myth

This myth begins with a well-preserved introductory passage whose literal rendering is relatively assured but whose real meaning and implications are rather obscure and elusive — it depicts Dilmun as a land that is pure, holy, and radiant, a land where there are no birds to disturb the peace; where there are no wild animals preying on their victims; a land that knows neither sickness, aging, and (perhaps) death.

There now follows an address by goddess Ninsikilla, Dilmun's tutelary deity, in which she complains that the land Dilmun which he, Enki, had given her, lacked sweet water and crop-bearing fields and farms. Enki responds by blessing Dilmun with abundance of water brought out of the earth by the sun-god Utu.

The main action of the myth now begins with the depiction of Enki's sexual exploits. The first relates to his impregnation of the goddess Ninhursag in the marshland and the birth of his daughter Ninmu after nine days of gestation — each day, according to the author, representing a month. The second relates to Enki's impregnation of his daughter Ninmu on the river bank and the birth of his granddaughter Ninkurra after nine days of gestation. The third relates to his impregnation of his granddaughter Ninkurra on the river bank and the birth of his great-granddaughter, the goddess Uttu, after nine days of gestation.

This goddess Uttu would no doubt have gone forth to the river bank as did her mother Ninkurra and her grandmother Ninmu, and like them would have been impregnated by the sex-driven Enki, were it not for her great-grandmother Ninhursag who counselled her against it — the relevant passage is almost entirely destroyed, but to judge from what follows, Ninhursag had instructed her to stay in her house and to have nothing to do with Enki unless and until he brought her a gift of cucumbers, apples, and grapes. In any case when the text becomes intelligible, we find that Enki had obtained these products from a grateful gardener and playing the role of a gardener brought them to a joyful Uttu, into whose welcoming womb he poured so much of his semen that it overflowed her loins.

From this semen which was wiped off by the goddess Ninhursag from the loins of her great-granddaughter, the tale continues, she generated the sprouting of eight plants. But now Enki appears once again on the scene and this spelled disaster for both the plants and Enki. For Enki determined to decree the fate of the eight plants, and to do so, he decided that he first had to eat them. This destructive act so angered Ninhursag, the goddess who had generated them, that she pronounced the curse of death upon him, and then disappeared from the assembly of the gods.

Now comes the denouement of the plot of the myth. Fearing Enki's imminent demise and not knowing what to do about it, now that Ninhursag had vanished, the gods "sat in the dust." Whereupon the clever fox came to the rescue — speaking up before the great god Enlil, he claimed that he knew how to make Ninhursag return to the divine assembly, but would do so only if he received a suitable reward. Enlil promised to plant an orchard for him in Nippur, and the fox then did bring Ninhursag back to the gods, who persuade the goddess to have a change of heart. We next find her seating the ailing Enki in (or by) her vulva and asking him where he feels pain. Enki names one by one the eight organs that hurt him as a result of his eating the eight plants, and Ninhursag proceeds to give birth to the corresponding healing deities. Finally Enki, perhaps because he was grateful to Ninhursag for bringing him back to life, proceeded to bless the eight newly born deities, the last of whom, Enšag by name, he destines to be "the Lord of Dilmun."

So much for the plot of "Enki and Ninhursag: A Sumerian Paradise Myth." Let us now analyze it step by step and try to follow the author's train of ideas. The spark that kindled the author's desire for composing this myth was his conviction that he could explain the reason for the somewhat surprising theological tenet that the god who was in charge of Dilmun, a great commercial center in his day, was a rather minor deity by the name of Enšag — it must have been Enšag's father, the all-wise Enki, the god responsible for Dilmun's prosperity, brilliance, and purity, who made him Lord of Dilmun. This we learn from the very end of the myth, for it is virtually always the end of a composition that reveals the intent of its author. Just how and under what circumstances Enšag's appointment by Enki came about is the central theme of this rather complicated myth which includes some motifs, incidents, and episodes that are as yet enigmatic and obscure.

Let us start with the theological credos and tenets which, as evidenced by various extant literary sources, were probably current, and at the disposal of the author for constructing the plot of the tale. These include firstly the belief that Enšag, the god in charge of Dilmun, was the son of Enki and Ninhursag —*a priori*, therefore, it was not unlikely that these two deities played a major role in their son's appointment to this rather important office. Secondly, it was believed that Enki and Ninhursag were the parents of seven more deities: Abu, Nintulla, Ninsutu, Ninkasi, Nazi, Asimua, and Ninti.[4] These names, when analyzed closely, revealed to our author a rather curious and remarkable coincidence: each of these names contained a one-syllable word designating an organ of the body. Since these deities were all the children of Enki and Ninhursag, it was not unreasonable to conclude that the organ to which these names corresponded in part, belonged to one or the other of their parents. Thirdly, it was well known to our author that theologically speaking Enki and Ninhursag were bitter rivals —each, for example, claimed third place, that is, the spot following An and Enlil, in the hierarchy of the pantheon. It would not at all be surprising, therefore, if this struggle led to some serious injury on the part of one or the other. Given these theological credos relating to the genealogy of the gods, and the anthropomorphic views concerning their behavior, the author's train of thought when constructing the plot-scenario of the second half of the myth, the part beginning with Enki's self-indulgent consuming of the eight plants generated by Ninhursag, can be followed with a fair degree of confidence.

It is his rationale for Enki's sexual exploits depicted in the first half of the myth that is enigmatic and obscure — none of the extant Sumerian literary works help to illuminate and clarify the reason for the author's factitious description of the birth of the three goddesses Ninmu, Ninkurra and Uttu. Very little is known about these deities, and what is known seems quite irrelevant to their role in the plot of the myth. It is not unreasonable to assume that our mythographer knew what he was doing, and that he had his reasons for introducing these particular deities into his plot structure, but as of today they are totally out of our ken.[5]

Enki and Ninmah: The Creation of Man

The bitter rivalry between Enki and the goddess known by the names Ninmah or Ninhursag is also the dominating motif in the myth "Enki and Ninmah: The Creation of Man." Although the primary intent of the author in composing this creation myth is rather obscure because of the fragmentary state of preservation of the concluding thirty lines, it is reasonably certain that his main interest was to validate the superiority of Enki and his city Eridu over Ninmah-Ninhursag and her city Keš. In some obscure way this had to do with the enigmatic *umul*, a feeble, impotent, useless creature fashioned by Enki in the course of a disputatious contest with Ninmah-Ninhursag. Since the creation of so wretched a creature could hardly be the work of a great and wise deity in a sober, rational frame of mind, the author hit upon the idea of having the contest take place during a carousing banquet celebrating, rather ironically, though not inappropriately, the creation of the perfect man, a merry feast during which both Enki and Ninmah became drunk, belligerent and contentious. This myth, too, may therefore be divided into two sections, the second of which relates to the fashioning of the badly crippled *umul*, and the first to the creation of the model-man. In both sections it is possible to follow the author's thinking and reasoning as he invented the scenes and episodes that constitute the plot of the tale.

In the second section, for example, the author's prime purpose is to provide an answer to a twofold problem that must have been on the mind of many a Sumerian: the origin of the existence of a whole group of crippled humans who, despite their handicap, had found useful employment in society. Convinced that this must have related in some way to the rivalry between Enki and Ninmah, the two deities theologically endowed with the powers essential for the creation of man, he envisaged the following imaginative scenario. To celebrate the creation of the perfect man, the model human prototype, Enki arranged a sumptuous feast for the great gods, in the course of which he was acclaimed and exalted as the god of wide understanding and great deeds. Whereupon the resentful Ninmah, flushed with drink, and eager to humble Enki and discredit his handiwork, capriciously and arbitrarily created six crippled humans. But though he, too, was flushed with drink, Enki rose to the challenge and found suitable and useful work for all of them despite their handicap. But then, angered by Ninmah's persistent and belligerent rivalry, he proceeded to create the fatally defective *umul*, and demanded that she find useful employment for him just as he had done for the six damaged humans she had fashioned. Ninmah was unable to do so, and in some obscure way, this impotent *umul* helped to bring about the humiliation of the goddess who finally had to admit Enki's superiority.

The creation of man's perfect prototype, the event that motivated the unfortunate and fateful banquet scene, is the theme of the first section of the myth. Availing himself of the relevant current theological tenets, and transplanting human actions and emotions to the divine plane, our mythographer evolved the following scenario. In days of yore, after heaven had been separated from earth, the Anunna-gods who were born after this crucial event, having married and begotten offspring, complained bitterly about the hard labor they had to endure in order to support their families. Moved by their laments, Nammu, the primeval mother of all the gods, appealed to her son Enki, the all-wise water-god, who was lying asleep in the deep, to exercise his wisdom and find a way to relieve them of their drudgery. Obedient to his mother's wishes, Enki arose from his watery bed, brought forth sapient, sagacious creatures known as *sigensigdu*, and with the help of Ninmah, the goddess of birth, and seven assisting deities, man, the servant of the gods, was fashioned from the clay molded in the Abzu by Nammu, at the behest of her dutiful son.

Enki and Inanna: The Organization of the Universe

Unlike Ninhursag-Ninmah, the goddess Inanna was no rival of Enki, as is evident from the two myths in which Enki and Inanna are the principal characters. Although she troubled him from time to time with her complaints and demands, he was never seriously vexed with her and in fact finally yielded and let her have her way. In one of these tales, "Enki and Inanna: The Organization of the Universe," it was the author's primary intent to confirm and validate the vast powers and prerogatives that were attributed to Inanna by the theologians and mythographers of his day. To achieve his purpose, he introduced a dramatic scene toward the very end of the tale, in which an embittered Inanna is depicted as complaining angrily to Enki and claiming that she had been discriminated against, and neglected by him, when he was organizing the universe — he had assigned powers, duties, and functions to any number of deities, she contended, but she had received no comparable rights and prerogatives. Enki, according to the author, not only did not take offense at her insolent accusations, but actually went out of his way to soothe and placate her and to shower her with blessings and benedictions.

To properly motivate this concluding scene, the author deemed it essential to depict Enki's organization of the universe in considerable detail, and thus provided us with quite a number of theological credos and mythological motifs virtually unknown from any other extant literary source: Enki's blessing of Sumer, Ur, Meluhha, Dilmun and Martu, and his cursing of Elam and Marhaši; a detailed documentation of Enki's creative and resourceful deeds in providing for man's essential needs related to food, shelter and clothing, including the appointment of quite a number of deities to take charge of and supervise the varied and diverse cultural activities vital for man and his civilization. And since, unlike his superiors, the gods An and Enlil, Enki was never the leading deity of the Sumerian pantheon, his authority to organize the universe and appoint deities virtually at will, had to be justified and accounted for. The author therefore introduced his tale with several hymnal passages eulogizing Enki and stressing his very close relationship to An and Enlil, at whose behest and with whose cooperation he performed the extraordinary, far-sighted, and far-reaching tasks depicted in the main part of the myth.

Inanna and Enki: The Transfer of the Me *from Eridu to Erech*

In this myth, too, Enki and Inanna are the principal characters, but it is the goddess who plays the more prominent role. The intent of its author was to explain how the city Erech had regained its preeminence and leadership in the land, as well as to validate the cult practices relating to the adoration of its tutelary deity, Inanna. As he saw it, the rise of Erech to renewed greatness and glory could only have come about after it had acquired the precious *me*, the *sine qua non* of urban civilized life, and Inanna's cult of adoration could not have been instituted in the restored Erech without the sanction and blessing of her patron and ally, the god Enki. However, these *me*, according to theological belief current in his day, were in Eridu, in the Abzu, carefully guarded by Enki who would not willingly turn them over to another deity and city. Our mythographer, therefore, found it necessary to devise a plot that would account for the transfer of the *me* from his city Eridu to Inanna's city Erech. Accordingly, he contrived the following series of scenes and episodes, all revolving about Inanna's successful procurement of the *me* from their reluctant guardian: (1) a soliloquizing Inanna, confident of her charms, voicing her determination to journey to Eridu; (2) a festal welcome in the Abzu by Enki, featuring a carousing banquet in the course of which the drunken Enki presented to Inanna all the *me* under his charge; (3) Inanna's departure from Eridu in her "Boat of Heaven," loaded with the treasured *me*; (4) Enki's vain attempt to recover the *me* by dispatching his *sukkal*, Isimud, accompanied by a varied assortment of sea-monsters, to intercept the goddess at each of the seven stops between Eridu and Erech; (5) Inanna's safe arrival in her city, and her unloading of the *me* one by one in its "White Quay," amidst the jubilation of the Erechites; (6) Enki's gracious capitulation and reconciliation sealed with blessings and benedictions for its charming ambitious goddess.

Lugal-e: *The Deeds and Exploits of Ninurta*

Unlike Inanna who was young, charming, "sexy," aggressive, and ambitious, the goddess Nidaba was old, wise, literate, learned, and numbers-oriented. It is not surprising, therefore, that theologically speaking, she was entrusted with Sumer's richly stocked granaries on which the prosperity and well-being of the people depended. As for the time and circumstance of her appointment, there was at least one imaginative theologian, the author of *Lugal-e*, who was convinced that it was the heroic god Ninurta who invested her with this office after he had killed the monstrous demon Asag in the Kur, the cosmic realm below the earth, turned the Asag's corpse into a mountain that held back the dangerous waters of the Kur; gathered the fresh waters into the Tigris, thus making irrigation possible and farming productive, so that Sumer's granaries and storehouses were filled with the rich harvest of field, farm, and orchard. Then, deeming it essential to have some trustworthy deity to manage and supervise these vital granaries, Ninurta naturally chose Nidaba, the goddess noted for her skill with numbers, the designated sealkeeper of his father Enlil, the stewardess of his grandfather An. While, therefore, virtually the entire complex, multifaceted *Lugal-e* composition concerns the deeds and exploits, the power and glory of the heroic Ninurta, it was the investiture of the goddess Nidaba with her impressive skills related to stewardship that motivated the author to arrange and adapt some of the current Ninurta tales, hymns, and panygerics into its present form.

Enki and Eridu: The Journey of the Water-God to Nippur

This myth, which is quite obviously a "charter" type of tale, is one of the most poetic, imaginative, pictorially graphic compositions in the Sumerian literary repertoire. The primary intent of its author was to affirm and validate the greatness of Enki's temple, the renowned Abzu, his sea-house in Eridu. For though Enki was one of the four leading deities of the Sumerian pantheon, he still had to have the sanction and benediction of his superior, Enlil of Nippur, to assure its power and majesty. Beginning the composition, as expected, with a poetic image-laden description of the temple's attractive ornamentation and decoration, the author evidently felt that it would be more dramatic to have Enki's *sukkal*, Isimud, sing of its glory and splendor. He therefore composed a special chant for him that extolled the temple's architectural embellishments, and the resounding polyphony of its music, instrumental and vocal. Following Isimud's eulogistic, endearing chant, the poet introduced a scene that visualized Enki and his temple rising out of the deep sea, a sight wondrous and terrifying to behold. He next envisaged Enki loosening the boat from its mooring after loading it with food, drink, and musical instruments, and setting sail for Nippur. Arrived at Nippur's divine dining hall, the *giguna*, he prepared a banquet for the assembly of the gods that culminated in Enlil's eulogizing Enki's Abzu, especially as a house qualified to be in charge of man's arts and crafts.

Nanna and Ur: The Journey of the Moon-God to Nippur

This myth, like that concerned with Enki's journey to Nippur, is also an obvious "charter" type of tale, but unlike the latter, its style is repetitive and monotonous. The purpose of its author was to record, commemorate, and celebrate the divine base and support for the agricultural prosperity of Sumer as a whole. But since in accordance with the current theological credo this could have been achieved only with the approval and blessing of Nanna's father, Enlil of Nippur, the author conceived the idea that Nanna, the tutelary deity of Ur, Sumer's capital in his day, had journeyed to Nippur by boat with a rich assortment of gifts and thus obtained Enlil's coveted benediction. He therefore devised a series of scenes to depict this event, which included (1) a soliloquy by Nanna voicing his determination to journey to Nippur; (2) a detailed description of the construction of the various parts of his boat from different woods obtained from their places of origin inside and outside Sumer; (3) the loading of the boat with cattle large and small, birds, fish, oil, eggs, and reeds; (4) the ceremonial greeting of Nanna and his boat by the tutelary deities of the five places between Ur and Nippur where the boat docked in transit; (5) the arrival in Nippur and the unloading of the gifts before the rejoicing Enlil; (6) Nanna's request and Enlil's generous granting of the essential elements for Sumer's affluent agricultural economy.

Inanna and the Subjugation of Mt. Ebih

Not a few of the Sumerian myths mask and veil important political and military events in the history of Sumer. Thus, for example, "Enki and Ninmah: The Creation of Man" probably echoes a power struggle between the city states Eridu and Keš; "Enki and Inanna: The Organization of the Universe" and "Inanna and Enki: The Transfer of the *Me* from Eridu to Erech" were inspired by the restoration of Erech to its earlier power and influence. The complex composition "*Lugal-e*: The Deeds and Exploits of Ninurta" may reflect some favorable military and political events during the reign of Gudea of Lagaš. But there are two myths that clearly, plainly, and unmistakably mirror in the world of the gods, military and political events that actually took place in the course of Sumer's checkered history.

One of these, "Inanna and the Subjugation of Mt. Ebih," is a myth composed by a poet who conceived the attractive idea of celebrating the Sumerian conquest of Mt. Ebih, a mountainous region to the northeast of Sumer, by transferring the action to the world of the gods, and having the warlike Inanna symbolize the triumphant Sumerian people. To portray this momentous event with dramatic effect, the author envisaged and pictured the goddess and her actions in four sequential scenes: (1) a soliloquizing Inanna voicing her determination to subjugate the arrogant Mt. Ebih; (2) a respectful Inanna coming before the rather timorous heaven-god An who tries to discourage her from her rash undertaking; (3) an enraged Inanna attacking and devastating the insolent Mt. Ebih; (4) a triumphant Inanna extolling herself boastfully before her prostrate victim. To round out these dramatic scenes, the poet begins the composition with a eulogy of Inanna as the goddess of war and weaponry, appearing in the sky as the radiant Venus-star, and ends it with a song of self-praise by the goddess related to the building of her temple and the establishment of her cult in the conquered territory.

The Marriage of Martu

Unlike "Inanna and the Subjugation of Mt. Ebih," the myth revolving about the marriage of the god Martu does not celebrate a military victory of one people over another, but a sociopolitical alliance between two contrasting groups of people: the nomads and the urbanites. The nomads of this tale are the Martu, and the urbanites are the dwellers of Ninab, a city probably located in northern Sumer — an alliance between them must actually have taken place at some early date in the history of Sumer. But the author of this tale transposed this event to the divine world, and symbolized the alliance by a marriage between Martu, the tutelary deity of the nomadic Martu people, and the daughter of Numušda, the tutelary deity of urban Ninab. The events leading to this divine marriage are depicted by the author in a series of episodes that have no counterpart in any other Sumerian literary work. Briefly sketched, the logical and, on the whole, understandable plot runs as follows. Despite the rule that only married gods had to bring two bread offerings to An, while unmarried deities had to bring only one, Martu, for some reason, found that he had to bring two bread offerings although he was single. He therefore decided to marry, and his mother advises him not to marry a Martu girl, but to go seek a wife according to his heart's desire. He comes to the city Ninab, participates in a wrestling match in the presence of the god Numušda and his daughter, and emerges as victor and champion. Numušda offers him gold, silver, and precious stones as his prize, but Martu rejects them and demands the hand of his daughter instead. Despite a last-ditch attempt by her friends to dissuade her from marrying this barbarous nomad who eats raw food and buries not his dead, the daughter decides to wed him. And so it was that the nomadic Martu and the urban Ninabites became socially allied.[6]

Notes

1. Bibliographical references to these myths will be found in the forthcoming volume on Mesopotamian Mythology.
2. It is not quite certain that the name of the third deity was actually Enbilulu.
3. For Enlil disguised as a raven, cf. Miguel Civil, *AfO* 25 (1974/1977): 5ff. For Enki disguised as a gardener, cf. this paper, p. 291.
4. Actually only Ninkasi is known as the daughter of Enki and Ninhursag from other literary sources, while Nazi (Nanse) is known as the daughter of Enki but the name of her mother is not mentioned in any other extant source. It is not unreasonable to surmise, however, that to judge from our myth all eight were conceived as children of Enki and Ninhursag, despite the lack of evidence from other textual sources.
5. For rather far-fetched attempts to interpret this passage, cf. G.S. Kirk, *Myth* (Cambridge University Press and University of California Press, 1970), pp. 90ff.
6. The plot structure of virtually all other extant myths can be analyzed in a similar fashion. The one myth whose structure still remains quite enigmatic is "Inanna and Bilulu," since virtually nothing is known about the three minor deities who play a prominent role in the tale. The plot structure of the "Sumerian Deluge" myth remains obscure to some extent because of the fragmentary state of the first ninety lines.

SESSION VI
HEBREW AND ARAMAIC EPIGRAPHY

JONAS C. GREENFIELD, Session Chairman, *The Hebrew University of Jerusalem*

ALAN R. MILLARD, *The University of Liverpool*
An Assessment of the Evidence for Writing in Ancient Israel
ANDRÉ LEMAIRE, *Centre National de la Recherche Scientifique, France*
L'Inscription de Balaam trouvée à Deir ʿAlla: épigraphie
BARUCH LEVINE, *New York University*
The Balaam Inscription from Deir ʿAlla: Historical Aspects
EDWARD LIPIŃSKI, *Katholieke Universiteit Leuven*
Aramaic-Akkadian Archives from the Gozan-Ḫarran Area

Respondents

AARON DEMSKY, *Bar-Ilan University*
JOSEPH NAVEH, *The Hebrew University of Jerusalem*
ÉMILE PUECH, *Centre National de la Recherche Scientifique, France*
ALEXANDER ROFÉ, *The Hebrew University of Jerusalem*

Discussion

An Assessment of the Evidence for Writing in Ancient Israel

Alan R. Millard

IN 1982 WORKMEN preserving walls on the Ophel in Jerusalem made a rare discovery, a piece of a Hebrew inscription on stone dating from the time of the Monarchy.[1] The stone is so fragmentary that the purpose of the writing is uncertain. Nonetheless, it is further evidence that monumental inscriptions could be seen in the capital of Judah. Other discoveries in Jerusalem and elsewhere prove writing was practiced in ancient Israel for a variety of reasons. In 1972 I distinguished three classes of written document — the monumental, the formal, and the occasional.[2] The second and third classes are much better represented than the first, and the number of examples in each of them is continually growing. To catalogue each text would be tedious; a few examples will suffice to exhibit their form and range.

In the formal class, the fine engraving on an ivory plaque from Nimrud is now joined by the remarkable ivory pomegranate which André Lemaire discovered in a Jerusalem antiquities shop.[3] Letters engraved on it in a practiced hand form the words *qdš khnm*, 'holy of the priests,' with a broken passage which Lemaire has restored as *by*[*tyhwh*], but which could equally be reconstructed to give a different name. The standard examples of formal writing, the ostraca, are no longer the rarity they were in 1935, the year of the great Lachish find. The collection of over seventy examples from Arad, recovered through the late Yohanan Aharoni's insistence on "dipping" sherds, dwarfs all other groups except the Samaria hoard of 1910 (according to Lemaire, 102 ostraca from Samaria are kept in Istanbul, twenty-five of them illegible[4]). Yet the single ostracon is as valuable for the present study as a score, whether a letter, a list of names, or scribblings such as those from Kuntilet Ajrud.[5]

* In addition to his gratitude to the organizers of the Congress for their invitation, the writer thanks the Institute for Advanced Studies of The Hebrew University, under whose auspices he visited Jerusalem in 1984, and was provided with the opportunity and facilities to prepare this study.

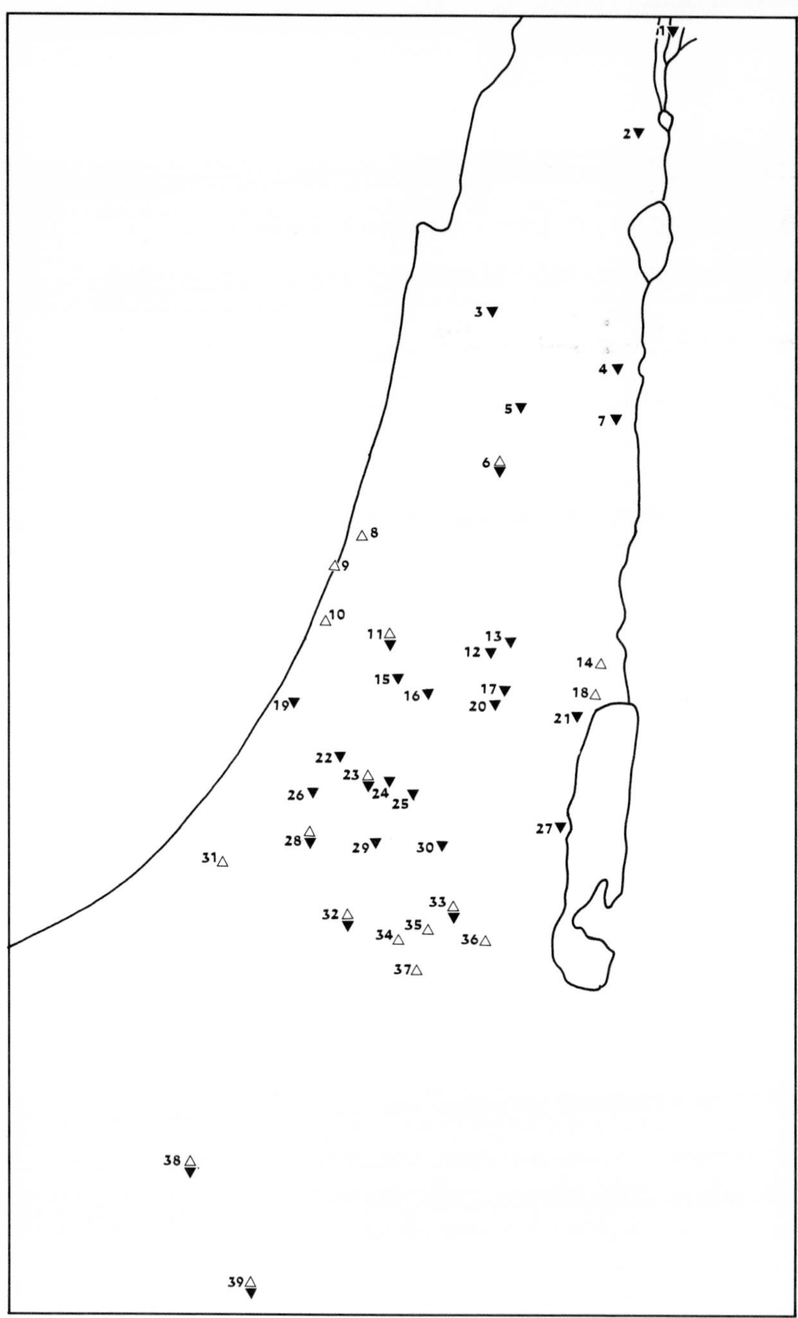

Distribution map of sites where Hebrew ostraca (△) and graffiti (▼) have been found

Beside the ostraca should be set the seals. Recent years have brought a refinement to the study of seals from the area, making clearer the distinction between Ammonite, Edomite, Hebrew and Moabite.[6] Several previously classed as Hebrew now stand in one of the other national categories on grounds of language and script, although neither criterion is always decisive. With the multiplication in the number of Hebrew seals, assuming the majority of them are authentic, their witness to writing in particular contexts grows stronger. Classed with the seal-stones are the impressions other seals have left on clay — the bullae which often carry the imprints of papyrus fibres on their backs. Bullae found in controlled excavations are important for they may reveal where seals were used and where sealed documents were stored. The fifty-one which Y. Shiloh's team found in a room of a seventh century B.C.E. building in the City of David in 1982 make a major contribution in this respect.[7] The occasional documents are the graffiti, names and notes written in ink or scratched on complete pots and pans, scribbled in tombs, on buildings or on more unusual surfaces such as a stalactite in a remote cave near the Dead Sea.[8]

Undoubtedly the scribes were responsible for the majority of these ancient Hebrew texts. They served monarchs, officials and the gentry where the royal court resided, writing such letters as Jezebel's to order Naboth's execution (1 Kings 21), or recording deliveries of produce as in the Samaria Ostraca, or preserving the words a Jeremiah might dictate (Jeremiah 36). In theory it is possible to argue that scribes sent from the capital cities on special missions wrote all of the ostraca which have been recovered. However, the content of most of them makes it hard to suppose anyone would take the trouble to travel journeys long by ancient standards in order to write notes of purely local and ephemeral interest. Therefore, it is satisfactory to assume there were scribes active in towns outside Samaria and Jerusalem. At major places like Lachish that is no surprise, but it is revealing to observe where Hebrew ostraca have been unearthed. On information at present available, there are fifteen sites which have yielded ostraca, apart from Samaria and Jerusalem. Among them are relatively small settlements, forts, or caravanserais like Ḥorvat ʿUza, Kuntilet Ajrud, and Khirbet Qumran. (For a list of sites yielding ostraca, see Appendix.) Should we assume there was a professional scribe operating at each, or can we suppose that military or government employees, or even private citizens, able to write, lived in them?

The question becomes more urgent with regard to the occasional texts. Again, it is not excluded that some of the pieces were carried from Jerusalem or another metropolis to the places where they were found. Once again, that is hard to accept for all the pieces, discovered at more than two dozen sites. (For a list of sites yielding 'occasional' texts, see Appendix.) Those written in ink are probably the products of scribes, or of people who were accustomed to write and equipped to do so; those scratched or pecked on pots may be the work of anyone who knew how to shape the letters, without pen and ink to hand. Together, the ostraca and graffiti come from thirty-five or forty sites. Yet if the larger collections of ostraca — Samaria, Arad,

Lachish — are set apart, the remainder, scattered across so many sites, afford a miserable picture of the scribes' work. Can it really be supposed that Israelite scribes did no more than write such trifles as the list of names from Tel Masos, or the incoherent complaint about a sequestrated cloak from Mesad Hashavyahu, or scribbled notes about the class of wine in various jugs? Were potsherds really their normal writing material, as one recent commentator has deduced?[9] Alongside the fragment of reused papyrus from the Wadi Murabbaʿat, the evidence of the seal impressions on clay stands against that opinion. Obviously, in Jerusalem, Samaria, Lachish and wherever else these bullae are found, papyrus documents once existed to leave the impress of their fibres on the clay, and sometimes the marks of the cords that bound the folded sheets. The bullae are identical in application to the clay sealings found in Egypt still attached to papyri of the Persian period.[10] They are clear testimony to Hebrew scribes practicing their craft on papyrus.

Egypt provides an analogy for the situation in ancient Israel which, although mentioned before,[11] is worth reinforcing. From the beginning of Egypt's history papyrus was the normal medium for administrative records, and, no doubt, already in the Old Kingdom, for preserving literary creations (although the earliest Egyptian literary texts extant on papyrus come from the Middle Kingdom). Short messages, memoranda, scribal exercises and notes of all kinds were written on potsherds or flakes of stone that were easy to find, cost nothing, and could be discarded freely. Very few sites have been excavated where the relationship between papyrus and ostraca can be seen clearly. The most prolific is the village of the tomb-workers at Deir el-Medineh, where documents dating from the Nineteenth and Twentieth Dynasties abound (that is ca. 1295–1069 B.C.E.). Diaries with entries for work done each day were kept on scrolls of papyrus, notes of tools issued were recorded on ostraca, as were requests for food, such as one from a workman to his mother: "Have some bread brought me, also whatever else you have, urgently, urgently!"[12]

From a later time, the famous community of Arameans and Jews at Elephantine has left both ostraca and papyri in Aramaic. They disclose a similar scribal habit. Banal information of passing interest was consigned to ostraca.[13] In the papyri, on the other hand, are legal deeds settling matrimonial affairs, ownership of property and rights of inheritance. There, too, are letters and drafts of letters received from rulers, officials and private citizens, or addressed to them. Among those on papyrus are documents that would need to be kept for consultation by the same and future generations.

The meager contents of the Hebrew ostraca parallel those of the ostraca from Deir el-Medineh and from Elephantine, and lead to the conclusion that in Israel also papyrus was the normal writing material for any text of value. Neither in Egypt nor in Israel is there a single ostracon that was certainly written to be kept in an archive or library, for someone to consult in the future. Even in the east, in Assyria, the small number of relevant texts appears to indicate a similar situation. While the large Assur Ostracon may imply a lack of papyrus in Uruk[14] (if the letter was actually carried north from that ancient center of cuneiform writing), papyrus was certainly used in Assyria in the seventh century B.C.E. in conjunction with clay tablets. There is pictorial evidence in the painting and reliefs of two scribes, one holding a clay tablet or a hinged writing board, the other a curling scroll, and there is written evidence in the reports of questions put to the god Shamash about "the man whose name is written on this piece of papyrus."[15] The term for papyrus is *niāru* for which, so far, no satisfactory etymology has been proposed, although we may suspect an Egyptian origin. Imported into the Levant and Mesopotamia papyrus may have been, a rarity it was not.[16] Circumstances might sometimes force a scribe to reuse a papyrus, partially washing off previous writing. However, it is worth noting that when this was done to the only ancient Hebrew example known, the last use was for an accountant's record, perhaps of less moment than the original letter had been, and the document was discovered in a remote cave.

Distribution maps for the extant examples of ancient Hebrew writing, added to the arguments for the production of very many others in antiquity, combine to make a strong case for writing as a well-known phenomenon during the Monarchy. However, the greater part of the material belongs after 750 B.C.E., in the last 150 years of Judah's history. Texts of all sorts from earlier dates are sparse, the Samaria Ostraca alone witnessing to the use of writing in Israelite administration. Faced with this pattern, we might assume the early Monarchy was a time of little writing, limited to the courts, not touching the consciousness of most Israelites at all. It is, of course, a fallacy to deduce directly from the absence of a feature in an archaeological horizon that it did not, or could not, exist in it. The rare early specimens of Hebrew epigraphy that do survive —graffiti from Hazor, perhaps a few pieces from Arad —point in the opposite direction. They give support to the argument that texts from the earlier period will seldom be found because of the general archaeological truth that only the last phase of a building's occupation and the remains of the last decades of a prosperous town yield many finds. Objects and texts dating from more than three generations before a destruction are comparatively uncommon. If a building was rebuilt after a number of years, little will be left from its first period of use, and very little from its initial years. This is demonstrable where documents bearing dates do survive in sufficient numbers to avoid the risk of statistical accident as in Assyria and Babylonia. By coincidence, very few ordinary legal and administrative deeds have survived at the major Assyrian sites Assur, Kalah and Nineveh from the ninth century B.C.E., the time of a similar dearth in Israel, although that was the age of the powerful kings Ashurnasirpal II and Shalmaneser III. Details of their reigns reach us through monumental inscriptions on stone and through foundation deposits. There is no reason to doubt that Assyrian scribes were drawing up deeds on clay tablets then as they did during the next two centuries; in fact, a handful of examples proves they did.[17] There is no good reason to project a different situation for Israel on this score, as rare specimens of early alphabetic writing prove it could be used freely from the earliest days of the Settlement. (The Gezer Calendar is the outstanding one; the ʿIzbet Ṣarṭah and other graffiti, and the inscribed arrowheads, enable us to trace the use of writing further back, and to see the same situation in force, with papyrus serving as the normal writing material, as I have argued in the Schaeffer volume.[18])

With the physical evidence before our eyes, there can be no question that writing was possible in Israel throughout the period of the Monarchy. Equally beyond dispute is the wide spread of writing; courtiers could see Hebrew on monuments in Samaria and Jerusalem, peasants could see it on seal impressions, jars and jugs in country towns, even in such remote farmsteads as those in the Buqeiʿah Valley. Anyone could see examples of the alphabet, but who could read or write it? In 1972, I suggested "writing was theoretically within the competence of any ancient Israelite ... and ... was, in fact, quite widely practiced," and went on to compare Israel with "classical Greece where the same simple script was the possession of every citizen."[19] Perhaps that was too optimistic a reaction to the commonly held idea that writing was limited to a small scribal class. Another writer has advanced several counter arguments. In Aristotle's Greece, he avers, "reading and writing were comparative luxuries, and were often treated with suspicion, if not total hostility." He relies on remarks made by Plato, Isocrates, and Aristophanes.[20] Yet literary sources such as those have to be read with care, lest they mislead. Classical scholars do not all reach that conclusion. Sir Frederick Kenyon noted that casual allusions in the Greek authors suggest there was nothing extraordinary about books in late fifth century B.C.E. Athens,[21] and Sir Moses Finley would agree: "In cities like Athens reading, writing and arithmetic appear to have been common attainments among the free population."[22] These opinions are drawn from the literary remains. Most telling is the testimony of epigraphy, the primary source for my remarks about ancient Israel. Inscriptions on stone are not such rare survivors in classical Greece as they are in ancient Israel, but their evidence helps little, for they could have been unintelligible to 99% of the population, as Hammurabi's Law Stele, the monuments of Karnak or the Rock of Behistun were to Babylonians, Egyptians and Persians. It is the wide range of other texts that is significant, as another classicist, Oswyn Murray, has observed. He wrote: "The varied subject matter of early inscriptions (laws, lists, private and public gravestones, artists' signatures, owner's names on pots) suggests widespread use of writing. By the late sixth century an institution like ostracism in Athens similarly presupposes large numbers of citizens able to write at least the name of a political opponent."[23] Common to Greece and to Israel are the casual or occasional texts, names on vessels and notes on potsherds. Here are visible the hands of schoolboys and workmen as well as of the trained scribes. These are the physical grounds for comparing Israel with Greece, irrespective of social or political systems.

Writing and Literature

The Hebrew documents are all mundane survivors from daily life apart from the monumental inscriptions, and with one exception. They reflect writing as primarily a utilitarian skill, which was the position when it was invented. From the absence of literary texts one may argue writing was little esteemed in academic circles. In fact, the oral element in "wisdom" compositions has given rise to the opinion "that the oral mode of communication was preferred even by those who could read and write." Yet this case is like the alleged bias against books of Plato and Socrates; all these teachers were intent on instilling attitudes of behavior and thought, and they were less concerned with relaying facts, which was the first purpose of writing. However, there are no grounds for supposing that any limit to what could be written ever existed after the initial stages in the invention of Near Eastern scripts. (In Egypt literary texts were created at least as early as the Pyramid age, and in Babylonia in the Jemdet Nasr period, about 3000 B.C.E.) Nothing suggests the alphabet had any smaller scope when the Israelites settled in Canaaan and adopted it.[24]

During the last decade two discoveries have proved there was writing and copying of literary texts in the Monarchy era. The first is the Balaam text from Tell Deir ʿAlla.[25] Whatever its origins, it is apparently the reproduction of a column of a scroll. (The omission of *ʾlwh*, 'to him,' before *ʾlhn*, 'the gods,' could well be a copyist's error.) Thus it illustrates nicely the appearance of the papyri we cannot recover. The column of a scroll was called a *deleth*, as the isolated occurrence in Jeremiah 36:23 has long told. Now Assyrian texts disclose that the cognate *daltu* denoted a single column or page in a context where clay and waxed tablets were normal writing surfaces.[26] In Greek the same word, *deltos*, has the same meaning. There can be no doubt the word written *dlt* in Lachish Ostracon IV carried the same sense.[27] Here is a term shared by writers of the cuneiform, West Semitic and Greek scripts, probably referring to the most common writing surface, a page, leaf, column or sheet of wood or papyrus.

The second hint about literary texts is Ostracon 88 from Arad. This snippet of a royal statement, whether a proclamation, a copy of an existing royal inscription or school exercise,[28] displays the possibility of someone having access to such a document, someone who was not in a palace or major temple, but stationed in a frontier fortress.

Comparisons with other Near Eastern societies enlarge this view. In Mesopotamia, at Ugarit and at Elephantine, archives belonging to private individuals included both legal deeds and literary compositions, often without distinction by category. These were the archives of priests and, frequently, of scribes. In several instances they used literary works in teaching the scribal art. To transfer this scene to ancient Israel is not unjustifiable. Even if Israelite society was more rural, less sophisticated than the urban communities of the Twin Rivers, the sea coast, or Periclean Athens, the evidence for writing in many places is nevertheless strong. Where there was writing there was certainly the possibility of literature, and of reading it. We may conclude that few ancient Israelites were out of reach of the written word, a situation certainly facilitated by the simplicity of the alphabet. Were there more material, a similar verdict might apply to neighboring states, to the cultures of the Ammonites, Arameans, Edomites, Moabites, Philistines and Phoenicians.

All these considerations help to deepen our concepts of Israelite culture, irrespective of the Scriptures. In the context of biblical archaeology and ancient documents reacting with each other and complementing one another, there are some specific benefits, and some further questions.

Passages in the Bible which mention writing gain credibility. The law book discovered in Josiah's eighteenth year, assuming it was more or less the present Deuteronomy, requires the king to copy and read the book of the law (Deuteronomy 17:18). That degree of education might not be exceptional for a king (although in Mesopotamian circles it would be noteworthy[29]), but Deuteronomy expects a degree of literacy to permeate society. A man divorcing his wife should have a written deed, no doubt a scribe's work, yet a written document of which both parties would be aware (Deuteronomy 24:1,3). There may be no more reality in these laws than in Hammurabi's 'Code,'[30] yet they presuppose a certain availability of writing. The extent of that presupposition is much greater in Deuteronomy's precepts than in Hammurabi's. True, Hammurabi expected people to go to read his stelae (reverse, col. XXV); Deuteronomy called for much more: the Israelites were to learn and teach the commands, always talk about them, and "write them upon the doorposts of your house and upon your gates" (Deuteronomy 11:20, cf. 6:9).

Is it credible that these words were written in a society which was totally incapable of performing them? The evidence of ancient Hebrew epigraphy suggests the answer is *no*; the lawgiver's commands could be fulfilled to a large degree.

In this light, too, the prophetic books deserve reappraisal. Oracles could have existed in writing alongside traditions from the time they were uttered. The prophets, indeed, could have recorded and edited their words themselves. What relationships could exist between written and oral traditions is a topic for further examination. Once something was in writing it may not have been so easy to alter or add to it as many have assumed. Certainly the consensus of ancient documents contradicts Ivan Engnell's thesis that such traditions were put into writing only at moments of national crisis.[31]

Archaeologists now reconstruct complex societies on the basis of material remains; they deduce from them distribution patterns and analogies. In Near Eastern archaeology there is often the great advantage of contemporary texts to give voice to the mute stones. In biblical archaeology there is the inestimable advantage of a cohesive body of ancient written tradition to bring life to the physical relics. This ancient tradition owes its survival to the readers and writers of ancient Israel. Ancient Hebrew written documents, recovered by archaeology, demonstrate both that there were readers and writers in ancient Israel, and that they were by no means rare. Few places will have been without someone who could write, and few Israelites will have been unaware of writing.

Notes

1. J. Naveh, "A Fragment of an Ancient Hebrew Inscription from the Ophel," *IEJ* 32 (1982): 195–198, Pl. 26A.
2. A.R. Millard, "The Practice of Writing in Ancient Israel," *BA* 35 (1972): 98–111; cf. rev. ed. in *The Biblical Archaeologist Reader*, vol. 4, eds. E.F. Campbell and D.N. Freedman (Sheffield, 1983), pp. 181–195.

3. A. Lemaire, "Une inscription paleó-hebraïque sur grenade en ivoire," *RB* 88 (1981): 236–239, Pls. V, VI.
4. Idem, *Inscriptions Hebraïques, I, Les Ostraca* (Paris: du Cerf, 1977), p. 37; see also I.T. Kaufman, "The Samaria Ostraca: An Early Witness to Hebrew Writing," *BA* 45 (1982): 29–39.
5. See the discussion by A. Lemaire, *Les écoles et la formation de la Bible dans l'ancien Israel* (Göttingen, 1981).
6. See the list drawn up by F. Vattioni, *Biblica* 50 (1969): 357–388, most recently supplemented in *Annali dell Instituto Orientali di Napoli* N.S. 28 (38) (1978): 227–254.
7. Reported by Y. Shiloh, *IEJ* 33 (1983): 131, Pl. 15D; and see idem, *EI* 19, forthcoming.
8. P. Bar-Adon, "An Early Hebrew Inscription in a Judean Desert Cave," *IEJ* 25 (1975): 226–232, Pl. 25.
9. S. Warner, "The Alphabet: An Innovation and Its Diffusion," *VT* 30 (1980): 89.
10. Clear examples in E.G. Kraeling, *Brooklyn Museum Aramaic Papyri* (New Haven, 1953), pp. 123ff., Pl. 21; each document bore a single seal, except for no. 10 which had two. Fourth century papyri from Wadi Daliyeh may have as many as seven seals; see F.M. Cross, *BA* 26 (1963): 111f.; 115, Fig. 3; 120, Fig. 5.
11. Millard, "The Practice of Writing" (see note 2), p. 109.
12. Translation by K.A. Kitchen, *Pharaoh Triumphant* (Warminister, 1982), p. 192.
13. See examples given by B. Porten, *Archives from Elephantine* (Berkeley, 1968), 274ff.
14. J.C.L. Gibson, *Syrian Semitic Inscriptions*, II (Oxford, 1975), pp. 98–110, giving an edition and translation.
15. The two scribes appear many times, on sculptured slabs; see R.D. Barnett and M. Falkner, *The Sculptures of Tiglath-pileser III* (London, 1962), Pl. 6; D.J. Wiseman, *Iraq* 17 (1955): 12, Pl.3.2; they are painted in a fresco at Til Barsip — A. Parrot, *Nineveh and Babylon* (London, 1961), opposite p. 279. The questions to Shamash were edited by J.A. Knudtzon, *Assyrische Gebete an den Sonnengott* (Leipzig, 1893), expecially nos. 98, 116; and E. Klauber, *Politisch-religiöse Texte aus der Sargonidenzeit* (Leipzig, 1913), especially nos. 49, 50, 52, 57.
16. Two rolls of papyrus were included in the list of gifts from Azuri [of Ashdod] and a neighbor received by Sennacherib in Nineveh during Sargon II's reign [*ABL* 568, see W.J. Martin, *Tribut und Tributleistungen bei den Assyrein, Studia Orientalia* 8 (1936): 40–49, and J.N. Postgate, *Taxation and Conscription in the Assyrian Empire* (Rome, 1974), pp. 111, 283f.]. They were destined for the palace scribe, together with one mana of silver and one garment. Other officials received comparable gifts.
17. See my study "The Survival of Cuneiform Texts," forthcoming.
18. A.R. Millard, "The Ugaritic and Canaanite Alphabets, Some Notes," *Ugarit-Forschungen* 11 (1979): 613–616.
19. Millard, "The Practice of Writing" (see note 2), p. 108.
20. Warner, "The Alphabet" (see note 9), p. 83.
21. F. Kenyon, *Books and Readers in Greece and Rome* (Oxford, 1932), p. 21.
22. M. Finley, *The Ancient Greeks* (Harmondsworth, 1966), pp. 94ff.
23. O. Murray, *Early Greece* (Glasgow, 1980), p. 95. A warning not to overestimate the value of inscriptional evidence is given by W.V. Harris, "Literacy and Epigraphy I," *Zeitschrift für Papyrologie und Epigraphik* 52 (1983): 97–111, dealing with the single site of Pompeii.
24. Millard, "Ugaritic and Canaanite Alphabets" (see note 18)
25. J. Hoftijzer and G. van der Kooij, *Aramaic Texts from Tell Deir ʿAlla* (Leiden, 1976); there are now many studies of this text; see the contributions by A. Lemaire and B. Levine in this volume (pp. 313–325, 326–339).
26. S. Parpola, "Assyrian Library Records," *JNES* 42 (1982): 2.
27. As H. Torczyner maintained in his edition, *Lachish I, The Lachish Letters* (London, 1938), p. 80; cf. Lemaire, *Inscriptions Hebraïques, I* (see note 4), p. 111; W.F. Albright favored 'door,' *BASOR* 61 (1936): 14, and in *ANET* 321, ed. J.B. Pritchard; as did R. de Vaux, *RB* 48 (1939): 194f.; and J.C.L.

Gibson, *Syrian Semitic Inscriptions*, I (Oxford, 1971), p. 42; and see Y. Yadin, *EI* 19, in press.

28. Y. Aharoni, *Arad Inscriptions* (Jerusalem, 1981), pp. 103–104; Lemaire, *Inscriptions Hebraïques* (see note 27), p. 221; cf. Y. Yadin, "The Historical Significance of Inscription 88 from Arad: A Suggestion," *IEJ* 26 (1976): 9–14; A.R. Millard, "Aramaic and Hebrew Epigraphic Notes," *PEQ* 110 (1978): 26.
29. See R. Labat, "Un prince éclairé," *CRAIBL* (1972): 670–671.
30. See J.J. Finkelstein, *The Ox that Gored, Transactions of the American Philosophical Society* 71.2 (1981): 17ff.
31. I. Engnell, *Gamle Testamentet* (Oslo, 1946), pp. 42f.; J.T. Willis, ed., *Critical Essays on the Old Testament* (London, 1970), Ch. 1, also published as *A Rigid Scrutiny* (Nashville, 1969); cf. S. Mowinckel, *Prophecy and Tradition* (Oslo, 1946).

Appendix: Index of Hebrew Ostraca and Graffiti from the Period of the Monarchy

In addition to the common abbreviations for periodicals, note the following:

D Diringer, D. *Le iscrizioni antico-ebraiche palestinesi.* Florence, 1934.
IR *Inscriptions Reveal.* Israel Museum Catalogue 100. Jerusalem, 1973.
L Lemaire, A. *Inscriptions Hebraïques I. Les Ostraca.* Paris, 1977.
M Moscati, S. *L'epigrafia ebraica antica.* Rome, 1951.

The numbers after the place names refer to those on the map on p.302.

Ostraca

ARAD (33): Y. Aharoni, in *Arad Inscriptions*, ed. A.F. Rainey (Jerusalem, 1981); *IR*, nos. 49–56, 61–63, 65–72, 166, 147–235.

AROER (37): A. Lemaire, *Semitica* 30 (1980): 19–20, Pl. 1; reported *IEJ* 32 (1982): 162, Pl. 23B.

BEER-SHEBA (32): Y. Aharoni, *Beer-Sheva* I (Tel Aviv, 1973), pp. 71–73; *IR*, nos. 74, 271–273.

GEZER (11): Reported *BA* 34 (1971): 117; *IEJ* 23 (1973): 248.

JAFFA (9): Reported *IEJ* 24 (1974): 136.

JEMMEH, TELL (31): Reported *IEJ* 24 (1974): 274.

JERUSALEM (17): "Ophel Ostracon": S.A. Cook, *PEQ* 56 (1924): 180–186, Pl. VI; *IR*, no. 138; *L*, pp. 239–243. Kenyon Ophel excavations: A. Lemaire, *Levant* 10 (1978): 156–161, Pl. XXIII. City of David excavations: reported *IEJ* 29 (1979): 246. Upper City excavations: N. Avigad, *Discovering Jerusalem* (Nashville, 1983), p. 41f., and *IEJ* 22 (1972): 195–196, Pl. 42 B.

KADESH-BARNEA (38): A. Lemaire and P. Vernus, *Or.* N.S. 44 (1980): 341–345, Pls. 71–73; R. Cohen, *BA* 44 (1981): 98f., 105–107.

KUNTILET AJRUD (39): Z. Meshel, *Kuntilet Ajrud* (Jerusalem: Israel Museum Catalogue 175, 1978).

LACHISH (23): H. Torczyner, *Lachish I, The Lachish Letters* (London, 1938); *IR*, nos. 77, 78; Y. Aharoni, *IEJ* 18 (1968): 168–169, Pl. XII; *L*, pp. 85–143; A. Lemaire, *Tel Aviv* 3 (1976): 109–110, Pl. 5:2; D. Ussishkin, *Tel Aviv* 10 (1983): 157–159, Pl. 41.

MASOS, TEL (34): V. Fritz and A. Kempinski, *Ergebnisse der Ausgrabungen auf Hirbet el-Mšaš (Tel Māśōs)* (Wiesbaden, 1983), pp. 133–137, Taf. 78, 79; *L*, p. 275.

MESAD HASHAVYAHU (10): J. Naveh, *IEJ* 10 (1960): 129–139, Pl. 17; *IR*, no. 33; *L*, pp. 259–269.

QASILE, TELL (8) B. Maisler, *JNES* 10 (1951): 265–267; *IR* no. 42; *L*, 251–258.

QUMRAN, KHIRBET (18): Reported, R. de Vaux, *L'archéologie et les manuscrits de la Mer morte* (London, 1961), p. 2.

SAMARIA (6): G.A. Reisner, *Harvard Excavations at Samaria*, I (Cambridge, Mass., 1924), pp. 227–246; *IR*, nos. 34–38; *L*, pp. 23–81; S.A. Birnbaum, in *Samaria-Sebaste*, III, eds. J.W. Crawfoot et al. (London, 1957), pp. 11–18, Pl.I; *IR*, no. 41; *L*, pp. 245–249.

SHARI'A, TELL ESH- (28): Reported *IEJ* 24 (1974): 265.

'UZA, ḤORVAT (36): Reported *IEJ* 32 (1982): 262; one published, I. Beit Arieh: *PEQ* 115 (1983): 105–108.

VERED YERICHO (14): Reported, *Ḥadashot Arkheologiyot* 82 (1983): 42. (Hebrew; reference by courtesy of J. Naveh)

Graffiti

ARAD (33): Y. Aharoni, *Arad Inscriptions*, pp. 105–118; *IR*, nos. 4, 8, 64.

AREINI, TELL EL- (22): A. Ciasca, *Or. Ant.* 1 (1962): 38, Pl. IX.12; *IR*, no. 114.

ASHDOD (19): M. Dothan and D.N. Freedman, *'Atiqot* 7 (1967): 84f., Fig. 26.4, Pl. XV. 8.

BATASH, TEL (15): Reported *IEJ* 29 (1979): 243.

BEER-SHEBA (32): Y. Aharoni, *Beer-Sheva*, I, pp. 73–75; idem, *Tel Aviv* 2 (1975): 160, 162, Pl. 33.1; *IR*, nos. 73, 119–121.

BEIT-LEI, KHIRBET (25): J. Naveh, *IEJ* 13 (1963): 74–92, Pls. 9–13; *IR*, no. 79.

BEIT MIRSIM, TELL (29): W.F. Albright, *AASOR* 21, 22 (1943): 73–74, Pl. 60.2–6.; cf. *AASOR* 12 (1932): 77; *D*, pp. 290–302.

BETH-SHEAN AREA (4): N. Tsori, *IEJ* 9 (1959): 191–92, Pl. 20D (spindle-whorl, inscription uncertain).

BETH SHEMESH (16): D. Mackenzie. *PEFA* 2 (1913): 86–88; *D*, p. 300; *IR*, no. 105.

DAN (1): *IR*, no. 113.

EN-GEDI (27): B. Mazar, *IEJ* 12 (1962): 146; *IR*, no. 115.

ESHTEMOA (30): Reported *IEJ* 21 (1971): 174; cf. *IR*, no. 101.

GEZER (11): Reported, *RB* 77 (1970): 395.

GIBEON (12): J.B. Pritchard, *Hebrew Inscriptions and Stamps from Gibeon* (Philadelphia, 1959); idem, *BASOR* 160 (1960): 518–519; F.S. Frick, *BASOR* 213 (1974): 46–48; *IR*, no.106.

ḤAMME, TELL EL- (7): R. Gophna and Y. Porat in *Judaea, Samaria and the Golan, Archaeological Survey 1967–1968*, ed. M. Kochavi (Jerusalem, 1972), p. 214.

HAZOR (2): Y. Yadin, *Hazor*, II (Jerusalem, 1960), pp. 70–75; *IR*, nos. 109, 111, 112.

ḤESI, TELL EL- (26): W.M. Flinders Petrie, *Tell el Hesy* (London, 1891), p. 50; *D*, pp. 297–299.

'IRA, TEL (35): Reported *IEJ* 31 (1981): 243.

JERUSALEM (17): Kenyon Ophel excavations: J. Prignaud, *RB* 77 (1970): 50–67; P.R.S. Moorey and P.J. Parr, eds. *Archaeology in the Levant, Kenyon Volume* (Warminster, 1978), pp.136–148; Upper City: *IEJ* 20 (1970): 131; City of David: *IEJ* 29 (1979): 246.

JEMMEH, TELL (31): F. Petrie, *Gerar* (London, 1928), p. 19, Pl. 43.2–4, *D*, pp. 298–299.

KADESH-BARNEA (38): R. Cohen, *IEJ* 32 (1982): 71, Pl. 8D; *Kadesh-Barnea* (Jerusalem: Israel Museum Catalogue 233, 1983), XVIII, 34.

KUNTILET AJRUD (39): Z. Meshel, *Kuntilet Ajrud* (Jerusalem: Israel Museum Catalogue 175, 1978).

LACHISH (23): D. Diringer in *Lachish*, III, ed. O. Tufnell (London, 1953), pp. 356–357, Pl. 52; *M*, p. 111, Pl. 29.3; D. Ussishkin, *Tel Aviv* 5 (1978): 81–88, Pls. 26–32; *Tel Aviv* 10 (1983): 159–160, Pl. 41.

MANASSEH REGION (5): A. Lemaire, *Semitica* 32 (1982): 15–17, Pl. 3.

MAQARI, KHIRBET EL- (21): F.M. Cross and J.T. Milik, *BASOR* 142 (1956): 13–14.

MEGIDDO (3): G. Schumacher, *Tell el Mukesellim*, IA (Leipzig, 1908), pp. 107, 109; *D*, p.301.

NASBEH, TELL EN- (13): C.C. McCown, *Tell en-Nasbeh*, I (New Haven, 1947), pp. 167–169, Pl. 57; N1, 112.

QÔM, KHIRBET EL- (24): W.G. Dever, *HUCA* 40–41 (1969–70): 139–204; cf. *IR*, nos. 139–141, 104.

RAMAT RAḤEL (20): Y. Aharoni, *Excavations at Ramat Raḥel 1959 and 1960* (Rome, 1962), p. 15, Pl. 10.1; *1961 and 1962* (Rome, 1964), p. 35, Pl.40.8.

SAMARIA (6): G.A. Reisner, *Harvard Excavations at Samaria*, I, p. 238, Pl. 55a,b; *D*, pp. 64–65; S.A. Birnbaum, in *Samaria-Sebaste*, III, eds. J. W. Crowfoot et al., pp. 16–25, Pls. I,II.

SHARI'A, TELL ESH- (28): Reported *Encyclopedia of Archaeological Excavations in the Holy Land*; IV (Jerusalem, 1978), p. 1062.

UNKNOWN SITES IN THE HEBRON AREA: N. Avigad, *IEJ* 22 (1972): 1–5, Pls. 1, 2; *IR*, no. 103; A. Lemaire, *Semitica* 25 (1975): 43–46, Pl.3; 27 (1977): 21, 22, Pl.4; and 32 (1982): 17–19, Pl.4; *RB* 83 (1976): 55–58, Pl. 1; and *Maarav* 2 (1980): 159–162.

ELSEWHERE: N. Avigad, *IEJ* 22 (1972): 5–9, Pl.3; *IR* no. 107.

L'inscription de Balaam trouvée à Deir ʿAlla: épigraphie

André Lemaire

Dès leur découverte en mars 1967 par les fouilles hollandaises dirigées par H.J. Franken, les fragments inscrits sur plâtre de Deir ʿAlla ont suscité un très vif interêt parmi les biblistes et les sémitisants d'autant plus que bientôt circulait le bruit, confirmé peu après par l'*editio princeps* de J. Hoftijzer et G. Van der Kooij en 1976,[1] que ces fragments mentionnaient le "voyant Balaam fils de Beor" bien connu par la tradition biblique.[2]

Le caractère sensationnel de cette découverte et sa rapide annonce préliminaire avaient suscité une grande attente mais celle-ci fut quelque peu déçue lorsque l'*editio princeps* permit de mieux se rendre compte du caractère très fragmentaire de ces inscriptions et de leurs nombreuses difficultés d'interprétation, désillusion qui transparut dans certains comptes rendus, en particulier dans celui de S.A. Kaufman:

> I fear that the "Aramaic Texts from Deir ʿAlla" constitute one of those inscriptions that are destined to remain enticingly obscure. It is almost as if the words of the inscription were meant to be self-descriptive: *šm.ḥsk.wʾl.ngh.*, "There is a darkness there, no light."[3]

Aujourd'hui, dix-sept ans après la découverte et huit ans après l'*editio princeps*, après les illusions et les désillusions, le temps semble venu d'un jugement plus équilibré. Utilisant le travail considérable de l'*editio princeps* et les nombreux commentaires ou comptes rendus parus depuis,[4] nous essaierons ici d'en examiner les principaux aspects du point de vue épigraphique.

Contexte archéologique et présentation matérielle de l'inscription

Le contexte archéologique de ces inscriptions a été présenté, de façon préliminaire par H.J. Franken,[5] sa description étant quelque peu précisée ensuite par ses fouilles ultérieures ainsi que par celles de M. Ibrahim et G. Van der Kooij.[6] Cependant l'interprétation de ce contexte archéologique n'aboutit pas, au moins pour le moment, à une conclusion claire.

Le premier problème qui se pose est celui de l'identification du Tell lui-même. Tell Deir ʿAlla est situé en Jordanie (coordonnées géographiques 208–178), à environ 5 km à l'est du Jourdain non loin du débouché du Wadi Zarqâ, ancien Yabboq, dans le Ghor. D'après la tradition talmudique conservée en *Shebiʿit* IX, 2, beaucoup de commentateurs, et en particulier Y. Aharoni,[7] avaient proposé d'identifier Deir ʿAlla (=Tarʿala) avec Soukkôt mais cette identification a été rejetée par H.J. Franken.[8] En fait, à la suite de F.M. Abel[9] et de R. de Vaux,[10] Soukkôt semble plutôt à situer à Tell Aḫsaṣ (en arabe "huttes de branchage"), à environ 2,5 km à l'ouest de Deir ʿAlla commandant le gué de Umm Sidré et nous avons nous-même récemment proposé d'identifier plutôt Deir ʿAlla avec Penuel qui semble lié à un sanctuaire dans la tradition biblique et dans la liste de Shéshonq Ier.[11]

Les fragments de plâtre inscrits ont été trouvés dans la phase M, probablement détruite par un tremblement de terre et par le feu (*ATDA*, p. 7). Lors des fouilles ultérieures, cette phase M a été appelée phase IX et une analyse préliminaire de la poterie semble montrer que cette phase est "probably to be dated in the eighth century B.C.E."[12]

Les principaux fragments inscrits ont été regroupés en deux combinaisons suivant leur lieu d'origine et leur possibilité de joint. Les fragments de la combinaison I ont été trouvés à peu près au milieu du *locus* 34 (=EE 334/5) et ceux de la combinaison II à l'extérieur (*locus* 57) de l'angle nord-est du *locus* 34, soit à environ 3 m de là. Les fragments de la combinaison II semblent avoir été très proches de leur lieu d'origine tandis que ceux de la combinaison I pourraient en avoir été un peu plus éloignés. Il semble y avoir eu un mur entre le *locus* 34 et le *locus* 57 mais il se pourrait qu'il y ait eu une porte ou un passage dans ce mur non loin de l'endroit où on a trouvé la combinaison I.[13] Les fragments inscrits, dont aucun n'a été trouvé *in situ*, pourraient avoir été, à l'origine, situés sur une stèle ou sur un mur ou encore, plus précisément, sur le chambranle de la porte et du passage entre les *loci* 34 et 57.

Parmi les morceaux de plâtre tombés, en plus des fragments inscrits le plus souvent à l'encre noire mais aussi parfois à l'encre rouge, on a retrouvé les restes d'un dessin représentant un sphinx ailé marchant vers la gauche. Ce dessin semble avoir été situé au-dessus et à gauche de la combinaison I puisqu'on reconnaît sur le fragment XIV, le même gros trait rouge horizontal qui se trouve au sommet de la combinaison I et se continue sur la gauche; il coupe un autre gros trait rouge vertical qui marque la fin des lignes de la combinaison I et apparaît aussi sur les fragments VIII et XII. Cet encadrement en haut et à gauche de l'inscription n'est pas sans évoquer la préparation de la copie d'une colonne d'un manuscrit tandis que l'emploi de l'encre rouge pour l'encadrement, le titre et certains passages importants (rubriques) était déjà bien connu en Egypte. Il est plus difficile de préciser si tous les fragments appartiennent à une même inscription et à une même colonne: le fait que la combinaison I représente la partie supérieure d'une colonne et que la combinaison II en semble la partie inférieure paraît le suggérer, mais sans confirmation décisive.

De telles inscriptions à l'encre sur plâtre sont rarissimes en Palestine à l'époque ancienne. En fait, on en rapprochera essentiellement les inscriptions de Kuntillet ʿAjrud en cours de publication et qui datent probablement de la première moitié du VIIIe siècle av. J.-C.[14] En effet, en plus des inscriptions et des dessins à l'encre sur pithos, on a retrouvé sur ce site plusieurs fragments de plâtre inscrits en phénicien à l'encre noire ou rouge, dont un encore *in situ* sur le chambranle nord du passage conduisant de la "salle-aux-bancs" à la cour. Comme à Deir ʿAlla, elles sont parfois accompagnées d'un dessin.[15]

Paléographie

Après l'étude de J. Naveh,[16] la longue analyse de G. Van der Kooij[17] et quelques remarques faites par d'autres commentateurs,[18] il apparaît assez clairement que cette inscription se rattache à l'épigraphie araméenne cursive du VIII–VIIe siècle av. J.-C., tout en notant que le rapport entre la paléographie araméenne et la paléographie ammonite reste discuté.[19]

Etant donné le petit nombre d'inscriptions araméennes anciennes écrites à l'encre, la datation paléographique ne peut que rester approximative: probablement milieu ou deuxième moitié du VIIIe siècle av. J.-C, datation qui semble corroborée par les données archéologiques. On notera, de plus, que cette cursive régulière et, semble-t-il, conventionnelle est probablement l'oeuvre d'un scribe expérimenté et convient tout à fait à la copie d'une oeuvre littéraire.

Le placement des fragments: lecture et restauration du texte

Le travail de restauration du texte à partir des fragments tombés est un travail long et difficile. Il a été bien commencé par G. Van der Kooij qui, s'appuyant surtout sur le lieu de découverte et sur l'aspect extérieur des fragments, a réussi à regrouper de nombreux fragments en deux grandes combinaisons, mais la combinaison I était composée de quatre ensembles sans que soit précisé le lien exact entre ces quatre ensembles dans le sens de la largeur.

En 1977, nous avons proposé de remonter les fragments C et D de la combinaison I par rapport aux fragments A et B, ce qui permettait de restituer une partie plus grande du titre et rendait plus cohérent le début en joignant, en largeur et en hauteur, Ia à Ic. Ce placement a été accepté par les commentateurs postérieurs. Nous avons aussi proposé de rapprocher deux fragments isolés VIIId et XIIc de telle manière qu'on lise *wblʿm.br bʿr.*[20]

Cette dernière proposition a été reprise et améliorée par Jo Ann Carlton qui fit remarquer que les deux fragments VIIId et XIIc prenaient place entre Ia et Id, ce qui permettait de remplir une grande partie de la lacune des lignes 3 à 5. Ce placement a été publié par P.K. McCarter[23] et accepté par B.A. Levine.[22]

Indépendamment de cet arrangement qui nous semble justifié, Helga et Manfred Weippert ont proposé de situer horizontalement Ia et Ic par rapport à Ib et Id en faisant remarquer que, à la ligne 6, la lacune du milieu devait être très petite et ne contenir que deux lettres, que l'on pense à la divinité *š(gr)* ou à *š(mš)*.[23] Cette proposition nous semble convenir au sens des lignes 5 à 7 et même confirmée par le placement, à la ligne 4, des fragments VIIId et XIIc. Elle a, de plus, l'avantage de nous indiquer la longueur approximative des lignes, environ 31 cm, avec de 46 à 48 lettres par ligne.

Il nous reste à examiner les propositions de G. Garbini.[24] Celui-ci pense que les combinaisons I et II se situent l'une en dessous de l'autre sur une même colonne pour aboutir à un total de 50 lignes:

1. Pour lui, les lignes 2 à 4 de la combinaison II sont la continuation des lignes 14 à 16 de la combinaison I, mais, s'il obtient aux lignes 6 à 7, une phrase qui semble donner un sens: *wʿyn/ʿlmh.rwy.ddn*, "et le regard/de la jeune fille enivrera les amoureux," il corrige la dernière lettre de la ligne 15, qu'il lit *k* alors que la lecture *n* est assurée, et n'obtient pas de suite vraiment significative. Ce placement ne nous semble donc pas s'imposer.
2. Il propose ensuite de placer le gros fragment Xd dans la partie centrale des lignes 11 à 14 de la combinaison I, mais son interprétation ne révèle aucune suite significative tandis que G. Van der Kooij avait remarqué que Xd se situerait plutôt près de IIe.[25] Ce placement ne nous semble donc pas s'imposer.
3. Il propose enfin de placer les deux fragments avec trait vertical rouge de fin de ligne, VIIIe et VIIIb, à la fin des lignes 9 et 10 de la combinaison I (=22, 23 de sa nouvelle numérotation globale), mais la lecture *bʿš* du fragment VIIIc reste très incertaine et ce placement conjectural tandis que, si le *rʾš* du fragment VIIIb peut être rapproché de *rʾšk* à la ligne 11, la lecture *ʾšt(k)* du début de cette ligne 11 paraît incertaine et ce placement nous semble rester très hypothétique.

Si nous laissons de côté ces propositions incertaines concernant la combinaison II, il nous semble possible de proposer quelques nouveaux placements de petits fragments pour la combinaison I:

D'après G. Van der Kooij,[26] les fragments du groupe III devaient être situés au sommet de la combinaison I; comme ils sont écrits à l'encre rouge, ils ne peuvent être placés qu'au début de la ligne 1 ou à la fin de la ligne 2. Nous proposons donc de placer:

— au début de la ligne 1: IIIh (lu *ṡṗ* plutôt que *ẏ*-, avec la hampe du *p* se trouvant au sommet de Ic), puis IIIa (lu *ṙb* plutôt que *ṭb* car les restes du premier signe peuvent très bien convenir à la tête d'un *r* dont la hampe se trouverait au sommet de Ic), IIIe (lu *lʾ*) et IIId (*ʿm*); ce placement permet de lire: *spr blʿm (.br bʿ)r. ʾš.ḥzh. ʾlhn*, c'est-à-dire le titre de l'inscription, le début de la ligne 1 pouvant être marqué par un alinéa[27] sans qu'il soit nécessaire de restaurer un pronom démonstratif de 2 ou 3 lettres comme l'ont proposé plusieurs commentateurs.[28] Un tel titre peut d'ailleurs être rapproché de Nahum 1, 1b: *sēpher ḥᵃzōn naḥūm hā ʿelqošī.*

— à la fin de la ligne 2:IIIc (*ṫ*), suivi de IIIf (*ysr*), IIIg (*h*) et IIIb (*y*), ce qui permettrait de lire *lhtysrh ypʿ* t, cette proposition restant plus conjecturale que la première.

— à la fin du fragment Ic, ligne 4, il semble qu'on puisse placer le petit fragment IIh (lu *.wy*);[29] ce placement permet de lire et de restituer au milieu de la ligne 4: *.wy(mrw.)lblʿm...*; on notera que (*wyʾmrw*) était déjà supposé par A. Caquot — A. Lemaire (1977) et restitué par P.K. McCarter (1980), B.A. Levine (1981) et H. et M. Weippert (1982).

— au début de la ligne 11: le petit fragment VIIa (*ʿl*), ce qui permet de lire à la fin de la ligne 10 et au début de la ligne 11: *gry.š/ ʿl*, lecture que nous avions déjà restituée en 1977.[30] On pourrait même se demander s'il ne faudrait pas ensuite placer, à la gauche de VIIa, les fragments VIIb et VIIc mais ce placement nous semble trop incertain pour que nous le retenions ici.

En plus de ces nouveaux placements, nous voudrions aussi proposer quelques corrections de lecture pour la combinaison I à la lumière d'un nouvel examen des photographies infra-rouge:[31]

— à la ligne 2, le début de la parole divine est très incertain; la quatrième lettre, lue *l* par G. Van der Kooij, nous semble tout aussi bien pouvoir être lue *n*, la forme de la tête d'un *n* étant très proche de celle de la base d'un *l*. Nous sommes donc tentés de lire au début: *ypʿ nhrʾ. ʾḥrʾh.*, "la dernière lumière est apparue," la lecture *nhrʾ* restant conjecturale.

— à la ligne 4, avec P.K. McCarter et B.A. Levine, il semble préférable de lire *ʾlwh*, plutôt que *ʾlqh* proposé par G. Van der Kooij.

— à la ligne 6, les traces du début du fragment Id semblent plutôt correspondre à un *š* (trait a2 selon la terminologie de G. Van der Kooij) qu'à un *r*; dès lors il semble paléographiquement préférable de restituer *š(m)š* plutôt que *š(gr)*.

— à la ligne 8, il nous semble possible de reconnaître clairement une liste d'oiseaux; en 1977, nous avions déjà proposé de lire *ṣdh*, "la chouette,"[32] plutôt que *ṣrh* lu par G. Van der Kooij; les photographies nous semblent confirmer la lecture d'un *d* et montrer que le mot précédent peut aussi bien être lu *nṣṣ*, "le faucon," que *nḥṣ* lu par G. Van der Kooij.

A la suite de toutes ces remarques, il nous semble possible de lire ou de restituer avec une grande probabilité la majeure partie des neuf premières lignes:

Texte

1. SPR BLʿM[.BR Bʿ]R.ʾŠ.ḤZH.ʾLHN[.]hʾ wyʾtw. ʾlwh. ʾlhn.blylh.w[ymllw.ʾlw]h
2. kml[y]ʾ. ʾl.wyʾmrw.lb[lʿ]m.brbʿr.kh.YPʿ NHRʾ.ʾḤRʾH. ʾŠ.LHTYSRH.YPʿT
3. wyqm.blʿm.mn.mḥr—[———]l.ymn.—[———]l—l— h.wlyk[h?l.lyʾkl].wbk
4. h.ybkh. wyʿl.ʿmh.ʾlwh.wy[ʾmrw.]lblʿm.br bʿr.lm.tsm[.w]lm tbkh.wyʾ
5. mr.lhm.šbw.ʾḥwkm.mh.šg[yh.lḥyh?]wlkw.rʾw.pʿlt.ʾlhn.ʾl[h]n.ʾtyḥdw.
6. wnṣbw.šdyn.mwʿd.wʾmrw.lš[m]š.tpry.skry.šmyn.bʿbky.šm.ḥšk.wʾl.n
7. gh.ʿdm.wʾ[l.]šmr ky.thby.ḥt.[bʿ?]b.ḥšk.wʾl.thgy.ʿd.ʿlm.ky.ssʿgr.ḥr
8. pt.nšr.wq[ʾ?].rḥmn.yʿnh.ḥ[sd.w]bny.nṣṣ.wṣdh. ʾprḥy. ʾnph.drr.nšrt.
9. ywn.wṣpr[.kl.ʿp š]myn.w[ʿl. ʾrq?]lmṭh.bʾšr.rḥln.yybl.ḥṭr.ʾrnbn.ʾklw.
10. [y?]ḥd.hpš[y?....

Traduction

1. *INSCRIPTION DE BALAAM (FILS DE BEO)R*, L'HOMME QUI VOYAIT LES DIEUX. Voici que les dieux vinrent auprès de lui à la nuit *et (ils l)ui (parlèrent)*
2. selon ces *paro(le)s* et ils dirent à Balaam fils de Beor ainsi: "LA DERNIÈRE *LUMIÈRE EST APPARUE*, UN FEU POUR *LE CHÂTIMENT EST APPARU!*."
3. Et Balaam se leva le lendemain (.......... *plusieurs)? jours* (..........) et il ne *pou(vait pas manger)* et il pleu-
4. rait intensément et son "peuple" entra chez lui et ils di(rent) à Balaam fils de Beor: "Pourquoi jeûnes-tu et pourquoi pleures-tu?" Et il
5. leur dit: "Asseyez-vous, je vous montrerai *combien gra(nd est le malheur)* et venez voir les oeuvres des dieux. Les dieux se sont réunis,
6. et les Puissants *ont fixé le terme*, et ils ont dit à *Sha(ma)sh*: 'Couds, ferme les cieux par ton nuage, (qu'il y ait) là l'obscurité et non l'é-
7. clat, ————————?————————*car tu provoqueras la terreur (par un nua)ge* d'obscurité, et que tu ne fasses plus de bruit à jamais, mais (à ta place?) le passereau, *la chauve-*
8. *souris*, l'aigle et *le péli(can), les vautours, l'autruche, la ci (gogne et) les fauconneaux* et la chouette, les poussins du héron, la colombe, le rapace,
9. le pigeon et le moineau, (*tout oiseau des ci)eux et (sur terre?) en bas*, à l'endroit où le bâton (= la houlette) menait (paître) des brebis des lièvres mangent
10. *(en)semble libre(ment.....*

Si nous avons à peu près bien compris ces neuf lignes, après le titre (*spr blʿm...*), cette inscription raconte une vision d'annonce de châtiment que le voyant Balaam transmet ensuite à son peuple. Du point de vue stylistique, on distingue un récit avec dialogue (lignes 1b à 5a) suivi d'une description de la catastrophe qui va se manifester à la fois dans les cieux (disparition du soleil et multiplication des oiseaux) et sur terre. Un tel texte n'est pas sans évoquer plusieurs passages prophétiques de la Bible annonçant et décrivant la venue du "jour du Seigneur."

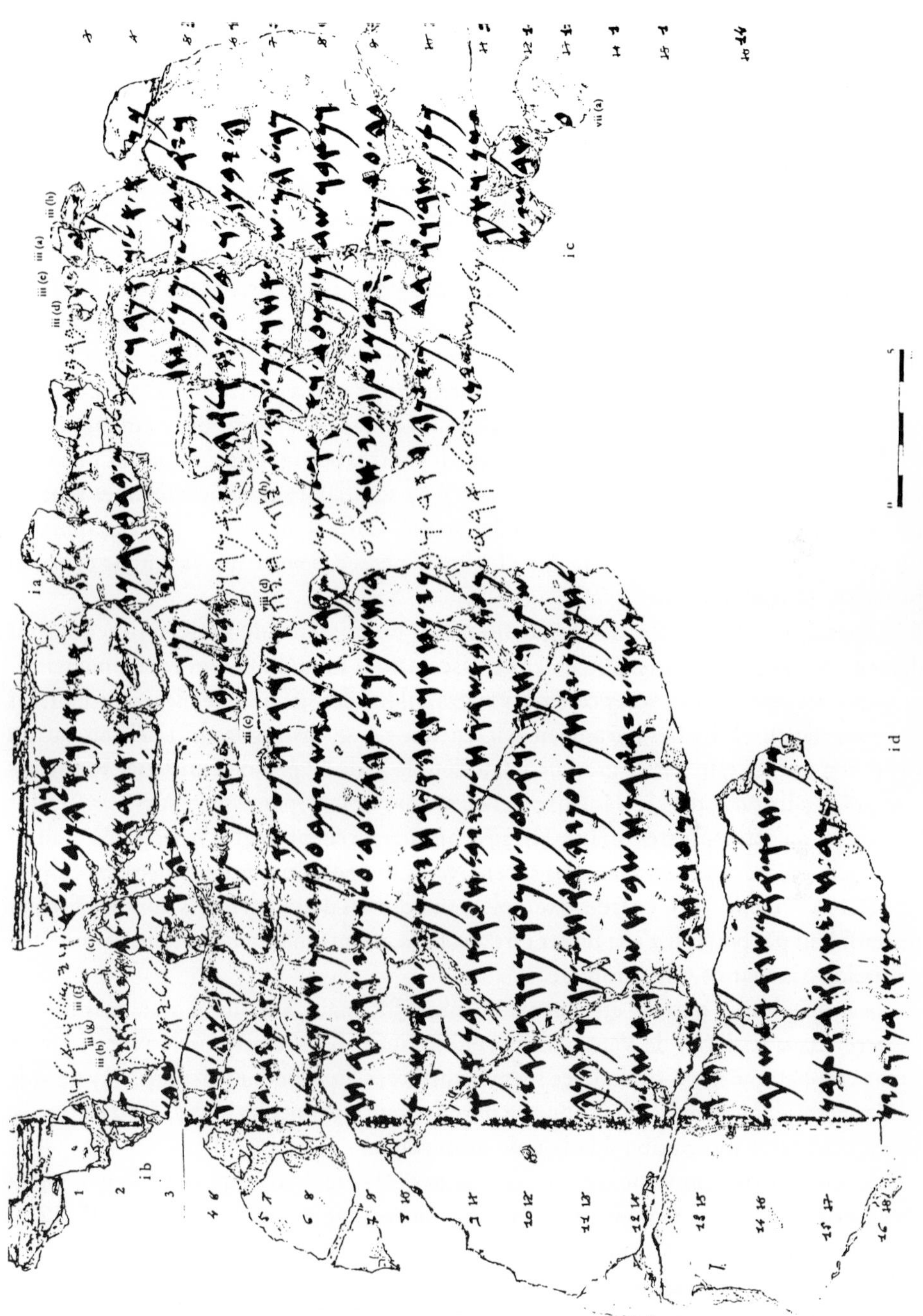

Reconstitution de la combinaison I

La langue

La langue de cette inscription a été discutée. La majorité des commentateurs (J. Hoftijzer, A. Caquot — A. Lemaire, J. Fitzmyer, S.A. Kaufman, K. Jackson, St. Segert) y ont vu de l'araméen ancien quitte à souligner la présence de certains traits dialectaux archaïsants et de "cananéismes," ou même à parler d'une langue mixte (cf. H.P. Müller et, avec nuance, P.K. McCarter). D'autres (F.M. Cross, J. Naveh, J. Greenfield) ont plutôt pensé à un dialecte cananéen transjordanien, peut-être au Gileadite, proche de l'ammonite et du moabite, quitte à parler aussi d'une langue mixte (cf. B.A. Levine). D'autres enfin ont pensé à une nouvelle langue ouest-sémitique, peut-être "midianite" (A. Rofé) ou proche du nord-arabe (G. Garbini).

Remarquons d'abord que géographiquement Deir ʿAlla semble se rattacher à la province de Galaad qui, dans la deuxième moitié du IXe siècle, semble avoir été un enjeu entre les royaumes de Damas et de Samarie et qui, à partir de 732 av. J.-C.., est devenue la province assyrienne de Galʿazu/Galaad à la suite des campagnes de Tiglat-Phalazar III.[33] Remarquons aussi que les autres petites inscriptions sur pierre et sur vase trouvées dans la phase M de Deir ʿAlla sont clairement araméennes tant du point de vue de la paléographie que de la langue. Enfin le fait que la paléographie de l'inscription sur plâtre soit araméenne incline à penser, *a priori*, que la langue est aussi probablement araméenne.

Cependant ce sont les traits linguistiques du texte même de l'inscription qui sont déterminants quant à la langue de cette inscription. Examinons-les rapidement:

1. *La phonologie* ou plutôt la représentation graphique des sifflantes et des interdentales est exactement celle de l'araméen ancien qui ne se distingue de l'hébreu ou du cananéen ancien que par la graphie *q*, au lieu de *ṣ*, du *ḏ proto-sémitique. Parmi les exemples allégués par J. Hoftijzer, deux, au moins, paraissent sûrs: *qqn* (I,15) "maigres, à l'étroit, rétrécis" (cf. Hb *ṣwq*, araméen récent *ʿwq*) et *hqrqt* (I,15), "a fait fuir" (cf. à Sfiré *qrq* et en araméen récent *ʿrq*). On peut ajouter à ces deux exemples *qbʿn* (I,10), "hyéne."[34] Ces trois exemples, surtout les deux premiers dont les formes ne semblent pas pouvoir s'expliquer en cananéen, montrent donc clairement que "the phonology is that of Old Aramaic."[35]

2. *La morphologie* a parfois été appelée "mixte"[36] mais, sans qu'il soit possible ici d'entrer dans le détail de l'analyse morphologique, il est clair que le pluriel en *-n*, l'état emphatique avec -ʾ final, les formes suffixées du pronom personnel *-ky* et *-wh*, la forme réfléchie *ʾtyhḏw* (I, 5), pour ne prendre que les traits les plus caractéristiques, rattachent cette inscription à la langue araméenne.

La seule forme morphologique qui paraît étrange en araméen ancien serait l'attestation du *niphʿal*, mais cette attestation ne semble probable qu'en II, 12 et encore la lecture et l'interprétation de ce passage sont loin d'être assurés. De plus, l'existence d'un *niphʿal* en araméen ancien ne serait pas si extraordinaire car la conjugaison à préfixe *n*- est attestée dans la plupart des langues sémitiques: en hébreu, en phénicien, en ougaritique, en cananéen d'El-Amarna, en accadien et en arabe.

3. *La syntaxe*, selon P.K. McCarter, "seems to be that of authentic literary

Canaanite."[37] Cette affirmation est vraie mais elle est tronquée: elle ne tient pas compte du fait que la syntaxe de l'araméen ancien[38] est presque identique à celle du cananéen ancien. Ainsi les deux traits syntaxiques souvent relevés comme des "cananéismes," la paronomase infinitive et l'inaccompli narratif précédé du *w*-consécutif, sont bien attestés en araméen ancien, le premier à Sfiré et à Nérab, le second dans la stèle de Zakkur. La syntaxe de cette inscription peut donc être tout aussi bien "that of authentic literary Aramaic" que "that of authentic literary Canaanite."

4. *Le lexique*, lui aussi, a été appelé mixte[39] mais cette affirmation paraît être fondée sur une équivoque. Du fait de l'écriture consonantique, il est le plus souvent impossible de distinguer un mot du lexique araméen d'un mot du lexique cananéen ou même du lexique d'une autre langue sémitique: ainsi *spr, ʾš, ʾlh, ʾl, lylh, ʾmr, kh*...Cependant, outre *qrq* et *qq* déjà mentionnés dans la phonologie, quelques mots semblent assez nettement araméens ainsi *ʿll*, "entrer" (I, 4), *ḥnyṣ*, "goret, cochon" (cf. Hb. *ḥzyr*, "porc", *nhr*?, "lumière" (cf. Hb *ʾwr*), *nṣṣ*, "faucon" (cf. Hb *nṣ*), *ṣdh*, "chouette" (cf. Hb. *kōs* ou *tinšemet*: Dt 14, 16; Lv 11, 18.30); l'exemple le plus clair est incontestablement *br*, "fils," qui lorsqu'il apparaît exceptionnellement en phénicien, dans l'inscription de Kilamuwa, ou en hébreu biblique, en Prov. 31:2 et, peut-être, en Ps. 2:12, est clairement un aramaïsme! A côté de ces mots clairement araméens, il y a un certain nombre de mots beaucoup plus usuels en araméen qu'en cananéen: ainsi *ḥzh, ʾth/y, mlh/y, ḥwh, ybl, ʿbd*... Les deux seuls mots qui paraissent quelque peu étranges en araméen sont *pʿlt* et *rʾw* dans la phrase: *lkw.rʾw.pʿ lt.ʾlhn*. (I, 5b) mais il s'agit probablement d'une phrase "liturgique" archaïsante pouvant comporter des mots rares.

Ainsi, si l'on se rappelle avec S.A. Kaufman[40] que l'araméen ancien de Syrie était plus proche du cananéen ancien que de l'araméen récent, il apparaît assez clairement que la langue de l'inscription sur plâtre de Deir ʿAlla était de l'araméen ancien.

La fonction de cette inscription

La fonction concrète de cette inscription est difficile à cerner du fait qu'elle n'a pas été trouvée *in situ* et que son contexte archéologique, en particulier la fonction des deux *loci* dans lesquels les fragments ont été trouvés, n'est pas très claire. Peut-être cette fonction pourrait-elle apparaître plus clairement lors du rapport définitif de fouilles?

En attendant ce rapport définitif, remarquons que le lieu où cette inscription a été trouvée et le fait qu'elle ait été écrite à l'encre ne semblent pas la rattacher au genre des inscriptions monumentales. De plus, il est clair que cette inscription, aussi bien par son titre que par ce qu'on peut saisir de son contenu, est probablement la copie d'un manuscrit: le *spr blʿm br bʿr* que l'on avait, en quelque sorte, affiché.

Nous avons rappelé que des inscriptions phéniciennes écrites à l'encre sur du plâtre avaient été trouvées à Kuntillet ʿAjrud et cela dans le contexte probable d'un enseignement plus ou moins "scolaire" donné à cet endroit comme le montrent les abécédaires, les formules de début de lettre et les dessins sur les pithoi.[41] L'inscription sur plâtre de Deir ʿAlla, affichage d'un texte littéraire probablement classique, pourrait avoir joué un rôle analogue c'est-à-dire se situer dans le contexte d'un enseignement (prophétique? ou lié à un sanctuaire?) donné à cet endroit et on soulignera, comme à Kuntillet ʿAjrud, la présence d'un dessin au-dessus et à gauche de l'inscription ainsi que d'un début d'abécédaire incisé sur un bol trouvé non loin de là.

L'interprétation de cette inscription dans le contexte probable d'un enseignement donné à cet endroit peut s'éclairer quelque peu à la lumière de quelques passages bibliques: ainsi, Dt 6,9: *ūk^{e}tabtām ʿal-m^{e}zūzot bēytekā ūbiš^{e} ʿāreykā*, "et tu les écriras sur les montants de porte de ta maison et dans tes portes de ville" (en référence à l'enseignement (cf. v. 7 *w^{e}sinnantām*) des "paroles" du Seigneur; Dt 27, 2–3: *wah^{a}qēmotā l^{e}kā ʾ^{a}bānīm g^{e}dolōt w^{e}sadtā ʾotām baśśīd w^{e}kātabtā ʿ^{a}leyhēn ʾet-kol-dibrēy-hattōrāh hazzoʾt*, "et tu dresseras pour toi de grosses pierres et tu les enduiras de chaux et tu y écriras toutes les paroles de cette *instruction*" (cf. aussi Dt 27, 4.8); Jos 8,32: *wayyiktāb-šām ʿal-haʾ^{a}bānīm ʾēt mišnēh tōrat Mošeh*, "et il écrivit là sur les pierres le double de l'*instruction* de Moïse"; tandis que la référence à une sorte d'école "prophétique" pourrait tenir compte du cycle d'Elisée et plus particulièrement de 2 R 6, 1–2.

En conclusion, quelque soit la fonction précise de ce texte à Deir ʿAlla et ses difficultés d'interprétation, l'inscription sur plâtre de Deir ʿAlla nous donne le premier exemple d'un texte littéraire en araméen ancien, plus précisément d'un texte littéraire prophetique. Bien plus, le personnage principal de ce texte, Balaam fils de Beor, nous est aussi connu par la tradition biblique qui semble ainsi attester de contacts avec la littérature araméenne ancienne.

Notes

1. J. Hoftijzer and G. Van der Kooij, *Aramaic Texts from Deir ʿAlla (ATDA)* (Leiden, 1976).
2. Nombres 22–24, 31:8–16; Dt. 23:5–6; Jos. 13:22; 24:9–10; Mi. 6:5; Neh. 13:2; cf. dernièrement H. Rouillard, "La péricope de Balaam (Nombres 22–24): la prose et les oracles" (Thèse, Paris, 1983).
3. S.A. Kaufman, *BASOR* 239 (1980): 74.
4. H.J. Franken, "Texts from the Persian Period from Tell Deir ʿAlla," *VT* 17 (1967): 480–481; J. Naveh, "The Date of the Deir ʿAlla Inscription in Aramaic Script," *IEJ* 17 (1967): 256–258; F.M. Cross, "Epigraphic Notes on the ʿAmmān Citadel Inscription," *BASOR* 193 (1969): 13–19, spéc. p. 14, n. 2; J. Naveh, *The Development of the Aramaic Script* (Jerusalem, 1970), p. 67, n. 214; F.M. Cross, "Notes on the Ammonite Inscription from Tell Siran," *BASOR* 212 (1973): 12–15, spéc. p. 14; J. Hoftijzer, "De ontcijfering van Deir-ʿAlla-teksten," *Oosters Genootschap in Nederland* 5 (Leiden, 1973): 113–134; F.M. Cross, "Ammonite Ostraca from Heshbon: Heshbon Ostraca IV–VIII," *AUSS* 13 (1975): 1–20, spéc. p. 10–17; H.J. Franken, "The Problem of the Identification in Biblical Archaeology," *PEQ* 108 (1976): 3–11, spéc. p. 10–11; J. Hoftijzer, "De aramese teksten uit Deir ʿAlla," *Phoenix* 22 (1976): 84–91; id., "The Prophet Balaam in a 6th Century Aramaic Inscription," *BA* 39 (1976): 11–17 (à corriger en "eighth-seventh century" d'après *BA* 39 (1976): 87; A. Caquot et A. Lemaire, "Les textes araméens de Deir ʿAlla," *Syria* 54 (1977): 189–208 (*infra* C-L); E.

Hammershaimb, "De aramaiske indskrifter fra udgravningerne i Deir ʿAllā," *Dansk Teologisk Tidsskrift* 40 (1977): 217–242; H. Ringgren, "Bileam och inskriften från Deir ʿAlla," *Rel. och Bibel* 36 (1977): 85–89; A. Caquot, "Un Nouveau témoignage sur le prophète Balaam," *RHR* 198 (1978): 143–144; J.A. Fitzmyer, *CBQ* 40, (1978): 93–95; J. Lust, "Balaam an Ammonite," *Ephemerides Theologicae Lovanienses* 54 (1978): 60–61; A.R. Millard, "Epigraphic Notes, Aramaic and Hebrew," *PEQ* 110, (1978): 23–26; H.P. Müller, "Einige alttestamentliche Probleme zur aramäischen Inschrift von Dēr ʿAllā," *ZDPV* 94 (1978): 56–57; E. Puech, *RB* 85 (1978): 114–117; G. Rinaldi, "Balaam al suo paese," *Bibbia e Oriente* 20 (1978): 51–59; J.B. Segal, *PEQ* 110 (1978): 69; G. Garbini, "L'iscrizioni di Balaam bar Beor," *Henoch* 1 (1979): 166–188; J. Naveh, *IEJ* 29 (1979): 133–136; D. Pardee, *JNES* 38 (1979): 296–297; A. Rofé, *The Book of Balaam (Hb)* (Jerusalem, 1979), spéc. p. 59–70; G.W. Ahlström, "Another Moses Tradition," *JNES* 39 (1980): 65–69; J.C. Greenfield, *JSS* (1980): 248–252; K. Jackson, "The Ammonite Language of the Iron Age" (Ph.D. diss., University of Michigan, 1980), p. 9–13; S.A. Kaufman, "The Aramaic Texts from Deir ʿAlla" (Review Article) *BASOR* 239 (1980): 71–74; P.K. McCarter, "The Balaam Texts from Deir ʿAlla: the First Combination," *BASOR* 239 (1980): 49–60; H.P. Müller, "Der neu gefundene Bileam-text aus Deir ʿAlla," dans *XX. Deutscher Orientalistentag*, Hrsg. W. Voigt, *ZDMG* Suppl. (1980): 128–130; S. Segert, *Wiener Zeitschrift für die Kunde des Morgenlandes* 72 (1980): 182–189; F. Vattioni, "*Peṭôr* (Nomb. 22:5; Dt. 23:5)," *AION* 40 (1980): 465–471; M. Dahood, *Biblica* 62 (1981): 124–127; M. Delcor, "Le texte de Deir ʿAlla et les oracles bibliques de Balaʿam," *VT* Sup. 32 (1981): 52–73; J.C. Greenfield, "Aramaic Studies and the Bible," id., 110–130, spéc. p. 115; A. Lemaire, *Les écoles et la formation de la Bible dans l'ancien Israël. OBO* 39 (1981): 92, n. 67; B.A. Levine, "The Deir ʿAlla Plaster Inscriptions," *JAOS* 101 (1981): 195–205; J. Naveh, "Inscriptions of the Biblical Period," dans *Thirty Years of Archaeology in Eretz-Israel, 1948–1978*, ed. B. Mazar (Jerusalem, 1981), p. 75–85, spéc. p. 82 (Hb.); H. Weippert, "Der Beitrag ausserbiblischer Prophetentexte zum Verständnis der prosareden des Jeremiabuches," dans *Le Livre de Jérémie, le prophète et son milieu, les oracles et leur transmission. Bibliotheca Ephemeridum Theologicarum Lovaniensium* 54 (1981): 83–104, spéc. p. 88–97; A. Catastini, "Le iscrizioni di Kuntillet ʿAjrud e il prophetismo," *AION* 42 (1982): 127–134, spéc. p. 133–134; M. Delcor, "Balaʿam Pâtôrâh, interprète de songes au pays d'Ammon d'après Nombres 22:5. Les témoignages épigraphiques parallèles," *Semitica* 32 (1982): 89–91; A.R. Millard, "In Praise of Ancient Scribes," *BA* 45 (1982): 143–153; H.P. Müller, "Die aramäische Inschrift von Deir ʿAlla und die älteren Bileamspruche," *ZAW* 94 (1982): 214–244; J. Naveh, *Early History of the Alphabet* (Leiden, 1982), p. 107–110; H. Ringgren, "Prophecy in the Ancient Near East," dans *Israel's Prophetic Tradition, Essays in Honour of P.R. Ackroyd*, ed. R. Coggins et al. (Cambridge, 1982), p. 1–11, spéc. p. 10; M. Weinfeld, "The Balaam Oracle in the Deir ʿAlla Inscription," *Shnaton* 5/6 (1981–82): 141–147 et p. LXVII (Hb.); H. et M. Weippert, "Die 'Bileam' —Inschrift von Tell Dēr ʿAllā," *ZDPV* 98: 77–103.

5. *ATDA* (voir note 1), p. 3–16.
6. H.J. Franken and M.M. Ibrahim, "Two Seasons of Excavations at Tell Deir ʿAlla, 1976–1978," *ADAJ* 22 (1977–78): 57–80, spéc. p. 60–71; M.M. Ibrahim and G. Van der Kooij, "Excavations at Tell Deir ʿAlla, Season 1979," *ADAJ* 23 (1979): 41–51, spéc. p. 48–50.
7. Y., Aharoni, *The Land of the Bible* (London, 1974), p. 241–242 et 384.
8. Franken, "The Problem of Identification..." (voir note 4): 10–11; id., "The Identity of Tell Deir ʿAlla, Jordan," *Akkadica* 14 (1979): 11–15.
9. F.M. Abel, *Géographie de la Palestine*, II, 3e ed. (Paris, 1967), p. 470.
10. R. de Vaux, "Notes d'histoire et de topographie transjordaniennes," *Bible et Orient* (Paris, 1967): p. 115–149, spéc. p. 130.
11. A Lemaire, "Galaad et Makir," *VT* 31 (1981): 39–61, spéc. p. 51–52.
12. Ibrahim and Van der Kooij, "Excavations at Tell Deir ʿAlla" (voir note 6), p. 48–50.
13. Franken and Ibrahim, "Two Seasons at Deir ʿAlla" (voir note 6), p. 65.
14. cf. A. Lemaire, "Date et origine des inscriptions hébraïques et phéniciennes de Kuntillet ʿAjrud,"

Studi Epigrafici e Linguistici 1 (1984): p. 131–143.

15. Z. Meshel, *Kuntillet ʿAjrud, A Religious Centre from the Time of the Judaean Monarchy on the Border of Sinai* (Jerusalem, 1978), p. 9f; 14–15.
16. Cf. surtout Naveh, "The Date of the Deir ʿAlla Inscription" (voir note 4), p. 256–258; id., *Early History of the Alphabet* p. 109 (voir note 4).
17. *ATDA* (voir note 1), p. 42–96.
18. C-L, p. 190–192; Puech, *RB* 85 (1978) (voir note 4), p. 115–116.
19. Selon Naveh, *Early History of the Alphabet* (voir note 4), p. 105–111, les Ammonites utilisèrent simplement l'écriture araméenne tandis que pour Cross,"Notes on the Ammonite Inscription" (voir note 4), p. 12–15; id., "Ammonite Ostraca from Hesbon" (voir note 4), p. 10–17, leur écriture, dépendante à l'origine de l'écriture araméenne, eut ensuite un développement particulier et plus lent. En fait, J. Naveh, lui-même, reconnaît que certaines formes particulières de lettres telles que le *ʿayin* carré attesté sur les sceaux (cf. aussi le *hé* à deux traits horizontaux et déjà N. Avigad, "Ammonite and Moabite Seals," dans *Essays in Honor of N. Glueck. Near Eastern Archaeology in the Twentieth Century* (New York, 1970): 284–295, spéc. p. 285) et le *hé* de l'inscription de la bouteille de Tell Siran semblent propres à l'épigraphie ammonite. Malheureusement il s'agit là d'écritures que l'on peut qualifier de "monumentales" et nous connaissons encore très mal les caractéristiques de l'écriture ammonite cursive; dès lors, il nous est difficile d'exclure totalement l'hypothèse que l'inscription de Deir ʿAlla puisse éventuellement se rattacher à la paléographie ammonite. Cependant le fait qu'aucune des formes des lettres de cette inscription ne s'écarte de l'évolution normale de la cursive araméenne au VIIIe siècle (cf. Naveh, *The Development of Aramaic Script* (voir note 4), p. 10–15, rend l'hypothèse d'un rattachement à la paléographie ammonite peu vraisemblable.
20. C-L, p. 193–194.
21. McCarter, "The Balaam Texts" (voir note 4), p. 51.
22. Levine, *JAOS* 101 (1981): 195.
23. Weippert, "Die 'Bileam'" (voir note 4), p. 82.
24. Garbini, "L'iscrizioni di Balaam" (voir note 4), p. 168–171.
25. *ATDA* (voir note 1), p. 158.
26. *ATDA* (voir note 1), p. 147.
27. Cf. déjà C-L, p. 194; Ringgren, "Bileam och Inskriften" (voir note 4), 85; Rofé, *The Book of Balaam* (voir note 4), p. 61; McCarter, "The Balaam Texts" (voir note 4), p. 51. Si nous n'avons encore aucune attestation claire de la pratique de l'alinéa dans les inscriptions de cette époque, cette pratique est bien attestée dans les textes de Qumrân et l'absence de témoignage de cette pratique en hébreu de l'époque royale et en araméen ancien pourrait très bien être accidentelle [cf. J.M. Oesch, "Textgliederung im Alten Testament und in den Qumranhandschriften," *Henoch* 5 (1983): 289–321, spéc. p. 294]. Le même problème se pose pour l'inscription du tunnel de Siloé où *hnqbh* paraît être le titre; en effet, malgré É. Puech, "L'inscription du tunnel de Siloé," *RB* 81 (1974): 196–214, spéc. p. 199, mais avec V. Sasson, "The Siloam inscription," *PEQ* 114 (1982): 111–117, il est impossible de lire quoi que ce soit dans l'espace de 2 ou 3 lettres avant *hnqbh*.
28. Cf. Garbini, "L'iscrizioni di Balaam" (voir note 4), Kaufman, *BASOR* 239 (voir note 3); Levine, *JAOS* 101 (1981) (voir note 4); Müller, "Der neu gefundene Bileam-Text" (voir note 4); et Weippert, "Die 'Bileam'" (voir note 4).
29. Ce que G. Van der Kooij croyait être la fin de la hampe de gauche d'un *h* peut aussi bien être la fin d'un trait de séparation dont la partie supérieure se trouverait à la fin du fragment Ic, ligne 4.
30. C-L., p. 200.
31. Nous tenons à remercier ici G. Van der Kooij qui nous a très aimablement communiqué ces photographies.
32. C-L., p. 198.
33. Cf. A. Lemaire et J.M. Durand, *Les inscriptions araméenes de Sifré et l'Assyrie de Shamshi-Ilu*, Hautes

Études Orientales 20 (1984), p. 114, 122; H. Tadmor, "The Southern Border of Aram," *IEJ* 12 (1962): 114–122.

34. C-L, p. 200.
35. McCarter, "The Balaam Texts" (voir note 4), p. 50.
36. Ibid., p. 51.
37. Ibid.
38. Cf. R. Degen, *Altaramäische Grammatik der Inschriften des 10–8. Jh. V. Chr.* (Wiesbaden, 1969), p. 82–137, spéc. p. 114–117.
39. McCarter, "The Balaam Texts" (voir note 4), p. 51.
40. Kaufman, *BASOR* 239 (voir note 3), p. 73.
41. Cf. déjà Lemaire, *Les écoles et la formation de la Bible* (voir note 4), p. 25–32.

The Balaam Inscription from Deir ʿAlla: Historical Aspects

Baruch A. Levine

THE RECENT DISCOVERY of inscribed plaster fragments fallen onto the floor within the walls of the Iron Age temple at Deir ʿAlla, has caused a curious sensation: on these fragments a literary composition is preserved in which the name of Balaam son of Beor (written: *blʿm br bʿr*) is repeatedly mentioned. He is designated a divine seer (*ḥzh ʾlhn*). This fact alone, quite apart from the intriguing character of the text as a whole, enhances the realism of biblical poetry and historiography. An epic figure known only from the Hebrew Bible (and from post-biblical interpretive literature) was, in fact, renowned in the Jordan Valley during the pre-exilic biblical period at a site just north of the lower Jabbok (Zerqa), some 12 km north-northeast of its juncture with the Jordan. This area, known in the Bible as the Valley of Succoth (Psalms 60:8, 108:89), is not all that remote from the Plains of Moab, the site of Balaam's encounter with the Israelites, which biblical historiography assigns to an earlier period.

The discovery of the Deir ʿAlla fragments has raised the question of just how the biblical Balaam saga and the Balaam text from Deir ʿAlla are related to one another, for surely a relationship exists. It is this awareness of connection that is basic to the field we call biblical archaeology, and to the comparative method in the study of ancient civilizations.

The study of the Balaam text from Deir ʿAlla is affected by four principal types of evidence: historical, archaeological, epigraphic and biblical. In each class of evidence we encounter difficulties of interpretation, and suffer, at the present time, from grossly inadequate information. In fact, this is perhaps the most uncertain time to venture historical hypotheses regarding the Balaam text! The pottery from Phase M, H.J. Franken's designation for the level in which the plaster fragments were found, has not yet been published. Thus, his assertion that the ceramic assemblage characteristic of Phase M is distinct from that found west of the Jordan during the same period cannot as yet be evaluated.[1]

The stratigraphy of Tell Deir ʿAlla is far from clear, due to natural conditions, and to the limited excavations carried out. Work has been resumed under G. van der Kooij, who accomplished the palaeographic study of the inscription for the 1976 publication, and a Jordanian archaeologist, M. Ibrahim. The present excavations are concentrated on the higher levels of the mound, and thus promise to provide us with information about the strata most relevant to the Balaam text. We are awaiting publication of the report of J.B. Pritchard's excavations at nearby Tell es-Saʿidiyeh, and that of Mohammed Kh. Yassine, at Tell el-Mazār. One hopes that additional plaster inscriptions may be uncovered at one or another of these sites. Within the near future we should, in any event, know much more about the material culture of the immediate area.

Historically, we know less about life in Gilead during the eighth and seventh centuries B.C.E. than we do, on the basis of Egyptian, Assyrian and Aramean sources, about the preceding centuries, and the same imbalance characterizes the biblical record. Finally, the state of the fragments has made their reading an uncertain enterprise, and even the alignment of the fragments has proved to be precarious. Palaeographic analysis has yielded diverse dates, and disagreement persists even on the language of the text. An extensive literature has arisen on the subject of the Balaam text, and the divergence of views expressed only further reinforces our uncertainties regarding its proper interpretation.

In historical terms, the primary question confronting us is whether the Balaam text was a product of the period *prior* to the Assyrian subjugation of Gilead, a series of events probably extending from 734 to 721 B.C.E. under Tiglath-Pileser III and Sargon, or whether it was a product of the period *subsequent* to these pivotal events. The Assyrian campaigns must be regarded as a watershed in any attempt to ascertain whose temple it was at Deir ʿAlla that had the Balaam text inscribed within its rooms; to know for whom this text speaks, and by whom it was authored. In the wake of the Assyrian campaigns there were mass deportations of the inhabitants of Gilead, and the demography of the Valley of Succoth changed radically. Before the Assyrian campaigns the population was probably predominantly Israelite, although direct evidence bearing on this conclusion is admittedly sparse. Settlement patterns are often complex, and the population may well have been mixed. On the other hand, it is quite clear that after the Assyrian deportations there is less likelihood that the population of the area was predominantly Israelite, and consequently, it is less likely that our text would have been the work of Israelite authors.

I prefer to outline my hypothesis on the historical provenience of the Balaam text at this point, so that the discussion to follow may be accepted as an attempt to deal with specific historical problems.

I submit that the Balaam text may well preserve a literary composition antedating the Assyrian subjugation of Gilead. Palaeographic analysis allows for this conclusion, though it by no means compels its acceptance. I further submit, with greater assurance, that the language of the Balaam text from Deir ʿAlla is *not* Aramaic, as we know it from the eighth and seventh centuries B.C.E., but rather a regional language. Whatever limited features of the language that point us in the direction of Old

Aramaic can be explained either as originally dialectal, or as the result of language contact with Aramaic, introduced into the area by Arameans. Nothing in the Deir ʿAlla language suggests that the Balaam text is culturally remote from contemporaneous Hebrew, Moabite or Ammonite creativity.

In literary form and with respect to its themes and diction, the Balaam text bears striking affinities to biblical literature, and of course, to the biblical Balaam saga itself; to the point of suggesting that the biblical saga is of Transjordanian origin! There is also a great similarity between "Combination II" of the Balaam text (according to Hoftijzer's delineation) and the Sheol oracle of Isaiah 14. Many such similarities are documented in my earlier study, where I stopped short of attempting to explain these affinities in literary-historical terms.[2]

It is possible that the Balaam text from Deir ʿAlla speaks for the predominantly Israelite population of Gilead before the Assyrian subjugation. When further evidence becomes available this hypothesis will be tested, but for the moment it should not be excluded, *a priori*, simply because of the context of the text itself. This is a polytheistic text, of a mythological character, in which the Syro-Canaanite deity El is prominent, and in which a goddess, Shagar weʿIshtar, plays a role. It is my assessment, nonetheless, that Israelite culture was more pervasive in the pre-exilic period than was Israelite monotheism, and that the existence of non-Yahwistic, Israelite temples in Judah, in northern Israel or in Transjordan (which was at various periods incorporated within the northern Israelite kingdom) should not be denied, in principle or in fact. Judging from the content of the Balaam text, one may conclude that the Iron Age temple at Deir ʿAlla was an El temple.

Having prefaced these general remarks, I may now begin a more detailed analysis of the text in historical perspective.

It would be well to engage the language question at this point. The Aramaic label that was affixed to the Deir ʿAlla text has, in my opinion, impeded a proper historical and cultural assessment of its provenience.

In Phase M at Deir ʿAlla, four brief Aramaic inscriptions were found. One of them, on a clay jar, reads: *zy ś/šr*⟨ʾ⟩, "belonging to X," attesting the Aramaic relative pronoun. The same name appears on the handle of a stone jar. A third inscription preserves a partial abecedary and the fourth is too fragmentary to be intelligible. Both Franken and Hoftijzer, as well as others it seems, have assumed a direct connection between these Aramaic inscriptions and the language of the literary Balaam text.[3] This assumption is unsound methodologically. One would only expect to find Aramaic administrative notations at a site governed by Arameans, or at a later time by Assyrians, if that proved to be the case. The name *ś/šr*⟨ʾ⟩ is not likely a divine name, as Franken and Hoftijzer suggest, but rather an official name. It does not occur in the Balaam text, nor should it logically be restored there as the name of a goddess. There is no warrant for adducing the presence of these Aramaic administrative notations as evidence for the language of the Balaam text.

As uncertain readings are reexamined, it becomes evident that there are fewer clear indications of Aramaic factors in the Deir ʿAlla language. An instructive example occurs near the beginning of "Combination I." Once, a preferred reading was: *kmly*ʾ ʾ*l*, "according to these words," the sense being that the "gods" (ʾ*lhn*) spoke to Balaam. Just as my study was going to press, I benefited from a suggestion by É. Puech that *kmś*ʾ ʾ*l* should be read "according to the revelation of El." Later, I learned that A. Rofé had suggested the same reading, and now I find that the Weipperts have adopted it as well, and it is gaining wider acceptance.[4] In terms of linguistic assignment, the effect of this reading has been to eliminate the only putative attestation of the Aramaic post-positive determination in the Balaam text!

An example of another type illustrates how the Aramaic label may condition the mind of the exegete, and lead one to seek validation for an undemonstrated conclusion. According to my understanding of the text, the second feminine suffix, -*ky*, which is suggestive of Old Aramaic and of later dialects, but surely not an unequivocal indication of such, does not actually occur in the Balaam text. There are three attestations of *ky*, in close succession, and I prefer to take all of them as the particle *ky*, "for" or "that," and as initiating discrete clauses:

1. *ky šm ḥsk w*ʾ*l ngh*, "So that darkness and no brilliance will be there."
2. *ky thby ḥtt*, "That you may instill dread!"
3. *ky ss* ʿ*gr ḥrpt nšr*, "For the swift [and] crane will shriek insult to the eagle."

As far as I can determine, the only phonetic feature of the Deir ʿAlla language that is common to Old Aramaic is the representation of the phoneme *Ḍod* as *Qoph*, rather than as a *Ṣade* or *ʿAyin*, as is normal in the Canaanite languages. Thus, we have the verbal form *hqrqt*, "She put to flight," late in "Combination I," and probably a few more examples. Most important is the word *nqr*, which occurs three times in "Combination II." It means "corpse, the dead," and is cognate to the Hebrew *hapax nēṣer* in Isaiah 14:19, unrelated to נצר, "shoot." Deir ʿAlla *nqr* and Hebrew נצר of Isaiah 14:19 may be derived from a root *nḍl* (or *nḍr*), given the Syriac form *neṣlā*ʾ, "carrion." In this connection, J. Naveh has overstated his case for claiming that no such sound-shift is attested in the Balaam text.[5]

What does the occurrence of this sound-shift, usually regarded as critical in the differentiation of Old Aramaic from the Canaanite languages of the eighth and seventh centuries B.C.E., truly indicate? It is, in my judgment, an error to base the linguistic assignment of the Balaam text solely on one criterion. We should evaluate the overall linguistic character of a given text. Similarly, the probable occurrence of Ethpeʿel froms (such as *lytmlk*, "He will not consult") is not conclusive in morphological terms. Nor does a text become Aramaic because it uses a number of verbs uncharacteristic of the Canaanite languages and known mostly from Aramaic, such as ʿ*bd*, "to do, make" (Aramaic connotation), *qrq*, "to flee," ʿ*ll*, "to enter," and the verb *ḥwy*, "to show, tell." The form *ḥad*, "one," is not a clear indication of Aramaic, and as Naveh has pointed out, *br* (instead of *bn*), "son," occurs only in the name of Balaam, and no more makes this text Aramaic than does the name *klmw br ḥy(*ʾ*)*, "Kilamuwa son of Ḥayya," render a Phoenician text from Samal Aramaic![6]

On balance, what is most revealing about the language of the Balaam text is its dominant syntax, which is based on the consecutive tense, with the *Waw* of succession, as W. Moran calls it (or the *Waw* conversive, if you will). This tense system is not at home in Aramaic. It does no good to cite the several occurrences of the consecutive tense in the inscription of Zakur of Hamath, dated to the end of the ninth or the beginning of the eighth century B.C.E., as evidence for the currency of this tense system in Aramaic. If anything, the occurrence of this tense in the Zakur inscription reflects the earlier, native culture of the kingdom of Hamath, prior to its Aramaization, when the language of the area was a form of Canaanite (or northwest Semitic, if you will), coexisting with a form of Hittite. Indeed, the Zakur inscription is a salient example of the expansion of the Aramaic language, but not, in and of itself, a paradigm of Old Aramaic![7]

Although the Deir ʿAlla language exhibits some phonetic and morphological peculiarities when compared to Hebrew, Moabite and Ammonite, as well as Phoenician, it is much closer to the Canaanite group than it is to Old Aramaic, as preserved in the Sefire inscriptions, for example. Historically, this analysis, if correct, is quite significant because it endorses the conclusion that the Balaam text is a native literary creation of the immediate region, not one imported from Syria or elsewhere.

A word about palaeography is now in order. Scholars such as van der Kooij, Naveh, Cross and now Puech have utilized palaeographic criteria in dating the Balaam text and, to the extent that script has a bearing on language and cultural provenience, to determine whose text this was. The script derives from the Aramaic script group. Cross, and now Puech, suggest that it exhibits characteristics of Ammonite script.[8]

This discussion has only indirect bearing on the language question, because script and language are different phenomena. At a site such as Deir ʿAlla, so close to Ammonite territory, one might expect Ammonite scribes to be at work, just as one would expect to find Aramean scribes at this site, which was at certain periods under Aramean administration. It is not unknown for one group or people to employ the script of another, for political or sociological reasons. The determining factors in ascertaining the cultural provenience of a given literary text are language and diction, in addition to specific content, of course.

The value of palaeographic analysis for dating a given script must also be stated cautiously. Van der Kooij subjected the script to painstaking analysis, character by character, even describing the movement of the nib used to write on the plaster in forming each character. He does not relate to any historical event, such as the Assyrian campaigns, but provides a qualified date of 700 B.C.E., give or take twenty-five years, as is customary. Naveh dates the script to around the middle of the eighth century B.C.E., perhaps a bit earlier, and Puech now suggests a date of ca. 725 B.C.E., plus or minus twenty-five years, favoring a pre-Assyrian provenience. Cross fixed a date of ca. 700 B.C.E., and has verbally stated that the Balaam text postdated the Assyrian campaigns, and that he does not consider it an Israelite creation.[9]

Palaeographic analysis alone cannot answer the most pressing historical questions regarding the Balaam text, certainly not in the present state of the overall evidence.

At best, it can project sequences, differentiate between lapidary and cursive scripts and their respective rates of change and development, and trace the emergence of new forms, geographically.

I have already referred to the tentative state of the archaeological evidence. On the basis of what is presently known (April 1984), it seems that Phase M at Deir ʿAlla, though it may have survived the Assyrian campaigns by a brief span, is primarily a pre-Assyrian phase and most probably not one initiated after 721 B.C.E. This seems to be Franken's conclusion, although his discussion is difficult to follow on this point.[10] The radio-carbon testing of a charred grain sample from Phase M yielded a date of ca. 800 B.C.E., plus or minus seventy years, with a 66% probability.[11] According to Franken, the lower limit of Phase M is ca. 650 B.C.E., because it was at about that time that wheel-turned pottery, absent from Phase M, was introduced to the area. The pottery changed between Phases M and N, according to Franken, and there may even have been an intermediate M–to–N phase. This matter will undoubtedly be clarified by the current excavations at the site. It is quite possible that the Ammonites did not move into the area until quite late in the seventh century B.C.E., and not very soon after the Assyrian subjugation of the area, as has been supposed.

What is at stake in this discussion is a clear indication of the demography of the Valley of Succoth at the time the Balaam text appeared on the inner walls of the Deir ʿAlla temple. There were two radical changes in the demography of the immediate area, one at the end of the Late Bronze Age (ca. 1200 B.C.E.) and the other as a consequence of the Assyrian deportations, occurring near the end of the eighth century B.C.E.

The Late Bronze Age culture of the lower Jabbok is called Canaanite for lack of a more precise term. We know that Egypt was interested in the area, as evidenced by the scarab of Taossert found at Deir ʿAlla, dating to the thirteenth century B.C.E.[12] The Late Bronze Age II temple at Deir ʿAlla was destroyed ca. 1200 B.C.E. —exactly how is not presently known. Construction at Deir ʿAlla was resumed early in the twelfth century. Clear historical information about the Valley of Succoth begins to appear only late in the tenth century B.C.E. I prefer, pending the publication of the Late Bronze Age II pottery and the Iron Age material, not to discuss in detail what has been reported about the finds of the early Iron Age at Deir ʿAlla. We are told that, after a brief Israelite period, there was an extended period characterized by Philistine-type pottery, perhaps of local manufacture. Then followed the period of the United Monarchy.

Very soon after the breakup of the United Monarchy, Jeroboam I fortified Penuel (1 Kings 12:25). Very shortly thereafter, early in the last quarter of the tenth century B.C.E., Shishak overran the Valley of Succoth, and his stele at Karnak, so effectively illuminated by Mazar, mentions no less than six sites in the area: Adam, a site named Kadesh, Penuel, Succoth, Mahanaim and Zaphon. Whether Deir ʿAlla is indeed ancient Succoth, or some other mound a few kilometers away, is not yet certain and matters little for the present discussion.[13]

At the time of Shishak's campaign, the Valley of Succoth was a fertile, densely populated area fed by the waters of the Jabbok as they poured down into the Jordan.

In effect, Shishak went out of his way to reach this area, undoubtedly so as to reassert Egyptian interests here, and perhaps as punishment imposed on Jeroboam who had in some way displeased the Egyptians, after having found refuge in Egypt during the last days of Solomon. According to the latest information available to me, there is as yet no evidence of a Shishak destruction-level at Deir ʿAlla, but such evidence has turned up at Nimrin, a site south of Deir ʿAlla in the direction of Jericho and the Dead Sea. Further excavations may clarify this matter considerably.[14]

As Mazar emphasizes, the importance of the Valley of Succoth declined sharply after Shishak's campaign, and we have very little information about the area in the biblical record. The focus of international attention shifted to Ashtaroth in the Bashan and to Ramoth Gilead, both important stations on the international route linking up with the King's Highway and proceeding northward to Damascus.

With interruptions and setbacks, Aramean expansion, beginning in the early ninth century B.C.E. under Ben-Hadad II and continuing until near the end of the century under Hazael, eventually encompassed all of Gilead. At the end of the ninth century the campaigns of Adad-Nirari III weakened Aram-Damascus considerably, and for a time Israelite hegemony was reasserted under Joash and Jeroboam II. But sometime before the campaigns of Tiglath-Pileser III, Rezin, the Aramean king, probably regained control of Transjordan. We do not know how extensive the Aramean presence was in the Valley of Succoth during this period, but the discovery of the Aramaic administrative notations in Phase M at Deir ʿAlla indicates at least an official presence, if we are correct in dating Phase M prior to the Assyrian subjugation of Gilead

H. Tadmor has meticulously summarized what is known of the effects of the Assyrian subjugation in Bashan and Gilead, showing that the forces of Tiglath-Pileser III reached all the way south to Moab. There were mass deportations from Gilead and Galilee.[15]

In the period prior to the Assyrian campaigns we have some evidence of a strong Israelite factor in the population of Gilead. Possibly as many as four kings of northern Israel were Gileadites! Pekah son of Remaliah was a Gileadite and came to power with the assistance of a group of important Gileadites (2 Kings 15:25). It is also probable that Menahem son of Gadi (that is, a resident of the territory of Gad) was a Gileadite, which would make his son, Pekahiah, a Gileadite as well (2 Kings 15:14–17, 23). Come to think of it, Shallum son of Jabesh (2 Kings 15:13) must have been a Gileadite, from Jabesh of Gilead.[16] We would thus have a sequence of four kings in northern Israel who were Gileadites, from Shallum to Pekah, ruling from 748/47 to 733/32 B.C.E. Without overstating the implications of this political reality, it is safe to say that even during periods of Aramean hegemony in Transjordan, Gilead was part of the political configuration of the northern Israelite kingdom.

In summary, a date prior to the Assyrian campaigns for the Deir ʿAlla plasters would not be incompatible with the evidence currently available. At the present time, pending further evidence, the strongest argument for a Transjordan-Israelite provenience, as against a non-Israelite provenience, is the character of the Balaam text itself, especially its close affinity to certain biblical literary traditions. It is this complex of affinities which can be explored productively at the present time, always with an eye to historical questions but in a manner that does not presuppose as certain one set of historical conclusions. We turn now to the *literary-historical* provenience of the Balaam text from Deir ʿAlla.

In the light of a restoration proposed independently by both G. Hamilton and É. Puech, and pursuant to my earlier interpretation, we may now read, near the beginning of "Combination I," the following:

> (*wyḥz mḥzh*) *kmś*ʾ ʾ*l*, "He [Balaam] beheld a vision according to the revelation of El."

This reading, with its specific reference to the deity El, links the two "Combinations" of the Balaam text to one another more firmly than was previously possible. Near the beginning of "Combination II" we read:

> (*ddn*) *yrwy* ʾ*l wyʿbd* ʾ*l byt ʿlmn*, El sates himself with lovemaking; then El fashioned a netherworld.

El emerges as the dominant deity in the Balaam text, one who shows compassion by revealing to Balaam, through his divine messengers, the imminence of disaster. Subsequently, El provides a proper burial and residence for the rejected, though heroic seer, Balaam. The exact relationship of the goddess Shagar weʿIshtar to El is not explicit; but El is clearly concerned with her fate.

All this means that the Iron Age temple at Deir ʿAlla was most probably an El temple. This should hardly surprise us, either during the eighth or the seventh century B.C.E. in the Valley of Succoth, whatever the demography of the region. El is by far the most frequent element in the Ammonite theophoric onomasticon, as known primarily from the seventh century B.C.E.[17] Biblical traditions inform us that El was specifically associated with the Valley of Succoth in earlier centuries. This is most clearly epitomized in the Genesis narratives, which relate that Jacob became *Yisrael* at Penuel (Genesis 32:25–32)! This narrative qualifies as a *hieros logos* of Penuel, much in the same way that Genesis 28:10–22 represent a *hieros logos* of Bethel. The *Sitz-im-Leben* of the Penuel episode is most logically the period prior to Shishak's invasion, although in its present form it is probably a later composition.

The entire complex of El traditions associated with the Patriarchs is topically relevant to the present discussion, but is far too involved to be dealt with here in any detail. Suffice it to say that in contrast to Baal, who was utterly rejected in monotheistic circles early in the monarchic period, the last persons properly to be given Baalistic names being Saul's sons, El was generally welcomed, and the attitude toward El remained positive. El was synthesized or fused with Yahweh, the God of Israel. Some of the Genesis traditions betray an awareness that the Patriarchs (or, to put it less traditionally, the earliest Israelites) were devoted to El. This hindsight is not expressed with any disapproval, as evidenced by the startling statement in Exodus 6:2–4.

In the Balaam text from Deir ʿAlla, El is the proper name of a deity and certainly not a common noun, or a way of referring to the God of Israel!

The classification of the Iron Age temple at Deir ʿAlla as an El temple leads one to conclusions of both historical and literary relevance. In historical perspective, it means that there was more than one pattern to cult practice and religious life in pre-exilic Israel. Yahwistic temples and cult sites could be "polluted" by the introduction of pagan rites or the like, and this situation is repeatedly called to our attention by biblical prophets and historiographers. There was another pattern whereby temples and cult sites dedicated to pagan gods coexisted with Yahwistic ones. There was a Baal temple in (or outside of) Samaria, which was put out of commission by Jehu (2 Kings 10:18f.) and subsequently, after Athaliah's backsliding, by the priests under Jehoiada (2 Kings 11:17f.).

As for Gilead, we know that there was a temple of Yahweh in Nebo around the middle of the ninth century B.C.E. Mesha tells us that, upon conquering Nebo, then an Israelite stronghold, he dragged "the vessels of Yahweh" before Ashtar-Kemosh, at his capital of Dibon.[18] The presence of an El temple in Gilead during the eighth century B.C.E. does not mean that Israelite monotheism was not established there, but only that it coexisted, in this case, with an autochthonous El cult of probable great antiquity.

The northern Israelite prophet of the eighth century B.C.E., Hosea, twice speaks of Gilead in his denunciations of improper worship and societal wickedness. Both passages are somewhat cryptic but, if studied in depth, may prove to be relevant to our discussion. Our starting point is Hosea 6:4. Continuing with deletions until verse 10, we read the text as follows:

4. What can I do for you Ephraim,
   What can I do for you, *Israel*,
   When your goodness is like morning clouds,
   Like dew early gone? ...
6. For I desire goodness, not sacrifice,
   Obedience to God, rather than burnt offerings!
7. But they, *in Adam* have transgressed the covenant,
   There they have been false to Me.
8. Gilead is a city of evildoers,
   Tracked up with blood!
9. The gang of priests is
   Like the *ambuscade* of bandits
   Who murder on the road to Shechem,
   For they have encouraged depravity.

10. *At Beth Shean* I have seen
A horrible thing:
Ephraim has fornicated there,
Israel has defiled himself![19]

Hosea is condemning the undue emphasis on cult and worship to the utter disregard for "steadfast love," a theme frequent in biblical prophecy, and in which sexual depravity, even if not actual, serves as a poignant way of expressing Israel's infidelity. What is significant is the fact that Hosea, like other prophets, targets certain towns as focal points of iniquity. He includes sites on both sides of the Jordan, starting with Adam and Gilead, projected as a town not a region (perhaps intending Jabesh-Gilead), and going on to encompass two major sites west of the Jordan, Shechem and Beth-Shean.

The geographic scope reflected in this list of places points to ancient realities affecting economy, trade and culture. *En route* from central Gilead to the Mediterranean, one could cross the Jordan at Adam. The route branched off west of the Jordan, northward to Beth-Shean, then westward to Megiddo, where it linked up with the "Via Maris." Another branch of the same route continued in a westerly direction to a point between Shechem and Tirzah, also linking up with the "Via Maris," either by way of Samaria or Dothan. Beth-Shean was also a station on the route from Jabesh-Gilead, which extended from the King's Highway in Transjordan to the "Via Maris." At various points, these routes exploited rifts in the northern mountains.[20]

Hosea 11 tells the same story, albeit in much less detail. In verse 11 we read:

As for Gilead, it is worthless,
And to no purpose have they
Been sacrificing oxen in Gilgal.
The altars of these are also
Like stone heaps upon a plowed field.

It is not our purpose to suggest that Hosea is necessarily referring to the pattern of pagan worship we have proposed as applicable to an El temple at Deir ʿAlla, during the eighth century B.C.E. It is sufficient, in terms of our argument, to note that he is speaking of an Israelite society in the Gilead of his time, and that, in so doing, he perceives a societal configuration on both sides of the Jordan that is parallel with the political configuration discernible in the history of the northern Israelite monarchy during the same period.

Our literary analysis begins with the observation that the closest biblical parallels to the Balaam text from Deir ʿAlla are, as one would expect, the biblical Balaam oracles and the narrative saga. I am not speaking merely of topical parallels but of close affinities in diction. This prompts me to suggest the existence of an El repertoire, emanating from centers of the El cult, upon which biblical writers drew for their materials. Some of those centers were in Transjordan, and this would explain how a complex of traditions and oracles about Balaam, originating at sites such as Deir ʿAlla, found its way into biblical literature. Monotheistic writers fused El with Yahweh, by using אל in parallelism with יהוה, or with such terms as אלהים/אלה. Often אל was used as a common noun or as an epithet of Yahweh. It is difficult, of course, to ascertain where in the Hebrew Bible אל was intended by the ancient writers to designate a deity, Syro-Canaanite El. It is, however, precisely in those biblical poetic passages most similar in diction to the Balaam text from Deir ʿAlla that this is most likely the case! Let us begin with the Sheol oracle of Isaiah 14, which I have compared to "Combination II" of the Balaam text.

There are salient dictional affinities for comparison: Isaiah 14:19 refers to "the wrap of the slain" (לובש הרוגים), while "Combination II" has (*mn*) *mškb mtksn lbš*, "From the bed, they cover themselves with a wrap." Further compare Isaiah 14:11: "Your covering is the worm" (ומכסיך תולעת). Isaiah 14:18 states "They all repose in honor, each in his own 'house'" (כלם שכבו בכבוד), while "Combination II" has *tškb mškby ʿlmyk*, "you will repose on your eternal bed."

A remarkable parallel is provided by the term נצר, "carrion, corpse" in Isaiah 14:19 "You have been cast from your grave like loathsome carrion." (ואתה השלכתה מקברך כנצר תצב). In "Combination II," the term *nqr*, as it is expressed in the phonetic system of the Deir ʿAlla language, occurs three times. Two of the occurrences appear in clear contexts:

1. *nʾnḥ nqr blbbh*, "The corpse moans in his heart."
2. *lbb nqr šḥh*, "The heart of the corpse is desolate."

These affinities would suggest that the two compositions derive from the same repertoire, and indeed the Sheol oracle of Isaiah 14 is El literature! Long ago M.D. Cassuto speculated that the term אל in Isaiah 14:13–14, in the boastful speech of the pagan king, was not a common noun referring to the God of Israel, but a reference to the well-known Syro-Canaanite deity, El.[21] The passage reads:

> I will ascend to the heavens;
> I will set my throne above the stars of *El* (ממעל לכוכבי־אל);
> I will mount the back of a dense cloud;
> I will be comparable to Elyon (אדמה לעליון)!

In contrast to words attributed to a pagan king, the tone of the Balaam oracles is passionately monotheistic. The biblical poets sing a paeon of praise to Yahweh, and carefully synthesize El with Yahweh. In the first instance, this is shown through poetic parallelism (Numbers 23:8):

> How can I curse what אל has not cursed?
> How can I condemn what Yahweh (יהוה) has not damned?

Nonetheless, the derivation of the Balaam oracles from an El repertoire glares through the Yahwistic fusion. In citing the following verses, I render the Hebrew אל as *El* in italics, to show that one could just as well read these verses (Numbers 23:19) as referring to the deity, El:

> *El* is not person that he would deceive,
> No mortal man, that he would retract.

And Numbers 23:22 and 24:8:

> *El*, who freed them from Egypt,
> Has horns like a wild ox!

And Numbers 23:24:

> It is promptly told to Jacob,
> To Israel — what *El* has done.

The third and fourth oracles open with a statement about Balaam himself (Numbers 24:3–4):

> The oration of Balaam, son of Beor
> The oration of the man whose vision is clear;
> The oration of one who hears *El*'s oracles,
> Who beholds the vision of Shaddai —
> Prostrate, but with eyes wide open!

In the opening statement of the fourth oracle, the following words are added (Numbers 24:15–16):

> Who possesses knowledge of Elyon

In addition to the El theme, there are other links between the biblical Balaam saga and the Deir ʿAlla text. In both, divine beings "come" to Balaam at night, and in both he beholds visions and relates to others what has been disclosed to him. He tells what the gods are doing, conveyed by the verb פעל/*pʿl*. In both, Shaddai or Shaddai-gods play a role.

Apart from the sources being discussed here because of their direct bearing on the Balaam text from Deir ʿAlla, there are other inroads of the El repertoire in biblical literature. One example, of a later period, is the book of Job which, exclusive of the prologue and epilogue, may well be of Transjordanian origin. One also recalls the opening lines of Psalm 19:

The heavens relate the glory of *El*;
The firmament tells of his handiwork.

Although biblical Balaam oracles may antedate the version of the Balaam text from Deir ʿAlla, the latter has the advantage of showing us an example of El literature as it was, unaffected by the Yahwistic monotheism of the biblical writers. Given the history of Transjordan as it has been outlined here, one may suppose that contacts across the Jordan, in both directions, were normal throughout the tenth to the late eighth centuries B.C.E., allowing for continuous cultural interaction. Biblical writers drew on native, Transjordanian traditions, and it is probable that Transjordanian writers, no less skilled and artistic —whether Israelite or not —were affected by literary movements west of the Jordan, primarily in northern Israel.

Bible scholars will now be required to focus attention on the Transjordanian factor in biblical literature, just as we have been seeking to identify Judean and north Israelite factors. The discovery of the inscribed plaster fragments at Deir ʿAlla has initiated a new era in Bible scholarship, as well as in the study of the ancient cultures of Transjordan. It is hoped that increased archaeological activity on the soil of ancient Transjordan, especially in the Zerqa Valley, will provide valuable materials for study to all students of Near Eastern antiquity.[22]

Notes

1. J. Hoftijzer and G. van der Kooij, eds., *Aramaic Texts from Deir ʿAlla* (Leiden, 1976). See H.J. Franken, "Archaeological Evidence Relating to the Interpretation of the Text," ibid., especially his comments on the pottery on pp. 11–12. See also, H.J. Franken and M.M. Ibrahim, "Two Seasons of Excavation at Tell Deir ʿAlla," *Annual of the Department of Antiquities, Jordan* 2 (1977–78): 57–80, with a note by J. Hoftijzer; M. Ibrahim, J. Sauer, K. Yassine, "The East Jordan Valley Survey, 1975," *BASOR* 222 (1976): 41–66. An interesting attempt to synthesize the biblical record with external evidence is provided by O. Ottosson, *Gilead: Tradition and History* (Lund, 1969).
2. B.A. Levine, "The Deir ʿAlla Plaster Inscriptions," *JAOS* 101 (1981): 196–205.
3. For comments on these Aramaic notations, see Hoftijzer and van der Kooij, *Aramaic Texts* (note 1), pp. 15, 267f., 274f., and 285f.
4. Cf. A. Rofé, *The Book of Balaam* (Jerusalem, 1979), p. 61, s.v. line 2 (Hebrew); H. and M. Weippert, "Die Bileam-Inschrift von Tell Der ʿAlla," *ZDPV* 98 (1982): 77–103, especially 83, s.v. line 2. Now see J. Hackett, *The Balaam Text from Deir ʿAlla* (Scholars Press, 1984), p. 25, line 2, and commentary, and p. 33.
5. Cf. J. Naveh, *IEJ* 29 (1979): 133–136, which is a review of Hoftijzer and van der Kooij, *Aramaic Texts* (see note 1). Also see Levine, "The Deir ʿAlla Inscriptions" (note 2), p. 200, s.v. lines 27, 35; and p. 201, s.v. line 03. See also Hackett, *The Balaam Text* (note 4), Ch. IV: The Dialect, pp. 109–124.
6. The occurrence of Aramaic *bar*, "son," is explained in this manner by Naveh, *IEJ* (note 5), p. 136, as an official representation of the name of the seer perceived as an Aramean.
7. See discussion of this question by J. Hoftijzer, in Hoftijzer and van der Kooij, *Aramaic Texts* (see note 1), p. 296, n. 23.
8. See the careful treatment of the script by G. van der Kooij in Hoftijzer and van der Kooij, *Aramaic Texts* (see note 1), pp. 23–170. This study includes a detailed description of the method of writing

used at Deir 'Alla. In addition to Naveh's review of 1979 and his early analysis of the script in *IEJ* 17 (1967): 256–258, we have two statements by F.M. Cross Jr., "Epigraphic Notes on the Amman Citadel Inscription," *BASOR* 193 (1969): 13–19, especially p. 14, n. 2, where he tends to agree with Naveh's early dating in the eighth century B.C.E. with reservations, and "Notes on the Ammonite Inscription from Tell Siran," *BASOR* 212 (1973): 12–15, where he alters his view. Also see É. Puech. "L'Inscription de la Statue d'Amman et la Paléographie Ammonite," *RB* 92 (1985): 5–24.

9. The reader is directed to the response by É. Puech (below pp. 354–365), and to the remarks made by F.M. Cross Jr. (below, p. 369).
10. See the discussion by Franken, in Hoftijzer and van der Kooij, *Aramaic Texts* (note 1), pp. 12f.
11. Ibid., p. 16 under "Note."
12. See J. Yoyotte, "Un Souvenir du 'Pharaon' Taossert en Jordanie," *VT* 12 (1962): 464f.
13. See B. Mazar, "Shishak's Campaign to Eretz-Israel," in *Canaan and Israel: Historical Essays* (Jerusalem, 1974), pp. 234–244, especially 236–237. (Hebrew)
14. Nimrin is perhaps biblical בית נמרה (Numbers 32:36, Joshua 13:27 and Numbers 32:3).
15. See H. Tadmor, *Encyclopaedia Biblica*, vol. VIII (Jerusalem, 1982), s.v. *Tiglat-Pil'eser*, pp. 415f., especially 423f. (Hebrew).
16. The name of the town is יב[י]ש in 1 Samuel 11:1, 3, *passim*; in 1 Samuel 31:12, etc.
17. See K.P. Jackson, *The Ammonite Language of the Iron Age* (Scholars Press, 1983), pp. 95f., and his study, "Ammonite Personal Names in the Context of the West Semitic Onomasticon," in *The Word of the Lord Shall Go Forth. Essays in Honor of D.N. Freedman* (Philadelphia, 1983), pp. 507–521.
18. See H. Donner and W. Röllig, *Kanaanäische und Aramäische Inschriften*, vol. I (Wiesbaden, 1962), p. 33, no. 181, lines 17–18, as restored: *w'qḥ mšm '[t k]ly YHWH*, "I took from there [Nebo] the vessels of Yahweh," etc.
19. H.L. Ginsberg has suggested that in transmission of Hosea from northern Israel to Judah, archetypal *Yods*, originally standing for ישראל, were misunderstood as referring to יהודה. This explains the proposed reading ישראל, "Israel," in v. 4. See *Encyclopaedia Judaica*, vol. VIII (1970), p. 1015, in H.L. Ginsberg, "Hosea, Book of." For this reading, and for the reading בית־שאן instead of בית־ישראל in v. 10, see *The Prophets* (Jewish Publication Society of America: New York, 1978), to Hosea 6:4f., and notes, pp. 774–775. For the reading באדם, "in Adam," instead of Masoretic כאדם, "to a man," see E. Sellin, "Die Geschichtliche Orientierung der Prophetie des Hosea," *Neue kirchliche Zeitschrift* 36 (1925): 607–658, especially 624–625. In v. 9, Masoretic וכחני probably misrepresents a form of the verb חבא, "to conceal," as suggested by Sellin and others. Cf. H. Tadmor, "The Historical Background of Hosea's Prophecies," in Y. Kaufmann Jubilee Volume, ed. M. Haran (Jerusalem, 1962), pp. 84–88.
20. See Y. Aharoni and M. Avi-Yonah, *The Macmillan Bible Atlas* (New York, 1968), map no. 10, p. 17.
21. See M.D. Cassuto, *Encyclopaedia Biblica*, vol. I (1955), pp. 283–284, s.v. אל, p. 2 (Hebrew). Also see O. Eissfeldt, "El and Yahweh," *JSS* 1 (1956): 25–37.
22. I am grateful to Profs. H.L. Ginsberg and B. Mazar for the pleasure of discussing this study with them. Prof. Sauer was kind enough to share with me his extensive knowledge of the archaeological history of ancient Transjordan.

Aramaic-Akkadian Archives from the Gozan-Ḫarran Area

Edward Lipiński

THE WELL-KNOWN IMAGE of two scribes, one writing in Akkadian on a clay tablet and the other in Aramaic on leather or parchment, is almost contradicted by the bilingual archives which the Brussels Royal Museums of Art and History purchased in 1972. These archives comprise Neo-Assyrian, Neo-Babylonian and Aramaic deeds, all written on clay tablets. The parchments sealed by the clay dockets are, of course, irremediably lost. All the documents date roughly from the seventh century B.C.E.

Although the tablets were in the hands of two different persons prior to their purchase, a quick examination immediately showed that the Aramaic tablets at least,[1] and probably the others as well, came from the same source. This common origin was evidenced in particular by the appearance — in both collections — of a contract passed between the same parties, in the same year, and sealed by the same stamp seal of the borrower.[2]

The clay tablets were generally in good condition, but some of them were coated with hardened mud, while others were completely blackened by cinders. They were subsequently treated and cleaned at the British Museum. In consequence, the deciphering of the parts coated with mud was made possible and some provisional readings, which were in the meantime quoted in a few publications of mine,[3] could be improved upon. Unfortunately, a couple of Aramaic tablets suffered from this operation, and the impression of a cylinder seal, which appeared on one of them, vanished almost completely. For these few deeds, therefore, we have to rely mainly on photographs and on previously made provisional copies.

The publication of the Akkadian texts — forty-one Neo-Assyrian deeds, two Neo-Babylonian letters and one Neo-Babylonian contract — was entrusted in 1982 to Prof. P. Garelli, to whom I owe the information concerning this part of the archives.[4] I am charged with editing the twenty-four Aramaic clay tablets, one

(0.3633) of which bears only two seal impressions without text visible on its top. Two of the Neo-Assyrian deeds in cuneiform have Aramaic epigraphs as well (0.3693 and 0.3698), one of which became visible only after the tablet had been cleaned. Prof. Denyse Homès-Fredericq is preparing the publication of the seal-impressions[5] and other authentication marks, such as fingernail or shell impressions. These marks are apposed on most Akkadian and Aramaic tablets and are integral elements of bilateral transactions.

The Brussels tablets offer a remarkable diversity of authentication signs. Impressions of cylinder seals occur both on cuneiform tablets, which generally offer a broader surface, and on Aramaic tablets, either on the top or on the obverse — and even on the lateral side of a triangular docket, where we can see a mythological scene, perhaps that of Gilgamesh slaying the heavenly bull.[6] Stamp seals are definitely the most common, appearing on both tablets written in Akkadian and in Aramaic. Quite often the seal is apposed twice, or even three times. From the thematic point of view, there seems to be a certain preference of symbols incorporating the moon-crescent and the *Sibitti*, the seven planets. In fact, this motif occurs in various seal impressions with only minor variations. The *Sibitti* occur also with another symbol (0.3683), while the moon-crescent appears also in a cultic scene (0.3705) or above an animal, apparently a horse (0.3656) or, elsewhere, a wild goat (0.3715). The widespread use of this emblem of the moon-god can probably be explained by the vicinity of Ḫarran, the main center of his cult in the Aramaic regions of northern Mesopotamia. However, we have also the representation of a bird, without any divine symbols attached to it (0.3699), or even the Egyptian *ankh* sign combined with the *neb* sign (0.3713), as on Egyptian scaraboids, although all the parties to the case bear good Aramaic names.

Sometimes the borrower or the seller had no personal seal. In such cases, the nail marks were used as personal authentication signs. They could be apposed several times in a horizontal line, or in a bundle pattern on the top of the tablet, or in any particular order. It was also possible to use some small objects, such as shells, as identification signs.

The study of the Akkadian deeds by Prof. Garelli shows beyond doubt that most of the texts come from the same archives, and reveals that at least two tablets belonging to this group of texts have been published previously: one by J.N. Postgate,[7] and the other in the splendid volume edited by O.W. Muscarella.[8] It would not be surprising if other clay tablets from these archives were to surface somewhere else.

Many texts, both Akkadian and Aramaic, bear date formulas with names of Assyrian eponyms. They are dated between 697 and 620 B.C.E. The initial date relates to Nabû-dūra-uṣur, governor of Parnunna. The latter date is that proposed by Margarete Falkner[9] for *Dadî* the *masennu* (*Ddy mšn*), mentioned in two or three Aramaic deeds, in three different months: the eighth month, *yrḥ ʾsmnh* (0.3716, 8–9), the month of Tammuz, *yrḥ t*[*mz*] (0.3656, 8–9) (where the restoration is almost certain, for this month name is used in the Aramaic deeds while *tišrî* is called *šbʿ*, Assyrian *seba*, "seven"), and finally *yrḥ zb*[ ] (0.3657, 5) (either a month of sacrifice(s), *zb*[*ḥ*] or *zb*[*ḥn*], or a month *zbn* related to the Syriac noun *zabnā*, "time," and to the month name *zibnu*, attested east of the Tigris in Old Babylonian times).

An Aramaic judicial text (0.3714), which on palaeographic grounds should be dated ca. 700 B.C.E., bears the name of *l*'[*m*] *pd mp*[*sr*?] who, in all likelihood, is to be identified with the *limmu* ᵐ*Pa-da m*[*u*?-*x-x-x*] of Carchemish tablet BM 116230 (reedited by J.N. Postgate[10]). The name of the eponym is neither Akkadian nor Aramaic, for the spelling *pd* excludes any connection with the Old Aramaic verb *pdy*, "to ransom."[11] It might be an Anatolian name, to be compared, for instance, with ᵐ*Pa-a-ta*.[12] The name of the eponym is followed by a title, the first letters of which are *mp*[ ] on the Aramaic tablet, while a part of the cuneiform sign *m*[*u*-] might appear after the eponym's name on the Carchemish tablet. These letters do not correspond to any known title of Assyrian eponyms, unless we suppose that the man was a *mupassiru*, "messenger," and that this is the true reading of the Neo-Assyrian logogram DUL_4 É. GAL, traditionally read *nāgir ekalli*, "the herald of the palace." The similar case of the logogram AGRIG, used to designate the high dignitary *masennu* in Assyria, shows that this hypothesis is at least well worth considering.

The eponym Pada cannot be a post-canonical *limmu*, for his name provides the dating of a judicial decision in favor of Ḥaddiy, who was active from the earliest period of our archives down to 665 B.C.E. An objection to an early dating of the document could arise on archaeological grounds, for the Carchemish tablet was found by Sir Leonard Woolley in "building D," on the doorsill between rooms four and five.[13] A bronze seal with the cartouche of Psammetichus I was found in room four and several seal impressions with the cartouche of Necho were discovered in room five,[14] which must have included a group of documents written on papyrus and sealed with these Egyptian bullae. Thus, these two rooms could be considered as part of a chancellery connected with the Egyptian troops stationed at Carchemish between 610 and 605 B.C.E. The fact that the clay tablet dated from the eponymy of Pada was discovered on the doorsill between these two rooms might, therefore, be viewed as an indication of its very late date. However, Woolley discovered only one single level in this building, and he attributed this fact to the exceptional solidity of the structure, which was used over a long period without having to be rebuilt. In consequence, this clay tablet, together with a small fragment of another tablet, might be a remnant of older archives kept in "building D" and later removed by the Egyptians. R. Campbell Thompson, who edited the tablet,[15] was actually convinced that it antedates the period of Ashurbanipal. One thing is certain, the tablet cannot be anterior to the conquest of Carchemish by Sargon II in 717 B.C.E. The Aramaic tablet suggests a somewhat lower date for Pada, shortly after 700 B.C.E., in order to coincide with the time of Ḥaddiy. The appearance of this eponym on a tablet from Carchemish and in an Aramaic document from our archives is perhaps not a coincidence, if one notes that the Brussels tablets come from the Gozan-Ḫarran area, as we shall see.

The earliest part of the archives belonged to Ḥaddiy, whose name was engraved on the seal impressed on one of the tablets (0.3686). Ḥaddiy's name is spelt *Ḥdy* in Aramaic deeds, *Ḫa-an-di-i* on the Neo-Assyrian tablets, and *Ḫa-an-di-ia* in the Neo-

Babylonian texts. The identity of the person is certain and the different spellings of his name leave no doubt about its meaning and onomastic pattern. The name has no connection with the god Haddu or Hadad, and cannot be considered a hypocoristicon.[16] The doubling of *d*, reflected in the dissimilated phonetic spelling *-an-di-*, and the final *-iy* instead of *-ay*, marked by *-di-i* and *-di-ia*, indicate that the name was coined according to the Aramaic adjectival pattern *qattīl* and that *ḥāddīy* therefore means "gladdening," "rejoicing," "cheering." It is an obvious allusion to the birth of a child which makes the family rejoice.

Ḥaddiy was a businessman and a *šaknu ša ekalli* of the queen, who obviously had a palace in the area referred to in our archives. Ḥaddiy was already active in the time of Sennacherib (704–681 B.C.E.), when Naqīyā-Zakūtu, the influential wife of Sennacherib, was queen. And he continued to function in the time of her son Esarhaddon and in the first years of her grandson Ashurbanipal, down to 665 B.C.E. This is the lowest date appearing in an Aramaic document issued on behalf of Ḥaddiy and dated from the eponymy of Mannu-ki-šarri. The same eponym also gives the date of the earliest Neo-Assyrian deed in which Ḫarranay, the son of Ḥaddiy, appears as one of the parties to the case.

His name is spelt ᵐKASKAL-*a-a* in the Neo-Assyrian deeds and *Ḥrny* in the Aramaic documents. This name, which seems to have enjoyed a certain popularity in the seventh century B.C.E., does not necessarily signify that the person was a "native of the city of Ḫarran,"[17] which was no doubt a holy city known for its temple of the moon-god Sin, called *Šiʾ* or *Bʿl-Ḥrn*, "the Lord of Ḫarran," by the Arameans. The name Ḫarranay is likely to have expressed the devotion to this great god.

Ḫarranay was a businessman dealing, *inter alia*, in tin but he does not appear to have succeeded his father Ḥaddiy to the office of palace governor. At least, his name is never followed by a title. Instead, he may have held a financial office in a temple. In fact, he could dispose of silver that was *rēšāti*[18] of Ishtar from Arbela, *rsh zy ʾšr rbʾl*, and lend it at 50% interest (0.3650). Despite the accurate study of the economy of Neo-Assyrian temples by Stefan Zawadzki,[19] the exact meaning of *rēšāti* is not yet very clear, but it cannot differ widely from Old Hebrew *rēʾšīt*, "first-fruits" or "the choicest of the fruits,"[20] which were displayed on the altar and later assigned to the priests as part of their cultic income.[21] The real problem starts when *rēšāti* is used to characterize silver or copper. Some years ago I defended the opinion that it was first-quality metal guaranteed by the temple, generally by the temple of Ishtar of Arbela.[22] This interpretation was consistent with the biblical use of *rēʾšīt* and provides a solution to one of the puzzling features of the Neo-Assyrian documents, where silver, the *rēšāti* of Ishtar of Arbela, appears as loans from Balāwāt, Kalḫu, Nineveh and even the western province of Gozan.

Now, however, a new element suggests reconsideration of the problem. In fact, a Neo-Assyrian sale contract from our archives, when describing the exact location of the real estate to be sold, mentions a sanctuary of Ishtar of Arbela in our Gozan-Ḫarran area. It appears therefore that documents from this region mentioning the *rēšāti* of Ishtar of Arbela do not refer to the main sanctuary of Arbela itself, distant several hundred kilometers, but to a local shrine which could lend small quantities of silver to persons living in the vicinity. Instead of being only pure silver guaranteed by the temple, it could have been silver given to the local sanctuary as a particular kind of offering instead of first-fruits or the choicest of the fruits. In this case, *rēšāti* would have lost its original meaning and would also designate the equivalent of the fruits in precious metal.

Stefan Zawadzki and Brigitte Menzel surmise that the temples sold the superfluous part of the "first-fruits" and that the capital realized from these sales was considered as *rēšāti*.[23] Although the texts referred to might be interpreted in a different way,[24] this hypothesis is in itself feasible. It remains somewhat questionable if one compares the Assyrian *rēšāti* to the Hebrew *rēʾšīt*, that an Israelite, who was not a priest or a Levite, was strictly forbidden to eat.[25] It is surely a much easier solution to consider the precious metals as a substitute for goods in kind.

J.N. Postgate, to whom Zawadzki's study was unavailable, suggests rather that the wealthy used the temples as a sort of safe-deposit in which to store their capital.[26] In exchange for this service, the capital was technically designated as one or another kind of temple offering, for instance *rēšāti*. When this silver was lent either by the creditor or by the temple officials acting on his behalf as financial agents, it was stipulated that this silver was, for instance, *rēšāti* of Ishtar of Arbela. In this hypothesis, Ḫarranay would merely be a despositor who had attained religious and physical protection for his funds.

One wonders if this reconstruction is not too elaborate. R. Bogaert suggested three possible explanations of the existence of temple goods (in our case the *rēšāti*) that are both the property of the god and apparently of the creditor.[27] The creditor could be a functionary of the temple, acting on its behalf, or an intermediary not of the temple personnel, or a cessionary who has borrowed directly from the temple in order to lend money to others. Brigitte Menzel's discussion of this problem takes the three possible explanations into account, but leaves the issue open.[28]

Actually, the texts mentioning silver as *rēšāti* of Ishtar of Arbela do not seem to provide us with the answer. Instead we find it in the third part of our archives which belonged to *Šhrnwry*, whose name is spelt in five different ways in the Neo-Assyrian deeds. His activity is to be dated to the last years of the Assyrian Empire, in the days of Ashur-eṭel-ilāni and Sîn-shar-ishkun. Contrary to the archives of Ḥaddiy and of Ḫarranay, where the Akkadian texts are more numerous, there are only six cuneiform texts from the time of Śehr-nuri, and eight Aramaic tablets bearing his name. The texts do not indicate whether he was a relative of the two other men or a son of Ḫarranay. It is nevertheless certain that he was active in the same region. Like Ḫarranay, he lent silver that was *rēšāti*, though not of Ishtar of Arbela, but of Hadad, *rsh l-Hdd*. From the Neo-Assyrian deeds quoting a classic penalty formula, we know that Hadad of Gozan was the storm-god worshipped in this region.

It is extremely interesting to observe that the Aramaic deed does not say that the silver was the property of Śehr-nuri. The formula says: "Silver, *rēšāti* (*rsh*) belonging to Hadad, Śehr-nuri has given to Amnan, son of Matiʿadad, from Maʿallānāh, three shekels of silver" (0.3716). The rate of interest is then 100%. The same formula appears on another tablet: "Silver, *rēšāti* (*rsh*) belonging to Hadad, one (shekel), Bēsi has given to Baban" (0.3652). The rate of interest is the same. Now, it emerges from a third tablet that Śehr-nuri borrowed this silver from the temple at a rate of only 25%: "Silver, [x] shekels, belonging to Hadad, to be debited to Śehr-nuri. The interest [amounts] to its quarter" (0.3647). The silver is not called *rēšāti* in this case and the document bears no seal impression, but the names of four witnesses are duly recorded on the reverse.

These formal differences certainly reveal a special relationship between Śehr-nuri and the temple of Hadad. Besides, it seems from these deeds that both he and Bēsi were cessionaries who borrowed silver directly from the temple in order to lend it out to others at a much higher interest rate. It is surprising that we should find the debt and credit note of Śehr-nuri, as well as the credit note of Bēsi in one and the same archive. This could indicate that these tablets were all kept together in the temple precincts, as in the case of the debt notes from Balāwāt.[29] In that case, one could wonder whether the two men were only cessionaries or also temple officials using the capital of the temple for their own business transactions. Besides silver, Śehr-nuri lent barley and straw, and he dealt in small cattle. These deals had no special relation to the temple, and the presence of the aforementioned documents apparently in the same archive could possibly be explained in a different way. Śehr-nuri may have recuperated his debt-note after having repaid his loan and the interest. In fact, the sum lent to him seems to have been scratched from the tablet. As for Bēsi, he may have transferred his credit note over to Śehr-nuri for some reason.

Although the answer to this particular question remains speculative, the Aramaic deeds seem to reveal, to a certain extent, the system lying behind the apparent contradiction of silver described as the property of two different creditors, a deity and a man. The fact that the silver is described in bilateral acts as *rēšāti* of the deity means that this had a certain importance and that both of the mortal parties to the case were aware of its origin. We can hardly see how this was possible if that silver was not marked in a recognizable way or if the business was not transacted within the precincts of the temple. The temple of Hadad, to which our deeds refer, was not necessarily located in Gozan proper, for Hadad of Gozan also had shrines elsewhere, for instance at Sikan, as we learn from the bilingual inscription from Tell Feḫḫerīye.[30] If it is not evident that the moneylenders (in our case Śehr-nuri and Bēsi) were temple officials, they had at least a kind of monopoly over the loan transactions of the temple. Otherwise people would have borrowed money directly from the temple at a much lower rate of interest. Perhaps a cause of the very high interest rate imposed by our moneylenders was the political situation of the moment. With Śehr-nuri, in fact, we reach the rather dark and uncertain period of Ashur-eṭel-ilāni and Sîn-shar-ishkun, in which money-borrowing may have become expensive.

The main city in the area where Ḥaddiy, Ḫarranay and Śehr-nuri were active was Maʿallānā(t), mentioned several times both in the Akkadian and in the Aramaic deeds of our archives. This place-name does not seem to appear in any other source and it was not the city where our men carried out their business. There is little doubt, however, that the archives came from the Gozan-Ḫarran area. The name of Ḫarranay and the mention of the place *Tll zy Qpn Ḥrn* (0.3648) point to the region north of Ḫarran, while the worship of Hadad of Gozan, mentioned in several Akkadian texts, suggests a place relatively close to Gozan. This is confirmed by several additional indications. A certain *A-za-ri-iá-u* appears in one of the Akkadian deeds and he is certainly an Israelite. We know from the Bible[31] that inhabitants of Samaria were deported to the area of "the Habur, the river of Gozan," and this is confirmed by various Neo-Assyrian texts.[32] The mention of Ishtar of Arbela occurs not only in our archives but also in two texts from Gozan or its neighborhood, published by Ungnad.[33]

The Gozan-Ḫarran area might even be suggested by the mention of an Egyptian called *ʾsḥr* (*nś-ḥr*) in a document from the end of the seventh century B.C.E., when the Egyptians tried to aid the last remnants of Assyrian power at Ḫarran under Ashur-uballiṭ II. This tablet cannot be connected directly with the archives of Ḥaddiy, Ḫarranay and Śehr-nuri, and it bears no date. Palaeographically, it could also date to the mid-seventh century B.C.E., but the mention of *ʿEsḥor šᵉmeh zar kīn*, "Eshor, by name, a reliable foreigner," suggests the presence of an Egyptian who was not a deportee moved to this region by the Assyrian authorities. The last sentence, if we read it properly, specifies: *halū bayit šallēm be-Ḥadarāh*, "See, he has paid a house in Ḥadarāh" (0.3648).

Exceptionally, this Aramaic tablet is not a contract, but an informal message sent to two men "at Tilul of the Qipān of Ḫarran" by an unnamed correspondent living apparently in Ḥadarāh or in its vicinity. One of the two addressees, Mati ʿadad, bears the same name as the father of one of Śehr-nuri's customers, who lived in Maʿallana(t). If the letter reached the addressees, it should have been found at Tilul. This is why Tilul is likely to be the place of our archives.

The Tilul where Ashurnasirpal II had built a palace[34] is too distant, for it lies either in Katmuh (to the west and northwest of modern Cizre, occupying the eastern side of the Kashiaru)[35] or in the region south and southwest of Cizre.[36] The specification "Tilul of the Qipān"[37] clearly indicates that there were several places called Tilul. One might wonder if modern Viranşehir, called Antipolis and Constantia in Greek, but Tella in Syriac,[38] is not our Tilul. Unfortunately, I do not think we are able to answer this question with our present knowledge of the historic geography and toponymy of the region.

Notes

1. First report by E. Lipiński, "Les tablettes araméennes de Bruxelles," in *Études sémitiques* (Actes du XXIXᵉ Congrès International des Orientalistes), ed. A. Caquot (Paris, 1975), pp. 25–29.
2. 0.3656 and 0.3716.
3. In particular, E. Lipiński, "Textes juridiques et économiques araméens de l'époque sargonide," in

Acta Antiqua Academiae Scientiarum Hungaricae 22 (1974): 373–384 [= *Wirtschaft und Gesellschaft im Alten Vorderasien* (Budapest, 1976)]. It should be pointed out that the *ḥrqy* from 0. 3650, quoted even more recently, is to be corrected in *ḥrny*.

4. P. Garelli reported on these tablets during the 30th Rencontre Assyriologique Internationale in Leiden, on July 5, 1983.
5. Denyse Homès-Fredericq, "Glyptique sur les tablettes araméennes des Musées Royaux d'Art et d'Histoire (Bruxelles)," *Revue d'assyriologie* 70 (1976): 57–70. Mrs. Homès presented a similar report on the seal impressions of the Akkadian tablets at the Rencontre in Leiden, on July 5, 1983.
6. 0.3645. A different explanation is proposed by Homès-Fredericq, ibid., p. 67. The animal seems to me to be an overturned bull, and the scene would then be similar to the one represented on a terracotta panel in the Royal Museums of Art and History in Brussels. A color reproduction can be found in *Musées Royaux d'Art et d'Histoire. Galerie de l'Asie antérieure et de l'Iran anciens* (Brussels, 1967), p. 2.
7. J.N. Postgate, "Assyrian Texts and Fragments," *Iraq* 35 (1973): 13–36 and pl. XII–XV (see pp. 34–35 and pl. XII, no. 6).
8. O.W. Muscarella, ed., *Ladders to Heaven* (Toronto, 1981), pp. 126–127.
9. M. Falkner, "Die Eponymen der spätassyrischen Zeit," *AfO* 17 (1954–56): 100–120 (see p. 119).
10. J. N. Postgage, *Taxation and Conscription in the Assyrian Empire*, Studia Pohl: Series Maior 3 (Rome, 1974), pp. 360–362.
11. E. Lipiński, *Studies in Aramaic Inscriptions and Onomastics* , vol. I, Orientalia Lovaniensia. Analecta 1 (Leuven, 1975), pp. 129–131; R. Zadok, *The Jews in Babylonia during the Chaldean and Achaemenian Periods according to the Babylonian Sources* (Haifa, 1979), p. 15; P. Swiggers, "Notes on the Hermopolis Papyri I and II," *Annali dell'Istituto Orientale di Napoli* 41 (1981): 143–146 (see p. 146).
12. E. Laroche, *Les noms des Hittites* (Paris, 1966), p. 138, no. 956.
13. C.L. Woolley, *Carchemish. II. The Town Defences* (London, 1921), p. 128, no. 1 and Pl. 26a.
14. Ibid., pp. 125–126.
15. Ibid., pp. 135ff.
16. Therefore, one should correct the interpretation proposed by R. Zadok, *On West Semites in Babylonia during the Chaldean and Achaemenian Periods. An Onomastic Study*, 2d. ed. (Jerusalem, 1978), p. 47.
17. K.L. Tallqvist, *Assyrian Personal Names* (Helsingfors, 1914), p. 86b.
18. J.N. Postgate, "Review of B. Menzel's *Assyrische Tempel*," *JSS* 28 (1983): 156 rightly observes that the correct Neo-Assyrian normalization of SAG.MEŠ is probably *rēšāti*, since the spelling *re-šá-a-ti* is given by ND 10026:5, published by J.V. Kinnier Wilson, *The Nimrud Wine Lists* (London, 1972), Pl. 45. This is supported by the Aramaic transcription *rsh*, which would stand normally for *rēšā(t)*, although the *mater lectionis* or vowel-letter *h* may also be used to mark -*ē* at the end of a word.
19. St. Zawadzki, *Podstawy gospodarcze nowoasyryjskiej świątyni* (Poznań, 1981), with a special chapter on SAG.MEŠ (pp. 51–56). A synthesis of the economic components is lacking; see Brigitte Menzel, *Assyrische Tempel* I–II. Studia Pohl: Series Maior 10/I–II (Rome, 1981). The texts with SAG.MEŠ are collected in vol. II, T 181–193, Nos. 73–131. An additional text has been published by Postgate, "Review of Menzel's *Assyrische Tempel*" (see note 18), p. 155.
20. As suggested by *rēʾšît bikkūrê hāʾădāmā*, "the choicest of the first fruits of the soil," in Exodus 23:19; 34:26; cf. Ezekiel 44:30.
21. Numbers 18:12–13; Deuteronomy 18:3–5.
22. E. Lipiński, "Les temples néo-assyriens et les origines du monnayage," in *State and Temple Economy in the Ancient Near East*, ed. E. Lipiński (Orientalia Lovaniensia. Analecta 6), vol. II (Leuven, 1979), pp. 565–588.
23. Zawadzki, *Podstawy gospodarcze* (see note 19), pp. 54–55; Menzel, *Assyrische Tempel* I (see note 19), pp. 12, 22.
24. Lipiński, *State and Temple Economy* (see note 22), pp. 574–580.
25. Mishna, *Bikkūrīm* II, 1. The death penalty might be incurred by the non-priest who consumed them

of set purpose. However, if he consumed the first-fruits offered to the temple in error, only 20% of their value had to be added as restitution for the sin.

26. Postgate, "Review of Menzel's *Assyrische Tempel*" (see note 18), pp. 155–159.
27. R. Bogaert, *Les origines antiques de la banque de dépôt* (Leyde, 1966), p. 62, cf. pp. 72–73.
28. Menzel, *Assyrische Tempel* (see note 19), pp. 11–21 and in particular pp. 19–21.
29. Ibid., pp. 14–16.
30. A. Abou-Assaf, P. Bordreuil and A.R. Millard, *La statue de Tell Fekherye et son inscription bilingue assyro-araméenne* (Paris, 1982).
31. II Kings 17:6; 18:11; I Chronicles 5:26.
32. In particular *ADD* 234; *CT* 53, 46 (= *ABL* 633); ND 2619 [*Iraq* 23 (1961), p. 38 and pl. XIX].
33. J. Friedrich, G.R. Meyer, A. Ungnad and E.F. Weidner, *Die Inschriften vom Tell Halaf. Beih. AfO* 6 (1940), nos. 112 and 113. It is not certain that these tablets were found at Tell Halaf; cf. ibid., p. 47. They may have been brought by workmen from the surrounding area. Authors usually do not pay attention to Ungnad's introductory remarks, for instance, Zawadzki, *Podstawy gospodarcze* (see note 19), pp. 55 and 73; Menzel, *Assyrische Tempel* I (see note 19), pp. 10 and 18.
34. L.W. King, *Annals of the Kings of Assyria*, vol. I (London, 1902), p. 226:35 and 37 (*Ti-lu-li*); p. 326:87 (DU_6-*u-li*). The place is also mentioned in *ADD* 850, rev. 2.
35. J.N. Postgate, "Katmuḫu," *Reallexikon der Assyriologie* V (1976–80): 487–488.
36. K.H. Kessler, *Untersuchugen zur historischen Topographie Nordmesopotamiens* (Wiesbaden, 1980), pp. 9–15.
37. For the problems related to the exact location of Qipān, see F.M. Fales, "Il paese di Q/Kipani," *Revista degli Studi Orientali* 45 (1970): 21–28.
38. R. Payne Smith, *Thesaurus syriacus*, vol. II (Oxford, 1901), col. 4438.

Respondents

Aaron Demsky

On the Extent of Literacy in Ancient Israel

It is a credit to biblical archaeology that this session is devoted to the study of Northwest Semitic inscriptions. Over the past twenty years a growing number of inscribed sherds have come to light because of careful dipping and patient examination by field archaeologists; previously, such artifacts would have been overlooked. Palaeography, the handmaiden of archaeology, is coming into its own as a scientific discipline aiding the archaeologist in dating his finds and illuminating their historic and linguistic context.

These discoveries, which naturally become the highlight of every excavation, open new vistas of research for the historian of the biblical period. For more than what the inscriptions tell us about battles, burial customs, military correspondence, wine-growing and taxation, they begin to give us an inkling of writing practices in ancient Israel and among her neighbors. They raise questions of broad cultural interest, such as the extent of literacy in the ancient world, the social and technical aspects inherent in the media of communication at that time and, of course, the shaping and transmission of the books of the Bible.

Prof. Millard, studying the epigraphic data, has cogently argued for widespread literacy in ancient Israel, especially during the later period of the monarchy.[1] I wholeheartedly agree with his conclusions. Similarly, following an inductive method based on the epigraphic finds, E. Dhorme already in 1930,[2] and more recently J. Naveh,[3] have demonstrated the extent of the use of writing. Furthermore, Prof. Cross has emphasized that literacy spread rapidly after the alphabet was standardized at the beginning of the Iron Age.[4] Hopefully, we will be able to substantiate these conclusions, placing them in their historic and social context.

In my forthcoming monograph on *Literacy in Ancient Israel* to be published by the Bialik Institute, I attempt to present a comprehensive study of this complex cultural-historical problem. In essence, it seems to me that we must cull both the literary evidence found in the Bible and that of the Hebrew epigrapha in order to understand how the phenomenon of literacy permeated the various levels of Israelite society.

Scribal Culture and Literate Societies

The starting point of this study is the fact that ancient societies that have left written documents fall into one of two general categories. The first was characterized by literacy limited to a class of professional scribes, and the second by widespread literacy which permeated through all classes of society.[5] Fortunately, the ancient Near East during the second and first millennia B.C.E. affords an opportunity to study both types in juxtaposition. This milieu presents the scholar with what is probably one of the best examples of limited literacy, in Mesopotamia and ancient Egypt, which I have termed "scribal culture." It manifests itself not only in the mastering of the technique of writing but in a fully developed organization, educative process and ideology of being literate. It is also in this historic context that one can study the earliest examples of literate societies. These emerged at the end of the second millennium B.C.E. For reasons technical, historic and social, it was those societies in Canaan and Syria that were most affected by the medium of writing. In particular, ancient Israel, having adopted the Canaanite alphabet early in its history and having left the most detailed record of its culture, is the best subject for the study of an ancient literate society.[6] In comparing cultural phenomena, we must bear in mind that every pattern of literacy has its unique characteristics and social setting and must be understood in its own historical context, even though there were periods of contact and mutual influence.[7]

In discussing a "literate society," it is necessary to differentiate between reading ability, which is passive, and writing, which one learns because of a need and demands some practice. It is quite plausible that more people could read their own name, a simple letter or some official announcement than were able to write such texts. It is this basic ability to read which defines the broadest form of literacy in ancient Israel. Interestingly, in the two instances known to me where the question of literacy is raised in ancient Hebrew documents (Isaiah 29:11–12, Lachish letters 3, lines 8–9), it is the ability to read which is mentioned.

For the average Israelite, education was informal and sporadic, dependent upon individual abilities and the professional needs of his family. Public education was the development of a later period. It is not unlikely, however, that within the framework of the family or the occupational unit, the child did learn the fundamentals of writing.[8]

On the other hand, among professional groups which are known to have received a formal education, as in the case of the scribes, or even the priesthood in Israel, this differentiation between reading and writing abilities has less bearing. Given a set period of education and a planned curriculum for professional training, the students without doubt learned both skills equally well. Therefore one must bear in mind that the meaning of literacy varies according to the social context discussed.

Measuring the Extent of Literacy

In discussing the problem of the extent of literacy in ancient Israel, one is always asked: Are there any sources for such a study? Inevitably, that "boy" at Succoth (Judges 8:14) is recalled.[9] In essence the sources for this research, so central to an understanding of biblical society, are *not* the scattered verses about literate children (Isaiah 10:19) but rather the total product of written evidence, both sacred and profane, which was composed by mature people in Israel and among her neighbors.

It seems to me that we can overcome the methodological difficulty in determining the extent of popular literacy even at a time when no direct, absolute or objective criteria exist.[10] I propose five criteria which suggest that at least during the last two hundred years of the monarchy, ancient Israel can be termed a literate society, that is, where literacy was not limited to a closed group of professional scribes:

1. One is struck by the relatively high frequency of inscribed personal seals having no iconographic motifs, dating from the end of the Judean monarchy. It has been suggested that this was due to the Josianic reform and ban on graven images.[11] However, if we assume that the seal served a basically administrative function, declaring ownership or control, and esthetic considerations were secondary, then we must conclude that *the choice of a written word in place of a symbol or picture* indicates a growing spread of literacy.
2. Following the guidelines of F.M. Cross and J. Naveh,[12] who have discerned gradations of expertise in writing hands, it is now possible to distinguish between a formal, professional script, a free cursive script used by the intelligentsia, and a vulgar script adopted by the common folk for simple notations. *The relative ubiquity of the vulgar script* on seals, jar handles (el-Jib) and graffiti (Kh. Beit Lei, Kh. el-Qôm) would therefore be a second indicator of literacy in ancient Israel.
3. The Hebrew epigraphic finds present an array of *inscriptions that were written by and for craftsmen and farmers* clearly not of the scribal and priestly classes. This material reflects the adaptation of writing by wider circles in society such as potters, ivory joiners and builders. Special note should be made of the number of inscriptions concerning viticulture, reflecting a growing number of literate vintners.[13]
4. Contemporary with most of the epigraphic data is the flourishing of the Classical or so-called Writing Prophets of the late eighth–early sixth centuries B.C.E.[14] Moved by the imperative to write down their prophecies, they clearly saw the potential of preparing inscriptions to illustrate and popularize their message (for example, Isaiah 8:1; Ezekiel 37:16; Habakkuk 2:2). In essence the prophetic presentation or act is a striking example of *the bridging process between a literate group and a lay audience.*
5. The fifth suggested criterion of a literate society is paradoxically *the critique of writing*, noting its limitations — particularly in the educative process as well as in its exploitation for deceitful purposes by professional scribes.

In comparing the extent of literacy in ancient Israel with the widespread use of writing in classical Greece, Millard takes note of some counterarguments that "reading and writing were comparative luxuries and were often treated with suspicion, if not total hostility."[15] This supposed wariness of literacy by the great book men (philosophers and dramatists) of Classical Greece is more complex than meets the eye. It is the result of critical reflection on the differences between oral and literate means of thinking and transmission. For Plato, writing has its limitations. For him, it is actually a hindrance and not an aid to memory. Furthermore, in the educating process, it is only the dialectic, oral method which can impart the essential principles of truth. These conclusions were reached in a society where elementary alphabetic literacy was commonplace and should not be taken as evidence for limited literacy.[16]

Similarly, rabbinic Judaism, founded on a literate means of expounding the Bible, suppressed contemporaneous written compositions in favor of Oral Law. Already by the late Second Commonwealth period, elementary education had been organized along communal lines and children were studying in the *Beth Sepher* — the House of the Book. However, advanced studies were pursued in the *Beth Midrash* or *Beth Talmud* along dialectic lines under the tutelage of teachers who were "living books," or rather "a basket full of books" (TB Megillah 28b). Even the great masters in the highest academies were not allowed to bring their written notes, called *mĕgīlôt sĕtārīm* ("secret or private rolls"), to class. Despite the fact that writing was widespread, "there was an overriding injunction against putting the oral law in writing."[17]

Returning to the biblical period, it is the Classical, Writing Prophets of the eighth to sixth centuries B.C.E. who were the first to recognize and criticize the misuse of writing in the hands of jurists and wisemen. For example, Isaiah cries out:

> Ha! Those who write out evil writs
> And compose iniquitous documents.
> To subvert the cause of the poor
> To rob of their rights the needy of my people. (10:1–2)

Even more emphatically, Jeremiah reprimands the established class of literati:

> How can you say "We are wise,
> And we possess the instruction of the Lord"?
> Assuredly, for naught has the pen labored,
> For naught the scribes! (8:8)[18]

It is in the presence of a literate laity and in its wake the emergence of a new literati — be it the philosophers and dramatists of classical Greece, the Rabbis of the Roman period or the Classical Prophets during the late monarchy — that we find a reflective critique of established uses or writing. In contrast, the patterns of limited literacy found in Mesopotamia and Egypt produced only paeans to the scribe and praise for the scribal art.

In summary, it is the epigraphic fruits of biblical archaeology in conjunction with the study of the biblical text, tempered by the careful and critical use of historic method, that will help clarify the complex problems of the biblical period such as the extent of writing in ancient Israel.

Notes

1. A.R. Millard, "The Practice of Writing in Ancient Israel," *BA* 35 (1972): 98–111 and supplemented by his paper at this Congress (see p. 301–312).
2. E. Dhorme, "L'ancien Hébreu dans la Vie Courante," *RB* 39 (1930): 62–73.
3. J. Naveh, "A Palaeographic Note on the Distribution of the Hebrew Script," *Harvard Theological Reveiw* 61 (1968): 68–74.
4. F.M. Cross, "The Origin and Evolution of the Alphabet," *EI* 8 (1967): 12ff.
5. For this distinction and relevant comparative material and methods, see J. Goody and I. Watt, "The Consequences of Literacy," in *Literacy in Traditional Societies*, ed. J. Goody (Cambridge, 1968), pp. 27–68.
6. A slightly later example of a literate society is Athens of the fifth and fourth centuries B.C.E.; see F.D. Harvey, "Literacy in Athenian Democracy," *Revue des Études Greques* 79 (1966): 585–635.
7. See the enlightening study by R. Pattison, *On Literacy — The Politics of the Word from Homer to the Age of Rock* (New York, Oxford, 1982).
8. A. Demsky, "Education in the Biblical Period," *Encyclopaedia Judaica*, vol. 6 (1971), cols. 382–398.
9. For example, see the discussion in C.H. Kraeling and R.M. Adams, eds., *City Invincible, A Symposium on Urbanization and Cultural Development in the Ancient Near East* (Chicago, 1960), pp. 119ff. However, it has long been argued that the *naʿar* at Succoth was no more than a city clerk familiar with the names of the free citizens and taxpayers responsible for local decisons, and therefore a reliable source of information for Gideon's punitive force. Furthermore, it seems that Succoth was a non-Israelite enclave at that time. On the term *naʿar* as adult servant, cf. 1 Samuel 9:2, 9; 2 Kings 4:14, etc., and as administrator, see J. McDonald, "The Status & Role of the *Naʿar* in Israelite Society," *JNES* 35 (1976): 158; also H. Reviv, *IEJ* 27 (1977): 193–194. I owe the clarification of this term to Prof. A. Malamat. See also A. Demsky, "A Proto-Canaanite Abecedary Dating from the Period of the Judges and Its Implications for the History of the Alphabet," *Tel Aviv* 4 (1977):57.
10. On the methodological problem, see R.S. Schofield, "The Measurement of Literacy in Pre-Industrial England," in *Literacy in Traditional Societies* (note 5), pp. 311–325.
11. A. Reifenberg, *Ancient Hebrew Seals* (London, 1950), pp. 17, 19, 24.
12. Naveh, "Distribution of the Hebrew Script" (see note 3); F.M. Cross, "Epigraphic Notes on Hebrew Documents of the Eighth–Sixth Centuries B.C.: II. The Murabbaʿât Papyrus and the Letter Found near Yabneh-Yam," *BASOR* 165 (1962):34–46; idem, "III. The Inscribed Jar Handles from Gibeon," *BASOR* 168 (1962): 18–23.
13. See A. Demsky, "Dark Wine from Judah," *IEJ* 22 (1972): 233–234; idem, "A Note on *yyn ʿšn*," *Tel Aviv* 6 (1979): 163.
14. Y. Kaufman, *Toledoth Haʾemûnāh Hayisraelit*, vol. 3 (Tel Aviv, 1955), pp. 1–55 passim; idem, *The Religion of Israel*, tr. M. Greenberg (Chicago, 1960), pp. 349–362.
15. S. Warner, "The Alphabet: An Innovation and Its Diffusion," *VT* 30 (1980): 83.
16. See Goody and Watt, "The Consequences of Literacy" (note 5), pp. 49–55.
17. S. Lieberman, "The Publication of the Mishnah," in *Hellenism in Jewish Palestine* (New York, 1950, 1962), pp. 83–99.
18. Translations according to the New Jewish Publication Society version (Philadelphia, 1978).

Joseph Naveh

I fully agree with the conclusion drawn by Prof. Millard that in pre-exilic Judah there was a widespread use of writing. In fact, I would go even further, and actually I did so already in 1968 in a short article devoted to the distribution of the Hebrew script (*HTR* 61: 68–71), where I suggested that one has to consider the people of Judah in the late seventh century and early sixth century B.C.E. as a literate society. A society can be considered literate if, in addition to professional scribes, there are people both of the higher and lower middle classes who can write. Such a situation must surely be reflected in the styles of writing, that is, in addition to the formal cursive of the scribes, one can discern the free cursive handwriting of the educated person who is not bound by calligraphic rules, on the one hand, and the vulgar cursive writing of the unskilled person, on the other.

This assumption does not exclude the existence of such a literate society even earlier, but it certainly applies to a later period. From a practical point of view, it means that not every ostracon is an official document, and not every hoard of bullae necessarily reflects a royal archive.

Persons who knew how to read and write, or at least some of them, presumably learned these skills in schools. But I do not believe that "on every high hill and under every green tree" there was a school. At any rate, the Kuntillet ʿAjrud inscriptions and the plaster texts from Deir ʿAlla certainly were not writing exercises.

In my opinion there is not sufficient evidence for assuming that the Deir ʿAlla plaster texts were written by Israelites. True, they belong to the mid-eighth century B.C.E. and their language is certainly not Aramaic, but rather a Canaanite dialect. However, this does not necessarily indicate that the language is Hebrew, even poetic Hebrew. The script is certainly not Hebrew but Aramaic (according to Prof. Cross it is Ammonite, an Aramaic offshoot). At any rate, I would recommend avoiding fargoing conclusions based on these very fragmentary and often obscure texts.

Émile Puech

L'inscription sur plâtre de Tell Deir ʿAlla

Ma réponse se limite à l'inscription sur plâtre de Deir ʿAlla et porte sur les points suivants: datation et paléographie (araméenne ou "ammonite"?), langue et lecture, rapprochement avec la soi-disant 'école' de Kuntillat ʿAjrud.

Datation et paléographie

Depuis les premières indications données par le fouilleur,[1] la datation de l'inscription sur plâtre de Deir ʿAlla a été remontée de la période perse à la période du Fer. Sans doute les données du contexte archéologique ont-elles joué un rôle,[2] mais c'est surtout des critères paléographiques et leur discussion par les épigraphistes qui ont provoqué ce changement. L'*editio princeps* propose une date *ca* 700 av. J.C., ±25 ans[3], alors que J. Naveh, suivi par F.M. Cross, a proposé une datation *ca* 750 ou même plus tôt.[4] Dans une recension, j'avais opté pour une date *ca* 725,[5] datation paléographique qui invite l'historien à chercher des arguments de vraisemblance historique. Il est en effet préférable d'attribuer cette inscription à la période précédant la conquête assyrienne, *ca* 732, même si la destruction de la couche archéologique est due à un tremblement de terre.

En outre, depuis l'invention de l'alphabet, on doit *a priori* postuler l'existence de scribes ammonites, moabites, édomites aussi bien qu'israélites, judéens, araméens ou phéniciens, dans ces diverses entités géographiques et régionales, de scribes attachés soit au pouvoir central (palais), soit à des temples, soit à d'autres institutions plus ou moins publiques, écoles, notariats, etc. *A priori* donc, il importe de vérifier si précisément, comme l'indiquent les éditeurs et la plupart des commentateurs, l'inscription de Deir ʿAlla est paléographiquement araméenne ou si elle ne porte pas des caractéristiques de l'écriture locale, ammonite ou galaadite, pour donner un nom, cf. Juges 8, 14.

Les inscriptions de la région font encore passablement défaut mais les plus proches pour une comparaison sont les inscriptions ammonites qui se singularisent quelque peu paléographiquement des inscriptions moabites, israélites ou araméennes. Compte tenu des précautions nécessaires dans l'utilisation de l'écriture lapidaire pour dater et classer une inscription à l'encre, il s'avère que le texte sur plâtre de Deir ʿAlla se place en ligne directe de l'inscription de la citadelle d'Amman, *ca* 800,[7] et non des inscriptions araméennes qui connaissent une évolution parallèle très proche mais avec toutefois des différences. Écriture lapidaire: stèle de Zakkur, *ca* 800, de Sfiré, *ca* 740, cursive: briques de Hama, milieu 8e s., poids de Ninive, 2e moitié du 8e s. ou l'ostracon de Nimrud, fin du 8e s. (Figure 1).[7a]

En effet on ne retrouve pas à Deir ʿAlla des *ḥet* à une barre ou des *he* à trois barres parallèles ou même des *qof* à tête cursive, ni de *ʿaïn* ouverts comme sur les poids de Ninive. Non seulement toutes les lettres se situent dans l'évolution normale de l'écriture locale "ammonite", mais encore certaines d'entre elles ne s'expliquent que dans cette tradition locale: *e.g.* le *ṭet* ovale à barre unique (citadelle et sceaux), le *ṣade* avec le 'v' couché à droite (citadelle et Deir ʿAlla, nulle part ailleurs).[8] Les *bet*, *dalet* et *reš* fermés et les *alef, ḥet, kaf, lamed, mem* et *taw,* archaïques, en particulier, ont leurs devanciers directs dans l'inscription de la citadelle d'Amman et le *he* de Deir ʿAlla avec deux de ses barres écrites en 's' prépare la forme rectangulaire de celui de Siran. Force est donc d'admettre l'existence d'une tradition d'écriture locale à Deir ʿAlla, d'une guilde de scribes probablement attachés au temple, tradition très fortement influencée par la tradition ammonite, si elle n'est pas elle-même ammonite,[9] se développant selon son rythme propre et parallèlement à la tradition araméenne, sa voisine du nord, dont elle subit inévitablement des influences. Les deux courtes inscriptions de langue araméenne, portant le nom d'un même personnage, trouvées dans ce niveau, ne suffisent pas à contrebalancer cette conclusion paléographique concernant la grande inscription sur plâtre, pas plus que l'inscription sur bol récemment mise au jour immédiatement sous ce niveau.[10]

Langue et lecture

Mes remarques se limiteront à la première combinaison ainsi dénommée par les éditeurs, mais étant donnés le nouvel arrangement et la mise en place de fragments supplémentaires, il s'agit de la première partie du texte conservé (Fig. 2).

Transcription (les capitales délimitent les rubriques)

1) YSRY [.] SPR [.B]LʿM [.] B[RBʿ]R. ʾŠ.ḤŻH. ʾLHṄ. [.]hʾ wyʾtw. <ʾlwh>.ʾlhn. blylh [.w]ẏḥz[.] mḥ̇zh.
2) kmśʾ. ʾl.wyʾmrw. lb[lʿ]m. brbʿr.kh. YPʿL ḂLʾ. ʾḤRʾH. ʾŠ.LR [ʾ]Ṫ[.]MH.ŠṀʿT.
3) wyqm. blʿm.mn.mḥr [.]ḣṅ[.]ʾḥ̇[r.].l̇ṫ. yzmn. ṙ[ʾšy.] q̇ḣl̇ [.ʾ]l̇ẇḣ.wlyṁ[yn.yṣ]ṁ.wbk
4) h.ybkh.wyʿl. ʿmh.ṩlqh. [wyʾmrw.] lblʿm. brbʿr.lm.tṣm[.] ẇl̇ṁ.tbkh.wyʾ
5) mr.lhm.šbw. ʾḥ̇wkm.mh.šd[yn.ypʿlw.] wlkw.rʾw.pʿlt.ʾlhn.ʾl[h]n.ʾtyḥdw.
6) wnṣbw.šdyn.mwʿd.wʾmrw. lš[gr.]tpry.skry. šmyn. bʿbky. šm. ḥšk.wʾl.n
7) gh.ʿṭm.wʾl.smrky. thby. ḥtṫ[.bʿ]b.ḥšk.wʾl thgy. ʿd. ʿlm.ky.ssʿgr.ḥr
8) pt.nšr.wqṅ.rḥmn.yʿnh.ḥ̇[sdh.]bny.nṩṣ.wṣdh.ʾprḥy.ʾnph.drr.nšrt.
9) ywn.wṣpr[....š]myn.w[.....].mṭh.bʾšr.rḥln.yybl.ḥtr.ʾrnbn.ʾklw.
10) [y]ḥd.ḥpš [............]ṅ.štyw.ḥmr.wqbʿn.šmʿw.mwsr.gry.š
11) [gr 1/2l.]lḥkmn.yqḥk.wʿnyh.rqḥt.mr.wkhnh.
12) [1/2l.]lnśʾ.ʾzr.qrn.ḥšb.ḥšb.wḥšb.ḥ
13) [šb. 2/3l.].wšmʿw.ḥršn.mn.rḥq
14) [2/3l.]wkl.ḥzw.qqn.šgr.wʿštr.l
15) [3/4l.]k̇nmr.ḥnyṣ.hqrqt.bn
16) [3/4l.]ṁšn.ʾzrn.wʿyn

Traduction

1) ADMONITIONS DU LIVRE DE [BA]LAAM, FI[LS DE BEO]R, L'HOMME QUI VOIT LES DIEUX. Voici, les dieux vinrent vers lui la nuit [et il] vit une vision

2) comme un oracle de El et ils dirent à Ba[laa]m, fils de Beor: IL SERA RENDU SANS POSTÉRITÉ/AVENIR (?) L'HOMME DESTINÉ À VOIR CE QUE TU AS ENTENDU.

3) Et Balaam se leva le lendemain; *voici qu'apr[ès...]* il invita *les chefs de l'assemblée chez lui*, mais [deux] jours [il jeû]na et il pleura

4) abondamment et *monta son oncle Ṣelqah.* [Ils dirent] à Balaam, fils de Beor: Pourquoi jeûnes-tu et pourquoi pleures-tu? Il leur

5) répondit: Asseyez-vous, je vais vous montrer ce que les Puis[sants vont faire] et allez voir les oeuvres des dieux. Les dieux se sont réunis

6) et les Puissants ont tenu une assemblée et ils ont dit à Ša[gar:] Couds, ferme les cieux, par ton nuage (qu'il y ait) là la ténèbre et non l'é-

7) clat, leur obscurité et non ta clarté; tu provoqueras la terreur [par le nu]age de

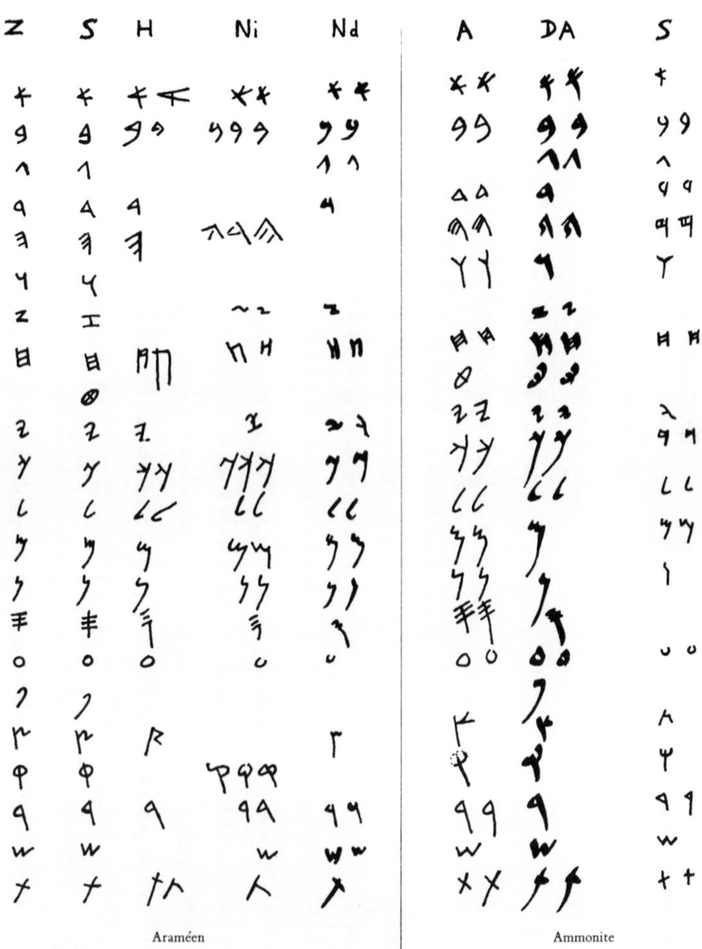

Fig. 1

Tableau comparatif de l'écriture araméenne et ammonite:

légende: Z = stèle de Zakkur; S = stèles de Sfiré; H = briques de Hama; Ni = poids de Ninive; Nd = ostracon de Nimrud; A = inscription de la citadelle d'Amman; DA = inscription sur plâtre de Deir ʿAlla; S = inscription de la bouteille de Siran

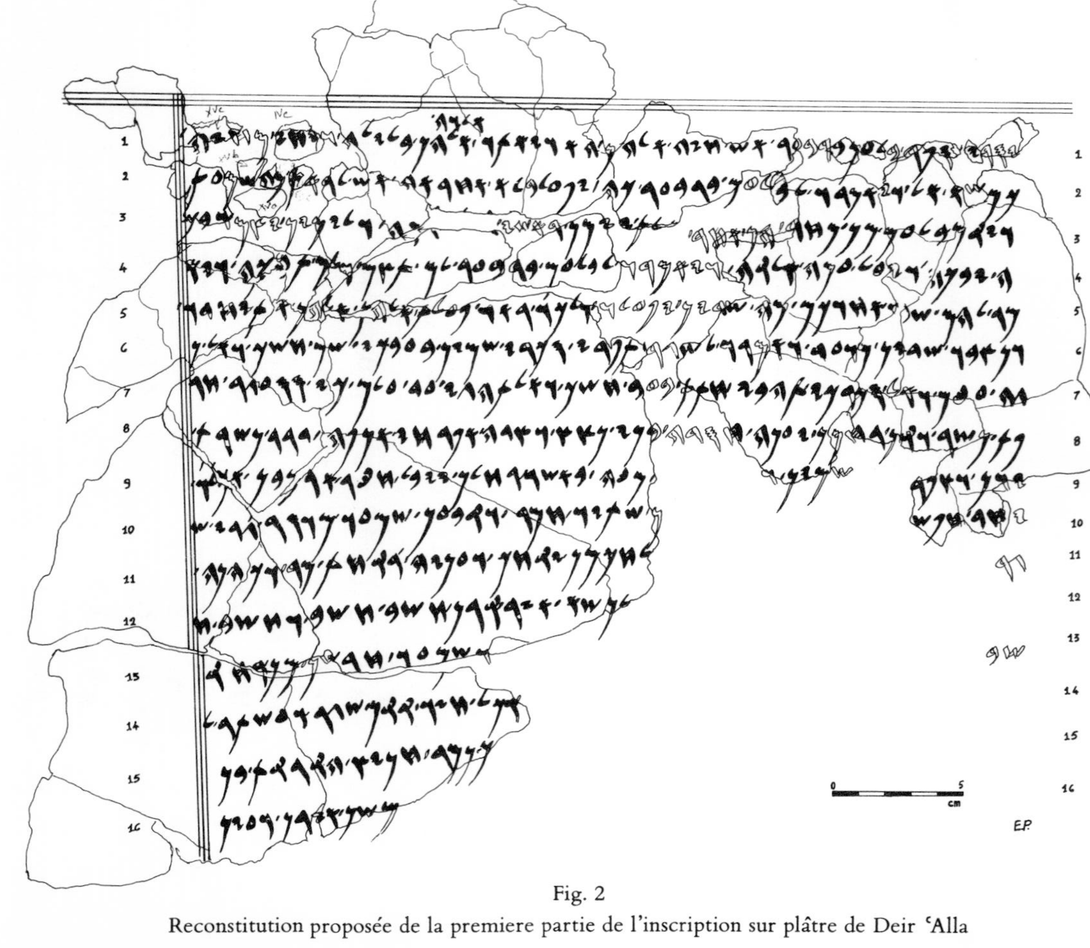

Fig. 2
Reconstitution proposée de la premiere partie de l'inscription sur plâtre de Deir 'Alla

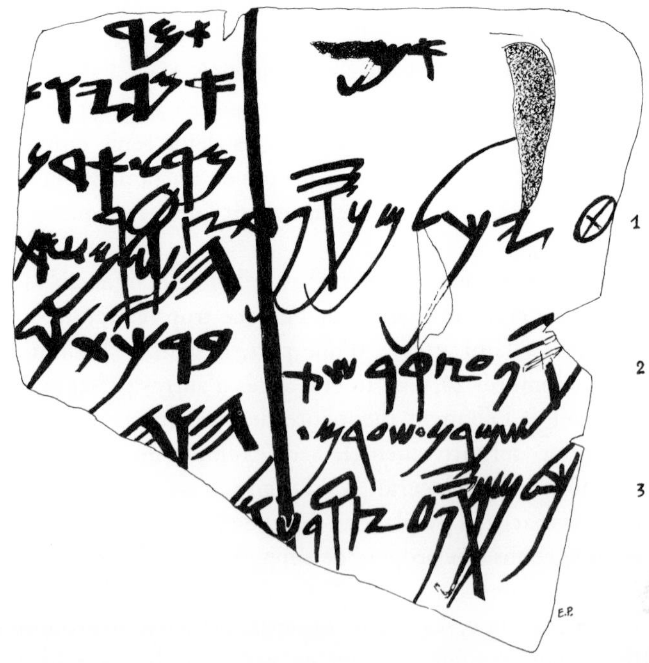

Fig. 3
Fragment inscrit de Kuntillat ʿAjrud

ténèbre et tu ne feras plus de bruit à jamais, car le passereau rail-

8) lera le rapace, la nichée des vautours l'autruche, *la ci*[*gogne*] les petits du faucon, la chouette les poussins du héron, la colombe les aigles,

9) le pigeon et le moineau [les - s (?) *du ci*]*el* et [- -]*le bâton*, à l'endroit où la houlette menait paître les brebis, des lièvres mangent

10) [en]semble,...[ ]s boivent du vin, et les hyènes écoutent l'enseignement des adversaires de Ša-

11) [gar le sot (?)] se moquera des sages et la pauvresse se parfume de myrrhe et *la prêtresse*

12) [ ]à celui qui présente la libation de la corne. Réfléchis bien et considère attentivement,

13) [ ]et les sourds entendent le loin

14) [ ]et tous voient l'oppression de Šagar et Aštar pour

15) [ ]*comme* la panthère fait fuir le goret *dans*

16) [ ]... les libations et *l'oeil/la source*

Nous acceptons le rapprochement des fragments proposé par Caquot et Lemaire. Parallèlement et indépendamment d'autres collègues, j'avais replacé les fragments VIIId et XIIc aux lignes 3 et 4. Je proposerais de placer les fragments à l'encre rouge IIIh, e et d au début de la première ligne, assurant ainsi matériellement la lecture *spr.blʿm.brbʿr,*[11] et avec des réserves, les fragments IIIc, g, XVa à l'encre rouge, XVb à l'encre rouge et noire, et IVc, XVc à l'encre noire à la fin des lignes 1 et 2, permettant de lire ainsi, lig. 1: [.*w*]*yḥz*[.]*mḥzh,* lig. 2: *ʾš.lr*[ʾ]t[.]*mh*[.]*šmʿt*. La lecture *wyḥz mḥzh* est appuyée aussi par le fragment Ve, ligne 2: *wyḥz.m*[*ḥzh,* mais qu'on ne peut placer ici vu la trace d'une ligne supérieure, et par les deux seuls emplois bibliques de l'expression dans le livre des Nombres, à propos de Balaam, 24, 4 et 16: *neʾum šoméʿa ʾimrê-ʾel ʾašer maḥazeh šadday yéḥézéh,*[12] confirmant l'appartenance des deux textes à une même tradition.

Une lecture *kmlyʾ.ʾl* (Caquot–Lemaire) au début de la ligne 2[13] est exclue à cause des traces trop basses pour un *lamed* et de l'espace trop restreint pour-*ly*. Je lis avec quasi-certitude *kmśʾ.ʾl*[14] qui atteste, d'une part, le nom de la divinité El, attendue d'ailleurs d'après Nombres 24, 4 et 16 et d'après d'autres passages concernant cette région (voir Penuel et l'élément théophore de plusieurs noms ammonites) et qui, d'autre part, élimine définitivement le seul exemple invoqué en faveur de l'état emphatique araméen.[15] On placerait XVd, ligne 2.

Pour respecter la marge, il y a place au début de l'inscription pour au moins trois au quatre lettres, et certains ont proposé de suppléer *zh* ou la forme araméenne *znh.*[16] Mais ces restaurations sont suspectes et l'une d'entre elles suppose résolue la question d'appartenance linguistique, justement au centre du débat. Je propose de placer ici le fragment IIIb, à l'encre rouge, portant un *yod*, et de lire soit [*dbr*]*y,* parfait pour l'espacement et connu d'expressions hébraïques similaires, *e.g.* 2 Rois 22, 13: *ʿl dbry spr hzh,* 16: *ʾt kl dbry hspr ʾšr...*; 23, 2: *ʾt kl dbry spr hbryt hnmṣʾ*, voir 2 Ch. 34, 30; Jér. 29, 1: *wʾlh dbry hspr ʾšr šlḥ yrmyh*; Is. 29, 18: *dbry spr;* Esd., 7, 11: *spr dbry mṣwt yhwh*, I Rois 11, 41: *ʿl spr dbry šlmh*, soit, si l'on veut placer tous les fragments à l'encre rouge, IIIf–b, *ysry,* "admonitions" (?) (la présentation matérielle de ce fragment le situe en cet endroit, d'après l'éditeur).

Dans notre reconstitution, on note que la première rubrique occupe la première moitié de la première ligne et que la deuxième rubrique occupe la deuxième moitié de la deuxième ligne, mais le sens de cette deuxième rubrique n'est pas clair. Après *ypʿl* on lit à la suite des éditeurs *blʾ* (*lʾ* certain et *b,* très probable).[17] La finale pourrait se comprendre *ʾš lrʾt mh šmʿt,*[18] avec *ypʿl* au *nifʿal*[19] que l'on rendrait littéralement: "il sera fait sans *postérité/avenir* l'homme sur le point de voir ce que tu as entendu." Il s'agit donc d'un oracle de malheur, les parallèles 'voir—entendre' sont fréquents dans les visions prophétiques de la Bible. La forme *ʾḥrʾh* est comprise comme *ʾḥrʾ–h* (suf. masc. sing.).

Ligne 3: une partie de la ligne est trop mal conservée pour proposer une restitution d'ensemble pour le moment, mais la disposition des fragments permet au moins de connaître la grandeur des lacunes. On lit *he* ou *ḥet* la première lettre cassée, puis au milieu de la ligne après des *lamed* ou *taw*, *yod* certain (Pl. 9, 1a de l'édition) et *zmn.*, certain lui aussi. A la fin, *wbk* est précédé d'une lettre à longue hampe qu'on propose de lire *mem* et de comprendre *yṣm*, cf. ligne 4, la séquence *lm tṣm wlm tbkn*. Ce verbe serait précédé du mot *wlym*[*yn*, probablement au duel, vu l'espace disponible. Auparavant, les traces pourraient convenir à]*l.ʾlwh* (malgré les décalages de la reconstitution, voir la fin de la ligne 4, par exemple). Au milieu de la ligne, la lecture *yzmn* donne la clé de ce passage en expliquant l'action prophétique qui suit (Balaam jeûne et pleure) et la réaction des invités au repas —symposium (pourquoi jeûnes-tu et pourquoi pleures-tu?). En effet, le verbe *zmn* au *piʿel–paʿel* en hébreu mishnique et en araméen signifie "convoquer, inviter", spécialement à un repas; ce sens serait donc à envisager aussi à haute époque. Le *puʿal* est connu en Esdras 10, 14 et Néh. 10, 35 et 13, 31.[20] (Oserait-on suggérer, à titre d'hypothèse, une lecture: *hn*[.]*ʾḥ*[*r.*].*lt.yzmn.r*[*ʾšy.*] *qhl*[.*ʾ*]*lwh.*, "voici, après..., il invita les ch[efs de] l'assemblée chez lui"!).

A la ligne 4, le mot *ʾlqh* n'est pas certain mais une lecture *ʾlwh* parfois proposée[21] n'est pas à retenir, le *qof* semble paléographiquement assuré alors que l'*alef* l'est moins; dans ce cas, n'aurait-on pas la séquence *wyʿl ʾlwh ʿmh*, cf. ligne 1? Une lecture *ṣlqh* serait sans doute meilleure. On connaît en effet un Ammonite *ṣlq,* preux de David, II Sam. 23, 37=I Ch. 11, 39, à côté de *ʾlqʾ*, il est vrai, mais de Harod, II Sam. 23, 25. Le mot *ʿmh* peut signifier "avec lui", "son clan/peuple" ou "son oncle". Dans le cadre d'un repas où Balaam semble avoir invité 'ses' gens, probablement sa famille, le sens "son oncle" convient apparemment le mieux, en particulier si on l'appose à *ṣlqh*, nom propre ammonite. On restituerait ensuite [*wyʾmrw*] *lblʿm.* Il est probable que le sujet pluriel du verbe, supposé par *lhm*, ligne 5, est à lire dans les mots mal conservés, lig. 3, (*rʾšy qhl*?).

On complète ainsi ligne 5: *mh.šd* [*yn.ypʿlw.*]*wlkw.rʾw.pʿlt. ʾlhn*[.]*ʾl*[*h*]*n., ʾtyḥdw* avec le vocabulaire du contexte immédiat, *pʿlt*, lig. 5 et *šdyn*, lig. 6.[22]

Ligne 6: le nom d'une divinité féminine est exigé dans la lacune à cause du verbe *tpry* et des suffixes *-ky*. Caquot–Lemaire préfèrent lire *šmš*, féminin en ugaritique *špš*, mais rarement en hébreu et en araméen. On retiendra la lecture *šgr*, mentionnée lig. 14, car on se demande ce que le Soleil a affaire avec les ténèbres et les nuages.[23] Il n'est pas question d'une éclipse solaire mais de l'obscurcissement du ciel par de sombres nuages. En revanche, *šgr* accompagne *ʿštr*, lig. 14, et on imagine mieux que la déesse commandant les nuages (et la pluie) aille de pair avec *ʿštr* de laquelle relèvent les rites de fécondité (Dt. 7, 13; 28, 4, 18, 51). Faut-il rattacher *bʿbk* à ce qui précède ou à ce qui suit? On préférera le lire avec la suite, ce que suggèrent les couples antonymiques *ḥšk wʾl ngh* et *ʿṭm wʾl smrky*; pour *ʿb*, "sombre nuage", voir Is. 25, 5 et Job 22, 14. On lit sûrement *ʿṭm* avec les éditeurs et Weippert et non *ʿdm* ou *ʿlm.*[24] Le mot *ʿṭm* se rattache à la racine *ʿṭh* qui signifie, en hébreu, "s'envelopper" mais "détruire" en syriaque, "couvrir, cacher" en arabe et "être sombre" en akkadien, *eṭû*, *eṭûtu* signifiant justement "l'obscurité". Le mot est ici avec le suffixe masc. pluriel. en parallèle antithétique avec *smrky*[25], suf. fém. sing. On comprendrait "couds, ferme les cieux, par ton nuage (qu'il y ait) là l'obscurité et non l'éclat, (que soit) leur ténèbre et non ta clarté.

Ligne 7: on accepte la proposition de Caquot–Lemaire de restaurer *ḥtt* qu'on complétera par [*bʿ*]*b.ḥšk*, "tu provoqueras la terreur par le nuage d'obscurité".[26]

Ligne 8: Dans la liste des noms d'oiseaux, on suivra Caquot–Lemaire pour la lecture *wṣdh*, "la chouette" mais Weippert pour *qn.rḥmn.yʿnh,* "la nichée des vautours l'autruche" et on lirait *ḥet* la première lettre cassée, probablement pour *ḥsdh,* "la cigogne",[27] puis *bny nṣṣ*, "les petits du faucon", avec Lemaire, communication ci-devant.

Ligne 9: *šmyn* déjà proposé dans ma recension.

Ligne 10: on lit *yḥd* au début et on comprend *gry šgr* à la fin, "les adversaires de Šagar", non "des chacals", Caquot–Lemaire.

Ligne 12: *lnśʾ. ʿzr.qrn* est à comprendre au sens cultuel, après la mention *wkhnh*, "la prêtresse", ligne 11. L'offrande *ʿuzr* est bien attestée à Ugarit, en phénicien et en punique, comme l'a récemment montré H. Cazelles.[28] Le *ʿuzr* concerne généralement un liquide (stimulant). On ne sera donc pas surpris de trouver ici la mention de *qrn*, "la corne", pour le liquide justement, et le verbe *nśʾ*, au participe, du vocabulaire cultuel cananéen et non *qrb*, araméen. Ce mot au pluriel est peut-être à lire encore, ligne 16.

Ligne 15: On lirait *kaf* devant *nmr*, "comme la panthère".

La lecture de cette première partie de l'inscription montre assez éloquemment que la langue n'a rien de fondamentalement araméen, même si l'un ou l'autre mot ou forme araméens s'y sont glissés, tels *ʿll* (?), *qrq*, *ḥwy* (?), *yhb* (?), du fait du voisinage immédiat du royaume de Damas. Faut-il faire appel à l'origine araméenne de Balaam, comme le voudrait le texte biblique, Nb. 22, 5 et 23, 7? Cela ne s'impose pas. Quoi qu'il en soit, le devin devait parler un langage compris des gens du pays, ce que semble appuyer la présence de l'oncle ammonite *ṣlqh*, ligne 4. Le pluriel en *nun* n'est pas étranger en Transjordanie puisqu'il est attesté sur la stèle de Mésha, en moabite. On note l'absence de l'état emphatique et du relatif *zy*, typiques de la langue araméenne, mais le *ʾetpeʿel*, *ʾtyḥdw*,[29] et le phonème *ḍad* rendu par *qof*, en *hqrqt*, comme dans l'araméen archaïque. Le suffixe fém. *-ky* n'est pas exclusivement araméen puisqu'il est attesté en phénicien et en punique et déjà dans les gloses cananéennes d'el-Amarna, et la forme *-(w)h* dans *ʾlwh*, *ʿmh*, *ʾḥrʾh* est probablement connue aussi en moabite.[30] L'absorption du phonème ẓ > ṭ présupposée par la lecture *ʿṭm*, n'est pas vérifiée dans notre interprétation *ʿṭ-m*[31]. En revanche, on rencontre dans ce texte bien des caractéristiques cananéennes, dans la conjugaison, *nifʿal, wyqtl*, le vocabulaire, *rʾh, nśʾ*, *pʿl*, *ʿzr* et des expressions communes avec le passage des Nombres 22–24 (*wyḥz mḥzh, šdyn, ʾl, wyʾtw ʾlwh ʾlhn blylh // wybʾ ʾlhym ʾl blʿm lylh*, Nb. 22, 20, *wyqm blʿm mn mḥr //wyqm blʿm bbqr*, Nb. 22, 13, 21, *qbb*, Nb. 22, 11, 17,...) qui dénotent une tradition locale commune, connue par le scribe de Deir ʿAlla et par la Bible. L'élément *br* dans le nom ne dénote pas nécessairement l'origine araméenne du devin, ni sa langue. On connaît Kilamuwa, *bar* Ḥayʾa, dans une inscription phénicienne de Zendjirli ou des Bar–Abbas, Bar-Kosba, etc., qui n'ont rien d'araméens, contrairement aux Bar-Hadad, ... Ce mot est trop commun pour servir de trait caractéristique.[32] En outre, le nom Balaʿam peut être ammonite, l'élément *ʿm* y est fort utilisé, ʿAmminadab, Elîʿam,... à la base même de l'ethnie, ʿAmm.[33]

Dans l'état actuel de la recherche, l'oracle du devin Balaam appartient à cette région, ce que l'onomastique, la langue de cette première partie et la paléographie prouvent sans conteste, mais on ne peut en conclure que cette tradition est spécialement ou exclusivement israélite.[34] Elle est avant tout un "produit" local[35] et la situation géographique et historique expliquent suffisamment les influences linguistiques et scribales araméennes du voisin du nord, transformé parfois en occupant. A titre d'hypothèse, on verrait assez bien les influences araméennes sur le langage et la paléographie dater de l'époque de la longue occupation ou domination araméenne sur la région au IXe s. et l'emprunt de ces traditions par l'Israël du nord sous la domination de Jéroboam II, au début du VIIIe s., voir aussi Michée 6, 5.

Deir ʿAlla et l'"école" de Kuntillat ʿAjrud

Enfin, on n'oserait rapprocher Deir ʿAlla et Kuntillat ʿAjrud au sujet des écoles de scribes, car je ne crois pas à une école de scribes à Kuntillat ʿAjrud où on y aurait appris à écrire. L'exemple du pithos avancé récemment par A. Lemaire dans son livre "Les écoles et la formation de la Bible..."[36] s'oppose aux conclusions qui en sont tirées, (figure 3). Il n'y a pas sur ce pithos de témoignage d'un apprentissage de l'écriture de l'alphabet par un élève. La prétendue copie, alphabet 2, est antérieure à celle des alphabets 1 et 3, attribués à une même main, celle du maître pour Lemaire. Cette dépendance serait encore plus difficile dans la mesure où la copie, selon la lecture de cet auteur, porterait un ordre différent *ʿaïn-pe* au lieu de *pe-ʿaïn*. Les alphabets 1 et 3 n'appartiennent pas à une même "école" et ne sont pas contemporains de l'alphabet 2, voir le *šin* particulier de 1 et 3 qu'on retrouve à Arad.[37] En outre, l'alphabet 2 est bien disposé à droite d'une ligne verticale servant de marge au texte écrit antérieurement aux alphabets 1 et 3 qui le chavauchent. De plus, l'alphabet 1, écrit sur l'anse (*ṭet* et *yod*), montre que l'espace disponible était plus restreint que lorsque l'auteur de l'alphabet 2 écrivit le sien. Il en résulte que l'alphabet 2 est donc antérieur aux deux autres, écrits par la même main, et ne peut donc pas être la copie de l'élève.

Il n'y a pas non plus deux mots répétés (maître–élève) mais *šmrn* et *šʿrm*. Enfin la salle aux banquettes n'est pas une salle de classe mais de dépôts d'offrandes, comme l'a suggéré le fouilleur.[38]

On n'allait pas de Palestine à Kuntillat ʿAjrud dans le Sinaï pour apprendre à écrire mais ceux qui passaient par Kuntillat ʿAjrud savaient écrire. Les alphabets peuvent avoir une tout autre signification.

Notes

1. H.J. Franken, Texts from the Persian Period from Tell Deir ʿAlla, *VT*, 17, 1967, 480s.
2. H.J. Franken–M.M. Ibrahim, Two Seasons of Excavations at Tell Deir ʿAlla, 1976–1978, *ADAJ*, 22, 1977–1978, 57–79 et M. Ibrahim–G. van der Kooij, *Archiv für Orientforschung*, 29, 1983–1984, 260–263, 262s, phase IX =phase M avec de la céramique du VIII e s. et un changement de technique céramique après la phase M.
3. J. Hoftijzer–G. van der Kooij, Aramaic Texts from Deir ʿAlla, *Documenta et Monumenta Orientis Antiqui, XIX,* Leiden 1976.
4. J. Naveh, The Date of the Deir ʿAlla Inscription in Aramaic Script, *IEJ,* 17, 1967, 256–258; F.M. Cross, *BASOR*, 193, 1969, p. 14, note 2, mais *BASOR*, 212, 1973, p. 12, début VI e s., p. 14, début VIIe s. J. Naveh, Inscriptions of the Biblical Periods, dans *Recent Archaeology in the Land of Israel,* ed.

by H. Shanks–B. Mazar, Jerusalem, 1984, p. 65, considère l'écriture ammonite comme araméenne.

5. *RB*, 85, 1978, 116.
6. A. Caquot–A. Lemaire, Les textes araméens de Deir ʿAlla, *Syria*, 54, 1977, 189–208. On saura gré aux auteurs pour leur importante contribution dans la compréhension de ce texte.
7. Cette écriture n'a rien de typiquement araméen comme le voudrait F.M. Cross, *BASOR*, 193, 1969, p. 14, qu'il date ca. 875–825 ou *BASOR*, 212, 1973, p. 13, voir É. Puech–A. Rofé, L'inscription de la citadelle d'Amman, *RB*, 80, 1973, 531–546. L'écriture des sceaux ammonites en particulier et de l'inscription de Siran confirme cette évolution, voir H.O. Thompson–F. Zayadine, *BASOR*, 212, 1973, 5–11.

7a. Voir maintenant É. Puech. L'inscription de la statue d'Amman et la paléographie ammonite, RB, 92, 1985, 5–24, 12s, où l'ostracon de Nimrud est identifié comme ammonite et non araméen.

8. On ne partage pas les remarques de Caquot–Lemaire, *op. cit.,* p. 191, sur *ḥet* et *ṣade*.
9. F.M. Cross, *BASOR*, 193, 1969, p. 14 et note 2, en fait un texte ammonite.
10. J. Hoftijzer, Note on a Newly Found Text Fragment on a Bowl from Deir ʿAlla, *ADAJ*, 22, 1977–1978, 79–80, en fait un texte araméen mais la lecture de ce fragment peut être tout à fait différente.
11. Eliminant *ʾ]mr[y.blʿ]m* de P.K. McCarter, The Balaam Texts from Deir ʿAlla: the First Combination, *BASOR,* 239, 1980, 49–60, 51.
12. Eliminant la reconstruction *[.wyʾmrw.ʾlw]h* présupposée par Caquot–Lemaire et acceptée par H.-M. Weippert, Die "Bileam"-Inschrift von Tell Der ʿAllā, *ZDPV*, 98, 1982, 77–103 et McCarter, *op. cit.,* *[.wymllw.l]h.* Cette lecture est aussi celle de J.A. Hackett, The Dialect of the Plaster Text from Deir ʿAlla, *Orientalia*, 53, 1984, 57–65.
13. Acceptée par McCarter.
14. Proposition faite indépendamment par A. Rofé, *The Book of Balaam (Nb. 22, 2–24, 25): A Study in Methods of Criticism and the History of Biblical Literature and Religion*, with an Appendix: Balaam in the Deir ʿAlla Inscriptions, Jerusalem 1979, suivi par Weippert et B.A. Levine, The Deir ʿAlla Plaster Inscriptions, *JAOS*, 101, 1981, 195–205.
15. Caquot–Lemaire, suivis par M. Delcor, Le texte de Deir ʿAlla et les oracles bibliques de Balaam, *Sup. VT*. 32, 1980, 52–73. G. Garbini, L'iscrizioni di Balaam Bar-Beor, *Henoch*, 1, 1979, 166–188, lit *kmlʾ.ʾl* et H.P. Müller, Die aramäische Inschrift von Deir ʿAlla und die älteren Bileamsprüche, *ZAW*, 94, 1982, 214–244, 216, propose *kmt?ʾ.ʾl*, suivant Hoftijzer. L'autre exemple invoqué par Hoftijzer, *škmtʾ*, ligne 3s, repose sur une mauvaise lecture.
16. Müller suivi par Millard (communication orale). Levine, *op. cit.*, lit *zh.*
17. Ainsi Weippert, mais *zdʾ*, Garbini, est exclu ainsi que *gdʾ*, Caquot–Lemaire.
18. McCarter, *op.cit., 51*–52, lit *zy š]mʿt* mais cette restitution suppose résolu le problème de la langue. En II, 8, cette forme n'est pas à retenir.
19. Ch.-F. Jean–J. Hoftijzer, *Dictionnaire des inscriptions sémitiques de l'ouest*, Leiden 1965, (cité DISO) p. 232, *s.v.* Le *nifʿal* est connu en phénicien et on ne voit pas de sens clair à la forme *qal* dans ce passage puisque les sujets précédents sont au pluriel.
20. Voir *DISO*, *s.v.*, signification incertaine. Une lecture *ymn*, McCarter, *op. cit.,* pp. 51s, n'est pas à retenir, pas plus que la finale *wlyk* [*l.lʾkl.*].
21. McCarter, Levine, Lemaire (*supra*).
22. Partiellement avec McCarter et Levine, *šd[yn.pʿlw.*]. L'espace suppose une lettre supplémentaire et le sens demande un imparfait de préférence. Une lecture *šg (yn/t)*, Caquot–Lemaire, n'est pas à retenir car elle introduit *a priori* un aramaïsme patent sans preuves suffisantes.
23. Ringgren a déjà fait cette remarque, d'après une note de Delcor, *op. cit.,* p. 55, note 15. On ne voit pas non plus ce que viendrait faire le Shéol dans ce passage, McCarter.
24. *ʿdm*, Caquot–Lemaire, sans parallélisme en sémitique, suivis par Garbini, ou *ʿd/ṭm*, Müller, *ʿlm*, McCarter.
25. Tous les commentateurs ont lu *smrky*. L'interprétation "ton timon" de Caquot–Lemaire ne fait pas

de sens dans ce contexte, pas plus que *skr*, "verrous" dans le premier emploi, suivis par Weippert.

26. La lecture *ḥt*, Weippert, est trop courte et ne rend pas compte de la trace suivante.
27. McCarter a proposé de lire *ḥsd* mais il faut ajouter un *he* pour l'espace. Pour les oiseaux, *cf.* G.R. Driver, Birds in the Old Testament, *PEQ,* 87, 1955, 5–20 et 129–140.
28. H. Cazelles, *ʾUzr* Ugaritique et *ʾzr* phénico-punique à travers des travaux récents, dans *Atti del I congresso internazionale di studi fenici e punici, Roma 1979*, Rome 1983, 673–75. Notre interprétation était faite quand on a pris connaissance de celle de Müller, mais ce dernier n'y a pas joint *qrn*.
29. L'occurrence des *ʾitpeʿel* ou *ʾitpaʿal* est discutée par J.C. Greenfield, recension dans *JSS*, 25, 1980, 248–252, p. 251, mais acceptée par Levine.
30. J.C. Greenfield. *op. cit.*, 250 et F.M. Cross–D.N. Freedman, *Early Hebrew Orthography*, New Haven 1952, p. 38.
31. Ce phénomène invoqué par Hotfijzer a été contesté avec raison par J.C. Greenfield, *op.cit.*, p. 251, pour *ẓ* > *ṣ* dans *ʿṣh* et *ytʿṣ* en II, 9.
32. On connaît l'usage de *bn* dans des inscriptions araméennes, voir pour une époque plus récente J. A. Fitzmyer–D. Harrington, *A Manual of Palestinian Aramaic Texts,* Rome 1978, 312, s.v. et de *br* dans des textes hébraïques, voir P. Benoit—J.T. Milik–R. de Vaux, *Les grottes de Murabbaʿât,* Oxford 1961, 294 s.v.
33. Voir en outre l'anthroponyme *ṣlqh* et la fréquence de l'élément *ʾl* dans l'onomastique ammonite, K.P. Jackson, Ammonite Personal Names in the Context of West Semitic Onomasticon, dans *The Word of the Lord Shall Go Forth* (Essays in Honor of D.N. Freedman in Celebration of His Sixtieth Birthday), ed. by. C.L. Meyers–M. O'Connor, Winona Lake, 1983, 507–521, 518, s.v.
34. Voir B. Levine, communication *supra.* L'auteur en fait une production locale mais de population israélite. A bon droit, il ne retient pas la dénomination araméenne pour la langue et propose de distinguer le langage religieux, avec des aramaïsmes dans ce texte, des fragments araméens trouvés dans le même niveau qui peuvent appartenir à la langue administrative, au moins depuis la domination de Reçin de Damas.
35. Greenfield, *op. cit.*, conclut aussi à un dialecte cananéen et, selon toute vraisemblance, ammonite, p. 251. Il n'y a pas de preuves suffisantes pour en faire un dialecte araméen, fut-ce poétique, comme le voudrait McCarter, *op. cit.*, pp., 50s.
36. A. Lemaire, *Les écoles et la formation de la Bible dans l'Ancien Israël, OBO* 39, 1981, 25–32.
37. Y. Aharoni, *Arad Inscriptions,* Jerusalem 1981, Insc. 103; F.M. Cross, Two Offering Dishes With Phoenician Inscriptions from the Sanctuary of Arad, *BASOR*, 235, 1979, 75–78. On se demanderait si un quelconque rapport ne doit pas être établi entre Arad et Kuntillat ʿAjrud.
38. Z. Meshel, The Israelite Religious Centre of Kuntillet ʿAjrud, *Bulletin of the Anglo-Israel Archaeological Society,* 1982–1983, 52–55, p. 52.

Alexander Rofé

It is my conjecture that the Deir ʿAlla inscription is Midianite. This is not a desperate proposal of an unknown language for an unintelligible piece of writing, but rather an attempt to apply the method of history of tradition current in Bible criticism to what meaning can be made out of these already famous fragments.

If the inscription covered a stele, or stelae in a sanctuary as indicated by Franken and Hoftijzer, then its function should have been that of a *hieros logos*. In that case the two "combinations" would relate to each other as the two parts of one story: in the first — a doom prophecy of drought and waste (with many biblical analogies); in the second — the prevention of calamity with some sort of ritual act. Most expressions in the second part are ambiguous; indeed, they may refer either to death, the grave and the netherworld, or to a merry making of love. But at the beginning of this portion (line 4) we read: "Young woman, be sated with love" (עלמה רוי דדן), and further on (line 8) we find "from testicles of men and from thighs" (מן פחזי בני אש ומן שקי). Therefore the sequence of the second "combination" seems better to befit love affairs than the eternal rest of death. And since in line 7 there is also a "house to benefit a guest, and to benefit a bridegroom there" (בית ליעל הלך וליעל חתן שם), the most natural solution at hand is that the stele commemorates the institution of sacral prostitution at this temple, in order to enhance fertility and avert drought and desolation.

Turning now to the biblical tradition, one finds two distinct phases in the tradition about Balaam. At first, in the oldest sources, he is an Aramean, a prophet to the Lord, indeed not one affected by undue modesty but still faithful to the Lord's command. Later, in the Priestly Document, he is considered a wicked sorcerer, of Midianite origin, identified as the one who set the Moabite-Midianite girls to whore with the Israelites at the sanctuary of Baal Peor. What caused this shift in the tradition about Balaam? And where lie the origins of the Priestly Document's new conceptions?

If we have understood the meaning of the second "combination," we already possess half of the answer: the Priestly Document describes Balaam in the way he was conceived by a non-Israelite people settled in the Central Jordan Valley by the end of the eighth century B.C.E. But then in turn, on the basis of the Priestly Document, we are able to identify this foreign people, the people who so fondly conceived of Balaam as the founder of their cult of sacral prostitution: the Midianites.

The Midianites are placed in this area by several biblical passages. The war of Midian in Joshua 13 and that of Gideon in Judges 6–8 are fought respectively in and toward central Transjordan. In the story of Joseph, a Midianite caravan traveling to Egypt crosses the Dothan Valley. Perhaps at the time of the inscription, Deir ʿAlla was a way station on the spice-road leading from South Arabia to the Mediterranean coast, Phoenicia and Egypt.

Discussion

F.M. Cross: I would like to clarify my statement that literacy spread like wildfire. It appears that literacy did not spread slowly, since the period of transition between a rigidly conventionalized pictographic script and the exceedingly deft cursive was only 400–500 years. I believe Profs. Naveh and Millard agree with me on the speed involved.

Concerning the analysis of the Deir ʿAlla script, I am in agreement with Émile Puech, regardless of the name he applies to it — a national script of Transjordan, Ammonite with national peculiarities or whatever. This script has traits uncommon to the Aramaic of Damascus or of Syria, and its typological features are not identical with the mainstream of Aramaic in the central Aramaic areas.

I believe that the language of Deir ʿAlla is in the Canaanite sphere. Here, too, much depends on terminology. I again agree with Puech and Naveh that no definite article is found here. And I think the morphology of the verb is pure Canaanite (though some such occasional features are also found in Aramaic). What is important is that we agree on how to describe the material. Very frequently our viewpoints are not as different as the labels we use to describe them.

M. Weinfeld: At first I associated the Deir ʿAlla inscription with Kuntilet Ajrud where we have a syncretism of Yahweh, Asherah and Baʿal. I thought that perhaps Deir ʿAlla was another instance of syncretism, possibly Israelite. However, we do not have there any indication of the tetragrammaton, so probably it is just pure "foreign" material. In regard to the date of the Deir ʿAlla inscription, I previously ["The Deir ʿAlla Inscriptions," *Shnaton* 5–6 (1981–1982) (Hebrew)] pointed out the similarities to Neo-Assyrian inscriptions and also to biblical material relating to threats and curses about desolation, which I would date to the time of the Assyrian invasion ca. 720 B.C.E.

Concerning the *delet*, "column of writing," mentioned by Alan Millard, in the special session at the Knesset, we heard Prof. Yuval Neʾeman referring to a passage from Baba Meẓiʿa, the "middle" of the three "gates" in Seder Nezikin. *Baba* is like *delet*. I think these concepts originate in pages or pericopes; *delet* may originally have meant a page or a column in a papyrus, but later some kind of pericope or tractate. We can understand the three *babas* only on the basis of such concepts, starting with *delet*.

Concerning Dr. Demsky's response, *naʿar* and its Akkadian equivalent *ṣuḫāru* do not refer to a young boy, but rather to a professional, in this case a scribe, as is well attested in later literature. Metatron, the *safra rabba*, the "heavenly great scribe," is also called a *naʿar*.

J. Balensi: Quelle est l'exacte identité des habitants de Deir ʿAlla à l'époque de l'inscription de Balaʿam? La réponse jaillira d'une étude comparative des cultures matérielles de la Vallée du Jourdain. Mener à bien une telle étude exige d'être familiarisé avec les archives matérielles des deux rives; ce qui malgré tout n'est pas impossible. Et nous pressentons que la réponse doit être cherchée du côté de la proposition de É. Puech. Deux remarques s'imposent à propos de la communication de B. Levine.

D'une part, nous savons qu'au Bronze Récent II il y avait à Deir ʿAlla un sanctuaire, mais nous ne sommes pas sûrs qu'il y ait eu un village. En revanche au Fer I, il semble qu'il y ait eu un village, mais le sanctuaire n'est pas connu. Il est alors difficile de postuler une continuité du lieu de culte. Cette lacune nous oblige à la prudence aussi longtemps que de nouvelles fouilles ne viendront pas renouveler le débat.

D'autre part, quels sont les arguments qui permettent de parler d'une Deir ʿAlla "philistine?" Les tablettes demeurent à ce jour une énigme et seraient, de toute façon, antérieures à la destruction qui marque la fin du Bronze. La céramique dite "Philistine" publiée par Franken, issue des quatre phases A à D (Fer I) est originale et présente un décor proche du "Monochrome" (Myc. IIIC local); rien ne peut être encore affirmé quant à son origine. Elle diffère sensiblement de la céramique du sud de la Plaine du Sharon. Les tessons "Philistins" de Deir ʿAlla peuvent accuser une influence égéenne sur le Levant (répercussion de l'immigration, ateliers locaux) mais on ne saurait ignorer que certains motifs, comme les oiseaux ou les demi-cercles concentriques, appartienment aussi au répertoire "Midianite." Je ne vois pas qu'on puisse parler aujourd'hui de Deir ʿAlla comme site philistin, quand bien même on assimilerait "Philistins" à Peuples de la Mer.

Pour revenir à l'inscription de Balaam, le problème est surtout ethnique et géo-politique, L'identification du site avec la Succoth biblique a été avancée. Les habitants (Phase M = IX) étaient-ils israélites du Nord, araméens, ammonites, ou pourquoi pas, une communauté mêlée? Que leur culte gêne par son hétérodoxie est un fait au regard des prescriptions bibliques. Pourtant l'argument ne porte pas: ou bien les prescriptions sont celles du culte postexilique et l'argumentation tombe du fait du décalage chronologique; ou bien le culte "israélite" de Deir ʿAlla est entaché d'idolâtrie. Dernière hypothèse: Deir ʿAlla n'était pas israélite.

La recherche n'a de sens que dans le cadre d'une étude régionale. D'une part, dans une meilleure compréhension globale des différences culturelles entre le versant oriental de la Samarie et le piémont de Galaad. D'autre part, dans l'originalité mieux admise de la Deir ʿAlla du 8ᵉs., quand la synthèse sera possible pour cette rive orientale du Jourdain avec les publications de T. es-Saʿidiyeh, T. Mazār et Pella. Ce qui ne saurait tarder.

D. Barag: There is need for a note of caution in judging the extent of the practice of writing prior to the eighth century B.C.E. mainly on the basis of sigillography. Prof. Avigad and others have shown that very few Hebrew seals are to be ascribed to a date prior to that century, while very large numbers date from the eighth century, perhaps not even very early in that century, and mainly from the seventh century B.C.E. and later. This concerns not only Judah and Israel but practically seems to be the general case. The number of known stamped jar handles from excavations is slowly increasing and, as far as I know, no tenth or ninth century B.C.E. level has yet yielded a handle bearing a private or, for that matter, royal seal.

B. Levine: Let's talk about syncretism. What I have tried to point out is that there was more than one pattern of cultic practice. The Bible is constantly talking about the infiltration or pollution of cults at established Yahwistic sites, and this is a constant target for prophetic denunciation. Such cults could have coexisted. I am quite certain that if there was a temple to Yahweh at Samaria — and there might have been — there was also a temple to Baʿal, whether within the city or outside. This is not syncretism. For syncretism to have taken place, there would have to be a situation in which the name of Yahweh occurs alongside that of some other god or goddess, that is, some form of a pantheon. This obviously is not the case at Deir ʿAlla.

A. Lemaire: I agree with what has been said on literacy, but we cannot think of schools in antiquity as we do of them today. Only the finding of true schoolboy abecedaries, exercise letters and the like at a given site can indicate the existence of a school. The finds at Kuntilet Ajrud and at Kadesh-Barnea point to the existence of schools there.

F.M. Cross: The new material from Tell Mazār in Jordan is exceedingly important and belongs to the same group of inscriptions. There is a parallelism between the Heshbon and Tell Mazār material current in the sixth century B.C.E. and then shifting to a fully conventional Aramaic script in the fifth century B.C.E. Not only must the Deir ʿAlla material be compared to the ʿAmmān Citadel inscription, but we must link up the sequence to these later Transjordanian scripts. I have dated in print the Deir ʿAlla material to 700 B.C.E. plus or minus twenty-five years, after the Assyrian conquest. And this material is of non-Israelite origin.

I think the key to judging the speed of the spread of literacy is the rate at which a script evolves. Just as language tends to evolve faster in urban areas, so scripts change with extreme use. The transition in the character of Hebrew script between the tenth and the ninth centuries B.C.E. was rapid and the development of the cursive extraordinary. The use of seals is, in part, a cultural pattern, and I do not think it can serve as an indication of the spread of literacy in Israel.

J.C. Greenfield: The separation of reading and writing is complex. Probably everyone who could read could also write enough to append his own signature; but some could possibly sign without knowing how to read. Nevertheless, in the light of Millard's paper and the responses, I tend to assume that, on the whole, literacy included both skills. In general in regard to literacy, I would like to emphasize that in most societies in which writing exists, we find its use simultaneously for commercial, legal and communication needs as well as for the transmission of literary texts. In the biblical period, the Book of Jeremiah refers to both the writing of a land transfer document and a bill of divorce on the one hand, and to the writing down of the prophets words on the other.

Concerning the Deir ʿAlla plaster inscription, I doubt whether it has even one Aramaic trait. I would rather agree that it was written in a dialect which may be a branch of Ammonite or in some other Canaanite dialect. Suffice it to say that the Deir ʿAlla inscription remains for me a pagan text totally outside of the Israelite orbit, despite the efforts of B. Levine to bring it under the wings of ʾEl. I wish to record my sense of awe of those scholars who have achieved an integrated understanding of this difficult and fragmentary text, its context and religious background.

Baruch Levine mentioned Job. It was long ago pointed out that Job often replied in the language or dialect in which he was addressed. In other words, the Book of Job is not necessarily in pure Hebrew but in a variety of languages skillfully manipulated by the author. In the same way, one does not necessarily have to take everything in the Book of Job as of Yahwistic or Israelite content.

Now I would like to refer to M. Weinfeld. Are you really sure that there was syncretism at Ajrud? Are you sure that the reference is to the goddess Asherah, even though the Hebrew grammar is not in character. Perhaps the reference to Baʿal was made by a Phoenician who passed by, and should not be connected to the main shrine.

Finally, I would like to note our gratitude to E. Lipiński for continuing to share with us information about the Aramaic-Assyrian archives from the Gozan-Ḫarran area. The Aramaic texts on which he is working are indeed difficult, but the discovery of their Assyrian counterpart has made their interpretation easier. Nonetheless, as Lipiński has shown, comprehensive knowledge and hard work are needed to interpret them.

SESSION VII
THE DEAD SEA SCROLLS

PART I: THE HALAKHA AND THE DEAD SEA SCROLLS

HARRY M. ORLINSKY, Session Chairman, *Hebrew Union College–Jewish Institute of Religion*

LAWRENCE H. SCHIFFMAN, *New York University*
Purity and Perfection: Exclusion from the Council of the Community in the *Serekh Ha-ʿEdah*
JOSEPH M. BAUMGARTEN, *Baltimore Hebrew College*
Halakhic Polemics in New Fragments from Qumran Cave 4
ELISHA QIMRON, *Ben-Gurion University of the Negev*
JOHN STRUGNELL, *Harvard University*
An Unpublished Halakhic Letter from Qumran

PART II: EARLY CHRISTIANITY AND THE DEAD SEA SCROLLS

PIERRE BENOIT, O.P., Session Chairman, *École Biblique et Archéologique Française*

HARTMUT STEGEMANN, *Universität Göttingen*
Some Aspects of Eschatology in Texts from the Qumran Community and in the Teachings of Jesus
DAVID FLUSSER, *The Hebrew University of Jerusalem*
The Sons of Light in Jesus' Teaching and in the New Testament

Discussion

Purity and Perfection: Exclusion from the Council of the Community in the *Serekh Ha-ʿEdah*

Lawrence H. Schiffman

The *Serekh Ha-ʿEdah* ("Rule of the Congregation") 1:25–2:11 contains a description of the council of the community which the Dead Sea sect expected to constitute in the end of days. This description begins with a summary of the functions of this assembly which include: serving as the highest court of the sect, deciding the sectarian interpretation of Jewish law and declaring war. The text continues with a list of those leaders and sages of the sect who are expected to take their places in the assembly, and then turns to the subject of this study, those who are to be excluded from the council because of impurity, physical impairment or advanced age (1QSa 2:3–11):

וכול איש מנוגע [באחת מכו]ל טומאות האדם אל יבוא בקהל אלה
וכול איש מנוגע ב[אלה לבלתי] החזיק מעמד בתוך העדה וכול
מנוגע בבשרו נכא[ה רגלים] או ידים [פס]ח או [עו]ר או חרש או
אלם או מום מנוגע [בבשרו] לראות עינים או איש ז[קן] כושל
לבל[ת]י התחזק בתוך העדה אל יב[ואו] אלה להתיצב [בתוך] דעת
[אנו]שי השם כיא מלאכי קודש [בעצ]תם
ואם יש [דבר לאחד מ]אלה לדבר אל עצת הקודש [ו]דורש[יהו] מפיהו ואל
תוך [העדה לוא] יבוא האיש כיא מ[נוגע ה]וא

And any man who is afflicted[1] [with any one of][2] the human uncleannesses[3] shall not enter into the congregation[4] of these.[5] And anyone who is afflicted with [these so as not to][6] take (his) stand[7] among the congregation:[8] And any who is afflicted in his flesh,[9] crippl[ed in the legs][10] or the hands, [lam]e or [blin]d[11] or deaf or dumb, or if he is stricken[12] with a blemish [in his flesh] visible to the eyes; or a tottering o[ld] man who [can]not maintain himself[13] among the congregation; these may not en[ter] to take (their) stand [among][14] the congregation of the [me]n of renown, for holy angels [are in their coun]cil. But if one of these has [a matter][15] to say to the council of holiness,[16] [then] he shall examine [him] directly [lit. "from his mouth"] but among [the congregation] the man [shall not] enter for h[e is af]flicted.[17]

Our passage is made up of several parts: 1QSa 2:3f. contains a blanket prohibition to the effect that anyone who is impure may not enter into the council of the community; 2:4–7 prohibits those afflicted with various physical deformities or diseases from participation in the council; 2:7 prohibits the aged from taking part; 2:8f. indicates that the reason for these prohibitions from participation in the council of the community in the end of days is the presence of the holy angels in the council. Finally 2:9–11 provides that an official take a deposition in the event that such a person desires to present a matter to the council. Each one of these regulations will be considered in detail.

The Impure

1QSa 2:3f. prohibits anyone who is stricken with any of the "impurities of man" from entering the council of the community in the end of days. The key to this prescription is the interpretation of the words *ṭumʾot ha-ʾadam*. J. Licht correctly notes that the text is referring here to a variety of ritual impurity, rather than to some kind of a blemish or deformity. He maintains that this phrase refers to all forms of impurity. The phrase is derived from *ṭumʾat ʾadam* which occurs in Leviticus 5:3 and 7:21. Our author adapted the phrase and used it in the plural. The context in Leviticus 5:3 indicates that this phrase refers to impurity of the dead as well as those impurities which are imparted to a person by virtue of the various bodily fluxes. It is no doubt the intention of the author of the *Serekh Ha-ʿEdah* to include these varieties of impurity, hence the use of the plural. Therefore, we may safely conclude that our text includes all forms of ritual impurity which a person may contract.[18]

This entire prescription can be compared with a passage in the War Scroll (7:3–6). Indeed, as noted by Y. Yadin,[19] the regulations which were in effect for the eschatological council of the community were similar to those for the eschatological battle. That passage (DSW 7:4f.) provides that:

או איש מנוגע בטמאת בשרו כול אלה לא ילכו אתם למלחמה

...or a man who is afflicted with an impurity of his flesh, all these shall not go with them to battle.

This sentence is similar in wording to our text except that *ṭumʾat besaro*, "an impurity of his flesh," appears where the *Serekh Ha-ʿEdah* uses *ṭumʾot ha-ʾadam*. DSW 7:5f. juxtaposes these impurities to another type, that of one who had a seminal emission:

וכול איש אשר לוא יהיה טהור ממקורו ביום המלחמה לא ירד אתם

And any man who is not pure in regard to his sexual organs[20] on the day of battle shall not join them in battle....[21]

Yadin notes the dependence of this regulation on Deuteronomy 23:11f. According to him, those who have experienced seminal emissions are not excluded completely from the battlefield, yet they cannot take part in battle until they have been purified.[22] Yadin notes that this formulation is less severe than that regarding women and children who are excluded from the camp. He therefore suggests that those impure as a result of seminal emissions "may have served away from the actual battlefield."[23] While Yadin was certainly correct in noting that the formulation appears less severe, the source in Deuteronomy would indicate that those who had experienced seminal emissions were to be excluded from the camp until they had completed their required ablutions.

Yadin suggests that the expression *ṭum'at besaro* is meant to include all the forms of disease listed in Leviticus 13. Indeed, this verse does contain the word *besaro* and may be the basis of the non-Pentateuchal term *ṭum'at besaro*. According to verse 46, such temporary diseases result in exclusion from the desert camp of Israel. On the other hand, it is possible that this phrase in the War Scroll refers to all impurities other than that resulting from seminal emission. Nevertheless, *ṭum'ot ha-'adam* in *Serekh Ha-ʿEdah* most probably refers to all impurities, including that resulting from a seminal emission. If so, the laws for battle (not conscription) are in this case the same as those for the council of the community.

A parallel to this prescription is found in TS 45:7–12:

ואֿ[יש] כי יהיה לו מקרה לילה לוא יבוא אל כול המקדש עד אשר
[יש]לים שלושת ימים וכבס בגדיו ורחץ ביום הראישון וביום
השלישי יכבס בגדיו ורחץ ובאה השמש אחר יבוא אל המקדש ולוא
יבואו בדנת טמאתמה אל מקדשי וטמאו ואיש כיא ישכב עם אשתו
שכבת זרע לוא יבוא אל כל עיר המקדש אשר אשכין שמי בה שלושת ימים

And if a m[an] has a nocturnal emission he may not enter the entire sanctuary until he [com]pletes three days. And he shall launder his clothes and wash on the first day, and on the third day he shall launder his clothes and wash. Then after the sun has set, he may enter the sanctuary. They may not enter my sanctuary in their time of impurity so as to render it impure. And when a man has sexual relations with his wife he may not enter the entire city of the sanctuary wherein I cause my name to dwell for three days.[24]

Yadin has discussed the connection between this regulation and that of DSW 7:6.[25] He noted that the sect interpreted the laws of the camp from the Bible to refer to the "city of the sanctuary" (*ʿir ha-miqdash*), which, in his view, is the entire city of Jerusalem. B. Levine, on the other hand, has argued that the city of the sanctuary is in fact the Temple Mount,[26] a view already taken by L. Ginzberg based on the Zadokite Fragments.[27] In any case, we certainly have a similar prescription. Yadin cited as the basis of the purificatory rituals described here the account of Israel's purification in preparation for the Sinaitic revelation in Exodus 19:10–15, a passage which also served as the basis for the requirement of purification for the sectarian assembly in the end of days which is described in 1QSa 1:25–27. For our purposes, the passage shows that a seminal emission renders a man impure and forbidden to enter the sacred precincts. In the same way, in Yadin's view, such people were unable to participate in the battle at the end of days and in the Messianic Council of the Rule of the Congregation.

Yadin considers the Temple Scroll to be part of the corpus of the documents of the Dead Sea sect. There has been some dispute on this point.[28] If one takes the view that the Temple Scroll reflects the work of a similar and in some way related group, which was part of the Qumran sect's library, then it is not in fact certain if the sect would have subscribed to all the regulations of this scroll. Nonetheless, the Temple Scroll and the other Qumran manuscripts certainly demonstrate the close affinities among the various sectarian circles of the Second Commonwealth.

TS 45:15–18, further down the same page as the passage we have just discussed, supplies further information:

וכול איש אשר יטהר מזובו וספר לו שבעת ימים לטהרתו ויכבס
ביום השביעי בגדיו ורחץ את כול בשרו במים חיים אחר יבוא
אל עיר המקדש וכול טמא לנפש לוא יבואו לה עד אשר יטהרו
וכול צרוע ומנוגע לוא יבואו לה עד אשר יטהרו

And any man who becomes pure from his issue (gonorrhea), shall count for himself seven days for his purification, and launder his clothes on the seventh day, and wash all his flesh in living waters. Afterwards, he may enter the city of the sanctuary. And anyone who is impure by impurity of the dead may not enter it (the city of the sanctuary) until they (sic) are purified. And any *ṣarua*ʿ and one stricken may not enter it (the city of the sanctuary) until they are purified.[29]

This passage enumerates several classes of individuals excluded from the sanctified precincts until they have completed their purification rituals. These include the gonorrheac, one who had contracted the impurity of the dead, one afflicted with the various forms of disease listed in Leviticus 13, and one who had contracted the skin disease so often and inaccurately translated as "leprosy." These impurities are most probably the very same ones termed *ṭum*ʾ*at besaro* in the War Scroll. These persons are impure by virtue of causes other than that of seminal emission, and they are to observe the laws of purification listed in the Torah before reentry to the city of the sanctuary. These same people are forbidden even to enter the military camp according to the War Scroll.

That the Tannaim also forbade those with gonorrhea and *ṣara*ʿ*at* from entering the Temple precincts is a foregone conclusion based on the Torah's explicit laws in this regard. Numbers 5:2–3, as pointed out by Yadin, required that such people be excluded from the camp.[30] This was taken by the Tannaim to prescribe that gonorrhea restricted those afflicted with it from entering the Temple precincts. In fact, the Tannaim forbade the one afflicted with *ṣara*ʿ*at* from entering the entire city of Jerusalem.[31] Deuteronomy 23:11 had indicated to the Tannaim that one who had had a seminal emission was to be excluded from the Temple Mount.[32] There was no question that all such people could neither serve as priests nor participate in the fulfillment of the commandment of pilgrimage.

The situation is somewhat different regarding one who had contracted the impurity of the dead. Numbers 5:2 had classed the *ṭame' la-nafesh* with the gonorrheac and the person afflicted with *ṣaraʿat*. Yet the Tannaim saw the *ṭame' la-nafesh* as disqualified only from entry to the Temple courtyard (*ʿazarah*).[33] Nonetheless, such a person would have been excluded from priestly service and from fulfilling the commandment of pilgrimage to the Temple.

The Exclusion of the Physically Deformed

Several categories of physical deformity disqualify those afflicted from participation in the sectarian assembly of the end of days. This entire passage is based on Leviticus 21:16–24 which requires that the priests serving in the sanctuary not be afflicted with particular deformities or blemishes.

The phrase *nekhe raglayim*, "crippled in the legs," occurs in 2 Samuel 4:4. The Targum translates *laqe be-tarten riglohi* as "crippled in both legs." Because Jonathan's surviving son was crippled in both legs, he was disqualified from serving as king. This interpretation suggests that our text would refer to one who was crippled in both legs. Despite the use of the root *psḥ* as a description of this condition by the author of 2 Samuel, it is clear that the author of the *Serekh Ha-ʿEdah* does not consider these terms to be synonymous. While the phrase *nekhe yadayim*, "crippled in the hands," does not occur in the Bible, it is likely that this phrase refers to one who is deprived of the use of both hands.

These two categories of prohibition are clearly derived from the regulation of Leviticus 21:19 that a priest suffering from a *shever ragel* or a *shever yad* is prohibited from performing the sacrificial service. The problem is that the exact meaning of these terms in the Bible cannot be determined. From the translations of the Vulgate and the Septuagint,[34] and from Tannaitic sources,[35] it would appear that the reference is to fractures which have not healed properly and which have left the priest somewhat deformed.[36] If so, the *nekhe raglayim* and *yadayim* ought to be similarly interpreted. We have no way of knowing if the sect would have included in this category similar deformities which were congenital, as did the Tannaim.

The Tannaim had no trouble in distinguishing the *pisseaḥ*, whom we will discuss below, from the one suffering the *shever ragel*.[37] The former was one who limped, either in one or both legs. The latter, however, was deformed outwardly. In other words, the one with the *shever* would be disqualified even if he walked perfectly, whereas the *pisseaḥ* was disqualified even if his legs looked normal. If the sect's exegesis made the same distinction as that of the Tannaim, we could conclude that the *nekhe raglayim* and *yadayim* suffered either in one or both limbs, and that the distinction was that the *pisseaḥ* walked with a limp whereas the *nekhe raglayim* was outwardly deformed.

From biblical passages it seems that the *ʿiwwer* is blind in both eyes and therefore cannot see at all.[38] One cannot speculate as to how blindness was defined, but some passages seem to indicate that inability to find one's way was the decisive factor, not reading as in our society.

Nonetheless, the Tannaim interpreted the blindness which is mentioned in Leviticus 21:19 as referring even to one blind only in one eye. Indeed, they widened the meaning of the term *ʿiwwer* to include those suffering from other eye ailments and deformities,[39] besides those mentioned in Leviticus 21:20. We cannot be certain how the sect took this verse, and, therefore, what the specific definition of the blind man was. It would seem probable, though, that the sect in its stringency would have interpreted the Torah to exclude those with the greatest variety of deformities and blemishes from the priestly service in the Temple.

Our list of disqualifications in the *Serekh Ha-ʿEdah* deviates from the pattern of Leviticus 21 in including the *ḥeresh*, "deaf," and *ʾillem*, "dumb." These have been included as a result of scriptural exegesis which taught the sect that these two categories were also to be disqualified from the priestly service. The combination *ʿiwwer* and *pisseaḥ* occurs in a number of passages, including Leviticus 21:18. It should be noted that Deuteronomy 15:21 classes *ʿiwwer* and *pisseaḥ* as blemishes which disqualify a first-born animal from sacrifice. The difficult account of 2 Samuel 5:6–8 relates that when David attacked Jerusalem, the Jebusites taunted him saying that the blind and the lame would turn back his advance. In commemoration of his victory, it was said, presumably at a later date, that the blind and the lame may not enter the Temple (*ha-bayit*). This passage must have greatly influenced our text. Further basis for the sect's views, however, was Exodus 4:11 which links the *ʿiwwer* with the *ʾillem* and *ḥeresh*. The sect reasoned, basing itself on this passage, that the same disqualification applied to the *ḥeresh* and *ʾillem* as applied to the *ʿiwwer* in Leviticus 21:18.[40]

The nominal use of *ḥrš* in the Bible makes it clear that it is one who does not hear.[41] In other words, both ears do not function. The biblical deaf person was often unable to speak since he had been deaf from youth. This is how a root which normally means "to be silent" could be the basis of a noun describing a deaf person. Tannaitic opinion recognized two kinds of *ḥeresh*. One type neither hears nor speaks, and is, therefore, considered legally incompetent. This person was congenitally deaf and therefore never learned to speak. The second is one who is deaf but does speak. Such a person had learned to speak before becoming deaf.[42]

Tannaitic halakha disqualified the *ḥeresh* from performing the priestly service in the Temple.[43] While it is most probable that this refers to one who neither speaks nor hears, some later traditional scholars think it might have applied also to one who could speak but could not hear.[44] Further, the *ḥeresh* was exempt from the obligation of pilgrimage to the Temple on the three festivals.[45] This appears to refer only to the one who neither speaks nor hears and who, therefore, is mentally incompetent.[46] Nevertheless, some Tannaim understood this exemption to include those who could speak but could not hear (as well as those who could hear but could not speak). Some Amoraim ruled that one who was deaf even in one ear was exempted from this commandment.[47] It is difficult to determine on the basis of these parallels how far the sect might have gone in its disqualifications. It should again be emphasized that the sect's desire to insure ultimate perfection and purity might have led them to exclude even the most minimally unfit.

The term *ʾillem* in the Bible denotes one who cannot speak.[48] The Tannaim understood this to refer to one who heard but could not speak.[49] In other words, such a person was physically unable to speak, as opposed to the type of *ḥeresh* who could not speak as a result of his inability to hear. Some Tannaim ruled that such persons were exempt from the requirement of pilgrimage on the three festivals.[50] The sect learned from Exodus 4:11 that the *ʾillem*, like the *ʿiwwer*, was to be excluded from priestly service, and, hence, from participation in the eschatological council.

The term *menugaʿ*, "afflicted," occurs four times in our text from the *Serekh Ha-ʿEdah*. The first occurrence (line 3), as we have already seen, refers to those stricken with forms of ritual impurity. The second (line 4) is in a general statement which introduces the list of disqualifications due to physical deformity. The third (line 5) and fourth (line 6) refer to various types of blemishes, termed *mumim* by the Bible and the Rabbis. The first of these types of blemishes is referred to by the phrase *menugaʿ bivsaro*, "afflicted in his flesh." This phrase clearly represents an exegesis of the phrase *ʾasher bo mum* in Leviticus 21:17. Our text uses *bivsaro* as an explanation of the Bible's *bo* which was somewhat vague. One afflicted with such a condition, in the view of the sectarians, was prohibited not only from performing the priestly service in the Jerusalem Temple, but also from participating in the sectarian eschatological assembly.

Some Tannaim did, however, accord certain subsidiary priestly privileges to priests with blemishes.[51] While the Tannaim differentiated the permanent blemish (*mum qavuaʿ*) from the temporary blemish (*mum ʿover*), they saw both as prohibited by this verse.[52] This seems to be the interpretation of the sect.

In line 7f. the *Serekh Ha-ʿEdah* excludes also one afflicted with a blemish in his flesh "visible to the eyes" (*li-reʾot ʿenayim*). This phraseology exactly matches that of the Tannaim, but it seems that the meaning of the usages in the two literatures is not the same. To the Tannaim, certain conditions prohibited those afflicted from performing the priestly service, *mipene marʾit ha-ʿayin*.[53] The exact meaning of this phrase is itself difficult to determine. The correct view seems to be that these people were excluded because of the unattractiveness of these conditions.[54] To the Tannaim, these were not conditions which the Torah had excluded. To the sect, though, the phrase *lirʾot ʿenaw* designated those afflicted with the temporary blemishes, those termed *mum ʿover* by the Tannaim. Both the Tannaim and the sect took the view that the Torah had prohibited priests with these conditions from performing the Temple service. The sect saw such people as excluded from the eschatological council of the community as well.

A parallel to our passage may be cited from DSW 7:4. Among those who are excluded from participation in the eschatological battle are:

וכול פסח או עור או חגר או איש אשר מום עולם בבשרו

...every lame man or blind man, or cripple or a man who has a permanent blemish in his flesh.

This passage is extremely helpful for the interpretation of our text, since many of the same people are disqualified in both lists. The *ḥigger* ("cripple") of the War Scroll is the *nekhe raglayim* of the *Serekh Ha-ʿEdah* who has an improperly healed fracture which leaves him deformed. Even if he walks properly, his presence will in some way defile the military camp, so he may not go to war. The lame (*pisseaḥ*), as above, is the one who limps, even if his limbs are formed properly. Such a person, not only for practical military reasons, but also for reasons of sanctity, cannot go to war with the armies of the sect. In regard to these deformities, the sect has the same requirements for the eschatological council as it has for the battles of the end of days. The correspondence has led J. Carmignac to suggest that the War Scroll version is dependent on that of the "Rule of the Congregation."[55] Yet in regard to blemishes, the laws are not the same. Only a permanent blemish disqualifies one from battle, while even a temporary blemish prevented participation in the council of the community at the end of days.

Some note should be taken of the usage of *ḥigger* in Tannaitic texts. The Tannaim encountered difficulty in differentiating the *pisseaḥ* from the *ḥigger*, and various later commentators have offered explanations.[56] Suffice it to say that the *ḥigger* was exempted from the commandment of pilgrimage.[57] An Amora took this law as applying even if his condition affected only one leg,[58] and priests with this condition were disqualified from priestly service.[59] We have already seen how the sect distinguished these two categories.

The passage from the War Scroll makes no mention of the blind, the one with a fractured arm which has healed improperly, the deaf and the dumb. While it is most likely that such people were not intended to go to war with the sect, this is not stated explicitly. It is possible that the author of the War Scroll did not see the deaf and dumb as excluded by the law of purity, since he did not make the connection with Exodus 4:21 which we have noted above.

There is also a parallel to our passage in CDC 15:15–17. As is, this passage is extremely fragmentary in the medieval manuscripts. J.T. Milik has identified a manuscript of this text from cave IV, which has been given the siglum 4QDb. Milik has suggested the following restored translation,[60] without publishing the text:

Fools, madmen (*mšwgʿ*), simpletons and imbeciles (*mšwgh*), the blind [lit., those who, being weak of eye, cannot see], the maimed (*ḥgr*), the lame, the deaf, and the minors, none of these may enter the midst of the community, for the holy angels (are in the midst of it).

Now this passage must be compared with our listing. It seems to us that the initial mention of the fools and madmen is actually the end of the previous sentence, as can be shown from comparison with the medieval fragments in our possession. The remaining designations are the subject of the prohibition. While Milik sees this text as excluding the classes of people listed from entrance to the sect, comparison with our text and the conclusions to be reached below would recommend a different interpretation. Most probably, this text, upon publication, will be seen to refer to entrance into the assembly of the sect, a privilege denied to those listed. This passage is certainly referring to the present age. Indeed, all those prohibited from the eschatological assembly are the very same ones who could not attend the *moshav ha-rabbim* in the present, for in the present the sect lived in such a way as to emulate and prepare for the way of life of the end of days. Detailed analysis of this passage, however, will have to await its publication in the original Hebrew.

A partial parallel to the disqualification of the deformed may also be cited from TS 45:12–14:

כול איש עור לוא יבואו לה כול ימיהמה ולוא יטמאו את
העיר אשר אני שוכן בתוכה כי אני ה׳ שוכן בתוך בני
ישראל לעולם ועד

No blind man may enter it [the city of the sanctuary] for their entire life so that they will not render impure the city in which I dwell. For I am the Lord Who dwells among the children of Israel for ever.[61]

This passage is found immediately after the excerpt from the Temple Scroll quoted above. It prohibits the blind from entering the sacred precincts. Yadin has already noted that this passage is based on Leviticus 21:18. He suggested that the actual meaning of the passage is that all of the deformities listed in the Leviticus passage disqualify the subject from entry to the city of the sanctuary and that the blind man was only given as an example.[62]

It is difficult to maintain that the material dealing with the other deformities has been omitted by scribal error from our manuscript of the Temple Scroll, since a second fragment apparently preserves the very same text.[63] It is possible to propose an alternate restoration for the fragment such that it would include one or two additional deformities, but Yadin's restoration in light of the 11Q manuscript of the complete scroll is certainly most probable. Yet it is difficult to see how the word *ʿiwwer*, "blind man," could have been used as a general term by the author of the Temple Scroll. It is more likely that the omission of the other deformities found in Leviticus 21 from the Temple Scroll is to be explained as an oversight of the author(s).[64]

The Aged

Our passage also excludes from the assembly an elder who stumbles so as not to be able to take his stand there. The absence of the technical use of the root *kšl* in the Bible makes the precise definition of this term difficult on philological grounds.[65] Indeed, the usual usage of this verb in biblical literature is to designate moral or religious stumbling. Only comparison of this regulation with similar prescriptions in other Qumran texts will avail.

Several passages make clear that to the sect, the age of sixty was the appropriate age for retirement from serving as judge, military leader, or sectarian official. CDC 10:7–10 explicitly states that judges must not serve beyond the age of sixty because senility sets in at this age. After a description of the ten men who must be appointed as judges, the text specifies their ages:

...מבני חמשה ועשרים שנה עד בני ששים שנה ואל יתיצב עוד
מבן ששים שנה ומעלה לשפוט את העדה כי במעל האדם מעטו ימו
ובחרון אף א־ל ביושבי הארץ אמר לסור את דעתם עד לא ישלימו
את ימיהם

...from twenty-five years old[66] to sixty years old. But let no one over sixty years old take his stand[67] to judge the congregation. For because of man's transgression,[68] his days[69] diminished, and because of God's wrath[70] with the inhabitants of the earth, He decided to remove[71] their understanding before[72] they complete their days.

What exactly is meant by "God's wrath with the inhabitants of the earth"? It is tempting to suggest that it refers to Adam's fall, yet *ha-ʾadam yosheve ha-ʾareṣ* ("the inhabitants of the earth") could not properly be used to describe Adam and Eve but must mean mankind in general. Jubilees 23:11 and Rabbinic parallels[73] suggest that it was in the times of Abraham that senility began to appear and man's life span was no longer as great as before.

The War Scroll, in the beginning of the very same column to which we have referred so often in this study, limits the age of military service to those under sixty years of age. Specifically the passage tells us that (DSW 7:1):

וסורכי המחנות יהיו מבן חמשים שנה ועד בן ששים שנה

The camp prefects shall be from fifty to sixty years old.

This age is the highest of all those mentioned in the Scroll, and it is apparent that the role of *sorekhe ha-maḥanot* was given to the oldest men still serving in the eschatological army. While it would be understandable that older men would not be efficient in a military context, their exclusion must also have been the result of the desire to insure perfection and purity in all the military operations of the sect.[74]

The biblical laws of Levitical service indicate that the Levites were prohibited from serving after the age of fifty. Numerous passages fix this age limit: Numbers 4:3, 23, 30, 35, 39, and 47. Yet Yadin points out that Numbers 8:25f. allows those beyond age fifty to discharge certain lesser tasks. So too, in the War Scroll men were not allowed to go into battle after age fifty but were allowed to function as *sorekhe ha-maḥanot*, camp prefects, until the age of sixty.[75]

Yadin has suggested that the sect determined that military service ended at age sixty by means of a legal *midrash* of Leviticus 27:3 which interprets Numbers 8:25.

While Numbers 8:25 indicates that some sort of service is possible for Levites after age fifty, it does not specify for what length of time it may continue. Leviticus 27:3, however, states: "Then thy valuation shall be for the male from twenty years old even unto sixty years old." Rabin explains that sixty represents the "limit of full value."[76]

The very same maximum age was in effect for the priest in charge of mustering the assembly, probably to be identified with the *paqid*. CDC 14:6 prescribes:

והכהן אשר יפקד אש הרבים מבן שלושים שנה עד בן ששים

And the priest who shall muster[77] the assembly[78] [shall be] from thirty to sixty years old.[79]

In view of the parallels regarding judicial and military service, it seems that the *ʾish zaqen koshel* is one who has passed the age of sixty years. From that age on he is not to be allowed to take a stand among the council of the community. For the sect, apparently, priests were to cease their service at the age of sixty. This is probably another correspondence between the law of disqualification from the priesthood and that of entry into the eschatological council of the sect.

Tannaitic law provides that the *zaqen* ("elder") is exempt from the commandment of pilgrimage.[80] Such an elder is undoubtedly to be understood as one who has grown too old to be able to walk sufficiently well to make the pilgrimage.[81] It is also possible that this definition ought to be applied to the "tottering old man" of the *Serekh ha-ʿEdah.*

The Presence of the Angels

Our text gives a specific reason for its requirements of purity, absence of those with specific deformities, and the aged. According to the *Serekh Ha-ʿEdah,* the angels are regarded as being in the assembly. DSW 7:6 gives the very same reason for the requirement that those impure from a seminal emission do not participate in the eschatological battle.

כיא מלאכי קודש עם צבאותם יחד

For holy angels are together with their armies.

B. Bokser suggests that this is actually a reworking of Deuteronomy 23:15 which explains the requirement of ritual purity in the military camp as resulting from the presence of the Lord. Bokser maintains that the divine presence is represented here by the angels.

A parallel to this very concept occurs in DSW 12:7f. where it is stated that the angels are fighting alongside the members of the sect:

כיא קדוש א־דוני ומלך הכבוד אתנו עם קדושים גבו[רים
ו]צבא מלאכים בפקודינו וגבור המלח[מה] בעדתנו וצבא רוחיו
עם צעדינו

For the Lord is holy, and the King of Glory is with us. A people of holy ones, her[oes and]a host of angels is mustered with us, and the Mighty One of wa[r] is in our congregation, and the hosts of His spirits marches with us [lit. "is with our steps"].[82]

It was a cardinal belief of the sect that just as the world below is divided into the domains of the two spirits, those of good and evil, so is the world of the angels. Just as the teacher of righteousness and the wicked priest represented the forces of good and evil to the sect in the present age, so the Prince of Lights (the angel Michael) and his enemy, Belial, represented the very same forces on high. These forces would be arrayed against each other in the end of days, just as they are in the present pre-Messianic age.[83]

The great eschatological battle would be fought, therefore, both in heaven and on earth. The actual battle would be a simultaneous and mutual one, in which the angels and men would fight side by side. After the long series of engagements described in the War Scroll, the forces of good would be victorious. For this reason the sect believed that in the end of days the angels would be present in the military camp described in the War Scroll. At the same time, the eschatological council would also involve both the earthly and heavenly sons of light.

The appearance of the very same reason for the prohibitions in our text from the *Serekh Ha-ʿEdah* and in the War Scroll may allow another important conclusion. DSW 7:3–4 provides that women and children are to be excluded form the military camp:[84]

וכול נער זעטוט ואשה לוא יבואו למחנותם בצאתם מירושלים
ללכת למלחמה עד שובם

No young boy[85] or woman shall enter their encampments when they go forth from Jerusalem to go to battle until they return.

It is most likely that the very same regulation was in force regarding the eschatological council. Although women and children would be part of the sect, as is evident from 1QSa 1:6–11, their presence among the angels in the council of the community would not be allowed, as it was not in the military camp of the battle inaugurating the end of days.[86]

Deposition by the Disqualified

That those disqualified from the eschatological council were still expected to be part of the sect in the end of days can be seen from the last prescription of our text. It indicates that if one of those disqualified from the council wished to present a matter for consideration by that body, it was to be done by deposition. The text does not indicate who would take the deposition, but it is to be assumed that some official, perhaps the *mevaqqer* ("examiner"), would discharge this function.

This passage most probably provides insight into the conduct of the sect in the present age as well. Apparently, in the everyday life of the sect, those who were impure or disqualified for reasons of physical deformity were not permitted into the sectarian assembly, the *moshav ha-rabbim*. Such people, however, could be members of the sect and were allowed representation by deposition. Such deposition was given to the *mevaqqer* who then presented it before the sectarian assembly. In this way the opportunity was granted for all members of the sect to be heard in the assembly, without compromising the all-important requirement of ritual purity and perfection of the highest level.

Indeed, this seems to be the ruling of CDC 14:11f. for the present age:

> ולכל דבר אשר יהיה לכל האדם לדבר למבקר ידבר לכל ריב ומשפט
>
> And regarding any matter about which any man has to speak to the examiner, let him speak regarding any [legal] case or judgement.[87]

Those who could not consult the council, the *moshav ha-rabbim* in the present age, would give depositions to the examiner. Only in this manner could the petitions or questions of such individuals be considered. Once again, we have seen that the life of the sect in the present was to mirror its legislation for the end of days.

Conclusion

The Dead Sea sect, in seeking to achieve the highest standards of purity and perfection in the end of days, maintained the exclusion of certain classes of those afflicted with impurity, physical deformities or old age from the eschatological assembly. These prohibitions were derived from Leviticus 13 and 21, passages regarding the disqualification of priests from Temple service. After all, the sect saw itself as constituting a sanctuary through its dedication to a life of holiness and purity. It therefore extended the Torah's legislation regarding the priesthood to the eschatological assembly. It is most probable that the very same regulations were in force in the present age, in which the sect lived in preparation for and in expectation of the dawn of the eschaton. Indeed, the sect expected that very similar regulations would be in effect regarding the camp in the eschatological war. The author(s) of the Temple Scroll believed that prescriptions of the same sort would govern the Temple to be constituted in his (their) view in the pre-Messianic period. The eschatological council described in the *Serekh Ha-'Edah* would represent what the Qumran sect believed was the highest standard of purity and perfection. Only in this way could the sectarians, together with the holy angels, live the life of the future age.

Notes

1. Translating in light of Psalm 73:5 which is the only case of the *puʿal* of *ngʿ* in the Bible. Note that *ʾadam* occurs in that verse. On the other hand, the use of this root in the *qal* in Leviticus 5:3 which has clearly influenced our passage might require a translation, "who has come in contact with..." J. Licht, *Megillat Ha-Serakhim* (Jerusalem, 1965), ad loc., notes that this verb in Tannaitic usage refers only to houses and garments (cf. M. Negaʿim 13:6–7, etc.) but not to people.
2. Restored with the traces by Licht, *Ha-Serakhim* (see note 1) and by H. N. Richardson, "Some Notes on 1QSa," *JBL* 76 (1957): 115.
3. Translation in new JPS of Leviticus 5:3, see below.
4. Cf. Deuteronomy 23:2–9, Lamentations 1:10 and Nehemiah 13:1. While prevalent exegesis has taken this usage as referring to the prohibition on marriage, Lamentations 1:10 and our text seem to take this as referring to a prohibition on entry into the Israelite sancta, represented by the Temple in Lamentations and the sectarian eschatological assembly in our passage.
5. D. Barthélemy and J.T. Milik, *Qumran Cave I, DJD* I (Oxford, 1955), ad loc.; J. Carmignac, *Les Textes de Qumran* II (Paris, 1963), p. 23, amended to *ʾel* (cf. Deuteronomy 23:2–4), but Licht regards this as unnecessary in light of the sect's tendency to avoid the use of the divine name. Y. Yadin, *Megillat Ha-Miqdash*, vol. I (Jerusalem, 1977), p. 225, understands *ʾlh* as the divine name *ʾeloah*. Cf. Barthélemy. Richardson suggests that the scribe would have written *ʾlwh* (*plene*) had he intended this divine name.
6. Restoring with the unclear traces, see Licht, *Ha-Serakhim* (note 1).
7. Cf. line 7, DST 4:36 and 5:29 in Licht, *Ha-Serakhim* (note 1).
8. Licht suggests that this sentence is a remnant of another version of the following statement which was copied in error. He also suggests that this may be a general statement preceding the details which follow. The second interpretation is followed here.
9. Cf. Leviticus 13:2 for *besaro* and *negaʿ*.
10. Restored with unclear traces, see Licht, *Ha-Serakhim* (note 1).
11. Licht notes that the letters *pš* and *ʿw* are not written clearly.
12. All these deformities are treated in detail below.
13. Restored with traces, see Licht, *Ha-Serakhim* (note 1).
14. Cf. note 7.
15. Restored with traces, see Licht, *Ha-Serakhim* (note 1).
16. Restored with traces, see Licht, *Ha-Serakhim*. Cf. DSD 6:12, CDC 14:11.
17. Carmignac takes the next line of 1QSa as the continuation of this sentence.
18. Cf. Sifra Wa-Yiqra, *pereq* 12:8, ed. I.H. Weiss (Vienna, 1861/2), pp. 23b–c; Midrash Ha-Gadol, ed. S. Fisch (Jerusalem, 1972), to Leviticus 7:21; M. Kasher, *Torah Shelemah*, vol. 27 (Jerusalem, 1975), p. 77, n. 147. On the exclusion of the impure from priestly service, see Philo, *Special Laws* I, 118.
19. Yadin, *Ha-Miqdash*, vol. 1 (see note 5), pp. 221–223.
20. See the detailed note of Y. Yadin, *The Scroll of the War of the Sons of Light against the Sons of Darkness*, trans. B. and C. Rabin (Oxford, 1962), p. 291; as well as J. Carmignac, *La Règle de la Guerre*, vol. I (Paris, 1958), p. 106; and B. Jongeling, *Le Rouleau de la Guerre* (Assen, 1962), pp. 196f.
21. Trans. in Yadin, ibid.
22. Yadin, ibid., p. 73. Cf. the forthcoming study of B. M. Bokser, "Approaching Sacred Space."
23. Yadin, ibid., p. 290.
24. For detailed commentary, see Yadin, *Megillat Ha-Miqdash*, vol. II (Jerusalem, 1977), pp. 135f. Cf. Leviticus 22:4. Note that TS 46:16–18 provides for a special place to the east of the city for those who were impure as a result of seminal emissions. Yadin was correct in taking this to refer to the city of the sanctuary. On the purificatory ablutions of the Temple Scroll, see J. Milgrom, "Studies in the Temple Scroll," *JBL* 97 (1978): 512–518.
25. See the detailed discussion in *Ha-Miqdash*, vol. I (note 5). pp. 221–224.

26. B. Levine, "The Temple Scroll: Aspects of Its Historical Provenance and Literary Character," *BASOR* 232 (1978): 5–23; J. Milgrom, "'Sabbath' and 'Temple City' in the Temple Scroll," *BASOR* 232 (1978): 25–27, and Yadin's response to Levine in "Is the Temple Scroll a Sectarian Document," in *Humanizing America's Iconic Book* (Society for Biblical Literature Centennial Addresses, 1980), pp. 153–169.
27. L. Ginzberg, *An Unknown Jewish Sect* (New York, 1976), pp. 73f.
28. See L.H. Schiffman, *Sectarian Law in the Dead Sea Scrolls, Courts Testimony and the Penal Code* (Chico, CA, 1983), pp. 13f.; and Levine, "The Temple Scroll" (note 26).
29. For detailed commentary, see Yadin, *Ha-Miqdash*, vol. I (note 5), ad loc. Note that the gonorrheac and the one afflicted with *saraʿat* are assigned special places outside of the city of the sanctuary in TS 46:16–18. Both these classes are assigned similar places outside of all cities according to TS 48:14–17. Detailed prescriptions regarding the impurity of the dead are spelled out in TS 48:11–50:9. See the detailed discussion in ibid., pp. 249–263. Cf. also Leviticus 22:4.
30. Yadin, *Ha-Miqdash*, vol. I (see note 5), pp. 226f.
31. Sifre Zuṭa, Naso᾽ 5:2, ed. H.S. Horovitz, *Sifre deve Rav* (Jerusalem, 1966), p. 228; cf. TB. Pesaḥim 67a. Yadin, ibid., p. 226 notes that according to Josephus, *War* V, 227 and *Ant.* III, 261, both classes were forbidden from the city of Jerusalem. Yadin takes the view that this same regulation is intended by the Temple Scroll.
32. A *baraita* in TB Pesaḥim 68a; L. Finkelstein, ed., *Sifre Devarim*, 255 (New York, 1969), p. 281.
33. Tos. Kelim, Bava Qamma 1:8, Sifre Zuṭa, Naso᾽5:2 (see note 31), p. 228, cf. Yadin, *Ha-Miqdash*, vol. I (see note 5), p. 227.
34. The Septuagint has σύντριμμα for *shever*. Vulgate has *fracto*. On this and the following deformities, cf. Philo, *Special Laws* I, 80, 81, 117, 118.
35. Sifra, ᾽Emor Parashah 7:11, ed. Weiss (see note 18), p. 98c, *baraitot* in TB Bekhorot 45a.
36. J. Preuss, *Biblical and Talmudic Medicine*, trans. F. Rosner (New York-London, 1978), p. 193.
37. See *Ḥigger*, in *Enṣiqlopedyah Talmudit*, vol. 12, pp. 610–612.
38. Leviticus 19:14, Deuteronomy 27:18, 28:29, Isaiah 42:18, 59:10, Job 29:15. On blindness in biblical and Rabbinic literature, see Preuss, *Biblical and Talmudic Medicine* (note 36), pp. 270–276.
39. Sifra, ᾽Emor Parashah 3:5, ed. Weiss (see note 18), p. 95b; *baraita* in TB Bekhorot 44a.
40. Cf. Carmignac, *Textes* II (note 5), p. 23, n. 65.
41. Psalms 38:14; Isaiah 29:18; 42:18.
42. M. Terumot 1:2, Tos. Terumot 1:2, and the detailed discussion in A. J. Peck, *The Priestly Gift in Mishnah* (Chico, CA, 1981), pp. 30–37. Cf. TB Ḥagigah 2b, TB Gittin 71a and *Ḥeresh*, in *Enṣiqlopedyah Talmudit*, vol. 17, pp. 495–499.
43. M. Bekhorot 7:6; Sifra, ᾽Emor Pereq 3:2, ed. Weiss (see note 18), p. 95c.
44. *Ḥeresh*, in *Enṣiqlopedyah Talmudit* (see note 42), p. 536.
45. M. Ḥagigah 1:1.
46. This view is supported by the occurrence of the grouping *ḥeresh shoṭeh we-qaṭan* in this mishnah.
47. TB Ḥagigah 2b–3a, TP Ḥagigah 1:1 (75d–76a). Cf. D. Halivni, *Meqorot U-Mesorot, Seder Moʿed* (Jerusalem, 1974/75), pp. 575–577.
48. Exodus 4:11; Isaiah 35:6; Psalms 38:14.
49. See note 42.
50. See note 47.
51. *Baraita* in TB Yoma 23b, Tos. Soṭah 7:16, Sifre Be-Midbar 75, ed. Horovitz (see note 31), p. 70, and parallels in S. Lieberman, *Tosefta Ki-Fshutah*, vol. VIII (New York, 1973), p. 682, n. 132–134. Cf. *Baʿal Mum*, in *Enṣiqlopedyah Talmudit*, vol. 4, pp. 115–117.
52. Sifra, ᾽Emor Parashah 3:5, ed. Weiss (see note 18), p. 95b, cf. M. Bekhorot 7:1, Tos. Bekhorot 5:1; and J. Neusner, *A History of the Mishnaic Law of Holy Things*, part III (Leiden, 1979), pp. 199, 203.
53. M. Bekhorot 7:3 and 5; Tos. Bekhorot 5:2. Cf. Neusner, ibid., pp. 200f., 203.
54. So I. Lipschutz, *Tiferet Yisra᾽el* (Koenigsberg, 1850), to M. Bekhorot 7:3. Cf. Licht, *Ha-Serakhim* (see

note 1), 1QSa 2:7.

55. Carmignac, *Textes* II (see note 5), p. 103, n. 7; idem, *Règle*, (see note 20), p. 105.
56. See *Ḥigger* (note 37).
57. M. Ḥagigah 1:2.
58. TB Ḥagigah 3a.
59. Sifra, ʾEmor Parashah 3:7, ed. Weiss (note 18), p. 95b, which takes Tannaitic Hebrew *ḥigger* as equivalent to biblical *pisseaḥ*. Indeed, the Targumim translate *pisseaḥ* as *ḥaggir*. According to the Sifra, a priest is disqualified even if he is a *ḥigger* in only one leg. Cf. Sifre Be-Midbar 75 (see note 31); TP Megillah 1:10 [ed. Krotoschin (Jerusalem, 1959/1960) 12, 72b].
60. J. T. Milik, *Ten Years of Discovery in the Wilderness of Judaea* (London, 1959), p. 114; cf. Licht, *Ha-Serakhim* (note 1), 1QSa 2:5–6.
61. For commentary, See Yadin, *Ha-Miqdash*, vol. II (note 24), p. 136. Note that the Scroll makes no provisions for special places in which to quarantine the blind or any other deformed individuals either for the city of the sanctuary or other cities.
62. See detailed discussion in Yadin, *Megillat ha-Miqdash*, vol. I (note 5), pp. 224f. and in *Megillat ha-Miqdash*, vol. II (see note 24), p. 136.
63. Rockefeller 49.976, in Yadin, *Megillat ha-Miqdash*, vol. II (note 24), pp. 132f.
64. Note that according to Matthew 21:14, Jesus healed the blind and the lame in the Temple. Cf. Luke 14:21.
65. Note that in Daniel 11:35 this verb occurs with *maskilim*, a term which was used by the sect to refer to those who had achieved high standards of both scholarship and conduct. Cf. L.H. Schiffman, *Halakhah at Qumran* (Leiden, 1975), p. 25, n. 24.
66. For the minimum age of twenty-five and for a complete discussion of the ages of the judges at Qumran, see Schiffman, *Sectarian Law* (note 28), pp. 30–37.
67. For the forensic use of the *hitpaʿel* of *yṣb*, see Numbers 11:16; C. Rabin, *The Zadokite Documents* (Oxford, 1954), ad loc. Note also Job 33:5 where it is used for answering a charge (BDB).
68. Rabin in regard to CDC 19:23 comments that this is an "abstract noun used for inf. constr. (a procedure not uncommon in medieval Hebrew of all periods)." He translates our passage, "When man sinned ... when God waxed wroth...." He is taking the preposition *be-* in a temporal sense while our translation reflects a causal relation, the *bet pretii* (Ges. sec. 119p).
69. Phonetic spelling of the plural possessive (without *yod*) is common at Qumran.
70. S. Schechter's emendation [S. Schechter, *Fragments of a Zadokite Work* (reprint New York, 1970)] to *be-ḥarot* (cf. Psalms 124:3) is ill-advised in light of the parallelism with *maʿal*, a noun, not an infinitive. In the Bible, the phrase *ḥaron ʾaf* occurs either with the Tetragrammaton or with a pronoun, only once with *ʾelohim* (Ezra 10:14) and never with *ʾel*. No doubt, our text is following the Qumran custom of avoiding the Tetragrammaton.
71. M.H. Segal, "Sefer Berit Dameseq," *Ha-Shiloaḥ* 26 (1912): 499, suggests that we read *la-sir, hifʿil* with elided *heʾ*. His view is supported by what we now know about this phenomenon at Qumran [Licht, *Ha-Serakhim* (see note 1), p. 46; cf. Ges. sec. 53q] as well as by the similarity of the letters *waw* and *yod* in the Dead Sea Scrolls [see Schiffman, *Halakhah at Qumran* (note 65), pp. 30f., n. 61]. This is certainly the simplest interpretation. Nevertheless, if Rabin is correct in seeing this clause as a quotation from Jubilees 23:11, his analysis as a *qal* and translation: "He commanded that their understanding should depart..." would be better. Rabin notes that the Latin: *et erunt transeuntes ab ipsis spiritus intellectus eorum* [see R. H. Charles, *The Ethiopic Version of the Hebrew Book of Jubilees* (Oxford, 1895), ad loc.] supports his view. He suggests that the peculiar Hebrew form of accusative with infinitive may lie behind this Latin text. Rabin rejects reading *la-sir* since then *ʾamar* "could only mean 'He intended.'" I fail to see why this understanding of *ʾamar* would be objectionable.
72. See Proverbs 8:26 in Segal, ibid. Rabin compares Targumic *ʿad laʾ* and Christian Palestinian Aramaic, *ʿadlaʾ de-*, as opposed to Syriac, Galilean, Babylonian, *ʿad delaʾ*. His suggestion that the Hebrew has here conditioned the Aramaic usage is unlikely in light of the already established

influence of Aramaic on Qumran Hebrew [Licht, *Ha-Serakhim* (see note 1), pp. 44f.].

73. Cf. L. Ginzberg, *The Legends of the Jews*, vol. V (Philadelphia, 1968), p. 276, n. 36. On the notion that Abraham was the first to show signs of old age, see ibid., p. 258, n. 272.
74. Cf. 1QSa 1:19 which Licht takes as referring to those between fifty and sixty.
75. Members of the *mishmarot* (or *maʿamadot*) also served past the age of fifty according to DSW 2:4f., but no retirement age is specified, see Yadin, *War Scroll* (note 20), p. 78.
76. To CDC 10:7.
77. Read *ʾet* in Schechter, *Zadokite Work* (see note 70). Rabin's restoration to *brʾs*, based on DSD 6:14, is no more convincing and, as he indicates, "excludes the otherwise attractive rendering 'who musters.'" *ʾEt* is used regularly in CDC. Cf. E.Y. Kutscher, *Ha-Lashon We-Ha-Reqaʿ Ha-Leshoni shel Megillat Yeshaʿayahu Ha-Shelemah Mi-Megillot Yam Ha-Melaḥ* (Jerusalem, 1959), p. 316; and G.W. Nebe, "Der Gebrauch der sogennanten nota accusativi ʾet in Damaskusschrift XV, 5.9 und 12," *Revue de Qumran* 8 (1973): 257–264.
78. The process of mustering is described several lines above on the same page of CDC. Apparently, members were arranged in order and their names listed. On these lists, see Schiffman, *Halakhah at Qumran* (note 65), pp. 66f. For the connection of this method of sectarian organization with military tactics, see Yadin, *War Scroll* (note 20), pp. 60f.
79. Cf. Schiffman, *Sectarian Law* (note 28), p. 34f.
80. M. Ḥagigah 1:1.
81. Maimonides, *Perush Ha-Mishnayyot*, ad loc. and M. Ḥagigah 2:1. To the Tannaim, the requirement was only that one be able to make the trip from Jerusalem by foot.
82. The translation has been adapted from that in Yadin, *War Scroll* (see note 20), p. 317. See the commentaries of Yadin, Carmignac and Jongeling (note 20) for complete philological notes.
83. Yadin, ibid., pp. 229–242; J. Licht, "An Analysis of the Treatise of the Two Spirits in DSD," *Aspects of the Dead Sea Scrolls. Scripta Hierosolymitana* IV (1958): 87–100. The same idea is found in DSD 11:8, see Barthélemy and Milik, *Qumran Cave I* (note 5).
84. Trans. in Yadin, *War Scroll* (see note 20), p. 291.
85. Yadin notes that this refers to a boy below the age of twenty-five. Cf. 1QSa 1:12 and Schiffman, *Sectarian Law* (note 28), pp. 30–32. On *zaʿaṭuṭ*, cf. Yadin's note, ibid., ad loc.
86. Cf. Yadin, *Ha-Miqdash*, vol. 1 (note 5), p. 237 according to whom the Temple Scroll envisages that no woman will be permitted to live in the city of the sanctuary, taken by him as Jerusalem.
87. Cf. The similar phraseology in DSD 6:9f.

Halakhic Polemics in New Fragments from Qumran Cave 4

Joseph M. Baumgarten

In the eyes of modern students the epithet בוני החיץ, "builders of the wall," which the Qumran sect applied to its opponents, seems a most fitting description of its own ideological posture vis-à-vis contemporary halakhah. The geographic isolation of the Qumran settlement goes hand in hand with its social isolation and the avoidance of religious dialogue with those on the outside. In what had been regarded as a manifesto of the Teacher of Righteousness, the *Maskil* is admonished not to "rebuke the men of the Pit nor dispute with them." While it is his duty to instruct the men of the *Yaḥad* in all that is revealed from time to time, he must "conceal the teaching of the Law from men of falsehood" (1QS 9:16–17). This detachment from controversy may well be taken to have been characteristic of the formative stages of the sect, but it could hardly be expected to have been maintained throughout its history. We know this from the sectarian literature. Prof. Yadin has called attention to the reference in 4Q177 to a "second book of the Torah," quite possibly identical with the Temple Scroll, which was despised by certain antagonists who "spoke disdainfully about it."[1] A fragment of a *pesher* on Psalm 37 may also refer to this Torah "which he sent to him," the recipient being perhaps none other than the Wicked Priest.[2] A priest, even if wicked, may be expected to be somewhat conditioned by historical precedent to the discovery of hidden scrolls, and if in addition he has Sadducean learnings, he may even have an inherent respect for laws which are "written and deposited."[3] No such illusions could be entertained about the Pharisaic reaction to purported supplements to the Mosaic Law. It is therefore not at all surprising to note that the Damascus Document, in its effort to soften the resistance of the "builders of the wall" to its halakhic novella, does not resort to citing the Temple Scroll. Rather it attempts to support its rules by exegesis from the Torah of Moses, "for in it everything is specified" (CDC 16:1). This approach, too, was hardly a total success, as we surmise from the charge that "they have opened their mouth against the ordinances of the covenant of God with a blasphemous tongue saying, They are not correct; abomination they speak against them" (CDC 5:11–13).

Our knowledge of the issues involved in such polemics has been significantly broadened by the recent publication of *Qumran Grotte 4* III. We should like to deal here with one text, 4Q513, which, though quite fragmentary, has halakhic ramifications not fully appreciated by the editor.[4] His readings of the fragments to which we will refer are reproduced on page 394.

Maurice Baillet has observed correctly that there is a salient concern in this text with ritual purity. This is quite evident in fragments 1 and 2 where, according to the editor's restorations, the phrase מהמה הטמאה occurs three times. What is not evident is how this phrase relates to the subject of the fragments, which is the same as that of 4Q159 (Ordinances) — the proper standardization of weights and measures, particularly the equalization of the בת for liquids with the איפה for grain, in conformance with Ezekiel 45:11.[5] The suggestion that this phrase merely metaphorically expresses disapproval of deviations from the standardized measures[6] lacks cogency. The first step toward understanding the intent of the text is to note that both here and in Ezekiel the measures are used to separate the priestly *terumah*,[7] which had to be scrupulously protected from any source of ritual defilement. Measuring vessels, because of their constant use for all kinds of transactions, constitute a ready source of contamination. This is especially so in the case of liquid measures, because if they are used to pour liquids into an impure receptacle, the measuring vessels themselves become ritually unclean. In rabbinic halakhah this problem was alleviated by the tannaitic ruling that the נצוק, the liquid stream, does not constitute a link for defilement.[8] This ruling, however, was repudiated by the Zadokites, as indicated in M. Yadayim and corroborated by a Cave 4 text cited by Milik.[9] A further difference was that mishnaic halakhah did not require the *terumah*, whose rate is not fixed in the Torah, to be set aside by measurement. In fact, one ruling forbids the use of weights, measures and counting.[10] Sectarian interpretation apparently followed closely the admonition in Ezekiel 45:13 to avoid loose estimates and to separate 1/60 of the grain and 1/100 of the oil. Since the use of utensils for measuring *terumah* was thus mandatory, it was appropriate to warn the user about their being a potential source of ritual impurity.

The susceptibility of liquids to impurity is likewise indicated in fragment 13, where the words שמן and משקה are found in a context dealing with טמאה. We pointed out some years ago that the Essene avoidance of oil derived from its role as a transmitter of defilement, as stated in CDC 12:16 and now confirmed by 11Q Temple 49:11, where it is stated that the floor and walls of a house in which a corpse had been must be scraped to remove stains of "oil, wine and damp spots of water."[11]

Since the subject of fragment 13 is ritual purity, we can hardly accept the editor's reading of the first line ומערות איא, "et la nudité du père de," assumed to be an allusion to some form of incest. What remains of the first letter of the second word may be taken to be part of a *gimel*, thus giving us גבא, "rock-pool." According to CDC 10:12–13, the waters of a גבא, a pool in a rock not sufficient to cover a person, are unfit for immersion. Instead, the waters themselves are rendered unclean by the man in need of purification. In mishnaic Hebrew גבא occasionally appears together with מערות, both denoting natural pools lacking the minimal size of a מקוה.[12] That our fragment likewise deals with purification is confirmed by the words in the following line: כפורי רצון, employed for cleansing rites in 1QS 3:11.[13] We would therefore suggest that the intent was to prohibit the use of water of shallow rock pools for purification.

According to Josephus, it was due to such differences over the proper form of purification that the Essenes kept themselves apart even when they sent offerings to the Temple. Thus we read in *Ant.* 18, 19, according to the preferred text (without οὐκ) preserved in the MSS:

> They send votive gifts to the Temple, but complete their sacrifices employing a different ritual of purification. For this reason they are prevented from using those precincts of the Temple that are frequented by the common people and complete their sacrifices by themselves.[14]

It is interesting in this connection to note that fragment 10 of our text preserves the words בני ישראל followed in the next line by the prohibition ואין לערב במ◦, "one must not intermingle with them," as well as in successive lines the words בטהרה, "in purity," and המקדש, "the Sanctuary." One is tempted to restore the sense of the text in accordance with Josephus, as pertaining to the intermingling of the sect with other Jews; but a word of caution is in order. Line 8 refers to מבני אה[רון], "the sons of Aaron," the priests. Ezekiel 46:20–24 is concerned with keeping the meat of the sin and guilt offerings, reserved for the priests, separated from the lay people. A similar concern is now found in 11Q Temple 35:12, employing the verb לערב, "to mingle," as in 4Q513. This and the use in fragment 11 of the strong expression זמה, "depravity," following בני ישראל and the phrase "if they eat of them," would seem to favor the assumption that it is the intermingling of priestly and lay sacrifices which is the object of criticism in the text.

The critical position of the sect vis-à-vis the Temple priesthood has till now been known to us primarily from the *pesher* on Habakkuk, which alludes to the hostile activities of the Wicked Priest. As to specific transgressions attributed to the priests, the *pesher* mentions their lust for riches (9:4–5), and their uncleanliness (8:13, 12:8), two of the three nets of Belial known to us from the Damascus Document (4:14–5:11). Fragment 2, Col. II of our text now completes the accusation with its reference to זנות, "fornication," charged against the priesthood, because of which they are deemed unworthy to eat *terumah* and to touch the sacred purities.[15] The nature of this "fornication" is not explicated. In the Damascus Document the term זנות is applied to polygamy and niece marriages. The Aramaic "Testament of Levi" calls upon Levi, as the archetypal priest, to take a wife from his own family, and not to profane his seed with "harlots."[16] The main Greek text of the "Testament of Levi" is not quite as restrictive but applies the term "fornication" to marriage with non-Israelite wives (9:10):

> Beware of the spirit of fornication; for this shall continue and shall by thy seed pollute the holy place. Take, therefore, to thyself a wife without blemish or pollution, while thou art young, and not of the race of strange nations.

The problem of intermarriage in priestly families already emerged in the early post-exilic period. A son of Jehoiada, the high priest, who had married the daughter of the Samaritan satrap, Sanballat, was driven out by Nehemiah (Nehemiah 13:28). A century later Manasses, a brother of the high priest Jaddua, was disqualified by the elders because of his marriage to the daughter of another Sanballat. The elders feared that this union might become a stepping-stone toward widespread intermarriage and intercourse with foreigners (*Ant.* 11, 307).

We note that fragment 2 also alludes to illicit relations with foreigners: בעלות לבני הנכר (1.2), echoing the phraseology of Malachi 2:11: בעל בת אל נכר, "consorting with aliens." However, the word בעלות is feminine and we may presume that it refers to the female partners in such relations. One possibility is that it is descriptive of the promiscuity of the harlots involved in the fornication of the priests. Yet, a priest is forbidden to take a harlot regardless of whether she previously consorted with aliens or Israelites (Leviticus 21:7). It appears much more likely that the phrase refers to illicit marriages involving women who belonged to the households of the priests. According to Leviticus 21:9, the harlotry of the daughter of a priest is not only a capital offense, but is said to profane her father. Some rabbinic exegetes understood this loosely in the sense of his disgrace in the eyes of the public,[17] but there are indications that the illicit relationship of a priest's daughter with a heathen was regarded as sufficient cause for the suspension of her family's priestly privileges. One striking example involved the priestly house of Bilgah, which was permanently deprived of certain accommodations in the Temple because Miriam, the daughter of Bilgah, had defiantly married a Greek officer.[18] This anomalous application of collective guilt is explained in the Talmud as reflecting popular attitudes. Another illustration, closer to the milieu of the sectarian writings, may be found in the lessons drawn from the story of Dinah and Shechem in Jubilees ch. 30.

The author of Jubilees uses the ravishing of Dinah as a springboard for the most severe denunciation of intermarriage in general, but it is evident that he was particularly concerned about marriages between women from priestly families and the heathen. Thus he says: "They shall burn the woman with fire because she has profaned the name of the house of her father" (30:7); both the penalty and the phraseology are derived from the law about harlotry of the daughter of a priest, in Leviticus 21:9. Of those who give their daughters to gentiles he declares: "There will be no respect of persons and no receiving at his hands of fruits and offerings and burnt-offerings and fat nor the fragrance of sweet savour so as to accept it" (30:16). One can infer that the author is alluding to members of the priestly aristocracy.

Recently, Roger Beckwith has directed attention to a priestly marriage in the middle of the third century B.C.E. which is likely to have been viewed with misgivings in proto-Essene circles.[19] A sister of the high priest Onias II was married to Tobias, who can be identified as a descendant of Tobiah the Ammonite in the days of

1 et 2 i

1 (f. 2 i)]◦[

(1) f. 1 12···]השקל גרה עש[רים בשקׄ(]ל הקודש [מׄחצית

וׄגם

])השקל מעה שתים [עשרה 13 זׄוׄזׄ]ם שנים [מׄהׄמה הטמאה(

מ[המה הטׄמׄ]אה

]האיפה וה[בת תׄכון א)חד]עשרה עשרנים 14 כאיפת ה[דׄגן בת היין והסאה

]ש(לושת העש[רנים ו)שליׄשת ה]עשרון מהמה 15 הטמ[אׄה ומעשר האיפה

]העשרון] *vacat* [

2, col. II

marge supérieure?

להגׄיעם בטהרת]הקו[דׄש כיא טמאׄיׄם] המה]

בעלוׄת לבני הנכׄר וׄלכול הזנות אשׄר] אשר]

רׄא]ה [לו להׄאׄכילם מכול תרומת השׄ◦]]

בהם

ולבגׄ] מ[לאכׄי ולכפר בׄמׄהׄ לרצון על יׄ]שראל]

הזׄנות מאכׄליהם נשא עוון כי החל כו]]

המה מ] [וׄרׄ] [◦ אשמה בחללם]]

ומח] [ם] [הׄיׄם לׄ]]

4 3

1 (f. 4)]יׄוׄ[ ]◦[

(1) f. 3 [מׄקׄרא]קודש........[הנף עמר]

א]

[ביום שבת לׄ··] [מלבד שבׄתׄות]

[לעשות זכרון ע]ל [ל תעות עורון ה]

[אשר הר]א[הׄ ענני] [ולא מתורת משה]

(5) [◦] [יׄם ו◦]

[לׄ]

10 11

Col. II Col. I

]אׄ [ ]◦אׄ[

]וא[תׄ בני ישראל]

]ו[אין לערב במ◦]

אותם בטׄ]

]ו[את השׄ◦]

בטׄהׄרה ר]

המקדש]

מבני אהׄ]רון

נׄ] [מׄי הותנה

יׄ] [ן

◦] [רׄון

11

[אם יׄאוׄכׄלו מהמה

[תׄ בני ישראל

[◦וׄן זמה

[לם ב]כו[ל

12

]·· וב]ש[מׄן [

למנ[חׄה וללבׄנׄה ◦]

[ואין להטׄ◦]

[◦ח יׄזבח] [לׄ]

13

[וׄמׄעׄרׄוׄתׄ :אׄיׄאׄ

[לכפורי רצוןׄ

[◦ עושים ומגאליׄ]ם[

מגו[אלים בשמןׄ ◦]

[◦ טמאתםׄ ◦]

[◦וׄים למשק]ה

[ל כאם א]

[מׄכול ש]

Fragments of Text 4Q513 referred to in this paper

Nehemiah (Nehemiah 2:19). It was from this union that Joseph and the Hellenist Tobiads originated. Although Josephus does not record any protest against this marriage, Beckwith notes that it was in violation of the law forbidding Ammonites to come into the congregation of the Lord. The passage (Deuteronomy 23:3–4) in which this law occurs is cited in 4QFlorilegium.[20] Moreover, we wonder whether in likening the marriage of one's daughter or his sister to a gentile, to giving one's seed to Molech, the author of Jubilees may have been alluding to the identity of the latter as the "abomination of the Ammonites" (1 Kings 11:7).

However this may be, the term "fornication" employed in our fragment was capable of being used to denote any variety of priestly intermarriage. Where the illicit union involved the priests themselves, they were of course regarded as unclean and unfit to touch the priestly portions, a restriction which can be paralleled from rabbinic sources.[21] Even where the marriage involved their daughters who had "consorted with aliens," such priestly houses were no longer qualified to eat the sacred *terumah*, and whoever delivered it to them was viewed as an accomplice to the profanation. So much for matters of purity. We come now to a small but very significant fragment pertaining to the calendar.

That fragment 4 has some bearing on the controversy concerning the date of the Omer offering was recognized by the editor. This is apparent from the mention of הנף עמר and the denunciatory phrases תעות עורון, "error of blindness" and לא מתורת משה , "not from the Law of Moses." The accusation that Israel has been blind to the true implications of the Law of Moses is found likewise in CDC 16:1–2.[22] In the phraseology of the sect it means that they are not only ignorant of the נסתרות, the esoteric aspects of sectarian religious law, but "they defiantly violate the נגלות" (1QS 5:12), the obvious and open meaning of the Torah. Baillet, while noting that the sect set the Omer on Sunday the 26th of the first month, does not find it possible to follow the argument implicit in our fragment. Concerning the words מלבד שבתות in 1.3, he merely observes that they derive from Leviticus 23:38, and are also found in CDC 11:18. The latter passage, however, provides the key for discerning the halakhic issue involved in the polemics (CDC 11:17–18):

> Let no man offer upon the altar on the Sabbath [anything] except the burnt-offering of the Sabbath; for thus it is written: "apart from your Sabbaths."

The point at issue there is the profanation of the Sabbath occasioned by the offering of extraneous sacrifices. It can be taken for granted that the sacrifices intended were not voluntary offerings of individuals, which by universal consensus could not be brought on the Sabbath. Rather we must assume that they were communal sacrifices ordained for certain festival occasions.[23] But what occasions? Since the structure of the idealized solar calendar of Jubilees and Qumran is now known, it has been noted that its salient feature is the elimination of any possible coincidence of the dates of any of the biblical festivals with the Sabbath.[24] The only exceptions are the two seven-day festivals, Passover and Sukkot, whose fourth day coincides with the Sabbath. It is conceivable that the law in the Damascus Document pertains to this Sabbath of the intermediate days, on which no additional (*Musaph*) sacrifice was to be brought,[25] although this would leave the biblical quota of seven days of burnt offerings (Leviticus 23:8, 37) unfulfilled.[26] However, this approach, based on the premise that sectarian halakhic pronouncements necessarily presuppose the sect's own calendar, must not be reevaluated in the light of fragment 4.

This fragment is clearly concerned with the grave violation of the Sabbath resulting from the occurrence of the Omer ceremony on that day, but this could never happen according to the Qumran calendar. The 26th of the first month is always a Sunday. Neither is this possible according to any school of exegesis which takes the crucial words ממחרת השבת in Leviticus 23:15 as designating the day following the weekly Sabbath. The ones accused of the "error of blindness" must necessarily be the precursors of the Rabbis who, like the Septuagint translator, took these words to mean the day following the first day of Passover, which in the lunar-solar calendar may indeed fall on Friday. When this happened the harvesting of the sheaves of barley, otherwise biblically prohibited on the Sabbath (Exodus 34:21), was ostentatiously conducted on Friday after sundown. The procedure is familiar to us from the graphic account in M. Menaḥot 10, 3:

> When it grew dark, he [the reaper] said to them [the messengers of the court] "Is the sun set?" and they answered "Yea!" ... three times for every matter ... Wherefore was all this? Because of the ביתוסים who used to say: The Omer is not to be reaped at the close of the Festival-day.[27]

The point of contention here is not merely the question of the proper date for the Omer offering, but the public desecration of the Sabbath involved in reaping the barley. It is this practice which evoked the sharp rebuke found in fragment 4.[28] According to the author of this text, the Sabbath must never be violated for the sake of any holiday ritual since the holidays were ordained to be מלבד שבתותיכם, apart and distinct from your Sabbaths. This principle is applied in the Damascus Document to the question of extraneous festival sacrifices, although the Sabbath and *tamid* burnt-offerings were sanctioned by the Torah. *A fortiori*, was it applicable to reaping, a form of labor never allowed elsewhere on the Sabbath, and whose permissibility for the Omer was not unanimously approved even by rabbinic opinion?[29]

The sectarian calendar, which sets the Omer on the 26th of the first month, of course eliminates this entire problem. It has been pointed out in this connection by S. Leiman[30] that the flat statement attributed in the Mishnah to the ביתוסים, that the Omer is never to be reaped at the close of the first day of Passover, would not be accurate according to those who understood the Sabbath in Leviticus 23:15 to be that which falls during the week of Passover. Thus, if the first day of Passover happened to be a Sabbath, the Omer would indeed be cut "at the close of the Festival-day." However, according to the Qumran calendar, the connection between the Omer and Passover is entirely severed,[31] and the statement in the Mishnah becomes completely accurate. This and the contents of fragment 4, which supply the sectarian counterpart to the demonstrative affirmation of the Pharisaic practice in the Mishnah, would make desirable a reevaluation of the possible identification of the ביתוסים in M. Menaḥot with the Essenes, proposed some years ago by Y.M. Grintz.[32] We have elsewhere assessed the grounds for a similar evaluation of the possible identification of the צדוקים in M. Yadayim, who complained about Pharisaic leniencies in the sphere of ritual purity, with the בני צדוק of Qumran.[33] Both questions are admittedly complicated by the widespread confusion of Boethusians and Sadducees found in rabbinic sources, as pointed out by M.D. Herr,[34] but are ripe for further investigation.

In conclusion, 4Q513, despite its very fragmentary state of preservation, serves to put into sharper focus a number of disputed halakhic matters which were of concern to the Qumran exegetes. The fragment dealing with the Omer provides one of those rare opportunities to follow the polemics from both sides of the חיץ which separated the sect from its Pharisaic antagonists. M. Menaḥot, M. Parah, and M. Yadayim, it turns out, have preserved authentic historical records of efforts to counteract sectarian criticism of Pharisaic teachings. In view of the lingering tendency in a good deal of contemporary scholarship to question the relevance of tannaitic literature for the religious history of the Second Temple period,[35] it may not be superfluous to observe that we have consistently found rabbinic sources to be the most indispensable frame of reference for the investigation of Qumran literature.

Notes

1. *DJD* 5 (Catena A), p. 68; Y. Yadin, *Megillat ha-Miqdaš*, vol. I (Jerusalem, 1977), p. 303.
2. *DJD* 5, 171, p. 45; the text is fragmentary and its restoration by no means certain.
3. B. Qiddushin 66a; cf. S. Lieberman, *Greek and Hellenism in ʾEreṣ Yisraʿel* (Jerusalem, 1962), p. 215 (Hebrew); J.M. Baumgarten, *Studies in Qumran Law* (Leiden, 1977), pp. 21–22.
4. M. Baillet, *Qumran Grotte 4* (*DJD* 7) (Oxford, 1982), Text 513, pp. 287–295.
5. *DJD* 5, 159, Col. II, line 13, p. 7.
6. Baillet, *Qumran Grotte 4* (see note 4), p. 288.
7. Col. II, line 3; Ezekiel 45:13.
8. M. Makhshirin 5,9 and Yadayim 4, 7.
9. *DJD* 3, p. 225. Attention to this text was drawn by Yadin, *Megillat ha-Miqdaš* (see note 1), vol. II, p. 150; cf. our discussion in "The Pharisaic-Sadducean Controversies about Purity and the Qumran Texts," *Journal of Jewish Studies* 31 (1980): 157–170.
10. M. Terumot 1, 7; cf. Ter. 4, 6 and Abot 1, 16, where measurement of the harvest as a whole and the tithes is encouraged. As to the whether the *terumah* of one tenth of the levitical tithe requires measurement, cf. TB Betzah 13b and TP Ter. 42d.
11. J.M. Baumgarten, "The Essene Avoidance of Oil and the Laws of Purity," *Revue Qumran* 6 (1967): 183–193; Baumgarten, *Studies in Qumran Law* (see note 3), pp. 88–97; see also *JBL* 97 (1978): 587.
12. M. Miqwaot 1, 4; Tos. Miqw. 1, 7.
13. Cf. 1QS 3:4 לוא יזכה בכפורים ולוא יטהר במי נדה. The fact that כפורים appears in parallel with מי נדה, the sprinkling waters used for purification with the ashes of the red heifer (Numbers 19:13, 20, 21), suggests the possibility that fragment 13 may be particularly concerned with the substitution of

the water from rock pools for the "living waters" (Numbers 19:17), required for sprinkling; cf. M. Parah 6:5 המפנה את המעין ... לתוך הגבים פסולים and the metaphorical use in TP Berakhot 7d: "Your waters are waters of rock pools (מי מערה) and your ashes are wood ashes."

14. For a reappraisal of this passage, see Baumgarten, *Studies in Qumran Law* (note 3), pp. 57–74.
15. Restoring at the beginning of line 3 [רא]וי], cf. 11QT 66:9, and at the end of the line תרומת הק[דשים] derived from Leviticus 22:12: ובת כהן כי תהיה לאיש זר הוא בתרומת הקדשים לא תאכל . The last extant letter on the line is *qof* of which the right vertical stroke is visible.
16. R.H. Charles, *The Greek Versions of the Testament of the Twelve Patriarchs* (Oxford, 1908), p. 247, col. b, lines 16–20.
17. B. Sanhedrin 52a.
18. M. Sukkah 5, 8; Tos. Sukkah 4, 28; TB Sukkah 56b.
19. R.T. Beckwith, "The Pre-history and Relationships of the Pharisees, Sadducees and Essenes: A Tentative Reconstruction," *Revue Qumran* 11 (1982): 20–30.
20. The application of Deuteronomy 23:3–4 in 4QFlorilegium is for exclusion from the sanctuary rather than intermarriage; cf. "The Exclusion of *Netinim* and Proselytes in 4QFlorilegium," *Revue Qumran* 8 (1972): 87–96; and Baumgarten, *Studies in Qumran Law* (see note 3), pp. 75–87.
21. See TB Yebamot 99b, where a priest who married a wife "not fit for him" was excluded from receiving *terumah* in the granaries; cf. Targum on Malachi 2: 12 ואם כהין הוא לא יהי ליה מקריב קורבנא בבית מקדשא.
22. Cf. 1 Enoch 89:54: "They went astray in everything and their eyes were blinded."
23. Cf. L. Schiffman, *The Halakha at Qumran* (Leiden, 1975), pp. 128–131, who believes that the law in CDC was directed against the permission to offer the regular daily burnt offerings on the Sabbath. However, as he recognizes, this would contradict both Numbers 28:10 and Jubilees 50:10. Cf. Yadin, *Megillat ha-Miqdaš* (see note 1), p. 105; and B.Z. Wacholder, *The Dawn of Qumran* (Cincinnati, 1983), pp. 49–50, where the attribution to Yadin of the view that the sect did not permit the *tamid* on the Sabbath must be corrected.
24. K.G. Kuhn, in *Theologische Literaturzeitung* 85 (1960): 649–655; cf. Baumgarten, *Studies in Qumran Law* (see note 3), pp. 10, 114; and R.T. Beckwith, "The Earliest Enoch Literature and Its Calendar," *Revue Qumran* 10 (1981): 379–381.
25. Wacholder, *The Dawn of Qumran* (see note 23), p. 50.
26. Yadin, *Megillat ha-Miqdaš* (see note 1), pp. 105–106, believes that the sect excluded the Sabbath from the reckoning of the seven-day holidays, as reported by Al-Qirqisani concerning the Zadokites. Conceivably, they took the eight day of ʿAṣeret (Leviticus 23:36) as a model for the completion of the missing day, although no such supplement is found in the Torah in the case of Passover. A comprehensive survey of the different schools of exegesis is provided by D. Hoffman, *Das Buch Leviticus* (Berlin, 1906), pp. 159–215.
27. See also Tos. Menaḥot 10, 23 (Zuckermandel 434); cf. M. Ḥag 2, 4.
28. Fragment 3, detached from and textually separated from the sequel in fragment 4, also mentions the Sabbath day. Baillet notes the word זכרון, which he takes as most likely derived from Leviticus 23:24 זכרון תרועה. It is interesting that this phrase was used in talmudic exegesis to apply to the omission of the sounding of the Shofar when Rosh Ha-Shanah coincided with the Sabbath; when this occurred there was to be only the "*remembrance* of the blasts" of the Shofar (M. Rosh ha-Shanah 4, 1; TPR. H. 59b; TBR. H. 29b). Unfortunately, the preserved portion of fragment 3 does not suffice to determine the context in which זכרון is used.
29. According to TB Menahot 72b, Rabbi (Judah ha-Nasi) did not concur with the sanction to cut the Omer on the Sabbath. See also the comments of the Tosaphists, TB Men. 72a, rubric מנין.
30. This observation was part of an as yet unpublished paper presented before the Society of Biblical Literature.
31. No satisfactory rationale for the Qumran designation of the Sunday *following* the *maṣṣot* festival for the Omer ritual has, to my knowledge, been offered. Unless we are to suppose that this was merely

the incidental by-product of a desire to date Pentecost on the 15th of the third month, we would suggest that it reflects the same principle as that involved in the avoidance of the coincidence of the Sabbath with the holidays, that is, no festival must overlap with any other festival; hence, the Omer ritual is not to be held on Sunday (19/I) which falls during the week of *maṣṣot*.

32. Y.M. Grintz, "The Men of the Yaḥad, Essenes, Bet-Sin," *Sinai* 32 (1953): 11–43 (Hebrew), renewing the suggested identification of the Boethusians and the Esssenes first proposed by Azariah di Rossi in 1575. .

33. Baumgarten, "The Pharisaic-Sadducean Controversies" (see note 9), pp. 166–168.

34. M.D. Herr, "Who Were the Baethusians?," *Proceedings of the Seventh World Congress of Jewish Studies, Talmud, Halacha and Midrash* (Jerusalem, 1981), pp. 1–20 (Hebrew). The indication that fragment 4 of 4Q513 is part of a protest against the Sabbath violation involved in the Pharisaic version of the Omer ritual, although the latter was not in accord with the Qumran calendar, considerably mitigates the calendaric objections to Grintz's proposed identification. It harmonizes quite well with the story in Tos. Sukkah 3,1, about the Boethusians placing rocks on the willow branches before the Sabbath "because they did not accept the ruling that the beating of the willows supercedes the Sabbath." There are moreover indications that the Essene separation from the Temple was, at least in later times, not as absolute as has hitherto been supposed; cf. Baumgarten, *Studies in Qumran Law* (see note 3), pp. 57–74.

35. See, for example, a recent review of A. Oppenheimer, *The Am Ha-aretz*, in *JBL* 97 (1978): 596–597, in which the author is taken to task for his "rabbinocentric bias" and "his readiness to accept rabbinic dicta as reliable historical sources even for the Hasmonean period."

An Unpublished Halakhic Letter from Qumran

Elisha Qimron and John Strugnell

THE WORK PRESENTED HERE is a halakhic letter from Qumran (4Q394–399) which we have called מקצת מעשי התורה (henceforth its abbreviation MMT). This is one of the most important documents from Qumran. That it was highly considered by the sect itself can be inferred from the fact that six manuscripts of the work have been found in 4Q. Its importance for the history of the Hebrew language was already recognized by J.T. Milik, who cited — under the siglum 4QMishn(ique) — some passages of MMT in his introduction to the Copper Scroll.[1] Y. Yadin[2] and J.M. Baumgarten[3] refer to these passages in explaining one halakha, which appears also in early rabbinic literature as an item of controversy between the Sadducees and the Pharisees. F.M. Cross has studied the palaeography of one manuscript of the work.[4]

A few years ago J. Strugnell, in an attempt to accelerate the publication of the large number of 4Q manuscripts for which he was responsible, initiated various forms of collaboration with other scholars, and as a result several advanced publications will appear reasonably soon. Two years ago he invited E. Qimron to help in the edition of MMT. J. Sussman, of The Hebrew University, kindly consented to give his advice in halakhic matters and has supplied numerous references. It is hoped that a preliminary edition of the whole document will be finished within a year or so.

Description of the Letter

MMT is a letter from a leader of the Qumran sect (possibly the Teacher of Righteousness himself) to the leader of its opponents (possibly Jonathan or Simon). Unfortunately, the beginning of the letter is not preserved, and we can only guess who the writer and the addressee were. The phrase from which we have derived our title for the work, מקצת מעשי התורה, is taken from the epilogue, and means "some of the precepts of the Torah."

As S. Lieberman, D. Flusser and others have shown, the word מעשים can mean "precepts" or the like, and the verb עשה can mean "perform the precepts [of the Torah]."[5] Accordingly, the surviving sections of the work contain principally a list of halakhot. The exact date of the work is also unknown as the opening formula is missing. However, from the moderate tone of the polemic, and from the fact that the author still hopes that his opponent will be persuaded to accept the sect's viewpoint, we assume that the text is of an early date in the development of the Qumran schism. This assumption is not inconsistent with the palaeographical results. MMT may then be the earliest Qumranic work, probably written immediately after the separation of the sect. It should be noted that a polemic-halakhic letter such as our work is unique in early Hebrew literature.[6]

Six manuscripts of the work were found in Cave 4 at Qumran. They are all very fragmentary but supplement each other.[7] In all they provide a composite text of some 120 lines. At the beginning of this text there is (in one manuscript) a calendar which will be published separately by J.T. Milik. Our composite text, together with the calendar, may well preserve most of the original work which apparently contained four main sections: (1) an opening formula (now wholly lost and of undeterminable length); (2) the calendar (only partly preserved, but which can be reconstructed); (3) a list of several special Qumranic halakhot (entitled אלה מקצת דברינו) in which the sect differed from its opponents. More than twenty of these halakhot are preserved partly or completely, and only a few seem to have been wholly lost. Each halakha begins with the formula ו(אף) על X אנחנו אומרים ש-, "and (also) concerning X we say that." The word in parentheses is optional, while the X denotes the subject discussed; (4) an epilogue discussing the reasons for the sect's withdrawal from the rest of the people, and suggesting to its opponent and his people that they should return to the "true way." This section also contains some special Qumranic theological principles and ideas.

The following is a list of twelve out of about twenty halakhic topics discussed in the letter:

1. A prohibition against accepting sacrifices from gentiles.
2. אותו ואת בנו — Slaughter of pregnant animals.
3. אסורי ביאה בקהל — Those forbidden from entering the congregation.
4. The law of the red heifer (פרה אדומה).
5. The banning of the blind and the deaf from the purity of the Sanctuary.
6. Purity of streams of liquid (MH נצוק).
7. A prohibition against bringing dogs into Jerusalem.
8. The fruit of the fourth year (נטע רבעי) to be given to the priests.
9. The tithe of cattle to be given to the priests.

10. Regulations concerning the impurity of a leper.
11. The impurity of human bones.
12. A prohibition of marriages between priests and Israelites.

The Character of the Letter

The letter is of a distinct polemic nature (see the polemic formulae, such as והמה (באים), ואתם יודעים, אנחנו חושבים, אנחנו אומרים). From the list of controversial halakhot, we can discern the major topics of controversy between the sect and its opponents. Three in regard to law are noted here: (1) the cultic calendar — this stands before the proper halakhic section of the work; (2) ritual purity (especially in connection with the Temple), and the sacrificial cult; (3) laws on marital status — in fact only one *halakha* on this topic remains, but the evidence in one of the small fragments indicates that the text immediately following probably continued with other marital halakhot.

The importance of all these halakhic topics to an ongoing communal religious life does not need emphasizing. For the importance of the calendar one need only read the articles by S. Talmon.[8] As for laws on ritual purity and the Temple cult, it is well known that they were assigned a central position among the earliest halakhot. We may note also that most of the disputes with the Sadducees in early Rabbinic sources involved matters of ritual purity. Two or three of the halakhot on ritual purity expressed in our work are cited also in early Rabbinic literature as the opinion of the Sadducees in their controversies with the Pharisees. MMT thus becomes an important piece of evidence in establishing the identity of the Sadducees (and Boethusians) mentioned in Rabbinic sources. The last area, that of marital status, is of course also a central part of the halakha,[9] and any dispute in such matters could create barriers to communal religious life.

The sect's halakha was more strict and literalistic than that of its opponents. On many questions its members (or its leadership) were not willing to compromise, and this is why they separated themselves from the majority of the Jewish people. This fact is stated explicitly in the epilogue:

> פרשנו מרוב הע[ם...] מהתערב בדברים האלה
> ומלבוא ע[מם ע]ל גב אלה
> We have separated ourselves from the majority
> of the peo[ple...] from intermingling in these
> matters and from participating with them
> in these [matters].

Here we have the earliest evidence for the term פרש being used to designate withdrawal from the general community. Its application with regard to the Qumran sect confirms the view of S. Lieberman that the term פרושים originally designated any sect which withdrew from the rest of the people.[10] D. Flusser has maintained that the sages were called פרושים by their opponents, who sought to depict them as a separatist sect.[11] We also find here the words על גב, which are used in Rabbinic literature in contexts referring to participation in purity.[12] A similar passage in Mishna Yebamoth 1:4, summarizing the disputes between the Schools of Hillel and Shammai, also contains the words על גב (but obviously not the term פרש):

אף על פי שאילו פוסלין ואלו מכשירין לא נימנעו בית שמאי מלישא
נשים מבית הלל ולא בית הלל מבית שמאי, כל הטהרות והטמאות שהיו
אלו מטהרין ואלו מטמאין לא נמנעו עושין טהרות אלו על גב אלו

Though these declared ineligible what the others declared eligible, the [men of the] School of Shammai, nevertheless, did not refrain from marrying women from [the families of] the School of Hillel, nor the [men of the] School of Hillel [from marrying women] from [the families of] the School of Shammai. [Similarly in respect of] all [questions of ritual] purity and impurity, where these declared clean what the others declared unclean, neither of them abstained from using those things pure according to the principles of others.

Note that a verb like נמנע could have been present in the lacuna in the passage in MMT, before מהתערב.[13]

As an illustration of the character of the halakhot in MMT, let us examine one of them — the law of the red heifer:

ואף על טהרת פרת החטאת השוחט אותה והסורף אותה והאוסף
את אפרה והמזה את [מי] החטאת, לכול אלה להערי[בו]ת השמש
להיות טהורים בשל שא יהיה הטהר מזה על הטמה

And (also) concerning the purity [ritual] of the [red] heifer of the sin-offering he who slaughters it and he who burns it and he who gathers its ash and he who sprinkles the water of purification — all these should become pure [only] at sundown, so that the pure should sprinkle upon the impure.

This halakha, which is based on Numbers 19, centers around those who take part in the preparation of the ashes of the red heifer and the sprinkling of the purifying water. It declares that they must wait after their immersion until sundown before performing their tasks. The purity of those who participated in the red-heifer ritual was the subject of much controversy during the Second Temple period. The Rabbinic sages of that time saw fit purposely to defile the priest who was to burn the heifer, and then to immerse him; immediately thereafter, he had to perform his tasks without waiting for sundown. This was contrary to the practice of the Sadducees,[14] as we read in Mishna Parah 3:7:

ומטמין היו את הכהן השורף את הפרה מפני הצדוקים, שלא יהוא
אומ׳: במעורבי שמש היתה נעשת

They [the Sages] defiled [deliberately] the priest who was to burn the heifer, on account of the Sadducees so that they would not [be able to] say: only by those on whom the sun had set (after their immersion) was it [the heifer] prepared.

The contrast with the Rabbinic view relates to a broader problem: Is the טבול יום (in Rabbinic terminology)[15] considered clean or unclean? From this halakha on the *Parah*, and from several halakhot in the Temple Scroll, one can infer that the Qumran sect considered the טבול יום unclean. This topic has been treated recently by Y. Yadin[16] and J.M. Baumgarten.[17] Let us only add one more example of this principle from MMT, and discuss another source of the controversy.

In MMT we find several halakhot concerning the purification of the leper. One of them rules that the leper must wait until sundown at the end of the eighth day of his purification process before he may eat from the sacred food (cf. Leviticus 14:10ff.), contrary to the view of the Rabbis, who did not require waiting until sundown on the eighth day. J. Sussman has drawn our attention to the fact that Yom Tov Lipman Heller, in his commentary on Mishna Parah 3:7, had already postulated that such would have been the view of the Sadducees concerning the leper, in conformity with their position on the purity of the red heifer!

One of the sources regarding this controversy was the passage concerning nocturnal impurity in Deuteronomy 23:12:

> והיה לפנות ערב ירחץ במים וכבא השמש יבא אל
> תוך המחנה

Bernard Revel demonstrated[18] that, contrary to the Rabbinic view, the Karaites interpreted the phrase לפנות ערב as designating the time immediately preceding sundown. They deduced from this passage that immersion, permitting contact with purities, should only be performed immediately before sundown, thus eliminating in effect the status of טבול יום. It is likely that this was also the regular custom among priests, as noted by H. Albeck.[19]

In the light of this practice it comes as no surprise that the passage of Deuteronomy was differently construed in both the Samaritan Pentateuch and the Temple Scroll. The SP reads in Deuteronomy 23:12: לא יבוא אל תוך המחנה כי אם רחץ בשרו במים ובא שמש ואחרי כן יבוא אל המחנה. And the TS 45:9–10 reads: וביום השלישי יכבס בגדיו ורחץ ובאה שמש. אחר יבוא אל המקדש. The same construction is found in the TS 51:5: וכבס בגדיו ורחץ במים ובאה השמש. אחר יטהר.

The adverb אחר in all three passages refers not only to ובאה השמש but to the whole sequence of verbs which precede it. If not we would expect a construction such as: 'וכבס בגדיו ורחץ במים וכבוא השמש יבוא אל המקדש.' However, this construction, with וכבס ... רחץ ... ובא השמש followed by אחר, is also found elsewhere in MT (for example, Leviticus 14:18; 22:6–7). Due to the tendency to harmonize texts, it influenced the form found in SP Deuteronomy 23:12 and the Temple Scroll.

Linguistic Observations

The most surprising expression is undoubtedly העריבות שמש. The word העריבות is a *hifʿil* verbal noun from the root ערב. There are three types of *hifʿil* verbal nouns in

Hebrew: הַקְטִילָה, הַקְטָלָה and הֶקְטֵל. הֶקְטֵל is a MH offshoot of the BH infinitive הַקְטֵל; הַקְטָלָה is the Aramaic infinitive; הַקְטִילָה is a special Hebrew development modelled on that Aramaic form. In Qumran Hebrew we find types 1 and 3: הניפת העומר (TS 18:10) and הנף העומר (TS 11:10 et al.), whereas the Aramaic form הקטלה is know to us only from the Isaiah Scroll (להנפה 30:28, as in MT). These three types occur in Hebrew also with the root ערב (העריבות, הערבה, הערב).

As is known, the construct and suffixed form of the Aramaic infinitive ends in the feminine *-ut*, for example: להודעה but להודעותני. E.Y. Kutscher has shown that such *-ut* construct forms occur also in Hebrew; for example, להשמעות אזנים (Ezekiel 24:26); הכרות פניהם in the Isaiah Scroll [equals הכרת פניהם in the MT (Isaiah 3:9)]; שתיקותיך as against שתיקה in MH; and so שפיכות דמים as against שפיכה.[20]

The form הקטילות itself is, however, known to us only from later Hebrew sources: להפיצותם in Daniel al-Qumissi's *Commentary on the Twelve Prophets* (ed. Markon, p. 56), and להצליחותנו in Midrash Tanḥuma (*Lešonenu* 23, p. 128). The form הקטילה is rare in standard MH, but it does occur in the Samaritan tradition, in Ben-Sira and in an inscription from Jaffa (perhaps it is a dialectal feature).[21]

Historically speaking, the phrase להעריבות השמש (which is similar to MH's הערב שמש[22] as against בוא שמש in BH) must have originated before MH, since MH generally uses the word חמה instead of שמש. We also see that the phrase הערב שמש was originally used adverbially, exactly as כבוא השמש in BH. On the use of *lamed* to denote the future in adverbial expressions of time, compare למחר, "tomorrow," or לעתיד לבוא in MH, and לערב (in the Temple Scroll 49:22).[23]

Another special phrase is פרת החטאת, "the red heifer." This is the mishnaic expression (for example Mishna Parah 2:1, 4:1), which replaces the single word חטאת or פרה found in BH. Perhaps one of the manuscripts originally intended to use the biblical term, since in it the word פרת is added between the lines.

The phrase בשל שא occurs several times in MMT. It is attested only once in the Bible, in the form בשל אשר (Qoh. 9:18); it also does not exist in standard MH, but appears in a Bar Kokhba Letter.[24] Commentators on Qohelet compare it to the Aramaic expression בדיל ד, which is used in the Aramaic Targum to translate למען and לבלתי (= בדיל דלא). M. Bar Asher has drawn our attention to the fact that the Aramaic attestations of these items are far later than MMT, and therefore that the view of Qohelet commentators (that בשל אשר is a loan translation from Aramaic) is not very probable.

The initial impression created by the language of MMT is that it differs from that of the other Dead Sea Scrolls, and is very similar to MH.[25] However, a closer examination of the linguistic components proves that the similarity to MH is restricted to vocabulary and to the use of the particle ש, whereas in areas of grammar (spelling, phonology, morphology, and syntax) there is a very great similarity to the Hebrew of the other Dead Sea Scrolls. An especially large number of MH words occur in the halakhic part of MMT. Some of these words appear frequently in halakhic discussion, for example:

מקבל, "[a vessel] receiving poured liquid"
פרת החטאת, "the red heifer"
העריבות שמש, "sundown"
על גב, "in participation"
טהרה, "purity, pure food and purity laws"
אומרים, "decide, have an opinion on halakha"

It is not only MH words, but also Aramaic words, which are more frequent in MMT than in any other Qumranic text; for example מדע, "knowledge," and מקצת, "some."

We believe that the language of MMT, more than that of any other Qumranic text, reflects the spoken Hebrew of Qumran, which was apparently closer to MH than the standard written Qumran Hebrew. However, it was distinct from MH both in its grammar and in its vocabulary, and it contains elements not known to us from any other phase of Hebrew (though some of them are known from Aramaic). It seems, then, that we should describe the language spoken at Qumran as a special Hebrew dialect.

Three factors may account for the use of this "spoken" language in MMT: (1) the genre of the work — a letter; (2) the language of its addressee; (3) the topic — halakha.

In conclusion, our letter is one of the most important Qumranic works. Its contribution to the history of halakha and of the Hebrew language, and to other fields, cannot be exaggerated.

Notes

1. J.T. Milik, *DJD* III (Oxford, 1962), pp. 221–225.
2. Y. Yadin, *The Temple Scroll*, vol. II (Jerusalem, 1983), p. 213.
3. J.M. Baumgarten, "The Pharisaic-Sadducean Controversies about Purity and the Qumran Texts," *JSS* 31 (1980): 163–164.
4. F.M. Cross, "The Development of the Judaean Scripts," in *The Bible and the Ancient Near East, Essays in Honor of William Foxwell Albright* (Garden City, New York, 1961), p. 149, line 4, and pp. 186ff.
5. The use of the word מעשה in connection with laws occurs in Exodus 18:20 (see the interpretation in TB Baba Meṣiʿa 30b, the Targum Yerushalmi, and Ibn Ezra). For מעשים, "precepts" in post-biblical literature, see S. Lieberman, *Tarbiz* 2 (1931): 377–379; S. Abramson, *Lešonenu* 19 (1954): 61–66; D. Flusser, *Die rabbinischen Gleichnisse und der Gleichnisserzähler Jesus* (Bern, Frankfurt-am-Main, Las Vegas, 1981), pp. 101ff.; J.M. Baumgarten, *Studies in Qumran Law* (Leiden, 1977), pp. 82–83; J. Licht, *Megillat Ha-Serakhim* (Jerusalem, 1965), p. 135 (Hebrew). The expression has been recently discussed by M. Friedman, *Tarbiz* 51 (1982): 193ff. One could add many further examples of מעשים and עשה with the meaning "precepts" and "perform the precepts."
6. For similar letters in Greek-speaking Judaism, see 2 Maccabees 1 and some of the epistles of Paul.
7. The variant readings of the several manuscripts are very interesting, but cannot be dealt with here.
8. For example, S. Talmon, "The Calendar Reckoning of the Sect from the Judaean Desert," *Scripta Hierosolymitana* 4 (1965): 164–199.
9. See L. Ginzberg, *An Unknown Jewish Sect* (New York, 1976), p. 128.
10. S. Lieberman, *Tosefta Kifshuta*, Berakhoth, pp. 53–54.

11. D. Flusser, "Jerusalem in the Second Temple Literature," ed. A. Even-Shoshan (Jerusalem, 1974), pp. 270ff. (Hebrew)
12. S. Lieberman, *Tosefta Kifshuta*, Beṣah, pp. 950ff.
13. Note the form ומלבוא after a verb of prevention. Such a construction is known from Aramaic and MH, but is as yet unattested in the Hebrew literature of the Second Commonwealth. Here we have side by side the BH usage (מהתערב) and the MH usage (ומלבוא).
14. See Tos. Parah 3:7–8; and Lieberman's notes, in *Tosefet Rishonim*, pp. 218–219. Note that this passage from MMT does not confirm Geiger's opinion (based upon the Targum Yerushalmi) that the Sadducees maintained that all the parts of the ritual of the *Parah* must be performed by priests [see M. Bar-Ilan, הפולמוס בין חכמים לכהנים (Ph.D. diss., Bar-Ilan University, 1982), pp. 129–146].
15. That is, one who had bathed but had not then waited until sundown.
16. Y. Yadin, *The Temple Scroll*, vol. I (Jerusalem, 1983), pp. 329–334.
17. Baumgarten, "The Pharisaic-Sadducean Controversies" (see note 3), pp. 157–161.
18. B. Revel, *The Karaite Halakah* (Philadelphia, 1913), p. 35.
19. See H. Albeck's commentary on Berakhot 1:1, and his additions, p. 325.
20. E.Y. Kutscher, *Hebrew and Aramaic Studies* (Jerusalem, 1977), pp. 131–133. (Hebrew)
21. E. Qimron, *Lešonenu* 42 (1978): 94 (and n. 65).
22. For the indefinite form שמש, see G. Sarfatti, in *Studies in Hebrew and Semitic Languages Dedicated to the Memory of Prof. E.Y. Kutscher* (Ramat-Gan, 1980), pp. 140ff.
23. See M.H. Segal, *Mishnaic Hebrew Grammar* (Oxford, 1927), § 296.
24. *DJD* II, pp. 165–166 (and the editor's note).
25. Cf. Milik, *DJD* III (note 1), pp. 221–227.

Some Aspects of Eschatology in Texts from the Qumran Community and in the Teachings of Jesus

Hartmut Stegemann

THIS PAPER CONCERNS "aspects of eschatology" in some Qumran manuscripts from the Second Temple period and in the teachings of Jesus. How can one treat such a subject within the context of a congress on *archaeology*? As a matter of fact, archaeologists like the late Père de Vaux and Prof. Yigael Yadin have contributed much to research on the Qumran finds. Nevertheless, one cannot dig down to eschatology.

The ancient Jewish historian, Flavius Josephus, wrote twenty books on τῶν ιστοριῶν τῆς Ιουδαϊκῆς ἀρχαιολογίας, surveying the history of Israel from the creation of the world up till his own time. Let us therefore use this broader, traditional understanding of the term "archaeology," and travel back to the distant past of Judaism in the Second Temple period.

Our efforts may result not only in specific information concerning the Qumran texts, but finally in a rather unusual, new appreciation of the teachings of Jesus that differs from most scholarly descriptions of him, whether Jewish or Christian. Even if we can only look for the main structures and implications of this new understanding and sketch it with broad strokes, this should suffice to stimulate discussion, perhaps even to reach some agreement.

* Sections 4–7 of this paper were not read at the Congress. I am obliged to my Goettingen New Testament colleague, Dr. Gerd Luedemann, and to my daughter, Stefanie Stegemann, for some improvements of my English style, and to my assistant, Phillip R. Callaway, for a decisive revision of the language of this paper.

Introduction

According to Luke 16:17, Jesus said: Εὐκοπώτερον δέ ἐστιν τὸν οὐρανὸν καὶ τὴν γῆν παρελθεῖν ἢ τοῦ νόμου μίαν κεραίαν πεσεῖν, "...it is easier for heaven and earth [that is, the whole world] to pass away, than for one dot of the law to become void."[1] This high esteem for the Torah is thoroughly Jewish. No member of the Qumran community, nor a Pharisee, nor any of the Talmudic sages could have improved upon it. Jesus was doubtless a pious Jew with all his heart and with all his soul. The problem of his recorded estimation of the Torah is that it is limited to a formal aspect only. What was Jesus' specific *interpretation* of this imperishable Torah?

Most *Christian* scholars tend to characterize Jesus somewhat as he is presented in the New Testament gospels.[2] Most *Jewish* scholars prefer to adopt rabbinical sources as background materials for their historical approach to Jesus.[3] Neither of these two approaches is totally wrong, but both are largely misleading. Today, our main sources for trustworthy knowledge of Palestinian Judaism in the time of Jesus are the Qumran texts. Therefore, they should now be used as the *primary* background materials for understanding the teachings of Jesus.

The remains of more than 800 scrolls were found in eleven Qumran caves.[4] Not even half of them are published to date.[5] But one can already say that most of the texts of these scrolls are not specific products of the Qumran community itself. About one-third of these scrolls are copies of biblical books, all of which were composed before the origin of the Qumran community, which dates, in my opinion, from the middle of the second century B.C.E.[6] Another third of the Qumran manuscripts consists of copies of non-biblical books, which were composed independently of the Qumran community, that is before the emergence of this group or in groups outside of it. Only about one-third of all these manuscripts may, strictly speaking, be Qumranic. As there are often several copies of the same document,[7] only slightly more than one hundred different texts from the Qumran caves may be characterized as specifically Qumranic.

Such specifically Qumranic texts are *Serekh ha-yaḥad*, the Damascus Documents,[8] the *Hodayot*, the *Pesharim* as well as many other fragmentary scrolls, most of which were unknown to modern scholarship before the Qumran discoveries. Pre-Qumranic are not only the Book of Tobit, the Book of Ben Sira, and the biblical Daniel Apocalypse, but also some of the Enoch writings like the Astronomical Book and the Book of the Watchers,[9] Jubilees[10] and the so-called Genesis Apocryphon,[11] the basic literary concept of *Milḥama*,[12] most of the collections of psalms including apocryphal hymns,[13] several prayers[14] and liturgies,[15] and finally the text of the Temple Scroll,[16] which may come from the fourth or third century B.C.E. at the latest.[17]

It is particularly interesting that not a single apocalyptic book can be attributed with certainty to a member of the Qumran community. Only two Aramaic texts, the Enochic Book of Giants and a description of the New Jerusalem prepared in Heaven, may possibly be designated as apocalypses and may possibly have originated in the Qumran community[18] — in any case, less than 2% of all the specifically Qumranic texts. Therefore, the Qumran community can in no way be regarded as an "apocalyptic movement."[19]

As a matter of fact, the Qumran writings give us not only much information about the Qumran community itself, but also a broad look at the ideas of Palestinian Judaism of the Second Temple period in general. The non-biblical Qumran texts were composed in the time from the fifth or fourth century B.C.E. down to the days of Jesus or to the first half of the first century C.E. No document from the rabbinical tradition is as old as the writings from the time of the Qumran community.

Even the specifically Qumranic texts are not "sectarian," but come from one of the most influential groups within Judaism of that time, the Essenes.[20] At Khirbet Qumran, there was just one settlement of this group. Less than 1% of all its members lived there.[21] If something like an Essene "headquarters" existed, one would expect to find it in Jerusalem,[22] not at Qumran. The designation "Qumran community" may only technically indicate that the best source for our current knowledge of the Essenes are the Qumran texts. In fact, members of this group probably lived in most Jewish towns, quarters, and villages throughout Palestine.[23] Is it not possible that some of them settled in Egypt[24] and in Mesopotamia as well? Furthermore, most of the Essenes were most likely married: not a single writing among all the Qumran scrolls published to date requires a celibate way of life.[25] The popular scholarly description of the Qumran community as a small group of "monks" living in "splendid isolation" on the shores of the Dead Sea is in fact nothing but science fiction.

During the last two centuries of the Second Temple period, according to my own theories from 153/152 B.C.E. to 68 C.E., the so-called Qumran community probably had slightly fewer members than the Pharisees: Josephus refers to more than 4,000 Essenes in comparison to more than 6,000 Pharisees in his time.[26] Nevertheless, the Essenes exerted a deep influence on the piety of Palestinian Judaism, as did the Pharisees.

As there was no established "orthodoxy" during the Second Temple period, the Qumran community, or the Essenes, cannot be designated as a "schismatic sect," but only as one of the larger groups of Second Temple Judaism. To speak of it, and the specifically Qumranic texts, as "sectarian" is no less than a "dogmatic" and misleading fiction of some scholars, indicating an incorrect and unhistorical view of Palestinian Judaism. Jewish orthodoxy was established after the destruction of the Second Temple not before 9 Ab 70 C.E.[27]

The center of the religious orientation of this Essene Qumran community was the Torah, as was basically the case for most Jewish groups after Ezra. Therefore, they could call their own community בית התורה, "the house of the Torah" (CD XX,10). But their canon of holy scriptures already included a second part of similar value, the prophets, whose books were also regarded as מצוות of God. The members of this group were obliged to think and to act כאשר צוה ביד מושה וביד כל עבדיו הנביאים, "according to that which He [God] had commanded by Moses and by all His servants, the prophets" (1Q S I, 2–3). Indeed, the books of the biblical prophets — including ספר תהלים — were the foundation for the "eschatology" of this group.

What is the meaning of "eschatology"? Eschatology belongs to a specific idea of history, which runs in a "linear" way from a "beginning" to an "end," for example, from the creation of the world to its replacement, from God's covenant with Israel in the past to a "new covenant" in the future, or from the Davidic empire to a worldwide messianic empire in days to come. "Eschatological orientation" means that people consider themselves involved in the ultimate stages on the way to the turning point, which is the "end" of the now current history. This "end" signifies for them the completion of salvation as well as the final extermination of all evil. Basic for each concept of "eschatology" is a pattern, in which specific elements of the "beginning" and of the "end" of a given history correspond to one another. 'Ἰδού, ποιῶ τὰ ἔσχατα ὡς τὰ πρῶτα, "See, I make the last things according to the first things," is an extremely apt description of this mode of thinking in the Early Christian letter of Barnabas 6:13.[28] Frequently, the end will be more perfect than the beginning had been.

There were several different concepts of eschatology in most of the Jewish groups of the Second Temple period. Eschatology was a basic element of orientation for the Qumran community. But in my opinion, its importance was second only to that of the Torah. The Torah itself remained always the most important element of their orientation and their main text for the halakha. The prophets could, however, offer advice about living according to the Torah, even for those living in the final days before the turning point that leads to salvation.[29]

Let us turn now to some aspects of eschatology in texts from the Qumran community and in the teachings of Jesus.

Eschatological Interpretation of Biblical Books

Eschatological orientation is documented already for pre-exilic prophets like First Isaiah and Jeremiah.[30] In post-exilic Jewish literature, many passages in the written tradition are quoted in an actualizing eschatological manner: the new author discovers a correspondence between himself or the data of his actual experience and sayings of traditional authorities.

But the Qumran community introduced a totally new theory, which they attributed to their מורה הצדק: the biblical prophets wrote their books not in relation to their own times but focusing on the future. This future of the prophets was at the same time the present period of the Qumran community and the last period of the existence of evil in this world prior to God's final judgment.[31] This kind of interpretation of the biblical prophetic books is found in about fifteen *pesharim*,[32] most if not all of which were written by members of the Qumran community during the first century B.C.E. The hermeneutical principle of the Qumran community was as follows: if you want to understand what happens in connection with us in the present end of days, read the books of the biblical prophets; they report it directly!

The Qumran community never interpreted the books of the Torah in this pesharic manner. One finds only midrashic texts like 4Q Patriarchal Blessings,[33] the sheet of

4Q Testimonia,[34] and many scattered quotations in different types of Qumran texts,[35] where single verses from the Torah are interpreted with regard to eschatology. From the point of view of the Qumran community, some passages in the Torah may be related to the "end of days," as the Torah deals with every aspect of Israelite experience in this world. But the commandments of the Torah were, according to their belief, everlasting and not only related to a specific period of history.

Jesus' eschatological interpretation of the books of the prophets may have been similar to that of the Qumran community. It was his time alone which the ancient prophets had in mind. Likewise, Jesus did not write commentaries, but gave his interpretations orally.[36] The main difference between him and the Qumran community in the realm of eschatology was, however, that he started an eschatological understanding of the entire Torah. In my opinion, this view is the key for comprehending the historical teachings of Jesus. Unfortunately, it has not yet been used sufficiently in New Testament research. Jesus thought that the end of time would have to correspond to the beginning of all time. He did not see the eschatological fulfillment in the appearance of a Messiah and a new Davidic empire,[37] nor of a new Moses with an amended Torah,[38] but rather a state of affairs as it was in the world before the fall, that is, according to the descriptions in Genesis 1–2. God and mankind will be together again and all evil will be destroyed.

Many of Jesus' sayings in the gospels demonstrate that he viewed himself and his followers as already living in the situation of eschatological fulfillment. The process of destruction of evil had just begun, but was not yet finished. For example, the sayings on anxiety in the Sermon on the Mount (Matthew 6:25–34; cf. Luke 12:22–32) correspond to the situation of גן עדן (Genesis 2): God himself gives to the human beings whatever they need — food and clothes. As a result of the fall, Adam had to cultivate the land in order to harvest its fruits (Genesis 3): the followers of Jesus get their bread effortlessly from God by means of a daily prayer (Matthew 6:11; Luke 11:3). The women, who caused the fall and who became guilty through their ancestor Eve, are now again religiously accepted like men according to the situation of Genesis 1:27. They are no longer disqualified. One could draw up a long list of such examples in the traditions from Jesus, all of which demonstrate (a) the eschatological interpretation of the Torah; (b) the correspondence of beginning and end; and (c) Jesus' conviction that the eschatological fulfillment had already started.[39]

Of all the groups in Palestinian Judaism, the Essenes were the most progressive in the eschatological interpretation of holy scriptures at that time. They may have influenced Jesus. Nevertheless, he took the next step by understanding Judaism's central document, ספר התורה, eschatologically. This was the basic idea of all his teaching, activity, and living in accordance with the situation of fulfillment presupposed by him.[40]

Evil in the World and Its Elimination

From the time of the Judean and Israelite kings down to the post-exilic centuries, there were in general two kinds of evil in the world: (a) the sin of people, and (b) enemies oppressing Israel.

The Qumran community introduced a rather new view: all evil in the world is inaugurated exclusively by wicked spirits. Their head is בליעל, and their aim is to make people violate God's commandments.[41] The Essenes thought that the wicked spirits were created by God himself, as he was the only creator of all beings.[42] But when they turned out to be bad, God decided to eliminate them. In the future, מועד הפקודה, "the time of the visitation," will come, and then God will destroy the wicked spirits entirely and forever (1Q S IV, 18–19). Humanity will be liberated from sin and, one day, will become pure and holy through an act of God himself. Then there will be only his רוח in the world, no other רוחים or רוחות. Of course, these ideas provide only hope for the future, for at present the pious are afflicted by בליעל and prevented by his evil spirits from a life in full accordance with God's will.

Jesus had precisely the same concept of evil as did the Essenes: Satan and his spirits are the source of every evil and sin as well as illness and distress in the world. The only difference between them was, according to Jesus, that the eschatological act of destruction of evil in the world had already begun. The power of Satan is broken in a first stage: he is pushed out of Heaven,[43] and his spirits must yield to the acting God. According to the formulation in Luke 11:20 (cf. Matthew 12:28), Jesus said: εἰ ἐν δακτύλῳ θεοῦ τὰ δαιμόνια ἐκβάλλω, ἄρα ἔφθασεν ἐφ υμὰς ἡ βασιλεία τοῦ θεοῦ, "... if it is by the finger of God [that is, by God's own might[44]] that I cast out demons, then the kingdom of God has come upon you." Jesus did not heal illness or exorcise demons in order to demonstrate his personal power or because he had pity on sick people. Rather, all his involvement in healing was merely a demonstration of the superiority of God's power in this world against the might of Satan and his wicked spirits. What the members of the Qumran community hoped would come, had started already, according to Jesus, during his lifetime — the expulsion of all evil from this world by the might of God himself.[45]

God as King and His Way of Ruling

One of the main ideas about God in the biblical books is his designation as "king." What was the concept of "king" in Judaism of the Second Temple period?

There were two central, political aspects in this concept, as is demonstrated clearly by the Statutes of the King in the Temple Scroll: (a) the king is the military leader of his people; (b) he is the supreme judge in his country.[46]

Both of these aspects are relevant also for the idea of God as king in the eschatology of the Qumran community. At the present time, God may appear to be a *deus otiosus*, who does not act against the evil in the world. But at the end of days, he will again be the decisive actor.

In texts like the *Milḥama* scroll[47] and *Hodayot* III, 34–36, God is the גבור, the "hero," who controls the eschatological war. He is the chief commander of his angelic troops, the צבא השמים, who act as warriors and destroy all evil in heaven and on earth. God will demonstrate militarily that he alone is the almighty king, a kind of מלך המלכים in the world. This is the main aspect of the divine foreign policy.

In the domestic policy, the king was a judge. A good king demonstrates his quality by means of fair trial. However, he can act as a judge only if there are problems to be solved. In a world which is entirely good, a judge is superfluous. The religious perspective of the Qumran community in this regard was as follows: God is a king, and therefore, he must act as a judge. In order to enable himself to become a judge, he created evil. If there was no evil in the world, God would lack the juridical aspect of a king. For this purpose, the wicked spirits were created; but they will be punished in the final judgment by God himself. This is one of the very few theories in ancient Jewish literature that explains why there must be evil in the world according to God's will.[48]

The idea of "king" in post-exilic Jewish literature is slightly different from the biblical descriptions of kings in pre-exilic times. In the post-exilic period, the "king" functioned primarily as a military leader; his role as judge was of secondary importance. This is demonstrated for the political king, for example in the Statutes of the King in the Temple Scroll (T LVI, 12–LIX, 21), as well as for the messianic king in the Psalms of Solomon from the first century B.C.E. (PsSol 17:21–43). The third biblical aspect, that the king will support the widows and orphans, the poor and oppressed people, plays no role at all in such post-exilic texts. Consequently, this third aspect was neglected in the common Jewish concept of "king" at the time of Jesus as well, even if New Testament scholars like to appeal to it. The literary sources of that period do not support such a view.

It is rather difficult to find the precise understanding of God as "king" in the teachings of Jesus concerning the βασιλεία τοῦ θεοῦ. After a first look into the New Testament gospels, one is inclined to say that Jesus saw God as a judge, because there are so many of his sayings related to the final judgment. A tradition-critical examination reveals, however, that most of those sayings, if not all of them, belong to secondary stages of tradition.[49]

Therefore, the conclusion is, according to the teachings of Jesus, that God as "king" acted primarily in a military fashion, his enemy being the evil in this world.[50] Not one saying of Jesus explains the origin of this evil; but many state that it is being expelled now by the might of God.

John the Baptist still announced a final judgment, the destruction of the whole world by fire.[51] But Jesus saw the military power of God already active in the world without any particular final judgement.[52] This concept may have been influenced partly by specifically Qumranic ideas of God as a military king, whose adversaries were the evil spirits. But Jesus' treatment of both of these aspects was more popular than that in the highly elaborate texts of the Qumran community.

The Motif of a New Creation in the Framework of Eschatology

According to the Torah and the other books of the Bible, the central point of God's creative activity was the creation of heaven and earth along with all of their constituent beings at the beginning of time. In the Bible, there are very few passages from the exilic and post-exilic periods referring to God's creative activity between the beginning of time and the end of days in the future.[53]

The same ideas can be found in several non-biblical Qumran scrolls, especially in the specifically Qumranic texts. In all of them, there are many sayings concerning God as the creator of heaven and earth, of angels and human beings. But there is no creative activity of God thereafter until the end of days, when he will again demonstrate this creative power. In the present, God does not act as creator.

The only eschatological evidence in the voluminous Temple Scroll states that God himself will create a new temple at the end of days (T XXIX, 9–10). Until that time, the temple built by men will be his dwelling place on earth. Such a divine creation of a building never is mentioned in biblical texts, and in the surviving text of the Temple Scroll there is no hint as to the specific function of that future temple. Perhaps, there will be only a kind of divine indwelling with the Chosen People in the future.

Other notions of this kind can be found in specifically Qumranic texts from the second century B.C.E. According to 1Q *Hodayot* XIII, 11–12, God will replace the קימי קדם, "what had been established in the past," by נהיות עולם, "everlasting things," a future act which is defined as לברוא חדשות," to create [things] anew." According to 1Q S IV, 25, the specific state of this world is determined both by good and wicked spirits. This state of affairs will persist unchanged until the end of days, when God will עשה חדשה, "make [things or conditions] new."[54]

According to the non-biblical Qumran texts, the world as it is will endure until the end of days without any further creative activity of God. Still, God will act again as creator in the future and will make new conditions for many fundamental things.

In those teachings of Jesus that can be traced back to his own historical situation, there is no specific saying concerning God as creator. But Jesus' descriptions of God have two aspects, both related to the motif of a new creation in texts from Qumran. On the one hand, God is acting again directly in the present as he did in the past, creating new conditions for salvation and for human life. On the other hand, there are many elements, particularly in the parables concerning the kingdom of God, that are oriented to the biblical creation motifs.[55] Therefore, one may suppose that there is something like an eschatological "new creation" present in the teachings of Jesus, even if the key expression "(new) creation" or some characterization of God as an eschatological "creator" does not occur. Nevertheless, his creative activity is again as actual as it was at the beginning of time, and as it was expected for the future by members of the Qumran community.

Purification and the Temple Idea

A central idea in the Torah is that Israel will be holy and pure in the middle of a world that is unhallowed and impure. The temple is not only God's abode on earth and a place of prayer and worship, but also the main instrument, established by God himself, for the atonement of sins through offerings on the altar.

These ideas were expanded and further pursued in the post-exilic Temple Scroll in a highly elaborate fashion. In this text, Israel as a whole is ideally secluded from all the other peoples of the world. This is the only way for them to exist as the holy people of their God without interference from the outside world.[56]

Some Jewish communities in the second century B.C.E., like the Essenes and the Pharisees, took the next step by separating themselves voluntarily from the masses of people in Israel.[57] The aim of all these groups was to live in holiness and purity according to the commandments of the Torah, in fact excelling the purity of Israel as a whole, as most of the Jews of that time were viewed by these groups as violators of the Torah. This was a sort of "inner emigration," each of these "separating" groups considering itself to be the only true representative of "Israel" in contrast to all other groups and the masses in Israel.

One main difference between the Essenes and the Pharisees during the Second Temple period was that the latter continued to participate in the temple cult at Jerusalem, while the former believed that all offerings made at this place were impure. The offerings were disqualified as impure, because they were carried out under the authority of non-Zadokite Hasmonean high priests from the time of Jonathan (152–142 B.C.E.). Therefore, the Essenes established their own community to represent the temple. The religious service conducted by the members of this community was regarded as representing all the offerings prescribed by the Torah.[58]

Nevertheless, there was no Jewish group in Palestine at that time which would have rejected the idea of the temple as the central institution for the acquisition of holiness and purity.[59] Until the end of days, the basic importance of the temple, its priests, its altar, and its offerings would not change. At any rate, there should be a new Jerusalem, with a new temple as God's dwelling place among his people, later in the new world, in days to come, but not at present.

Jesus did not challenge the ideas that Jerusalem was the omphalos of the world or that the temple was the dwelling place of God. But according to him, there was no longer any need for sin offerings in this temple. He thought that God, as a just king, had already begun to expel all evil from this world, and everyone was now invited to become a citizen of his kingdom. Wherever this kingdom of God had been established, that is, at least in association with Jesus himself and within the group of his followers, all sin and uncleanliness had been wiped out by the power of God. By continuing to sacrifice guilt offerings at the temple, other people demonstrated that they did not recognize this eschatological change. The historical background of the passages in the gospels on the so-called cleansing of the temple (Mark 11:15–18 and John 2:13–22) may have been nothing other than Jesus' prophetic protest in order to hinder the performance of such offerings in view of the changed conditions.[60]

Regarding this point, the most serious discrepancies emerged between Jesus and all the other contemporary Jewish groups in Palestine. But these discrepancies resulted solely from the eschatological fulfillment situation as starting point in the teachings of Jesus, not from any general opposition to the Torah or to specific interpretations of its meaning by any of the other groups. Where sin no longer exists, because evil has been destroyed or expelled, there is no longer any need for sin offerings to reinstate holiness and purity. According to Jesus, God himself had begun to purify everything.[61] In the teachings of Jesus, one encounters precisely the same idea of holiness and purity as is found in the Torah. However, Jesus argues that God himself now provides for these conditions and, therefore, the hitherto existing instruments insuring holiness and purity have been definitely invalidated.

The Basic Function of the Torah for the Qumran Community and for Jesus

No traditionally minded Jew after Ezra could accept any basic source for the knowledge of God's will other than the books of the Torah. In groups like the Qumran community, the biblical books of the prophets could enrich the possibilities of thinking about God's activities. Whenever contradictions arose between different sources, the text of the Torah had to provide the final argument.

This function of the Torah as the sole and definitive authority for religious orientation was challenged in Judaism of the Second Temple period by the authors of apocalyptical books. For the main intention of every apocalypse written in this period was to install a new authority besides the Torah.[62] Formally, such a new authority was established by Enoch, Noah, Abraham, Daniel, Ezra, or some other famous person from the past. But behind all of these figures stands the authority of Heaven, that is finally God himself, the real source of each of these revelations.

Each apocalypse claims heavenly authority for some specific matter, which is not presented precisely in this way in the Torah, for example a solar calendar with 364 days per year (1 Enoch 72–82), a description of the interior parts of Heaven and its angelic inhabitants (1 Enoch 1–36), a new concept of history (Daniel), etc. Wherever such an apocalypse was written by Jews during the Second Temple period, the Torah was no longer accepted as the sole and unique source of God's will. It had to be completed by further knowledge. Therefore, the Qumran community never composed such books, and if it used them, this was never done for their basic instructions.

This was also the orientation of Jesus. He did not base his teaching on apocalypses,[63] but only on biblical books, mainly on the Torah as the central source through which one knows God's will. If he concentrated on Genesis 1–2 specifically, this resulted from his eschatological orientation that there must be a basic correspondence between the beginning and the end of history. However, in order to gain this conviction, Jesus did not require any source for the knowledge of God's will other than the Torah alone. Reading these books from the eschatological fulfillment perspective would suffice.

Therefore, the Qumran community and Jesus basically agreed with one another in their acceptance of the Torah as the central and decisive authority for their beliefs. The only difference between them was how to read these books. And this they did in a rather different manner, due to their different attitudes toward the eschatological fulfillment situation.

The Actuality of an "Eschatological" Interpretation of the Torah

Members of the Qumran community started an eschatological interpretation of the books of the biblical prophets. But they could not treat the books of the Torah in the same way, as they regarded them as the basic documents of God's will, valid for all time.

An inevitable implication of each eschatological interpretation of the Torah itself as a whole is that the relevance of most parts of these books will be changed. In particular, the Sinai covenant is now related only to a specific period of the history of the world concluding with the end of days. Everything which is written in the books of the Torah remains the will of God, but now it is related to specific circumstances only.

From Jesus' point of view, one can learn many everlasting aspects of God from the Mosaic Sinai covenant, such as that He is merciful and will help even sinners to live in holiness and in accordance with His will. Such characteristics of God, which one can find in every part of the Torah, are unchangeable and will survive even the end of days. Therefore, according to Jesus, the Torah as a whole remained the central source for all human knowledge of God, in spite of his eschatological interpretation of these books. The specific election of Israel, however, is completed with the end of days, since now all mankind is under the same conditions. These conditions are freedom from every evil as in the time before the fall, and the sole, sovereign authority of God in this world.

This new orientation had already been inaugurated by John the Baptist, as is demonstrated by his saying in Matthew 3:9/Luke 3:8: at the end of days, there is no longer any specific situation applying to Israel alone as the children of Abraham, but everybody will now be involved in the same way in God's activity in the world. This is the very new and specific situation of the eschaton. John the Baptist and Jesus did not leave the borders of Palestinian Judaism physically. Nonetheless, their eschatological views had a worldwide orientation.[64] Whatever happens from their time onward, will involve all of heaven and earth; no one on earth will escape the incipient events.

Later some Christian communities tried to restrict the activity and teaching of Jesus during his lifetime fundamentally to the people of Israel, as is shown for example in Matthew 10:6 and 15:24. But historically, there was no ideological limitation of this kind for Jesus himself[65] — perhaps only a practical one, since the period of his activity was rather short.

This world-embracing orientation within the teachings of Jesus is also demonstrated at a secondary stage of tradition by passages like "the rejection at Nazareth" (Luke 4:16–30).[66] But it was precisely Jesus' world-embracing orientation, even if viewed historically, that became the main root of the missionary approach to the gentiles in the Early Church, as is shown best in the epistles of Paul. Paul's eschatological orientation includes also the idea that the Christian community — as a part and as an aspect of the "body of Christ" — is a domain in this world free from sin and evil.[67] As a matter of fact, this is the continuation of a central idea of Jesus himself, which stood in sharp contrast to the traditional view of the Essene Qumran community as well as to that of other Jewish groups of that time, such as the Pharisees and their successors, the rabbis.

Therefore, a specific kind of eschatological orientation became the crucial point of divergence between Christianity and Judaism even up to the present. Neither a different evaluation of the Torah nor any messianic claim of Jesus was responsible for the separation of the two groups. On the contrary, the separation resulted from giving different answers to the question whether the eschaton had already started or not.[68]

From the Christian point of view, the situation of eschatological fulfillment had already begun in the days of Jesus, even if much of the evil in this world had not yet been destroyed by God's power. Jews believe, however, that eschatological fulfillment will take place in the future only, not having been resolved in part in the past. Until today, both religions are strongly divided from one another by their different views of history. This is exactly the reason for the "actuality" of "eschatology" that continues until the present, having been introduced by Jesus the Jew almost two thousand years ago.[69]

Conclusion

Let me conclude my argumentation with a summary that offers both a rough impression of the main ideas of Jesus and of their background.

When God created the world, everything was "good" as attested in the Torah itself (Genesis 1:31). Following the fall (Genesis 3), all people became sinners, and from that time on the world was oppressed by evil. Despite this situation, God elected the people of Israel, gave them a covenant, and offered them the possibility of extinguishing their guilt by means of the temple cult and obedience to the law.

Accordingly, Israel could be sacred and pure within a world which was viewed as corrupt and unclean. This was God's special arrangement with Israel alone as witnessed by the Torah.

But at "the end of time," the power of God will overwhelm the whole world and gradually exterminate all evil. Wherever the power of God is victorious, evil is eradicated. This was, in fact, the belief of Jesus: during his time, the eschatological activity of God had already started to dawn. Since God had already begun to rule as the sole king in the world, there was no longer any need for guilt offerings in the temple of Israel, purification, or commandments insuring human obedience to the divine will. These special instruments were valid only under the conditions of sin and evil in the world.

Jesus proclaimed a kind of "realized eschatology," a concept that he had developed to a certain extent against the background of specific ideas of the Qumran community. But, in contrast to its understanding, he offered a new way of reading the Torah. As the Torah remains the basic document of God's will, revealed by God himself to Moses on Mount Sinai, nothing can be wrong or changeable in it. No further authority is needed to supplement it. Nevertheless, the basic conditions had changed since Mount Sinai, that is with the end of days, during which evil is being removed from this world by the power of God. There is no longer any need for the use of weapons against this evil, nor of sin offerings and priests, nor of commandments and purification. Everything is now pure, for God is the only remaining actor in this world.

Jesus' main objection to his contemporaries was simply that many of them, such as some Pharisees, did not recognize the eschatological change of these basic conditions. They failed to take account of the new actualizing understanding of the Torah, continuing to read it and perform its prescriptions just as they had always done. They did not believe in a God acting in the present, only in a God who had acted in the past and who would act again in the future. This was the basic issue between Jesus and contemporary Judaism.

Neither John the Baptist nor Jesus was an Essene. Nonetheless, some of Jesus' central ideas are now more comprehensible with the help of the Qumran writings.

Let us end with an expression of the hope that the vast amount of still unpublished Qumran manuscripts will become available to scholarship as soon as possible. I am sure that they will help us, much more than any other source of ancient times, to rectify our views of Palestinian Judaism during the time of Jesus. Whether Jerusalem was the headquarters of the Essenes in the past or not remains disputable. But unquestionably, Jerusalem is the headquarters of their surviving scrolls today. Let us stimulate in Jerusalem further research on these scrolls. They are certainly worth the trouble!

Notes

1. Even if the formulations of Luke 16:17 (cf. Matthew 5:18) can not be traced back to Jesus, the basic thrust of this saying was characteristic for his position. The sayings of Matthew 5:21–48 did not originally confront the Torah as a whole, but only a specific issue regarding the Mount Sinai covenant. The logion Matthew 11:12–13, and Luke 16:16 may have had a similar background.
2. This includes the messianic claim of Jesus, as well as the motif that his death might be an atonement for the sins of other people.
3. This results in a picture of Jesus as a "rabbi," or a kind of a "prophet," or a miraculous "healer."
4. The quantity of manuscripts from the eleven caves is as follows: 1Q: 72+3 =75 MSS; 2Q: 32; 3Q: 15; 4Q: about 580; 5Q: 25; 6Q: 31; 7Q: 19; 8Q: 5; 9Q: 1; 10Q: 1; 11Q: about fifteen; XQ: 4 — a total of about 823 manuscripts.
5. The texts from Caves 1–3+5–10+XQ (208 manuscripts) are all published, except for some parts of 1Q Genesis Apocryphon. Most of the manuscripts from 11Q are also published, but some of them only preliminarily. From 4Q, Nos. 128–157 (=*DJD* VI), 158–186 (=*DJD* V), and 482–520 (=*DJD* VII) are published definitively. Of the remaining approximately 483 4Q manuscripts, some are published preliminarily or in part, as for example some of the 4Q Enoch manuscripts by J. T. Milik, 1976 — altogether about forty manuscripts. Therefore, there remain about 440 unpublished manuscripts, more than 250 of them representing non-biblical texts.
   The editions of most of the published manuscripts are registered by J. A. Fitzmyer, *The Dead Sea Scrolls. Major Publications and Tools for Study* (Missoula, Mont., 1975). To these add: *DJD* VI (1977); *DJD* VII (1982); J. T. Milik, *The Books of Enoch* (1976); Y. Yadin, *The Temple Scroll* (1977, Hebrew edition; 1983, English edition), and some smaller preliminary editions.
   The scholars who are in charge of publishing the remaining 4Q manuscripts are Frank M. Cross, J. T. Milik, Jean Starcky, John Strugnell, and (instead of the late P. W. Skehan) Eugene Ulrich. See their articles for some preliminary editions of 4Q manuscripts.
6. See H. Stegemann, *Die Entstehung der Qumrangemeinde* (Bonn, 1971).
7. There are, for example, eight manuscripts of *Hodayot*, seven of *Milḥama*, or eight of the so-called Angelic Liturgy from the Qumran caves.
8. CD I–VIII + XIX–XX and CD IX–XVI represent two different books.
9. According to J. T. Milik, *The Books of Enoch* (1976), pp. 5–7, the oldest manuscript of the "Astronomical Book" was written about 200 B.C.E. and the oldest manuscript of the "Book of the Watchers" in the first half of the second century B.C.E.
10. The Book of Jubilees is cited as an authority from the past in CD XVI, 3–4, a text formulated in the second third of the second century B.C.E.
11. There are no specifically Qumranic elements in 1Q Genesis Apocryphon.
12. The basic literary concept of "*Milḥama*" may have been contemporary with the biblical book of Daniel. See P. von der Osten-Sacken, *Gott und Belial* (1969), p. 72.
13. There are at least four examples: 4Q Ps^{f}, 11Q Ps^{a} (=*DJD* IV, 1965), 11Q Ps^{d}, and 11Q PsAp^{a}. In my opinion, the biblical Book of Psalms was the literary foundation of those collections, but their non-biblical hymns are not specifically Qumranic, perhaps pre-Qumranic. These collections of Psalms were regarded as "non-canonical" by the Qumran community, a fact which is demonstrated in 11Q Ps^{a} by the palaeo-Hebrew tetragrammata in the square-script context of this manuscript. See the edition of J. A. Sanders, *DJD* IV (1965); and cf. Y. Yadin, *The Temple Scroll*, I (Hebrew edition, 1976), p. 300, n. 10; (English edition, 1983), p. 392, n. 10.
14. For example 4Q 504–506 (*Dibre ham-m^{e}ʾorot*).
15. For example the "Angelic Liturgy." Two fragments of it have already been published by J. Strugnell, *VT Suppl.* 7 (1960): 318–345; most of the 4Q manuscripts can be found in Carol Ann Newsom, "4Q Serek Šîrôt ʿOlat HaŠŠabbāt (The Qumran Angelic Liturgy). Edition, Translation, and Commentary," Ph.D. diss., Harvard University, 1982.

16. Y. Yadin, *The Temple Scroll* (Hebrew edition, 1977; English edition, 1983).
17. See H. Stegemann, "'Das Land' in der Tempelrolle und in anderen Texten aus den Qumranfunden," in *Das Land Israel in biblischer Zeit*, ed. G. Strecker (1983), pp. 154–171, especially pp. 156f., 167f.; idem, "Die Bedeutung der Qumranfunde für die Erforschung der Apokalyptik," in *Apocalypticism in the Mediterranean World and the Near East,* ed. D. Hellholm (1983), pp. 495–530, especially p. 507, n. 37, and pp. 515f. .
18. In Stegemann, "Apokalyptik" (see note 17), the "Angelic Liturgy" and the 4Q ʿAmram-texts were also listed under this rubric. But these two texts are not apocalypses. Cf. also J. Carmignac, "Qu'est-ce que l'Apocalyptique? Son emploi à Qumran," *Revue de Qumran* 10 (1979–1981): 3–33.
19. This is a rather popular but inaccurate characterization of the Qumran community, used in particular by some German scholars.
20. Differences between findings in the specific Qumran texts and the descriptions of the Essenes by Philo Alexandrinus and by Flavius Josephus may result from the following considerations: (a) both of these authors were only acquainted with rather late stages of development of the Essenes; (b) their information remained fragmentary, as they were not members; (c) their depictions are tendentious; (d) there may have been several "branches" within the Essenes; and (e) during the history of this group some changes may have taken place. But there should no longer be any doubt that the Qumran writings came from the Essenes.
21. Common meals were obligatory for the members of local Essene groups, cf. 1Q S VI, 2; Philo Alexandrinus, *Quod omnis probus liber sit*, §§86,91; idem, *Apology* (Eusebius, *Praeparatio Evangelica* VIII 11.1–18), §§5, 11f.; Flavius Josephus, *Wars* 2:5 (§§129–133, 138f.). But in the main room of the building at Khirbet Qumran [see R. de Vaux, *Archaeology and the Dead Sea Scrolls*, 2d ed. (1973), p.111] not more than about twenty-five persons could have had their meal at one time. As a parallel, much less than 1% of all Dominican Fathers in the world (fifteen out of 7,000) are residents of their monastery, St. Etienne in Jerusalem. Nevertheless, their École Biblique and its imposing library are famous throughout the world.
22. None of the Qumran texts presents an argument against living in Jerusalem for the members of this group. Positively, cf. CD XII, 1–2, and Flavius Josephus, *Antiquities* XVIII 1:5 (§19); idem, *Wars* I 3:5 (§§78–80); V 4:2 (§§142–145): "Gate of the Essenes" in Jerusalem.
23. See Flavius Josephus, *Wars* 2:4 (§124 sq). Cf. Philo Alexandrinus, *Quod omnis probus liber sit*, §76; idem, *Apology* (see note 21), §1. A few settlements like Khirbet Qumran probably existed on the shores of the Dead Sea, all of whose inhabitants were Essenes, but most of the members of this group lived in towns or villages together with other people. Ancient authors like Philo, Josephus, or Pliny may have restricted their descriptions to a few specific settlements.
24. Perhaps, the "Therapeutae" in Egypt, described by Philo Alexandrinus, *De vita contemplativa*, were nothing other than a specific branch within the complex group of the Essenes, even though Philo himself does distinguish them from one another.
25. Cf. H. Hübner, "Zölibat in Qumran?" *New Testament Studies* 17 (1970/71): 153–167. In the Qumran texts that appeared after this publication, there is no evidence which contradicts the view of Hübner.
26. The number of Essenes: Philo Alexandrinus, *Quod omnis probus liber sit*, §75; and Flavius Josephus, *Antiquities* XVIII 1:5 (§20). The number of Pharisees: ibid., XVII 2:4 (§42).
27. According to Tos. B^{e}rakot 2:6, Jewish orthodoxy started at Jabneh in the time of Rabban Gamliel II, that is about 80 C.E. There is no reason to challenge the historical accuracy of this tradition.
28. The best example of research on this subject is still the book of H. Gunkel, *Schöpfung und Chaos in Urzeit und Endzeit* (1895), citing Barnabas 6:13 as its "motto," on p. II.
29. For the eschatology of the Qumran community, see Stegemann, "Apokalyptik" (note 17), pp. 521–524. As far as I know, there existed only one group in Judaism of the Second Temple period whose basic orientation was (a) eschatology; and (b) a "canonical" rank of other documents besides the Torah and the biblical prophets. This was the so-called συναγωγὴ Ασιδαίων (עדת החסידים)

(1 Maccabees 2:42; cf. 7:13, and 2 Maccabees 14:6), probably including הברית החדשה בארץ דמשק (CD VI, 19, VIII, 21/XIX, 33f., and XX,12). This group flourished from about 172 to 153 B.C.E., and then split into two branches, the Essene Qumran community and the Pharisees. During the first stage of its existence, about 150 B.C.E., the Qumran community took over a shortened edition of the rules of its predecessors, which is still represented by CD IX–XVI in a fragmentary condition. In this text, not only ספר מחלקות העתים (= the Book of Jubilees) is of "canonical" rank (CD XVI, 3f.), but also ספר ההגי (CD X,6, XIII,2, XIV, 7f., cf. 1Q Sa I,7), which was the basis for the jurisdiction of this group with precedence over the Torah (see CD XIV,7f.). But the Qumran community soon changed this perspective. In its own rules, which were composed in the second half of the second century B.C.E., and which are represented particularly by 1Q SI–XI, books like ספר ההגי are no longer mentioned. Everything is now based on the Torah and on the biblical prophets alone. In the first volume of his edition of the Temple Scroll, Yigael Yadin discusses the possibility that ספר ההגי is identical with the text of the Temple Scroll; see his Hebrew edition (1976), p. 301; English edition (1983), pp. 393f. This possibility cannot be rejected, but considering the name of the ספר ההגי [see L. Ginzberg, *Eine unbekannte jüdische Sekte* (1922; reprint 1972), pp. 70–72], I would favor the opinion that it was a kind of "mishnah," or better something similar to the medieval *Shulchan Arukh*, that is a kind of "catechism." There are several other Qumran texts besides the Temple Scroll which also might be discussed as identical with ספר ההגי, for example 4Q Ordinances $^{a-c}$ [= 4Q 159, in *DJD* V (1968), pp. 6–9, and 4Q 513–514, in *DJD* VII (1982), pp. 287–298], or some of the still unpublished 4Q texts from the lot of John Strugnell.

30. See for example H.-P. Müller, *Ursprünge und Strukturen alttestamentlicher Eschatologie*, *BZAW* 109 (1969). Also H.D. Preuss, ed., *Eschatologie im Alten Testament* (1978).
31. See 1Q pHabakuk II, 7–10, and VI, 12–VIII, 3.
32. The Hebrew texts of all these *pesharim* are now readily accessible in Maurya P. Horgan, *Pesharim: Qumran Interpretations of Biblical Books*, Catholic Biblical Quarterly Monograph Series 8 (1979).
33. Preliminary edition, J.M. Allegro, "Further Messianic References in Qumran Literature," *JBL* 75 (1956): 89–95. Additional text, H. Stegemann, "Weitere Stücke von 4Q pPsalm 37, von 4Q Patriarchal Blessings, etc.," *Revue de Qumran* 6 (1967/69): 193–227, especially 211–217: quotations of Genesis 36:12, and from Genesis 49:4.
34. 4Q 175, in *DJD* V, ed. J. M. Allegro (1968), pp. 57–60. This sheet represents quotations from Exodus 20:21, Samaritans (= Deuteronomy 5:28–29, 18:18–19 MT), Numbers 24:15–17, Deuteronomy 33:8–11, and from non-canonical Psalms of Joshua.
35. Cf. for example the quotations of Exodus 15:17–18 in 4Q Florilegium I,3; of Numbers 24:17 in CD VII, 19–20 and in 1Q *Milḥama* XI, 6–7; or of Deuteronomy 32:33 in CD VIII, 9 = XIX, 22.
36. Cf. for example the relation to the Books of Isaiah and of the Psalms in Luke 6:20–23/Matthew 5:3–12, or in Luke 7:22/Matthew 11:5, even though there are some difficulties in tracing some elements from these sayings back to the historical Jesus.
37. Passages like Mark 8:27–30 and parallels, and Mark 11:1–10, must be attributed to later stages of tradition in Christian communities.
38. The secondary character of such traditions in the gospels is clearly demonstrated by F. Hahn, *Christologische Hoheitstitel* (1963), pp. 380–404.
39. More examples of this kind in the teachings of Jesus are listed by M. Hengel, "Jesus und die Thora," *Theologische Beiträge* 9 (1978): 152–172; and by H. Stegemann, "Der lehrende Jesus," *Neue Zeitschrift für Systematische Theologie und Religionsphilosophie* 24 (1982): 3–20, especially 13ff. A secondary, but nice illustration of this pattern is the passage Mark 10:1–12, playing off Genesis 1:27 against Deuteronomy 24:1.
40. A specific mark of this fulfillment situation is the activity of the "spirit of God" in the present. Jewish groups like the Essenses believed that God had restricted the operation of his spirit in the past to the time of the prophets, but that he would act again in the future, for example 1Q S IV, 21, even if there are many sayings about the presence of this spirit in specific Qumran texts like 1Q

Hodayot. However, as is demonstrated by early Christian texts like the epistles of Paul, or Mark 1:10 and parallels, the spirit of God acts now again in the present. Jesus himself had probably already propagated this idea (cf. Luke 4:18).

41. See for example 1Q S III, 21–24, or 1Q *Hodayot* frg. 6:2–3.
42. See 1Q S III,15.25.
43. Cf. Luke 10:18, and John 12:31. These sayings presuppose the idea that Satan governs his spirits from a position in heaven, as in the biblical Book of Job 1:6ff.
44. This formulation corresponds to Exodus 8:19. Further parallels: A. Deissmann, *Licht vom Osten*, 4th ed. (1923), p. 260, with n. 8.
45. There are still a few miracle stories in the New Testament gospels that represent Jesus as a healer, but the praise for this healing is addressed to God, for example Mark 2:12, Luke 7:16, or Luke 13:13. Even if none of these stories was formulated by Jesus himself, the idea itself corresponds to his own conviction.
46. See Temple Scroll LVI,12–LIX, 21.
47. For example 1Q *Milḥama* XII, 10/XIX, 2.
48. This theory is illustrated best by 1Q S II,13–IV, 26. The key word appears in III, 14.18.26 and in IV, 6.11.19.26. See also 1Q *Hodayot* IV, 38, and XV, 17f.
49. For example, Mark 4:29 appears to be a secondary addition to Mark 4:26–28, and Matthew 13:49–50 are secondary to Matthew 13:47–48.
50. The view of the might of God as a military power in the teachings of Jesus is still much depreciated in New Testament scholarship, but it receives much support from the Qumran texts.
51. Matthew 3:11/Luke 3:16. Cf. Matthew 3:7–10/Luke 3:7–9.
52. In the teachings of Jesus, the aspect of judgment was incorporated in the power of the "kingdom of God"; the punishment is exclusion from this kingdom, see for example Mark 10:25, whereas entrance into this kingdom precludes any further punishment or even any trial, see for example Mark 10:14 or Matthew 5:3/Luke 6:20.
53. The biblical evidence is discussed in a suitable manner by K.-H. Bernhardt, "ברא," in *Theologisches Wörterbuch zum Alten Testament*, I, eds. G. J. Botterweck and H. Ringgren (1973), pp. 773–777.
54. In the specific Qumranic texts, there is no speculation on the new creation in the future, neither why there is any need for it, nor what will be the real objects of this future creation.
55. For example, Jesus picked up motifs from nature to illustrate God's way of acting, for instance in the "Parable of the Sower" (Mark 4:3–8 and parallels). As God was the creator of nature, natural experience itself demonstrates the propriety of God's will. Just as there are different fates for plants created by God, there are also different fates for human beings independent of their own inclinations, established by the will of God alone and not questionable in any way. The Jewish background of this idea is now well attested in specific Qumranic texts like the *Hodayot*, or *Serekh Ha-yaḥad*.
56. Stegemann, "'Das Land'" (see note 17), pp. 158–162.
57. This kind of separation "from the uncleanness of the people" is well attested in rabbinic sources, and well known in the case of the Pharisees. The lecture given by Dr. Qimron at this Congress (see pp. 400–407), however, offers the first example of this kind in the case of the Qumran community. A passage in the still unpublished manuscript of 4Q MMT, from the second century B.C.E., reads: מרוב הע[ם ו]מהתערב בדברים האלה ומלבוא ע[מם ע]ל גב אלה פרשנו. For a translation and discussion of this passage, see Dr. Qimron's article. The Pharisees could have written the very same words.
58. See for example 1Q S VIII, 3ff.; and cf. G. Klinzing, *Die Umdeutung des Kultus in der Qumrangemeinde und im Neuen Testament* (1971).
59. In the Jewish diaspora, there may have been another orientation in cultic connections. Even if Jewish temples were built at Elephantine and Leontopolis, the main orientation was detached from the temple and its cult, as is demonstrated, for example, by Philo Alexandrinus. But there is only poor evidence for such perspectives in Palestinian Judaism of the Second Temple period.

60. The basic tradition for this prophetic protest may be represented substantially by the elements common to Mark 11:15–18 and John 2:13–22. There is no historical obligation to fix this event close to the death of Jesus, as the gospel of Mark suggested, or just at the beginning of his teaching, as according to John, for both Mark and John are led by technical ideas in this case.
61. For example Mark 7:1–23. One can trace back to Jesus himself not only v. 15, but also some other elements of this passage.
62. See I. Gruenwald, *Apocalyptic and Merkavah Mysticism* (1980), p. 3ff.; and Stegemann, "Apokalyptik" (see note 17), especially pp. 505f., 524, and 526, no. 2.
63. This argument challenges the popular opinion that Jesus conceived "the kingdom of God" according to the idea of "the two worlds" in some apocalypses. But neither was the concept of "the two worlds" confined to apocalyptic books (for example, Pseudo-Philo, *Antiquitates Biblicae*), nor was Jesus dependent on this concept at all, as it conflicts with most of his "parables on the kingdom" and some of his specific sayings.
64. The "fire" of judgment in the teaching of John the Baptist (Matthew 3:11 /Luke 3:16) probably was expected to be an eschatological *Weltenbrand*, that is a conflagration consuming the universe, as demonstrated already by 1Q *Hodayot* III, 29–32. Therefore, the perspective of John the Baptist would have been worldwide, and consequently also the perspective of his adherent, Jesus.
65. Indeed, the "Call of the Twelve" by Jesus (Mark 3:13–19 and parallels) must imply a specific orientation to Israel, as "the Twelve" were none other than the representatives of the traditional twelve tribes of Israel. But the election of "the Twelve" probably occurred in the first Christian community after the death of Jesus and was not carried out by the historical Jesus himself. Also Jesus "Son of Man" sayings may imply a specific orientation to Israel, but all of them are better attributed to early Christian communities than to Jesus himself; see Ph. Vielhauer, *Aufsätze zum Neuen Testament* (1965), pp. 55–140.
66. According to this passage, the Jewish participants in a Sabbath service at the synagogue of Nazareth "wondered at the gracious words" of Jesus, when he proclaimed himself to be the messiah (Luke 4:17–23), that is they accepted this claim. But as soon as Jesus continued to demonstrate from the holy scriptures that salvation from God comes first to gentiles and not to Israel, they were "filled with wrath" and tried to kill Jesus (Luke 4:28–30). This is a rather late and somewhat legendary story. But its world-embracing perspective may still be rooted in the teachings of Jesus.
67. For example Romans 6:1–23.
68. Jewish scholars sometimes are inclined to the view that Jesus himself was a good Jew, and that Paul founded Christianity as a separate religion. In fact, this division was not caused by Paul, who was a much better disciple of Jesus than is usually taken for granted, but by Jesus himself. Also, Jesus did not tend to split Judaism, but as his eschatological claim was rejected, or not accepted, or as it remained unknown to Jewish people, the split became inevitable.
69. David Flusser has already stated this quite accurately in his book *Jesus in Selbstzeugnissen und Bilddokumenten*, Rowohlts Monographien 140 (1968), p. 87: "Er [Jesus] ist der einzige uns bekannte antike Jude, der nicht nur verkündet hat, dass man am Rande der Endzeit steht, sondern gleichzeitig, dass die neue Zeit des Heils schon begonnen hat"; cf. J. Jeremias, *Neutestamentliche Theologie I. Die Verkündigung Jesu* (1971), p. 110. See also George E. Ladd, *The Presence of the Future* (1974), especially the chapter, "The Kingdom Present as the New Age of Salvation," pp. 195–217.

Appendix

In the discussion of this paper, Prof. Weinfeld kindly pointed to similar rabbinical traditions in which it is said that the Torah will be somewhat reduced in the days of the Messiah, in the other world, or after resurrection, as some commandments will not be required in the time of future salvation. The oldest source of this kind is the Babylonian Talmud, Nidda 61b. Others are *P^{e}siqtha* 50a and 97a. These and others are listed by Paul Billerbeck [in *Kommentar zum Neuen Testament aus Talmud and Midrasch*, eds. H.L. Strack and P. Billerbeck, vol. 1 (1926, reprinted 1956), pp. 246ff]. There are parallels of argumentation, but no historical relationship to the teachings of Jesus. In such rabbinical traditions, the reduction of the Torah will always take place in a future world, never during the present as is attested for Jesus.

The Sons of Light in Jesus' Teaching and in the New Testament

David Flusser

THE IMPORTANCE OF the discovery of the Dead Sea Scrolls for the New Testament and the understanding of the beginnings of Christianity has been recognized. Although Jesus' moral teaching is deeply rooted in the frame of rabbinic Judaism, his words and concepts often have striking parallels in the writings of the Dead Sea Sect identified usually with the Essenes. It has also already been noted that John the Baptist was near to Essenism, though it seems that he was not truly an Essene. Thus a difficult question arises, namely to what extent Essene elements in Jesus' words reached Jesus through John the Baptist and how much Jesus adopted from the Essenes directly. The answer is not clear-cut. In another contribution, I attempted to show that Jesus' Beatitudes have a literary parallel in the Essene Thanksgiving Hymns, but even in this case it is impossible to decide whether the Beatitudes depend directly on the Essene literature or whether Jesus was influenced by John the Baptist. One fact is evident —Jesus' Beatitudes are influenced by Essene poetry as reflected in the Thanksgiving Hymns either directly or indirectly.

It is very probable that Jesus himself knew the Essene Thanksgiving Hymns. Otherwise it is very difficult to understand why his own Thanksgiving Hymn (Matthew 11:23–30; Luke 10:21–22) is not only composed according to the same patterns as these Essene Hymns, but even contains their terminology and is similar to them in theological views. The self-awareness of Jesus in his Hymn is parallel to the self-awareness of the author of the Thanksgiving Scrolls, and at the same time the hymn in the Gospels is an expression of Jesus' high self-appreciation.

That Jesus met the Essenes and not only knew of them through John the Baptist becomes clear from his Parable of the Unjust Steward (Luke 16:1–2). There Jesus

* The above is an abstract of Prof. Flusser's lecture. The complete paper will appear in D. Flusser, *Judaism and the Origins of Christianity* (Jerusalem: Magnes Press, in press).

speaks about the Sons of Light in a critical way. When we compare this parable with the Dead Sea Scrolls, we recognize that Jesus opposes Essene economic separatism. In contrast to the Essene Sons of Light, who opposed economic ties with the men of iniquity (that is, the outside world), Jesus recommends to his disciples to acquire friends among the men of iniquity.

From Jesus' criticism of the economic separatism of the Essenes we can also conclude that he knew the Essenes themselves, though it is probable also that John the Baptist himself was not a partisan of the strict Essene separatism (and of their economic communalism).

At any rate the Sons of Light in Luke 16:8 are the Essenes and not Christians or Jesus' disciples. Luke 16:8 is the only verse in the first three Gospels where the term "Sons of Light" appears. The second stratum of Christianity represented mainly by Paul and John the Evangelist uses the term "Sons of Light" as designating the Christians themselves. This shows the difference between Jesus and his disciples and the second, Pauline and Johannine, stratum of Christianity.

Discussion

Y. Yadin: We had today מקצת דברי התורה as Dr. Qimron calls his document. For those who are not accustomed to the study of Qumran, I believe the five lectures we heard today illustrate how diverse, provocative and interesting the subject is.

First, I would like to relate to Prof. Schiffman's lecture. There is general agreement that the Qumranites sought to attain purity in the community already in the days of Belial for otherwise they believed that they would not be prepared for the end of days.

Concerning the use of the word עוור, its appearance alone without other blemishes was not a scribal mistake or oversight. Rather, עוור was used as a type heading for an entire group of uncleanliness, a sort of אב טומאה, encompassing all other types of uncleanness deriving from physical blemishes.

Both Prof. Levine and Prof. Stegemann disagree with my main chronological and theological conclusions concerning the Temple Scroll. I think it was composed somewhere around 150–125 B.C.E., that is, in the second half of the second century B.C.E., and that it is a sectarian document. Levine and I have agreed to disagree. Prof. Stegemann dates the Scroll to the end of the third century B.C.E.

The use in the Temple Scroll of the words עיר המקדש is paralleled, as far as I know, only in one other document — the Damascus Document. Both these documents — in nearly the same words — prohibit anyone after having sexual intercourse from entering and living in this "city of the temple" without previously undergoing three days of arduous purification. Only in these two sources — aside from the New Testament — is there a strict prohibition of polygamy. These two documents are also exclusive in their strict regulations for purifying the house of a deceased person.

In the letter presented by Dr. Qimron, the following phrase appears: כי ירושלים היא מחנה הקדש אשר בחר ה'. In my treatment of the Temple Scroll, I argued that the Essenes or the Temple Scroll's author interpreted all the prohibitions of uncleanness referring to the camp in the wilderness as applying to עיר המקדש — the city *per se*. Here we have a clear-cut definition of עיר המקדש.

I would like to make two or three short comments on Prof. Baumgarten's interesting lecture. I find it difficult to read in Fragment 2, col. II, line 2: בעלות לבני הנכר as *bĕʿūlōt*, since it is written without a *waw*. This spelling in Qumran is unknown to me. However, in הנף עמר, עמר is also spelt without the *waw*. Possibly the actual reading of בעלות should be reconsidered, especially since the term בעל in the Damascus Document and in other Qumran texts has a completely different meaning, that is, "experience."

In Fragment 4, I doubt whether the mention of הנף עמר and מלבד שבתות are sufficient to deduce that the former was actually prohibited on the Sabbath — though we know that, according to their calendar, it never occurred. In another connection, מלבד שבתות occurs with reference to other festival sacrifices (excepting the perpetual *tamid* and the Sabbath sacrifices). In regard to Fragment 13, I always thought, and I understand that Baumgarten agrees, that תגלאת שמן does not mean a mere stain of oil, for in Qumranite jargon, גאל actually means "ritually contaminated." In any event, this phrase here is another very important indication of the connection of the Essenes with the Dead Sea Scrolls, for Josephus clearly states that they avoided using oil because an unclean speck of it could contaminate.

Lastly, I would like to say a word about Qimron on Qumran. Qimron's rendering of the word מהתערב (in פרשנו מרוב הע]ם ...] מהתערב בדברים האלה) as "intervene," should rather be translated, "intermingle in uncleanness." (In the version of the lecture printed above, Dr. Qimron has corrected this accordingly — Eds.) Furthermore, יבוא אל המחנה אחר יבוא אל המקדש ואחרי כן is quite clear. The main point is that for the Qumranites, washing the clothes and cleansing the body were not sufficient. They did not recognize this semistatus of טבול יום, insisting that only after the sun set would men be pure. Therefore, אחרי יטהר most probably refers to בא השמש. If so, צדוקים in the Mishnaic usage would either be a generic term for all sorts of heretics — including the Dead Sea group — or because the latter called themselves בני צדוק. Hence Schechter's wisdom in calling the Damascus Document "Zadokite" rather than "Sadducee."

M. Weinfeld: Prof. Schiffman, there is a midrash that at "Matan Torah" there were no פסחים, עוורים, no invalids. Possibly we have here a comparison of the eschatological period to the ideal period of the Matan Torah, in that the entire congregation was to be whole and sound in body. In Acts 2, also, after the first congregation was founded, the episode about the healing of the lame is related.

Concerning Prof. Flusser's lecture, I would like to make a philological point. In rabbinic law, the words הון/ממון are interchangeable.

I would like to ask Prof. Stegemann a question. Pharisaic tradition also includes the belief that when the Messiah comes most of the precepts of the Torah will not be in force. Could we say, therefore, that the Pharisaic sect preserved a similar attitude to that of Jesus, whereas the Qumran sect believed that the Torah could never be cancelled? We should take into consideration the possibility that Pharisaic tradition influenced Paul when he said that after Jesus' coming (that is, for him the Messiah's), the Torah would be unnecessary.

I would like to add to Yadin's comment on מחנה and עיר. Here, too, we may find an origin in biblical literature, for example, Leviticus 14. Y. Kaufman has already noted that the מחנה in the desert was a prototype of the עיר (especially Jerusalem) in Eretz-Israel.

על ענין זה אנו אומרים mentioned by Dr. Qimron is reminiscent of Jesus's saying: "You say like this and I say like this," and is probably a manner of polemic exchange apparently referring to deciding or interpreting.

B. Levine: We have not seen the full 120 line text presented by Dr. Qimron, but it sounds more like something we would expect to read in the early second century of the Christian era, rather than a few hundred years before. The use of על ענין is very Rabbinic. Concerning עיר המקדש, the term מחנה, a biblical term, has its own typology in Qumran literature; in Rabbinic literature, we have מחנה לויה, מחנה כהונה and so forth. Since this is a very ambiguous, and rather ubiquitous, term, we will have to wait till the final publication to decide on the matter.

L.H. Schiffman: I would like to respond to Prof. Yadin's comments on עוור. It seems to me that of all those blemishes mentioned in the *Serekh Ha-ʿEdah* and in various other texts, the עוור is the least likely to have been included in the list. Therefore, if we accept Prof. Yadin's view, it is like the Rabbinic רבותא — the least obvious case is mentioned, taking for granted that the other blemishes are known.

I would now like to make a point concerning Prof. Baumgarten's lecture. I have noted in my *The Halakhah at Qumran* that כי־אם עולת השבת means that nothing can be sacrificed on the Sabbath except the עולה. The text does not state קרבנות or קרבנות השבת but specifically עולה. The עולה is the תמיד, a sort of replacement, מוסף, for the daily sacrifice in the morning and that in the afternoon. This was very radical on their part, and hard to understand. But in the light of what we have heard today, and of the now-published Temple Scroll, I will have to reevaluate the matter.

As for the Sadducees or Zadokites, we often fall into the trap of regarding these two terms as referring to groups which are absolutely defined. We often fall into the same trap in regard to Rabbinic texts on various types of Pharisees. If the descriptions have something in common with the Boethusians, we think of them as Boethusians. Although we have learnt from the new Qumranic literature that there was a multiplicity of groups, the fact is often still not acknowledged.

J.M. Baumgarten: I have great hesitations about the Sabbath sacrifices because the Book of Jubilees specifically permits the *tamid* offering on Shabbat, and it would be unusual, although possible, for the Damascus Document and Jubilees to disagree on such a point.

Prof. Yadin's has commented on my taking the Qumranites to have understood the passage on מלבד שבתותיכם as referring to the sacrifices. From the preamble to the chapter אלה מועדי ה׳, "these are the festivals which you should proclaim," מלבד שבתותיכם, "they should never overlap with the Sabbath but should be separate." Thus, we might be able to understand why this particular day was chosen for הנף עמר, on the twenty-sixth of the month, after Pesaḥ. In this way, the Qumranites avoided the overlapping of any holiday with another, just as holidays are not supposed to overlap with the Sabbath.

I believe that we can settle the matter of the oil, for I never meant that it was only a matter of dry-cleaning and staining. However, there is more here than just a concept of טומאה in the abstract. Something tangible had to be removed, as indicated in the Temple Scroll, by the scraping of the walls and the like.

E. Qimron: In regard to my citation על ענין פלוני, the latter two words are inferred only and therefore placed in brackets. As for מלהתערב, I accept Prof. Yadin's translation.

As to the singling out of the blind; they are not part of a list, for we have a halakha in MMT which specifically states that the blind and the deaf are not to serve, not because they are impure due to a physical defect, but because their handicap prevents them from knowing the law.

SESSION VIII
REVEALING BIBLICAL JERUSALEM

PHILIP J. KING, Session Chairman, *Boston College*

A.D. TUSHINGHAM, *Royal Ontario Museum*
From Charles Warren to Kathleen Kenyon
YIGAL SHILOH, *The Hebrew University of Jerusalem*
The City of David: 1978–1983
BENJAMIN MAZAR, *The Hebrew University of Jerusalem*
The Temple Mount
NAHMAN AVIGAD, *The Hebrew University of Jerusalem*
The Upper City

Respondents

GABRIEL BARKAY, *Tel Aviv University*
PIERRE BENOIT O.P., *École Biblique et Archéologique Française*
MAGEN BROSHI, *The Israel Museum*
AMOS KLONER, *Israel Department of Antiquities and Museums*
H. DARRELL LANCE, *Colgate Rochester Divinity School*

Discussion

Revealing Biblical Jerusalem: An Introduction

Philip J. King

In 1903 Immanuel Benzinger wrote:

> That to a certain extent Jerusalem has always been looked upon as the centre of Palestinian research is not strange. For the correct understanding of its history, this city, like few others, imposes upon us the necessity of acquiring an accurate knowledge of its topography. But in this city topographical research also meets with such enormous difficulties as are found nowhere else. These grow out of the city's history. More frequently than any other city has Jerusalem been conquered, and destroyed, and almost levelled to the ground; and upon the ruins of the old a new city always rose again.[1]

Written eighty years ago, this description is still an appropriate introduction to this session on "Revealing Biblical Jerusalem."

Jerusalem has a universal appeal, especially in the religious realm. It is the city where the Jews built their Temple, where Christians mark the Resurrection, where Muslims commemorate the Prophet's Ascension. As early as the second century C.E., Christian pilgrims arrived in Jerusalem to retrace the footsteps of Jesus. From the time of the construction of the Dome of the Rock in 691, they were joined by Muslim pilgrims who continued to come through the Islamic period to modern times. When Jews were not spitefully denied entrance to Jerusalem, they, too, made their pilgrimages. During the nineteenth century alone, about a million pilgrims visited the Holy Land.

Despite the large number of travelers to the Holy Land, Palestine was *terra incognita* from the scientific point of view until the nineteenth century. Much of the credit for the development of historical-geographic research in Palestine belongs to the American, Edward Robinson, the first scientific explorer of Palestine. His work in the nineteenth century inaugurated a new era in the topographical research of Palestine.

In his book, *The Development of Palestine Exploration,* Frederick Bliss, the first American excavator in Palestine, singled out four leaders whom he described as "the great quartette"; they were Edward Robinson, Titus Tobler, Victor Guerin and Claude Conder, representing respectively America, Germany, France and England. Tobler, the father of German exploration in Palestine, made a topographical study of Jerusalem and its environs, including the architectural features of the walls, gates and main buildings of Jerusalem. He also described in detail the complex construction of the Church of the Holy Sepulchre. Of Guerin's impressive seven-volume work on the geography, history and archaeology of Palestine, one complete volume is devoted to the study of Jerusalem. Conder's name is identified with the monumental surveys of the Palestine Exploration Fund. Each of these pioneer explorers acknowledged his indebtedness to Robinson. Conder's tribute was typical: "The results of his [Robinson's] travels form the groundwork of modern research, and showed how much could be done towards recovering the ancient topography.... It is in his steps that we have trod."[2]

The results of Robinson's explorations appeared in his classic, *Biblical Researches in Palestine.* Not by accident did the word *Biblical* appear in this title; Robinson used it deliberately. As his biographer, Roswell Hitchcock, explained: "The one adjective in our language which he loved the most, was 'biblical.' It was the watchword of all his studies."[3] The objects of Robinson's research were the physical geography of the Holy Land and the identification of biblical sites. His own expertise in the biblical languages and in the geography and history of the Bible was complemented by the special competence of his traveling companion, Eli Smith, an American missionary in the Near East. Smith's firsthand acquaintance with the Holy Land and his fluency in Arabic enabled these two explorers to veer from the well-trodden paths to visit areas seldom seen by other travelers. Smith's knowledge of Arabic was especially useful in discovering the correct Arabic forms of place-names. By matching modern Arabic and ancient Hebrew place-names, Robinson and Smith were able to identify over a hundred biblical places. In that way they laid the foundation for biblical archaeology and geography.

In his *Biblical Researches in Palestine* Robinson stated: "My one great object was the city [Jerusalem] itself, in its topographical and historical relations ... in short, everything connected with it that could have a bearing upon the illustration of the Scriptures."[4] Approaching Jerusalem for the first time, Robinson observed: "From the earliest childhood I had read of and studied the localities of this sacred spot; now I beheld them with my own eyes; and they all seemed familiar to me, as if the realization of a former dream."[5]

Robinson was severely critical of fanciful oral traditions emanating from monasteries and repeated by pious pilgrims. His rejection may have been too sweeping when he stated that "all ecclesiastical tradition respecting the ancient places in and around Jerusalem and throughout Palestine, is of no value, except as far as it is supported by circumstances known to us from the Scriptures, or from other contemporary testimony."[6] This negative attitude antagonized many of his contemporaries.

Robinson was skeptical about the genuineness of the Church of the Holy Sepulchre as the site of Golgotha and the tomb of Jesus. No direct evidence is available to authenticate the Holy Sepulchre, but the tradition remains probable. The New Testament clearly indicates that at the time of Jesus' death the place of the crucifixion and the location of the tomb were outside the city walls, as Jewish custom required. Kathleen Kenyon's excavations in Jerusalem have confirmed that at the time of Jesus' death Golgotha and the tomb enshrined within the Holy Sepulchre were situated outside the Second Wall of Jerusalem.

Robinson is associated in a special way with three prominent architectural features of Jerusalem. He and Smith were the first in modern times to explore Hezekiah's tunnel. It was a precarious feat; in Robinson's words: "Most of the way we could indeed advance upon our hands and knees; yet in several places we could only go forward by lying at full length and dragging ourselves along on our elbows."[7] Robinson also discovered the remains of Jerusalem's Third Wall, built by Herod Agrippa I and mentioned by Josephus.

The arch which bears Robinson's name commemorates his contribution to the rediscovery of Jerusalem. Robinson was the first to identify the row of stones jutting out near the southwestern corner of the enclosure wall of the Temple platform. He thought this spring of an arch supported a bridge leading across the Tyropoeon Valley and extending to the Upper City. Benjamin Mazar's excavations adjacent to the Temple Mount established that Robinson's Arch actually supported a monumental staircase from the Temple Mount down to the street in the valley.

In addition to the "great quartette," several other nineteenth century travelers to the Holy Land made their contribution to the history and archaeology of Jerusalem. The primary literary sources for this era are vast. Scholarship owes a great debt to Y. Ben-Arieh who has sifted through the *fontes* and synthesized them in his excellent study, *The Rediscovery of the Holy Land in the Nineteenth Century*.

In the field of cartography, F.W. Sieber and Frederick Catherwood played an important role. Sieber produced the first modern map of Jerusalem, depicting such architectural features of the city as the walls and the mosques. Little biographical information is available concerning Catherwood, who was trained as an architect and surveyor. He was also a great archaeological explorer. His detailed study and drawings of the Dome of the Rock are especially valuable. Using a camera lucida, he copied the outlines of prominent buildings in Jerusalem and produced a panorama and a map of the city. Robinson credited Catherwood's work as having been useful in his own investigations of Jerusalem.

Two well-known artists, David Roberts and William Bartlett, made their own lasting contribution to nineteenth century Jerusalem. Although Roberts' landscapes are somewhat romantic, they shed light on the architecture of ancient sites and excited interest among westerners in the Bible lands. Bartlett's expressive but unembellished depictions are an authentic presentation of Jerusalem and the Holy Land.

George Williams was another leading figure in the exploration of Jerusalem. His book, entitled *The Holy City*, contains valuable information about the plan of Jerusalem and the course of its walls. Totally unsympathetic to Robinson's skeptical views about the Holy Sepulchre, Williams supported the traditional position.

Jewish travelers were also among the nineteenth century visitors to Jerusalem. Two rabbis stand out: David Beth-Hillel and Joseph Schwarz. Beth-Hillel served as Robinson's guide in Jerusalem. In acknowledging Beth-Hillel, Robinson commented that he "had published a book full of extravagant descriptions of Jerusalem."[8] The geographer Schwarz settled in Jerusalem and devoted himself to the exploration of Palestine. In his *Sefer Tebuot Ha'aretz*, he commented on the site of the ancient Temple:

> This spot [the Western Wall] is visited by travelers of all nations; and no one can ever quit the place unmoved and with indifference. It is no vain fancy! I have indeed often seen there non-Israelitish travelers melt into tears. No one can describe the feelings experienced on this sacred spot.[9]

Despite the serious efforts of the nineteenth century travelers, explorers, artists and archaeologists, much work remained to be done. The reconstruction of Jerusalem's history had not been completed, nor all the scholarly disagreements resolved. The major excavations of the past two decades have made an extraordinary contribution to the understanding of Jerusalem's history. The material evidence unearthed in this period is clarifying both biblical and extra-biblical sources. These excavations have also revealed information totally unknown until now.

Nahman Avigad's excavations in the Jewish Quarter established that the Western Hill had been populated and enclosed by a city wall already in the First Temple period, at least from the eighth to the early sixth century B.C.E., contrary to Kathleen Kenyon's conclusion that the Western Hill was settled only in the Hellenistic period. Benjamin Mazar's excavations, close to the retaining walls of the Temple Mount, confirm many of the details in Josephus' description of the city. Yigal Shiloh's investigation of the City of David, while confirming some of Kathleen Kenyon's conclusions, has revealed new information. Evidence has come to light for human settlement in Jerusalem, on the eastern spur, as early as the fourth millennium B.C.E.

Robinson's lifelong ambition was to write a biblical geography, a systematic work on the physical and historical geography of Palestine, based on his own topographical studies. He projected a two-volume work, the first to be divided into physical, historical and topographical geography. He completed only the physical geography before his death. Robinson's friend and biographer, Roswell Hitchcock, lamented: "There lives no man to finish it; and when one shall be born to do it, God only knows."[10] He wrote that in 1863, the year of Robinson's death.

In the intervening years scholars from many fields and many countries have played a significant role in the completion of Robinson's comprehensive biblical geography. Many of those scholars are here today, in the audience and on the platform. An impressively large number of them are among our Israeli hosts at this Congress. To them and to all, sincere gratitude.

Notes

1. I. Benzinger, "Researches in Palestine," in *Explorations in Bible Lands During the 19th Century*, ed. H. Hilprecht (Edinburgh, 1903), pp. 596f.
2. "Lieut. Conder's Address," *PEFQS* (1876): 37f.
3. H. Smith and R. Hitchcock, *The Life, Writings and Character of Edward Robinson* (New York, 1863), p. 82.
4. Ibid., vol. 1 (reprint Jerusalem, 1970), p. 227.
5. Ibid., p. 221.
6. Ibid., p. 253.
7. Ibid., p. 339.
8. Ibid., p. 353.
9. J. Schwarz, *A Descriptive Geography and Brief Historical Sketch of Palestine*, trans. by I. Lesser (Philadelphia, 1850), p. 260.
10. Smith and Hitchcock, *Life, Writings and Character* (see note 3), p. 79.

Revealing Biblical Jerusalem: From Charles Warren to Kathleen Kenyon

A.D. Tushingham

THE RESULTS OF THE pre-Kenyon excavations are well known and excellent summaries can be found in many places. I need only mention, among the more recent, the summary and critique of earlier work given by Kathleen Kenyon in the first chapter of her *Digging Up Jerusalem* (1974); the catalogue of excavations provided by Shiloh in *Jerusalem Revealed* (1975); and the historical studies on Jerusalem in the *Encyclopedia of Archaeological Excavations in the Holy Land* (1975–1978).

The results of the Kenyon expedition's work in Jerusalem from 1961 to 1967 were reported yearly in the *Palestine Exploration Quarterly* and in Kenyon's *Digging Up Jerusalem*, but have not yet appeared in a full and detailed publication, although, I am happy to say, this fault is in process of being rectified. Since the deaths of Kathleen Kenyon and Père de Vaux, I, as the one surviving director of the project, have chaired a Jerusalem Publications Committee which is actively pursuing research and publication. The first volume is now in press and contains full reports on my excavations in the Armenian Garden, and on the investigations of the so-called Third Wall by E.W. Hamrick; there are also studies by Dr. John Hayes of the wares imported from the Greco-Roman and Byzantine world, and of the weights of the Monarchy period and some of the weights of the Greco-Roman period by R.B.Y. Scott. Work on other areas excavated by Kenyon is in progress or planned. In the light of this renewed activity, it is possible to present fuller studies of individual areas, supported by full documentation.

No doubt, the reports here of Shiloh, Mazar and Avigad, and the commentaries of Père Benoit, Barkay, Broshi, Kloner and Lance (see below) will introduce new data and new interpretations of evidence which, like some of the Kenyon conclusions, have been set forth up to now only in preliminary reports or more or less popular publications. This Congress presents an ideal opportunity to do the same for the Kenyon expedition. In what follows, therefore, I give a summary of the important work done before 1961, a statement of the aims and accomplishments of the Kenyon excavations and, finally, comments on two areas where the results of the Kenyon investigations have, I believe, much to contribute to the ongoing archaeological dialogue.

I would first like to note what I believe to be the most significant accomplishments of the pre-Kenyon era of Jerusalem investigation. Charles Wilson, in his *Ordnance Survey of Jerusalem* (1865), provided an accurate map of the Old City with contour lines carefully recorded and extrapolated — a *sine qua non* for all subsequent studies. Charles Warren, in his investigations from 1867 to 1870 under and around the Sacred Area, provided information which still remains unique in many respects but which has been corroborated in many ways by the no less indefatigable excavations of Mazar. Warren's contribution to our knowledge of underground Jerusalem extended to many other parts of the city; his recording of rock contours, his investigation of the water works deriving from the Spring of Gihon, and his tracing of the wall stretching from the southeast corner of the Haram southward along the crest above the Kidron — all had much to do with determining the locale and the directions of further research.

Bliss, with Dickie between 1894 and 1897 and with Macalister from 1898 to 1900, complemented Warren's work by tracing elements of the city walls around the Southwest and Southeast Hills and by explorations in the lower course of the Tyropoeon Valley. It is to the late Père Vincent that we are indebted for recording and attempting to date the Parker expedition's 1909–1911 discoveries of the various canals leading from the Gihon Spring, as well as for his noting and commenting on many other discoveries in and around the city over nearly seventy years. In 1913–1914 and 1923–1924, Weill undertook extensive excavations on top of the southern end of the Southeast Hill and identified what he thought to be surviving traces of tombs of the kings of Judah. From 1923 to 1925, Macalister and Duncan traced lines of fortification along the eastern crest of the City of David, which were confidently dated to the period of the Monarchy and later, and excavated large areas on the northern part of that hill to bedrock. In 1925–1927, with a further attempt in 1940, Sukenik and Mayer investigated the defense line which runs east-west some 450 m north of the present north wall of the city and which has been considered, by some scholars before and since, as constituting Josephus' Third Wall. In 1927–1928, Crowfoot and Fitzgerald cut a great transverse trench across the Tyropoeon Valley — not only again documenting the vast amounts of debris filling that valley but also discovering traces of Byzantine buildings and an imposing gate (the "Crowfoot" gate) which obviously belonged to a western line of defense for the Southeast Hill.

While in this brief catalogue we have singled out some of the important pioneers, we must at least name, if only in passing, others whose contributions cannot be slighted: Robinson, Conder and Maudslay, de Saulcy, Clermont-Ganneau, Germer-Durand, Guthe and Schick, Bagatti and Saller, Corbo and Milik, and many more of the devoted members of the religious orders all indicate the international and interfaith concern with the physical and emotional relics of a respected and beloved past in the Holy City.

In a different category we must place the investigations made under the Mandatory government, particularly by Robert Hamilton and C.N. Johns for the Department of Antiquities of Palestine. Their work on the north wall of the city and in the Citadel, respectively, provides new evidence which shows their use of a more precise stratigraphic method than that available to (or understood by) their predecessors, and their ability to use, in addition to coins and architectural criteria (which could be misleading), the results of a more accurate appreciation of the evolution of pottery styles.

A further step forward in stratigraphic technique, in meticulous recording and in the use of ceramic evidence for dating, is represented by the application of the Wheeler/Kenyon methodology to the problems of Jerusalem by Kathleen Kenyon in the years 1961–1967. She gives a succinct account of the outstanding problems which she felt still required answers in 1960 in her *Digging Up Jerusalem* (pp. 47–54). I may summarize them:

1. The problem of a complex hydraulic system deriving from the Spring of Gihon but apparently inaccessible from inside the city, whose walls at the crest of the hill were considered to be contemporaneous. Her great Trench I, down the east slope of the City of David, solved this question and for the first time located a series of defensive systems on that slope which could be firmly dated from about 1800 B.C.E. to Roman and Byzantine times.
2. The problem of the walls found by Bliss and Dickie, specifically their bearing on the expansion of the walled city from its origins on the Southeast Hill to the Western Hill. Her excavations in and on the eastern and western slopes of the Central Valley and around the Pool of Siloam have provided new evidence which cannot be disregarded, for the southern part of the Western Hill in particular.
3. The problem of the north wall of the city from the earliest period to at least the time of the Roman colony of Aelia Capitolina. Some answers to these questions have been found (from sites H, P, A XVIII and A XXIV) for the north wall in the Canaanite and succeeding Hebrew monarchy periods. Site C, south of the Church of the Redeemer, inside the Old City, provided new evidence for the lines of Josephus' First and Second walls and, incidentally, on the question of the authenticity of the traditional sites of the Crucifixion and Entombment of Christ marked by the Church of the Holy Sepulchre. The 1964 excavations of the Jordan Department of Antiquities at the Damascus Gate, on behalf of the Jerusalem Municipality, directed by Hennessy of the British School, have, we believe, established the line of Josephus' Third Wall. The new evidence discovered by Hamrick in 1965 for the dating of the defense line some 450 m north of the present city wall to a time later than Herod Agrippa (the builder of the Third Wall), should settle the long-standing dispute as to its date and its purpose. It is best interpreted as a barrier wall built by the Jewish insurgents in the year or two preceding the siege and capture of the city by the Romans under Vespasian and Titus.

4. The question of the pre-Hasmonean occupation on the northern part of the Western Hill. The work of Johns at the Citadel gave only slight clues for a possible pre-exilic occupation. Our excavations in the Armenian Garden were intended to supplement the evidence provided by Johns, but also to reveal fresh insights into the extent and construction of the Palace of Herod and of the headquarters of the Tenth Legion which succeeded it.
5. If the north line of Hadrian's Aelia Capitolina coincided at least in part with the present north wall of the city, as demonstrated by Hamilton, what was the south line? The excavations east of the Dung Gate, in site S, were intended to find answers to this question, while site C — just north of David Street — quite surprisingly provided interesting details on the forum which occupied roughly the area now called the Muristan.

Regarding nearly all of the above-noted problems and the solutions suggested or demanded by our discoveries, there is additional evidence resulting from Israeli excavations since 1967. The new discoveries have been reported promptly but, like ours, without the supporting evidence whose presentation is a costly and time-consuming effort. I am confident that the speakers who follow me will produce some of that evidence. I hope they will bear with me when I confess that I shall be using only the published reports available to me when I discuss their discoveries in the light of our more mature consideration of some of the evidence from Kenyon investigations.

In what follows, I shall concentrate on two areas which, besides being of great interest in themselves, have drawn the eager attention of our Israeli colleagues: the archaeological history of the City of David, and of the Western Hill. I must leave Prof. Mazar's magnificent achievements around the Temple Mount out of my purview; the Kenyon expedition's contributions in that area are at best peripheral and indirect — although by no means unimportant: they were often frustrated for multitudinous reasons which, I am sure, will be understood by Mazar and Shiloh.

Over the last seven years, Shiloh has been excavating on the eastern slopes of the City of David and has made very significant discoveries. He has confirmed Kenyon's dating of the earliest known city wall of Jerusalem to about 1800 B.C.E., and has traced continuations of the later walls down to the destruction of the city in 587 B.C.E. He has also recognized the existence and purpose of the great stone terraces which, under the Canaanite precursors of the Israelites and under David and his successors, extended down the eastern slopes of the hill. Kenyon considered them to be foundations of houses and to constitute what, after the Davidic capture of the city, was called the Millo. Shiloh, I think, interprets the Canaanite elements of these terraces as an intrinsic component of a Canaanite citadel or acropolis complex at the northeast corner of the city.

I should, however, like to make a few comments on the great sloping revetment which Shiloh interprets as an element of the Ophel or Citadel of Jerusalem built by David. This sloping stone structure, called by its discoverers, Macalister and Duncan, the "Jebusite ramp," consists of two sections (see opposite p. 49 of their 1926 publication). The plan shows no connection between the northern part of the ramp and the rectangular tower dated by them to the Davidic-Solomonic period, but in their Plate V the curving line of the northern portion extends to meet their outer wall (also attributed to the Jebusites). What seems to be the logical continuation of the northern portion is considered to be an earlier sloping glacis which was later converted into the rectangular tower. A comparison of their Fig. 48 with Kenyon's Pl. 81, however, suggests strongly that the southern part of the "Jebusite ramp" actually abutted the tower and so must be later than it; as this tower is now, following Kenyon, generally considered to be Maccabean, the southern portion of the ramp must be at least Maccabean or later. The fact that this portion does not descend below the line where the Kenyon excavations commenced — which must have been the level reached by the Macalister excavations — indicates that whatever the confusion introduced by the reconstruction of this part of the ramp by the Palestine Department of Antiquities after the Macalister and Duncan excavations, there can be no doubt that there must be a sharp distinction between the history of the southern and northern part of the ramp. I believe, however, that it was this discrepancy between the southern and northern portions which led Shiloh to think there was a conflict between his discoveries and Kenyon's.

There *is* a northern portion of the stone stepped structure which, as Shiloh has now demonstrated, descends without a break *below* the level of the latest artificial terraces; it abuts the earlier Canaanite terraces and perhaps incorporated them as part of the Davidic citadel. Why, then, did not this fact become clear to Kenyon?

I have discussed this matter with Henk Franken of Leiden, who has assumed responsibility for the publication of the results of the Kenyon expedition on the east slope of the City of David. He points out that the northern side of Kenyon's Trench I is a projection eastward and downward of the north face of the Macalister rectangular tower. This line is about 7 m south of the northern and earlier ramp. Nowhere does Shiloh's ramp appear in the north section of Kenyon's Trench I. Near the top of the slope where she did continue her excavations further toward the north, she found the Late Bronze Age terraces immediately below remains of the 587 B.C.E. destruction with no intervening ramp. Obviously, she had no reason to believe that any part of Macalister's ramp descended below the post-exilic level. There is no conflict between the interpretations of Kenyon and Shiloh because they were dealing with two different architectural features.

There is, however, one consequence of Shiloh's discoveries which may modify Kenyon's interpretation of the eastern defense walls of the City of David from their first construction about 1800 B.C.E. down to the eighth–seventh centuries B.C.E. It will be remembered that she had identified these low down on the eastern slope in Trench I. Excavation higher up the slope and about 40 m north of Trench I, in square A XXIV, revealed no construction earlier than the eighth century B.C.E. The line followed by the city wall up the slope before the eighth century B.C.E. must, therefore, run south of square A XXIV. In squares H and P, on the top of the hill, almost due west of square A XXIV, were walls which must in some way be associated with the Canaanite and early Israelite defenses. Along the southern side of site H runs a massive structure built of large blocks embedded in and faced with thick white mortar. Its northeast corner is about 11 m west of the crest of the Kidron, and the north side of the structure is about 21 m long. It may be the base or podium of a major feature of the early north defense line, but it is not itself the north wall for there is no evidence that it stretched across the whole width of the hill. Evidence for dating this construction directly is scanty but its destruction *may* coincide, at least approximately, with the Davidic conquest.

We are on surer ground when we consider the remains of a casemate wall, lying directly on bedrock and running just inside the crest above the Kidron Valley (see Kenyon's Pl. 37). On typological grounds, at least, we are tempted to date it to the time of Solomon and compare it with similar constructions found at Megiddo, Hazor and Gezer of that period. Some 10 m further south is site P, and directly east of P is square A XVIII. In A XVIII, bedrock had been quarried on a sheer vertical line, and above it, resting directly on bedrock, ran the wall dated by Kenyon to the time of Nehemiah. At the base of the scarp, beneath a midden of the Nehemiah period which lapped up against the foot of the Nehemiah wall, was a deposit of tumbled masonry representing the Babylonian destruction of important buildings of the Monarchy period, including a proto-Aeolic capital. The vertical scarp is therefore pre-exilic and it is logical to assume that the city wall of the early Monarchy period ran along its crest. The fact that the Nehemiah wall is the earliest wall preserved at this point can only mean that the debris at the foot of the scarp represents the collapse outward of all earlier structures on this line at the time of the Babylonian destruction. We may, then, conjecture that the casemate wall found in site H continued at least as far south as site P and even abutted the Davidic fortress posited by Shiloh, if, as seems probable, it rose to the crest of the slope at this point.

If this somewhat long and tentative interpretation of our discoveries in sites H, P and A XXIV be accepted, we must modify Kenyon's hypothetical oblique course of the Israelite east wall (her Wall NB) up the steep slope of the City of David in several respects. Such a wall must have existed originally, for Kenyon noted (p. 94) that the houses of the Middle Bronze Age town merely climbed up the slope above and inside the eastern wall without the benefit of a terrace system. It is probable, however, that experience quickly demonstrated the difficulty of building and maintaining a city wall on such a slope. The solution to this problem reached by the Jebusites, and adapted by David, was to construct a fortress at this weak point, using a system of heavy stone terraces which could provide a better foundation for a defense line on the steep slope. It was not a perfect solution, as is witnessed by the archaeological evidence of frequent collapses and repairs, but it remained in use for some 500 years until, with the growth of the city and in anticipation of Assyrian attacks, new defensive works were required on the east slope. These, including wall NA of some 7 m width, were carried due north to include areas which had previously been excluded from the walled city. Only then, when the Davidic citadel ceased to have a primary defensive role, were private houses built on the steep but solid slope of the ramp (Kenyon, pp. 130–131, 144–151). No doubt, when Shiloh and Franken provide complete publication of the work carried out over the last twenty-two years on this east slope of the City of David, new precision and new evidence will be at hand for the reconstruction of the architectural history of this important area.

The important discoveries of Avigad on the Western Hill, in the Jewish Quarter, are now well known. His proof that the city already possessed a suburb on the Western Hill during the period of the Monarchy has revolutionized all of our thinking. The broad defense wall — 7 m thick — discovered by Avigad follows, as everyone admits, a rather strange course which has left the definition of the area enclosed within it open to considerable guess work. Avigad himself (p. 43 and map) projected the line of the wall southward to run down the crest of the hill — some 140 m inside the present western city wall — and to cross the Central Valley to join up with the walls of the original City of David at its southern point, enclosing the traditional Pool of Siloam. The northern end of the wall was considered to have curved toward the east to follow the traditional line of Josephus' First Wall and to cross the Central Valley and then abut the western wall of the Temple Mount. A course along the line of Josephus' First Wall was to some extent substantiated by Avigad's later discovery of part of an Iron Age tower on the same line, which was apparently besieged by the Babylonians at the end of the Monarchy. Subsequently, Geva in 1979 proposed extending the western limit of the settlement there as far west as the crest above the Hinnom Valley.

The evidence is now quite definite that the area excavated on top of the Western Hill eastward from the crest of the Hinnom Valley bears no indication of a pre-exilic city wall or occupation. In the Armenian Garden, our excavations and those of Bahat and Broshi have demonstrated that the whole area was quarried, and it is clear from the deposits sealing the quarries that they were being exploited right down to the last days of the city before its destruction by Nebuchadnezzar. There are, indeed, walls of this period resting on bedrock but none of them appears to have been free-standing, and all seem to have run in a north-south direction. There are no cisterns of the period nor any other evidence of permanent settlement. It is best, therefore, to interpret these walls as retaining walls for the spoil heaps of earth removed from the rock surface before quarrying or as by-products of the quarrying operation itself.

The existence of quarries of the pre-exilic period north of the line of Josephus' First Wall has also been demonstrated by the Kenyon excavations in area C (Kenyon, pp. 227–235); those quarries have been traced northward in the excavations of Ute Lux-Wagner and Karel Vriezen under the Church of the Redeemer, and by Broshi in the vicinity of the Church of the Holy Sepulchre. We can assume that such quarries also existed in the area of the Citadel. Johns, for instance, refers (p. 138) to a very deep "quarry-pit" at the base of his sounding E; Amiran and Eitan, however, make no specific reference to quarries. There is reason to believe that all of these quarries belong to the same period as our quarries in the Armenian

Garden — the last years of the Monarchy. We must conclude that any city walls of the pre-exilic period on the Western Hill must lie not only south of David Street but also well to the east of the crest above the Hinnom Valley. How far inside these limits the defense lines of the quarter there must be drawn remains uncertain, but it is difficult to believe that any part of the southern extension of the Western Hill down to Siloam was included if the crest of the hill was not.

Ever since the excavations of Johns in the Citadel, there has been general agreement that the northern part of the Western Hill, if not the whole of it down to its southern extremity, was enclosed by city walls from Hasmonean times on. Basically, the evidence is that defensive walls existed in the Citadel before the building of the great towers of Hippicus, Phasael and Mariamme by Herod the Great. Johns defined two masonry types (his first and second builds) as distinctive of the pre-Herodian period, the former preceding the latter.

The earliest city wall found in our 1962–1967 excavations in the Armenian Garden was structurally of Johns' first period (see Johns, Pls. L.3:LI.1), but it must be emphasized that we found only foundational courses. The stratigraphy leaves no doubt that this wall belongs to the period of Herod the Great. The deposits in question constitute the fill of the great podium upon which Herod built his palace; the wall which retained them to the west was also the city wall. These deposits contain not only domestic pottery of the period of Herod the Great, but also imported pottery which is datable to the last quarter of the first century B.C.E. A coin of Herod the Great was found in a consolidation wall of this first podium.

No trace was found in our excavations of walls representing Johns' second or third builds. Amiran and Eitan, on the basis of their excavations in the Citadel, accepted Johns' dating of the two earlier periods to the Hasmonean period, although Johns himself recognized that, structurally, his second build could be Herodian; and Paul Lapp (pp. 52–53), in his analysis and critique of Johns' dating, based on pottery criteria, suggested that it "may date to the early part of Herod's reign or possibly the time of Antipater...."

I confess that I have not had time to digest Geva's 1983 report on his 1979–1980 excavations in the Citadel, nor to compare the results with the work of Johns and Amiran and Eitan. I can only say that the results appear to differ so much from what has been found in the Armenian Garden, and on the traditional Mount Zion to the south, that we may have to consider a much more complicated history of the defensive systems on the Western Hill than we have had to envision up to the present.

Bahat and Broshi, in their excavations in the Armenian Garden, identified as Hasmonean a very broad wall underlying the present Turkish wall and extending beyond it on both sides. Later, Broshi, in his article "Along Jerusalem's Walls," modified this conclusion and posited the existence of two walls — an earlier, termed "Hasmonean," founded on bedrock and with a width of 5.3 m, and a later "Herodian Outer Rampart" built up against the western face of the earlier wall and extending its width to a total thickness of 8 m. No evidence is given for dating these walls, but the earliest structural remains inside them appear to be no earlier than the podium of Herod's palace.

Our excavations in the Armenian Garden produced similar results. I have noted that the earliest wall was that which bounded Herod's great palace podium and it projected 2.5 m east of the present Turkish wall. This wall, however, and the eastern wall of the podium collapsed outward to west and east, necessitating a rebuild of the outer walls and the insertion of a new fill. The new wall on the crest of the Hinnom was built, like Broshi's, west of the earlier one but — as we could not dig west of the Turkish wall — we learned nothing of its construction or width. However, it can be dated quite clearly on the basis of the second podium fill; the evidence of the pottery and coins is that this rebuilding was no earlier than the time of Herod Agrippa and, for a variety of reasons, it seems probable that it is to be attributed to Agrippa. It appears that we have found, in our excavations, a clear parallel to Broshi's double wall, but we can date the inner element to the time of Herod the Great and the outer element probably to Herod Agrippa.

In this regard we should note, also, the discoveries of Broshi south of the Armenian Garden on the traditional Mount Zion (1975). Here he distinguished two first century B.C.E. periods of building, the first assigned to the "eve of Herod's accession" and possibly destroyed by the earthquake of 31 B.C.E., the later of the two ascribed to the period from Herod the Great to the destruction of the city in 70 C.E. He has apparently found no earlier, Hasmonean, buildings or defenses in this area.

One could add to the above the evidence, discovered on the Southwestern Hill south of the traditional Mount Zion by Bliss and Dickie (p. 39), for a wall of bossed ashlars similar to Johns' second build, which both Johns (pp. 150–152) and Kenyon (pp. 202–204) considered to be probably its continuation, and hence of the pre-Herodian period. Kenyon (p. 235) also notes a tower excavated by Bliss and Dickie (p. 30) which could be of the Herodian period, but whether of Herod the Great or Herod Agrippa is uncertain. Doubt already expressed as to the dating of the bossed masonry in the Citadel, and the apparently complete absence of pre-Herodian defenses in the Armenian Garden and on the traditional Mount Zion, force us to await new excavations on the Southwest Hill to establish the true ascription of elements in the Bliss–Dickie circumvallation, based on stratigraphic and other evidence, more accurately datable than styles of stone-cutting. We should also note that the evidence from Kenyon's excavations on the lower eastern slopes of the Western Hill and in the vicinity of the Pool of Siloam, together with the probable Maccabean date of the "Crowfoot" gate in the Central Valley, raises grave doubts as to the validity of the assumption of including the whole Western Hill down to the Pool of Siloam within the city walls as early as the Hasmonean period.

I have presented some of the evidence from the Kenyon excavations and the subsequent Israeli excavations as it bears on problems in two areas only. Possibly, in the papers that follow mine, I shall discover that some of the problems have already received solutions on the basis of information not at my disposal. I hope, in turn, that our colleagues will have the patience to await the full publication of the Kenyon expedition before assuming that everything valuable has already appeared in print. Personally, I believe that the archaeological history of the city of Jerusalem is of sufficient importance to withold final judgment on details until all he evidence is at hand.

Select Bibliography

Amiran, R. and Eitan, A. "Excavations in the Jerusalem Citadel." In *Jerusalem Revealed*, edited by Y. Yadin. Jerusalem, 1975, pp. 52–54.

Avigad, N. "Excavations in the Jewish Quarter of the Old City, 1969–1971." In *Jerusalem Revealed*, edited by Y. Yadin. Jerusalem, 1975, pp. 41–51.

——. "Jerusalem, the Jewish Quarter of the Old City." *IEJ* 27 (1977): 55–57.

Avi-Yonah, M. and Stern, E., eds. *Encyclopedia of Archaeological Excavations in the Holy Land.* Vol. II, English ed. Jerusalem, 1975–1978.

Bahat, D. and Broshi, M. "Excavations in the Armenian Garden." In *Jerusalem Revealed*, edited by Y. Yadin. Jerusalem, 1975, pp. 55–56.

Bliss, F.J. and Dickie, E.C. *Excavations at Jerusalem 1894–1897.* London: Palestine Exploration Fund, 1898.

Bliss, F.J. and Macalister, R.A.S. *Excavations in Jerusalem During the Years 1898–1900.* London: Palestine Exploration Fund, 1902.

Broshi, M. "The Jerusalem Ship Reconsidered." *International Journal of Nautical Archaeology and Underwater Exploration* 6 (1977): 349–356.

——. "Along Jerusalem's Walls." *BA* 40 (1977): 11–17.

——. "Excavations in the House of Caiaphas, Mount Zion." In *Jerusalem Revealed*, edited by Y. Yadin. Jerusalem, 1975, pp. 57–60.

Crowfoot, J.W. and Fitzgerald, G.M. *Excavations in the Tyropoeon Valley, Jerusalem, 1927. Palestine Exploration Fund Annual* 5 (1929).

Geva, H. "The Western Boundary of Jerusalem at the End of the Monarchy." *IEJ* 29 (1979): 84–91.

——. "Excavations in the Citadel of Jerusalem, 1979–1980." *IEJ* 33 (1983): 55–71.

Hamilton, R. "Excavations Against the North Wall of Jerusalem, 1937–38." *QDAP* 10 (1940): 1–54.

Johns, C.N. "The Citadel, Jerusalem." *QDAP* 15 (1950): 121–190.

Kenyon, K.M. *Digging up Jerusalem.* London: Ernest Benn, 1974.

Lapp, P. *Palestinian Ceramic Chronology.* New Haven: American Schools of Oriental Research, 1961.

Lux, U. "Vorläufiger Bericht über die Ausgrabungen unter der Erlöserkirche im Muristan in der Altstadt von Jerusalem in den Jahren 1970 und 1971." *ZDPV* 88 (1972): 185–201.

Macalister, R.A.S. and Duncan J.C. *Excavations on the Hill of Ophel, Jerusalem, 1923–1925. Palestine Exploration Fund Annual* 4 (1926).

Shiloh, Y. "Notes and News." *IEJ* 27 (1977) – *IEJ* 33 (1983).

Sukenik, E.L. and Mayer, L.A. *The Third Wall of Jerusalem.* London: Oxford University Press, 1930.

——. "A New Section of the Third Wall, Jerusalem." *PEQ* (1944): 145–151.

Vincent, L.H. *Underground Jerusalem.* London: Horace Cox, 1911.

Vincent, L.H. and Stève, A.M. *Jérusalem de l'ancient testament.* 2 vols. Paris: Gabalda, 1954, 1956.

Vriezen, K. "Zweiter vorläufiger Bericht über die Ausgrabung unter der Erlöserkirche im Muristan in der Altstadt von Jerusalem (1972–74)." *ZDPV* 94 (1978): 76–81.

Warren, C. *Underground Jerusalem.* London: R. Bentley, 1876.

——. *Plans, Elevations, Sections, Etc. Showing the Results of the Excavations at Jerusalem, 1867–70.* London: Vincent Brooks, Day and Son, 1884.

Weill, R. *La cité de David.* 2 vols. Paris: Gabalda, 1920, 1947.

Wilson, C. *Ordnance Survey of Jerusalem.* London, 1865; reprint Jerusalem: Ariel, 1980.

Wilson, C. and Warren, C. *The Recovery of Jerusalem.* London: R. Bentley, 1871.

The City of David: 1978–1983

Yigal Shiloh

THE RENEWED EXCAVATIONS in the City of David, the mound of ancient Jerusalem, began in the summer of 1978 and are being carried out on behalf of the City of David Society. To date, twelve areas, totaling about 3.5 dunams in area, have been exposed down to bedrock. Twenty-five occupational strata have come to light, representing a time span from the Chalcolithic period down to the Middle Ages. The discussion here will be limited to a few major discoveries from the Bronze and Iron Ages, that is, from the Canaanite and Israelite cities and mainly from one of the most important excavation areas, Area G. The broad variety of problems in Area G are representative of those we encountered in the other excavation areas. We hope, through the discussion of this subject, to demonstrate the multidisciplinary method which has served as the cornerstone of our archaeological research in the City of David, as is the case at other archaeological excavations in Israel.

The form of the ancient mound, on the slopes of which the settlement developed, above the Gihon spring, is best seen on the eastern slope. Most of our excavations have been carried out along the length of this slope, from Area G in the north, through Areas E, D, B and K, to Areas A and H in the south. Figure 1 shows the strata of the mound uncovered in the various areas, and the relative quantity of finds from the various periods in each area. Thus, we learn of the unequal distribution of the presence of the various strata within a single area. The major causes for such unequal continuity of occupational strata in each area lie, *inter alia*, in the fact that we have before us a hilly site, the buildings of which, in most periods, were constructed on bedrock or on built-up terraces. The inhabitants in each period tried to lay their foundations on the bedrock, reutilizing or demolishing earlier supporting walls. Only by exposing broad areas, in well-controlled, contiguous trenches, were we able to obtain accurate information and reduce the margin of error to a minimum. On a mound of this type, the fact that "no evidence for a settlement of a given period has been found" (to date) does not necessarily indicate that there was no settlement in that period in the area in question.

The City of David and the Old City, looking north: (1) the lower, outer city wall of the Bronze and Iron Ages; (2) the lower city of the Israelite period; (3) the stepped stone structure — the southeastern corner of the "Ophel"; (4) the "Millo" area (?); (5) the Temple area; (6) the Gihon spring; (7) the entrance to "Warren's Shaft" (1983)

In light of the archaeological discoveries made till now in and around Jerusalem, the area of the City of David was included within the city since its foundation at the beginning of the Early Bronze Age and down till the end of the Byzantine period (except for a short time in the Late Roman period). The various parts of Area E have been excavated in recent years under the supervision of Alon de Groot, Yair Shoham and Eilat Mazar. In the area above the city wall of the Bronze and Iron Ages, which was excavated for a length of some 120 m, terraces bearing the major structures of Strata 12 to 10, of the eighth to sixth centuries B.C.E., have been exposed. Most of our efforts in the summer of 1984 will be concentrated in those areas, inside the city-wall, where we can reach the strata of the tenth century B.C.E. and the city of the Early and Middle Bronze Ages.

In Area G, the area closest to the acropolis of the ancient city, the British archaeologists Macalister, Duncan and Kenyon had already been at work. The stepped stone structure and the large square tower, uncovered by Macalister, have variously been ascribed and dated by the several excavators here and by other scholars, such as Vincent, Simons and Avigad. When we started in 1978, we had to dig through the rubble and fills of the Byzantine, Roman, Hellenistic and Persian periods, before we could reach the conclusions we are about to present. These conclusions are based on both stratigraphic and ceramic analyses. We can only thank the staff and the

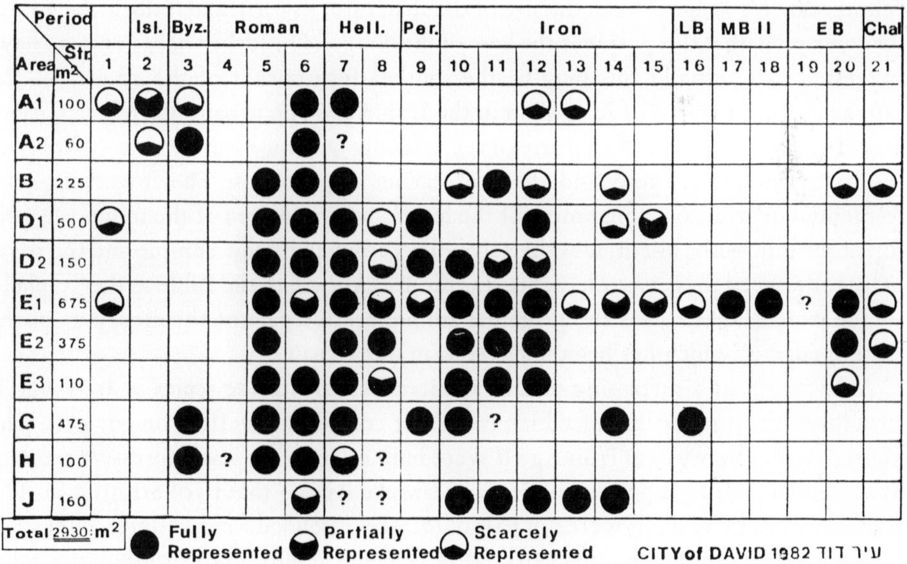

Period			Isl.	Byz.	Roman			Hell.		Per.	Iron						LB	MB II		EB		Chal
Area	Str / m²	1	2	3	4	5	6	7	8	9	10	11	12	13	14	15	16	17	18	19	20	21
A1	100	◔	◕	◔			●	●					◔	◔								
A2	60		◔	●			●	?														
B	225					●	●	●			◔	●	◔		◔						◔	◔
D1	500	◔				●	●	●	◔	●			●		◔	◕						
D2	150					●	●	●	◔	●	●	◕	◕									
E1	675	◔				●	◕	●	◕	◕	●	●	●	◔	◕	◕	◔	●	●	?	●	◔
E2	375					●		●	●		●	●	●								●	◔
E3	110					●	●	●	◕		●	●	●								◔	
G	475			●		●	●	●		●	●	?			●		●					
H	100			●	?	●	●	◕	?													
J	160						◕	?	?		●	●	●	●	●							

Total 2930:m²
● Fully Represented
◕ Partially Represented
◔ Scarcely Represented
CITY of DAVID 1982 עיר דוד

Fig. 1.
Strata and distribution of remains in the City of David (1978–1982)

volunteers for their persistence in excavating here, as the problems and difficulties involved in working in Area G were often neither scientific nor technical. The excavations here were supervised by David Tarler and Jane Cahill. The main architectural elements are shown in the photograph on p. 455. In the upper part of the photo (1) are the remains of the latest fortifications in the area, the "First Wall," which protected the southern flank of the city in Second Temple period, and which continued in use in Byzantine times. The stepped stone structure is in the center (2) and is preserved to a height of 18 m. The strip of buildings at the base of the stepped stone structure flourished in the seventh to sixth centuries B.C.E. down till the destruction of the city in 586 B.C.E. In the foreground (5) are the remains of the terraces and the network of stone compartments which formed the platform of the Canaanite acropolis.

The stepped stone structure is most impressive in its form and the extent of its preservation. Its stratigraphic position within the series of strata is very clear. The structure is located above the remains of the Canaanite citadel of the fourteenth to thirteenth centuries B.C.E., and below the building remains of the ninth to sixth centuries B.C.E. (see Fig. 2). On the basis of the ceramic, stratigraphic and architectural analyses, we assume that it should be ascribed to the phase of the renewed building of Jerusalem in Stratum 14, when it became the capital of the Israelite kingdom in the tenth century B.C.E. This structure served as a broad retaining wall, stepped and sloped, and built so as to support the upper area at the top of the hill, and to seal the earlier strata on the slope below. At the top of this artificial podium, the fortress known as "David's Citadel" was apparently built, serving the city from the tenth century on. We assume, from the size of the structure, its form and its location within the town plan, that this part was the base of the citadel. On earlier occasions, we have suggested that actually this may be the southeastern corner of the citadel — the "Ophel," the acropolis of Jerusalem in the Iron Age. The urban plan of the City of David in the tenth to ninth centuries B.C.E. has now become clearer in the light of the results of our excavations and those of earlier expeditions. The lower city, the residential quarter, occupied most of the lower, southern area of the mound. At the top of the hill, to the north, was the acropolis, crowned by the Temple and the royal palace. Between these two elements was the area known in the Bible as the "Ophel" — the citadel, which was the principal administrative part of the city, part of the eastern edge of which has been uncovered in our Area G.

A discovery of a surprising nature awaited us beneath the series of Iron Age II structures, the dismantling of which called for considerable effort on our part. The massive retaining walls of Iron Age II were built over the no less impressive remains of a monumental stone podium of the Late Bronze Age — that is, of Stratum 16. The Canaanite retaining walls were not part of terraces intended for dwellings, but rather they served as a supporting network, with the intervening spaces filled with fieldstones. The sparse pottery recovered in the sections cut through these stone compartments dated no later than the fourteenth to thirteenth centuries B.C.E. To date, an area of some 250 sq m has been exposed down to the early podium. It should be remembered that the southern half of Area G was excavated already by Kenyon, years ago, and that she found there what was, in our opinion, the southern edge of the podium of the Canaanite citadel. Kenyon, too, ascribed these terraces to LB II, in broad terms, but we cannot accept her view that they were terraces for dwellings in that period. Rather, we regard them as a part of the retaining walls and stone

Area G, aerial photograph looking west: (1) the Second Temple city wall and towers; (2) the stepped stone structure; (3) "The House of Ahiel"; (4) the "Burnt Room"; (5) retaining walls and stone compartments of the podium of the Late Bronze II citadel (1983)

compartments forming the podium of the Canaanite citadel on the south. The section in Fig. 3 presents one profile of the series of stone compartments, oriented on a north-south axis on the central terrace, one of the three successive terraces descending to the east and, very sharply, to the south.

The major conclusion stemming from analysis of these data is that the citadel of the tenth century B.C.E. was actually built over the impressive remains of the podium of the Canaanite citadel, and even utilized some of its walls. The main innovation in the planning of the city in this century was thus the incorporation of the area north of the early acropolis. This acropolis continued to serve the same role, and it became the "Ophel" of the Israelite period. The appended area to the north included the new palaces and Temple. Whereas an "Ophel" was a regular feature in royal centers in the Iron Age — as at Samaria or Dibon — the addition of the area of the Temple Mount to the north was unique to Jerusalem, and it served the specific needs of urban planning in the new capital. It would seem that, in keeping with this concept, we should go back and look for the location of the "Millo" (the built-up fill at the saddle separating the citadel from the Temple Mount which was an architectural feature peculiar to Jerusalem) at the site proposed long ago. This saddle is situated approximately where the present road separating the Temple Mount excavations from the northern part of the lower city runs. It can reasonably be assumed, following Mazar,

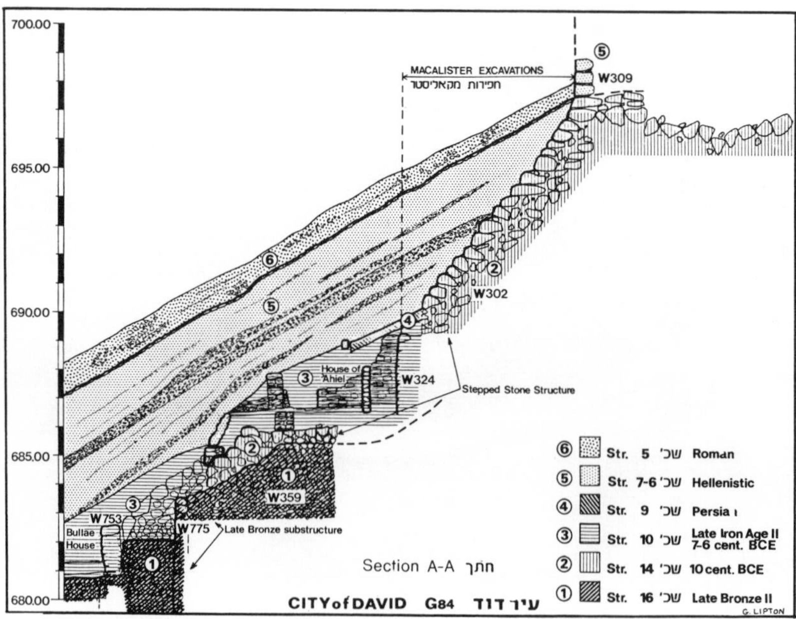

Fig. 2.
Area G, Strata 16-5: General schematic section AA, looking south

that the impressive remains of a large Iron Age II structure uncovered at the southeastern corner of the Temple Mount excavations — which Mazar has denoted the "Millo House" according to 2 Kings 12: 21 — was indeed part of the complex of buildings located in this central quarter of the Israelite city.

A change in the architecture resembling that on the Western Hill of biblical Jerusalem was made in this part of the city during the seventh century, or possibly already in the eighth century B.C.E. The base of the stepped stone structure was covered over by a series of terraces, which, this time, did serve as the base for a strip of dwellings. We have distinguished three clear units here, denoting them according to the major finds in each: the largest of them, a broad "four-room house," is called the "House of Ahiel." North of it was the "Burnt Room" and, on the lower terrace, was the "House of Bullae" (see Fig. 4 and the photograph on page 455). These buildings flourished down till the destruction of the city by the Babylonians in 586 B.C.E. When the city was destroyed, the houses here collapsed, and the entire eastern slope was covered with a thick layer of debris. Subsequently, this slope remained outside the fortified area of the city. The rubble reached a depth of two to three meters, up to the roof level of the first storey of the structures. The "Burnt Room" received its name from the charred layer some 70 cm thick which we came upon when we finished clearing the rubble from the stone walls and the upper floor of the

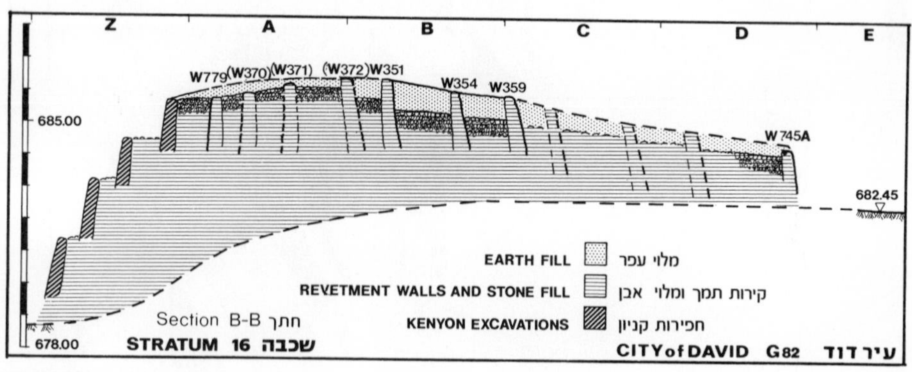

Fig. 3.
Area G, Stratum 16: Schematic section BB, looking west on the low terrace of the Late Bronze Age II structure

structure in which it is located. Of the plethora of finds here, we should mention that which provides the clearest and most dramatic evidence of the frightful events which preceded the Israelite city's destruction — a large quantity of arrowheads, mostly made of iron and with a flat profile, but some with "Scythian" pattern in cast bronze.

The eighth to sixth centuries B.C.E. are represented in the City of David by three distinct strata and their pottery assemblages. Stratum 12 was the main building phase on the eastern slope, ascribed to the days of Hezekiah in the second half of the eighth century B.C.E. Stratum 10 is apparently to be dated to the days of Josiah, in the second half of the seventh century and down to the destruction of the city in 586 B.C.E. Between these two strata, we discerned an intermediate stratum — Stratum 11 — of the first half of the seventh century B.C.E. This stratigraphic series, anchored at either end on historical dates, is also based on large pottery assemblages rich in quantity and

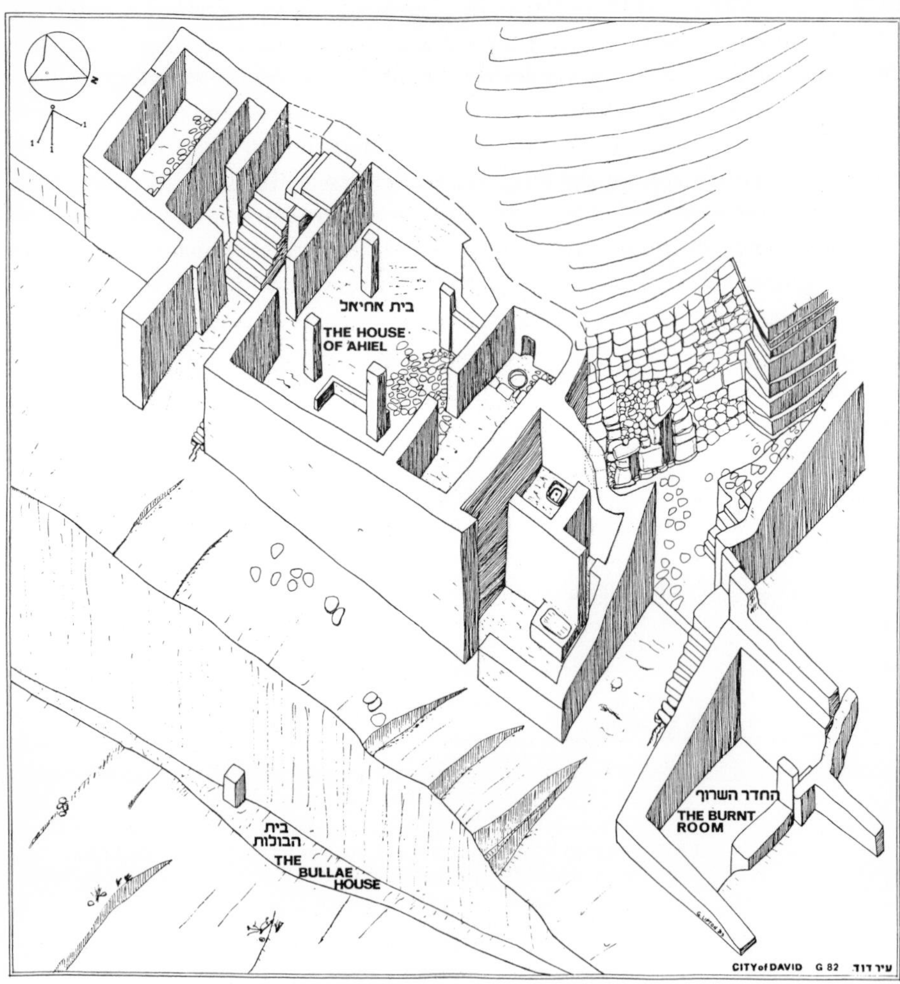

Fig. 4.
Area G: Isometric reconstruction of the strip of buildings in Stratum 10

in the variety of types which represent each of the pottery phases of the Late Iron Age. The distinct stratigraphy, as well as explicit historical documentation and the rich groups of complete pottery vessels — such as the group from Stratum 10 — should enable us to make a significant, innovative contribution to the chronology and typology of the pottery of the end of the Iron Age. The destruction layer in the City of David — Stratum 10 — has clear parallels in Lachish Stratum II, En-Gedi Stratum V, Arad Strata VII–VI, Ramat Raḥel Stratum VA, Aroer Stratum II and others. The material from Stratum 12, which we ascribe to the eighth century B.C.E., has numerous parallels, such as Lachish Stratum III.

Among the variegated auxiliary research studies relating to our excavations, I wish to point out two examples, one in the realm of zoo-archaeology and the other in the realm of palaeontology. Over the years of excavation, we have carefully accumulated a large group of animal bones found in loci which were stratigraphically sealed and well defined and thus of definite chronology. Liora Hurowitz, who is engaged in the study of this material, has so far identified over 1,300 bone fragments from various animals, from the Early Bronze Age down to Byzantine times. We assume that upon publication, her study will prove to be of considerable importance for the zoo-archaeology of Israel and of the ancient Near East in general, especially in the light of the broad range of animals identified, all from a single site and dating from a fairly uninterrupted sequence of periods.

During our excavations in the "Burnt Room," many lumps of carbonized wood were found. Some of them were from the roof-beams and others, we have tentatively assumed, were from wooden furniture. A painstaking examination of the smaller pieces revealed that some of the fragments had been beautifully carved in the same manner as the ivories of this period, and with the well-known palmette motif. Prof. Fahn, of the Department of Botany at The Hebrew University, identified some of the more crudely worked pieces as of *Pistacia atlantica*, the locally found Terebinth tree. The more finely worked pieces are of *Buxus* (boxwood) unknown in Israel. The boxwood could only have been imported from northern Syria or southern Anatolia, and thus we have further confirmation of commercial ties with northern Syria in the Iron Age.

But here at this Congress, we are dealing with archaeology and the Bible. The main type of finds connecting the Bible with archaeology in the Iron Age is epigraphic. In this realm, too, the City of David excavations have been blessed with a number of especially impressive discoveries. The epigraphic material is being studied and prepared for publication jointly by Prof. Joseph Naveh and myself. For the first time, large incised inscriptions on stone were found, which may have been affixed to various buildings in the city. One of the most interesting finds is an easily legible ostracon, from Stratum 10 in Area G. It bears a list of names, including the name Ahiel, and is a fine example of the script appearing on Judean ostraca toward the end of the Iron Age. Palaeographically, it is identical with the "Ophel Ostracon" discovered by Macalister in 1925. An even more significant find is a large and well-preserved group of clay bullae bearing Hebrew seal-impressions, from Stratum 10. This group was found in a building which was subsequently denoted the "House of the Bullae." It is located on the lower terrace at the eastern edge of Area G (see Fig. 4).

Despite the fact that excavation here was by means of a very narrow, deep sounding, the stratigraphic series is clear. The podium of the Canaanite citadel was bolstered in Stratum 10 by a massive retaining wall, W.753, which was the western wall of locus 967 — the "House of the Bullae." This entire complex had been covered over by layers of earth and gravel forming the Hellenistic glacis. The stratigraphic position of the plastered floor of the "House of the Bullae" was easily determined — it was the final floor in use in the Iron Age and is represented in the destruction layer of the City of David. Though only a small part of the "House of the Bullae" has been cleared, many variegated finds were uncovered: stone cult stands(?), iron and stone implements, arrowheads and a rich group of pottery vessels. The pottery assemblage is typical of Stratum 10 in the City of David and hence also of other Judean sites on the eve of the Babylonian destruction as mentioned above.

The first bullae were found during the sifting of the earth removed from the floor in the "House of the Bullae" — a procedure employed whenever a floor or other living surface was encountered. After papyri documents had been completed, they were rolled up and tied with a string, the knot or the string being covered by a small blob of clay which, when impressed with a seal, became a bulla. Well-preserved examples of sealed documents were found in the Jewish military colony at Elephantine-Yev, in Upper Egypt, from the Persian period. It is not so easy to distinguish in an excavation such small, crumbling objects, no larger than your thumbnail. Our bullae were found scattered within an area of about a square meter in the northwestern corner of the house. We have fifty-one clay bullae, all bearing seal-impressions. On four of them the seal has a graphic motif but no trace of script. All the other seal-impressions bear the legible Hebrew names of their owners. On the backs of the bullae we can see the clear impression of the strings which had tied the documents, as well as of the fibers of the papyrus itself.

On the face of the bullae we generally find the common formula of Hebrew seals with no accompanying decorative motif — a feature typical of the seventh to sixth centuries B.C.E. The formula is: "Belonging to X the son of Y." Thus, we read on one bulla, "לבניהו בן הושעיהו," "[Belonging] to Benayahu the son of Hoshayahu." The bullae have yielded a corpus of eighty-two Hebrew names, some of which occur several times. Almost two-thirds of the names include a theophoric element.

Another good example are the two bullae bearing the identical legend "לאלנתן בן בלגי," "[Belonging] to Elnathan the son of Bilgai." Though the inscriptions are identical, these bullae were made with two different seals. Comparative palaeographic analysis clearly shows that the two seals were carved by one and the same artisan, and we assume that both belonged to the same owner. The script appearing on these bullae, as well as on the others of the group, is typical of the final phase of the development of the glyptic script of the seventh to sixth centuries B.C.E. This can be seen quite readily, for instance, in the forms of the letters *alef*, *dalet*, *heh*, *waw*, *het*, *lamed* and *mem*.

This find represents one of the largest single groups of Hebrew names ever encountered in controlled archaeological excavations. Even so, all these names remain "anonymous," so to speak, for only one of them could possibly be identified with a known figure in the Bible. The same negative phenomenon has long been known in Hebrew epigraphy, even taking into account the hundreds of examples of Hebrew seals and seal-impressions extant from the Iron Age in Israel. Only recently, Prof. Avigad suggested — and quite rightly so, in my opinion — that the names he found on a seal and on two bullae from an unclear source could be identified with persons known to have been active at the court of Jehoiakim, King of Judah. They are "Berahyahu the son of Neryahu the Scribe," "Seryahu the son of Neryahu," possibly a brother of the first, and "Jerahmeel the son of the King." All three are mentioned in Jeremiah 36.

Now, we too can possibly identify one of our seal owners: "לגמריהו בן שפן," "[Belonging] to Gemaryahu the son of Shaphan," whose name appears on a bulla from the City of David. A scribe of this name was also active at the court of Jehoiakim, King of Judah, as is mentioned in Jeremiah 36:9–11, in that king's fifth year, that is, 604 B.C.E. Such an identification, of course, adds a dramatic and emotional dimension to our research of the finds from our excavations. We assume that the group of documents represented by the bullae was not merely some private, family archive, in which we would expect to find much repetition of just a few names within the family. Rather, it may be regarded as an archive of some public bureau, located at the "House of the Bullae" in the City of David. The appearance here of the name of the scribe Gemaryahu the son of Shaphan, and the location of the building,

1

2

Two bullae from the "House of the Bullae," Area G, locus 967 (1982)
1. ["Belonging] to Benayahu son of Hoshayahu"
2. ["Belonging] to Gemaryahu son of Shaphan"

adjacent to the lower city on the one hand, and to the citadel, the "Ophel" and the Temple Mount on the other, would strengthen our contention.

The fact that this is the first time that such a large group of bullae was recovered from a controlled and orderly excavation and is accompanied by clear architectural, stratigraphic, palaeographic and historical evidence, contributes to the significance of this discovery. The chronological conclusions regarding the find derived from all these fields are in accordance.

For detailed bibliography, see: Y. Shiloh, *Excavations at the City of David, I, 1978–1982. Qedem* 19. Monographs of the Institute of Archaeology. Jerusalem: The Hebrew University of Jerusalem, 1984.

The Temple Mount

Benjamin Mazar

THE EXTENSIVE EXCAVATIONS conducted from 1968 to 1978 adjacent to the southern retaining walls of the Temple Mount, and additional investigations in the enclosed area of the Haram, enable us to arrive at some basic conclusions regarding the elaborate design of the Herodian construction project and the development of the temenos during the Second Temple period. Archaeological work has been carried out mainly south and southwest of the enclosure, an area which, facing the gates of the Temple enclosure, was a focal point in the Herodian period.

Special attention was given to the access to the enclosure, especially to the broad staircase leading up to the Double Gate in the southern wall, and to the monumental flight of stairs on the west, supported by Robinson's Arch and leading to the Royal Stoa. The Royal Stoa, which towered high above the southern part of the outer Temple court, was a remarkable feature of Herod's construction plan. Our investigations have served to confirm the detailed and relatively accurate description of the Royal Stoa given by Josephus Flavius in his book, *Antiquities*. The principal part of the structure was the long, rectangular hall with four rows of columns, 162 in number. It was built on the model of the Roman basilica and served for important communal and commercial functions (especially for the cultic requirements of the Temple). The Royal Stoa in the Herodian period, until the destruction of Jerusalem by the Romans, constituted an organic part of the huge quadrangular sacred enclosure, which had porticos built all around, including the basilica to the south. This type of temenos, with a temple in its center, was common in the neighboring lands as well. An interesting example of a similar but much less extensive enclosure has been discovered at Cyrene. According to Sjoquist, its origin is to be found in the Caesareum of Alexandria, built in 48 B.C.E. as the official center of the imperial cult. It seems that Herod's architects took the model of the Caesareum into consideration, devoting their attention mainly to the Royal Stoa, described by Josephus as "a structure more noteworthy than any other under the sun."

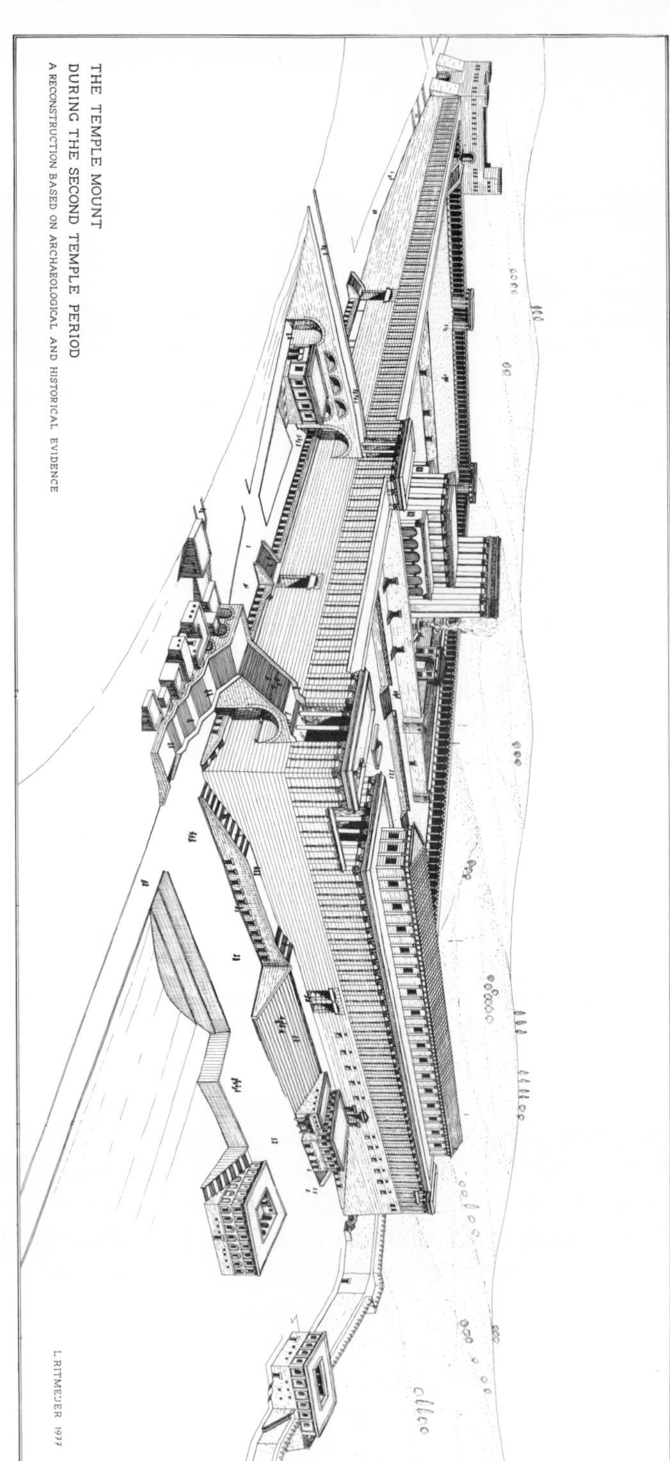

Fig. 1.
The Temple enclosure in the Herodian period

It is most difficult to determine, even in general outlines, the stages in the historical development of the Temple Mount and its fortifications during the long era of the Second Temple, from Zerubbabel at the end of the sixth century B.C.E. up to the commencement of Herod's building project at the end of the first century B.C.E. The literary sources are insufficiently clear, and archaeological data are very few and problematic. Nevertheless, some observations may be helpful in formulating a hypothesis based upon comprehensive examinations of the relevant literary material.

A fundamental assumption is that the *bīrāh* of the biblical sources of the Persian period was the citadel of Jerusalem on "Mount Zion" (that is, the Temple Mount), including in its fortifications the Second Temple complex. The Hebrew term *bīrāh*, Aramaic *birtha* derived from Assyrian *birtu* (castle, fort, citadel), was used in that period to describe a royal acropolis (as at Susa or Ecbatana) and administrative citadels at the centers of the western provinces, including Jerusalem, Samaria and Tyre of the Tobiads. In the anachronistic story in 1 Chronicles 28–29, David presents Solomon with a plan for the *bīrāh* (v. 19), including the sanctuary and its adjacent courts and structures. The following (29:1) is noteworthy: "The work is immense, for the *bīrāh* is not for men but for Yahweh God." The author had in mind the *bīrāh* on the Temple Mount, including the sanctuary and its fortifications, just as Nehemiah did in his request to the king to supply him with timber from Lebanon for the gates of the *bīrāh* of the Temple (הבירה אשר לבית), as well as for the gates of the city and his own palace (Nehemiah 2:8). It seems that in the Hellenistic period, too, the citadel was separated from the city, but included the Temple in its fortified enclosure. According to the "Letter of Aristeas," the citadel was located on a lofty spot close to the city and served to protect the Temple precinct; and Hecataeus of Abdera mentions a stone wall with a pair of gates, and within its enclosed area, a square altar and a great edifice. The description of the ideal temple complex in Ezekiel 45, apparently based on a conception originating in the priestly circles of the Persian period, regarded the sacred complex as a square of 500 cubits, fortified by a sturdy wall with three gates. These gates are described according to an old model, reminiscent of the Solomonic pattern. The same measurements are given in the Mishnah (Middot 2,1), and even Josephus relied on the generally accepted tradition that the sacred enclosure had a perimeter of four stades, each side one stade long. These data are apparently an indication of the original limits of the square *bīrāh*, built in post-exilic times over the ruins of the pre-exilic royal acropolis, which included the complexes of the Temple and the palace of the kings of Judah.

My colleague, Leen Ritmeyer, has made observations on the present-day platform of the Temple Mount, regarding traces and indications of the early square. The starting point is the bottom step of the staircase at the northwestern corner of the raised Islamic platform. It seems to be a remnant of a massive wall with marginally drafted masonry, possibly the northwestern corner of the *bīrāh*. This masonry can be distinguished from the Herodian style. An important indication of its earlier date is the distance of 262.50 m between the step and the eastern wall, when measured along the line of the present-day raised platform. The projected northeast corner would then lie about 8 m north of the Golden Gate. Since the eastern wall of the enclosure is known to be pre-Herodian in origin, the southeast corner of the square should be sought some 262.50 m south of the northeast corner. At that very point a "bend" was observed by Charles Warren, which we take to indicate a change in masonry, thus lending support to the idea that the southeast corner of the earlier platform was indeed located there. Whether the bossed, marginally drafted masonry of this section of the wall is Hellenistic or Persian-Achaemenian is difficult to establish; nevertheless, this wall is certainly connected in some way with the early square. From the determination of three corners and three walls, a square of 262.50 m per side can be formed. Assuming that the cubit of the literary sources is the "great" or Phileterion cubit of 525 mm, we can cite additional indications in the south and west to support the theory that the early platform was 500 cubits square.

A problem in itself is the location of the Seleucid "Akra." The Akra is considered as a revolutionary innovation of the Hellenistic period in Jerusalem. It was built by Antiochus Epiphanes in 168 B.C.E. as a stronghold for his garrison and for the pro-Seleucid aristocracy; it was condemned by the Jewish population as "an ambush for the Temple," used by the garrison to violate its sacred character. Numerous attempts have been made to locate the Akra, both in the Lower and Upper City. It would now seem that the most suitable place would be in the extreme north of the City of David; to be more precise, on the southern spur of the Temple Mount. Such a suggestion was already put forward by Charles Watson nearly eighty years ago, placing the stronghold in the area of the Aqsa Mosque. In our estimation, the Akra was built immediately south of the fortified Temple enclosure, on an elevated spot so that the entire city could be seen and the approach to the Temple gates controlled. The area of the Huldah gates is just such a spot.

Further evidence for locating the Akra there is provided by Charles Warren's discovery of an elaborate cistern (No. 11) described as having three large tanks. In a recent unpublished paper, J. Schwarz of Bar-Ilan University considers the location of the three cisterns on the Temple Mount, mentioned in the Mishnah Erubin. According to his manuscript, one of the three cisterns was apparently called בור חקר, "cistern of (the) Akra." This cistern can be identified with Warren's cistern No. 11 and we may place the ancient Akra in its vicinity.

The Books of Maccabees and the works of Josephus are important though inadequate sources for the history of the extensive building activities of the Hasmoneans on the Temple Mount. Concerning the early Hasmoneans, we may note that Jonathan ordered the walls and defenses around "Mount Zion" to be rebuilt in square ashlars. In 141 B.C.E., Simon occupied the Akra and razed it to the ground; he fortified the walls of the Temple Mount "by the side of the citadel," and occupied it with his men. It is not impossible that the author had in mind the extension of the old eastern wall, from the "bend" to the "seam." North of the "seam," a stretch of Hasmonean masonry has been observed, apparently a corner construction of headers-and-stretchers. This may have belonged to Simon's project, the purpose of which was to enlarge the Temple enclosure southward as to include the area of the former Akra. In

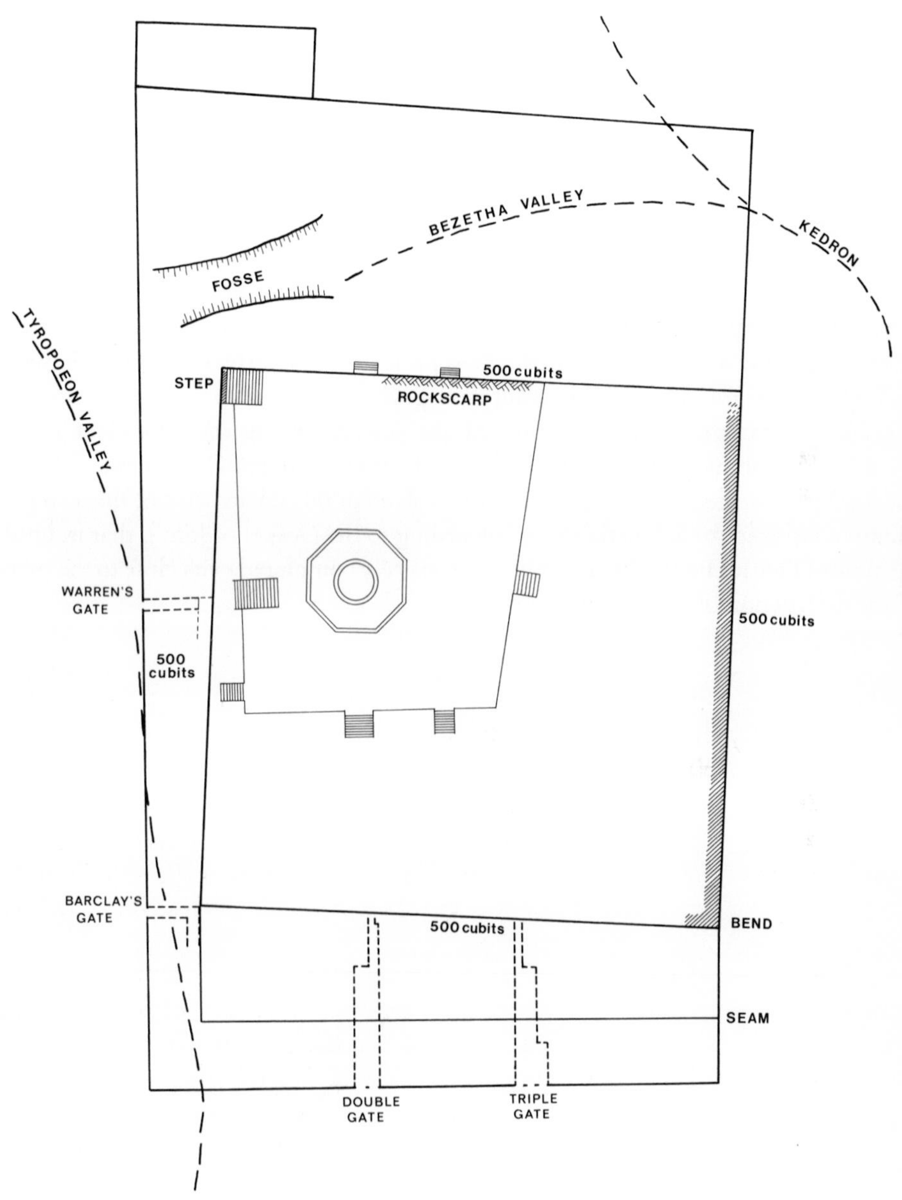

Fig. 2.
The Temple Mount (with indications of the early square)

a later period, Herod enlarged the eastern wall south of the "seam," adding 32 m more for the projected Royal Stoa.

The extensive enterprises of the later Hasmoneans on the Temple Mount, especially of John Hyrcanus I and Alexander Jannaeus, up to the siege and conquest by Pompey in 63 B.C.E., are only occasionally mentioned in the literary sources (particularly Josephus and Strabo). These enterprises included the filling in of the Tyropoeon Valley bed to link the new Upper City with the Temple enclosure; the building of a "bridge" over the Tyropoeon; the strengthening of the fortification of the Temple Mount with massive towers and gates, as well as a fosse on the north which, together with the Tyropoeon and Kidron Valleys, created a strong defensive perimeter around the sacred precinct.

The Temple Mount seems to have undergone further, limited construction in the short period prior to Herod's colossal project, which brought about a decisive change in the topography of the entire area. Most of the pre-Herodian structures were razed or reconstructed at that time, for the new project doubled the size of the Temple enclosure. The grandeur of this enterprise gave expression to Herod's visionary concept — that the religious center of the Jewish people should reflect in its remarkable plan the architectural character of the magnificent Caesareum of Alexandria. The enormous construction effort involved in this renaissance of the Temple Mount continued for forty-six years (according to the Gospel of John), that is, until the time of Pontius Pilate. In fact, it was not entirely completed even close to the time of the destruction of the Temple in 70 C.E.

The Upper City

Nahman Avigad

WE HAVE HEARD AT THIS Congress lectures on the history of archaeological research in Jerusalem, and on the City of David and the Temple Mount, which form the nucleus of the Holy City. It is now my pleasure to relate to you about another, more recent part of Jerusalem known as the "Upper City."

This "Upper City," so named by Josephus, is situated on the second and larger hill of ancient Jerusalem, known as the Southwestern Hill, covering the area of the present Jewish Quarter, the Armenian Quarter, the Citadel and the traditional Mount Zion. The Jewish Quarter, holding a key position on the Western Hill, is the only one of these sites which had not previously been excavated and was *terra incognita* in the real sense of the word. We knew nothing of its stratigraphy, chronology or material remains, nor was it explicitly described in any of the sources.

However, this Southwestern Hill has been a subject of constant discussion in archaeological literature. The major problems concerning the historical topography of Jerusalem could not be solved here for want of archaeological excavation. This part of Jerusalem remained enigmatic until excavations commenced following the reunification of Jerusalem in 1967.

Our excavations changed things radically, contributing not only to the solution of some of the problems under discussion, but also revealing a totally unknown facet of ancient Jerusalem, adding new dimensions to the topography, stratigraphy, and urban and cultural history of the city.

Our finds, covering a wide range of topics and periods, are summarized in my recent book *Discovering Jerusalem*. Here, I confine myself to discussing only one major topic: the topography of Jerusalem in the First Temple period. Although I have clearly expressed my views on this subject in my book, my case is outlined here once again in the light of queries which have been raised, as well as some new material relating to this subject.

The topography of Jerusalem has been a controversial issue ever since excavations in Jerusalem began more than 100 years ago. The question was whether Jerusalem was confined to the narrow limits of the City of David until the end of the First Temple period, or whether it spread over both the Southeastern Hill and the Southwestern Hill already in that period. Two major theories concerning this question were prevalent:

1. *The two-hill theory* (or "maximalist view") was based primarily on Josephus, who described the first or "early" wall of Jerusalem as having encompassed both hills, and as having been built by David, Solomon and the successive kings. It was held that only so large a city could have suited the capital of Israel and Judah. Furthermore, biblical references to the *Mishneh* ("the second quarter") also point to the existence of residential quarters outside the walled City of David.

2. In contrast, the adherents of the *one-hill theory* (or "minimalist view") regarded the rival theory as purely hypothetical, without substantial foundation and devoid of any archaeological evidence. Josephus' early date for the wall was regarded as unrealistic, or as sheer fantasy. A city of such extent (about 150 acres) was regarded too large for the Iron Age in Judah. In recent decades, the one-hill theory also took into account the reported negative results of Kenyon's trial excavations on the Southwestern Hill. These, it was held, revealed no evidence of a permanent, pre-exilic occupation at the excavated sites. Accordingly, pre-exilic Jerusalem must have been confined to the Eastern Hill alone.

Naturally, several intermediate theories developed, including only parts of the Southwestern Hill within pre-exilic Jerusalem, and some even considered the possibility of two separate cities, one on each hill.

Nowadays, subsequent to our excavations, the one-hill theory can be disregarded entirely. Actually, that theory was based on sound method — the results of archaeological excavations in contrast to the then hypothetical concept of a two-hill city based on the testimony of an ancient historian, a testimony which was regarded by many scholars *a priori* as unreliable. No wonder that this one-hill theory was more widely accepted.

Jerusalem would have remained in our minds as a small, limited town but for our excavations. We not only proved that the conclusions drawn from those earlier investigations on the Southwestern Hill were wrong, and that there was a permanent occupation on the site, but also that Josephus was basically right in relating his "early" wall to the time of the Monarchy. This development should serve as a reminder to us all not to draw far-reaching conclusions solely from limited probes. In our excavations, for instance, we encountered several spots where Herodian (or even Byzantine) layers were resting on bedrock. All earlier remains had simply been removed by later building activity. What erroneous conclusions could have been drawn in such situations concerning the earliest settlement on this site?

Moreover, Kathleen Kenyon found in several pits thick layers of earth containing quantities of Iron Age pottery. However, in interpreting this material it was not taken into account that such large quantities of earth bearing Iron Age pottery could not possibly have been brought from so far away as the City of David. Actually, this pottery must have come from the Western Hill itself, and thus there must have been a settlement there in pre-exilic times.

Our present state of knowledge of the Southwestern Hill in the pre-exilic period will be summarized in the following. In the Jewish Quarter excavations, evidence for a permanent occupation in Iron Age II or the Israelite period was found in the bottom stratum resting on bedrock. Expansion of the city to the Western Hill apparently began in the early eighth century B.C.E. Initially, this was an undefended settlement, spreading over most of the hill, as indicated by occasional finds from other parts of the Western Hill, as far as the Citadel and "Mount Zion." In the late eighth century B.C.E., this settlement was encompassed by a city wall and annexed to the walled City of David. This new part of the city should probably be identified with the *Mishneh*, the "second quarter," or "second city" mentioned in the Bible.

A section of this city wall, 65 m long, was uncovered in the northern part of the Jewish Quarter. It is a massive wall, 7 m thick, and thus has come to be known as the "Broad Wall." We have ascribed this wall, associated with eighth and seventh century B.C.E. pottery, to Hezekiah, whom, the Bible relates, in preparing for the Assyrian siege, fortified the city and built another wall "outside." Hezekiah also built "Hezekiah's tunnel" and the Siloam Pool. The plan of the "Broad Wall" and its location show that it cut through earlier buildings of the undefended city, reminding us of Isaiah's description concerning the defensive measures taken in Jerusalem in preparation for the war: "...and you counted the houses of Jerusalem, and you broke down the houses to fortify the wall" (Isaiah 22:10). Here then is vivid visual evidence of this very passage.

When discovered, the location, direction and continuation of this segment of the city wall came somewhat as a surprise and caused quite a headache. It did not seem to fit in. We tentatively suggested that it continued southward to enclose only a part of the Western Hill. But with the discovery of further fortifications to the north, the situation was clarified. These latter remains of Israelite and Hasmonean towers and defense walls are located on the northern line of the "First" or "early" wall, described by Josephus as leading from the tower of Hippicus (near the Citadel to the west) to the Temple Mount in the east, on a course south of the so-called Transversal Valley.

Our "Broad Wall" (see Fig. 1) was apparently a part of this wall at an early stage, making a bay-like turn along the contour of the hill in order to skirt a ravine existing between the two summits of the Southwestern Hill. At a later stage, in the seventh century B.C.E., this part of the wall was straightened out across the ravine, and the use of the bay-like section of the "Broad Wall" was discontinued. The factors behind this change remain unknown, but perhaps it was connected with the need for a new gate. The topography there was most suited for a gate, and there seems to have been one here in the "First Wall" (no. 1) as well as in the Hellenistic wall (nos. 6–7). The form of the Israelite gate (nos. 2–3), as reconstructed in Figure 2, is tentative and based on only a few remains.

At the foot of this gate tower we found evidence of a fire, and a group of arrowheads — the remains of a battle which had raged here at the wall of Jerusalem apparently during the Babylonian siege in 586 B.C.E. Tentatively, we would identify this northern gate, some 20 m north of our "Broad Wall," with the "Middle Gate" mentioned in Jeremiah 39:3 as the meeting place of the Babylonian generals after the breaching of the north wall of Jerusalem.

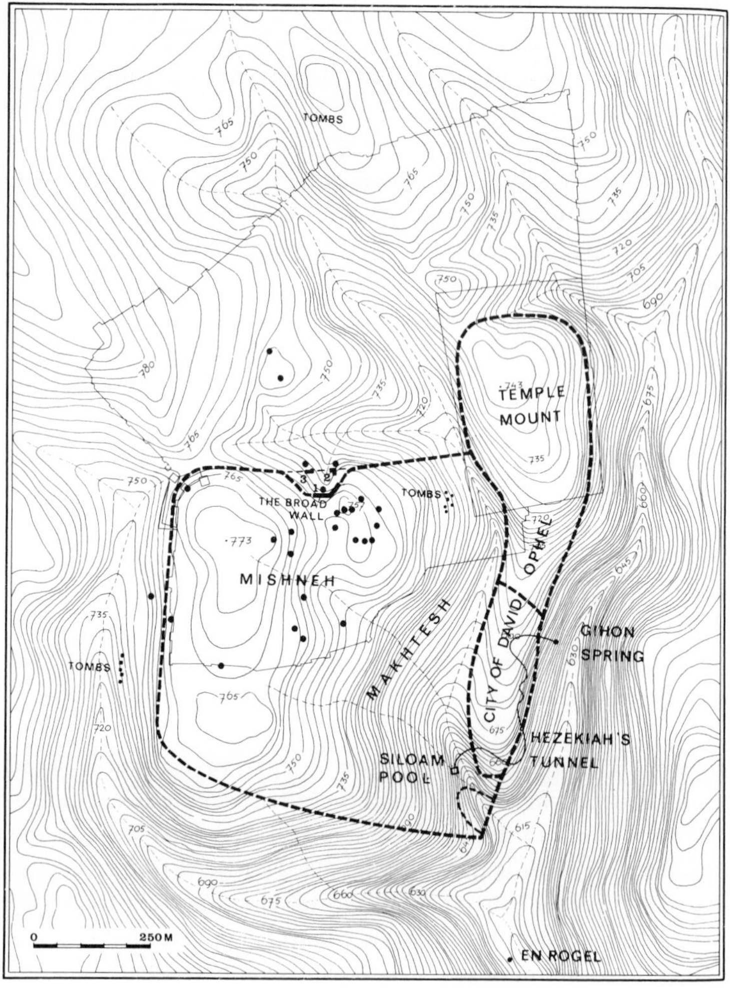

Fig. 1.
Map of Jerusalem at the end of the monarchic period. The dots represent excavated Israelite sites

The discovery of defense walls and towers at this spot, dating from the Israelite and Hasmonean periods, is of the greatest significance, revealing the following facts: (1) Josephus was correct in describing the course of the northern "First Wall" on this line, as well as in ascribing it to the period of the Monarchy. (2) The Israelite and Hasmonean remains are built side-by-side, abutting one another, indicating that: (3) the Hasmoneans built their defenses on the same line as their predecessors and, where possible, they integrated earlier remains into their new defenses.

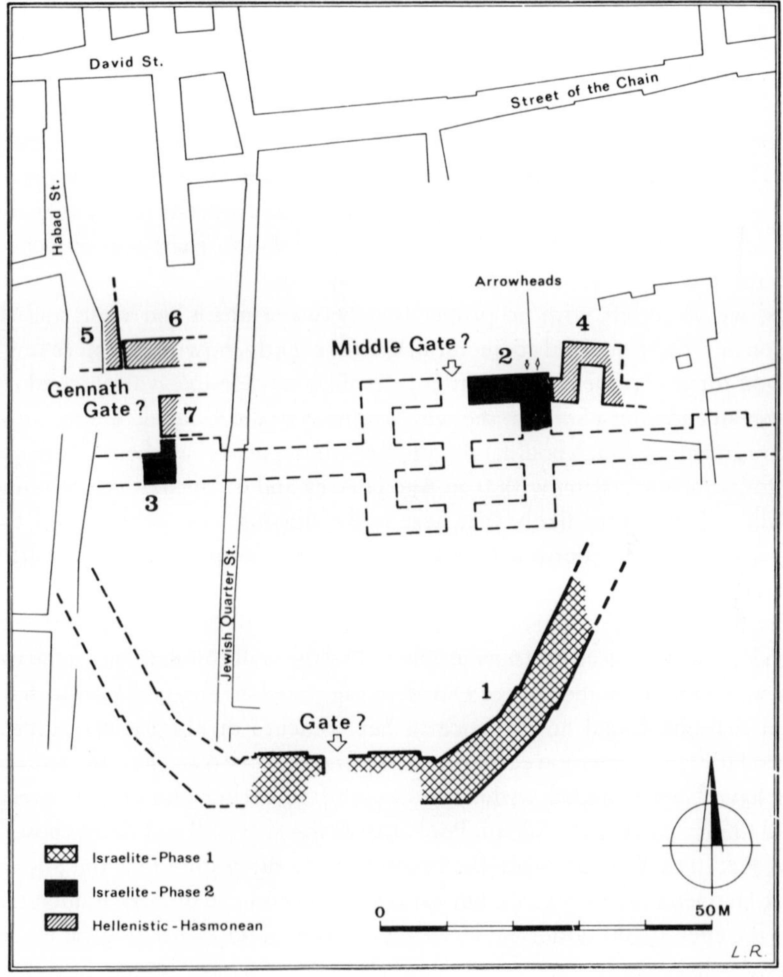

Fig. 2.
Plan of the remains of the Israelite and Hasmonean fortifications, with conjectural reconstruction of the "Middle Gate"

We are inclined to assume that the same correlation observed for the north wall holds good for other parts of the "First Wall" on the west and south, and that the Israelite and Hasmonean walls more or less followed the same course, though not necessarily as closely as in the northern part. After all, a line of defense is generally determined by topographic considerations, which remain more or less constant over long periods. Fortunately, the course of the Hellenistic or Hasmonean wall on the west and south is generally known, for several wall fragments of that period have been uncovered there, and they exactly follow the course described by Josephus.

With this in mind, we are confident that the northern wall did continue to the west, to join the well-attested Hasmonean wall running along the crest above the Hinnom Valley, close to the present Turkish wall. Within the Citadel, Amiran and Eitan found a well-stratified Iron Age floor. Hillel Geva, of our staff, sought the Israelite wall which we anticipated there; but because his excavation was limited to a narrow pit, he failed to reach the appropriate level. In discussing the western boundary of Jerusalem, Geva has also relied on a section of a wall uncovered by Tushingham in his excavations in the Armenian Garden and dated by him to the Iron Age. It was well built with large boulders certainly appropriate for a city wall in this period. But the width of the wall is unknown and Tushingham is convinced that it was no more than a terrace wall built over a quarry.

Thus, we were left with no proper link between north and west, and the line drawn on our map remained conjectural. Quite recently, however, a mere few weeks ago, good fortune came to our assistance from a salvage excavation conducted by Renée Sivan and Giora Solar in the western moat of the Citadel. There, they came across fragmentary rough boulder masonry reminiscent of that of our "Broad Wall." It was found in association with Iron Age pottery and is approximately in line with our wall. It seems very likely that here is the missing link — the proof that our northern wall indeed continued far to the west, enclosing the entire width of the Southwestern Hill.

Approaching the Tyropoeon or Central Valley on the other flank of the Southwestern Hill, we are faced by a new problem. Did the wall continue across the valley to join the southern tip of the City of David, as suggested in our plan? Kathleen Kenyon claimed that she found no evidence in her trenches on the eastern slope of the Western Hill for occupation earlier than the first century C.E. Thus, the entire valley cannot have been included within the walls of an earlier city. To counteract the one-hill theory placing the Siloam Pool outside the city wall and thus exposed to the enemy, Kathleen Kenyon made the revolutionary suggestion that the Siloam Pool was not an open reservoir at all, but rather a subterranean cistern, hidden from the eyes of the enemy. She admitted, however, there was no archaeological evidence to support this hypothesis.

Of greater significance is the fact that Kenyon did find at this spot, near Birket el-Hamra, a thick accumulation of earth probably supported by a still hidden wall, and it contained much Iron Age pottery. Now, how could a thick Iron Age deposit possibly have accumulated on a spot which, according to Kenyon, was outside the city in the pre-exilic period? By closing the Valley with our wall, as suggested on our plan, we place the Siloam Pool within the protection of the walled city and can thus explain two apparently contradictory statements in the Bible concerning the location of the Siloam Pool.

The pool must have been located within the walled city, for otherwise it could not have fulfilled its purpose. Actually, it is located *extra muras* — that is, outside the walls of the City of David. This seems very strange, but it surprisingly fits the description in 2 Chronicles 32:30, according to which Hezekiah directed the water "to the west side of the City of David." According to 2 Kings 20:20, however, Hezekiah made the pool and the conduit, and brought the water "into the city." Indeed, with our new defense wall, crossing the valley, and also assigned to Hezekiah, the pool would be located within the city.

There is still another description, that of Isaiah 22:9–11, relating that "the pool" — not explicitly the Pool of Siloam, but obviously referring to it — was located "between the two walls" (בין החומותיים). And here, indeed, the pool would be located between two walls — the old one of the City of David, and the new one of the Western Hill. Thus, three sources describe one and the same location for the pool, but in three different ways. Therefore, there must have been a wall there.

In conclusion, the archaeological evidence seems to point to the fact that, in the period of the late Monarchy, the city wall uncovered in the Jewish Quarter encompassed the entire plateau of the Western Hill. This complements the "maximalist," two-hill theory which, however, advocated a somewhat higher chronology for such a greater Jerusalem. It can only be hoped that future excavations along the southern line of the wall will provide more evidence culminating in a final solution of the problem.

Respondents

Gabriel Barkay

I would like to present here a third alternative to the "maximalist-minimalist" controversy concerning Israelite Jerusalem — a "super-maximalist" approach which would include even areas in the Christian and Muslim Quarters of the Old City. Reexamination of the earlier excavations in those areas is quite revealing. Pottery of Iron Age II was found in relatively large quantities in excavations throughout the extensive area between Avigad's Wall and the northern wall of the Old City: in the Muristan (Kenyon's Area C); beneath the Church of the Redeemer (by Ute Lux); near Via Dolorosa (by Clermont-Ganneau and M. Magen); in the Church of the Holy Sepulchre (by Corbo, Broshi and the Armenian Patriarch); and along the northern Old City wall (by Hamilton) and at Kikar Zahal.

How is the discovery of such quantities of Iron Age pottery in that area to be interpreted? Is this material from dumps? But if so, then why is it so far from the settled area? And if it was brought from the City of David, why is there no pottery of the Bronze Age? The pottery from these widespread areas is generally domestic in nature, and not of funerary type. Nor should it be ascribed to mere quarrying activities. Indeed, at several spots (for example the Church of the Redeemer and the nearby Holy Sepulchre), fragmentary floors, occupation levels and even building fragments of the Iron Age could be discerned.

The overall, cumulative picture obtained from this material reveals a series of extramural, scattered suburbs. The presence of a very few tombs and of quarries indicates that initially settlement here was sparse and sporadic, but that later it gathered momentum.

Another important factor for determining the extent of the city toward the end of the Iron Age are the necropolises. Over 110 Iron Age II tombs are known today in Jerusalem (only eight of which have truly been published). North of Damascus Gate, a group of fifteen such burial-caves has come to light, including some of the finest examples from that period known in the entire country (in the area of St. Étienne, investigated by G. Barkay and A. Kloner). Two other tombs in that area, with Iron Age finds *in situ*, have been published by A. Mazar. All along the Hinnom Valley, there is an extensive necropolis of this period. All together, some forty Iron Age II tombs have been examined in the western necropolis, and nine have been excavated recently (by G. Barkay). In the latter, rich finds have come to light, including a repository of over a thousand items (two of which were silver plaques, inscribed in the ancient Hebrew script and rolled up).

Pierre Benoit, O.P.

To Y. Shiloh: I do not question the intriguing stepped structure Y. Shiloh found north of Kenyon's trench, nor the Canaanite and Israelite walls in the plot north of Weill's excavations. But concerning the so-called Warren's Shaft, may I ask him if he sees any possibility or prospect of better dating this whole hydraulic system around the Gihon Spring? Until recently, many scholars thought that this system was Canaanite and that the shaft could be the *ṣinnor* through which Joab climbed into the city. Because there are similar structures in other cities such as Hazor, Megiddo and Gibeon, all well dated to the Israelite monarchy, have we not to lower the old-fashioned date of Warren's Shaft? And how should we interpret the *ṣinnor*?

To N. Avigad: Avigad has discovered clear evidence of pre-exilic fortifications on the northern flank of Jerusalem dating to the eighth and seventh centuries B.C.E. I understand he thinks that this line proceeded further to the west, up to the present Citadel, and then turned along the Hinnom Valley to Siloam, joining the wall of the Eastern Hill there. This west–south wall, until now attributed to the Hasmoneans, would have been planned and built before the Exile. This seems logical, but I wonder whether it has an archaeological basis. To my knowledge, neither the excavations of Bliss and Dickie nor those of Johns, Amiran and Eitan in the Citadel, nor those of Tushingham in the Armenian Garden or, more recently, the soundings of Broshi and Bahat, have revealed any evidence for an Iron Age wall along the western and southern line of Josephus' First Wall. Does this not refute the maximalist extension of Jerusalem before the Exile?

To A.D. Tushingham: Perhaps Tushingham has an alternative solution (in French, "solution de rechange"). As far as I know from what he wrote (and from what we shall soon read in the final report on his work in the Armenian Garden), he observed layers of debris sloping to the west, that is, toward the Hinnom Valley, as is to be expected, but also to the east, which is more intriguing. If I understand him correctly, this led him to conclude that under the buildings of the Armenian Patriarchate there was a valley, or at least a depression, oriented north–south and separating the platform of Herod's palace from the plateau of the Jewish Quarter. If such did exist, would it not be possible to imagine that Avigad's Iron Age city wall did not reach the Citadel, but turned to the south at the western edge of the Jewish Quarter, just east of this supposed valley, utilizing it as a sort of moat?

To B. Mazar: Among Mazar's wonderful finds were Herodian, Byzantine and Umayyad buildings, but did he not also find many Rhodian jar-handles, which would attest a Hellenistic presence? This is all the more interesting in view of the fact that Avigad found no occupation on the Western Hill during the Persian period or the first half of the Hellenistic period, that is, prior to the Hasmoneans. Is this not significant for the location of the Akra? Such scholars as Vincent, Abel and Avi-Yonah proposed locating this Syrian fortress on the Western Hill, but Josephus seems to place it on the Eastern Hill. Do not the recent excavations urge us to look for the Akra on the Eastern Hill, near the Temple?

Magen Broshi

On Kenyon's Methodology

I would like to draw attention to a methodological lesson which should be emphasized. Few scholars have contributed to Palestinian archaeology as much as the late Dame Kathleen Kenyon — and not the least were her contributions in the field of methodology. But on one point she seems to have been wrong — in her belief in the principle of *pars pro toto*, "a part representing the whole." It may be valid in medicine (a drop of blood can provide an accurate picture), but this does not apply in archaeology. Here, evidence is often so fragmentary that we generally find ourselves in the position of the three blind men and the elephant in the Indian fable.

Concerning Kenyon in Jerusalem, one could cite several instances where she failed to understand the nature of the site she was excavating (for example, the Umayyad palaces southwest of the Temple Mount, the Herodian podium in the Armenian Garden, or the stepped stone structure in the City of David). This was not due to any failure on her part as a keen observer, but rather to the very limited areas exposed by her. "Quantity," of course, also raises problems, and "quality" should not be sacrificed for the sake of "quantity." But the advantages of excavation areas larger than mere trenches should always be kept in mind.

Amos Kloner

During the past decade, discoveries and studies have substantially added to our knowledge of ancient burial practices and cemeteries surrounding Jerusalem. We now know of rock-cut tombs all around the ancient city during two historical periods — the last two centuries of the Judean Monarchy, and the last two and a half centuries of the Second Temple period. Their distribution enables us to calculate the expansion of the city during these periods. On the other hand, we know very little about burials in Jerusalem and its vicinity during the Persian and early Hellenistic periods.

The discovery of tombs immediately below the city walls south of the Citadel and along its western slope clearly indicates and emphasizes that Jerusalem had spread to the Western Hill during the late Iron Age.[1] Tombs north of the present-day northern wall and Damascus Gate also evidence the development and expansion of the suburbs of the city in that direction.[2] The tombs situated on the premises of St. Étienne, the largest and most carefully hewn burial places known from the time of the Judean Monarchy, are — it is suggested — royal tombs in which some of the late Judean kings were buried. Thus, we locate here the "Garden of Uzza." Could these be the caves to which Josephus referred in *War* V, 147 when describing the Third Wall (σπηλαίων βασιλικῶν)?[3]

Concerning the fortifications uncovered in the Jewish Quarter, two new discoveries should be mentioned (see the figure below and on p. 481). The wall found in 1983 in the eastern moat of the Turkish Citadel, running northeast-southwest, is dated to the Iron Age. A wall found at the end of 1976 along the western side of the Tyropoeon Valley, 12 m below the present El-Wad Street, was constructed in the same manner as the "Broad Wall" in the Upper City.[4] It was traced in a tunnel for a length of 26 m. Its minimal width is 3.75 m, and the preserved height along the tunnel is 0.90–1.50 m (about 2.00 m of the wall's height had apparently been demolished in the main shaft prior to notification to the Department of Antiquities and Museums). Most of the pottery found along the higher level of the wall's eastern face was late Hellenistic and early Roman. A few Iron Age sherds, as well as a base of a Persian vessel, were also found. This wall, originally constructed during the late Iron Age, was part of a fortification system encircling the Tyropoeon Valley. It was later reused, probably during the Persian and Hellenistic periods.

Notes

1. D. Davis and A. Kloner, "A Burial Cave of the Late Israelite Period on the Slopes of Mt. Zion," *Qadmoniot* 41 (1978): 16–19 (Hebrew); M. Broshi, G. Barkai (Barkay) and Sh. Gibson, "Two Iron Age Tombs Below the Western City Wall," *Cathedra* 28 (1983): 17–32 (Hebrew).
2. G. Barkai (Barkay), A. Mazar and A. Kloner, "The Northern Cemetery of Jerusalem in the First Temple Times," *Qadmoniot* 30–31 (1975): 71–76 (Hebrew); G. Barkay and A. Kloner, "Burial Caves North of Damascus Gate, Jerusalem, *IEJ* 26 (1976): 55–57; A. Mazar, "Iron Age Burial Caves North of the Damascus Gate, Jerusalem, *IEJ* 26 (1976): 1–8; A. Kloner, "Rock-cut Tombs in Jerusalem," *Bulletin of the Anglo-Israel Archaeological Society* (1982–83): 37–40.
3. A. Kloner, "The Third Wall and the Tombs of the Kings," in *Zev Vilnay's Jubilee Volume*, ed. E. Shiller (Jerusalem, 1984), pp. 204–208 (Hebrew).
4. Idem, "Hagay St., Fortifications," *Hadashot Arkheologiyot* 84 (1984): 45–47 (Hebrew).

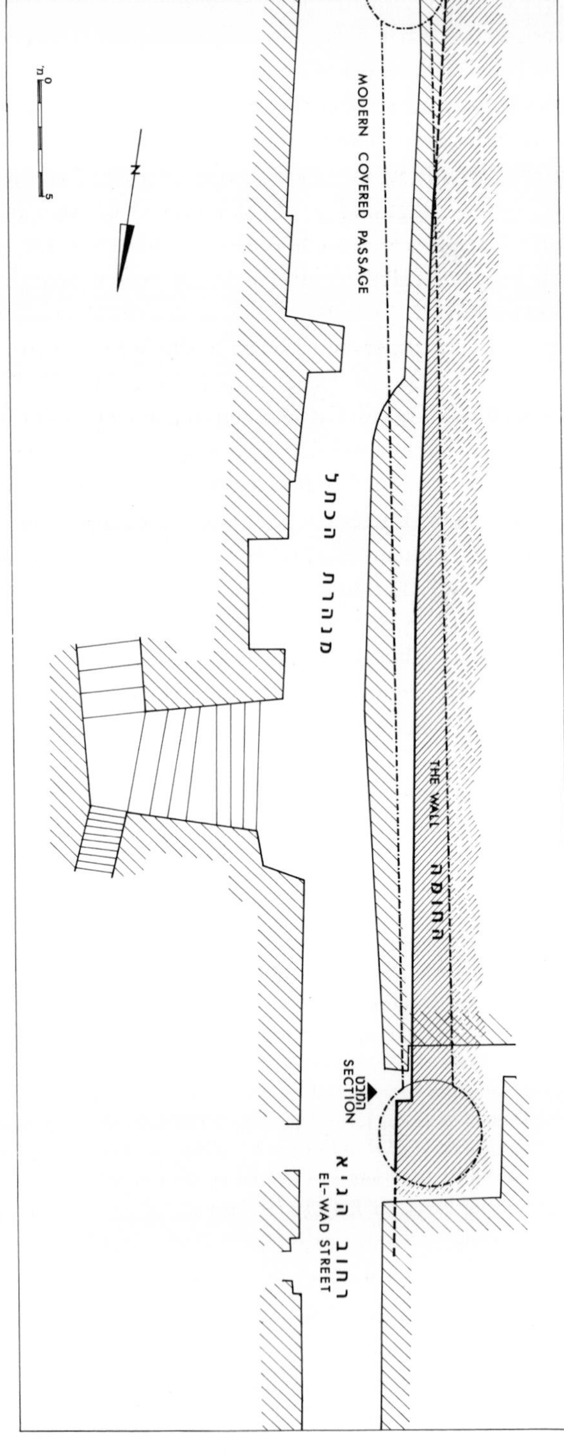

Fig. 1.
Schematic section of the northern part of the wall

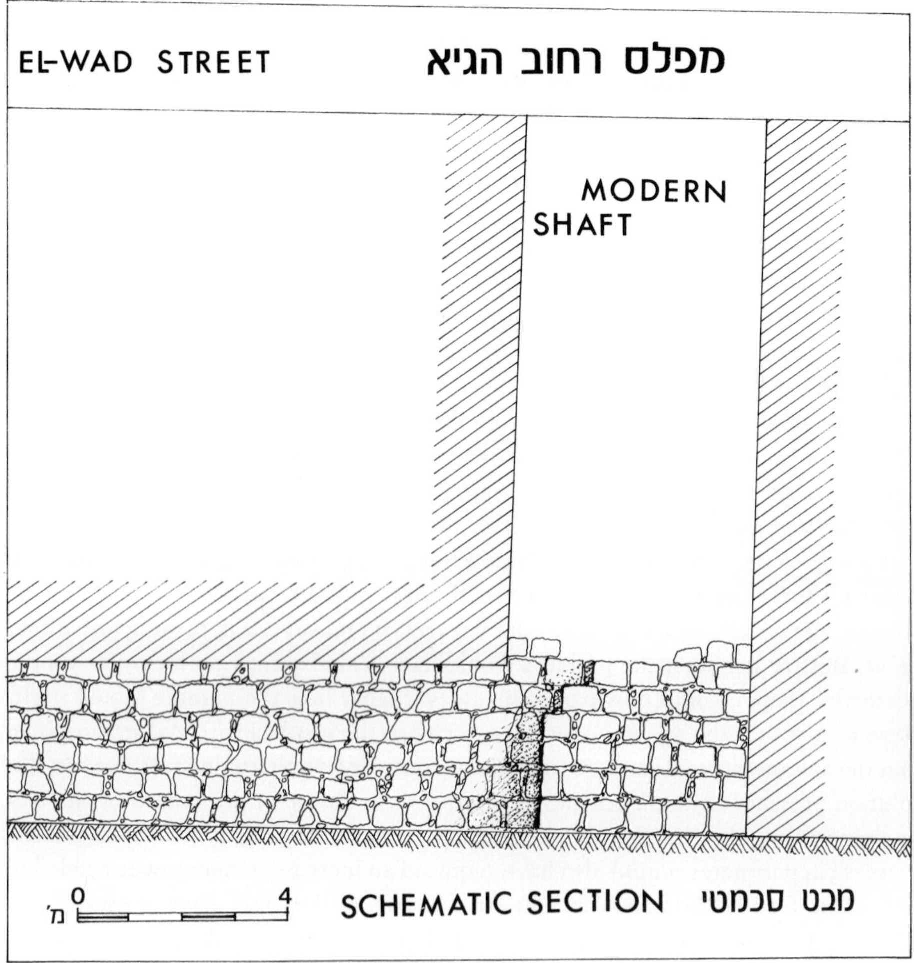

Fig. 2.
Plan of wall under El-Wad Street

H. Darrell Lance

Information on ancient Jerusalem recovered during the past quarter century has yet to be completely published, studied, and assimilated. It is still too early to achieve consensus on a number of problems, and there are additional questions that need to be posed before closure is attempted. I would like to raise two such questions deriving from the recent renewal of the debate on the site of the First and Second Temples on the Temple Mount.

My first question relates to topography. On its own resources, the rugged terrain of early Jerusalem would never have given rise to a major city. Only because David realized its political value was the site chosen as the capital. Solomon's designs to expand the city to make room for his palace and temple involved a daunting problem of engineering. The peak of the Temple Mount rose some 70 m above the level of David's Jerusalem; to encompass this, a wall would have to be far longer than the existing walls. Thus we come to my question. What was the strategy of Solomon's engineers in approaching the problem of walling the Temple Mount and ensuring its best defense?

Extending the walls northward to fortify the Temple Mount on the east and west would have presented little problem. On the east, the Kidron's escarpment was ideal for fortification, and the Tyropoeon side would not have been much more difficult. The wall would certainly have followed the eastern slope of the Tyropoeon rather than crossing it, as the Herodian platform does. It would be in the north that a viable defense would have been difficult to devise. The PEF map[1] of the bedrock under the Temple platform shows a cross-valley or ravine projecting into the Temple Mount just north of the Golden Gate. Solomon's architects would almost certainly have taken advantage of this feature to extend the east wall toward the west to begin the closure; and in fact, Warren's plans show traces of a massive wall turning just at that point. But farther west the builders would have had a serious problem, for on the northwest there is a hill (now partly cut away) higher than the Temple Mount itself. Beyond that hill, the ground continues to rise to the north. Prof. Mazar[2] proposed that the Solomonic wall ran some distance up onto this northern slope. However, this solution presents some difficulties. Firstly, it extends the entire length of the city wall, increasing the expense with no corresponding strategic gain. Furthermore, the increase in perimeter would also have required an increase in manpower needed to defend it. Finally, attackers at this part of the wall would have possessed the advantage as they would have had the higher ground. Prof. Avigad[3] proposes a solution which in my opinion is more plausible, placing the Solomonic wall on the level saddle between the Temple Mount and the threatening hill to the northwest. Warren's plans in fact indicate the presence of a ditch across this saddle which would have provided some added protection; however, there is no evidence for dating this ditch. Incidentally, a city wall placed at this logical spot contradicts Prof. Kaufman's[4] hypothesis that the Temple was located to the north of the Temple Mount peak. Such a location would have cramped the First Temple and its surrounding structures against the city wall. It also would have made the First Temple hard to shield from observation and attack from the north.

The second question that must be raised concerns the water supply for the Temple Mount. Both Bible and Mishnah indicate that considerable quantities of water were needed for the function of the Temple. It is generally assumed that for the First Temple this was met through the use of the many cisterns which underlie the surface, although Wilkinson[5] suggests that the Temple Mount may have been supplied by an aqueduct already in the First Temple period. Be that as it may, the aqueduct from

"Solomon's Pools" certainly serviced the Second Temple in its Herodian phase. Once onto the Temple Mount, the conduit split with one branch leading to the Israel Pool outside and the other bending to the south to what is now the Muslim place of ablution known as el-Kas. The presence of a water-channel on the Temple Mount is mentioned in several sources. Both Tacitus (*History* V, 12) and the probably earlier *Letter of Aristeas* (Para. 88–91) mention a copious natural spring on the Temple Mount, an obvious impossibility, though a casual observer might mistake the end of an aqueduct for a spring. The supply of water to the Temple Mount in Herodian times, however, did not reach either the traditional site of the Temple at the rock es-Sakhra or any building farther north; rather, it flowed toward the southern part of the platform, implying that it was there where the water-channel mentioned in the Mishnah was located. One should also note the presence in this area of several large cisterns, including the enormous one bearing the suggestive Arabic name *el-Bahr*, "the sea."

Both these questions might advise us to hold open the possibility, recently revived by Bagatti and Vogt,[6] that the site of the Temple may have been somewhere to the south of es-Sakhra.

Notes

1. C. Warren, *Plans, Elevations, Sections, Etc., Showing the Results of the Excavations of Jerusalem, 1867–70* (Palestine Exploration Fund, 1884), Pl. II.
2. B. Mazar, *The Mountain of the Lord* (New York: Doubleday, 1975), p. 56.
3. N. Avigad, *Discovering Jerusalem* (New York: Thomas Nelson, 1983), p. 58.
4. A.S. Kaufman, "Where the Ancient Temple of Jerusalem Stood," *BAR* 9, no. 2 (1983): 40–59.
5. J. Wilkinson, "Ancient Jerusalem: Its Water Supply and Population," *PEQ* 106 (1974): 36–37.
6. B. Bagatti, "La posizione del tempio erodiano di Gerusalemme," *Biblica* 46 (1965): 443–444; idem, *Recherches sur le site du Temple de Jérusalem (1èr – VIIè siècle)* (Jerusalem: Franciscan Printing Press, 1979), pp. 11–32, Pl. XIII; E. Vogt, "Vom Tempel zum Felsendom," *Biblica* 46 (1965): 443–444; idem,

Discussion

A.S. Kaufman: Prof. Mazar refers to a square measuring 500 cubits by 500 cubits, quoting Mishnah, Middot 2, 1. However, it should be realized that in the language of the Tannaim, such an area was not necessarily a square *per se* (cf. for example Mishnah Peah 3, 6; TP Taanit 10a). In modern terms, Middot 2, 1 would have been stated as an area of 250,000 square cubits. If a square had been intended, the text would have read: "length 500 cubits by breadth 500 cubits," as in the description of the "Court of the Women" in Middot 2, 5, universally accepted as a square.

According to Prof. Mazar, L. Ritmeyer was able to delineate three points of a square 262 m by 262 m in the present-day Temple area. One of the three points is a massive ashlar stone constituting most of the lowest step of the northwestern staircase leading to the raised platform surrounding the Dome of the Rock. To make the "Ritmeyer square" plausible, this archaeological find should be parallel to the eastern wall of the Temple area. However, these two features digress from the parallel by 1.7°. It is doubtful that the planners and executors of such a square could have miscalculated by 15 cubits over a length of 500 cubits, and so the identification, on this score alone, is doubtful.

D. Stronach: With reference to construction on the Temple Mount early in the Persian period, it is perhaps of interest to return to the question of the validity of the edict of Cyrus. Needless to say, certain of the expressions in the Book of Ezra (where it is "the Lord God of Heaven" who charges Cyrus with building "His house" in Jerusalem; Ezra 1:2) have cast doubt on the authenticity of the proclamation. At the same time, however, E.J. Bickerman has recently argued that such doubts are misplaced [see his "The Edict of Cyrus in Ezra I," in *Studies in Jewish and Christian History*, vol. I (Leiden, 1976), pp. 77f.]. In his judicious estimation, "Ezra 1 preserves a genuine edict of Cyrus" (p. 108), which was drafted by Cyrus' multilingual scribes and then rendered into Hebrew.

There is, in addition, a small neglected strand of evidence which may lend some support to Bickerman's conclusion. When Cyrus issued his edict, it included specific building instructions. Not only was the Temple to be built on secure foundations, but its walls were to have three courses of "great stones." Now such an instruction could be viewed as more appropriate to Cyrus than to any other Achaemenid monarch. His palaces at Pasargadae were built with stone socles up to three courses in height [cf. my *Pasargadae. A Report on the Excavations Conducted by the British Institute of Persian Studies from 1961 to 1963* (Oxford, 1978), p. 62], and the use of such costly, multicourse stone socles was abandoned in Iran after his reign.

If, as we have just heard, traces of Persian period construction may still be detectable on the Temple Mount, this is, of course, a matter of extreme interest. I hasten to say that I have not seen the largely buried stone block with drafted edgers, which is crucial to Prof. Mazar's reconstruction. The somewhat rounded edge of the boss on the block in question would not, in fact, be canonical in Achaemenid Iran, even if the considerable dimensions of the stone would equate with many from either the late sixth or early fifth century B.C.E. Indeed, it will be difficult to date with accuracy any of the larger blocks in the vicinity of the Temple Mount which may belong to the Persian period if it is no longer possible to inspect such features as mason's marks or — still more particularly — clamp shapes.

THE CLOSING SESSION

JOSEPH AVIRAM, Session Chairman
Israel Exploration Society
JAMES A. SAUER
President, American Schools of Oriental Research

CYRURS H. GORDON, *New York University*
The Ugaritic Texts: Half a Century of Research
EPHRAIM E. URBACH, *The Israel Academy of Sciences and Humanities*
The Search of the Past

The Closing of the Congress

Joseph Aviram: We have reached the final session of the Congress. Before Prof. Gordon delivers his lecture on "The Ugaritic Texts: Half a Century of Research," I would like to make an apology to him. When planning the Congress, we decided that all the name-tags would be written in both Hebrew and English. The people who prepared the tags were confused by some of the names, and a few errors did slip by. Unfortunately, Cyrus Gordon's was one of them. When he received his tag, he was shocked to see not *Koresh*, the Hebrew for Cyrus, but *saris*, Hebrew for "a eunuch." He went to the Hostess' Desk and complained, "You can call me whatever you like, but to call me *saris*, this is too much!"

Our second lecture tonight is on "The Search of the Past" by Prof. Ephraim Urbach. The Organizing Committee decided that it would be appropriate and refreshing to bring the Congress to a close with a lecture by a scholar who is not an archaeologist, but one who has been an active member of the Israel Exploration Society for many years, and who has watched and contributed much to its growth. Lately, Prof. Urbach has helped us in our fight against the proposed archaeology law. However, his most recent effort on behalf of the Society has been as an active member of the Organizing Committee of this Congress.

Someone told me that a few days ago on a radio program devoted to the Israel Exploration Society, Prof. Yadin called me "Mr. Exploration Society" or "Mr. Society." Indeed, I have been with the Society for the last forty-three years, and I cannot pass up this opportunity to add a little more about the *hevrah* to the pamphlet placed in your Congress kit.

During my four decades as Honorary Secretary of the Israel Exploration Society, one of the most impressive developments has been the increase in professional membership. In the 1940s, there were half a dozen local archaeologists in the Society, while today there are several hundred, both young and old. As for the general membership — then, we had about 120 members — now we have some 5,000. And those here who are not members can pay tribute to the Society on this occasion by joining our ranks. The Israel Exploration Society cooperates with almost all local archaeologists and archaeological institutions, and often acts as a roof organization for the archaeological community. Much of the Society's success over the years is due to the voluntary spirit of its active members, for we have never been blessed by an abundance of funds or endowments.

In recent years, the Israel Exploration Society has strengthened its ties with the American Schools of Oriental Research. Indeed, we of the Society have come to regard ASOR as a sort of older brother in the exploration of the Holy Land. It is thus with great pleasure that I now invite Prof. James Sauer, President of the American Schools of Oriental Research, to say a few words in his official capacity, and as an active participant in the Congress.

James A. Sauer: It is an honor to have been asked by Avraham Biran, Joseph Aviram and Yigael Yadin of the Organizing Committee of this first International Congress on Biblical Archaeology, to say a few words this evening. It has been a privilege to represent ASOR and the University of Pennsylvania at the Congress, and I know that I speak for all of the participants when I say that we have all benefited immensely from being here. The papers, responses, and discussions have all been stimulating, and it has also been worthwhile to meet informally with many of the participants during the numerous opportunities between sessions and at receptions.

I was pleased to find during the Congress that I could agree with most of the serious work being presented here. It was a relief, in particular, to find the discussion focused on the post-thirteenth century B.C.E. in agreement with my own views that the chronological heart of biblical history falls after that date. Yet, it has hardly been mentioned at this Congress that this post-thirteenth century B.C.E. emphasis constitutes a significant departure from the older Albright–Wright–Bright reconstruction of Israelite history and religion. Their approach was optimistic about finding direct connections between the biblical traditions of the Patriarchs and the archaeological evidence from the Near East in the second and third millennia B.C.E. By wisely concentrating on the thirteenth century B.C.E. and later, the Congress highlighted a number of the most striking successes of biblical archaeology, including the Philistine and Israelite evidence of the twelfth–eleventh century B.C.E., the Davidic–Solomonic remains of the tenth century B.C.E., the Neo-Assyrian evidence at Lachish in 701 B.C.E., the Neo-Babylonian evidence at Jerusalem in 586 B.C.E., the 70 C.E. Roman evidence at Jerusalem and Masada, and the period of Bar Kokhba in 135 C.E. As long as scholars have stayed within the ca. 1250 B.C.E.–135 C.E. period of time, and have applied the highest scientific standards and principles to their work, they have engaged in a biblical archaeology which is convincing. Thus, I salute the proper successes in this field, as represented by many of the papers at this Congress.

But, there must also be a word of caution against a narrowness of perspective and excess of enthusiasm among some of those who practice biblical archaeology. Should every ancient culture of the Near East from 3000 B.C.E. on be looked upon only from the viewpoint of potential biblical connections, this would constitute a distortion of overall historical realities. In addition, when speculative and sensationalistic claims are made without sufficient evidence, this damages the image of biblical archaeology, as well as archaeology in general. Such claims may attract public interest and funding, but they will lead to the isolation of biblical archaeology in the worldwide setting of archaeology as a discipline.

The biblical archaeological perspective which emphasizes the ca. 1250 B.C.E.–135 C.E. period is certainly a valid one. On the other hand, those centuries are one part of a very long historical continuum, which includes over half a million years of prehistory, and eighteen hundred years of Classical and Islamic history. As the President of ASOR, I have a policy of viewing all archaeological problems in the Middle East on the same, constructive and positive basis.

One specific issue which was raised during the Congress was the lack of agreed-upon terminologies in our field. In response to this problem, ASOR would like to suggest that a symposium be organized in the near future to work toward a consensus on terminology.

Once again, we the participants wish to thank everyone, especially the Israel Exploration Society, for making this International Congress on Biblical Archaeology a success. We congratulate the Israel Exploration Society on its 70th Anniversary, and we look forward eagerly to participating in those congresses which it may plan in the future.

Joseph Aviram: We can't close the Congress without expressing thanks and appreciation to all those who worked toward its success; foremost, the Organizing Committee and its Chairman, Prof. A. Biran. The Committee spent much time and effort to plan an interesting and fruitful program. Our thanks also go to the sponsoring institutions whose support was greatly valued. Mrs. Avigail Hyam, Secretary of the Israel Academy of Sciences and Humanities, was of great assistance, and Ophir Tours, and its staff, proved most efficient in the physical arrangements, and so far I have not heard any complaints. There were so many persons and institutions involved that I can only extend a general "thank-you" to them all. But I must especially mention Mrs. Janet Amitai, Secretary of the Organizing Committee, who labored day and night, and unceasingly urged us on, to assure the success which we have all enjoyed here.

Here this evening, there is, I believe, only one person who has been active in the Israel Exploration Society longer than I — Prof. Benjamin Mazar. He has been at the fore of the Society for more than half a century, and it was he who brought me into it. As you have seen during the past week, he still has much to give us, and on behalf of all the participants, I wish him עד מאה ועשרים, "May he live to be 120!"

Someone has already suggested that we hold such a Congress as an annual event. It took us two years to arrange this one, so an International Congress as an annual event is out of the question. But I recall that the Society's local conventions were initiated as an experiment forty years ago, and our next one will be the thirty-eighth! Maybe our international congresses will suffer a similar fate.

Twenty years ago, at the Jubilee of the Society, we also wanted to hold an international archaeological meeting, but we felt that the time was not yet ripe. And how right we were! These last twenty years have been so fruitful for the Society and, indeed, we can regard this present occasion as the zenith of its activities — a true *hag* on the Society's 70th Anniversary. Such congresses often open with the traditional blessing ברוך שהחיינו, "Thank God that we lived to see the day," but by the end of the Congress, one says ברוך שפטרנו, "Thank heavens it is over." Not so in the case of this Congress! From beginning to end, it has been a most pleasant time of social and scientific activities.

I hope you all have enjoyed the Congress. For those participating in the excursions, may your pleasure continue! For those going home — Bon Voyage!

At the close of our Congress, the Hora Jerusalem Dance Group will perform some Israel folk dances.

The Ugaritic Texts: Half a Century of Research

Cyrus H. Gordon

THE UGARITIC TABLETS began to emerge from the soil on May 14, 1929. Two international colloquia celebrated the fiftieth anniversary in 1979, while the discoverer, Claude F.-A. Schaeffer, was still alive to enjoy the occasion.[1] Now that five more years have passed and he is no longer among the living, the tablets that he and his successors have unearthed continue to enrich our knowledge of the Bible World.

The most important single aspect of Ugaritic is the script itself: our alphabet. The order of the letters was already fixed in essentially the same sequence as in the Hebrew/Phoenician,[2] Greek and Latin[3] alphabet. There is no telling what future discoveries hold in store, but as of now our alphabet is first attested in the Ugaritic tablets written about 1400–1200 B.C.E.

Attention was called to Ugarit when a nearby Mycenaean-type tomb was accidentally struck by a peasant's plowshare in 1928. A Mycenaean structure on Semitic soil foreshadowed the connections between the Aegean and Semitic spheres that were soon to be reflected in the tablets themselves.

Ugaritic has affected our understanding of the entire ancient Near East, from Mesopotamia to Egypt and from the Aegean to Arabia. But nowhere is the impact more profound than in Old Testament studies. Ugarit has so revolutionized Hebrew scholarship that it constitutes a simple test for determining whether a publication is up-to-date or antiquated. If a Hebrew commentary, history, grammar or dictionary abounds in references to Ugaritic, the book presumably reflects the present status of the subject. If Ugarit plays little or no part in the publication, it is either old or out of date.

Ugarit and Israel belonged to the same cultural sphere, often referred to as "Canaanite."[4] Their linguistic, literary and many other cultural features had much in common. Yet the differences were also profound and significant. To a great extent, Israel reacted against "Canaanite" values, particularly in ethics, morals and religion.[5] To stress the relationships, as we shall do, is not to deny the differences.

The "heroic age" of Ugaritology is over. Schaeffer, the pioneer discoverer, is gone and so are Charles Virolleaud, the pioneer copyist, translator and interpreter of the alphabetic texts,[6] and Jean Nougayrol, to whom we owe the publication of most of the syllabic tablets from Ugarit. Hans Bauer, the chief decipherer of the Ugaritic alphabet, is no longer among the living; nor is Édouard Dhorme, who made significant refinements in the decipherment.

Among the refiners of the interpretation we may single out the late Prof. Umberto (Moses David) Cassuto of The Hebrew University in Jerusalem. His contributions are characterized by sobriety and insight.

We shall not review the long list of interpreters, commentators, grammarians and other specialists who have established Ugaritology as a full-fledged branch of Semitic languages and literatures. Many of them are still active. In general the early Ugaritologists were confronted with new and comprehensive problems, whereas later ones have had to refine the results of their predecessors. A scholar bridging the pioneering spirit of the early generation and the refining spirit of the younger scholars was the late Prof. Mitchell Dahood, S.J. Whereas the author of *Ugaritic Grammar* (1940), in mentioning that *b*- and *l*- may mean "from" (often in Ugaritic and sometimes in Hebrew), gave enough examples to illustrate the phenomenon, Dahood would seek hundreds of examples. Such exhaustiveness means widening the margin of error. Pioneering Ugaritologists applaud Dahood for the new examples of such phenomena he pointed out correctly, while the critical perfectionists take him to task for his mistakes.[7]

With the refinement of Ugaritology, acceptable methods of research are changing. For example, at the start the etymological method was indispensable for defining the words of the new language. But now, with about 50% of the extensive Ugaritic corpus accurately translated, the contextual method has relegated etymology to a secondary role.

Ugaritic has a huge and steadily growing bibliography. *Ugarit-Forschungen* appears annually with original articles, while the *Newsletter for Ugaritic Studies* is published several times a year, featuring a current bibliography and brief articles, reviews and notices.

Most of the Late Bronze Age level at Ugarit (1400–1200 B.C.E.), whence the tablets have emerged, has been excavated and preserved for visitors. Some work, especially in the lower city outside the wall, goes on. But the productive successor is Ras Ibn Hani, a small port in the precincts of Latakia that once belonged to the Kingdom of Ugarit. It is from Ras Ibn Hani that a stream of alphabetic tablets continues to flow. About forty new tablets were found there in the 1983/84 campaign.[8]

There are many small dependencies of Ugarit that lie buried in the vicinity. Eventually, more alphabetic tablets will come from them. In any case, the archives in Ugaritic are not a closed book. Ugaritology will continue to be quickened by the ongoing excavation of additional tablets.

We shall illustrate, at a basic level, typical effects of Ugaritic on biblical Hebrew. In Psalm 84:12, לא ימנע־טוב להלכים בתמים, "he will not withhold good *from* those who walk in perfection," the preposition *l*- means "from," as in Ugaritic (*UT* §10.11), while in 2 Kings 23:33, ויאסרהו ... במלך בירושלים, "he stopped him ... *from* ruling in Jerusalem," the preposition *b*- means "from," as in Ugaritic (*UT* §10.5).

Ugaritic has thrown much light on Hebrew vocabulary. One word is particularly noteworthy in that it had not even been isolated prior to the discovery of Ugaritic: Ug. *spsg*, "white glaze" has at last been identified in Proverbs 26:23, כסף סיגים מצפה על־חרש שפתים דלקים ולב־רע,[9] "like white glaze (כ, 'like' + ספסג, 'white glaze' + enclitic -*m*) covered over a pot, so are enthusiastic-sounding lips when the heart is in evil case" (that is cheerful words masking a sorry heart within).

In 2 Kings 5:25 the *ktib* of מאן is מֵאָן, "whence?" while the *qre* is the normal מֵאַיִן. The reduction of the diphthong *ay* to *a* is attested in Ugaritic. Thus the place name "Yana" is written alphabetically *yn*[10] or syllabically GEŠTIN-*na*.[11] Accordingly, the word for "wine" in Ugaritic is not pronounced *yayn/yên* but *yan*. Similarly, the personal name בן־ענת is written syllabically DUMU $^{m\,d}$IGI-*at*.[12] IGI is the Sumerogram for "eye"; therefore "eye" was not pronounced *ʿayn/ʿên* but *ʿan* at Ugarit. The shift of *ay* to *a*, common in Eblaite, is also attested in Minoan where the word for "wine" is written *ya-ne*.[13] Our discussion of מֵאָן foreshadows further isoglosses embracing early Bronze Age Eblaite, Middle Bronze Age Minoan, Late Bronze Age Ugaritic and early Iron Age Hebrew.

The content of the literary texts from Ugarit overlaps the content of the Old Testament especially as concerns the Patriarchs in Genesis. Both the Kret and Danʾel Epics deal with the theme of continuing the royal line through a special god-given son (cf. Isaac). Furthermore, the Kret Epic highlights a theme that we may call the "Helen of Troy" motif, whereby only the destined bride can fill the needs of her royal husband. King Menelaus of Sparta must retrieve his wife Helen from an alien palace (King Priam's at Troy); King Kret of Ḫbr must retrieve his irreplaceable bride (Ḥry) from the palace of King Pbl of Udm; and "King"[14] Abraham must retrieve his Sarah (who alone is destined to bear the heir) from the palace of Pharaoh and later from the palace of Abimelech, King of Gerar. It was Ugaritic literature that bridged the gap between Homer and the Bible in this regard.[15] Moreover, it turns out that all three Late Bronze Age epics (Ugaritic, Greek and Hebrew) are royal epics concerned with the ruling class.

The diffusion of concepts among the peoples of the Eastern Mediterranean is extensive. For some time it has been clear that the Three Graces appear at Ugarit before they are attested in Greek mythology.[16] While the Greek versions vary, the earliest (in Hesiod) makes them daughters of Zeus. They are beautiful goddesses of fertility named Aglaia ("Brightness"), Thalia ("Bloom") and Euphrosyne ("Mirth"). They are anticipated by Baal's three beautiful daughters: Bt ʾAr ("Girl of Light") corresponding to Aglaia, Ṭly ("Dew") corresponding to Thalia[17] and Arṣy ("Earth"). A Ugaritic bilingual equates Arsy with the Mesopotamian underworld goddess Al-la-tu(m). Perhaps the happy-sounding name of Euphrosyne is a euphemistic substitute for the ominous underworld deity.

The pre-Islamic Arabs knew of Three Daughters of Allah, who are named in the *Qurʾān* (53:19ff.): Allat, Al-ʿUzza and Manat. Allat = Al-la-tu(m) = Arṣy. It stands to reason that a phenomenon appearing in the pre-biblical tablets from Ugarit, and in the *Qurʾān* of the seventh century C.E., might crop up in between. In Job 40:29, in the course of overwhelming Job, God asks him rhetorically whether he can vanquish the mighty Leviathan and play with it as with a pet bird. The implication is that although Job cannot, God can. God goes on to ask Job: "Canst thou bind him for thy girls?" This implies that Job cannot tie up Leviathan as a plaything for his three beautiful daughters,[18] whereas God has done so for His girls. The threeness of Job's daughters suggests that God's girls were also three in number. But in any case, in the mythology that reverberates in the poetry of Job, God has daughters to be compared with the Three Graces.

Ugaritic literature is even closer to the Bible in form than in content. The structure of both literatures has as its unit the verse consisting of parallel stichs. To take a familiar example: Danʾel is described as exercising his basic royal duty as follows:

ydn dn almnt, He judges the case of the widow.
yṯpṭ ṯpṭ ytm,[19] Adjudicates the cause of the fatherless.

Every word in this passage occurs also in Hebrew in keeping with phonetic law. Besides, the same thought is expressed in Isaiah 1:17 with three out of the four above roots duplicated:

שפטו יתום, Judge the fatherless.
ריבו אלמנה, Plead the cause of the widow.

"Judging" in these passages does not imply legal impartiality. What we call the "social justice" of the Prophets is not so much justice as mercy for the underdog. More precisely, it means that in any conflict of interest, the weaker must be saved from the stronger. A landlord evicting a widow is *a priori* wrong, and the widow *a priori* right, regardless of the legalities. This ideal is expressed in the literature of Ugarit and elsewhere[20] in the Bible World as the moral duty of rulers. But only in Israel was it extended to the entire community. *Noblesse oblige* was incumbent on Danʾel, *qua* ruler. But God's People are enjoined, one and all, by the Prophets to act nobly. This is the key to understanding much of the contribution of the Bible. Israel took the highest standards of the elite of the Bible World and applied them to all the people. Israel was to be a Holy People, a nation of priests. Commonness has no place in such a scheme.

The alphabet of Ugarit was used to record a number of languages: Hurrian and Babylonian as well as Ugaritic. There was also a short version of the Ugaritic ABC, running from right to left like Hebrew.[21] This shortened alphabet had only twenty-two letters (or thereabouts) like the Hebrew/Phoenician alphabet, and texts written in it have been found at several Palestinian sites, making it conceivable that the Hebrew conquerors of the Land at the end of the Late Bronze Age and the beginning of the early Iron Age were exposed to the script and to literature expressed in it. That would partly explain the close literary affinities between Ugaritic and Hebrew literature.[22]

The fact that the Ugaritic alphabet was used to express a variety of languages shows that the cultural milieu favored the spread of the system of writing among the various peoples in contact with each other. Since the Mycenaean Greeks were an important ethnic element on the scene, the times favored the transmission of the alphabet to the Greek World. That it actually happened then is not yet demonstrable. In no case should we pinpoint Ugarit as the specific place where the transmission took place. A more likely location would be Crete, where Northwest Semites and Mycenaean Greeks lived side by side and had long been accustomed to sharing the same linear syllabary[23] for their respective languages. Later, from Archaic Greek to Imperial Roman times, the dwindling Semitic population of Crete shared with their Greek neighbors the familiar alphabet for writing their respective languages.[24]

The Amarna Age, which embraced Ugarit, favored the application of cuneiform writing to different languages. So, while we cannot say that the Greeks used the alphabet during the Late Bronze Age, we can state that the atmosphere pervading the world of Late Bronze Age Ugarit favored the transmission and at least paved the way for it.

The age was one of multiple literacy. At Ugarit, not only the alphabet but also the Mesopotamian syllabary were used to record Ugaritic, Babylonian and Hurrian.[25] This reminds us to temper the theory of oral transmission in biblical criticism, starting with the earliest strata of the Old Testament. Obviously, oral factors are present in all linguistic expression. But the texts of the ancient Near East, and especially those from Ugarit, oblige us to recognize that no part of the Old Testament stems from an illiterate milieu. Virtually all its compositions originated in an intellectual, literary environment.

The techniques of writing known to the Hebrews varied. There were scrolls of skin or papyrus; lapidary inscriptions; clay tablets; seals, ostraca, and inscribed weights. Deuteronomy 27:2–3 states that the Tablets of the Law consisted of stones covered with plaster on which the text was inscribed. Stelae covered with white plaster on which the text and figures were painted are familiar from Egyptian collections in our museums. At Deir ʿAlla (cf. Kuntilet Ajrud) inscriptions were made with black ink, with red ink for the rubrics, on plaster in the Egyptian tradition. The Deir ʿAlla texts, dating from about 700 B.C.E., deal with Balaam, the same (non-Hebrew) prophet discussed in Numbers 22–24. Both versions, despite differences, belong to the same genre: tales of the prophets. Neither account reflects illiterate folklore. Literacy is the chief criterion dividing primitivism and civilization. The Hebrews, from the start, were part of an intellectual ecumene.

It is not only in literature that Ugarit explains the high level at which Israel embarked on its history. David, who liberated his people from Philistine domination and forged an empire from the Euphrates to the Egyptian border, also appears as a musical genius. He performed, composed, and excelled at every level of music, including the inventing of instruments.[26] It was he who imparted the aesthetic component of worship which endures long after the Tabernacle and Temple sacrifices have vanished. Synagogue and church foster liturgies ennobled by the Psalms of David without the slaughter of animals that formed the main part of the divine service in the Tabernacle, and continued in the Temples until 70 C.E. The fact that David has never been surpassed as a psalmist requires a historic explanation. The author of the Iliad is the greatest epic poet of all time. Such genius cannot be the beginning of a process but only its climax. The Gilgamesh Epic and its cuneiform heirs had brought the epic tradition to the shores of the Eastern Mediterranean long before the birth of Homeric epic. Bach cannot be considered the creator *ex nihilo* of the finest church music, but rather the apex of a development rooted in antiquity and developed through the Middle Ages and Renaissance down to his time. The same, *mutatis mutandis*, was true of David. His achievement can only be the climax of a long process.

Music is a part of every human culture, primitive or advanced. The art of the ancient Near East depicts song accompanied by a large assortment of instruments. Note, for example, the Royal Tombs at Ur, and the mural paintings in the Tombs of the Princes at Thebes. The poetry of the ancient Near East from Egypt to Mesopotamia provides us with librettos that went with the scores. But until the discoveries at Ugarit since 1929, there was a lingering suspicion that Canaan was a kind of backwash, on the fringes rather than a part of ancient Near Eastern civilization.

One of the tablets from Ugarit is a hymn to the goddess Nikkal. It is Hurrian and written in the Mesopotamian syllabary. The text is in two parts: the psalm itself, and the score. The latter consists of the names of the note-sequences (or "intervals") whereby the entire melody is recorded. As of now, the Ugaritic psalm is the earliest song in the world provided with its complete musical notation.[27]

The text dates from the thirteenth century B.C.E., at least two centuries before the birth of David. The Ugaritic song is not folk music, but the product of an academic, musicographic tradition. Music was one of the disciplines fostered at "The University of Ugarit." There were teachers, students and files of recordings. Thus Canaan even long before David's time cultivated a tradition whereby both librettos and scores were written, just as the psalms of David have musical specifications in the captions.[28]

Comparisons are not equations. Jerusalem (to say nothing of Bethlehem or Hebron) was not Ugarit. But they belonged to same Syro-Palestinian ecumene, in which the writing of David's psalms would not be anachronistic.

David's psalms are so called because they bear his name; note, for example, the formula לדוד, "concerning David."[29] There he is called "David," not "King David." The Ugaritic psalm has a colophon naming the writer: *qāt* ^{m}*am-mu-ra-pí*, "(from) the hand of ʿAmmurapiʾ."[30] Conceivably, this ʿAmmurapiʾ was only a scribe in the Ugaritic bureaucracy. But the last king of Ugarit was called ʿAmmurapiʾ. He ruled until the city fell early in the twelfth century B.C.E. The scribe or author of the Ugaritic psalm is not called "king" but neither is David called "king" in the psalms attributed to him.

Hebrew contains vocabulary borrowed from Sumerian, such as היכל, "temple, palace," כסא, "chair, throne" and a host of *nomina agentis* of the *qaṭṭâl* formation (like נגר, "carpenter," פחר "potter," etc.). Sumerian loans in Hebrew account for much of the terminology of advanced culture associated with the spread of Mesopotamian urbanism. At the beginning of this century, the Mesopotamian components of Hebrew tended to be attributed to the Babylonian Exile. The Jews learned much from Babylonia during their Exile and still use the Babylonian Nisan-to-Adar calendar. But by the time of the Exile, Sumerian had become a dead, classical language. Common Sumerian words in Hebrew had already been incorporated into Ugaritic; for example, *hkl, ksu, ngr*. Therefore, Sumerian vocabulary had entered the Northwest Semitic language of Syria-Palestine before (to use the terminology of the Old Testament) the Aramean Abraham and his retinue entered the land of Canaan and learned what we call Hebrew.

Thanks to Ebla, we know the enormous impact of Sumerian in Syria by the middle of the Early Bronze Age. The Sumerian component of Hebrew was there from the ground floor. To remove it would strip Hebrew of terminology essential for expressing aspects of urban and technical culture.

Cultural interchange tends to be a two-way street. Europe may have given America its present European civilization, but America has now for a long time been exerting influence on Europe. That the Sumerians were the first literate bearers of high civilization is agreed. But from the very start there was a Semitic input. A Sumerian word like *silim*, "well-being, peace," is derived from Semitic *šālôm/sālām*. Sumerian MA-NA, "mina" cannot be divorced from the Semitic מנה, "to count." In the Sumerian pantheon, there are very early Semitic elements such as the god Dagan (cf. דגון, the fertility god whose name is connected with דגן, "grain").[31]

Ugarit sheds light on the origin of the name of a major Akkadian deity known as Ea, identified with EN-KI in the Sumerian pantheon. This equation recurs in an Ebla bilingual identifying Sumerian EN-KI with Eblaite É-*um*.[32] The Ebla tablets have made it clear that the sign transliterated É is not the vowel *e* but representes a syllable opening with a laryngeal such as *h* or *ḥ*. This has been evident (but not adequately reckoned with) for a long time, since a word like É-GAL comes into

Semitic languages as *haykal>hêkal*. Now we have bilinguals from Ebla equating what appears in Hebrew as חדר, "room" with Eblaite É-*da-ru-um*.[33] EN-KI means "Lord of the Earth" which in Ugaritic is translated *bˁl arṣ*, בעל ארץ, "Lord of Earth." In Ugaritic mythology, the living Baal is hailed:

> *k ḥy aliyn bˁl*, for alive is Almighty Baal.
> *k iṯ zbl bˁl arṣ*,[34] for the Prince, Lord of Earth exists.

This is the most joyous moment in the Canaanite fertility cult, when Baal comes back to life so that nature can flourish. E-*um* at Ebla is not to be normalized *eum* but *ḥay(y)um*, "The Living One," for such is the epithet of the "Lord of Earth." Ugaritic thus provides us with an example of West Semitic derivation of the name of a major god in the Akkadian pantheon. É-*a*[=*Ḥay(y)a*] cannot be East Semitic, because *ḥyy*, "to live," is replaced in Akkadian by *blṭ*, "to live."[35]

In keeping with the urbanism of the Cuneiform World, we must view Ugarit as an intellectual center. In such cities, where scribes flourished, philology was the queen of the disciplines. At Ugarit students used sophisticated philological texts such as quadrilingual lexica: Sumerian-Babylonian-Hurrian-Ugaritic. The Ugaritic academy also engaged in the translation of literary works, involving Sumerian, Akkadian and Hittite.

Ugarit during the Late Bronze Age was heir to a long history of literate urbanism in Syria. A millennium earlier, Early Bronze Age Ebla nurtured bilingualism; though developments such as the Ugaritic quadrilinguals and the alphabet still lay in the future.

The Old Testament is the culmination of ancient Near Eastern civilization, literarily and in quality of content. Ugarit, more than any other excavated site, tells us how this was historically possible.

Notes

1. Gordon D. Young, ed., *Ugarit in Retrospect: 50 Years of Ugarit and Ugaritic* (Winona Valley, Indiana: Eisenbrauns, 1981); Afif Bahnassi, ed., *Colloque international des études ugaritiques* [= *Les annales archéologiques arabes syriennes*, vols. XXIX–XXX (Latakia, 1979–80)].
2. Modern scholars restrict the term "Phoenician" more than the ancient Greeks and Romans did. Since the decipherment early in the nineteenth century of what we call Phoenician, the term has come to be limited to the Northwest Semitic dialects of Tyre, Sidon, Byblos and other coastal cities in Lebanon (in addition to Syria and Israel), with their offshoots (colonies) throughout the Mediterranean. "Punic" often designates the "Phoenician" dialects in the Western Mediterranean, especially those of a later date. The Greeks and Romans applied "Phoenician" to any Northwest Semites who plied their trade by sea. Their broad definition includes even groups of Arameans. In Nero's time, the Romans called the Eteocretans "Phoenician" and "Punic" indiscriminately. Eteocretan happens to be Northwest Semitic with strong Aramaic affinities. Cf. Cyrus H. Gordon, "The Semitic Language of Minoan Crete," in *Amsterdam Studies in the Theory and History of Linguistic Science*, vol. IV, eds. Y. Arbeitman and A.R. Bomhard (Amsterdam: Benjamins, 1981), pp. 761–782.

Since "Phoenician" in classical sources is not the same as "Phoenician" in current Semitic linguistics, the confusion is disconcerting. That the Phoenicians never call themselves "Phoenician" in any of their inscriptions does not make matters easier. Scholars should face the problem and try to agree on an acceptable terminology.

3. While the Greek and Latin alphabets reflect essentially the Hebrew/Phoenician version, they do contain at least one factor linking them to an earlier and longer version such as the Ugaritic. Greek and Latin both incorporate *u* as an integral part of the sequence. In the Ugaritic alphabet (as in Greek and Latin), *u* appears later than *t*. Accordingly, the Greek and Latin ABC cannot be derived exclusively from the twenty-two letter Hebrew/Phoenician alphabet that ends in *t*.
4. The term is not really satisfactory. Note that *ugrty*, "(native) Ugaritic" (*UT* text 64:8, 9) is to be differentiated from the alien *knʿny* (*UT* text 311:7), "Canaanite" (cf. *UT* 19.1272).
5. The Tenth Commandment (against coveting) was evoked in opposition to the Canaanite stress on materialism and acquisitiveness. The adored Baal was a coveting god (75:I:38; 2001:rev. 7). The sex rites of the Canaanite fertility cult were termed "whoring" by the religious leaders of Israel.
6. The decipherment of Ugaritic is reviewed and analyzed in C.H. Gordon, *Forgotten Scripts*, 2d ed. (New York: Basic Books, 1982).
7. The most extensive of Dahood's voluminous contributions is his three-volume Anchor Commentary on *Psalms*.
8. My source of information is Gabriel Saade, author of *Ougarit: Métropole Cananéenne* (Latakia, 1978).
9. Not knowing ספסג and enclitic *-m*, the scribes garbled the consonants *kspsgm* into כסף סיגים, "silver of dross," which is impossible Hebrew.
10. *UT* 19.1112 and its gentilic *yny* in 19.1114.
11. Documented in C.H. Gordon, "The Decipherment of Minoan and Eteocretan," *Journal of the Royal Asiatic Society* (1975): 148–158. Note pp. 157–158.
12. Denis Kinlaw, "A Study of the Personal Names in the Akkadian Texts from Ugarit," (Ph.D. diss., Brandeis University, 1967; University Microfilms, Ann Arbor, Michigan), pp. 36, 264.
13. C.H. Gordon, *Evidence for the Minoan Language* (Ventnor, N.J., 1966), pp. 28–29.
14. That Abraham and Sarah are to produce kings is stated in Genesis 17:6, 16. In Genesis 23:6, where Abraham is called a נשיא, the Septuagint translates *basileus*, "king."
15. Treated in detail in C.H. Gordon, *The Common Background of Greek and Hebrew Civilizations* (New York, 1965).
16. Michael Astour, "La triade de déesses de fertilité à Ugarit et en Grèce," *Ugaritica* VI (Paris, 1969), pp. 9–23.
17. C.H. Gordon, "The Three Graces," *Newsletter for Ugaritic Studies* 31 (April 1984): 11.
18. Job 42: 14–15.
19. *UT* text 2 Aqht:V:7–8.
20. For example, Hammurapi, who states in the Prologue to his Code that his laws aim at preventing the strong from oppressing the weak.
21. For the Ugaritic alphabet (and its short version), see *UT* §§3.1–6.
22. That cuneiform literature was studied in Palestine before the Israelite Conquest is indicated by the tablet of the Gilgamesh Epic found at Megiddo.
23. Linear A has essentially the same syllabic signs for Minoan as Linear B has for Mycenaean Greek. Indeed it was the decipherment of Linear B that made it possible to pronounce Linear A before the Minoan language was identified.
24. The Greeks and Eteocretans at sites like Dreros and Praisos used the same letter-forms for writing their quite different languages.
25. See the rich documentation in *Ugaritica* V (Paris, 1968).
26. Amos 6:5.
27. See Raoul G. Vitale, "La tablette 'musicale' H. 6," *Colloque internationale des études ugaritiques* (note 1), pp. 42–62.

28. Psalms 4, 5, 6, 8, 12, 39, 45, 46, etc.
29. For example, Psalm 25.
30. The correct pronunciation is *ʿAmmurāpiʾ*, not *Hammurabi.*
31. Dagan was important at Ugarit. The two temples excavated at Ugarit were devoted to Baal and Dagan respectively. Moreover, Baal is called "Dagan's son" in the Ugaritic texts.
32. Giovanni Pettinato, *Materiale Epigrafici di Ebla — 4* (Naples, 1982), p. 290 (No. 803).
33. Ibid., p. 267 (No. 595).
34. *UT* text 49:III:20–21.
35. How É-*a* (nominative with mimation at Ebla: É-*um*) was associated with the sea, and is frequently depicted as dwelling in an underwater shrine, calls for discussion. A Mesopotamian scribe, not knowing West Semitic, would naturally explain the signs É-A as meaning "house of water" (for É = "house" and A = "water" in Sumerian). This is, so to speak, "scribal etymology," stemming from a written (and not oral) tradition.

The Search of the Past

Ephraim E. Urbach

MICHAEL HOWARD, REGIUS PROFESSOR of Modern History at the University of Oxford, wrote recently in an essay entitled "The Concept of Peace":[1]

> I regard the relative absence of internal disorder which in this country enables me to travel unhindered, to speak my mind freely and walk at least some of the streets in our cities without fear of being attacked as an advantage not to be despised; and the absence of war for the past forty years as something for which we should give heartfelt thanks to God every night. As an historian I am perhaps *unduly conscious* of the turmoils and tragedies through which mankind has passed, of the precariousness and evanescence of peace in the past, and of our extraordinary good fortune in enjoying such peace as we do possess. I am also conscious of the extent to which that peace is the result of the patient work of generations labouring to build up a just order within our societies, and ever-growing links between our societies. I wonder at what seems to me the amazing miracle of technology and organisation that enables so much of mankind to travel so freely over so much of the world unarmed and in perfect safety — something inconceivable only a hundred years ago. I am astonished and grateful, in fact, for how much peace we have got, and how successfully we prevent the conflicts which inevitably arise in various corners of the world from disturbing its global structure.

May I be allowed to say that even a historian who has reached the peak of an academic career — Regius Professor at Oxford — misses his point if he is conscious of the past only in the frame of his academic, artificial and cloistered environment. Otherwise he could not have made such a statement, in December 1983, when a bloody war is being fought between Iran and Iraq, not to mention the Russian invasion of Afganistan, the wars in Africa and Central America, and the cruelties and terrorist activities in so many parts of the world.

Does not such a view of the present blur the historian's description of the past? Was 1893 so much worse than 1983, as Howard suggests? Being unconscious of the turmoils and tragedies of the present cannot help in the assessment of the past. It only renders more difficult the answering of the question "Should the historian sit in judgment?" This question was formulated by the American historian, Henry Steele Commager, as follows:

> Should the historian sit in judgment over the great drama of the past and the men and the women who performed on that stage, exposing evil and celebrating virtue and damning and praising famous men? Or should he observe the historical processes with scientific detachment and record them as automatically as a tape recorder, rigorously excluding personal, national or religious considerations.[2]

The opinions of historians and philosophers of history on this issue have been divided since ancient times. The answers they have given are not only a result of different views on the purpose of history or the duties and responsibilities of scholars. Even historians who adhere to the aphorism that history is philosophy teaching by examples, and who see the danger implicit in moral neutrality, may still question the competence of any historian to judge the past because of shortcomings of one kind or another.

Where remote times are concerned all the relevant evidence is seldom available. Retrodiction — filling in gaps in the past for which no testimonies exist — and efforts made to reconstruct what must have occurred in intermediate phases are interesting exercises, but nobody denies that they are not a too reliable method for discovery of the past.[3] And there are many instances where the discovery of an unknown body of evidence has not only disproved such conjectures but also brought radical changes in judgment.

On the other hand, there is no less difficulty in assessing periods for which there are abundant and variegated sources, since the historian's horizon embraces almost the entire gamut of human affairs, in which politics and war — the traditional subjects of history — fall into place as only a small part of the great whole. There is not very much hope that a balanced historical view can be obtained from team work in intellectual activities, and certainly not in passing judgments.

But, notwithstanding all such doubts and difficulties, one cannot deny that the view that the successes and failures of the past provide some guidance for one's own times became in itself an influential factor in history. This is especially noticeable in the histories of peoples with a long record. In the Bible, historicism is not confined to the historical books: prophets remind the people of their past; the psalmists spell out the lessons of history and reference is made to it in prayers.[4] For the Chinese, history provided the instances and proofs of the principles operating in the affairs of men as taught by their laws and traditional wisdom.[5] Cicero called history *magistra vitae*. Tacitus thought that the function of history was "to hold out the reprobation of posterity as a warning and rebuke to all base conduct." Even a new nation is quick to adopt a similar attitude toward the past. "Nothing in the history of American Nationalism," writes Commager,[6] "is more impressive than the speed and the lavishness with which Americans have provided themselves with a usable past ... and what a past it was — splendid, varied, romantic and all but blameless...."

It is certainly true that values and principles have varied greatly from age to age, from society to society, and in the same society from one generation to another. It is also true that the historian, like the judge or statesman, can never emancipate himself from the formative influence of his race, nationality, religion, or class, of his heredity, or education. But making allowances for the standards of the age he is dealing with is also a kind of judgment for the historian — and the wish to understand and be just to the past may be doing an injustice to the present, because such an approach fosters the conviction that nothing is good or bad in itself.[7]

The chief professional preoccupation of the historian in our day is the tendency to revise, and the struggle against misuse of the past by consciously projecting the present for the benefit of practical or political action of the state, churches and groups whose aim is to direct or dominate society by means of great or lesser lies or clever inventions.[8] The task of judgment in history is difficult because the frontiers between fact and interpretation are confused and shifting, and what seems to be fact from one perspective becomes interpretation from another. One may even say that facts are never neutral; in the eyes of each of us they are impregnated with value judgments.

The task of judgment is made even more difficult if the historian claims that some general laws must underlie any legitimate historical explanation. The confusion of aims and methods in recent studies of the human condition, which are concerned more with persons and personal reactions, with quality rather than quantity, with the operation of the laws of the natural sciences, was named by Isaiah Berlin "one of the greatest fallacies of the last hundred years."[9]

The historian's task is pervaded by paradox. He is supposed to empathize with the past because without this capacity he cannot visualize either the past or the present, but at the same time he is also told to see them in perspective. If he neglects the former, he will never leave the present, and will simply parade in his writings contemporary actors dressed up in period costume; and if he neglects the latter, he will never leave the past, becoming not its student, but its accomplice in the tale. Another paradox facing the historian concerns his choice of literary genre as a means of conveying the truth. The form and style, the rhythm of narration, became the framework of deeper issues. There is an ongoing debate between the proponents of beauty with truth and the proponents of truth without beauty. But, as Peter Gay pointed out, style is not only a decoration, it is not the dress of thought, but part of its essence.[10] It reveals the historian's understanding of causes and the course of events, and it facilitates understanding on the part of a listener or reader. I need not say that we can find many instances and illustrations in various histories which confirm the existence of these paradoxes. I shall limit myself to only one which principally demonstrates the meaning of style in writing history but also has a bearing on the issue of empathy and distance. The theme and source of the example are connected — at least partly — with the topic of this Congress.

Hayim Tadmor, in his article "Autobiographical Apology in the Royal Assyrian Literature,"[11] dealt with the compositions of kings who, not being first in the line of succession, assumed their office in an irregular fashion. In this context, Tadmor does not fail to mention the Davidic and Solomonic succession-stories in the Books of Samuel and Kings. He finds that their only possible *Sitz-im-Leben* was the necessity to prove the legitimacy of the founders of the Judean Kingdom. Tadmor summarizes his results in the following way:

> The second millennium Hittite, North Syrian (or even Egyptian) "autobiographies," as well as the biblical apologetic accounts of the early first millennium, indicate that the genre of the apology was at home in the countries west of the Euphrates. The Neo-Assyrian examples of this genre were relatively novel in Mesopotamian historical writing and could be regarded as further evidence of the Western impact upon Assyria. Such a genre was foreign to the rather rigid and formalistic traditions of Southern Mesopotamia. It appeared in Babylonia — though in a different guise — with the coming of the Chaldean kings, Nabopolassar and Nabonidus. It was continued by the Persian conquerors of Babylonia and found its most masterful expression in the apology of Darius I.... We shall conclude with the brief apology of Xerxes.... Xerxes admits that he was not the firstborn son — his father had older sons — but Darius made him "greatest after himself"... Herodotus, commenting upon the choice of Xerxes as heir to Darius (VII, 3), adds yet another element: The influential queen-mother Atossa, the daughter of Cyrus and mother of Xerxes, thus joins our list of equally famed and highly influential queens from the West, like Bathsheba or Naqiʿa-Zakutu, who obviously were not the only *grandes dames* in history, ancient or modern, to have imposed their favorite sons upon aging monarchs....

Tadmor gives us a good case for the use of analogy in history but, as Braudel has said, analogy is like "*navigation en haute mer*" with all its dangers:[12] general patterns that recur, even if they are not simply false, are only superficially relevant.

The problems of succession and of the legitimacy of rulers, and the ways in which they reached their thrones, are familiar themes throughout world history. What may make them interesting to us is the explanation affected by the narrator of the events and their unusual aspects. Before following these features in the biblical narrative, let me relate a story from the year 546 B.C.E. in China:

> Minister Cui Zhu killed his lord, Duke Zhuang of Qi. The chief historiographer thereupon recorded on his official slip: "Cui Zhu committed regicide." Angry, Cui executed him. The brother of the historiographer, succeeding him, made the same entry and Cui killed him also. Then he had to kill a third brother. Finally, another younger brother took over and persisted in making the same record, and Cui had to give up and let the record stand. The part of the story that is even more interesting is that another historiographer in a different part of the country, on hearing that the chief historiographers were killed, arrived on the

> scene with his bamboo tablets in hand, ready to record the facts. Only when he found that the event had finally got recorded, did he return home.

What a difference from the Assyrian record! The main theme of the story is that the task of the historiographer is to write down the truth. Chinese historiography had a moral purpose, and in its best form does not arbitrarily follow the vicissitudinous tide of politics or ideological fashions. Since history records the rights and wrongs of the past it provides guidance for future behavior.

But in China, after the Confucian redaction of the annals, this tendency led to a systematic purification of anything considered to be unbecoming or unsuitable, so that it was eventually whittled down to a dry recounting of military campaigns, rebellions and mutinies.[13] The second feature of describing the past that we have mentioned, the narrative genre, is completely absent. Let us now come to the biblical succession narrative, in the first chapters of the Book of Kings. Here I confess that I am reading the story with its midrashic and talmudic interpretations. This implies a close reading of the text, which fills in many gaps and discloses some features that the Bible only hints at in expressions which may seem to us superfluous.

> Adonijah the son of Haggith exalted himself, saying "I will be his king".... And his father had not displeased him at any time in saying, "Why hast thou done so?" He also was a very goodly man, and his mother bare him after Absalom.(1 Kings 1:5–6)

The mention of Absalom in this context seems to be superfluous. But it is interpreted by the Midrash (Tanḥuma Shevuot §1) as an implicit criticism of David's passivity to the misdeeds of his sons, and a general inference is drawn that disorder in one's own house is more dangerous than battles against an external enemy.

In another unexplained episode King David, who easily agreed with the intervention of Nathan and Bathsheba on behalf of Solomon, charges Solomon before he dies and says: "Thou knowest also what Joab, the son of Zeruiah, did to me and what he did to the two captains of the hosts of Israel, unto Abner the son of Ner and unto Amasa the son of Jether, whom he slew.... Do therefore according to thy wisdom, and let not his hoar head go down to the grave in peace." The words of David "what he did to me" are unexpected, for Joab, as far as we have been told, had done nothing to wrong David.

As an answer to this question, an addition is introduced by the Midrash to the biblical account of the death of Uriah in 2 Samuel 11:15, where it is reported that David wrote in his letter to Joab: "Set ye Uriah in the forefront of the hottest battle that he may be smitten and die." Joab executed the assignment. In the source nothing is mentioned of any public reaction to this act, but the Midrash adds that afterwards the thirty-seven mighty men of valor stood up and threatened to punish Joab for it. In order to defend himself, Joab produced the letter of the king, and rumors started that the king had also ordered the execution of Abner. Solomon started to fulfill the charges of his father and Joab fled the tabernacle and caught hold of the horns of the altar. When Benaiah came in the name of the king and asked him to come out, Joab said, "Nay; but I will die here." Subsequently Benaiah reported to Solomon: "Thus said Joab and thus he answered me." This report can hardly refer to these words of Joab. Accordingly, our interpreters created a dialogue between Joab and Solomon in which the former proves that there was no legal justification for the accusation that he had wronged Abner and Amasa, and that his only sin was that he had supported Adonijah and not Solomon. A hint of this explanation is again detected by the Midrash in verse 28, "'... for Joab had turned after Adonijah and he turned not after Absalom.' What purpose does the second part of the verse serve? It hints that Amasa was guilty because he supported Absalom and his rebellion against his father, the anointed king, while he Joab had supported Adonijah before Solomon was chosen." The justification of Joab is given poetic expression in an Aramaic piyyut to the Fifth Commandment: לא תרצח, "Thou shalt not kill." The execution of Joab is considered to be a transgression against this commandment. It ends with the words, "The children of Israel were astonished and lamented over the execution of Joab." The justification of Joab continued to live on in a Yiddish paraphrase of the Book of Kings. The fact that the Bible makes no explicit comment on the actions of David and Solomon lends its narrative style to the interpretation described before, and allows a more just evaluation of the dramatis personae. It makes the search of the past more attractive while at the same time remaining faithful to the truth. The essence of that truth, both for the writers of the biblical narrative and for its midrashic interpreters, meant that history does not become something capricious and arbitrary.

Empathy and distance joined together may therefore render our judgment of the past more reasonable. Let me give an example of how this conjunction can be achieved.

The Mishna (Sanhedrin X) enumerates those who will have no share in the future world. Aside from those who deny resurrection and revelation it includes three kings, Jeroboam, Ahab and Manasseh. The Babylonian Talmud reports that Rav Ashi — reputed to be the redactor of the Talmud — was expounding the Mishna and when he reached the passage concerning the three kings, he said "tomorrow we shall commence to deal with our colleagues." King Manasseh appeared to him in a dream and complained "you called us 'your colleagues' — come and answer the following question," and they put to him a halakhic problem, which Rav Ashi did not answer. When Manasseh gave the solution, Rav Ashi asked him: "Since you are so wise, why did you worship idols?" Manasseh replied: "Had you been there, you would have caught up the shirt of your garment and would have run after me...." Next day Rav Ashi opened his lecture by saying: "Let us start with our great men, אחאב — אח לשמים אב לעבודה זרה, Ahab was a brother to Heaven and a father to idol worship."

Certainly, Rav Ashi would have distanced himself from anything connected with idolatry, but he understood the conditions of people living in a different age and made allowances for the syncretism of their times. The great Dutch historian, H. Huizinga, defined history as "the intellectual form in which civilization renders account to itself of its past."[14] However, society does not only want to know about its relationship with the past; it wants a past it can use. On the other hand, even those who say that they are not studying the past only "for its own sake" are obliged to adhere to disinterested inquiry and to support efforts in all branches of scientific research to discover what is not yet known. But at the same time the broadening of the field of historical inquiry and the multiplication of the sources have made it impossible for the historian to shut his eyes to his own ignorance. He is, as A.J. Toynbee has said, not more ignorant than his predecessors but he has gained one advantage over them. He has been brought face to face with his ignorance by the stupendous increase in his knowledge.[15]

However, Toynbee himself failed to adhere to this principle. Otherwise he could not have made so many facts fit into his *a priori* established historical system. Only the vigor and independence of a closely argued dialogue of interpretation, which works backwards from the known to the unknown, from the certain to the uncertain, and perceives both the similarities and the differences in history, may contribute to the clarification of the truth and save it from becoming propaganda. The search of the past cannot be final. Notwithstanding all its difficulties and intricacies, and the shortcomings of the historian, it will continue as long as human beings ask questions about the present and are concerned about the future. History, however, should avoid competition with religion and not describe its findings as a key to the salvation of mankind. Marxists have done this and the results are well known. Deuteronomy 32:5 addresses both religious preachers and educators and historians, to the first it says: **שאל אביך ויגידך זקניך ויאמרו לך**, "Ask your father and he will relate it to thee; thy elders and they will tell you." And to the searchers of the past it says: **זכור ימות עולם, בינו שנות דור ודור**, "Remember the days of old, consider the years of many generations."

Notes

1. M. Howard, "The Concept of Peace," *Encounter* 61/4 (1983): 18–24.
2. H.S. Commager, *The Search for a Usable Past and Other Essays* (New York, 1967), p. 305.
3. I. Berlin, *Concepts and Categories* (New York, 1979), p. 110.
4. J. Licht, "Biblical Historicism," in *History, Historiography and Interpretation*, eds. H. Tadmor and M. Weinfeld (Jerusalem, 1983), p. 111.
5. K.C. Chang, "Archaeology and Chinese Historiography," *World Archaeology* 13 (1981): 153.
6. Commager, *The Search for a Usable Past* (see note 2), p. 13.
7. C.V. Wedgwood, *Truth and Opinion: Historical Essays* (London, 1960), p. 49.
8. B. Croce, *History as the Story of Liberty* (London, 1941), p. 180ff.
9. I. Berlin, *Historical Inevitability* (London, 1954), p. 53.
10. P. Gay, *Style in History* (London, 1954).
11. H. Tadmor, "Autobiographical Apology in the Royal Assyrian Literature," in *History, Historiography and Interpretation* (see note 4), pp. 36ff.
12. F. Braudel, *Le monde actuel* (Paris, 1963), p. 54; and L. Confora, "Analogie et l'histoire," *History and Theory* 22:1 (1983), pp. 22–42.
13. K.C. Chang, "Archaeology and Chinese Historiography" (see note 5), p. 157.; M. Weber, *Gesammelte Aufsatze zu Religionssociologie*, vol. I (Tübingen, 1920), pp. 402ff. Yu Shan Han, *Elements of*

Chinese Historiography (Hollywood, 1955); P. van der Loon, "Die alten chinesischen Geschichtswerke und die Entstehunz historischer Ideale," *Saeculum* 8 (1957): 190–195.

14. H. Huizinga, "A Definition of the Concept of History," in *Philosophy and History: Essays Presented to Ernst Cassirer*, eds. R. Klibansky and H.J. Paton (Oxford, 1936), p. 91.
15. A.J. Toynbee, "The Limitations of Historical Knowledge," *The Times Literary Supplement* (January 6, 1956).

SOCIAL EVENTS
EXHIBITIONS
AND EXCURSIONS

Social Events

Reception and Visit at the Israel Museum

On Monday evening, April 2, 1984, the Israel Museum opened its doors to the Congress. The participants, divided into groups, were guided by the museum's curators through its archaeological section and to the Shrine of the Book. At the end of the evening a reception was held at which Mr. Martin Weyl, the director of the Museum, greeted the guests.

Reception at The Hebrew University of Jerusalem

On Wednesday evening, April 4, 1984, a reception was given for the Congress participants by Prof. Don Patinkin, the President of The Hebrew University of Jerusalem, at the Maiersdorf Faculty Club on the Mt. Scopus campus. Prof. Patinkin welcomed his guests, and His Excellency Dr. Robert S. Merrillees, the Australian Ambassador, himself an archaeologist, addressed those present.

Robert S. Merrillees: For biblical archaeology, the Israel Exploration Society and the City of Jerusalem, this Conference has been and still is a very special occasion. It has been no less important for me personally, for I have tonight decided to come professionally out of the closet. I see no further point in pretending to diplomats that I have no interest in archaeology, nor to archaeologists that I am no diplomat. In fact, this dissembling has served very little purpose over the last twenty years. My diplomatic colleagues have always had their suspicions that I was really a prehistorian in disguise, while my archaeologist friends have never had any doubts about my lack of diplomacy. However, I must confess to some uncertainty as to the capacity in which I am appearing before you this evening, and so I will try on this occasion to be both archaeological and diplomatic.

It is a great honor for Australia, and for me personally to have been invited to address you this evening. Not far from here is the Mount Scopus Commonwealth War Graves Cemetery, which is the resting place for Australian and other servicemen killed fighting the Turks in World War I. A permanent reminder of their passage through what became Palestine is the famous Shellal Mosaic in the Australian War Memorial in Canberra. Australians have since then had strong archaeological, military and political connections with this part of the world. My teacher, the late Prof. James Stewart, excavated with Sir Flinders Petrie at Tell El-Ajjul in 1934; Australian troops fought with the Allies against the Vichy French in this region during World War II; and Australia was one of the first nations to recognize the newly established State of Israel in 1949. It would be immodest of me to say how gratified I am by the Australian attendance at this conference, but it is very pleasing for us all to be surrounded by so many colleagues from all parts of the world, including some from Australia.

Ladies and Gentlemen, archaeology has never served to elucidate the past entirely for its own sake. It is after all the present generation that has determined where to investigate the past and how to interpret it. Indeed antiquarian research has been subject to so many nonacademic aims, directions and influences over the years, especially in western Asia, that archaeology and politics have now become two sides of the same coin. There is nothing in this association that should surprise or even alarm us, unless it is the devaluation of the currency, for the two professions have long had much in common, even if we have chosen not to recognize this, and all that has happened in recent times is that their convergence has become more evident and direct. It is to the coincidence of approaches that our Conference has been primarily devoted.

No more articulate or persuasive exponent of this point of view can be found than Prof. Yigael Yadin, whose lecture to the Conference has set the tone for the whole debate. He combines all the disciplines which must be brought to bear in contemporary antiquarian research, and inspired by his example I have revealed my dual credentials to you this evening. But we owe him more than simply a debt for the consummate way in which he has blended the multiple talents needed by today's archaeologist, for he is the author of one of the most influential popular works on archaeology produced in this country and in this century. His volume on *Masada, Herod's Fortress and the Zealot's Last Stand*, which has just been reprinted, was one of the three paperbacks I read before taking up my post in Tel Aviv. The excavations he conducted at Masada epitomized his skills as soldier, archaeologist and diplomat, and no less importantly reflected the qualities that have marked the work of the Israel Exploration Society since its inception seventy years ago — purpose, dedication and industriousness.

It is only fitting that in his book Yadin should have thanked his friend Joseph Aviram, the executive secretary of the Israel Exploration Society, which was one of the sponsors of the Masada excavation. But for Aviram's initiative and insistence,

Yadin doubted that he would have undertaken the enormous task of clearing this memorable site. We are all no less in Aviram's debt, for he has been the guiding spirit and guardian angel of our deliberations. His wise and gentle counsel has made it possible for this Conference to be held in the harmonious atmosphere that has pervaded our meetings. And if ever there were a handmaiden to Israeli archaeology it would be Mrs. Nehama Litani, whose good cheer, not to mention coffee and cookies, would alone justify a trip to Jerusalem and joining the Israel Exploration Society. We are also deeply grateful to the organizing committee, and especially its chairman, Prof. Biran, for having arranged this Conference and for the smooth functioning of all the sessions, wherever they have been held.

It has been especially valuable to have available to us the booklet produced to commemorate the 70th Anniversary of the Israel Exploration Society. Amongst other things, it serves to illustrate how transient are the names we use to label peoples and places. For while the Jewish Palestine Society became the Israel Exploration Society after the creation of the State of Israel, the name of the Palestine Exploration Society has remained unchanged in Britain. In our archaeological discipline names should ideally be means to an end, not an end in themselves, but since they are today so much exposed to political factors, we should properly aim for titles that are universalist, neutral and widely acceptable. This is much easier said than done for the area in which our archaeological activities lie. To describe this region I have assembled no less than eight names, which I now list in alphabetical order: Canaan, The Holy Land, Israel, The Land of the Bible, Palestine, The Promised Land, South or Southern Levant, and Southwestern Asia. Anyone who can get the archaeological community to agree on only one of these terms to the exclusion of the rest should in my view immediately take over the Middle East peace negotiations process.

The second popular book I read in preparation for my diplomatic assignment in Israel was *Jerusalem as Jesus Knew It. Archaeology as Evidence*, by the Rev. John Wilkinson, Director of the British School of Archaeology in Jerusalem. The application of archaological and scientific findings to textual data, especially the Bible, continues to cause difficulties, not to mention disputes, and leaves both scholar and layman perplexed by the seemingly contradictory or irreconcilable results of the attempted correlation. With great care and perceptiveness John Wilkinson has negotiated the archaeological and theological minefields of Christian antiquity and from his reflections has distilled the following memorable words:

> The particular point thus established (about the tangible existence of the resurrected Christ) is hard for a modern reader to accept, particularly at a time when honesty seems to require the application of scientific criteria to statements of every kind. Yet there are some statements to which such criteria are inappropriate. It would for instance be absurd to apply them to exclamations or to poetry, or to emotional expressions of joy or grief. An experience can be "real" in the sense that it is authentic, sincere, and important to the subject, and yet remain beyond the grasp of present day science.

As a theologian once remarked to me in Jerusalem, the pursuit of spiritual truth is no less valid or worthwhile than research into the sciences. Prof. Neeman did not say last night whether archaeology was considered an exact science or an inexact science — and in any case in my view it is not necessary to try to prove the Bible archaeologically exact or inexact.

If there is a sense in which this Conference belongs to anything or anyone, it belongs to Jerusalem and Mayor Kollek. In the minds of many they have been synonymous. All our sessions have taken place in this cosmopolitan city, which is the center of the three great monotheistic religions of the world. It is a beautiful location rich in history, associations and memories, whose preservation and enhancement have been entrusted to the benevolent, even worshipful direction of Mayor Kollek for over twenty-five years. But Jerusalem is much more than buildings, parks and cemeteries, for it does and must continue to embody the moving forces of our Conference — freedom of thought, tolerance, and enlightenment. Of the three volumes I read before coming to Israel, none is more evocative than *For Jerusalem. A Life by Teddy Kollek with His Son, Amos Kollek*, for it encapsulates all the beliefs, challenges and hopes that led to the creation of the State of Israel and continue to motivate many of its citizens today.

In his biography Kollek states that Jerusalem

> is not just a great city or an historical city. It is a place where everyone seems to feel he has a share, a stake — and a say. Because Jerusalem is a city holy to millions, every new house that goes up adds itself to history and thus often becomes controversial. Yet I feel that there is also a deep human value in preserving Jerusalem, independent of its political future, because I am overcome by sadness whenever a long-established thing of beauty and character disappears.

Perhaps Mayor Kollek is the most successful of all the archaeologists active in Israel, for he has never made any pretense about the way the past can be made to serve the present and has worked consistently and unashamedly to this end, without any loss of integrity.

Finally, it is my pleasant duty to thank our hosts, The Hebrew University of Jerusalem, for this splendid reception, and express the hope that from this Conference we will have derived greater awareness and understanding than before of the factors that shape our lives and increasingly govern our work.

Reception Given by the Mayor of Jerusalem

Mr. Teddy Kollek, the Mayor of Jerusalem, hosted a reception held at the Jerusalem Theater on Thursday evening, April 5, 1984, prior to the Closing Session. He greeted the Congress participants on behalf of the Municipality of Jerusalem.

Reception Given by the Municipality of Acre and the University of Haifa

A reception hosted by the Municipality of Acre and the University of Haifa was held in the Crusader Hall and Crypt in the city of Acre on Monday evening, April 9, 1984. During the reception young musicians from the city played for the guests. The research carried out by the University of Haifa in Acre was explained by the city's Mayor, Mr. Ely De Castro, and the University's rector, Prof. Uriel Rappaport. Dan Bahat delivered a brief lecture on the Crusader history of Acre. Prior to the reception, the Congress participants toured the city's well-preserved Crusader and Islamic remains.

Reception and Visit at the Haaretz Museum

The Congress came to a close on Tuesday evening, April 10, 1984 at the Haaretz Museum, which specially opened its doors for the occasion. The unusual reception, during which the guests were offered local falafel in pita prepared on the spot and the new "Tel Aviv" wine, was held as part of the city of Tel Aviv's 75th anniversary celebrations. The Mayor of Tel Aviv, Mr. Shlomo Lahat, and the Museum's director, Mr. Rechavam Zeevy, greeted the guests, and Prof. Cyrus Gordon said a few words on behalf of the Congress participants. After the reception, the guests visited at their leisure various pavilions of the Museum: "The Ceramics Pavilion," "The Copper Pavilion," "The Glass Pavilion," "The Kadmon Numismatics Pavilion," and "Man and His Work" (opened to the public for the first time). The curators of each pavilion were present to answer any questions.

Exhibitions

The efforts of the Organizing Committee to present an up-to-date review of the archaeological research carried out in Israel were coordinated with the archaeological institutions in the country. Consequently, the following exhibitions were specially planned for the Congress:

The Israel Department of Antiquities and Museums

On Saturday, April 7, 1984 at the Rockefeller Museum building, the Congress participants visited an exhibition of recent finds from the following excavations of the Israel Department of Antiquities and Museums:

Naḥal Ḥemar — Neolithic site
Biqʿat ʿUvda — Neolithic temple
Shiqmim — Chalcolithic village
Golan Chalcolithic sites
Yiftaḥʾel — Prehistoric site
ʿEnan — MBI tomb
Tell Beit Mirsim — Middle Bronze, Late Bronze and Iron Age cemetery
Storage jars from the period of the Israelite settlement found in Upper Galilee
Tel Shiloh — Israelite city
Iron Age fortresses in the Negev

The excavators of these sites and the Jerusalem district archaeologist were present to meet Congress participants.

Rockefeller Museum

Finds from Kadesh-Barnea and Achzib were specially exhibited in the entrance hall of the Museum. Their excavators were present during the visit on Saturday, April 9, 1984.

Finds from excavations carried out by the Israel Department of Antiquities and Museums, in the Rockefeller Museum building

The Israel Museum and Shrine of the Book

"News in Antiquities" was the name given to the exhibits of artifacts shown to the public for the first time in the various halls of the archaeological section of the Museum.

The Shrine of the Book opened an exhibition of twelve manuscripts from the Cairo Geniza dating from tenth–thirteenth centuries C.E. received on loan from the Jewish Theological Seminary of America. The exhibition comprised a representative choice of the material found in the Geniza: Bible, Apocrypha (Ben-Sira and Ecclesiasticus), Mishnah, Talmud and two autographs, one by the poet Yehuda Ha-Levi and the other by Maimonides.

Institute of Archaeology, The Hebrew University of Jerusalem

On Wednesday evening, April 4, 1984, the Congress participants visited the permanent study collection and a special exhibition at the Institute of Archaeology of the The

Hebrew University of Jerusalem. The exhibition consisted of unpublished selected finds from the following excavations carried out the by Institute:

Masada
The Upper City of Jerusalem
Hasmonean and Herodian Jericho
Yoqneʿam Regional Project
Hazor
Beth-Shean
Tell Qasile
Tel Mevorakh
Tel Batash
The City of David
Deir el-Balaḥ
Dor

The excavators of these sites and the staff of the Archaeometry Laboratory of the Institute were present to meet the Congress participants.

Nelson Glueck School of Biblical Archaeology of Hebrew Union College–Jewish Institute of Religion

The finds from the School's excavations at Tel Dan, ʿAroʿer, Tel ʿIra, Yeṣud Hamaʿalah and Anathoth were on exhibit throughout the duration of the Congress.

The Book Exhibit

The Israel Exploration Society, The American Schools of Oriental Research, Centre de Recherche Français de Jérusalem, the Israel Department of Antiquities and Museums, the Israel Museum, and the Institute of Archaeology of Tel Aviv University exhibited their publications for the duration of the deliberations of the Congress at the Jerusalem Hilton.

Excursions

In Jerusalem

The morning of Thursday, April 5, 1984, was set aside for visits to the three main excavations in Jerusalem: the City of David, the Upper City and the Ophel. The more than 700 Congress participants were divided into twelve groups, each guided by a member of these expeditions, and under the supervision of the directors of each excavation. On Saturday, April 8, 1984, the Congress participants visited the Citadel (Tower of David), where staff awaited them to explain the ongoing excavation and restoration being carried out at the site.

The City of David

The renewed excavations in the City of David have been carried out since 1978 on behalf of "The City of David Society for the Excavation, Preservation and Restoration of the City of David in Jerusalem." The Society was founded by the Institute of Archaeology of The Hebrew University, the Israel Exploration Society, The Jerusalem Foundation and a group of South African sponsors, headed by Mendel Kaplan. The archaeological activities of the City of David Society are spread over the entire Southeastern Hill of Jerusalem, south of the Temple Mount, and are directed by Yigal Shiloh of the Institute of Archaeology of The Hebrew University of Jerusalem.

The Ophel

The dream to excavate the area adjacent to the Temple Mount became a reality as a result of the Six-Day War in 1967. The excavations began in 1968 under the direction of Benjamin Mazar on behalf of the Institute of Archaeology of the The Hebrew University of Jerusalem and the Israel Exploration Society. Work continued all year round, without interruption, until 1977, when the site's reconstruction was commenced by The Jerusalem Foundation. Meir Ben-Dov assisted in organizing the Congress visit to the site.

The Upper City

The excavations in the Upper City of Jerusalem are located in the present Jewish Quarter of the Old City, on the "Western Hill" of the ancient city. They were started in 1969 under the direction of Nahman Avigad of the Institute of Archaeology of The Hebrew University of Jerusalem, and on behalf of the Israel Exploration Society and the Department of Antiquities and Museums in cooperation with the Jewish Quarter Reconstruction and Development Company.

The Citadel (Tower of David)
The first archaeological excavations in the courtyard of the Citadel near the Jaffa Gate of the Old City took place in 1934–1948 under the direction of C.N. Johns on behalf of the Mandatory Department of Antiquities. Since, the Israel Exploration Society has sponsored excavations in the Citadel carried out by Ruth Amiran and Avraham Eitan of the Israel Museum and The Hebrew University, by Hillel Geva of The Hebrew University, and recently by Renée Sivan and Giora Solar on behalf of the Jerusalem Municipality Museum located in the Citadel.

Outside Jerusalem

Between April 6–10, 1984, the Congress participants left Jerusalem for excursions in other parts of the country. At each site, the results of the excavation were explained by its director and staff.

Tel ʿAkko
Tel ʿAkko was a Canaanite/Phoenician port situated on the Mediterranean coast and is located outside the modern city of Acre. Excavations there are being carried out under the direction of Moshe Dothan of the University of Haifa.

Tel Beer-Sheba
Tel Beer-Sheba was the chief Israelite city in the Negev. Its city plan was revealed as a result of the excavations carried out by the late Yohanan Aharoni of Tel Aviv University between 1969 and 1977. Restoration of the site is being supervised by Zev Herzog of Tel Aviv University.

Tel Lachish
The renewed excavation of Tel Lachish was begun in 1974 under the direction of David Ussishkin of the Institute of Archaeology of Tel Aviv University. The Congress participants visited the Canaanite temple and palace, the city gate, the Israelite fort palace, the Assyrian rampart, and an area excavated by Gabriel Barkay for the specific purpose of clarifying the stratigraphy of this key site in the history of Judah.

Tel Beer-Sheba

Tel Lachish: The city gate of Levels IV–III from inside the city. Photograph by Michal Roche Ben-Ami

Hasmonean and Herodian Winter Palaces at Jericho

The magnificent Hasmonean and Herodian winter palaces located at the oasis of Jericho are being excavated by Ehud Netzer on behalf of the Institute of Archaeology of The Hebrew University of Jerusalem.

Tell el-Sultan

The Congress participants also visited the excavations at the ancient tell of Jericho, Tell el-Sultan, carried out by Garstang in the 1930s and by Kathleen Kenyon in the 1950s.

Theater and Amphitheater at Beth-Shean

The Roman theater at Beth-Shean was excavated in 1961–1962 by Shimeon Applebaum and in 1962 by Avraham Negev on behalf of the Israel Parks Authority. The amphitheater was uncovered during construction work carried out in the modern town. Its excavation was begun in 1980 by Gideon Foerster and Yoram Tsafrir of The Hebrew University. This amphitheatre is the first of its kind to be discovered in Israel and one of the rare examples found east of Italy.

Roman-Byzantine Thermae at Hammath Gader

The magnificent Roman-Byzantine thermae at Hammath Gader were excavated by Yizhar Hirschfeld and Giora Solar with the aim of reconstructing the site on behalf of the Israel Government Tourist Corporation.

Qaṣrin

The Qaṣrin museum, located in the modern city of Qaṣrin on the Golan Heights, is one of many local museums established throughout the country. Its exhibits include finds from the nearby synagogue and the Golan Chalcolithic sites. The Roman-Byzantine synagogue at Qaṣrin, built of local basalt stone, is being excavated by Zvi Maoz, Rachel Hachlili and Ann Killebrew on behalf of the Department of Antiquities and Museums. The Congress participants also visited one of the Chalcolithic villages excavated by Claire Epstein of the Israel Department of Antiquities and Museums.

Tel Dan

Tel Dan is identified as Canaanite Laish, conquered by the tribe of Dan, and is located on Israel's northern border. The excavations there have been carried out since 1966 by Avraham Biran on behalf of the Israel Department of Antiquities and Museums, and since 1972 on behalf of Hebrew Union College–Jewish Institute of Religion. The Congress participants visited the impressive arched brick gateway dating to the Middle Bronze Age, and the Israelite city gate and *bema*.

Jericho: The third Herodian palace

Beth-Shean: The Roman theater. By courtesy of the Israel Government Press Office

Qaṣrin: The synagogue. By courtesy of Zev Radovan

Tell Qasile

Tell Qasile, located within the grounds of Museum Haaretz, was the first "Israeli" excavation carried out — by Benjamin Maisler (Mazar) in 1948–1949 — after the establishment of the State of Israel. The renewed excavations are directed by Amihai Mazar of the Institute of Archaeology of The Hebrew University of Jerusalem on behalf of the Museum Haaretz. Tell Qasile was a Philistine port city and the finds at the site include Philistine temples which have not been discovered elsewhere in Israel. The Congress participants also visited the Tell Qasile Pavilion in the Museum.

Congress participants at Tell Qasile

Tel Dan: The arched brick city gate of the Middle Bronze Age

Hazor

The excavation of Hazor, the chief Canaanite city in the north, was carried out from 1955 to 1958 and in 1968 by Yigael Yadin. The visitors met Prof. Yadin at the museum in which most of the tell's finds are housed. On the tell, they saw the water system, and the Solomonic gate and casemate wall.

Chorazin

Chorazin, the town mentioned in the Scriptures as condemned by Jesus, is a Jewish town dating to the Byzantine period, built of local black basalt. The excavations and subsequent restoration of the site, including its synagogue and industrial and residential areas, are being supervised by Zev Yeivin on behalf of the Israel Department of Antiquities and Museums and the Israel Parks Authority.

Arad

At ancient Arad, the Early Bronze Age city's palaces, streets, houses and temples have been extensively excavated by Ruth Amiran of the Israel Museum. The Israelite fortress of Arad was excavated by the late Yohanan Aharoni on behalf of Tel Aviv University.

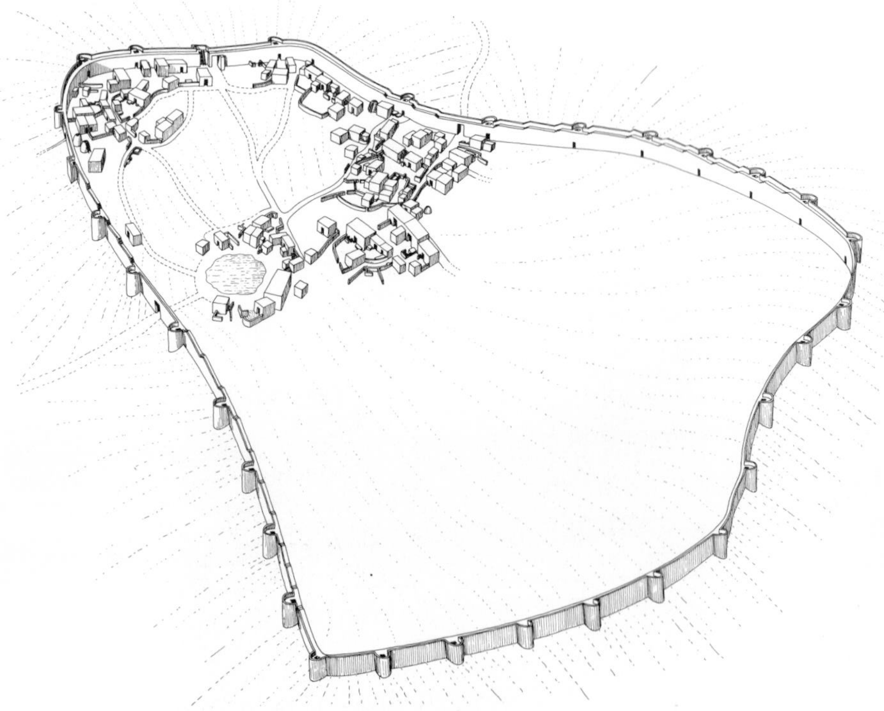

Arad: The Early Bronze Age city. By courtesy of Leen Ritmeyer

Tel Hazor: The water system. By courtesy of the Israel Government Press Office

Chorazin: The facade of the synagogue. By courtesy of Leen Ritmeyer and Moreshet Derech

Tel Megiddo

Tel Megiddo is located on the eastern slopes of Mt. Carmel. The finds, many of which are housed in the museum at the site, are of such importance to the study of an ancient mound that Megiddo should not be excluded from any archaeological study tour. The reconstructed remains at the site include walls, gates, palaces, temples, stables/stores and the water system.

Tel Dor

The excavation of Tel Dor, situated on the Mediterranean coast, was begun in 1980 by Ephraim Stern of the Institute of Archaeology of The Hebrew University of Jerusalem. At the time of the Congress, a well-preserved Hellenistic-Roman city wall, its main gate structure and residential quarters, and some Persian and Israelite buildings had been revealed. The finds from the site are housed, prepared for publication and exhibited in the nearby local museum located within the grounds of Kibbutz Naḥsholim.

Tel Megiddo: Model of the Israelite city. By courtesy of the Israel Government Press Office

Tel Dor: Area B at the end of the 1983 season. On the left (Area B1), the Hellenistic city wall and Hellenistic and Persian structures. On the right (Area B2), the Roman sewer and pavement and below Hellenistic and Persian remains

Aphek-Antipatris

Tel Aphek

The excavations at Aphek-Antipatris, which were begun in 1972, had revealed at the time of the Congress city fortifications, Middle Bronze and Late Bronze Age palaces and an Egyptian Governor's mansion dating to the Middle Bronze Age. The forum, Cardo and theater of the Roman city had also been uncovered; however, the Congress participants did not have time to visit this part of the site. The continuing excavations are carried out under the direction of Moshe Kochavi of the Institute of Archaeology of Tel Aviv University. The finds of the excavation are exhibited in the municipal museum of nearby Petaḥ Tikva.

Abbreviations

AAA	Annals of Archaeology and Anthropology
AASOR	Annual of the American Schools of Oriental Research
AfO	Archiv für Orientforschung
AHw.	W. von Soden, Akkadisches Handwörterbuch I–III (Wiesbaden, 1965–1981)
AIPHOS	Annuaire de l'Institut de philologie et d'histoire orientale et slaves
AJA	American Journal of Archaeology
ANET	Ancient Near Eastern Texts Relating to the Old Testament, ed. J.B. Pritchard (Princeton, 1969)
AOAT	Alter Orient und Altes Testament
ASAE	Annales du Service des Antiquités de l'Égypte
BA	Biblical Archaeologist
BAR	Biblical Archaeology Review
BASOR	Bulletin of the American Schools of Oriental Research
BCH	Bulletin de Correspondance Hellénique
BIFAO	Bulletin de l'Institut français d'archéologie orientale
BSA	Annual of the British School of Athens
CAH	The Cambridge Ancient History I–III, 3d ed (Cambridge, 1970–1977)
CdE	Chronique d'Égypte
CRAIBL	Comptes Rendus de l'Academie des Inscriptions et Belles Lettres
EA	J.A. Knudtzon, Die el-Amarna Tafeln, 2 vols. (Liepzig, 1915)
EI	Eretz-Israel: Archaeological, Historical and Geographical Studies
IEJ	Israel Exploration Journal
JAOS	Journal of the American Oriental Society
JARCE	Journal of the American Research Center in Egypt
JBL	Journal of Biblical Literature
JCS	Journal of Cuneiform Studies
JdS	Journal des Savants
JEA	Journal of Egyptian Archaeology
JEOL	Jaarbericht van het Vooraziatisch-Egyptisch Genootschap "Ex Oriente Lux"
JMEOS	Journal of the Manchester University Egyptological and Oriental Society
JNES	Journal of Near Eastern Studies
JRAS	Journal of the Royal Asiatic Society of Great Britain and Ireland
JSS	Journal of Semitic Studies
JSSEA	The Journal of the Society for the Study of Egyptian Antiquities

LdA	Lexikon der Ägyptologie
MDIAK	Mitteilungen des Deutschen Archäologischen Instituts Abteilung Kairo
MDOG	Mitteilungen der Deutschen Orient-Gesellschaft zu Berlin
Or.	Orientalia
PEQ	Palestine Exploration Quarterly
QDAP	Quarterly of the Department of Antiquities of Palestine
RB	Revue biblique
RdE	Revue d'Égyptologie
RE	Real-Encyclopädie der classichen Altertumswissenschaft
RHJE	Revue de l'Histoire Juive en Égypte
RlA	Reallexikon der Assyriologie
VT	Vetus Testamentum
ZA	Zeitschrift für Assyriologie und Vorderasiatische Archäologie
ZAS	Zeitschrift für ägyptische Sprache und Altertumskunde
ZAW	Zeitschrift für die alttestamentliche Wissenschaft
ZDMG	Zeitschrift der Deutschen Morgenländischen Gesellschaft
ZDPV	Zeitschrift des deutschen Palästina-Vereins
ZthK	Zeitschrift für Theologie und Kirche